Byron's holograph MS of the Latin poem 'Edleston', no. 173

Reproduced with permission, from the collection of John Murray Ltd.

LORD BYRON

The Complete
Poetical Works

EDITED BY
JEROME J. McGANN

VOLUME I

OXFORD
AT THE CLARENDON PRESS
1980

Oxford University Press, Walton Street, Oxford OX2 6DP

OXFORD LONDON GLASGOW
NEW YORK TORONTO MELBOURNE WELLINGTON
KUALA LUMPUR SINGAPORE HONG KONG TOKYO
DELHI BOMBAY CALCUTTA MADRAS KARACHI
NAIROBI DAR ES SALAAM CAPE TOWN

*Published in the United States
by Oxford University Press, New York*

© *Oxford University Press 1980*

British Library Cataloguing in Publication Data

Byron, George Gordon, *Baron Byron*
    [Poems]. The complete poetical works. (Oxford
    English texts)
    Vol. I
    I. Title   II. McGann, Jerome John   III. Series
    821'.7   PR4350

ISBN 0-19-812763-4 Pbk

*Printed in Great Britain
at the University Press, Oxford
by Eric Buckley
Printer to the University*

This Edition Of Byron's Works
Is Dedicated To The Man
Who, More Than Anyone Else, Has
Made It Possible

JOHN G. MURRAY

Primus Inter Pares

ACKNOWLEDGEMENTS

As editor of these volumes I stand *minimus inter pares*. The company of Byron scholars from the poet's day to our own is extensive and distinguished, and my debt to their work is incalculable. Those who are still working to preserve and elucidate the Byron canon will, I hope, forgive me if I thank them all here in this general way.

Still, certain people and institutions have been particularly kind and generous to me. John G. Murray, to whom this work is dedicated, has supported the project at every stage, so that any expression of thanks to him here must be helpless and inadequate. My special thanks go as well to Virginia Murray who, as archivist of the great Byron collection at John Murray Ltd., had to bear with my presence, and my perpetual requests, more than anyone ought. Leslie A. Marchand, the greatest Byron scholar of this century, brought me to work on this edition and I owe him a greater debt than I can ever hope to repay. To Cecil Y. Lang, one of the finest scholars and best friends I have ever known, I owe another unpayable debt. Finally, my wife Anne and my three children have been involved in this work from the beginning in so direct and intimate a way that I would not presume to thank them for their care and support.

Many other persons have been generous of their time and knowledge and possessions, and I am deeply grateful for the various kinds of help they have given me. I am only too well aware that they deserve something better than a place in a list of names: Thomas Ashton, Leo Braudy, Mrs. T. C. Bridal, Timothy A. J. Burnett, Virgil Burnett, Leonard Casley, Peter Croft, Nina Diakonova, Lucy Edwards, Paula R. Feldman, Arthur Friedman, Richard Gatty, W. F. Godden, Dorothy Kilgour, Gwin J. Kolb, Marjorie Levinson, Ernest J. Lovell Jr., the Earl of Lytton, Maynard Mack, H. M. Combe Martin, John S. Mayfield, Terry Meyers, Mr. and Mrs. Earle Miller, Mrs. Doris Langley Moore, Susan Morgan, Michael Murrin, H. F. Oppenheimer, Stephen Orgel, Francis Lewis Randolph, A. E. Raubitschek, Gordon N. Ray, Donald H. Reiman, William Ringler, Charles Robinson, Barbara Rosenbaum, Nicholas Rudall, Eduardo Saccone, Stuart M. Tave, Robert H. Taylor, Marcia Tillotson, Lindsay Waters, Barry Weller.

I have to thank as well a great many institutions along with their learned and dedicated directors and staffs. All have been unfailingly generous of their resources. The edition has been supported by grants from the American Philosophical Society, the John Simon Guggenheim Foundation, and the National Endowment for the Humanities. The University of Chicago and the Johns Hopkins University also supported me during several years when I was absent from my regular duties at those institutions. It is a pleasure to recall here as well the many libraries and museums which have put their facilities at my disposal, and whose staffs have been so helpful: the National Library of Athens; Balliol College Library; the Beinecke Library, Yale University; the Berg Collection, New York Public Library; Bibliotheca Bodmeriana; the Bodleian Library; Boston Public Library; the British Library; University of Chicago Library; William Andrews Clark Library; Library of Congress; Meyer Davis Collection, University of Pennsylvania Library; Fitzwilliam Museum; Gennadius Library; the Harrow School Library; the Houghton Library, Harvard University; the Henry E. Huntington Library; University of Iowa Library; the Johns Hopkins University Library; Keats House, London; Keats–Shelley Memorial House, Rome; Kent County Council; the King's School Library; University of Leeds Library; Manuscript Division, New York Public Library; the Pierpont Morgan Library; Newberry Library; University of Newcastle Library; Nottingham Public Libraries; University of Nottingham Library; the Carl H. Pforzheimer Library; Francis Lewis Randolph Collection, University of Pennsylvania Library; the Rosenbach Foundation; the Royal Library, Windsor; the Sterling Library, London University; the Robert H. Taylor Collection, Princeton University Library; the Humanities Research Center, University of Texas; Trinity College, Cambridge; University Library, Cambridge.

Finally, I want to thank the officers and the editorial and printing staffs of the Clarendon Press. My editors have been unfailingly patient and supportive, and my copy editor more helpful than I perhaps deserved.

Permission to print copyright materials and unpublished Byron poetry has been given for this edition by John G. Murray, Byron's legal representative and the controller of Byron copyrights.

CONTENTS OF COMPLETE WORKS

SHORT TITLES

Note. The Short Title list does not include the following: (*a*) the short title designations of the various collected editions cited and described in the Introduction; (*b*) sub-headings that designate specific editions of certain works by Byron. For example, many of the early printings of Byron's poems went through more than one edition. Often they went through many editions, and sometimes there are distinguishable issues within specific editions. My procedure has been to indicate these different editions by adding a number after the relevant short title: thus, *EBSR4* is the fourth edition (first issue) of *English Bards and Scotch Reviewers*. Further issues are distinguished by the addition of a lower-case letter: *EBSR4a* is the second issue of the fourth edition of *EBSR*, where *EBSR4* represents the first issue. On occasion I have placed the edition number in parentheses in order to avoid a possible confusion: *CHP(2)* is the second edition of the first two cantos of *Childe Harold's Pilgrimage; CHP(7)* is the seventh edition of the first two cantos.

References to *CHP*, with its different cantos and separate editions, can be confusing. The reader should know that, when the editorial reference does not involve making distinctions between editions, I refer to the first two cantos as *CHP I–II*, to the third canto as *CHP III*, and to the fourth as *CHP IV*. When separate editions or issues are to be distinguished in *CHP III* and *CHP IV*, these are written out (thus, *CHP III*, first edn.). The separate editions of *CHP I–II* are handled as noted above.

Finally, if a short title is used only in the apparatus and commentary of one specific poem, the short title is described in that commentary, and not in this list. Many of the relevant manuscripts and proofs, and a few books, fall under this procedure. Throughout the present edition identical symbols are used to stand for the manuscripts and proofs of many different poems. In all cases, the specific meaning of these sigla is set forth in the relevant commentary.

Unless otherwise indicated, Byron's works are listed here by the date of the first printing.

Age. The Age of Bronze; or, Carmen Seculare et Annus Haud Mirabilis (1823).

Anti-Jacobin. Poetry of the Anti-Jacobin, ed. Charles Edmonds (3rd edn., 1890).

Ashton. Byron's Hebrew Melodies, ed. Thomas L. Ashton (1972).

Astarte. Astarte. A Fragment of Truth Concerning George Gordon Byron, Sixth Lord Byron. Ralph Milbanke, Earl of Lovelace (privately printed, 1905).

Beppo. Beppo. A Venetian Story (1818).

Berg. The Berg Collection, New York Public Library.

Blessington. Lady Blessington's Conversations of Lord Byron, ed. Ernest J. Lovell, Jr. (Princeton, 1969).

BLJ. Byron's Letters and Journals, ed. Leslie A. Marchand (1973–   ). Vols. 1–6.

Blues. The Blues. A Literary Eclogue (1823).

BM. The British Library (formerly the British Museum).

BNYPL. Bulletin of the New York Public Library.

Bodleian–Lovelace. The collection of Lord Lytton, formerly the Lovelace Papers; on deposit at the Bodleian Library.

Bodmer. Bibliotheca Bodmeriana, Cologny/Geneva.

Borst. Lord Byron's First Pilgrimage. William A. Borst (New Haven, 1948).

Bride. The Bride of Abydos. A Turkish Tale (1813).

BSP. Byron, A Self-Portrait: Letters and Diaries, 1798–1824, ed. Peter Quennell (1950). 2 Vols.

Cain. Cain. A Mystery (1821).

Chew. Byron in England. His Fame and After-Fame. Samuel C. Chew (1924).

Chew, Dramas. The Dramas of Lord Byron. Samuel C. Chew (New York, 1915).

CHP. Childe Harold's Pilgrimage: Cantos I–II (1812); Canto III (1816); Canto IV (1818).

Corsair. The Corsair. A Tale (1814).

Curse. The Curse of Minerva (1812).

Dalgado. Lord Byron's Childe Harold's Pilgrimage to Portugal. D. G. Dalgado (Lisbon, 1919).

Dallas, Recollections. Recollections of the Life of Lord Byron. . . . R. C. Dallas (1824).

Decline and Fall. The History of the Decline and Fall of the Roman Empire, by Edward Gibbon. Ed. H. H. Milman (1846). 6 Vols.

Deformed. The Deformed Transformed. A Drama (1824).

DJ. Don Juan: Cantos I–II (1819); Cantos III–V (1821); Cantos VI–VIII (1823); Cantos IX–XI (1823); Cantos XII–XIV (1823); Cantos XV–XVI (1824); Canto XVII (written, 1823).

DJ Variorum. Byron's Don Juan. A Variorum Edition, ed. T. G. Steffan and W. W. Pratt (Austin, 1957). 4 Vols.

EBSR. English Bards and Scotch Reviewers, A Satire (1809).

ER. Edinburgh Review.

Escarpit. Lord Byron. Un Tempérament littéraire. Robert Escarpit (Paris, 1957). 2 Vols.

Finlay. A History of Greece . . . , by George Finlay. Ed. H. F. Tozer (1877). 7 Vols.

FP. Fugitive Pieces (1806).

Fuess. Lord Byron as a Satirist in Verse. Claude M. Fuess (1912).

Giaour. The Giaour. A Fragment of a Turkish Tale (1813).

Gleckner. Byron and the Ruins of Paradise. Robert Gleckner (Baltimore, 1967).

H and E. Heaven and Earth. A Mystery (1823).

Harvard. The Houghton Library, Harvard University.

HI. Hours of Idleness. A Series of Poems Original and Translated (1807).

Hints. Hints from Horace . . . (written, 1811).

HLQ. Huntington Library Quarterly.

HM1815. Hebrew Melodies (1815).

Hobhouse, Recollections. Recollections of a Long Life, by Lord Broughton (J. C. Hobhouse). Ed. Lady Dorchester (1909–11). 6 Vols.

Huntington. The Henry E. Huntington Library.

HVSV. His Very Self and Voice. Collected Conversations of Lord Byron, ed. Ernest J. Lovell, Jr. (New York, 1954).

Iley. The Life, Writings, Opinions, and Times of . . . *Byron* . . . [anon.] (London: Matthew Iley, 1825). 3 Vols.

Island. The Island; or, Christian and His Comrades (1823).

IT. Imitations and Translations from the ancient and modern classics. (ed.) J. C. Hobhouse (1809).

Joseph. Byron the Poet. M. K. Joseph (1964).

Kent. The Library of Kent County Council.

Kölbing. Lord Byrons Werke, in Kritischen Texten . . . Eugen Kölbing (Weimar, 1896). Vol. I (*The Siege of Corinth*). Vol. II (*The Prisoner of Chillon and other poems*).

K–SJ. The Keats–Shelley Journal.

KSMB. The Keats–Shelley Memorial Bulletin.

Lament. The Lament of Tasso (1817).

Lara. Lara. A Tale (1814).

Late Lord Byron. The Late Lord Byron. Doris Langley Moore (1961).

LBC. Lord Byron's Correspondence, ed. John Murray (1922). 2 Vols.

LBW. Lord Byron's Wife. Malcolm Elwin (New York, 1962).

Leeds. The Library of the University of Leeds.

Life. Letters and Journals of Lord Byron: with notices of his life. Thomas Moore (1830). 2 Vols.

LJ. The Works of Lord Byron. Letters and Journals, ed. Rowland E. Prothero (1898–1901). 6 Vols.

McGann (1). Fiery Dust. Byron's Poetic Development. Jerome J. McGann (Chicago, 1968).

McGann (2). Don Juan in Context. Jerome J. McGann (Chicago, 1976).

Manfred. Manfred. A Dramatic Poem (1817).

Marchand. Byron. A Biography. Leslie A. Marchand (New York, 1957). 3 Vols.

Marino Faliero. Marino Faliero, Doge of Venice. An Historical Tragedy (1821).

Mayne. Byron. Ethel C. Mayne (1912).

Medwin. Medwin's Conversations of Lord Byron, ed. Ernest J. Lovell, Jr. (Princeton, 1966).

Medwin (1824). Journal of the Conversations of Lord Byron. . . . Thomas Medwin (1824).

MLN. Modern Language Notes.

MLQ. Modern Language Quarterly.

MLR. Modern Language Review.

Monody. Monody on the Death of the Right Hon. R. B. Sheridan (1816).

Morgan. The J. Pierpont Morgan Library.

Morgante. The Morgante Maggiore of Pulci (1823).

Murray. The Archives of John Murray Ltd.

N1815. A Selection of Hebrew Melodies, No. I, ed. and arranged by Isaac Nathan (1815).

N1816. A Selection of Hebrew Melodies, Nos. I–II, ed. and arranged by Isaac Nathan (1816).

N1827–9. A Selection of Hebrew Melodies, Nos. I–IV, ed. and arranged by Isaac Nathan (1827–9).

N & Q. Notes and Queries.

Nathan. Fugitive Pieces and Reminiscences of Lord Byron. . . . Isaac Nathan (1829).

Newstead. The Roe–Byron Collection, and associated materials at Newstead Abbey and Nottingham, now held under the auspices of the Nottingham Public Library.

Ode to Napoleon. Ode to Napoleon Buonaparte (1814).

Origo. The Last Attachment. Iris Origo (New York, 1949).

Paston and Quennell. 'To Lord Byron'. *Feminine Profiles, based upon unpublished letters.* . . . George Paston and Peter Quennell (1939).

PCOP. The Prisoner of Chillon and other poems (1816).

Pforzheimer. The Library of the Carl and Lily Pforzheimer Foundation (N.Y.).

PMLA. Publications of the Modern Language Association.

Poems1816. Poems (1816).

POT. Poems Original and Translated. . . . (1808).

POVO. Poems on Various Occasions (1807).

Pratt. Byron at Southwell. Willis W. Pratt (Austin, 1948).

Princeton–Taylor. The Robert H. Taylor Collection, on deposit in the Princeton University Library.

Prophecy. The Prophecy of Dante (1821).

Reiman. The Romantics Reviewed. Contemporary Reviews of British Romantic Poets, ed. Donald H. Reiman. Part B, Byron (1972). 4 Vols.

RES. Review of English Studies.

Rutherford. Byron. A Critical Study. Andrew Rutherford (Stanford, 1961).

Sardanapalus. Sardanapalus. A Tragedy (1821).

Shelley and His Circle. Shelley and His Circle, 1773–1822, ed. K. N. Cameron, D. H. Reiman, et al. (Cambridge, Mass., 1961–   ). Vols. 1–6.

Siege. The Siege of Corinth (1816).

SiR. Studies in Romanticism.

Smiles. A Publisher and His Friends: Memoir and Correspondence of the Late John Murray. . . . Samuel Smiles (1891). 2 Vols.

SP. Studies in Philology.

Texas. The Humanities Research Center, University of Texas at Austin.

TLS. Times Literary Supplement.

Travels in Albania. Travels in Albania and Other Provinces of Turkey in 1809 and 1810. John Cam Hobhouse (new edition, 1858). 2 Vols.

Two Foscari. The Two Foscari. An Historical Tragedy (1821).

V and A. The Victoria and Albert Museum.

Vathek. The History of the Caliph Vathek. William Beckford (1786).

V of J. The Vision of Judgment (1822).

Werner. Werner; or, The Inheritance. A Tragedy (1822).

Wilmsen. Ossians Einfluss auf Byrons Jugendgedichte. Friedrich Wilmsen (Berlin, 1903).

Wise. Thomas J. Wise, *A Bibliography of the Writings in Verse and Prose of . . . Byron* . . . (1933). 2 Vols.

Yale. The Beinecke Library, Yale University.

EDITORIAL INTRODUCTION

Byron's Poetry. The State of the Text

MOST readers of Byron's poetry today approach it, directly or indirectly, through collected editions put together almost eighty years ago. The last thorough scholarly edition was done by E. H. Coleridge (1898–1904). In many ways this great edition will never be superseded, particularly in its bibliographical material, and in its extensive glosses upon the many topical references in Byron's work. But in many other ways Coleridge's edition no longer serves the student of Byron's poetry as well as it might, so that a new scholarly edition has been called for.

The main difficulty with Coleridge's—and with all other earlier and later collected editions—is textual, and resolves itself into two aspects: (*a*) the extent of the actual corpus is a good deal larger than what comes down to us as the received canon; (*b*) a substantial number of the poems in the corpus is more or less seriously corrupt.

Over the past eighty years various scholars have printed from time to time new poems by Byron, and others have appeared in sale and library catalogues. This body of material was large enough, but since undertaking the edition I have found a good many other new poems, and have been able to remove from the corpus several spurious or forged works. As a result, this edition collects approximately eighty-six new poems or poetic fragments (forty-five of which are unpublished in whole or in part); it removes five others which have been thought to be genuine; and it distinguishes, more clearly than heretofore, a body of *Dubia*, and an updated list of forged and spurious works. In addition, a great deal of important supplementary material—for instance, new 'rejected' stanzas of *Don Juan*—has also become available, and this has been incorporated into the new edition.

But an even more important problem in previous collected editions is the state of the received text. Coleridge published for the first time a fair number of new poems, mostly from manuscript, but almost every one of these is more or less seriously misprinted (apparently from bad copies made from Byron's barely legible

MSS). In addition, most of the poems published after Byron's death are textually corrupt. Most of these corruptions stem from the first comprehensive collected English edition, published in 1832–3 by Moore and Wright. Very few of these errors were corrected by later editors of the collected works, not even by Coleridge. Furthermore, uncorrected errors persist in poems published during Byron's lifetime. Finally, not even poems edited recently by skilled and careful modern scholars are completely dependable. The great 'Variorum' edition of *Don Juan*, for example, has itself perpetuated important errors, most notably in Cantos I and XVII. A crucial matter here was that the editors of the 'Variorum' did not make use of Byron's corrected proofs for Cantos I–IV.

These proofs illustrate another important reason for re-editing the poetry. A vast amount of manuscript and proof material bearing upon the texts was not known to earlier editors, or was not used by them, or was only partly utilized. Yet this material is often of the greatest importance for Byron's text, or for elucidating the poetry, and I have tried to present this material here in its true, and fullest, significance.

The Edition. Purposes, Scope, Format

This edition of Byron's works has two primary aims: to establish a complete collection of Byron's poetical works, and to reproduce a correct text of those works. Besides these two primary purposes, the edition offers a more elaborate textual apparatus than has been available in previously collected editions of the verse. A set of commentaries has been included to provide salient information about the bibliography, texts, sources, and contexts of the poems.

Abbreviations have necessarily been used extensively, here and throughout the edition. The reader is referred to a list of these on pp. xxi–xxv.

Byron's works in this edition are printed in the chronological order of their composition, but with certain necessary modifications:

(*a*) *CHP* and *DJ*. The separate cantos of these works were written and published over the space of several years, but both poems are printed entire and are placed in the chronological sequence by the date of the publication of their initial cantos.

(*b*) The sequence of early poems known traditionally as *Hours of Idleness*. These works comprise the poems which appeared in Byron's first four volumes, and they have been printed together in an arrangement explained in the commentary to the *HI* section.

(*c*) The lyrics which comprise the first Murray edition of *Hebrew Melodies*. These lyrics are printed as a group in the order of their appearance in that edition.

Certain other factors have obliged me to deviate slightly from an absolutely strict chronological arrangement in all cases. *EBSR*, for example, is placed at the beginning of the group of 1809 poems, though it was written in 1807–8 and published in the spring of 1809. Similar minor modifications have had to be made in the placement of a number of other large works; but I have placed all the shorter poems in strict chronological sequence, so far as my knowledge of the dating allowed.

A section of *Dubia* will appear in the last volume of the edition. The section includes poems whose authenticity is, for various reasons, neither disproven, nor established beyond reasonable doubt. For further discussion of the *Dubia*, as well as forged and spurious poems, see below, pp. xlv–xlvii.

Poems which have not hitherto been included in the standard collected editions (*C*, *C1905*, *More*: see below) are marked in the Table of Contents with an asterisk. But 'The Monk of Athos' (no. 148) and '[Epistle to Mr. Murray]' (no. 321) are so marked, though the titles are to be found in one or another of these editions, because the texts in the standard editions are seriously incomplete.

The History of the Text. General Remarks

This history, and thus the textual collations which have been carried out in the present edition, treats only manuscripts and editions which are textually relevant. The concept of textual relevance (defined below) is especially important for a poet like Byron. His works have been reprinted in various countries with great frequency, but most of these editions cannot assert a claim to textual relevance. In addition, numerous contemporary manuscript copies of Byron's works were made from the early editions, and whereas these manuscripts would be of crucial importance for an author (say) like Donne, they rarely have any textual relevance for Byron's works. The existence of these manuscripts is, however, noted in the appropriate commentaries, and when they do have textual relevance they are collated.

An edition is textually relevant (*a*) if it was authorized by Byron; (*b*) if it can reasonably claim to derive from a textually relevant manuscript even though the edition was not authorized; (*c*) if it is one of the specified collected editions discussed below.

A manuscript is textually relevant (*a*) if it was written or corrected by Byron; (*b*) if it was used as copy text for any printing authorized by Byron; (*c*) if it can claim to derive directly from an (*a*) or (*b*) manuscript which we do not or may not have.

Editions which are here regarded as having textual relevance, and hence which have been automatically included in the relevant collations, are the following:

1. All separately printed poems, or uncollected volumes of particular works, which were printed in any form (periodical, private printing, published work) during Byron's lifetime and with his authorization. These works are herein generically designated the 'early editions'.

2. Certain specific texts which are relevant only for particular poems or groups of poems, and which were issued without Byron's authorization during his lifetime, or after his death. This group includes certain important piracies, all critical editions, and a number of poems printed in various books and periodicals. Certain poems printed in various of the Galignani editions, in *1837*, in *Knight and Lacey* (all discussed below), are also part of this group.

3. The following collected editions *in toto*: *1815, 1817, 1818, 1819, 1821, 1823, 1825, 1827, 1828, 1829, 1829a, 1831, 1832, 1856, C, More.*

The History of the Text. Collected Editions

In the nineteenth century, the only collected editions which can claim textual relevance *in toto* are certain editions issued by Murray. All other collected editions are based, directly or indirectly, either on one of Murray's collected editions, or on one or more of the early editions, or on some combination of both. Nor are any of these other editions critical, in the scholarly sense.

The editions *1832, 1857*, and *C*, discussed below, are prima facie relevant because each attempted a more or less complete systematic correction of the derived text. But the Murray editions before

1832 have to be considered textually relevant because of certain historical conditions between *1815* and *1831*.

Byron did not read proof for any of the collected editions issued by Murray, not even for the first of these, which was produced while he was still in London (*BLJ* IV. 167). But he did read through the first collected edition, *1815*, and specifically pointed out some (but not all) of its errors, and he did the same for the new material added in *1817* (*BLJ* IV. 305 and V. 255). We also know that Byron sent Murray, at various times, corrections for certain poems which had already been printed. Not all of these corrections were incorporated in Murray's collected editions either before, in, or after *1832*, but Murray did make efforts to follow Byron's directions (see, for example, *Smiles*, I. 387). Nevertheless, substantive changes in these collections are few, and almost invariably when a change occurs (whether as revision or as error) it is preserved in the collected editions which follow its first appearance. Consequently, in citations in the apparatus for these collected editions I normally list these changes by citing two texts only: the edition of first appearance, and *1831*. If the textual change is not uniformly preserved between these two texts, the full details are given. *1832* is always cited, as are *C* and *More*. *1857* is only cited if it differs from *1832*.

A brief description of the contents of the textually relevant collected editions follows. The fullest bibliographical treatment of this subject is in E. H. Coleridge's bibliography (*C* VII. 89–136). My citations are to the items as numbered in *C*.

1815. The first Murray collected edition, in four vols. (*C*, item III). This comprised the contents of the following previously published volumes: *CHP I–II* (10th edn.), *Giaour* (14th edn.), *Bride* (10th edn.), *Corsair* (9th edn.), *Lara* (4th edn.), *Ode to Napoleon* 10th edn.), and *Hebrew Melodies* (1st edn.).

1817. In five vols. (*C*, item VII). This contains a 2nd edn. of *1815* augmented by a fifth vol. containing: *Siege* and *Parisina* (3rd edn.), *Poems 1816* (2nd edn.), *Monody* (1st edn.).

1818. In six vols. (*C*, item IX). This contains a 2nd edn. of *1817* augmented by a sixth vol. containing: *PCOP*, *Manfred* (2nd edn.), *Lament* (6th edn.). In 1818 and 1819 a seventh and eighth vol. were added to *1818* containing *CHP III* (Wise's third issue), *CHP IV* (Wise's fifth issue), *Beppo* (5th edn.), and *Mazeppa*.

1819. In three vols. (*C*, item XII). This contains the same material as *1818* except 'A Sketch' has been added and 'It Is the Hour' (from *Hebrew Melodies*) has been removed, and the works published in the *Mazeppa* volume have not been included, presumably by an oversight.

1821. In five vols. (*C*, item XVII). The same contents as *1819* except *Mazeppa* has been replaced.

1823. In four vols. (*C*, item XX). No new material. But in 1825 a fifth and sixth vol. were printed uniform with *1823* (*C*, item XXV) which contained: *Marino Faliero* (2nd edn.), and the three plays in the *Sardanapalus* volume.

1825. In eight vols. (*C*, item XXIV). This includes all the material in *1823* as augmented by its fifth and sixth vols.

1827, 1828, 1829, and *1829a*. (*C*, items XXXIII, XXXIV, XXXVII, XXXVIII). Contents of poetry unchanged from *1825*.

1830. In four vols. (*C*, item XLI). Contents the same as *1829a*.

1831. In six vols. (*C*, item XLIII). Vols. I–IV are a second edition of *1830*. Vols. V–VI contain a large body of new material, including: juvenilia from *POT* and other early vols. of *HI, EBSR, Hints, Curse, Waltz, Age, V of J, Morgante, Werner, Deformed, H and E, Island, Blues*, and a large group of shorter poems mostly picked up from Moore's *Life*, which had appeared in 1830–1. Other poems were taken from manuscripts or proofs (like *Hints*), or from the latest editions of separately issued volumes, or from *The Liberal*.

1832. In seventeen vols. (*C*, item XLVI). This is John Wright's edition, of which vols. I–VI contain Moore's *Life* and some of Byron's prose, and vols. VII–XVII contain the poetry. This is the first of Murray's collected editions to incorporate *DJ*, as well as a great deal of other new verse. A carefully edited work which served as the basis for most later collections.

1837. A one-vol. reprint of *1832*, with a few small additions (*C*, item LI). This edition was reprinted a number of times in the nineteenth century.

1856. In six vols., published 1855–6 (*C*, item LXX).
C. In seven vols. This is E. H. Coleridge's great edition (1898–1904). It considerably augmented the corpus and attempted a systematic correction of the text, as well as adding invaluable notes,

bibliographies, and commentaries. But his base text was *1831*, which was not the best choice. Moreover, *C* is an unreliable guide to poems which he first printed from manuscript. These are almost invariably miscopied. It was reprinted twice, without changes (in 1904 and 1922).

C1905. A one-vol. reissue of *C*, with several small changes, and one new poem. Frequently reprinted.

More. In one vol. P. E. More's careful edition (1905, and frequently reprinted). His base text was *1832*, a better choice than *C*'s, and he included all the new material collected in *C*, but without correcting the errors, because More did not generally work with manuscripts. It was reprinted, with minor revisions and corrections, in 1975, edited by Robert Gleckner (*More 1975*).

Two other twentieth-century editions must be mentioned, though neither has any relevance for the text. The first is the Oxford Standard Authors (*OSA*) text (1904 and frequently reprinted), edited by Frederick Page. It is based upon *1857*, a good choice so far as it goes; but Page made no serious efforts to correct the text beyond where it stood in *1857*, and the corpus is quite incomplete as well. It was reissued in 1970, edited by John Jump, who confined himself to correcting the text of *DJ* from Steffan and Pratt's 'Variorum' edition, and restoring a passage in *Cain*.

The other edition is the Everyman, which used *1832* as its base text. This edition (3 vols., 1910) has been frequently reprinted, and was twice re-edited: in 1948 by Guy Pocock, and again in 1963 by Vivian de Sola Pinto, when a few additions were made from Coleridge's edition. But the text is still seriously incomplete, nor was the base text critically edited at any point.

These two works are paradigmatic of all twentieth-century editions of Byron printed after *C* and *More*, including the re-edited version of *More*. Many of these editions are extremely useful, for notes or related matter; none have been critically edited, however, so that they all lack textual relevance.

The other collected editions which are textually relevant, but not *in toto*, are:

1. The several collected editions printed by John Hunt in 1824 and 1825. These were printed in a size uniform with Murray's octavo editions of *1819* and *1821*, and the volumes were variously numbered to accord with the Murray editions. Hunt's volumes

collected together the works he had printed for Byron, either in book form or in *The Liberal*. Only one of these Hunt collections is noted in *C* (item XXIII, herein designated *Knight and Lacey*). At least two other arrangements can be distinguished, however (at the British Library, shelf marks 11612. 1. 1 and 11613. c. 10). These are collated where appropriate. One of the three *Knight and Lacey* volumes (a set numbered vols. v–vii) is particularly to be noted: its vol. v contains a body of material not originally published by Hunt, including *HI*, *EBSR*, *Waltz*, *Curse*, and a number of shorter pieces, not all of them genuine.

2. The various editions issued by Galignani between 1818 and 1837 (herein designated as *Paris 1818*, *Paris 1819*, etc). These collected editions were the only ones before *1832* which were authorized by Byron and which contained anything like his complete works. Byron assigned to Galignani in 1818 the exclusive authority to issue his poems outside England (*BLJ* vi. 33, and see also *Smiles*, ii. 116). Galignani's editions are textually dependent upon early editions of Byron for most of their material, and in these instances they are not textually relevant. But Galignani also printed a number of poems from various other sources, including manuscripts, and in these cases they can be textually important.

The Present Text

Wherever possible, the present text returns to early editions of Byron for copy text. Many of Byron's poems were published in multiple editions during his lifetime, however; determining which of these editions will serve as copy text for a particular work has to be made on a poem by poem basis, and the relevant circumstances are explained in the commentaries. Nevertheless, certain general principles govern the choices of the present edition.

In the case of poems printed with Byron's authorization before he left England in 1816, I have tended to prefer a later rather than an earlier edition of the poems. I have done so because the evidence shows that Byron continued to correct proof for later editions of early poems like *CHP I–II*, *Giaour*, *Bride*, and *Corsair*. Extant proofs, plus standard collations and Byron's letters, all show that he altered and corrected continuously as these poems went through their early editions. I have tried to take as copy text the latest edition of these works which it can be shown, or reasonably deduced, Byron himself corrected.

After Byron left England in 1816 he was much less closely involved in the actual printing of his poems. I have therefore tended to prefer as copy text the early (normally, the first) editions of these poems. In any case, Byron's poems from 1816 onwards go through far fewer early editions. Where no such early printings are available, however, the copy text will be determined as follows:

1. *Life*, *1831*, *1832*, *1837*, *C*, and *C1905* are copy text for poems which first appeared in any of these works. Normally, the text of earliest appearance is copy text.

2. For poems which first appear in a printed source other than the early editions or the texts of group 1, the copy text will normally be the first printed text, though I have sometimes preferred the first text from group 1, or a manuscript. In any case, reasons for choice of copy text here will be clear from the data supplied in the commentaries.

3. For poems which exist only in manuscript form, the copy text is the manuscript of highest authority (see discussion below in 'Alterations in the Text').

These procedures have led me to alter the received texts of a large number of poems. All such alterations are discussed in the appropriate commentaries, but in two cases the alterations are perhaps sufficiently unusual to call for some notice here. The last three stanzas of the *Ode to Napoleon* are here printed as 'Additional Stanzas' rather than as part of the poem itself. This alteration carries out Byron's own explicit directions, and brings the poem into conformity with the early editions. The other instance is *Siege*, specifically the forty-five lines which have been printed as the opening passage in *1832* and all subsequent editions, including Kölbing's critical edition. Once again I have returned to the text as printed in the early editions, and to Byron's own executed intentions towards the text of the poem. The opening lines are here printed immediately after *Siege* as 'Lines Associated with *The Siege of Corinth*'.

Alterations in the Text

Substantive changes are introduced into the copy text on the basis of collations with manuscripts, proofs, or editions. When the copy text differs from another collated text, the copy text will be altered only when the other text has a manifestly higher authority.

For poems printed with Byron's authorization, the authority of the copy text is overridden in the following cases:

(*a*) when Byron can be shown to have specifically called for revisions after the establishment of the copy text (for example, in corrected copies of the copy text, in later texts, or in letters);

(*b*) when it can be shown that the present copy text has not faithfully reproduced what Byron wanted to be printed, or has not faithfully reproduced the text which was its printer's copy.

For poems published without Byron's authorization in his lifetime, or published after his death, or for poems which exist only in manuscript, the preferred substantive reading is that which can be determined by collation and other data to represent Byron's latest intent.

Punctuation and Other Accidentals

The opinion is still widespread that (in the words of P. E. More) Byron 'was perfectly reckless about [punctuation and other accidental] matters, and printed' texts represent the taste of Murray's advisers rather than that of the poet' (*More*, v). This judgement is seriously misleading and should not be allowed further currency.

It is true that Byron had no clear *principles* of punctuation and that he increasingly looked for help with them to friends like R. C. Dallas, Francis Hodgson, or, finally, to the house editors of his publisher, most notably to William Gifford. Thus, in matters of accidentals the manuscripts carry small authority, at least in most cases. Byron's characteristic method of publication was to submit a manuscript which was only irregularly or tentatively punctuated, to await the establishment of an accidental system (by Gifford, for example) in the course of printing, and then to make changes in the proofs or revises, often with the help of others.

None the less, the people who helped Byron to establish the punctuation and accidentals of his early editions were chosen by Byron himself. Moreover, although he said that he was ignorant of how to point his poems, he never said he did not care about these matters, and often complained to Murray about punctuation mistakes in his printed texts. That he should have sought help in pointing his poems from people he considered reliable (like Dallas) or expert (like Hodgson and Gifford) only testifies to his interest. Moreover, the many extant proofs show quite clearly that he cared a great deal about accurate punctuation and that he corrected punctuation in proof after proof.

For punctuation and other accidentals, then, the copy text is adhered to unless it is clearly inadequate to carry the sense of the verse. I have tried to preserve the accidental systems of Byron's choice and period rather than to modernize. Later editions, like *1857*, *C*, and *More*, have re-punctuated their base texts, *1837*, *1831*, and *1832*, sometimes frequently. But I have been guided by such changes only when the early editions, *1831*, or *1832*, do not offer good punctuation. I have supplied my own punctuation only in texts based on manuscripts or (very rarely) in cases where bad punctuation, or a plain mistake, remains current in the collated texts.

Special notice must be made of the poems published in volumes between 1809 and 1815. Most of these books went through numerous editions, and punctuation changes are frequent, even wholesale. In these cases, I have invariably chosen copy texts whose punctuation Byron saw, and had an opportunity to correct, in proof. In certain instances he saw and corrected in proof texts of these poems with radically different—and equally adequate—punctuation systems. As noticed earlier, my tendency has been to choose the latest of these texts.

Normalizing

Only a minimum of normalizing has seemed necessary. Spelling mistakes are corrected, but I have retained Byron's old spellings (like *chace* and *vilain*) as well as his inconsistent usage (like *grey* and *gray*). I have modernized the obsolete possessive forms *their's*, *it's*, etc., which in fact Byron's own texts tend increasingly to do after 1813. The use of quotation marks is emended according to modern style. During the course of printing *Bride*, Byron told Murray that the form *e'en* should be printed *ev'n* or *even* (*BLJ* III. 162) and I have followed this direction. In his manuscripts Byron made free use of the ampersand, but I have used *and* instead, which was the printed form he always used. Other alterations made without comment include: correction of reversed, dropped, and wrong-fount characters, and regularization of accidental irregularities in the printed form, for example, incorrect positioning of lines, or mistakes in line or stanza numbering. Ligatures (e.g. 'Phœbus') often appear in Byron's original texts, whereas modern usage normally separates the letters. The present edition has removed all such ligatures in order to conform to modern practice.

The editor has not normalized past participial forms like *unblest* and *stept*, not only because the early editions tend to keep them, but because their metrical value is clearly not the same as their more common modern forms, which Byron also uses. Byron's manuscripts show that he was able to distinguish the two forms during composition.

Special notice has to be taken of the so-called 'superfluous apostrophe', that is, the apostrophe in the unaccented past participial form ending in *ed*: *murmured* and *murmur'd*, *raped* and *rap'd*. Since *C*, the tendency has been to normalize these forms by removing the apostrophes. The present editor has returned to the earlier practice of preserving the distinction between the two forms.

The history of these apostrophized forms is long and complicated, and though they were beginning to fall into disuse in the early part of the nineteenth century, they persisted in the work of important writers until the modern period. Early nineteenth-century printer's manuals explicitly state that such forms, 'common only in poetical works . . . are under the arbitration of the author, who best knows where such contractions serve his purpose' (Johnson, *Typographia* (1824), II. 64).

T. G. Steffan, in editing *Cain* (Austin, 1968), pointed out that at least one formal rule governed the use of such apostrophes: verbs ending in a silent *e* in the present tense (like *gape* and *entwine*) tend to forbid the apostrophe. The reason for the prohibition quite clearly bears upon verse music, for to elide the *e* in the past participle of such verbs would be to suggest a change in the musical value of the vowel which precedes it, specifically, to shorten the vowel. By the same token, not all verbs are apostrophized whose present tenses lack the silent *e*: in Byron one finds both *reared* and *rear'd*, even in close proximity (see *CHP* IV, sts. 143 and 152). The decision to elide verbs without the silent *e* seems to have been, in other words, an *ad hoc* one.

Byron's manuscripts, however, do not mirror his earliest printed texts in the use or non-use of this form. Apostrophized forms can be found everywhere, but they are much less frequent than in the printed texts, and one judges that, in the matter of these accidentals, as in other matters, Byron was not especially competent. Consequently, though it may be shown that the superfluous apostrophe is, theoretically at least, a relevant tonal, even specifically musical, notation in verse, and that it was still recognized as such in Byron's day, the form may yet be irrelevant to Byron's verse.

The question is, was Byron indifferent to the superfluous apostrophe? Certain evidence does suggest that he was. His manuscripts, for example, are noticeably lacking in apostrophized forms, while his corrected copy of *FP* shows that he did not even bother to correct the elided forms of silent *e* verbs in that volume.

But this evidence must be weighed against certain other facts. In the first place, Byron's manuscripts, even his fair copies, were rarely taken as standards for accidentals either by himself or his publishers. In the second place, Byron's first four volumes (including *FP*) represent an exceptional event in his publishing career precisely because he was then dealing with a publisher, Samuel Ridge, whose lack of principles in the matter of accidentals was at least equal to Byron's own. Furthermore, the friends who helped Byron with these books were all amateurs like himself (John and Elizabeth Pigot, J. T. Becher). The publication of Byron's next book, *EBSR*, with James Cawthorne, was supervised by R. C. Dallas, who helped him with the accidental systems. Byron was grateful for this assistance, and the texts of *EBSR* do indeed show the presence of a principled editorial conscience. When Byron began publishing with John Murray he continued to benefit by the editorial help not only of friends like Dallas and Hodgson, but, even more crucially, of Murray's chief editor, William Gifford. The proofs for *Waltz*, *CHP*, *Ode to Napoleon*, *Giaour*, *Corsair*, and 'Fare Thee Well!' all show that great care was taken with accidentals, including the 'superfluous' apostrophes. Manuscript corrections in such forms are widespread in these proofs. One proof of 'Fare Thee Well!' carries a note by Byron requesting that Gifford be asked to edit the punctuation. In certain cases, separate proofs were sent to both Byron and Gifford.

Such editorial assistance, which Byron specifically sought, forbids us to think him indifferent about accidentals in general or superfluous apostrophes in particular. Byron knew his own laziness and incompetence, and he recognized that Gifford, foremost among several others, could supply his deficiencies. Thus, the case for retaining the superfluous apostrophes is essentially the same case for retaining the accidental systems as they were originally printed. The former is merely one aspect of the latter, and the evidence of the proofs shows clearly that no aspect of punctuation was a matter of indifference.

Finally, line numbers are editorially supplied, and any material in square brackets in text, apparatus, or Byron's notes has been added by the editor. The reader should also know that although most of Byron's poems originally used Roman numbers for separate stanzas, all stanza numbers in this text have been printed in arabic. This procedure has been adopted to avoid various ambiguities in the reference system used in the notes to the text.

Apparatus

Three general classes of variants may be appropriate to the textual apparatus: (*a*) variants in accidentals from manuscripts, proofs, or editions; (*b*) substantive variants from manuscripts, proofs, or editions; (*c*) cancellations or revisions in manuscripts or proofs. A complete record of these three classes of variants has seemed neither possible nor desirable for this edition.

Class (*a*) variants have been included only when they represent possible alternatives which radically affect the meaning of the verse.

All class (*b*) variants have been recorded with one exception: substantive variants which are clearly traceable to printing mistakes or editorial misjudgements. But variants of this sort have been recorded when their editorial history is such that they have acquired the status of a correct reading in normative editions like *1832*, *C*, and *More*.

All class (*c*) variants are recorded. The only exception is in the case of Byron's notes printed with the poems. Here I have not recorded a variety of distinctly minor variants. These include indifferent readings, like transposed terms and such minor verbal changes as *hath* and *has*, *you* and *ye*, *thine* and *thy*, *but* and *and*, *on* and *upon*, *for* and *since*, and the like. The apparatus for each poem is headed by a record of the collated texts. This record does not specify the textually relevant collected editions, but they are automatically included in all collations where they apply. In the apparatus itself, the traditional format has been used: line number, lemma, square bracket, variant, and the siglum or sigla. In the descriptions, if no variant is shown for any of the collated texts, this means the text conforms to the reading of the present edition. Angle brackets enclose material cancelled in the indicated text. In many cases cancellations within cancelled passages are indicated by angle brackets and the entire passage is then marked *cancelled*. A solidus (/) is used for several related purposes: (*a*) it separates uncancelled alternate readings; (*b*) it separates, in a cancelled passage, earlier and later cancelled material; (*c*) it separates a cancelled passage from a later uncancelled passage which was put in place of the cancellation. *Var.* means *variant* and *cor.* means *corrected by Byron in manuscript*. A centred question mark indicates an indecipherable word or words; a question mark attached to a word (e.g. blood?) indicates a doubtful reading. Ellipsis indicates the editorial omission of various sorts of obvious material.

These descriptive procedures have been chosen to give the greatest amount of information in the briefest form consistent with reasonable clarity. They do not, however, attempt to describe the physical manner in which changes were made on manuscripts—for instance, whether they are interlinear insertions, or marginal, or written above or below the line, etc. The descriptions, in other words, differ somewhat from those presented in critical editions like Ashton's of *HM* and Steffan and Pratt's of *DJ*. The aim here is to give an economical summary of the substance of the manuscript changes, and as clear a record as possible of the order in which they occurred. To have attempted a less abstract, more pictorial record would have swelled the apparatus beyond reasonable limits.

I offer several examples to illustrate the procedure. They are taken from Canto I of *Corsair*.

25 will] may *ML, cor. in M*
This means that 'will' in line 25 reads 'may' in *MS. ML* and that the variant was corrected to the received reading in the *M* text. It also means that all other collated texts conform to the received reading.

37 ⟨The future⟩ *ML*
This means a false start cancelled in *ML*.

298 sullen] ⟨fretful⟩ *ML*   ne'er] near *Proof 8–C, More*

This means that 'sullen' originally read 'fretful' in *ML* but was corrected in *ML* to the received reading; and that 'ne'er' reads 'near' in all texts from Proof 8 to the texts of *C* and *More*. But in all texts previous to Proof 8 the word is 'ne'er'. (The succession of the texts is established in the commentaries.)

317 And if my ⟨steel⟩ / ⟨purposed⟩ plan ⟨but hold tonight⟩ / hold firm and Fortune smile *ML*

This means that in *ML* Byron originally began line 317 'And if my steel', that he then cancelled 'steel' and continued the line with 'purposed plan', that he then cancelled 'purposed' and continued the line with 'but hold tonight', and that he finally cancelled the latter phrase and finished the line as indicated.

374 murmuring . . . ruder] ⟨fluttering . . . tempest⟩ *ML*

This means that the single words 'murmuring' and 'ruder' originally read 'fluttering' and 'tempest' in *ML*, but were there corrected to the received text.

375 it . . . prophetic] ⟨and low it seemed the rising⟩ *ML*

This means that the passage from 'it' to 'prophetic' originally read as the material in the angle brackets in *ML*, but was corrected there to the received reading.

Finally, an example from 'The Harp the Monarch Minstrel Swept'.

10 Till . . . grew] ⟨When Jesse's son⟩ And David's lyre was *A, B*

This means that in text *A* Byron began with a false start (the material in angle brackets), but then wrote 'And David's lyre was' for the received text's 'Till . . . grew'. It also means that text *B* follows the uncancelled reading of text *A*, but *only* the uncancelled reading. I have adopted this notation in order to avoid excessive repetition in the apparatus.

Commentaries

The commentaries on individual works contain a general note on the extant manuscripts, the facts in the poem's publishing history which establish the lines of its transmission, information about the poem's date, and, where necessary, evidence of authenticity. In the case of certain poems, like *Giaour*, the history of composition and early publication is of paramount importance and interest, and detailed commentary is provided. Commentary on bibliography and manuscripts is by no means exhaustive, but the current deficiencies in this kind of basic information about Byron's poems are so great that the editor has tried to give at least the minimum of accurate information on such matters. It should be noted that when manuscripts are referred to, or corrected proofs, the manuscripts and corrections are presumed to be in Byron's holograph unless specifically indicated otherwise.

The commentaries also deal briefly with sources and influences, both formal and substantive, as well as any biographical or historical information which bears upon the poem. The commentaries do not normally offer any literary criticism, though citations of relevant critical works are sometimes made when interpretation is especially problematical.

The new material set forth in these commentaries represents a considerable advance upon what is available in earlier collected editions. In many cases this material should alter, sometimes drastically alter, our sense of the content and context of certain poems. For example, the political dimensions—they almost amount to allegories—which lie hidden in Byron's tales of 1812–15 have not heretofore been sufficiently emphasized, I think. It is hoped that, in this respect, the commentaries on these poems will be of some interest to readers of Byron. *The Curse of Minerva* is another interesting case. This poem was not written—as we have always believed—before Byron returned to England in 1811. It was largely written after he returned, in November 1811, and that fact necessarily changes the context and meaning of the satire in various ways.

Notes

Both Byron's and the editor's notes for each poem follow the individual commentaries. Byron's notes are indicated by [B], added after the note; and in these cases the editorial note is placed after Byron's. Like previous editors—and, in particular, E. H. Coleridge —I have been forced to depart from this procedure in two cases: Cantos I–II, and Canto IV, of *CHP*. The author's notes for these (separately published) works are so extensive and complex that, in the interests of clarity, I have decided to place them immediately after the texts of the poems themselves. The editor's notes, as well as Byron's own brief glosses and notes to his notes, are placed—

as normally—after the commentary. Though this procedure is cumbersome in certain ways, and regrettable for that reason, the alternative formats proved to be much worse, because of the confusions they tended to create. My own notes supply certain information that seems necessary to elucidate passages whose meaning might be obscure because of unfamiliar references contained in them. Some readers will doubtless find various notes egregious— identifications of 'Thalia', or 'Tully', or 'the Seven Islands', for example. If the notes for these sorts of references offend, I hope it will be on the road to excess rather than otherwise. The glosses for particular words, on the other hand, have been more restricted. I have glossed only words and phrases that are not available in a good standard desk dictionary. Textual problems are always discussed, either in the notes, or in the commentary, or both. I have tried to identify all of Byron's explicit literary allusions and echoes, and as many of his less explicit ones as I have recognized. Byron is an extraordinarily allusive poet, however, with a literary memory few people (or poets) could hope to match. Though I have shamelessly plundered the work of earlier editors and scholars in this area particularly, I am well aware of the deficiencies that remain.

The explanatory notes do not always indicate when information has been taken from other editors and commentators, yet I have borrowed freely from the vast literature of older and more recent Byron studies in preparing the notes. The careful work of editors like Thomas Ashton, E. H. Coleridge, S. C. Chew, James Darmesteter, Eugen Kölbing, Willis W. Pratt, and T. G. Steffan has been particularly helpful. But I do cite Coleridge and other editors under certain circumstances: when the only source for the note known to me is the cited authority; when the information supplied in the note seems to me speculative rather than definitive.

Two special scholarly resources ought to be mentioned. Readers who wish further information about the early reviews of particular poems and volumes of poems should consult *Reiman* (see Short Title citation). An extremely useful bibliography of secondary materials about Byron, along with a fine essay on the history of Byron scholarship in English, is available in *George Gordon, Lord Byron: A comprehensive bibliography of secondary materials in English, 1807–1974*, by Oscar José Santucho, with A Critical Review of Research by Clement Tyson Goode, Jr. (Scarecrow Press, Metuchen, N.J., 1977).

Dubia

At the end of the edition is included a *Dubia* section of poems. This contains only poems which have some reasonable claim to authenticity, but which cannot be proved to be genuine. Each of these poems has its own separate commentary. The most comprehensive treatment of forged and spurious poems attributed to Byron is by Samuel C. Chew, 'The Byron Apocrypha', in *Byron in England* (1924). I list below only apocryphal poems which are not already treated by Chew.

1. 'Answer to ——'s Professions of Affection' ('In hearts like thine ne'er may I hold a place'). MS: fair copy in Lady Byron's hand (location: *BM*). Published as genuine in *C*, *C1905*, *More*. The poem is by Lady Byron *about* Byron; date, 1816.
2. *The Black Velvet Breeches* [Translated from Casti]. Three stanzas of a translation of Casti's Novella XIV published in Thomas Roscoe's edn. of J. C. L. Simonde de Sismondi's *Historical View of the Literature of the South of Europe*, 2nd edn. (1846), II. 79 n. The extract is said to be 'from an unpublished manuscript in the possession of the publisher' and 'believed to be by Byron'.
3. *Childe Harold*, a 'lost' stanza. Printed by Thomas Medwin in *The Angler in Wales* (1834).
4. 'A Danish Tale.' First published in *Morning Chronicle*, anonymously, 26 March 1808. It is tentatively attributed to Byron, on weak grounds, by Burton R. Pollin, *BNYPL* 73 (1969), 215–17.
5. 'An Edinburgh Eclogue' and 'A Meeting Sadder Than a Parting. To ——.' Two forgeries purporting to date *c.* 1808; MS. owned by John S. Mayfield.
6. 'An Epistle to Tom Moore.' A DeGibler forgery copied into the edition of Thomas Moore's *Odes of Anacreon* (1815). Location: Murray.
7. 'A Fight.' Forgery reproduced in facsimile by Paul Emile Schazmann, 'Un poème inédit de Byron', *Revue de France* (1 Dec. 1938), 427–30.
8. 'Fragments of an Unfinished Poem' (in 73 *ottava rima* stanzas); 'An Epitaph'; 'Life'. These three pieces were printed in at least two mid-nineteenth-century editions of Byron's works, one with the imprint of Milner and Sowerby (1865) and the other of Charles Daly (n.d.).
9. 'From thee such strains they breathe of woe.' MS. at Texas, possibly in Augusta Leigh's hand; but there is no reason to think the poem Byron's, though the Texas catalogue lists it as possibly by him.
10. 'If thy life's path is a dreary and rugged road.' MS. at Yale, a forgery purporting to date *c.* 1812.
11. 'In the hour when the weary spirit sinks.' Published in the *Metropolitan*,

10 (Aug. 1834), 353–4 as possibly by Byron; but it is by Benjamin
Disraeli (see *N & Q*, Sept. 1975, 392–3).

12. 'John Bull the other day in pensive mood.' MS. in unknown hand
(location: Marlay papers, University of Nottingham library). The copyist attributes it to Byron but the poem's circumstances make the attribution impossible.

13. 'Jove heard anxious mortals sigh.' A DeGibler forgery written in a copy
of *Anacreontis Teii Carmina Graece* . . . (1776), dated 1808 (location:
Murray).

14. 'The King of the Humbugs.' Published in facsimile and printed in *Good
Words* (Aug.–Sept. 1904), where it is firmly attributed to Byron and
dated July–Aug. 1821. It is a forgery. It was first published in *The Bookman* (Sept. 1903), 71–8, but with a facsimile of two stanzas only.

15. 'Literal Version of a Late Literal Effusion' ('Why by Jove my dear Murray'). Published once, by C. L. Cline (*TLS*, 7 Feb. 1942, p. 67) from a
MS. in an unknown hand found among the papers of Benjamin Disraeli,
at Hughenden Manor. More particularly, it was included among some
MS. notes on Romantic poets written by Isaac Disraeli. The poem is a
parody of Byron's '[Epistle to Mr. Murray]' (no. 322), and is certainly
not by Byron. It may well have been written by one of Murray's circle of
wits.

16. 'The Night of the Neckar' and 'The Persian Evening'. Two MSS. (location: Leeds) that are obvious forgeries (the paper is watermarked 1825).

17. 'The Poet's lyre, to fix his fame.' E. Pigot's MS. of these lines is on the
end flyleaf of her copy of *POVO*. They were published as Byron's and
said to be in his hand, in H. C. Roe's *The Rare Quarto Edition of Lord
Byron's 'Fugitive Pieces'* (1919), 27. The poem is an excerpt from William
Cowper's 'To the Rev. W. Cawthorne Unwin'.

18. 'Sonnet on Punch.' Seen only in an undated newspaper clipping in a
collection of newspaper materials dealing with Byron (location: *BM*).

19. 'This thieving love in great men is ambition.' Several stanzas in *ottava
rima* (MS. location: Gennadius Library), a DeGibler forgery. Published as
genuine in *The Griffon* (Summer 1970), 17–19, with a facsimile.

20. 'To Mary Chaworth' ('Ah Memory! torture me no more'). First printed
as Byron's in *Life*, I. 57, collected in *1831*, *C1905*, *More*. Byron's autograph MS. is at Newstead, but it is a copy of a poem written and published by Lady Tuite.

21. 'To Mr. Phillips the Bookseller.' The MS. is a DeGibler forgery
(location: Texas) written into vol. 4 of *The Works of Peter Pindar Esq.*
(1809), dated 1811.

22. 'Translation from Petrarch's *Africa*.' Mary Shelley's MS. copy, with
a few corrections by Byron or Thomas Medwin. Published in Ugo Fos-
colo's *Essays on Petrarch* (1823), 215–17, as Byron's; the translation is by
Medwin.

23. 'A Version of Ossian's Address to the Sun in "Carthon".' Collected in *C*, *C1905*, *More* from a previously published MS. that is, however, a De-Gibler forgery (location: Harvard).
24. 'What though beneath thee man put forth.' MS. in unknown hand (location: Leeds). Catalogued as possibly by Byron but there is no attribution on the MS. and no good reason to think it his.
25. 'When first I met thee warm and young.' Lady Melbourne's MS. copy in a letter to the Duchess of Devonshire (31 Jan. 1815). Attributed to Byron on the MS. by an unknown hand; the poem is by Thomas Moore (see B. H. Blackwell Catalogue 1022 (1975), p. 50).
26. 'Who killed Kildare' and 'Come fetch me a pint of wine'. MS. in unknown hand (location: Texas). Catalogued as possibly by Byron but on weak authority.
27. 'Woman and the Moon' and 'Unpublished Epistle from Lord Byron to John Murray' ('A Turkish Tale I shall unfold'). Published as Byron's by DeGibler in the *Albion*, 47 (20 and 27 March 1869). 141, 170. De-Gibler's MSS. are not forthcoming. For comment see T. G. Ehrsam, *Major Byron* (1951), 108–9.
28. 'Words to "God Save the King"' and 'Lines Upon Sir H[udson] Lowe in return for his *services* at St. Helena being admitted a Knight of the Bath'. Both of these poems are catalogued as 'Unidentified Manuscripts' in the Byron holdings at the Berg. Neither is in Byron's hand, and there seems no good reason to think he wrote them. The MSS. carry no attributions to Byron.

Finally, special notice must be made of a massive collection of Byron forgeries now in the possession of Dr. Francesco Attanasio, of Lugano, Switzerland. These forgeries were all made by one person (or perhaps two people in concert). They were made after 1831, and probably belong to the period 1832–40. The collection has hundreds of manuscript pages, with forgeries of both known and unknown poems. The forger was almost certainly an Englishman, and the collection contains letters (which may themselves be faked) bearing the names of John Raymond and J. Treseler. The collection descended to Dr. Attanasio through his uncle, but there is no further information about its provenance.

1   [Epigram on an Old Lady Who Had Some
      Curious Notions Respecting the Soul]

In Nottingham county there lives at Swine Green,
As curst an old lady as ever was seen;
And when she does die, which I hope will be soon,
She firmly believes she will go to the moon.

                         [1798]

2   [Then Peace to thy Spirit]

Then peace to thy spirit, my earliest Friend,
Beloved in thy life, and deplored in thine end;
Yet happy art thou to escape from the woe
Which awaits the survivors of friendship below.

I should not lament thee because thou art free   5
From the pangs that assail human nature and me;
Yet still I deplore thee in whom I have lost
The companion of childhood I valued the most.

Oh, if there is heaven thou surely art blest,
If death is eternal, at least then at rest.   10
Then away with the tears which we fruitlessly shed—
Let us mourne for the *living*, not weep for the dead.

Yet to think of the days we together have seen,
Of what thou now art, and of what we have been.

                         [1803?]

1. Copy text: *Life*
title   *untitled in Life*
  1 Swine] Swan *Life*, *C*

2. Copy text: *MS.*
title   *untitled in MS.*
  1 ⟨Oh⟩ Then *MS.*

3   # To My Dear Mary Anne

1.

Adieu to sweet Mary for ever,
   From her I must quickly depart;
Though the fates us from each other sever,
   Still her image will dwell in my Heart.

2.

The flame that within my breast burns,   5
   Is unlike what in Lovers' hearts glows;
The Love which for Mary I feel
   Is far purer than Cupid bestows.

3.

I wish not your peace to disturb,
   I wish not your joy to molest;   10
Mistake not my passion for Love,
   'Tis your friendship alone I request.

4.

Not ten thousand Lovers could feel
   The friendship my bosom contains;
It will ever within my Heart dwell,   15
   While the warm blood flows through my veins.

5.

May the Ruler of Heaven look down,
   And my Mary from evil defend;
May she ne'er know Adversity's frown,
   May her Happiness ne'er have an end.   20

6.

Once more my sweet Girl, Adieu!
   Farewell, I with anguish repeat,
For ever I'll think upon you,
   While the Heart in my bosom shall beat.

[1804]

3. Copy text: *C1905*, collated with *MSS. M, N; Paris1831*
title   *untitled in M*

4 will] shall *Paris1831*   5 breast] heart *C1905*   7 which] that *M*   10 joy]
joys *M*   12 alone *not in M*   21 Girl] Mary *Paris*1831   24 the] this *M*

4   [To Mary Chaworth. Fragment]

Since the feuds of our fathers descend on their race
And the children must part—till the parents embrace,
Though the tie that commands has dissevered our fate,
Oh! let not our bosoms inherit their hate.—

[1804]

5   [Fragment]

Whose influence mild and Globe of silver die
Performs a monthly circuit through the sky,
Or when he views the splendid orb of day
The wild enthusiast trembles at his ray.

[1804]

6   Fragment
Written Shortly After the Marriage of Miss Chaworth

Hills of Annesley, bleak and barren,
    Where my thoughtless childhood stray'd,
How the northern tempests, warring,
    Howl above thy tufted shade!

Now no more, the hours beguiling,   5
    Former favourite haunts I see;
Now no more my Mary smiling
    Makes ye seem a Heaven to me.

[1805]

4. Copy text: *MS. N*
    2 the children] ⟨command us⟩ *N*   3 Though] ⟨Let⟩   has dissevered] ⟨may decide on⟩
N   4 bosoms] ⟨hearts⟩ *N*

5. Copy text: *MS. M*
    1 Whose ⟨ ? form and shimmering sense⟩ *M*   3 Or ⟨that⟩ *M*   4 Thence? away
fragmentary line after 4

6. Copy text: *Life*, collated with *MS. G*
title *untitled in Life* Fragment; *1831*

7   [Extemporaneous Couplet]

> Bold Robert Speer was Bony's bad precursor,
> Bob was a bloody dog, but Bonapart's a worser.

[1805?]

8   [Ossian's Address to the Sun in 'Carthon']

> OH! thou that roll'st above thy glorious Fire,
> Round as the shield which grac'd my godlike Sire,
> Whence are the beams, O Sun! thy endless blaze,
> Which far eclipse each minor Glory's rays?
> Forth in thy Beauty here thou deign'st to shine!   5
> Night quits her car, the twinkling stars decline;
> Pallid and cold the Moon descends to lave
> Her sinking beams beneath the Western wave;
> But thou still mov'st alone, of light the Source—
> Who can o'ertake thee in thy fiery course?   10
> Oaks of the mountains fall, the rocks decay,
> Weighed down with years the hills dissolve away.
> A certain space to yonder Moon is given,
> She rises, smiles, and then is lost in Heaven.
> Ocean in sullen murmurs ebbs and flows,   15
> But thy bright beam unchanged for ever glows!
> When Earth is darkened with tempestuous skies,
> When Thunder shakes the sphere and Lightning flies,
> Thy face, O Sun, no rolling blasts deform,
> Thou look'st from clouds and laughest at the Storm.   20
> To Ossian, Orb of Light! thou look'st in vain,
> Ne'er cans't thou glad his agèd eyes again,
> Whether thy locks in Orient Beauty stream,
> Or glimmer through the West with fainter gleam—
> But thou, perhaps, like me with age must bend;   25

7. Copy text: *Dyce*

8. Copy text: *C* collated with *MS. T* and *Pratt*
   3 blaze] ⟨light⟩ *T*   6 quits] ⟨flies⟩ *T*   10 ⟨Now⟩ Who *T*   12 ⟨With years the Hills the ℈ must pass⟩ *T*   18 shakes] ⟨rolls⟩ *T*   22 Ne'er] Nor *C, More*
   23 stream] ⟨beam⟩ *T*

Thy season o'er, thy days will find their end,
No more yon azure vault with rays adorn,
Lull'd in the clouds, nor hear the voice of Morn.
Exult, O Sun, in all thy youthful strength!
Age, dark unlovely Age, appears at length,   30
As gleams the moonbeam through the broken cloud
While mountain vapours spread their misty shroud—
The Northern tempest howls along at last,
And wayworn strangers shrink amid the blast.
Thou rolling Sun who gild'st those rising towers,   35
Fair didst thou shine upon my earlier hours!
I hail'd with smiles the cheering rays of Morn,
My breast by no tumultuous Passion torn—
Now hateful are thy beams which wake no more
The sense of joy which thrill'd my breast before;   40
Welcome thou cloudy veil of nightly skies,
To thy black canopy the mourner flies:
Once bright, thy Silence lull'd my frame to rest,
And Sleep my soul with gentle visions blest;
Now wakeful Grief disdains her mild controul,   45
Dark is the night, but darker is my Soul.
Ye warring Winds of Heav'n your fury urge,
To me congenial sounds your wintry Dirge:
Swift as your wings my happier days have past,
Keen as your storms is Sorrow's chilling blast;   50
To Tempests thus expos'd my Fate has been,
Piercing like yours, like yours, alas! unseen.

                                              [1805]

9   Remembrance

'Tis done!—I saw it in my dreams:
No more with Hope the future beams;
My days of happiness are few:

27 yon . . . with] ⟨the . . . thy⟩ T   28 ⟨Sleeping⟩ in the Clouds, ⟨and heedless of the⟩
Morn T   31 ⟨Like yonder⟩ As T   32 While ⟨misty⟩ vapours ⟨all the mountains⟩
shroud T   34 ⟨The⟩ wayworn ⟨Stranger shivers in⟩ the Blast T   42 black] bright
C, More   44 Sleep ⟨with⟩ my T   45 Grief disdains her] ⟨Misery spurns thy⟩ T
47 warring] ⟨northern⟩ T

9. Copy text: 1832, collated with MS. G

Chill'd by misfortune's wintry blast,
My dawn of life is overcast,
Love, Hope, and Joy, alike adieu!—   5
Would I could add Remembrance too!

[1806]

10   To a Lady Who Presented the Author With the
Velvet Band Which Bound her Tresses

This Band, which bound thy yellow hair,
   Is mine, sweet girl! thy pledge of love;
It claims my warmest, dearest care,
   Like Relics left of Saints above.
Oh! I will wear it next my heart;   5
   'Twill bind my soul in bonds to thee;
From me again 'twill ne'er depart,
   But mingle in the grave with me.
The dew I gather from thy lip
   Is not so dear to me as this;   10
That I but for a moment sip,
   And banquet on a transient Kiss.
This will recall each youthful scene,
   E'en when our lives are on the wane;
The leaves of Love will still be green   15
When Memory bids them bud again.

1806

11   [A Woman's Hair]

Oh! little lock of golden hue
   In gently waving ringlet curl'd,
By the dear head on which you grew,
   I would not lose you for a *world*.

10. Copy text: *1832*, collated with *MS. N*

    12 Kiss] bliss *1832, C, More*   15 green] ⟨great⟩ *N*   16 [The poem is divided into quatrains in *1832, C, More*; *1832* and *More* print two final stanzas, which are, however, a separate poem, here no. 11.]

11. Copy text: *MS. N*, collated with *MS. NP, 1832*
title   *untitled in MSS.*

Not though a thousand more adorn   5
  The polish'd brow where once you shone;
Like rays which gild a cloudless morn
  Beneath Columbia's fervid Zone.

[1806]

12   [As Relics Left of Saints Above]

1.

As relics left of saints above
  Are said to guard from danger's blow,
And those who wear them safely move
  Through fields of blood and scenes of woe,

2.

Oh then bestow one look of thine   5
  To shield me from some battle blade,
Since thou hast been the only shrine
  Where all my vows were fondly made.

3.

If faith can save in danger's hour,
  No votary ever bent the knee,   10
Who felt devotion's warmest power
  So warmly as I feel for thee.

4.

And if their faith be blind as mine,
  And mine be as sincere as theirs,
Thy look will not be less divine   15
  If thou wilt deign to hear my prayers.

7 morn] sky *NP*

12. Copy text: *MS. M*
   6 shield ⟨guard⟩ *M*   14 be . . . theirs] ⟨no less be as sincere⟩ *M*

5.

Then yield that relic to my care,
All saintly relics mount above
And prove in miracles how far
Devotion ever yields to love.   20

[1806]

13   Impromptu on Seeing a Wedding

A woman's vow is far too long
Upon the Marriage Day;
For surely when a woman loves
She'll honour and obey.

[1806?]

14   [Suitors in Love and Law]

Women, 'tis said, when once found doubting
Are ruined spite of sighs and pouting;
But men in gowns are much acuter
When they doubt, woe betide the Suitor.

[1806?]

15   [Translation from Anacreon]

Εἰς ῥόδον.

Ode 5

Mingle with the genial bowl
The Rose, the *flow'ret* of the Soul,

18 ⟨That I the best effect may⟩ *M*   19 And prove] ⟨That shows⟩ *M*   20 ever]
⟨still must⟩ *M*

13. Copy text: *MS. F*

14. Copy text: *MS. F*
    1 Women] ⟨When women⟩ *F*

15. Copy text: *C*, collated with *MS. T, Pratt*
title   *Εισ ῥόδον* Ode 5th *T*

The Rose and Grape together quaff'd,
How doubly sweet will be the draught!
With Roses crown our jovial brows,   5
While every cheek with Laughter glows;
While Smiles and Songs, with Wine unite,
To wing our moments with Delight.
Rose by far the fairest birth,
Which Spring and Nature cull from Earth—   10
Rose whose sweetest perfume given,
Recalls our thoughts from Earth to Heaven.
Rose whom the Deities above,
From Jove to Hebe, dearly love,
When Cytherea's blooming Boy,   15
Flies lightly through the dance of Joy,
With him the Graces then combine,
And rosy wreaths their locks entwine.
Then will I sing divinely crown'd,
With dusky leaves my temples bound—   20
Lyaeus! in thy bowers of pleasure,
I'll wake a wildly thrilling measure.
There will my gentle Girl and I,
Along in sportive mazes fly;
We'll bend before thy potent throne—   25
Rose, Wine, and Beauty, all my own.

                                    [1805 or 1806]

16   [Translation from Anacreon. Ode 16]

Some Bards the Theban feuds recall,
And others Ilion's hapless Fall.
I too have trod the Field of War,
But not the rapid-circling Car,
No, nor the fiery-footed Steed,   5

3–4 ⟨Then doubly dear will be the draught | As that which⟩ *T*   3 together] ⟨in union⟩ *T*
5 crown] ⟨bind⟩ *T*   7 unite] incite *C, More*   9 ⟨Hail⟩ Rose *T*   10 Spring ⟨calls forth
/ awakes⟩ *T*   11 Rose ⟨the⟩ whose *T*   12 Recalls] Breathes *C, More*   13 ⟨Whence
een the Immortals might descend⟩ *T*   14 dearly] ⟨deign to⟩ *T*   16 Flies]
⟨Treads⟩ *T*   17 ⟨The budding Loves his ? / brows entwine⟩ *T*   18 their locks]
⟨his brows⟩ *T*   20 dusky] ⟨rose⟩ *T*   24 Along in] ⟨Through the⟩ *T*   in sportive
mazes] the mazes sportive *C, More*   25 We'll] Will *C, More*

16. Copy text: *MS. Υ*
title   *Εισ εαυτον* 16. *Υ*

Nor Falchion's edge hath made me bleed;
By Streams of heavenly force I die,
The Lightning of a rolling Eye.

1806

17   [Translation from Anacreon. Ode 34]

Though age the Herald of decay,
Has silver'd o'er my Tresses Gray,
And though my Locks are wreathed with Snow,
And though thy cheeks with Roses glow,
Yet fly me not, Capricious Girl!   5
What flowers in yonder Garland Curl,
The amorous Roses gently flush,
And near the Spotless Lily blush,
While each reflects a deeper hue
Than if their Beauties singly grew;   10
Thus next my hoary Locks of Snow,
Thy cheek will wear a brighter Glow.

[1806]

18   [Translation from Anacreon. Ode 47]

I love the old, the Jovial Sage,
Whose Soul expands unchilled by Age,
I love the lightly-bounding Boy,
Whose hours the dance and loves employ,

17. Copy text: *MS. T*, collated with *Pratt*
title   Εισ κορην Ode 34. *T*
   1 Though age ⟨has silenced oer⟩ the *T*
3–4   And though the roses heavenly blush
                         ⟨And though thy cheeks⟩ Thy youthful Cheeks with
                                         Beauty flush *cancelled T*
6 flowers] ⟨hues in⟩ *T*   7 The ⟨Lily⟩ amorous *T*   8 And near] ⟨Around⟩ *T*   9 ⟨Thus
next my locks of Snow / Thy locks will wear a brighter Glow⟩ *T*   deeper] ⟨fairer⟩ *T*
10 Beauties] ⟨Flowrets⟩ *T*

18. Copy text: *MS. T*, collated with *Pratt*
title   Αλλο ωδαριον Ode 47. *T*
   2 Whose ⟨fire is⟩ Soul *T*   3 the ⟨young⟩ lightly *T*   4 Whose ⟨hours are spent
in Dance, and Joy⟩ *T*

And when the Senior dances too   5
His very youth appears anew;
Age his many Locks may Sever,
But his heart will bloom forever.

[1806]

19   Epitaph on Mrs. [Byron]

Prone to take Fire, yet not of melting Stuff,
Here lies what once was woman—that's enough.
Such were her vocal powers, her temper such,
That all who knew them both exclaimed 'too much!'
Till tired with clamours worse than Ocean's roar,   5
Death kindly stept between and cried 'no more.'

[1806 or 1807]

20   Impromptu

Reply to Some Very Elegant Stanzas From a Lady
on 'Friendship'

Your Motto is L'Amitie,
At least, Eliza, so you say;
But should the Equinoctial Gales
Impel to Europe Indian Sails,
And should the happy Bark contain   5
Your absent Hall, that faithful Swain,
I think 'twould not be long before,
You changed that Motto, to L'Amour.—

[1806]

5 And] ⟨But⟩ T   6 ⟨Appears / His Youth must seem ? new⟩ T   8 But his heart]
⟨His heart his heart⟩ T

19. Copy text: MS. NP

20. Copy text: MS. NP
title ... Elegant ⟨lines⟩ Stanzas ... NP
   6 absent] ⟨much-loved⟩ NP

21   To These Fox Hunters in a Long Frost

Of unlearned men Lord Falkland did say
'I pity em much on a long rainy day.'
Ye Fox-hunters too are quite as much lost
When winter the ground has clothed in frost.

[1806–7]

22   To Miss H[ouson] An ancient Virgin who
tormented the Author to write something on her
sweet self

1.

You ask me so oft, and so warmly to write,
That I willingly would I declare,
But the Muses refuse with my Wish to unite,
So I think I had better forbear.—

2.

My Strains as the heedless Effusions of Youth,   5
Can never be pleasing to Age,
And I fear that the simple Relation of Truth,
Might astonish a Spinster so sage.—

3.

Was my Poem in praise of your Beauty or Wit,
How absurd it would seem een to you,   10
The Perusal for Strangers alone would be fit,
Who else could believe it was true?—

4.

Did I sing of that '*Balm Breathing*' Bondage of Love,
Which in *Sighs* for the *Captain* appears,
The Recital Contempt and Derision would move,   15
That Folly should grow with your Years.—

21. Copy text: *N & Q*

22. Copy text: *MS. T*, collated with *MS. Ta, Pratt*
title   *untitled in Ta*

5.

Then pray, my dear Maiden, torment me no more,
Oh Cease, if you're studious of Ease;
Desist for your *own* sake at least, I implore,
For I fear that my Song would displease.—   20

15 Nov. 1806

23   A Parody Upon 'The Little Grey Man' in
      Lewis' *Tales of Wonder*

Mary Ann was a spinster in Southwell well known,
The darling was she of her parents alone,
The plague of her fellows by day and by night,
So few in her presence could e'er find delight;
For no maiden surpassed or perhaps ever can   5
In prudish demeanor the prim Mary Ann.

Her dark sparkling eyes a gay boldness bedeck'd,
But a stiff education their glances had check'd.
On her mien her staymaker bestowed his best grace,
And her mind stood confess'd in the shape of her face; 10
Her form was *not* faultless, though aided by art,
Her carriage was stately, though melting her heart.

Few suitors had she, yet one Lover she knew;
Till a second appeared, to the first she was true.
So fearless to Tuxford he went, while the *maid*   15
Her fears of remaining *so* often betray'd,
Full oft to the walks in the Churchyard she went,
And thus to the Tempest her Sorrows found vent.

'Ah me!' would she sigh in a tone that would melt
The Bachelor near, could he ever have felt,   20
'Ah me!' would she sigh, 'past and gone is the Day

23. Copy text: *MS. S*, collated with *MS. T* and *Pratt*
title   *untitled in T*; [Prim Mary Ann] *Pratt*
1 a`... known] ⟨the Wonder of fair Southwell Town⟩ *T*   2 ⟨But⟩ The *T*   4 So]
⟨But⟩ *T*   5 ⟨But in stiffness none equalls / For no maiden in stiffness⟩ *T*   6 In ...
the] ⟨The ... of⟩ *T*   7–8, 11–12 *positions transposed in T and Pratt, corrected by B in S*
8 was ⟨stiff⟩ stately *T*   11 gay] ⟨fierce⟩ T   12 But ⟨Prudence⟩ a *T*   15 fearless
⟨that⟩ to *T*   18 Tempest] ⟨Wind⟩ *T*   20 The ⟨youth⟩ Bachelor *T*

When I hoped that my father would give me away;
My fancy what sad gloomy presage appalls,
Since the Captain no longer appears at our Balls'.

In Southwell there happened to be at this Time,   25
A singular Creature, a Dealer in Rhyme;
No very great praise of this Youth we afford,
His merit consisted in being a Lord.
A mighty aversion had he to a wife,
And he spoke to this nymph just three times in his life.   30

One evening so gloomy when only the owl
(A tempest impending) would venture to prowl,
Mary Ann who by chance had walk'd out in the gloom,
By a newly made grave squatted down on a tomb.
On the stone she reclined by the long sighing grass,   35
When who but his Lordship should suddenly pass.

His form it was stout, and his shoulders were broad,
He sang as he quietly pass'd on the road,
He bowed a low bow, nor affrighted was she,
She curtsied as if she would sink on her knee.   40
In a voice which had nothing surprising or new,
He cried to the maid, 'Madam, how do ye do.'

Near the Damsel the Youth for a time did remain,
She curtsied once more, and then sat down again.
His Lordship then said, at a loss for discourse,   45
'Would the weather were better, I fear 'twill be worse.
Such clouds are impending as darken the heaven,
'Twill be rain, so Miss Bristoe I wish you good even.'

A smile dimpled her cheek, as the maid look'd around,
The raindrops began to besprinkle the ground;   50
With a smile look'd the maid, though it scarcely was light,
And His Lordship had quite disappear'd from her sight.
In dread of a ducking, she quickened her tread,
Reached her home, eat her supper, and went to bed.

24 Since ⟨Lightfoot no more has⟩ appeared at ⟨the⟩ Balls. *T*   26 singular] ⟨Curious⟩ *T*
29 aversion ⟨he⟩ had he *T*   32 (A tempest impending)] 'A Tempest impending' *T*, *Pratt*
35 reclined] sat down *T*, *Pratt, cor. in S*   by ... grass] ⟨with a heart heaving Sigh⟩ *T*
37 it was] was *T*, *Pratt*   40 curtsied ⟨so low⟩ as *T*   42 Madam, how do ye do]
⟨Mary⟩ Madam ⟨pray⟩ how do ⟨you⟩ do *T*   43 ⟨He stopped for a time⟩ *T*   45 said
... for] ⟨muttered some common⟩ *T*   47 Such] ⟨The⟩ *T*   49 ⟨With⟩ A *T*

'Woe is me,' did she cry, 'Oh Lord what shall I do,   55
No Lover, no Suitor is coming to woo;
To be married I'm sure I do all that I can,
Nor care I to whom, so he is but a man.
Shall I wait for a husband much longer? Ah no!
In search of a spouse then tomorrow I go.'   60

A redspotted gown she put on the next morn,
A platted straw bonnet her head did adorn,
Her closely laced stays from the maker were new,
Her shoes were pea green, and her stockings were blue,
Her earrings the gift of Mamma, and at last,   65
A pelisse bound with velvet to guard from the blast.

The morning was cloudy, the sun shunn'd the day,
Her journey was short, but most dirty the way.
She wish'd for her Pattens, alas! 'twas too late,
She sigh'd as she cast a last look at the gate.   70
She listen'd, shrill rung on its wire the door bell,
And she thought that it sounded her funeral knell.

With caution she measur'd her steps through the street,
And in crossing almost faced about to retreat.
For mounting the pavement her step was too high,   75
She slipped and to help her no Hero was nigh.
As she rested the stone of the causeway upon,
She paused in surprise to be left quite alone.

For from thence though red groups (by the Chapter imposed)
Of raised brick and mortar are daily exposed,   80
In hods and in carts, and on ladders and trowels,
With a charge to the passing to guard their own poles;
To dinner retired had the workmen long been,
And Mary Ann tumbled, unhelp'd and unseen.

60 In . . . spouse] ⟨A Hunting for Spouses⟩ T   61 redspotted gown] ⟨velvet pelisse⟩ T
she . . . morn] the *next morn she put on* T, *Pratt*   62 A . . . bonnet] A Bonnet of purple
T, *Pratt*   63 ⟨The Snow of her Bosom a mantle concealed / Let the stays to the By-
standers eye be revealed⟩ T   64 were . . . were] ⟨are . . . are⟩ T   66 bound] lined
T, *Pratt*   67 the sun . . . day] ⟨and dirty the way⟩ T   71 shrill rung on its] ⟨how
shrill rung the ⟩T   72 her] ⟨a⟩ T   73 With caution ⟨and / she paced⟩ she measured T;
With caution measured *Pratt*   75 For . . . pavement] ⟨But . . . causeway⟩ T   76 slipped⟨fell⟩ T
77 stone] ⟨side⟩ T   79 For ⟨there in⟩ red T   80 Of raised] ⟨In heaps⟩ T
81 In hods ⟨and on trowels⟩ on ladder ⟨and poles / carts⟩ trowels T   83 had . . .
been] ⟨not a workman was seen⟩ T   84 Ann ⟨sulked⟩ tumbled T

Sore fatigued the maid rising, just said a short prayer,   85
Tied the string of her bonnet, which flow'd in the air.
Again she set out and sped slowly along,
And for want of amusement, she humm'd a short song.
But in thought the fair virgin digested a plan
To bring into notice the prim Mary Ann.   90

Arrived at the Major's she knock'd at the door,
Not opening, she lifted the knocker once more;
A servant then usher'd her into the house,
The Major was out, but at home was his spouse.
To her with complaint of ill usage began   95
In querulous anger the prim Mary Ann.

Says she, 'Mrs. Wylde, I am greatly enraged,
For a dreadful report has all Southwell engaged,
A report which I never can pardon, not I,
With vexation I really am ready to die.   100
And they say, Mrs. Wylde, but I hope 'tis not true,
That this dreadful report has arisen from you.'

In a well-acted rage, she continued to rail
(For Mary Ann's tongue hardly ever can fail).
At length Mrs. Wylde cut this eloquence short   105
By begging her merely to state the report.
'Then hear,' she replied, 'Mrs. Wylde, in a word,
They say I'm to marry this terrible Lord.

'The Creature is quite my aversion I swear,
Perhaps he may love, yet he still shall despair.   110
Indeed I suspect, he has form'd some design,
To proffer himself as a suitor of mine.
At a party last night his attentions increas'd,
And he stood by my chair for ten minutes at least.

'At this my Mamma was so greatly provoked,   115
No less than three times in one deal she revoked.
However, at once I will crush every hope,
Though the desperate wretch may remove by a rope.

85 said] swore *T, Pratt, cor. in S*   89 ⟨For her thoughts were digested as she⟩ *T*
93 house] ⟨Hall⟩ *T*   102 arisen from] ⟨been mentioned by⟩ *T*   107 ⟨Then till
I hear the account of this⟩ *T*   108 ⟨She raved⟩ *T*   109 swear] ⟨vow⟩ *T*
112 as a suitor] ⟨soon as a Lover⟩ *T*   113 ⟨For at Mr. Faulkners⟩ *T*   114 ten] ⟨five⟩
T   115 At this ⟨so⟩ my *T*

And do you Mrs. Wylde, contradict, I demand,
This shocking report, at my final command.'   120

The Lady whom thus in this style she address'd,
Replied, with a smile which could not be repress'd,
That she never *had* heard this most scandalous tale,
And wondered that such a report should prevail,
Or a stripling aspire to the hand of a maid   125
Who was seven years older as people had said.

At hearing this speech, Mary Ann gave a yell
Like the Little Grey Man, of fair Aix la Chapelle;
She rais'd up her bonnet, she rais'd up her chin,
And her mouth was distended displaying a grin,   130
On hearing this truth which she could not deny,
Though she almost was tempted to call it a lie.

Away then she went, and my tale must conclude.
Oh may such reports maids no longer delude,
Some people will laugh at such legends I fear,   135
For we must not believe every word which we hear;
And girls still giggle behind the light fan
At the tale of His Lordship and prim Mary Ann.

                                              1806

24 To Those Ladies Who Have So Kindly Defended the Author From the Attacks of Unprovoked Malignity

I.

What pity speaks in Beauty's Sigh!
When heartless Critics chide the Lay,
How dear the Beams of Beauty's Eye
Which chase the Clouds of hate away.—

119 And ⟨for⟩ do you . . . I ⟨require⟩ *T*   120 final] ⟨earnest⟩ *T*   125 Or ⟨an impudent Stripling of barely nineteen⟩ *T*   129 Bonnet ⟨displaying / from⟩, she *T*
133 must conclude] ⟨here must end⟩ *T*   134 ⟨While⟩ Oh *T*   135 Some] ⟨And⟩
For *T*; For *Pratt, cor. in S*   136 For . . . which] And . . . ⟨which⟩ that *T*; And
. . . that *Pratt, cor. in S*   137 ⟨Still stiff walks the Maiden⟩ *T*   And girls still] And
Girls will *T, Pratt*; ⟨And⟩ And girls ⟨will / should⟩ still *S*   138 At the] At *T*; At [the]
Pratt

24. Copy text : *MS. Υ*

4 Clouds of hate] ⟨envious clouds⟩ *Υ*

2.

In words from woman's Lip divine,   5
  What heavenly Consolation flows,
Since woman's words and Smiles are mine,
  I shall not fear a thousand Foes.

3.

Oh I forgive the lying Throng,
  From you alone I claim the Bays,   10
Since you approve my simple Song,
  Their censure is my warmest praise.

4.

'Twas not to soothe the Captious Fool,
  My youthful Lyre attuned its String,
To Matrons of the prudish School,   15
  Let venal Rhymers coldly sing.

5.

My Strains in glowing Stanzas roll,
  No withered Leaves my head Entwine,
The votive offering of my Soul,
  Was placed on Beauty's hallowed Shrine.   20

6.

And Beauty scanned the amorous page,
  And Beauty smiled her soft Applause,
Bade me despise the factious Rage,
  And Spurn despotic Envy's Laws.

7.

Shall I repress my Bosom's fire   25
  Lest prudes should pine for envied Bliss,
Lest Age should wake to young Desire,
  And faultering try the tasteless kiss?

8.

Must I unstring the Harp of Love,
  Lest hands depraved should sweep the Chords?   30

17 glowing Stanzas] (warmer numbers) *T*

Why should my verse to Sinning move?
Temptation's something more than words.

9.

Frail must the Virgin be who falls
    Seduced by artless Songs like these,
Internal Shame her Soul appalls   35
    Whom artless Songs of youth displease.

10.

The Minds of fair untainted Maids
    From Verse will still remain the Same;
Where Vice the burning Breast pervades,
    No Verse can quench the Subtle Flame.   40

11.

Then will I strike my Harp to Love,
    His Numbers are forever new,
To Me with fresh Delight they move
    When gently breathed for nymphs like you.

12.

Your Laurels will my Toils repay,   45
    Your frowns would check the tender Strain;
Then cheer with Smiles my Lyric Lay,
    I'll think I have not sung in vain.

1806

25   To a Knot of Ungenerous Critics

Rail on, Rail on, ye heartless crew!
My strains were never meant for you;
Remorseless Rancour still reveal,
And damn the verse you cannot feel.
Invoke those kindred passions' aid!   5

32 ⟨Does / Is Guilt inspired / stilled by glowing words?⟩ *T*   Temptation's] ⟨Sure Guilt
is⟩ *T*   39 Vice] ⟨Guilt⟩ *T*   40 quench] ⟨crush⟩ *T*

25. Copy text: *C*, collated with *MS. T, Pratt*
    6 whose] whole *Pratt*

Whose baleful stings your breasts pervade.
Crush, if you can, the hopes of youth,
Trampling regardless on the Truth!
Truth's Records you consult in vain,
She will not blast her native strain;   10
She will assist her votary's cause,
His will at least be her applause,
Your prayer the gentle Power will spurn.
To Fiction's motley altar turn,
Who joyful in the fond address   15
Her favoured worshippers will bless!
And lo! she holds a magic glass,
Where Images reflected pass.
Bent on your knees the Boon receive!
This will assist you to deceive—   20
The glittering gift was made for you,
Now hold it up to public view.
Lest evil unforeseen betide,
A Mask each canker'd brow shall hide
(Whilst Truth my sole Defence is nigh,   25
Prepared the danger to defy).
'There see the Maid's perverted name,
And there the Poet's guilty Flame,
Gloaming a deep phosphoric fire,
Threatening—but ere it spreads, retire!'   30
Says Truth, 'Ye Virgins, do not fear!
No Comet rolls its Influence here;
'Tis Scandal's Mirror you perceive,
Her dazzling Meteors but deceive—
Approach and touch—Nay, do not turn!   35
It blazes there, but will not burn.'—
At once the shivering Mirror flies,
Teeming no more with varnished Lies;
The baffled friends of Fictions start,
Too late desiring to depart.   40
Truth poising high Ithuriel's spear
Bids every Fiend unmask'd appear,
The vizard tears from every face,

15 Who] ⟨She⟩ T   19 Bent] ⟨Bow⟩ T   25 Defence] desire C   27 see] is C
31 Ye] Up C   32 No] The C   34 Her] These C   39 Fictions] Fiction C

And dooms them to a dire disgrace.
For e'er they compass their escape,   45
Each takes perforce a native shape—
The Leader of the wrathful Band,
Behold a portly Female stand!
She raves, impelled by private pique,
This mean unjust revenge to seek;   50
From vice to save this virtuous Age,
Thus does she vent indecent rage!
What child has she of promise fair,
Who claims a fostering Mother's care?
Whose Innocence requires defence,   55
Or forms at least a smooth pretence,
Thus to disturb a harmless Boy,
His humble hope, and peace annoy?
She need not fear the amorous rhyme,
Love will not tempt her future time,   60
For her his wings have ceased to spread,
No more he flutters round her head;
Her day's Meridian now is past,
The clouds of Age her Sun o'ercast;   65
To her the strain was never sent,
For feeling Souls alone 'twas meant—
The verse she seized, unask'd, unbade,
And damn'd, ere yet the whole was read!
Yes! for one single erring verse,
Pronounced an unrelenting Curse;   70
Yes! at a first and transient view,
Condemned a heart she never knew.—
Can such a verdict then decide,
Which springs from disappointed pride?
Without a wondrous share of Wit,   75
To judge is such a Matron fit?
The rest of the censorious throng
Who to this zealous Band belong,
To her a general homage pay,
And right or wrong her wish obey: 80
Why should I point my pen of steel
To break 'such flies upon the wheel?'

45 For e'er they] ⟨Ere they can⟩ T   48 portly] ⟨furious⟩ T   65 ⟨Besides the⟩ To T

With minds to Truth and Sense unknown,
Who dare not call their words their own.
Rail on, Rail on, ye heartless Crew!   85
Your Leader's grand design pursue:
Secure behind her ample shield,
Yours is the harvest of the field.—
My path with thorns you cannot strew,
Nay more, my warmest thanks are due;   90
When such as you revile my Name,
Bright beams the rising Sun of Fame,
Chasing the shades of envious night,
Outshining every critic Light.—
Such, such as you will serve to show   95
Each radiant tint with higher glow.
Vain is the feeble cheerless toil,
Your efforts on yourselves recoil;
New Glory still for me you raise,
Yours is the Censure, mine the Praise.   100

                                        1 Dec. 1806

26   L'Amitié Est L'Amour Sans Ailes

                        1.

Why should my anxious breast repine,
      Because my youth is fled?
Days of delight may still be mine;
      Affection is not dead.
In tracing back the years of youth,   5
One firm record, one lasting truth
      Celestial consolation brings;
Bear it, ye breezes, to the seat,
Where first my heart responsive beat,—
      'Friendship is Love without his wings!'   10

93 shades of envious] ⟨Clo⟩ shades of ⟨critic⟩ envious T   94 critic] ⟨envious⟩ T
99 New] Then C   100 ⟨Your censure is my greatest⟩ Praise. T

26. Copy text: 1832, collated with MS. N, MS. NM. Stanza numbers are not in 1832 and
later edns.
8 the seat] ⟨my friends / Lycus⟩ N

2.

Through few, but deeply chequer'd years,
  What moments have been mine!
Now half obscured by clouds of tears,
  Now bright in rays divine;
Howe'er my future doom be cast,   15
My soul, enraptured with the past,
  To one idea fondly clings;
Friendship! that thought is all thine own,
Worth worlds of bliss, that thought alone—
  'Friendship is Love without his wings!'   20

3.

Where yonder yew-trees lightly wave
  Their branches on the gale,
Unheeded heaves a simple grave,
  Which tells the common tale;
Round this unconscious schoolboys stray,   25
Till the dull knell of childish play
  From yonder studious mansion rings;
But here whene'er my footsteps move,
My silent tears too plainly prove
  'Friendship is Love without his wings!'   30

4.

Oh Love! before thy glowing shrine
  My early vows were paid;
My hopes, my dreams, my heart was thine,
  But these are now decay'd;
For thine are pinions like the wind,   35
No trace of thee remains behind,
  Except, alas! thy jealous stings.
Away, away! delusive power,
Thou shalt not haunt my coming hour;
  Unless, indeed, without thy wings.   40

11 few, but] ⟨many a⟩ N   13 Now ⟨half obscured by⟩ N   14 Now ⟨rained
on⟩ N   16–18 ⟨The last are / Passion is fled, forever gone | With love my future
hopes are one | Which still some Consolation⟩ N   21–2 ⟨When Grief, and I
though young have known | The Daimon's⟩ / ⟨When thoughtless boys unconscious play⟩ N
23 ⟨Strange ? ⟩ N   25 stray] ⟨play⟩ N   26 ⟨In / From yonder⟩ N   30 his]
⟨its⟩ N   31 ⟨On Caledonia's snow capt hills⟩ N   37 jealous] ⟨baleful⟩ N
38 ⟨Deprived of these, thou gentle⟩ N

5.

Seat of my youth! thy distant spire
    Recalls each scene of joy;
My bosom glows with former fire,—
    In mind again a boy.
Thy grove of elms, thy verdant hill,   45
Thy every path delights me still,
    Each flower a double fragrance flings;
Again, as once, in converse gay,
Each lov'd associate seems to say
    'Friendship is Love without his wings!'   50

6.

My Lycus! wherefore dost thou weep?
    Thy falling tears restrain;
Affection for a time may sleep,
    But, oh, 'twill wake again.
Think, think, my friend, when next we meet,   55
Our long-wish'd interview, how sweet!
    From this my hope of rapture springs;
While youthful hearts thus fondly swell,
Absence, my friend can only tell,
    'Friendship is Love without his wings!'   60

7.

In one, and one alone deceived,
    Did I my error mourn?
No—from oppressive bonds relieved,
    I left the wretch to scorn.
I turn'd to those my childhood knew,   65
With feelings warm, with bosoms true,
    Twined with my heart's according strings;
And till those vital chords shall break,
For none but these my breast shall wake
    Friendship, or Love deprived of wings!   70

42 scene of joy] ⟨gorgeous scene⟩ N   44 ⟨Again / I'm still a helpless⟩ N
47 fragrance] ⟨odour⟩ N   49 lov'd] dear *1831, 1832, C, More*   51 My . . .
dost] ⟨Dear . . . didst⟩ N   52 ⟨Oblivion is / Such tears⟩ N   55 ⟨Think how to
souls like ours endear'd⟩ N   56 ⟨Our winged pleasures will be sweet⟩ N   61–3 ⟨When
Fortune smiles, propitious power | Accept my grateful prayer, | If wealth on one could
blessings shower⟩ N   61 ⟨Once, Friendship, only once deceived⟩ / ⟨Once was my boyish
soul / Once, Friendship, in thy mark ? believed⟩ N   70 or Love] the power *1831, 1832,
C, More*

8.

Ye few! my soul, my life is yours,
    My memory and my hope;
Your worth a lasting love ensures,
    Unfetter'd in its scope;
From smooth deceit and terror sprung,   75
With aspect fair and honey'd tongue,
    Let Adulation wait on kings;
With joy elate, by snares beset,
We, we, my friends, can ne'er forget
    'Friendship is Love without his wings!'   80

9.

Fictions and dreams inspire the bard
    Who rolls the epic song;
Friendship and Truth be my reward—
    To me no bays belong;
If laurell'd Fame but dwells with lies,   85
Me the enchantress ever flies,
    Whose heart and not whose fancy sings;
Simple and young, I dare not feign;
Mine be the rude yet heartfelt strain,
    'Friendship is Love without his wings!'   90

                                                   [1806]

27 Soliloquy of a Bard in the Country, in an
    Imitation of Littleton's Soliloquy of a Beauty

'Twas now the noon of night, and all was still,
Except a hapless Rhymer and his quill.
In vain he calls each Muse in order down,
Like other females, these will sometimes frown;
He frets, he fumes, and ceasing to invoke   5

73 ⟨While⟩ N   78–9 ⟨Ours be the kindred flow of souls | Though⟩ N
78 ⟨Friendship be ours with / Elate with bliss / Above⟩ N   81 dreams inspire] ⟨fancy
cheer⟩ N   84 ⟨To others crowns belong⟩ N   88 Simple and young] ⟨Rude and
unskilled⟩ N

27. Copy text: C, collated with MS. T, MS. Ta
title   Soliloquy of a Bard in the Country C, Ta

The Nine, in anguish'd accents thus he spoke:
Ah what avails it thus to waste my time,
To roll in Epic, or to rave in Rhyme?
What worth is some few partial readers' praise,
If ancient Virgins croaking *censures* raise?   10
Where few attend, 'tis useless to indite;
Where few can read, 'tis folly sure to write;
Where none but girls and striplings dare admire,
And Critics rise in every country Squire—
But yet this last my candid Muse admits,   15
When Peers are Poets, Squires may well be Wits;
When schoolboys vent their amorous flames in verse,
Matrons may sure their characters asperse;
Or if a little parson joins the train,
And echos back his Patron's voice again—   20
Though not delighted, yet I must forgive,
Parsons as well as other folks must live:—
From rage he rails not, rather say from dread,
He does not speak for Virtue, but for bread;
And this we know is in his Patron's giving,   25
For Parsons cannot eat without a *Living*.
The Matron knows I love the Sex too well,
Even unprovoked aggression to repel.
What though from private pique her anger grew,
And bade her blast a heart she never knew?   30
What though, she said, for one light heedless line,
That Wilmot's verse was far more pure than mine!
In wars like these, I neither fight nor fly,
When *dames* accuse 'tis bootless to deny;
Hers be the harvest of the martial field,   35
I can't attack, where Beauty forms the shield.
But when a pert Physician loudly cries,
Who hunts for scandal, and who lives by lies,
A walking register of daily news,

6 in ⟨some⟩ anguished *T*   8 roll] ⟨rave⟩ *T*   9 ⟨What worth have all the Charms *?*
Rhymes / Verse can boast⟩ *T*   10 ⟨If all within a Country town are lost⟩ *T*   12 few]
⟨none⟩ *T*   13 none but] ⟨silly⟩ *T*   17 schoolboys] ⟨poets⟩ *T*   18 ⟨And all
bad riotous characters⟩ Matrons ... their ⟨naughty⟩ characters *T*   19 Or] ⟨And⟩ *T*;
And *C*, *T a*   21 ⟨I smile⟩ Though *T*   25 And this] ⟨His life⟩ *T*   26 eat] ⟨live⟩
T   27 The Matron ⟨too but⟩ knows *T*   28 Even] ⟨From their unkind / Her⟩ *T*
29 ⟨Her's be the harvest of the wellfought field⟩ *T*   30 ⟨What though she⟩ And *T*
33 In wars] ⟨In combat / From foes⟩ *T*   34 When ⟨Ladies rail⟩ tis ⟨useless⟩ to
deny *T*   39 ⟨To please⟩ A *T*

Train'd to invent, and skilful to abuse—   40
For arts like these at bounteous tables fed,
When S[mith] condemns a book he never read,
Declaring with a coxcomb's native air,
The *moral's* shocking, though the *rhymes* are fair,
Ah! must he rise unpunish'd from the feast,   45
Nor lash'd by vengeance into truth at least?
Such lenity were more than Man's indeed!
Those who condemn, should surely deign to read.
Yet must I spare—nor thus my pen degrade,
I quite forgot that scandal was his trade.   50
For food and raiment thus the coxcomb rails,
For those who fear his physic, like his *tales*.
Why should his harmless censure seem offence?
Still let him eat, although at my expense,
And join the herd to Sense and Truth unknown,   55
Who dare not call their very thoughts their own,
And share with these applause, a godlike bribe,
In short, do anything, except *prescribe*:—
For though in garb of Galen he appears,
His practice is not equal to his years.   60
Without improvement since he first began,
A young Physician, though an ancient Man—
Now let me cease—Physician, Parson, Dame,
Still urge your task, and if you can, defame.
The humble offerings of my Muse destroy,   65
And crush, oh! noble conquest! crush a Boy.
What though some silly girls have lov'd the strain,
And kindly bade me tune my Lyre again;
What though some feeling, or some partial few,
Nay, Men of Taste and Reputation too,   70
Have deign'd to praise the firstlings of my Muse—
If *you* your sanction to the theme refuse,

40 ⟨By ?⟩ Train'd *T*   42 When S[mith]] ⟨The ?⟩ *T*   43 ⟨Declaring though the rhymes were fair enough / perhaps are fair⟩ *T*   44 ⟨Yet neither⟩ The *T*   45 ⟨Ah! shall I ?⟩ pass the witch forsooth⟩ *T*   46 by ⟨Sat⟩ vengeance *T*   48 surely deign] ⟨deign at first⟩ *T*   49 must] ⟨will⟩ *T*   50 ⟨His / Why should⟩ I *T*   51 For . . . thus] ⟨Tis his subsistence / For daily dinners thus⟩ *T*   53 should ⟨Ideas his common⟩ his *T*   56 thoughts] ⟨souls⟩ *T*   57 ⟨With these some rumours⟩ And . . . a ⟨noble⟩ bribe *T*   61 Without improvement] ⟨None such ?⟩ their lives in⟩ ⟨Still / Unchanged in method⟩ *T*   63 ⟨Apollo, God of Medicine, and dames⟩ *T*   65 ⟨Revile⟩ The *T*   67 ⟨One who has never⟩ What *T*

If *you* your great protection still withdraw,
Whose Praise is Glory, and whose Voice is law!
Soon must I fall an unresisting foe,   75
A hapless victim yielding to the blow.—
Thus Pope by Curl and Dennis was destroyed,
Thus Gray and Mason yield to furious Loyd;
From Dryden, Milbourne tears the palm away,
And thus I fall, though meaner far than they,   80
As in the field of combat, side by side,
A Fabius and some nameless Roman died.

[1806]

28   Queries to Casuists

The Moralists tell us that Loving is Sinning,
   And always are prating about and about it,
But as Love of Existence itself's the beginning,
   Say, what would Existence itself be without it?

They argue the point with much furious Invective,   5
   Though perhaps 'twere no difficult task to confute it;
But if Venus and Hymen should once prove defective,
   Pray who would be there to defend or dispute it?

[1806?]

29   The Prayer of Nature

Father of Light! great God of Heaven!
   Hear'st thou the accents of despair?
Can guilt like Man's be e'er forgiven?
   Can vice atone for crimes by prayer?

75 Soon] ⟨Here⟩ T   76 A ⟨wondrous⟩ victim ⟨worthy of⟩ the blow T   79 ⟨Thus⟩
From T   82 ⟨Achilles and the meanest Greeks⟩ T   some nameless] ⟨the meanest⟩
T; some noble C

28. Copy text: C

29. Copy text: *1832*, collated with *Life*, MS. B
   4 vice] guilt *Life, 1831, 1832 C, More; cancelled in B*

Father of Light, on thee I call!   5
   Thou see'st my soul is dark within;
Thou who canst mark the sparrow's fall,
   Avert from me the death of sin.
No shrine I seek, to sects unknown;
   Oh point to me the path of truth!   10
Thy dread omnipotence I own;
   Spare, yet amend, the faults of youth.
Let bigots rear a gloomy fane,
   Let superstition hail the pile,
Let priests, to spread their sable reign,   15
   With tales of mystic rites beguile.
Shall man confine his Maker's sway
   To Gothic domes of mouldering stone?
Thy Temple is the face of day;
   Earth, ocean, heaven thy boundless throne.   20
Shall man condemn his race to hell
   Unless they bend in pompous form;
Tell us that all, for one who fell,
   Must perish in the mingling storm?
Shall each pretend to reach the skies,   25
   Yet doom his brother to expire,
Whose soul a different hope supplies,
   Or doctrines less severe inspire;
Shall these, by creeds they can't expound,
   Prepare a fancied bliss or woe;   30
Shall reptiles, groveling on the ground,
   Their great Creator's purpose know;
Shall these, who live for self alone,
   Whose years fleet on in daily crime,
Shall these by Faith for guilt atone,   35
   Exist beyond the Bounds of Time?
Father! no prophet's laws I seek,—
   Thy laws in Nature's works appear;—
I own myself corrupt and weak
   Yet will I pray, for thou wilt hear!   40
Thou, who can'st guide the wandering star

9 to] ⟨no⟩ *B*   15 Let priests ⟨before their Altar feign⟩ *B*   16 rites] rights *Life*,
1831, 1832, C, More   22 ⟨For ? of Frailty or ? of⟩ Form *B*   33 these] those *Life*,
1831, 1832, C, More   34 fleet] float *Life, 1831, 1832, C, More*   35 these] those
Life, 1831, 1832, C, More   36 Exist] And live *Life, 1831, 1832, C, More*

Through trackless realms of aether's space;
Who calm'st the elemental war,
  Whose Hand from pole to pole I trace:—
Thou, who in wisdom placed me here,   45
  Who, when thou wilt, can take me hence,
Oh! whilst I tread this earthly sphere,
  Extend to me thy wide defence.
To Thee, my God, to Thee I call!
  Whatever weal of woe betide,   50
By thy command I rise or fall,
  In thy protection I confide.
If, when this dust to dust's restored,
  My soul shall float on airy wing,
How shall thy glorious name adored   55
  Inspire her feeble voice to sing!
But, if this fleeting spirit share
  With clay the grave's eternal bed,
While life yet throbs I raise my prayer,
  Though doom'd no more to quit the dead.   60
To Thee I breathe my humble strain,
  Grateful for all thy mercies past,
My hope, my God, to Thee again,
  This erring life will fly at last.

29 Dec. 1806

30   [A Portrait]

Doats yet the hag that from her form so vile
A race shall quicken to enrich our isle,
Her poisonous blood thro' other channels roll
And spread pollution in each new born soul?
Forbid it Heaven—but yet a thought more wild   5
Ne'er fixed the fancy of the veriest child.

---

47 Oh] Ah *Life*, *1831*, *1832*, C, *More*   53 dust . . . restored,] Dust, to Dust restored B
63 My hope,] And hope *Life*, *1831*, *1832*, C, *More*   64 will] may *Life*, *1831*, *1832*, C,
More

30. Copy text: *MS. T*
  1 Doats] ⟨Dreams / Boasts⟩ *T*   her ⟨stern⟩ form *T*   6 fixed] sought *alternate read-*
ing in T

What bloodless spectre on what wizard dame
Ere shared the blessings of a holy flame?
Sooner, dire prodigy, will marble glow
Or flaming ashes melt in winter snow.   10
Big with like [thought] she roams from place to place,
See her each old one fold in close embrace,
And flattering hopes from drivelling tales inhale,
Tales that Dependents barter by wholesale;
Each herb, each philtre idling art employ   15
How to produce a much longed lovely boy.
Her phantom form now doubly rendered spare
With drugs on drugs—she almost lives on air.
Now costly viands, cordials lend their aid,
Now Matron throes weigh down the teeming maid,   20
Now sickenings, languors, faintings, longings press
But still instead of quickening she grows less.
Baffled at length, by Nature fairly spurned,
Her last fond hopes so basely overturned,
Boiling with ire which never tongue could tell,   25
Husband and earth and all she sends to Hell.

[1806 or 1807]

31–97   Hours of Idleness,

            A Series of Poems,
        Original and Translated

Μητ' αρ με μαλ' αινεε μητε τι νειχει.
                                    HOMER. Iliad, 10, [249]
        Virginibus puerisque Canto.
                                    HORACE. [Odes III. 1]
        He whistled as he went for want of thought.
                                    DRYDEN. [Cymon and Iphigenia, 85]

8 shared] ⟨felt / knelt / knew⟩   holy] ⟨mutual⟩ T   11 Big ⟨with the thought⟩ T
13 hopes . . . tales] visions from their tales *alternate reading in T*   17 now] is *alternate
reading in T*   18 With] ⟨By⟩ T   19 Now] ⟨And⟩ T   22 still] yet *alternate
reading in T*   23 At length outwitted and by Nature spurned *alternate reading in T*
24 basely] ⟨fairly⟩ T   25 ⟨With ? hate and ? no tongue can tell⟩ T

31–97. Copy text: *HI*, collated with *MS*. *T* (and see notes)

PREFACE

IN submitting to the public eye the following collection, I have not only to combat the difficulties that writers of verse generally encounter, but, may incur the charge of presumption, for obtruding myself on the world, when, without doubt, I might be, at my age,
5 more usefully employed. These productions are the fruits of the lighter hours of a young man, who has lately completed his nineteenth year. As they bear the internal evidence of a boyish mind, this is, perhaps, unnecessary information. Some few were written during the disadvantages of illness, and depression of spirits; under
10 the former influence, 'CHILDISH RECOLLECTIONS', in particular, were composed. This consideration, though it cannot excite the voice of Praise, may at least arrest the arm of censure. A considerable portion of these poems has been privately printed, at the request, and for the perusal of my friends. I am sensible that the partial,
15 and, frequently, injudicious admiration of a social circle, is not the criterion by which poetical genius is to be estimated, yet, 'to do greatly', we must 'dare greatly'; and I have hazarded my reputation and feelings in publishing this volume.

'I have pass'd the Rubicon', and must stand or fall by the 'cast of
20 the die'. In the latter event, I shall submit without a murmur, for, though not without solicitude for the fate of these effusions, my expectations are by no means sanguine. It is probable that I may have dared much, and done little; for, in the words of COWPER, 'It is one thing to write what may please our friends, who, because
25 they are such, are apt to be a little biass'd in our favour, and another, to write what may please every body, because they who have no connection, or even knowledge of the author, will be sure to find fault if they can'. To the truth of this, however, I do not wholly subscribe; on the contrary, I feel convinced, that these trifles will

1 submitting to] ⟨giving to⟩ laying before T   2 combat] ⟨encounter⟩ T   3 encounter] ⟨combat⟩ T   but, may] but moreover may T   4 might be] might ⟨have been⟩ T   6 a young] a very young T   lately] ⟨only now⟩ T   9 during] ⟨under⟩ T   10 former] latter T   11 This] ⟨These⟩ T   12 censure. A] Censure. —Some of the pieces also reflect upon old established methods of Study, and peculiarities of manners, in one of our principal Seats of Learning.—I am fully aware of the Danger, and obloquy, which may ⟨most⟩ probably be the consequence of not suppressing these opinions, but as they are the result of thorough conviction, I will not *revoke?* my Sentiments from a dread of Retaliation. T   13 has been] have been T   privately] ⟨already⟩ T   14 my] ⟨the author's⟩ T   sensible] ⟨well aware⟩ T   16 poetical genius] poetical merit T   21 solicitude . . . effusions] some share of vanity T   22–9 It is probable . . . these trifles] *MS. insert in T;* Well convinced, I am, these trifles T, *initial reading*   22 probable] ⟨by no means im⟩probable T   26 what may please] to please T

not be treated with injustice. Their merit, if they possess any, will be liberally allowed; their numerous faults, on the other hand, cannot expect that favour, which has been denied to others, of maturer years, decided character, and far greater ability. I have not aimed at exclusive originality, still less have I studied any particular model for imitation; some translations are given, of which many are paraphrastic. In the original pieces, there may appear a casual coincidence with authors, whose works I have been accustomed to read, but I have not been guilty of intentional plagiarism. To produce any thing entirely new, in an age so fertile in rhyme, would be a Herculean task, as every subject has already been treated to its utmost extent.—Poetry, however, is not my primary vocation; to divert the dull moments of indisposition, or the monotony of a vacant hour, urged me 'to this sin'; little can be expected from so unpromising a muse. My wreath, scanty as it must be, is all I shall derive from these productions; and I shall never attempt to replace its fading leaves, or pluck a single additional sprig from groves, where I am, at best, an intruder. Though accustomed, in my younger days, to rove a careless mountaineer on the Highlands of Scotland, I have not, of late years, had the benefit of such pure air, or so elevated a residence, as might enable me to enter the lists with genuine bards, who have enjoyed both these advantages. But they derive considerable fame, and a few, not less profit, from their productions, while I shall expiate my rashness, as an interloper, certainly without the latter, and in all probability, with a very slight share of the former, I leave to others 'Virum volitare per ora'. I look to the few who will hear with patience 'dulce est desipere in

31 liberally] handsomely *T*   32 cannot expect] ⟨will be seen⟩ *T*   has been denied] ⟨has not been extended⟩ *T*   33–57 I have . . . in loco.' *MS. insert in T*   33 ability. I have] ability.—I will not pretend ⟨to be callous⟩ an Insensibility to praise or censure, which is not inherent in my Nature, on the contrary I am 'Tremblingly alive' to both, but the Indulgence, which has been ⟨allowed⟩ extended to youth in other departments, can hardly exist in poetry, because in this one Instance, the pity for the Sensations of a young ⟨boy⟩ person in a public Situation and the desire to encourage his endeavours, is much increased by the/his personal appearance and exertions, in the other his works only are submitted to the dispassionate Reader, who as the Book not author is before ⟨his eye⟩ him does not hesitate to loudly condemn what he may disapprove, being totally unrestrained by the above considerations.— *T* 34 exclusive originality] ⟨or studied to avoid⟩ Originality, ⟨my ideas have been set down as they flowed / or studied to avoid Imitation / still less have⟩ *T*   still less] nor *T*   35 of which] though *T*   many are] many ⟨of the former⟩ are *T*   36 In the original] as to the original *T*   may appear] may be *T*   38–9 To produce] and to produce *T* 43 urged . . . sin] ⟨was all I aimed at⟩ *T*   44 My wreath] However my Wreath *T* all I] all ⟨the Benefit⟩ I *T*   45 replace] ⟨restore⟩ *T*   46 pluck] ⟨add / make an addition of⟩ *T*   48 rove] ⟨wander⟩ *T*   51–2 But they derive] However these derive *T*   53 productions, while] productions, but *T*   expiate] ⟨pay the penalty of *T*⟩ 55 others 'Virum] others 'victor Virum *T*   56–66 *MS. insert in T*

loco'.—To the former worthies, I resign, without repining, the hope of immortality, and content myself with the not very magnificent prospect, of ranking 'amongst the mob of gentlemen who 60 write', my readers must determine, whether I dare say 'with ease', or the honour of a posthumous page in 'The Catalogue of Royal and Noble Authors', a work to which the Peerage is under infinite obligations', inasmuch as many names of considerable length, sound, and antiquity, are thereby rescued from the obscurity, 65 which unluckily overshadows several voluminous productions of their illustrious bearers.

With slight hopes, and some fears, I publish this first, and last attempt. To the dictates of young ambition, may be ascribed many actions more criminal, and equally absurd. To a few of my own age, 70 the contents may afford amusement; I trust, they will, at least, be found harmless. It is highly improbable, from my situation, and pursuits hereafter, that I should ever obtrude myself a second time on the Public; nor even, in the very doubtful event of present indulgence, shall I be tempted to commit a future trespass of the 75 same nature. The opinion of Dr. JOHNSON on the Poems of a noble relation of mine, 'That when a man of rank appeared in the character of an author, his merit should be handsomely acknowledged', can have little weight with verbal, and still less with periodical censors, but were it otherwise, I should be loth to avail myself of the 80 privilege, and would rather incur the bitterest censure of anonymous criticism, than triumph in honours granted solely to a title.

57 resign] leave *T*   60 must] ⟨I leave to⟩ *T*   61 honour] ⟨favour⟩ *T* Catalogue of] Catalogue *T*   65–6 several . . . bearers] the Illustrious and sometimes well-spelt productions of their Bearers *T*   67 slight] ⟨some / few⟩ *T*   some] many *T* publish] ⟨submit⟩ *T*   and last] and probably last *T*   68 dictates . . . ambition] Desire of *Fame T*   69 a few] some few *T*   71 harmless.] *MS. originally ended here; the remainder of the Preface is a later insert in the MS.*   80 privilege, and] privilege, I *T*   80–1 incur . . . title] ⟨stand the⟩ just censure in obscurity, than triumph in honours granted ⟨merely⟩ to a Title only *T*

31   On Leaving Newstead Abbey

Why dost thou build the hall, Son of the winged days?
Thou lookest from thy tower to-day, yet a few years, and
the blast of the desart comes, it howls in thy empty court.
OSSIAN.

Thro' thy battlements, Newstead, the hollow winds whistle;
Thou, the hall of my fathers, art gone to decay;
In thy once smiling garden, the hemlock and thistle
Have choak'd up the rose, which late bloom'd in the way.

Of the mail-cover'd Barons, who proudly to battle,   5
Led their vassals from Europe to Palestine's plain,
The escutcheon and shield, which with every blast rattle,
Are the only sad vestiges now that remain.

No more doth old Robert, with harp-stringing numbers,
Raise a flame in the breast, for the war-laurell'd wreath;   10
Near Askalon's towers, John of Horistan slumbers,
Unnerv'd is the hand of his minstrel, by death.

Paul and Hubert too sleep, in the valley of Cressy,
For the safety of Edward and England they fell;
My fathers! the tears of your country redress ye;   15
How you fought! how you died! still her annals can tell.

On Marston, with Rupert, 'gainst traitors contending,
Four brothers enrich'd, with their blood, the bleak field;
For the rights of a monarch, their country defending,
Till death their attachment to royalty seal'd.   20

Shades of heroes, farewell! your descendant, departing
From the seat of his ancestors, bids you, adieu!
Abroad, or at home, your remembrance imparting
New courage, he'll think upon glory, and you.

Though a tear dim his eye, at this sad separation,   25
'Tis nature, not fear, that excites his regret;

31. Copy text: *HI*, collated with *FPM*, *POVO*, *POT*, *HI1820*
title   On leaving N—st—d *FPM*; On Leaving Newstead *POVO*   epigraph   *added in HI*

1–3 Through ⟨the cracks in these battlements loud the⟩ winds whistle,| ⟨For⟩ the hall of my
fathers ⟨is⟩ gone to decay; | ⟨And in yon once gay⟩ garden the hemlock and thistle *FPM*
5 mail-cover'd Barons, who] ⟨barons of old, who once⟩ steelcovered Barons, who *FPM*
9 doth] ⟨does⟩ *FPM*   11 Horistan] Horiston *POVO*, *HI*, *POT*; Horist⟨o⟩n
FPM   15 ye] ⟨ye⟩ you *FPM*; you *HI*   22 you] ⟨ye⟩ *FPM*   26 that
excites] ⟨which commands⟩ *FPM*

Far distant he goes, with the same emulation,
The fame of his fathers he ne'er can forget.
That fame, and that memory, still will he cherish,
He vows, that he ne'er will disgrace your renown;   30
Like you will he live, or like you will he perish;
When decay'd, may he mingle his dust with your own.

1803

32   Epitaph on a Friend

Ἀστὴρ πρὶν μὲν ἔλαμπες ἐνὶ ζωοῖσιν ἑῷος.
LAERTIUS.

Oh! Friend! for ever lov'd, for ever dear!
What fruitless tears have bath'd thy honour'd bier!
What sighs re-echo'd to thy parting breath,
While thou wast struggling in the pangs of death!
Could tears retard the tyrant in his course;   5
Could sighs avert his dart's relentless force;
Could youth and virtue claim a short delay,
Or beauty charm the spectre from his prey;
Thou still had'st lived, to bless my aching sight,
Thy comrade's honour, and thy friend's delight;   10
If, yet, thy gentle spirit hover nigh

28 ⟨In the grave, he alone can his fathers forget.⟩ FPM   29 That ... that] ⟨Your ...
your⟩ FPM

32. Copy text: HI, collated with FPM, POVO, POT, HI1820
title   Epitaph on a Beloved Friend FPM, POVO   epigraph   added in HI
    1 Oh! Friend!] Oh Boy! FPM, POVO   2 bath'd] ⟨wash'd⟩ FPM   5 retard]
⟨have turn'd⟩ FPM   6 avert] ⟨have check'd⟩ FPM
11–28   Though low thy lot, since in a cottage born,
            No titles did thy humble name adorn;
            To me, far dearer, was thy artless love,
            Than all the joys, wealth, fame, and friends could prove:
            For thee alone I liv'd, or wish'd to live,
            Oh God! if impious, this rash word forgive!
            Heart broken now, I wait an equal doom,
            Content to join thee, in thy turf-clad tomb;
            Where this frail form compos'd in endless rest,
            I'll make my last, cold, pillow on thy breast;
            That breast, where oft in life, I've laid my head,
            Will yet receive me mouldering with the dead;
            This life resign'd, without one parting sigh,
            Together in one bed of earth we'll lie!
            Together share the fate to mortals given,
            Together mix our dust and hope for Heaven.
                                            FPM, POVO

The spot, where now thy mould'ring ashes lie,
Here, wilt thou read, recorded on my heart,
A grief too deep to trust the sculptor's art.
No marble marks thy couch of lowly sleep,   15
But living statues, there, are seen to weep;
Affliction's semblance bends not o'er thy tomb,
Affliction's self deplores thy youthful doom.
What though thy sire lament his failing line,
A father's sorrows cannot equal mine!   20
Though none, like thee, his dying hour will cheer,
Yet other offspring soothe his anguish here:
But, who with me shall hold thy former place?
Thine image, what new friendship can efface?
Ah! none! a father's tears will cease to flow,   25
Time will assuage an infant brother's woe;
To all, save one, is consolation known,
While solitary Friendship sighs alone.

                                        1803

33   A Fragment

When, to their airy hall, my fathers' voice,
Shall call my spirit, joyful in their choice;
When, pois'd upon the gale, my form shall ride,
Or, dark in mist, descend the mountain's side;
Oh! may my shade behold no sculptur'd urns,   5
To mark the spot, where earth to earth returns:
No lengthen'd scroll, no praise encumber'd stone;
My epitaph shall be, my name alone:
If *that* with honour fail to crown my clay,
Oh! may no other fame my deeds repay;   10
That, only *that*, shall single out the spot,
By that remember'd, or with that forgot.

                                        1803

33. Copy text: *HI*, collated with *FPM, POVO, POT, HI1820*
title *untitled in FP, added in MS. in FPM*
    7 no . . . stone] of virtue and renown *FPM, POVO*   9 fail] ⟨fails⟩ *FPM*   12 with
that] fore'er *FPM*

34   The Tear

O lachrymarum fons, tenero sacros
Ducentium ortus ex animo; quater
Felix! in imo qui scatentem
Pectore te, pia Nympha, sensit.
                                        GRAY.

[1.]
When Friendship or Love
Our sympathies move;
When Truth, in a glance, should appear,
The lips may beguile,
With a dimple or smile,   5
But the test of affection's a Tear.

2.
Too oft is a smile
But the hypocrite's wile,
To mask detestation, or fear;
Give me the soft sigh,   10
Whilst the soul-telling eye
Is dimm'd, for a time, with a Tear.

3.
Mild Charity's glow,
To us mortals below,
Shews the soul from barbarity clear;   15
Compassion will melt,
Where this virtue is felt,
And its dew is diffus'd in a Tear.

4.
The man doom'd to sail,
With the blast of the gale,   20
Through billows Atlantic to steer,
As he bends o'er the wave,
Which may soon be his grave,
The green sparkles bright with a Tear.

34. Copy text: *HI*, collated with *FPM, POVO, POT, HI1820*   epigraph   *added in HI*

5.

The Soldier braves death,   25
For a fanciful wreath,
In Glory's romantic career;
   But he raises the foe,
   When in battle laid low,
And bathes ev'ry wound with a Tear.   30

6.

If, with high-bounding pride,
He return to his bride,
Renouncing the gore-crimson'd spear;
   All his toils are repaid,
   When, embracing the maid,   35
From her eyelid he kisses the Tear.

7.

Sweet scene of my youth,
Seat of Friendship and Truth,
Where Love chas'd each fast-fleeting year;
   Loth to leave thee, I mourn'd,   40
   For a last look I turn'd,
But thy spire was scarce seen through a Tear.

8.

Though my vows I can pour,
To my Mary no more,
My Mary, to Love once so dear;   45
   In the shade of her bow'r,
   I remember the hour,
She rewarded those vows with a Tear.

9.

By another possest,
May she live ever blest,   50
Her name still my heart must revere;
   With a sigh I resign,
   What I once thought was mine,
And forgive her deceit with a Tear.

31 If,] When *FPM*   32 return] returns *FPM*

10.

Ye friends of my heart,   55
Ere from you I depart,
This hope to my breast is most near;
    If again we shall meet,
    In this rural retreat,
May we meet, as we part, with a Tear.   60

11.

When my soul wings her flight,
To the regions of night,
And my corse shall recline on its bier;
    As ye pass by the tomb,
    Where my ashes consume,   65
Oh! moisten their dust with a Tear.

12.

May no marble bestow
The splendour of woe,
Which the children of vanity rear;
    No fiction of fame   70
    Shall blazon my name,
All I ask, all I wish, is a Tear.

1806

35   An Occasional Prologue,
Delivered Previous to the Performance of 'The Wheel of Fortune', at a Private Theatre

Since, the refinement of this polish'd age
Has swept immoral raillery from the stage;
Since, taste has now expung'd licentious wit,
Which stamp'd disgrace on all an author writ;
Since, now, to please with purer scenes we seek,   5

63 corse shall recline] body shall sleep *FPM*   dating Byron, October 26, 1806 *FPM*;
October 26, 1806 *POVO*

35. Copy text: *HI*, collated with *FPM*, *POVO*, *POT*, *HI1820*

Nor dare to call the blush from Beauty's cheek;
Oh! let the modest Muse some pity claim,
And meet indulgence, though she find not fame.
Still, not for her alone, we wish respect,
Others appear more conscious of defect;   10
To night, no Vet'ran Roscii you behold,
In all the arts of scenic action old;
No COOKE, no KEMBLE, can salute you here,
No SIDDONS draw the sympathetic tear;
To night, you throng to witness the debut,   15
Of embryo Actors, to the drama new;
Here, then, our almost unfledg'd wings we try;
Clip not our pinions, ere the birds can fly;
Failing in this our first attempt to soar,
Drooping, alas! we fall to rise no more.   20
Not one poor trembler, only, fear betrays,
Who hopes, yet almost dreads, to meet your praise,
But all our Dramatis Personae wait,
In fond suspence, this crisis of their fate.
No venal views our progress can retard,   25
Your generous plaudits are our sole reward;
For these, each Hero all his power displays,
Each timid Heroine shrinks before your gaze:
Surely, the last will some protection find,
None, to the softer sex, can prove unkind;   30
Whilst Youth and Beauty form the female shield,
The sternest Censor to the fair must yield.
Yet, should our feeble efforts nought avail,
Should, after all, our best endeavours fail;
Still, let some mercy in your bosoms live,   35
And, if you can't applaud, at least forgive.

[1806]

36   On the Death of Mr. Fox,
the Following Illiberal Impromptu Appeared in a Morning Paper

'Our Nation's foes lament on Fox's death,
But bless the hour, when PITT resign'd his breath;
These feelings wide, let Sense and Truth unclue,
We give the palm, where Justice points its due.'

To Which the Author of these Pieces, Sent the Following Reply.

Oh! factious viper! whose envenom'd tooth,
Would mangle still the dead, perverting truth;
What, tho' our 'nation's foes' lament the fate,
With generous feeling, of the good and great;
Shall dastard tongues, essay to blast the name   5
Of him, whose meed exists in endless fame?
When PITT expir'd, in plenitude of power,
Though ill success obscur'd his dying hour,
Pity her dewy wings before him spread,
For noble spirits 'war not with the dead',   10
His friends, in tears, a last sad requiem gave,
As all his errors slumber'd in the grave;
He sunk, an Atlas bending 'neath the weight,
Of cares o'erwhelming our conflicting state;
When, lo! a Hercules, in Fox, appear'd,   15
Who, for a time, the ruin'd fabric rear'd;
He, too, is fall'n, who Britain's loss supplied,
With him, our fast reviving hopes have died:

36. Copy text: *HI*, collated with *FP*, *POVO*, *POT*, *HI1820*
title   a Morning Paper *HI*, *POT*; the Morning Post *FP*, *POVO*; the following reply
POVO, *HI*, *POT*; the subjoined reply *FP*
    1 whose … tooth,] ⟨whose envenom'd tooth⟩ who, perverting Truth, *FPM*   2 per-
verting] in spite of *FP*; ⟨Would … truth,⟩ The Dead would mangle with envenomed tooth,
FPM   5–6 Shall therefore dastard tongues assail the name | Of him whose virtues
claim eternal fame? *FP*   5 *cor. in MS. in FPM*   12 As] And FP   13 sunk]
⟨died⟩ sinks *FPM*   14 ⟨oppressing our unhappy⟩ o'erwhelming our conflicting *FPM*
15 another Hercules) a Hercules in Fox appear'd *FPM*   17 ⟨dead! who still our England
propp⟩'d⟩ fall'n, who Britain's loss supplied, *FPM*   18 fast] *MS. cor. for* last *in all copies
of FP*   died] ⟨dropp'd⟩ died *FPM*

Not one great people, only, raise his urn,
All Europe's far extended regions mourn.   20
'These feelings wide, let Sense and Truth unclue,
To give the palm, where Justice points it due';
Yet, let not canker'd calumny assail,
Or round our statesman wind her gloomy veil.
Fox! o'er whose corse a mourning world must weep,   25
Whose dear remains in honour'd marble sleep,
For whom, at last, e'en hostile nations groan,
While friends and foes, alike, his talents own,
Fox! shall, in Britain's future annals, shine,
Nor e'en to PITT, the patriot's palm resign;   30
Which Envy, wearing Candour's sacred mask,
For PITT, and PITT alone, has dar'd to ask.

[1806]

37 Stanzas to a Lady, With the Poems of Camoens

1.

This votive pledge of fond esteem,
    Perhaps, dear girl! for me thou'lt prize;
It sings of love's enchanting dream,
    A theme we never can despise.

2.

Who blames it, but the envious fool,   5
    The old and disappointed maid?
Or pupil of the prudish school,
    In single sorrow, doom'd to fade?

3.

Then read, dear girl, with feeling read,
    For thou wilt ne'er be one of those;   10
To thee, in vain, I shall not plead,
    In pity for the poet's woes.

22 To] And *FPM*   23 Yet,] But *FP*   24 Or] And *FP*   28 While]
⟨And⟩ While *FPM*   32 has dar'd] ⟨would dare⟩ has dared *FPM*

37. Copy text: *HI*, collated with *MS. G, POVO, POT, HI1820*

4.

He was, in sooth, a genuine bard;
    His was no faint fictitious flame;
Like his, may love be thy reward;   15
    But not thy hapless fate the same.

[1806]

38   To M . . . . .

[1.]

Oh! did those eyes, instead of fire,
    With bright, but mild affection shine;
Though they might kindle less desire,
    Love, more than mortal, would be thine.

2.

For thou art form'd so heav'nly fair,   5
    Howe'er those orbs may wildly beam,
We must admire, but still despair;
    That fatal glance forbids esteem.

3.

When nature stamp'd thy beauteous birth,
    So much perfection in thee shone,   10
She fear'd, that, too divine for earth,
    The skies might claim thee for their own.

4.

Therefore, to guard her dearest work,
    Lest angels might dispute the prize,
She bade a secret light'ning lurk,   15
    Within those once celestial eyes.

38. Copy text: *HI*, collated with *MSS. N* and *G, FP, POVO, POT, HI1820*
title   To A——. *FP*

6 That though those orbs so wildly beam *N*   9 thy] the *G*   16 celestial] concealed *G*   dating   Friday, Nov. 7th 1806 *FP*; 1806 *POVO, HI, POT*

5.

These might the boldest sylph appal,
    When gleaming with meridian blaze;
Thy beauty must enrapture all,
    But, who can dare thine ardent gaze?   20

6.

'Tis said, that Berenice's hair,
    In stars, adorns the vault of heaven;
But they would ne'er permit thee there,
    Thou would'st so far outshine the seven.

7.

For, did those eyes as planets roll,   25
    Thy sister lights would scarce appear;
E'en suns, which systems now controul,
    Would twinkle dimly through their sphere.

Friday, 7 Nov. 1806

39   To Woman

Woman, experience might have told me,
That all must love thee, who behold thee;
Surely, experience might have taught,
Thy firmest promises are naught;
But, plac'd in all thy charms before me,   5
All I forget, but to adore thee.
Oh Memory! thou choicest blessing,
When join'd with hope, when still possessing;
But how much curst by ev'ry lover,
When hope is fled, and passion's over.   10
Woman, that fair and fond deceiver,
How prompt are striplings to believe her;
How throbs the pulse, when first we view
The eye, that rolls in glossy blue;
Or sparkles black, or mildly throws   15

39. Copy text: *HI*, collated with *FP*, *POVO*, *POT*, *HI1820*
  1 Woman,] Surely *FP*   4 Thy firmest] A woman's *FP*   8 Thou whisperest, as
our hearts are beating, | 'What oft we've done, we're still repeating.' *FP after line 8*

A beam from under hazel brows;
How quick we credit ev'ry oath,
And hear her plight the willing troth;
Fondly we hope, 'twill last for aye,
When, lo! she changes in a day: 20
This Record will for ever stand,
'Woman thy vows, are trac'd in sand.'

[1805?]

40   # To M. S. G.

[1.]

When I dream that you love me, you'll surely forgive,
    Extend not your anger to sleep;
For, in visions alone, your affection can live,
    I rise, and it leaves me to weep.

2.

Then, Morpheus! envelope my faculties fast,   5
    Shed o'er me your languor benign;
Should the dream of to-night, but resemble the last,
    What rapture celestial is mine.

3.

They tell us, that slumber, the sister of death,
    Mortality's emblem is given;   10
To fate how I long to resign my frail breath,
    If this be a foretaste of Heaven.

4.

Ah! frown not, sweet lady, unbend your soft brow,
    Nor deem me too happy in this;
If I sin in my dream, I atone for it now,   15
    Thus doom'd, but to gaze upon bliss.

21 This] The *FP*   22 'That woman's vows are writ in sand.' *FP*

40. Copy text: *HI*, collated with *MS. NP, POVO, POT, HI1820*

5.

Though in visions, sweet lady, perhaps you may smile,
  Oh! think not my penance deficient;
When dreams of your presence, my slumbers beguile,
  To awake, will be torture sufficient.   20

[1806]

41   Song

[1.]

When I rov'd, a young Highlander, o'er the dark heath,
  And climb'd thy steep summit, oh! Morven of Snow,
To gaze on the torrent, that thunder'd beneath,
  Or the mist of the tempest that gather'd below;
Untutor'd by science, a stranger to fear,   5
  And rude as the rocks, where my infancy grew,
No feeling, save one, to my bosom was dear,
  Need I say, my sweet Mary, 'twas centred in you?

2.

Yet, it could not be Love, for I knew not the name,
  What passion can dwell in the heart of a child?   10
But, still, I perceive an emotion the same
  As I felt, when a boy, on the crag-cover'd wild:
One image, alone, on my bosom imprest,
  I lov'd my bleak regions, nor panted for new,
And few were my wants, for my wishes were blest,   15
  And pure were my thoughts, for my soul was with you.

3.

I arose with the dawn, with my dog as my guide,
  From mountain to mountain I bounded along,
I breasted the billows of *Dee's* rushing tide,
  And heard, at a distance, the Highlander's song: 20
At eve, on my heath-cover'd couch of repose,
  No dreams, save of Mary, were spread to my view,
And warm to the skies my devotions arose,
  For the first of my prayers was a blessing on you.

41. Copy text: *POT*, collated with *HI1820*

4.

I left my bleak home, and my visions are gone,   25
   The mountains are vanish'd, my youth is no more;
As the last of my race, I must wither alone,
   And delight but in days, I have witness'd before;
Ah! splendour has rais'd, but embitter'd my lot,
   More dear were the scenes, which my infancy knew;   30
Though my hopes may have fail'd, yet they are not forgot,
   Tho' cold is my heart, still it lingers with you.

5.

When I see some dark hill point its crest to the sky,
   I think of the rocks, that o'ershadow Colbleen;
When I see the soft blue of a love-speaking eye,   35
   I think of those eyes that endear'd the rude scene;
When, haply, some light-waving locks I behold,
   That faintly resemble my Mary's in hue,
I think on the long flowing ringlets of gold,
   The locks that were sacred to beauty, and you.   40

6.

Yet, the day may arrive, when the mountains, once more,
   Shall rise to my sight, in their mantles of snow:
But, while these soar above me, unchang'd as before,
   Will Mary be there to receive me? ah no!
Adieu! then, ye hills, where my childhood was bred,   45
   Thou sweet flowing Dee, to thy waters adieu!
No home in the forest shall shelter my head,
   Ah! Mary, what home could be mine, but with you?

[1807 or 1808]

42   To——

[1.]

Oh! had my Fate been join'd with thine,
   As once this pledge appear'd a token;
These follies had not, then, been mine,
   For, then, my peace had not been broken.

42. Copy text: *HI*, collated with *POT*, *HI1820*
title   To a Lady *1831*, *1832*, *C*, *More*

2.

To thee, these early faults I owe,   5
   To thee, the wise and old reproving;
They know my sins, but do not know,
   'Twas thine to break the bonds of loving.

3.

For, once, my soul like thine was pure,
   And all its rising fires could smother;   10
But, now, thy vows no more endure,
   Bestow'd by thee upon another.

4.

Perhaps, his peace I could destroy,
   And spoil the blisses that await him;
Yet, let my Rival smile in joy,   15
   For thy dear sake, I cannot hate him.

5.

Ah! since thy angel form is gone,
   My heart no more can rest with any;
But what it sought in thee alone,
   Attempts, alas! to find in many.   20

6.

Then, fare thee well, deceitful Maid,
   'Twere vain and fruitless to regret thee;
Nor Hope, nor Memory yield their aid,
   But Pride may teach me to forget thee.

7.

Yet all this giddy waste of years,   25
   This tiresome round of palling pleasures;
These varied loves, these matron's Fears,
   These thoughtless strains to Passion's measures,

8.

If thou wert mine, had all been hush'd,
   This cheek now pale from early riot;   30
With Passions hectic ne'er had flushed,
   But bloom'd in calm domestic quiet.

9.

Yes, once the rural Scene was sweet,
    For Nature seem'd to smile before thee;
And once my Breast abhorr'd deceit,   35
    For then it beat but to adore thee.

10.

But, now, I seek for other joys,
    To think, would drive my soul to madness;
In thoughtless throngs, and empty noise,
    I conquer half my Bosom's sadness.   40

11.

Yet, even in these, a thought will steal,
    In spite of every vain endeavour;
And fiends might pity what I feel,
    To know, that thou art lost forever.

                                        [1806 or 1807]

43   To Mary, On Receiving Her Picture

[1.]

This faint resemblance of thy charms,
    Though strong as mortal art could give,
My constant heart of fear disarms,
    Revives my hopes, and bids me live.

2.

Here, I can trace the locks of gold,   5
    Which round thy snowy forehead wave;
The cheeks, which sprung from Beauty's mould,
    The lips, which made me Beauty's slave.

3.

Here, I can trace——ah no! that eye,
    Whose azure floats in liquid fire,   10
Must all the painter's art defy,
    And bid him from the task retire.

43. Copy text: *HI*, collated with *FP*, *POVO*, *POT*, *HI1820*

4.

Here, I behold its beauteous hue,
    But where's the beam so sweetly straying?
Which gave a lustre to its blue,   15
    Like Luna o'er the ocean playing.

5.

Sweet copy! far more dear to me,
    Lifeless, unfeeling as thou art,
Than all the living forms could be,
    Save her, who plac'd thee next my heart.   20

6.

She plac'd it, sad, with needless fear,
    Lest time might shake my wavering soul,
Unconscious, that her image there,
    Held every sense in fast controul.

7.

Thro' hours, thro' years, thro' time, 'twill cheer;   25
    My hope, in gloomy moments, raise;
In life's last conflict, 'twill appear,
    And meet my fond expiring gaze.

[1806?]

44   Damaetas

In law an infant, and in years a boy,
In mind a slave to every vicious joy,
From every sense of shame and virtue wean'd,
In lies an adept, in deceit a fiend;
Vers'd in hypocrisy, while yet a child,   5
Fickle as wind, of inclinations wild;
Woman his dupe, his heedless friend a tool,

14 so sweetly straying] of soft desire *FP, POVO*   16 Love, only love, could e'er
inspire. *FP, POVO*

44. Copy text: *HI*, collated with *MS. G, POT, HI1820*
title   My Character *G*

Old in the world, though scarcely broke from school;
Damaetas ran through all the maze of sin,
And found the goal, when others just begin: 10
Ev'n still conflicting passions shake his soul,
And bid him drain the dregs of pleasure's bowl;
But, pall'd with vice, he breaks his former chain,
And, what was once his bliss, appears his bane.

[1807]

45   To Marion

Marion! Why that pensive brow?
What disgust to life hast thou?
Change that discontented air;
Frowns become not one so fair.
'Tis not Love disturbs thy rest,   5
Love's a stranger to thy breast;
He, in dimpling smiles, appears,
Or mourns in sweetly timid tears;
Or bends the languid eyelid down,
But shuns the cold forbidding frown.   10
Then resume thy former fire,
Some will love, and all admire;
While that icy aspect chills us,
Nought but cool indiff'rence thrills us.
Would'st thou wand'ring hearts beguile,   15
Smile, at least, or seem to smile;
Eyes, like thine, were never meant
To hide their orbs, in dark restraint;
Spite of all thou fain would'st say,
Still in truant beams they play.   20
Thy lips,—but here my modest Muse
Her impulse chaste must needs refuse.
She blushes, curtsies, frowns,—in short she
Dreads, lest the subject should transport me;

45. Copy text: *HI*, collated with *MS. N*, *POT*, *HI1820*
   1 Marion] Harriet *N*   14 cool] cold *N*   22 Must needs her Impulse *chaste*
refuse *N*

And flying off, in search of reason,   25
Brings prudence back in proper season.
All I shall, therefore, say, (whate'er
I think, is neither here nor there,)
Is that such lips, of looks endearing,
Were form'd for better things, than sneeering;   30
Of soothing compliments divested,
Advice, at least's, disinterested;
Such is my artless song to thee,
From all the flow of flatt'ry free;
Counsel, like mine, is as a brother's,   35
My heart is given to some others;
That is to say, unskill'd to cozen,
It shares itself amongst a dozen.
Marion! adieu! oh! prithee slight not
This warning, tho' it may delight not;   40
And, lest my precepts be displeasing,
To those, who think remonstrance teazing,
At once, I'll tell thee our opinion,
Concerning woman's soft dominion:
Howe'er we gaze with admiration,   45
On eyes of blue, or lips carnation;
Howe'er the flowing locks attract us,
Howe'er those beauties may distract us;
Still fickle, we are prone to rove,
These cannot fix our souls to love;   50
It is not too severe a stricture,
To say they form a pretty picture.
But, would'st thou see the secret chain,
Which binds us in your humble train,
To hail you queens of all creation,   55
Know, in a word, 'tis ANIMATION.

[10 Jan. 1807]

27–8 *All* I shall therefore say of these | (Thy Pardon if my words displease) *N*
39 Marion] Harriet *N*
41–2   ⟨I think it will not be found fault by
            Those who may love the name of M-lt-by⟩
            And lest thy precepts be found fault by
            Those who ⟨esteem⟩ approve the frowns of M-lt-by *N*
52 form] make *N*   53 see] ⟨know⟩ *N*

46   Oscar of Alva

A Tale

[1.]

How sweetly shines, through azure skies,
　　The lamp of Heav'n on Lora's shore;
Where Alva's hoary turrets rise,
　　And hear the din of arms no more.

2.

But often has yon rolling moon,　　　　　　　　5
　　On Alva's casques of silver play'd;
And view'd, at midnight's silent noon,
　　Her chiefs in gleaming mail array'd.

3.

And, on the crimson'd rocks beneath,
　　Which scowl o'er ocean's sullen flow,　　　　10
Pale in the scatter'd ranks of death,
　　She saw the gasping warrior low.

4.

While many an eye, which ne'er again
　　Could mark the rising orb of day,
Turn'd feebly from the gory plain,　　　　　　15
　　Beheld in death her fading ray.

5.

Once, to those eyes the lamp of Love,
　　They blest her dear propitious light;
But now she glimmer'd from above,
　　A sad funereal torch of night.　　　　　　　20

46. Copy text: *HI*, collated with *MS.* scraps (*H*, 93–6, 105–8; *Hn*, 113–23, 125–36; *B*, 137–68; *P*, 179–84, 193–6; *Ne*, 257–60, 267–72; *Mo*, 285–8; *T*, 289–92; *S*, 293–6), *POT*

12 saw] view'd *HI*　　　13 While] When *HI, cor. on HI errata slip*　　14 mark] view *HI*

6.

Faded is Alva's noble race,
  And grey her towers are seen afar;
No more her heroes urge the chace,
  Or roll the crimson tide of war.

7.

But, who was last of Alva's clan?   25
  Why grows the moss on Alva's stone?
Her towers resound no steps of man,
  They echo to the gale alone.

8.

And when that gale is fierce and high,
  A sound is heard in yonder hall,   30
It rises hoarsely through the sky,
  And vibrates o'er the mouldering wall.

9.

Yes, when the eddying tempest sighs,
  It shakes the shield of Oscar brave;
But, there no more his banners rise,   35
  No more his plumes of sable wave.

10.

Fair shone the sun on Oscar's birth,
  When Angus hail'd his eldest born;
The vassals round their chieftain's hearth,
  Crowd to applaud the happy morn.   40

11.

They feast upon the mountain deer,
  The Pibroch rais'd its piercing note,
To gladden more their Highland cheer,
  The strains in martial numbers float.

12.

And they, who heard the war-notes wild,   45
  Hop'd that, one day, the Pibroch's strain
Should play before the Hero's child,
  While he should lead the Tartan train.

13.

Another year is quickly past,
    And Angus hails another son,   50
His natal day is like the last,
    Nor soon the jocund feast was done.

14.

Taught by their sire to bend the bow,
    On Alva's dusky hills of wind;
The boys in childhood chas'd the roe,   55
    And left their hounds in speed behind.

15.

But ere their years of youth are o'er,
    They mingle in the ranks of war;
They lightly wheel the bright claymore,
    And send the whistling arrow far.   60

16.

Dark was the flow of Oscar's hair,
    Wildly it stream'd along the gale;
But Allan's locks were bright and fair,
    And pensive seem'd his cheek, and pale.

17.

But Oscar own'd a hero's soul,   65
    His dark eye shone through beams of truth;
Allan had early learn'd controul,
    And smooth his words had been from youth.

18.

Both, both were brave, the Saxon spear,
    Was shiver'd oft beneath their steel;   70
And Oscar's bosom scorn'd to fear,
    But Oscar's bosom knew to feel.

19.

While Allan's soul belied his form,
    Unworthy with such charms to dwell;
Keen as the lightning of the storm,   75
    On foes his deadly vengeance fell.

20.

From high Southannon's distant tower
  Arriv'd a young and noble dame;
With Kenneth's lands to form her dower,
  Glenalvon's blue ey'd daughter came.   80

21.

And Oscar claim'd the beauteous bride,
  And Angus on his Oscar smil'd,
It sooth'd the father's feudal pride,
  Thus to obtain Glenalvon's child.

22.

Hark! to the Pibroch's pleasing note,   85
  Hark to the swelling nuptial song;
In joyous strains the voices float,
  And still the choral peal prolong.

23.

See how the Heroes' blood-red plumes,
  Assembl'd wave in Alva's hall;   90
Each youth his varied plaid assumes,
  Attending on their chieftain's call.

24.

It is not war their aid demands,
  The Pibroch plays the song of peace;
To Oscar's nuptials throng the bands,   95
  Nor yet the sounds of pleasure cease.

25.

But where is Oscar? sure 'tis late:
  Is this a bridegroom's ardent flame?
While thronging guests and ladies wait,
  Nor Oscar nor his brother came.   100

26.

At length young Allan join'd the bride,
  'Why comes not Oscar?' Angus said:
'Is he not here?' the Youth reply'd,
  'With me he rov'd not o'er the glade.

96 ⟨And all⟩ Nor yet the Sounds of ⟨Music⟩ pleasure cease. *H*

27.

'Perchance, forgetful of the day,   105
    'Tis his to chace the bounding roe;
Or Ocean's waves prolong his stay,
    Yet, Oscar's bark is seldom slow.'

28.

'Oh no,' the anguish'd Sire rejoin'd,
    'Nor chace, nor wave my Boy delay;   110
Would he to Mora seem unkind?
    Would aught to her impede his way?

29.

'Oh! search, ye Chiefs! oh! search around!
    Allan, with these thro' Alva fly;
Till Oscar, till my son is found,   115
    Haste, haste, nor dare attempt reply.'

30.

All is confusion,—through the vale,
    The name of Oscar hoarsely rings,
It rises on the murm'ring gale,
    Till night expands her dusky wings.   120

31.

It breaks the stillness of the night,
    But echoes through her shades in vain;
It sounds through morning's misty light,
    But Oscar comes not o'er the plain.

32.

Three days, three sleepless nights, the Chief   125
    For Oscar search'd each mountain cave;
Then hope is lost, in boundless grief,
    His locks in grey-torn ringlets wave.

105 ⟨It is not mine⟩ *H*   106 ⟨He⟩ *H*   114 ⟨Allan thy brother's name recall⟩ *Hn*
116 Haste ⟨nor bring to me⟩ *Hn*   121 ⟨And even through⟩ *Hn*   126 Oscar ⟨through⟩
searched *Hn*

33.

'Oscar, my Son,—thou God of Heav'n,
  Restore the prop of sinking age;   130
Or, if that hope no more is given,
  Yield his assassin to my rage.

34.

'Yes, on some desert rocky shore,
  My Oscar's whiten'd bones must lie;
Then grant, thou God, I ask no more,   135
  With him his frantic Sire may die.

35.

'Yet, he may live,—away despair;
  Be calm, my soul, he yet may live;
T'arraign my fate, my voice forbear,
  O God! my impious prayer forgive!   140

36.

'What, if he live, for me no more,
  I sink forgotten in the dust,
The hope of Alva's age is o'er,
  Alas! can pangs like these be just?'

37.

Thus did the hapless parent mourn,   145
  Till Time, who soothes severest woe,
Had bade serenity return,
  And made the tear-drop cease to flow:

38.

For still some latent hope surviv'd,
  That Oscar might once more appear;   150
His hope now droop'd, and now reviv'd,
  Till Time had told a tedious year.

131 ⟨Let me not⟩ *Hn*   133 on. . .shore] ⟨in. . .land⟩ *Hn*   134 My Oscar's
⟨cold Remains / mouldering ashes⟩ lie *Hn*   139 ⟨thy⟩ fate *B*   141 What] ⟨Yet⟩ *B*
143 age] line *B*   144 Alas!] Oh God, *B*   145 mourn] ⟨rave⟩ *B*   148 And
⟨bade⟩ the teardrops cease *B*   149 For] ⟨And⟩ *B*   150 That] ⟨And⟩ *B*

39.

Days roll'd along, the orb of light,
  Again had run his destin'd race;
No Oscar bless'd his father's sight,   155
  And sorrow left a fainter trace.

40.

For youthful Allan still remain'd,
  And now his father's only joy;
And Mora's heart was quickly gain'd,
  For beauty crown'd the fair-hair'd boy.   160

41.

She thought that Oscar low was laid,
  And Allan's face was wond'rous fair,
If Oscar liv'd, some other maid
  Had claim'd his faithless bosom's care.

42.

And Angus said, if one year more,   165
  In fruitless hope was pass'd away;
His fondest scruples should be o'er,
  And he would name their nuptial day.

43.

Slow roll'd the moons, but blest at last,
  Arriv'd the dearly destin'd morn;   170
The year of anxious trembling past,
  What smiles the lovers' cheeks adorn!

44.

Hark to the pibroch's pleasing note,
  Hark to the swelling nuptial song;
In joyous strains the voices float,   175
  And still the choral peal prolong.

153 the ... light] ⟨the orb of light / the orb of earth⟩ B   154 race] ⟨Course⟩ B
161 ⟨And Oscar would not come again⟩ B   162 was ... fair] was fair to see B
164 Might ⟨his⟩ win his heart, by ⟨ ? ⟩ fates decree. B   166 hope ⟨of Oscar⟩ was B

45.

Again the clan in festive crowd,
   Throng through the gate of Alva's hall;
The sounds of mirth re-echo loud;
   And all their former joy recall.   180

46.

But, who is he, whose darken'd brow
   Glooms in the midst of general mirth?
Before his eye's far fiercer glow,
   The blue flames curdle o'er the hearth.

47.

Dark is the robe which wraps his form,   185
   And tall his plume of gory red;
His voice is like the rising storm,
   But light and trackless is his tread.

48.

'Tis noon of night, the pledge goes round,
   The bridegroom's health is deeply quaft;   190
With shouts the vaulted roofs resound,
   And all combine to hail the draught.

49.

Sudden the stranger chief arose,
   And all the clamourous crowd are hush'd;
And Angus' cheek with wonder glows,   195
   And Mora's tender bosom blush'd.

50.

'Old man,' he cry'd, 'this pledge is done,
   Thou saw'st, 'twas duly drank by me,
It hail'd the nuptials of thy son,
   Now will I claim a pledge from thee.   200

179 The ⟨voice⟩ Sounds *P*   184 ⟨ ? the Blazes of⟩ *P*   194 are] was *P*   198 drank]
drunk *1831, 1832, C, More*

51.

'While all around is mirth and joy,
    To bless thy Allan's happy lot;
Say, had'st thou ne'er another boy?
    Say, why should Oscar be forgot?'

52.

'Alas!' the hapless sire reply'd,   205
    The big tear starting as he spoke;
'When Oscar left my hall, or died,
    This aged heart was almost broke.

53.

'Thrice has the earth revolv'd her course,
    Since Oscar's form has bless'd my sight;   210
And Allan is my last resource,
    Since martial Oscar's death, or flight.'

54.

' 'Tis well,' reply'd the stranger stern,
    And fiercely flash'd his rolling eye,
'Thy Oscar's fate, I fain would learn,   215
    Perhaps the Hero did not die.

55.

'Perchance, if those, whom most he lov'd,
    Would call, thy Oscar might return;
Perchance, the chief has only rov'd,
    For him thy Beltane yet may burn.   220

56.

'Fill high the bowl, the table round,
    We will not claim the pledge by stealth;
With wine let every cup be crown'd,
    Pledge me departed Oscar's health.'

57.

'With all my soul,' old Angus said,   225
    And fill'd his goblet to the brim;
'Here's to my boy! alive or dead,
    I ne'er shall find a son like him.'

58.

'Bravely, old man, this health has sped,
    But why does Allan trembling stand?   230
Come, drink remembrance of the dead,
    And raise thy cup with firmer hand.'

59.

The crimson glow of Allan's face,
    Was turn'd at once to ghastly hue;
The drops of death each other chase   235
    Adown in agonizing dew.

60.

Thrice did he raise the goblet high,
    And thrice his lips refused to taste;
For thrice he caught the stranger's eye,
    On his with deadly fury plac'd.   240

61.

'And is it thus, a brother hails,
    A brother's fond remembrance here!
If thus affection's strength prevails,
    What might we not expect from fear?'

62.

Rous'd by the sneer, he rais'd the bowl,   245
    'Would, Oscar now could share our mirth!'
Internal fear appall'd his soul,
    He said, and dash'd the cup to earth.

63.

'Tis he, I hear my murderer's voice,'
    Loud shrieks a darkly gleaming form;   250
'A murderer's voice!' the roof replies,
    And deeply swells the bursting storm.

64.

The tapers wink, the chieftains shrink,
    The stranger's gone,—amidst the crew
A form was seen, in tartan green,   255
    And tall the shade terrific grew.

247 fear] fears *HI*

65.

His waist was bound, with a broad belt round,
  His plume of sable stream'd on high;
But his breast was bare, with the red wounds there,
  And fix'd was the glare of his glassy eye.   260

66.

And thrice he smil'd, with his eye so wild,
  On Angus bending low the knee;
And thrice he frown'd, on a chief on the ground,
  Whom shivering crowds with horror see.

67.

The bolts loud roll, from pole to pole,   265
  The thunders through the welkin ring;
And the gleaming form, through the mist of the
    storm,
  Was borne on high by the whirlwind's wing.

68.

Cold was the feast, the revel ceas'd,
  Who lies upon the stony floor?   270
Oblivion prest old Angus' breast,
  At length his life-pulse throbs once more.

69.

'Away, away, let the leech essay,
  To pour the light on Allan's eyes';
His sand is done,—his race is run,   275
  Oh! never more shall Allan rise!

70.

But Oscar's breast is cold as clay,
  His locks are lifted by the gale;
And Allan's barbed arrow lay,
  With him in dark Glentanar's vale.   280

258 ⟨A sable plume high-streamed⟩ Ne   259 bare, with] ⟨there, and⟩ Ne   260 glare]
Stare Ne   268 borne . . . by] roll'd upon Ne   270 the ⟨Earth⟩ stony Ne
271 Old Angus prest, the earth with his breast, Ne, HI

71.

And whence the dreadful stranger came,
    Or who, no mortal wight can tell;
But no one doubts the form of flame,
    For Alva's sons knew Oscar well.

72.

Ambition nerv'd young Allan's hand,   285
    Exulting demons wing'd his dart,
While Envy wav'd her burning brand,
    And pour'd her venom round his heart.

73.

Swift is the shaft from Allan's bow,
    Whose streaming life-blood stains his side?   290
Dark Oscar's sable crest is low,
    The dart has drunk his vital tide.

74.

And Mora's eye could Allan move,
    She bade his wounded pride rebel:
Alas! that eyes, which beam'd with love,   295
    Should urge the soul to deeds of Hell.

75.

Lo, see'st thou not a lonely tomb,
    Which rises o'er a warrior dead?
It glimmers thro' the twilight gloom;
    Oh! that is Allan's nuptial bed.   300

76.

Far, distant far, the noble grave,
    Which held his clan's great ashes, stood;
And o'er his corse no banners wave,
    For they were stain'd with kindred blood.

292 drunk] drank *HI*   294 She ... pride] ⟨Love ... heart⟩ *S*
8118902   D

77·

What minstrel grey, what hoary bard,   305
    Shall Allan's deeds on harp-strings raise?
The song is glory's chief reward,
    But who can strike a murd'rer's praise?

78.

Unstrung, untouch'd, the harp must stand,
    No minstrel dare the theme awake;   310
Guilt would benumb his palsied hand,
    His harp in shuddering chords would break.

79·

No lyre of fame, no hallow'd verse,
    Shall sound his glories high in air,
A dying father's bitter curse,   315
    A brother's death-groan echoes there.

[1807]

47   To the Duke of D[orset]

n looking over my papers, to select a few additional Poems for this second edition, I found
the following lines, which I had totally forgotten, composed in the Summer of 1805, a short
time previous to my departure from H[arrow]. They were addressed to a young school-fellow
of high rank, who had been my frequent companion in some rambles, through the neighbour-
ing country; however he never saw the lines, and most probably never will. As, on a re-perusal,
I found them not worse than some other pieces in the collection; I have now published them,
for the first time, after a slight revision.

D[O]R[SE]T! whose early steps with mine have stray'd,
Exploring every path of Ida's glade,
Whom, still, affection taught me to defend,
And made me less a tyrant than a friend;
Tho' the harsh custom of our youthful band,   5
Bade *thee* obey, and gave *me* to command;
Thee on whose head a few short years will shower
The gift of riches, and the pride of power;
Even now a name illustrious is thine own,
Renown'd in rank, nor far beneath the throne.   10

47. Copy text: *POT*, collated with *HI1820*
    10 nor] not *HI1820, 1831, 1832, C, More*

Yet, D[o]r[se]t, let not this seduce thy soul,
To shun fair science, or evade controul;
Tho' passive tutors, fearful to dispraise
The titled child, whose future breath may raise,
View ducal errors with indulgent eyes,   15
And wink at faults they tremble to chastise.

When youthful parasites, who bend the knee
To wealth, their golden idol, not to thee!
And, even in simple boyhood's opening dawn,
Some slaves are found to flatter and to fawn;   20
When these declare, 'that pomp alone should wait
On one by birth predestin'd to be great;
That books were only meant for drudging fools,
That gallant spirits scorn the common rules';
Believe them not,—they point the path to shame,   25
And seek to blast the honours of thy name:
Turn to the few, in Ida's early throng,
Whose souls disdain not to condemn the wrong;
Or, if amidst the comrades of thy youth,
None dare to raise the sterner voice of truth,   30
Ask thine own heart! 'twill bid thee, boy, forbear,
For *well* I know, that virtue lingers there.

Yes! I have mark'd thee many a passing day,
But, now new scenes invite me far away;
Yes! I have mark'd, within that generous mind,   35
A soul, if well matur'd, to bless mankind;
Ah! tho' myself, by nature haughty, wild,
Whom Indiscretion hail'd her favourite child;
Tho' ev'ry Error stamps me for her own
And dooms my fall, I fain would fall alone;   40
Tho' my proud heart no precept, now, can tame,
I love the virtues, which I cannot claim.
'Tis not enough, with other Sons of power,
To gleam the lambent meteor of an hour,
To swell some peerage page in feeble pride,   45
With long-drawn names, that grace no page beside;
Then share with titled crowds the common lot,
In life just gaz'd at, in the grave forgot;

While nought divides thee from the vulgar dead,
Except the dull cold stone, that hides thy head,   50
The mouldering 'scutcheon, or the Herald's roll,
That well-emblazon'd, but neglected scroll,
Where Lords, unhonour'd, in the tomb may find,
One spot to leave a worthless name behind.—
There sleep, unnotic'd as the gloomy vaults,   55
That veil their dust, their follies, and their faults;
A race, with old armorial lists o'erspread,
In records, destin'd never to be read.
Fain would I view thee, with prophetic eyes,
Exalted more among the good and wise;   60
A glorious and a long career pursue,
As first in Rank, the first in Talent too;
Spurn ev'ry vice, each little meanness shun,
Not Fortune's minion, but her noblest son.

Turn to the annals of a former day,   65
Bright are the deeds, thine earlier Sires display;
One, tho' a Courtier, liv'd a man of worth,
And call'd, proud boast! the British Drama forth.
Another view! not less renown'd for Wit,
Alike for courts, and camps, or senates fit;   70
Bold in the field, and favour'd by the Nine,
In ev'ry splendid part ordain'd to shine;
Far, far distinguish'd from the glitt'ring throng,
The pride of Princes, and the boast of Song.
Such were thy Fathers, thus preserve their name,   75
Not heir to titles only, but to Fame.
The hour draws nigh, a few brief days will close,
To me, this little scene of joys and woes;
Each knell of Time now warns me to resign
Shades, where Hope, Peace, and Friendship, all were mine; 80
Hope, that could vary like the rainbow's hue,
And gild their pinions, as the moments flew;
Peace, that reflection never frown'd away,
By dreams of ill, to cloud some future day;
Friendship, whose truth let childhood only tell,   85
Alas! they love not long, who love so well.
To these adieu! nor let me linger o'er

Scenes hail'd, as exiles hail their native shore,
Receding, slowly, thro' the dark-blue deep,
Beheld by eyes, that mourn, yet cannot weep.   90

D[o]r[se]t! farewell! I will not ask one part
Of sad remembrance in so young a heart;
The coming 'morrow from thy youthful mind,
Will sweep my name, nor leave a trace behind.
And, yet, perhaps in some maturer year,   95
Since chance has thrown us in the self-same sphere,
Since the same senate, nay, the same debate,
May one day claim our suffrage for the state,
We hence may meet, and pass each other by
With faint regard, or cold and distant eye.   100
For me, in future, neither friend, nor foe,
A stranger to thyself, thy weal or woe;
With thee no more again I hope to trace
The recollection of our early race;
No more, as once, in social hours, rejoice,   105
Or hear, unless in crowds, thy well-known voice.
Still, if the wishes of a heart untaught
To veil those feelings, which, perchance, it ought,
If these,—but let me cease the lengthen'd strain,
Oh! if these wishes are not breath'd in vain,   110
The Guardian Seraph, who directs thy fate,
Will leave thee glorious, as he found thee great.

[1805]

48   Adrian's Address to His Soul, When Dying

Animula! vagula, blandula,
Hospes, comesque, corporis,
Quae nunc abibis in loca?
Pallidula, rigida, nudula,
Nec, ut soles, dabis jocos.

101 nor] or *POT*

48. Copy text: *HI*, collated with *MS, G, FP, POVO, POT, HI1820*

Translation

Ah! gentle, fleeting, wav'ring sprite,
Friend and associate of this clay!
   To what unknown region borne,
Wilt thou, now, wing thy distant flight?
No more, with wonted humour gay,   5
   But pallid, cheerless, and forlorn.

[1806]

49   Translation from Catullus

'Ad Lesbiam'

Equal to Jove, that youth must be,
Greater than Jove, he seems to me,
Who, free from Jealousy's alarms,
Securely, views thy matchless charms;
That cheek, which ever dimpling glows,   5
That mouth, from whence such music flows,
To him, alike, are always known,
Reserv'd for him, and him alone.
Ah! Lesbia! though 'tis death to me,
I cannot choose but look on thee;   10
But, at the sight, my senses fly,
I needs must gaze, but gazing die;
Whilst trembling with a thousand fears,
Parch'd to the throat, my tongue adheres,
My pulse beats quick, my breath heaves short,   15
My limbs deny their slight support;
Cold dews my pallid face o'erspread,
With deadly languor droops my head,
My ears with tingling echoes ring,
And life itself is on the wing;   20
My eyes refuse the cheering light,

1 wav'ring, fleeting *G*   2 of this] of *G*
dating in *FP only*

49. Copy text: *HI*, collated with *FP*, *POVO*, *POT*, *HI1820*

Their orbs are veil'd in starless night;
Such pangs my nature sinks beneath,
And feels a temporary death.

[1806]

50 Translation of the Epitaph on Virgil and Tibullus

by Domitius Marsus

He, who sublime, in epic numbers roll'd,
   And he, who struck the softer lyre of love,
By Death's unequal hand alike controul'd
   Fit comrades in Elysian regions move.

[1806]

51 Translation from Catullus

'Luctus de Morte Passeris'

Ye Cupids, droop each little head,
Nor let your wings with joy be spread,
My Lesbia's fav'rite bird is dead,
   Whom dearer than her eyes she lov'd:
For he was gentle, and so true,   5
Obedient to her call he flew,
No fear, no wild alarm he knew,
   But lightly o'er her bosom mov'd:

And softly fluttering here and there,
He never sought to cleave the air;   10
But chirrup'd oft, and free from care,
   Tun'd to her ear his grateful strain.
Now having pass'd the gloomy bourn,

50. Copy text: *HI*, collated with *MS. G, FP, POVO, POT, HI1820*
title *untitled in G*

51. Copy text: *HI*, collated with *FP, POVO, POT, HI1820*
  4 Whom] Which *FP, POVO*   11 But] He *C*   13 Now having] But now he's *FP*

From whence he never can return,
His death, and Lesbia's grief, I mourn,   15
    Who sighs, alas! but sighs in vain.

Oh! curst be thou, devouring grave!
Whose jaws eternal victims crave,
From whom no earthly power can save,
    For thou hast ta'en the bird away: 20
From thee, my Lesbia's eyes o'erflow,
Her swollen cheeks, with weeping, glow,
Thou art the cause of all her woe,
    Receptacle of life's decay.

[1806]

52   Imitated from Catullus

                    To Ellen

Oh! might I kiss those eyes of fire,
A million scarce would quench desire;
Still, would I steep my lips in bliss,
And dwell an age on every kiss;
Nor then my soul should sated be,   5
Still, would I kiss, and cling to thee;
Nought should my kiss from thine dissever,
Still, would we kiss, and kiss for ever;
E'en though the number did exceed
The yellow harvest's countless seed;   10
To part would be a vain endeavour,
Could I desist?—ah! never—never.

[16 Nov. 1806]

52. Copy text: *HI*, collated with *MSS. N* and *G, FP, POVO, POT, HI1820*
title   Imitated from Catullus. To Anna *FP;* Translation from Catullus *N*
    9 number] numbers *HI1820, 1831, 1832, C, More*   did] should *N*
dating   *in FP only*

53   Translation from Anacreon
                        To His Lyre

          I wish to tune my quivering lyre,
          To deeds of fame, and notes of fire;
          To echo from its rising swell,
          How heroes fought, and nations fell;
          When Atreus' sons advanc'd to war,   5
          Or Tyrian cadmus rov'd afar;
          But still, to martial strains unknown,
          My lyre recurs to love alone.
          Fir'd with the hope of future fame,
          I seek some nobler hero's name;   10
          The dying chords are strung anew,
          To war, to war, my harp is due;
          With glowing strings, the epic strain,
          To Jove's great son I raise again,
          Alcides, and his glorious deeds,   15
          Beneath whose arm the Hydra bleeds;
          All, all in vain, my wayward lyre,
          Wakes silver notes of soft desire.
          Adieu ye chiefs, renown'd in arms,
          Adieu the clang of war's alarms.   20
          To other deeds my soul is strung,
          And sweeter notes shall now be sung;
          My harp shall all its powers reveal,
          To tell the tale my heart must feel,
          Love, love alone, my lyre shall claim,   25
          In songs of bliss, and sighs of flame.

                                            [1805 or 1806]

53. Copy text: *HI*, collated with *MS. T, POT, HI1820, Pratt*
title Εισ Λυραν *MS. T*

  1 wish] sought *T, Pratt*   3 ⟨I strove to tune its⟩ rising swell *T*   4 ⟨To sing /
How Atreus / Nations⟩ How *T*   6 ⟨And the Theban⟩ Or *T*   9–12 *not in T, Pratt*
13 ⟨I sing the chords new strain⟩ *T;* The chords renewed, a second strain *T, Pratt*
14 raise] strike *T, Pratt*   18 Wakes] Makes *T, Pratt*   20 the ⟨clang of Hostile /
Blasts of⟩ clang *T*
21–4   The Trumpet's Blast with them accords,
                           To rouse the clash of hostile swords
                           Be mine the softer, sweeter Care,
                           To soothe the young, and virgin Fair, *T, Pratt*
26 sighs] ⟨winds⟩ *T*

54   [Translation from Anacreon]
Ode 3

'Twas now the hour when Night had driven,
Her car half round yon sable heaven,
Bootes only seem'd to roll
His Arctic charge around the Pole;
While mortals lost in gentle sleep,   5
Forgot to smile, or ceas'd to weep;
At this lone hour, the Paphian boy,
Descending from the realms of joy;
Quick to my gate, directs his course,
And knocks with all his little force;   10
My visions fled, alarm'd I rose,
'What stranger breaks my blest repose?'
Alas! replies the wily child,
In faultering accents, sweetly mild;
'A hapless infant here I roam,   15
Far from my dear maternal home;
Oh! shield me from the wint'ry blast,
The nightly storm is pouring fast,
No prowling robber lingers here;
A wandering baby, who can fear?'   20
I heard his seeming artless tale,
I heard his sighs upon the gale;
My breast was never pity's foe,
But felt for all the baby's woe,
I drew the bar, and by the light,   25
Young Love, the infant, met my sight;

---

54. Copy text: *HI*, collated with *MS. P, POT, HI1820*
title   From Anacreon *P*; Ode 3. *HI, POT*
     2 Her ⟨sable⟩ car half round ⟨the⟩ Heaven *P*   2a–b ⟨Bootes⟩ No moon in silver Robe
was seen, | Nor even a twinkling Star between, *P*   4 Arctic] ⟨silver⟩ *P*   5 ⟨Lost in the
balmy arms of Sleep⟩ / ⟨Mortals⟩ While ⟨man⟩ mortals *P*   6 ⟨Man ceased⟩ to smile *P*
9 ⟨To⟩ Quick *P*   10 And ⟨strikes⟩ with *P*   11 My visions fled, ⟨and I arose⟩ *P*
12 blest] ⟨soft⟩ *P*   14 In ⟨accents⟩ faultering *P*   15 A ⟨wandering⟩ Infant here I
⟨stray⟩ *P*   16 maternal] ⟨and native⟩ *P*   17 wint'ry] ⟨howling⟩ *P*   18 nightly]
⟨wintry⟩ *P*   19 lingers] ⟨wanders⟩ *P*   20 wandering] ⟨shivering⟩ *P*
21 Touched with the seeming artless Tale *P*   22 ⟨Compassion / The tear⟩ Compassion's
Tears oer doubt prevail *P*   23–4 Methought I viewed him cold, and damp | I trimmed
anew my dying lamp *P*   25 I drew] Drew back *P*   26 A ⟨winged⟩ Pinioned Infant
met my sight *P*

His bow across his shoulders flung,
And thence his fatal quiver hung,
(Ah! little did I think the dart,
Would rankle soon within my heart;)   30
With care I tend my weary guest,
His little fingers chill my breast,
His glossy curls, his azure wing,
Which droop with nightly showers, I wring:
His shivering limbs the embers warm,   35
And, now, reviving from the storm,
Scarce had he felt his wonted glow,
Than swift he siezed his slender bow;
'I fain would know, my gentle host,'
He cried, 'if this its strength has lost;   40
I fear, relax'd with midnight dews,
The strings their former aid refuse';
With poison tipt, his arrow flies,
Deep in my tortur'd heart it lies:
Then loud the joyous urchin laught,   45
'My bow can still impel the shaft;
'Tis firmly fix'd, thy sighs reveal it,
Say, courteous host, canst thou not feel it?'

[1805 or 1806]

55 Fragments of School Exercises, From the Prometheus Vinctus of Aeschylus

Great Jove! to whose Almighty throne,
Both Gods and mortals homage pay,

27 ⟨A⟩ His Bow across his shoulders slung *P*   28 And thence a ⟨quiver graceful⟩
gilded quiver hung *P*   29–30 *not in P*   31 ⟨I *?* again / my half extinguished
fire⟩ *P*   weary] little *P*   32 ⟨My fire receives his⟩ His ⟨tender⟩ shivering hands by
mine are prest *P*
32a–b   My hearth, I load with embers warm |
                         To dry the dewdrops of the Storm *P*
33 glossy curls] ⟨curling Locks⟩ *P*   34 ⟨Dripping⟩ with *P*   35–6 *not in P*
37 wonted] former *P*   39 ⟨Now will I bring⟩ *P*   know] ⟨learn⟩ *P*   41 ⟨Alas! I fear
thou / the rains of yonder Sky⟩ / ⟨My strings are drenched by yonder Sky⟩ Drenched by the
Rains of yonder Sky *P*   42 The strings are weak—but let us try *P*   43 tipt] ⟨tipt /
steep⟩ *P*   44 my ⟨heart / Bosom⟩ tortur'd *P*   46 ⟨'Unhurt, he cries⟩ *P*   47 ⟨It
st⟩ Tis ⟨strong I see⟩ thy sighs ⟨reveal't⟩ *P*   48 ⟨Tel⟩ Say courteous ⟨Stranger⟩ *P*

55. Copy text: *HI*, collated with *FP, POVO, POT, HI1820*

Ne'er may my soul thy power disown,
Thy dread behests ne'er disobey.
Oft shall the sacred victim fall,   5
In sea-girt Ocean's mossy hall;
My voice shall raise no impious strain,
'Gainst him who rules the sky and azure main.
★ ★ ★ ★ ★ ★ ★ ★ ★ ★ ★ ★ ★

How different now thy joyless fate,
Since first Hesione thy bride,   10
When plac'd aloft in godlike state,
The blushing beauty by thy side.
Thou sat'st, while reverend Ocean smil'd,
And mirthful strains the hours beguil'd;
The Nymphs and Tritons danc'd around,   15
Nor yet thy doom was fix'd, nor Jove relentless
frown'd.

Harrow, 1 Dec. 1804

56   The Episode of Nisus and Euryalus

A Paraphrase from the Aeneid lib. 9.

Nisus, the guardian of the portal, stood,
Eager to gild his arms with hostile blood;
Well skill'd, in fight, the quiv'ring lance to wield,
Or pour his arrows through th'embattl'd field;
From Ida torn he left his sylvan cave,   5
And sought a foreign home, a distant grave,
To watch the movements of the Daunian host;
With him Euryalus, sustains the post,

56. Copy text: *HI*, collated with *MS. B*, *POVO*, *POT*
title Fragment of a Translation from the 9th Book of Virgil's Aenead.
5–14   Him IDA sent, a hunter, now, no more,
              To combat foes, upon a foreign shore;
              Near him, the loveliest of the Trojan band,
              Did fair Euryalus, his comrade, stand;
              Few are the seasons of his youthful life,
              As yet a novice in the martial strife,
              The Gods to him unwonted gifts impart,
              A female's beauty, with a hero's heart. *POVO*
5 sylvan cave,] native grove; *HI*   6 Through distant climes, and trackless seas to rove .
HI

No lovelier mien adorn'd the ranks of Troy,
And beardless bloom yet grac'd the gallant boy;   10
Though few the seasons of his youthful life,
As yet a novice in the martial strife,
'Twas his, with beauty, valour's gifts to share,
A soul heroic, as his form was fair;
These burn with one pure flame of gen'rous love,   15
In peace, in war, united still they move;
Friendship and glory form their joint reward,
And now combin'd they hold the nightly guard.

'What God!' exclaim'd the first, 'instils this fire?
Or, in itself a God, what great desire?   20
My lab'ring soul, with anxious thought opprest,
Abhors this station of inglorious rest;
The love of fame with this can ill accord,
Be't mine, to seek for glory with my sword.
See'st thou yon camp, with torches twinkling dim,   25
Where drunken slumbers wrap each lazy limb?
Where confidence and ease the watch disdain,
And drowsy Silence holds her sable reign?
Then hear my thought: In deep and sullen grief,
Our troops and leaders mourn their absent chief;   30
Now could the gifts, and promis'd prize be thine,
(The deed, the danger, and the fame be mine;)
Were this decreed,—beneath yon rising mound,
Methinks, an easy path, perchance, were found,
Which past, I speed my way to Pallas' walls,   35
And lead Aeneas from Evander's halls.'
With equal ardour fired, and warlike joy,
His glowing friend address'd the Dardan boy.
'These deeds, my Nisus, shalt thou dare alone?
Must all the fame, the peril be thine own?   40
Am I by thee despis'd, and left afar,
As one unfit to share the toils of war?

18 they . . . nightly] the massy gate they *POVO*   19 instils this [has given this *B*
20 great desire] ⟨wish inspire⟩ *B*   22 Abhors] Disdains *B*   25 thou . . . with] ⟨you . . .
yon⟩ *B*   26 ⟨Who Wine & Sleep enrobe⟩ *B*   29 ⟨Then hear my plan, to yield
our troop relief⟩ *B*   33 ⟨Where gently rises / Beneath yon hill, a path perchance were
found⟩ *B*   37 warlike] ⟨equ⟩ *B*   38 Dardan] ⟨foreign⟩ *B*   39 ⟨Why
Friend⟩ *B*

Not thus, his son, the great Opheltes taught,
Not thus, my sire, in Argive combats fought;
Not thus, when Ilion fell by heavenly hate,   45
I track'd Aeneas through the walks of fate;
Thou know'st my deeds, my breast devoid of fear,
And hostile life-drops dim my gory spear;
Here is a soul, with hope immortal burns,
And *life*, ignoble *life*, for glory spurns,   50
Fame, fame, is cheaply earn'd by fleeting breath,
The price of honour, is the sleep of death.'
Then Nisus,—'Calm thy bosom's fond alarms,
Thy heart beats fiercely to the din of arms;
More dear thy worth, and valour than my own,   55
I swear by him, who fills Olympus' throne!
So may I triumph, as I speak the truth,
And clasp again the comrade of my youth:
But, should I fall, and he who dares advance,
Through hostile legions, must abide by chance;   60
If some Rutulian arm with adverse blow,
Should lay the friend, who ever lov'd thee, low,
Live thou, such beauties I would fain preserve,
Thy budding years a lengthen'd term deserve;
When humbled in the dust, let some one be,   65
Whose gentle eyes, will shed one tear for me;
Whose manly arm may snatch me back by force,
Or wealth redeem, from foes, my captive corse:
Or, if my destiny these last deny,
If in the spoiler's power, my ashes lie;   70
Thy pious care, may raise a simple tomb,
To mark thy love, and signalize my doom.
Why should thy doating wretched mother weep,

43 his son] ⟨my Sire⟩ *B*   44 ⟨His son, not thus in Argive⟩ *B*   47–8 *not in B*
49–50 ⟨Here is a Soul, which all, but Glory spurns | With hope of Fame, & life immortal
burns⟩ *B*   51 cheaply earn'd] ⟨cheaply bought / ? ⟩ *B*   52 price ... sleep]
⟨Bed. . .Bed⟩ *B*   53–4 Then Nisus, ah my Friend, why thus suspect | ⟨In⟩ Thy
⟨young⟩ youthful Breast admits of no defect, *B*   55 ⟨Thy Valour & thy worth⟩ *B*
59 dares advance] ⟨wields the lance⟩ *B*   60 Through] ⟨Gainst⟩ *B*   62 Should]
⟨Shall⟩ *B*   63–4 Live thou, ⟨nor share thy rash Companion's Fate | Thy youthful life,
deserves a longer Date *B*   63 such] ⟨thy⟩ *B*   66 shed] ⟨weep⟩ *B*   67 ⟨Whose
arm may snatch me, or whose wealth redeem⟩ *B*   68 my captive] ⟨his Nisus'⟩ *B*
69 ⟨Or if these last by destiny / by destiny these last⟩ *B*   70 the ... power] ⟨a foreign
Land / the victor's power⟩ *B*   71 ⟨Whose careful⟩ *B*   72 To mark ⟨Remembrance
of my / thy friendship⟩ *B*

Her only boy, reclin'd in endless sleep?
Who for thy sake, the tempest's fury dar'd,   75
Who for thy sake, war's deadly peril shar'd;
Who brav'd, what woman never brav'd before,
And left her native, for the Latian shore.'
'In vain you damp the ardour of my soul,'
Reply'd Euryalus! 'it scorns controul;   80
Hence, let us haste,'—their brother guards arose,
Rouz'd by their call, nor court again repose;
The pair buoy'd up on Hope's exulting wing,
Their stations leave, and speed to seek the king.
Now o'er the earth, a solemn stillness ran,   85
And lull'd alike the cares of brute and man;
Save where the Dardan leaders nightly hold,
Alternate converse, and their plans unfold;
On one great point the council are agreed,
An instant message to their prince decreed;   90
Each lean'd upon the lance, he well could wield,
And pois'd, with easy arm, his ancient shield;
When Nisus and his friend their leave request,
To offer something to their high behest.
With anxious tremors, yet unaw'd by fear,   95
The faithful pair before the throne appear;
Iulus greets them, at his kind command,
The elder first, address'd the hoary band.

'With patience,' (thus Hyrtacides began,)
'Attend, nor judge, from youth, our humble plan;   100
Where yonder beacons half expiring beam,
Our slumbering foes of future conquest dream,
Nor heed that we a secret path have trac'd,
Between the ocean, and the portal plac'd:

75 ⟨Was it for this / Did she / Was it⟩ B   76 war's . . . peril] ⟨thy . . . danger⟩ B
77 ⟨Whose very life with thine / ? ⟩ B   79 ⟨But he⟩ B   81 us haste—⟨they
call / they rouze⟩ their B   85 o'er] ⟨through⟩ B   86 ⟨And sleep⟩ B   87 ⟨Save
when the Dardan / anxious chiefs to ? Debate) / ⟨In nightly⟩ B   hold] ⟨sate⟩ B   88 ⟨In
anxious converse, or in deep Debate⟩ B   Alternate] Their anxious B   89 ⟨Yet in one
sentiment are all⟩ agreed B   90 ⟨A message to Aeneas is⟩ decreed B   instant] sudden B
92 And ⟨raised aloft / drooping held⟩ B   95 ⟨A project worthy notice / Of consequence & moment⟩ Trembling with ⟨modesty but not with⟩ diffidence, not awed by fear B
96 ⟨Nisus first summoned⟩ B   97 greets] ⟨bids⟩ B   98 The elder first] Nisus the
first B   101 ⟨Buried in sleep the vain Rutulians ly⟩ B   beacons half] ⟨fires are⟩ B
102 The vain Rutulians lost ⟨in slothful⟩ in slumber dream B

Beneath the covert of the blackening smoke,   105
Whose shade securely our design will cloak!
If you, ye chiefs, and fortune, will allow,
We'll bend our course to yonder mountain's brow;
Where Pallas' walls at distance meet the sight,
Seen o'er the glade, when not obscur'd by night;   110
Then shall Aeneas, in his pride return,
While hostile matrons raise their offspring's urn;
And Latian spoils, and purpl'd heaps of dead,
Shall mark the havock of our Hero's tread;
Such is our purpose, not unknown the way,   115
Where yonder torrent's devious waters stray;
Oft have we seen when hunting by the stream,
The distant spires above the vallies gleam.'

    Mature in years, for sober wisdom fam'd,
Mov'd by the speech, Alethes, here exclaim'd!   120
'Ye parent Gods! who rule the fate of Troy,
Still dwells the Dardan spirit in the boy;
When minds like these, in striplings thus ye raise,
Yours is the god-like act, be yours the praise;
In gallant youth, my fainting hopes revive,   125
And Ilion's wonted glories still survive';
Then in his warm embrace, the boys he press'd,
And quivering strain'd them to his aged breast;
With tears the burning cheek of each bedew'd,
And, sobbing, thus his first discourse renew'd:—   130
'What gift, my countrymen, what martial prize
Can we bestow, which you may not despise?
Our Deities the first, best boon have given,
Internal virtues are the gift of Heaven.
What poor rewards, can bless your deeds on earth,   135

110 Seen ⟨through the vales, though hid⟩ B   113 purpl'd ... dead] ⟨many a Hero⟩ purpled
heaps of ⟨slain⟩ B   115 Such] ⟨This⟩ B   116 ⟨We are⟩ B   118 above ... gleam]
⟨along ... beam⟩ B   119 sober] ⟨age &⟩ B   120 ⟨Alethes⟩ B   121 Ye ... rule]
⟨My ... ruled⟩ B   123 ⟨Whose⟩ B   124 ⟨My hopes revive⟩ B   god-like] ⟨glorious⟩
B   126 still] here B   127 warm embrace] ⟨arms by turns⟩ B   128 ⟨And
strained them trembling⟩ B   aged] ⟨thrilling⟩ B   129 tears ⟨bedewed⟩ the B
130 And ⟨thus⟩ sobbing B   131 gift ... martial prize] ⟨prize ... bet / blest reward⟩ B
132 ⟨Can here be given⟩ which ⟨may not be desp⟩ B   133 ⟨The first / best, the greatest,
Dieties will give / Our Deities the first & best will give⟩ / ⟨For virtue's Blessin / Internal
virtues in your Bosoms live⟩ B   135 can ... your] ⟨are offered here⟩ B   your]
⟨such⟩ B

Doubtless await such young exalted worth;
Aeneas, and Ascanius shall combine,
To yield applause far, far, surpassing mine.'
Iulus then; 'By all the powers above!
By those Penates, who my country love;   140
By hoary Vesta's sacred Fane, I swear,
My hopes, are all in you, ye generous pair!
Restore my father, to my grateful sight,
And all my sorrows, yield to one delight.
Nisus! two silver goblets are thine own,   145
Sav'd from Arisba's stately domes o'erthrown;
My sire secured them on that fatal day;
Nor left such bowls, an Argive robber's prey.
Two massy tripods, also shall be thine,
Two talents polished from the glittering mine;   150
An ancient cup, which Tyrian Dido gave,
While yet our vessels press'd the Punic wave:
But when the hostile chiefs at length bow down,
When great Aeneas wears Hesperia's crown,
The casque, the buckler, and the fiery steed,   155
Which Turnus guides with more than mortal speed,
Are thine; no envious lot shall then be cast,
I pledge my word, irrevocably past;
Nay more, twelve slaves and twice six captive dames,
To sooth thy softer hours, with amorous flames,   160
And all the realms, which now the Latins sway,
The labours of to-night, shall well repay.
But thou, my generous youth, whose tender years,
Are near my own, whose worth, my heart reveres,
Henceforth, affection sweetly thus begun,   165
Shall join our bosoms, and our souls in one;
Without thy aid, no glory shall be mine,

136 〈To yield applause far, far surpassing mine〉 *B*   139 〈Nisus I swear〉 *B*
140 〈Which yet the Dardan Prince〉 〈No joy is mine beyond my parents love〉 *B*   141 〈I
swear〉 *B*   144 〈No grie / Grief is no more, dispelled in praise〉 *B*   145 goblets are]
〈cups shall be〉 *B*   146 Saved 〈by my Sire〉 from *B*   148 Nor left 〈them〉 such *B*
150 Two talents 〈glittering〉 polished *B*   152 〈Where Carthage rises oer the foaming /
Where Ocean's billows Punic bulwarks lave / Where Ocean foam the Punic bulwarks lave〉 *B*
153 But when 〈beneath our yoke these〉 the *B*   156 〈Which Turnus guides along the
/ Whose coursers seem of more than mortal Breed〉 *B*   157 cast] 〈past〉 *B*
158 irrevocably] 〈this firm decree is〉 *B*   159 Nay more 〈my Nisus, twelve beauteous cap ·
tive〉 twelve *B*   163 thou . . . youth] 〈you . . . Boy〉 *B*   164 〈Proclaim〉 *B* heart]
〈Soul〉 *B*   165 affection] 〈our friendship〉 *B*

Without thy dear advice, no great design;
Alike through life, esteem'd, thou godlike boy,
In war my bulwark, and in peace my joy.'   170

To him Euryalus, 'no day shall shame
The rising glories, which from this I claim.
Fortune may favour, or the skies may frown,
But valour, spite of fate, obtains renown.
Yet, ere from hence our eager steps depart,   175
One boon I beg, the nearest to my heart:
My mother sprung, from Priam's royal line,
Like thine ennobl'd, hardly less divine,
Nor Troy, nor King Acestes' realms restrain
Her feeble age from dangers of the main,   180
Alone she came, all selfish fears above,
A bright example of maternal love.
Unknown the secret enterprize I brave,
Lest grief should bend my parent to the grave;
From this alone no fond adieus I seek,   185
No fainting mother's lips have press'd my cheek;
By gloomy Night, and thy right hand I vow,
Her parting tears would shake my purpose now:
Do thou, my prince, her failing age sustain,
In thee her much loved child may live again;   190
Her dying hours with pious conduct bless,
Assist her wants, relieve her fond distress:
So dear a hope must all my soul enflame,
To rise in glory, or to fall in fame.'
Struck with a filial care, so deeply felt,   195
In tears, at once the Trojan warriors melt;
Faster than all Iulus' eyes o'erflow,

169 esteem'd, thou godlike] ⟨beloved, gentle⟩ B   173 ⟨Fortune perchance may favour my renown⟩ / Fortune may favour, or ⟨may check renown / oblivion's frown⟩ B 174 ⟨Or Fate malignant on my / But Valour gain / spite of Fate attains / obtains Renown⟩ B   178 hardly] ⟨scarcely⟩ B   179–80 ⟨For me she spurned the dangers of the Main, | No ? her timid / feeble age restrain⟩ B   181–2 not in B   181 Alone] Hither HI   185–6 not in B   187 gloomy] ⟨sable⟩ B   188 parting] falling B   191 conduct] ⟨comfort⟩ B   192 Assist . . . fond] ⟨Succour . . . deep⟩ B   193–4 With this assurance ⟨Fate may will⟩ Fate's attempts are vain, | Fearless I dare the foes of yonder plain. B   195 Struck with ⟨his gentle love, & pious / filial Care⟩ B   so] ⟨thus⟩ B   197 ⟨With love, which now like / Faster than all Iulus' eyes oerflow / With love which he now / To hear this love which none like him⟩ B

Such love was his, and such had been his woe.
'All thou hast ask'd, receive,' the prince reply'd,
'Nor this alone, but many a gift beside; 200
To cheer thy mother's years shall be my aim,
Creusa's style, but wanting to the dame;
Fortune an adverse wayward course may run,
But blest thy mother, in so dear a son.
Now, by my life, my sire's most sacred oath, 205
To thee I pledge my full, my firmest troth,
All the rewards which once to thee were vow'd,
If thou should'st fall, on her shall be bestow'd.'
Thus spoke the weeping prince, then forth to view,
A gleaming falchion from the sheath he drew; 210
Lycaon's utmost skill had grac'd the steel,
For friends to envy, and for foes to feel.
A tawny hide, the Moorish lion's spoil,
Slain midst the forest, in the hunter's toil,
Mnestheus to guard the elder youth bestows, 215
And old Alethes' casque defends his brows:
Arm'd, thence they go, while all the assembl'd train,
To aid their cause, implore the gods in vain;
More than a boy, in wisdom and in grace,
Iulus holds amidst the chiefs his place, 220
His prayers he sends, but what can prayers avail!
Lost in the murmurs of the sighing gale!

The trench is past, and favour'd by the night,
Through sleeping foes, they wheel their wary flight;
When shall the sleep of many a foe be o'er? 225
Alas! some slumber, who shall wake no more!

200 ⟨My hapless mother / No mother / Thy / Nay⟩ *B*   gift] ⟨pledge⟩ wish *B*
202 ⟨Creusa's title only wants the Dame / In me, Creusa, but / though without the name⟩ *B*
style] ⟨name⟩ *B*   206 my firmest] ⟨& willing⟩ *B*   207 That all the gifts
⟨I promised thy return⟩ which *B*   208 ⟨On thy de / surviving race⟩ If thou shall
fall *B*   209 then forth] ⟨& sighed⟩ *B*   211 ⟨The steel⟩ Lycaon's . . . had ⟨formed⟩
the steel *B*   212 ⟨Not made alone⟩ *B*   213 ⟨A lion's tawny skin Mnestheus⟩ A tawny
skin the furious lyon's spoil *B*   214 midst] ⟨in⟩ *B*   215 ⟨Mnestheus gave / presented,
& a tempered Casque / helm⟩ / ⟨Alethes / His lord Alethes gave a tempered Casque⟩
Mnestheus presented, & the Warrior's Mask *B*   216 Alethes gave a doubly tempered
Casque *B*   218 ⟨Far as the portal⟩ To aid their journey, follow them in vain *B*
219 a boy, ⟨Iulus⟩ in *B*   221 ⟨And many a prayer he sends along the / but what can
prayers avail⟩ *B*   222 Dispersed & muttered on the sighing gale *B*   223 The . . .
past] They pass the trench *B*   226 some] ⟨they⟩ *B*

Chariots and bridles, mix'd with arms are seen,
And flowing flasks, and scatter'd troops between;
Bacchus and Mars, to rule the camp, combine,
A mingl'd Chaos, this, of war and wine.   230
'Now,' cries the first, 'for deeds of blood prepare,
With me the conquest, and the labour share;
Here lies our path, lest any hand arise,
Watch thou, while many a dreaming chieftain dies;
I'll carve our passage, through the heedless foe,   235
And clear thy road, with many a deadly blow.'
His whispering accents then the youth represt,
And pierc'd proud Rhamnes through his panting breast;
Stretch'd at his ease, th' incautious king repos'd,
Debauch, and not fatigue, his eyes had clos'd;   240
To Turnus dear, a prophet and a prince,
His omens more than augur's skill evince:
But he who thus foretold the fate of all,
Could not avert his own untimely fall.
Next Remus' armour-bearer, hapless fell,   245
And three unhappy slaves the carnage swell;
The charioteer, along his courser's sides,
Expires, the steel his sever'd neck divides;
And, last, his Lord is number'd with the dead,
Bounding convulsive, flies the gasping head;   250
From the swol'n veins, the blackening torrents pour,
Stain'd is the couch and earth, with clotting gore.
Young Lamyrus and Lamus next expire,
And gay Serranus fill'd with youthful fire;
Half the long night in childish games was past,   255
Lull'd by the potent grape, he slept at last;

227 ⟨Chariots & Bri / Reins Bridles Wheels & arms around⟩ *B*   228 And ⟨scattered
flasks / empty⟩ flowing *B*   229 to . . . camp] ⟨their empire here⟩ *B*   230 this]
⟨here⟩ *B*   231 ⟨The⟩ Said Nisus, now, for deeds *B*   233 lies] is *B*   234 Watch
thou, ⟨and he who⟩ while many a ⟨slumbering⟩ chieftain dies *B*   235 We'll carve . . .
the ⟨slumbering⟩ foe *B*   236 ⟨Lest in their slumber to the⟩ *B*   thy] the *B*   237 His
⟨voice the⟩ whispering *B*   239 king] ⟨prince⟩ *B*   241 ⟨A prophet⟩ *B*   prince]
⟨king⟩ *B*   242 ⟨He drew his omens from the expanding wing⟩ / ⟨His ski / frequent
omens⟩ *B*   more than] ⟨all an⟩ *B*   243 ⟨Alas that he who / But he who thus foretold
another's⟩ *B*   247 along] ⟨beneath⟩ *B*   248 ⟨The vengeful steel his severed head
divides] *B*   249 ⟨The⟩ And last ⟨his Master's Head⟩ his Lord *B*   250 Bounding
. . . gasping] ⟨Gasping . . . bounding⟩ *B*   251 ⟨For soil⟩ From the ⟨rush⟩ swoln *B*
254 gay] ⟨young⟩ *B*   255 ⟨On him the power of Bacchus stood confest⟩ By Bacchus
potent draught weighed down at last *B*   256 Half the long night in childish ⟨sports⟩
was past *B*

Ah! happier far, had he the morn survey'd,
And, 'till Aurora's dawn, his skill display'd.

In slaughter'd folds, the keepers lost in sleep,
His hungry fangs a lion thus may steep;   260
'Mid the sad flock, at dead of night, he prowls,
With murder glutted, and in carnage rolls;
Insatiate still, through teeming herds he roams,
In seas of gore, the lordly tyrant foams.

Nor less the other's deadly vengeance came,   265
But falls on feeble crowds without a name;
His wound, unconscious Fadus, scarce can feel,
Yet, wakeful Rhaesus sees the threat'ning steel;
His coward breast behind a jar he hides,
And, vainly, in the weak defence confides;   270
Full in his heart, the falchion search'd his veins,
The reeking weapon bears alternate stains;
Through wine and blood, commingling as they flow,
The feeble spirit seeks the shades below.
Now, where Messapus dwelt, they bend their way,   275
Whose fires emit a faint and trembling ray;
There, unconfin'd, behold each grazing steed,
Unwatch'd, unheeded, on the herbage feed;
Brave Nisus here arrests his comrade's arm,
Too flush'd with carnage, and with conquest warm: 280
'Hence let us haste, the dangerous path is past,
Full foes enough, to-night, have breath'd their last;

258 ⟨And to / till the Aurora's dawn in / dawning still played⟩ B   his skill display'd]
desportive played B
259–60   ⟨Thus the teeming fold the Lyon roams
                          In seas of gore the lordly savage foams⟩ B
                          By hunger prest, the Keeper's lull'd to sleep,
                          In slaughter thus a lyon long may steep, B
261 'Mid] Through B   262 With] ⟨In⟩ B   263 Thro' teeming ⟨folds⟩ herds
unchecked, unawed he roams B   264 gore] ⟨Blood⟩ B   265 ⟨Nor less
Euryalus / the other flashed his virgin sword⟩ B   267 ⟨His fall⟩ B   268 ⟨But⟩ Yet B
269 ⟨Behind a massy⟩ B   270 the] this B   271 the . . . his] he search'd his
inmost B   272 ⟨The blended wine & blood / wine & gore⟩ / ⟨The wine & blood
commixed, the weapon stains⟩ B   274 The . . . seeks] The Crimson Soul may seek B
275 ⟨Now to Messapus⟩ B   278 Heedless of Danger, on the B
279–82   ⟨Hence let us haste, said Nisus as he past
                          Full foes enough tonight have breathed their last,
                          This much he said, desirous to prevent
                          His rash young friend on further conquest bent⟩ B
279–80 Then Nisus said, desirous to prevent | His rash young friend, on further Con-
quest bent B

Soon will the Day those Eastern clouds adorn,
Now let us speed, nor tempt the rising morn.'

What silver arms, with various art embost;   285
What bowls and mantles, in confusion tost,
They leave regardless! yet, one glittering prize,
Attracts the younger Hero's wand'ring eyes;
The gilded harness Rhamnes' coursers felt,
The gems which stud, the monarch's golden belt;   290
This from the pallid corse was quickly torn,
Once by a line of former chieftains worn.
Th' exulting boy, the studded girdle wears,
Messapus' helm his head, in triumph, bears;
Then from the tents their cautious steps they bend,   295
To seek the vale, where safer paths extend.

Just at this hour, a band of Latian horse,
To Turnus' camp, pursue their destin'd course;
While the slow foot, their tardy march delay,
The knights impatient spur along the way: 300
Three hundred mail-clad men, by Volscens led,
To Turnus, with their master's promise sped;
Now they approach the trench, and view the walls,
When, on the left, a light reflection falls,
The plunder'd helmet, through the waning night,   305
Sheds forth a silver radiance, glancing bright;
Volscens, with question loud, the pair alarms,
'Stand, Stragglers! stand! why early thus in arms?
From whence, to whom?' he meets with no reply,
Trusting the covert of the night they fly;   310

283 ⟨Aurora⟩ Soon ⟨the young⟩ will B   284 ⟨Hence⟩ Now B   285 arms,
with various] ⟨shields with wondrous⟩ B   286 ⟨And arms & Robes⟩ Mantles
& Bowls in one confusion tost B   287 prize] ⟨eyes⟩ B   288 Hero's wand'ring]
⟨warrior's eager⟩ B   289 gilded] ⟨Silvery⟩ B   290 The ... stud] And
more than these B   292 ⟨Which a noble line of chiefs had⟩ worn B   294 ⟨Uncon-
scious of the Fate the⟩ from B   295 Then ⟨through the camp with cautious bend⟩
from B   296 ⟨Whence⟩ To ... where ⟨softer⟩ paths extend B   299 foot ... march]
⟨legions in the march⟩ B   302 promise] ⟨message⟩ B   304 light] ⟨bright⟩ B
305 ⟨The glittering helmet sparkles / sheds a gleaming light⟩ / ⟨The youth's / borrowed
helmet⟩ The borrowed helmet glancing through the night B   306 glancing] sparkling B
307–8 ⟨Stand, Stragglers, stand, why early thus in arms, | Whence from, & whither bound⟩ B
307 The voice of Volscens then the pair alarms B   310 Trusting the] ⟨To the
thick⟩ B

The thicket's depth, with hurried pace, they tread,
While round the wood the hostile squadron spread.

With brakes entangled, scarce a path between,
Dreary and dark appears the sylvan scene;
Euryalus, his heavy spoils impede,   315
The boughs and winding turns his steps mislead;
But Nisus scours along the forest's maze,
To where Latinus' steeds in safety graze,
Then backward o'er the plain his eyes extend,
On ev'ry side, they seek his absent friend.   320
'O God, my boy,' he cries, 'of me bereft,
In what impending perils art thou left!'
Listening he runs—above the waving trees,
Tumultuous voices swell the passing breeze;
The war-cry rises, thundering hoofs around   325
Wake the dark echoes of the trembling ground.
Again he turns—of footsteps hears the noise,
The sound elates—the sight his hope destroys,
The hapless boy, a ruffian train surround,
While lengthening shades, his weary way confound;   330
Him, with loud shouts, the furious knights pursue,
Struggling in vain, a captive to the crew.
What can his friend 'gainst thronging numbers dare?
Ah! must he rush, his comrade's fate to share!
What force, what aid, what stratagem essay,   335
Back to redeem the Latian spoilers' prey!
His life a votive ransom nobly give,
Or die with him, for whom he wish'd to live!
Poising with strength his lifted lance on high,
On Luna's orb, he cast his phrenzied eye,   340
'Goddess serene, transcending every star!
Queen of the sky! whose beams are seen afar;
By night, Heaven owns thy sway, by day, the grove,

311 depth] maze *B*   315 his heavy spoils] ⟨the branching trees⟩ *B*   316 ⟨His loaded
helm / heavy spoils⟩ *B*   turns] paths *B*   317 forest's] ⟨darkness'⟩ *B*   318 steeds in
safety] ⟨purebred coursers⟩ *B*   321 me] thee *B*   322 In what dire perils is my
Brother left *B*   323–6 *not in B*   327 ⟨Again he seeks the wood, he hears a⟩ noise *B*
329 There his lov'd Boy the ruffian Band surround *B*   330 Entangled in the tufted
forest found *B*   332 At length a Captive to the hostile crew *B*   334 Ah ... rush]
Rush in the midst *B*   337–8 *not in B*   339 ⟨To Luna's / Now to the orb he cast his⟩
Poising his lifted javelin on high *B*   340 phrenzied] rolling *B*   341 Goddess serene]
Thou Goddess ⟨far⟩ bright *B*   343 ⟨Whether as Dian on the / through the woods you rove⟩ *B*

When, as chaste Dian, here thou deign'st to rove;
If e'er myself, or sire, have sought to grace   345
Thine altars, with the produce of the chace;
Speed, speed, my dart, to pierce yon vaunting crowd,
To free my friend, and scatter far the proud.'
Thus having said, the hissing dart he flung,
Through parted shades, the hurtling weapon sung;   350
The thirsty point in Sulmo's entrails lay,
Transfix'd his heart, and stretch'd him on the clay;
He sobs, he dies,—the troop, in wild amaze,
Unconscious whence the death, with horror gaze;
While pale they stare, thro' Tagus' temples riven,   355
A second shaft, with equal force, is driven;
Fierce Volscens rolls around his lowering eyes,
Veil'd by the night, secure the Trojan lies.
Burning with wrath, he view'd his soldiers fall,
'Thou youth accurst; thy life shall pay for all';   360
Quick from the sheath his flaming glaive he drew,
And, raging, on the boy defenceless flew.
Nisus, no more the blackening shade conceals,
Forth, forth he starts, and all his love reveals;
Aghast, confus'd, his fears to madness rise,   365
And pour these accents, shrieking as he flies;
'Me, me, your vengeance hurl, on me alone,
Here sheathe the steel, my blood is all your own;
Ye starry Spheres! thou conscious Heaven attest!
He could not—durst not—lo! the guile confest!   370
All, all was mine,—his early fate suspend,

344 here . . . to] through the woods you *B*   345 ⟨If ere my Father to thy care was
dear⟩ *B*   346 ⟨Thy lofty altars with the⟩ *B*   350 ⟨The barbed point / Through
shades of darkness⟩ *B*   351 thirsty] barbed *B*   352 ⟨Pierc⟩ Transfixed *B*
355 pale . . . riven] ⟨fierce / wild . . . driven⟩ *B*   356 force] ⟨Skill⟩ *B*   358 No object
meets them, but the earth & skies *B*   359–60 He burns for vengeance, viewing in his
wrath, | Then ⟨Boy⟩ you, accursed, thy life shall pay for both *B*   361 Then from the
sheath his flaming brand he drew *B*   362 And ⟨maddening on the hapless⟩ raging *B*
364 starts] rush'd *B*   365 Aghast,] Pale & *B*   fears . . . rise] fear to madness grows *B*
366 And thus in accents wild, he greets his foes *B*
367–74   On me, on me direct your impious steel,
                                          Let me, and me alone, your vengeance feel,
                                          Let not a Stripling's blood by Chiefs be spilt,
                                          Be mine the Death, as mine was all the guilt.
                                          By Heaven & Hell, the powers of Earth & Air,
                                          Yon guiltless Stripling neither could, nor dare,
                                          Spare him, oh spare, by all the Gods above,
                                          A hapless Boy, whose only crime was love. *B*

He only lov'd, too well, his hapless friend;
Spare, spare ye Chiefs! from him your rage remove,
His fault was friendship, all his crime was love.'
He pray'd in vain, the dark assassin's sword,   375
Pierc'd the fair side, the snowy bosom gor'd;
Lowly to earth, inclines his plume-clad crest,
And sanguine torrents, mantle o'er his breast;
As some young rose, whose blossom scents the air,
Languid in death, expires beneath the share;   380
Or crimson poppy, sinking with the shower,
Declining gently, falls a fading flower;
Thus sweetly drooping, bends his lovely head,
And lingering Beauty hovers round the dead.

But fiery Nisus stems the battle's tide,   385
Revenge his leader, and Despair his guide;
Volscens he seeks, amidst the gathering host,
Volscens must soon appease his comrades's ghost;
Steel, flashing, pours on steel, foe crowds on foe,
Rage nerves his arm, Fate gleams in ev'ry blow;   390
In vain beneath unnumber'd wounds he bleeds,
Nor wounds, nor death, distracted Nisus heeds;
In viewless circles wheel'd, his falchion flies,
Nor quits the Hero's grasp, till Volscens dies,
Deep in his throat, its end the weapon found,   395
The tyrant's soul fled groaning through the wound.
Thus Nisus all his fond affection prov'd,
Dying, reveng'd the fate of him he lov'd;
Then on his bosom, sought his wonted place,
And death was heavenly, in his friend's embrace!   400

375 dark ... sword] ⟨furious Latian Lord⟩ fierce assassin's sword B   376 ⟨Pierced
the white bosom with his single sword / The snowy Bosom of the Trojan gored⟩ B
377–8 ⟨Euryalus is numbered with the dead, | Oer his fair limbs the purpling stream
is spread, | Drooping he bends to earth his lovely head⟩ B   377 Drooping to earth inclines
his lovely head B   378 Oer his fair limbs the purpling stream is spread B   379 As
some sweet ⟨flower, beneath untimely⟩ Lily by the ploughshare's broke B   380 expires
... share] sinks down beneath the stroke B   381 Or as some poppy bending with the
shower, B   382 Gently declining falls ⟨the⟩ a mourning flower B   383–4 ⟨Drooping
to earth inclines his lovely head | And / oer his fair limbs the purpling stream is spread⟩ B;
received lines not in B   385 stems] ⟨turns⟩ B   386 leader] object B
389–90 not in B   393 viewless] ⟨fiery⟩ / rapid B   395 its ... found] ⟨he plung'd
the Blade of Death⟩ B   396 ⟨The groaning Soul exhaled⟩ The ⟨tyrant's⟩ assassin's
soul B   397 ⟨Thus Nisus ? , sought his⟩ B   all ... affection] ⟨even in Death his Friend-
ship⟩ B   398 fate] Death B   399 bosom,] Breast he B   400 heavenly] lovely B

Celestial pair! if aught my verse can claim,
Wafted on Time's broad pinion, yours is fame!
Ages on ages, shall your fate admire
No future day, shall see your names expire;
While stands the Capitol, immortal dome!   405
And vanquish'd millions, hail their empress, Rome!

[1807]

57   Translation from the
            Medea of Euripides

[1.]
When fierce conflicting passions urge
    The breast, where love is wont to glow,
What mind can stem the stormy surge,
    Which rolls the tide of human woe?
The hope of praise, the dread of shame,   5
    Can rouse the tortur'd breast no more;
The wild desire, the guilty flame,
    Absorbs each wish it felt before.

2.
But, if affection gently thrills
    The soul, by purer dreams possest,   10
The pleasing balm of mortal ills,
    In love can soothe the aching breast;
If thus, thou com'st in gentle guise,
    Fair Venus! from thy native heaven,
What heart, unfeeling, would despise   15
    The sweetest boon the gods have given?

402 Yours are the fairest wreaths of endless fame *B*   404 your names] ⟨thy
deeds⟩ *B*   406 And countless millions, own their *B*

57. Copy text: *HI*, collated with *POT*, *HI1820*
  13 com'st in gentle guise] comest in disguise *HI1820, 1831, 1832, C, More*

3.

But, never from thy golden bow,
  May I beneath the shaft expire,
Whose creeping venom, sure and slow,
  Awakes an all-consuming fire;   20
Ye racking doubts! ye jealous fears!
  With others wage internal war;
Repentance! source of future tears,
  From me be ever distant far.

4.

May no distracting thoughts destroy   25
  The holy calm of sacred love!
May all the hours be wing'd with joy,
  Which hover faithful hearts above!
Fair Venus! on thy myrtle shrine,
  May I with some fond lover sigh!   30
Whose heart may mingle pure with mine,
  With me to live, with me to die.

5.

My native soil! belov'd before,
  Now dearer, as my peaceful home,
Ne'er may I quit thy rocky shore,   35
  A hapless, banish'd wretch to roam;
This very day, this very hour,
  May I resign this fleeting breath,
Nor quit my silent humble bower;
  A doom, to me, far worse than death.   40

6.

Have I not heard the exile's sigh?
  And seen the exile's silent tear?
Through distant climes condemn'd to fly,
  A pensive, weary wand'rer here;
Ah! hapless dame! no sire bewails,   45
  No friend thy wretched fate deplores,
No kindred voice with rapture hails
  Thy steps, within a stranger's doors.

7.

Perish the fiend! whose iron heart,
    To fair affection's truth unknown,   50
Bids her, he fondly lov'd, depart,
    Unpitied, helpless, and alone;
Who ne'er unlocks, with silver key,
    The milder treasures of his soul;
May such a friend be far from me,   55
    And Ocean's storms between us roll!

[1807]

58 Thoughts Suggested by a College Examination

High in the midst, surrounded by his peers,
MAGNUS his ample front sublime uprears;
Plac'd on his chair of state, he seems a God,
While Sophs and Freshmen tremble at his nod.
As all around sit wrapt in speechless gloom,   5
His voice, in thunder, shakes the sounding dome;
Denouncing dire reproach to luckless fools,
Unskill'd to plod in mathematic rules.

Happy the youth! in Euclid's axioms tried,
Though little vers'd in any art beside;   10
Who, scarcely skill'd an English line to pen,
Scans Attic metres, with a critic's ken.
What! though he knows not how his fathers bled,
When civil discord pil'd the fields with dead;
When Edward bade his conquering bands advance,   15
Or Henry trampled on the crest of France;
Though, marv'lling at the name of Magna Charta,
Yet, well he recollects the laws of Sparta;
Can tell what edicts sage Lycurgus made,
Whilst Blackstone's on the shelf, neglected, laid;   20

---

58. Copy text: *HI*, collated with *MS. Υ* (lines 59–62), *FP*, *POVO*, *POT*, *HI1820*
  2 Magnus] M—ns—l *FP*   5 As] ⟨Whilst⟩ *FPM*, *FPT*   11–12 Who with scarce
sense to pen an *English* letter, | Yet with precision, scan an *attic metre*. *FP*

Of Grecian dramas vaunts the deathless fame,
Of Avon's bard, rememb'ring scarce the name.

 Such is the youth, whose scientific pate,
Class honours, medals, fellowships, await;
Or, even, perhaps, the declamation prize,   25
If, to such glorious height, he lift his eyes,
But, lo! no common orator can hope,
The envied silver cup within his scope:
Not that our heads much eloquence require,
Th' ATHENIAN's glowing style, or Tully's fire. 30
A manner clear or warm is useless since
We do not try, by speaking, to convince;
Be other orators of pleasing proud,
We speak, to please ourselves, not move the crowd:
Our gravity prefers the muttering tone,   35
A proper mixture of the squeak and groan;
No borrow'd grace of action, must be seen,
The slightest motion would displease the dean;
Whilst ev'ry staring graduate would prate,
Against what he could never imitate.   40

 The man, who hopes t' obtain the promis'd cup,
Must in one posture stand, and ne'er look up;
Nor stop, but rattle over every word,
No matter what, so it can *not* be heard:
Thus let him hurry on, nor think to rest; 45
Who speaks the fastest's sure to speak the best:
Who utters most within the shortest space,
May, safely, hope to win the wordy race.

 The sons of science, these, who thus repaid,
Linger in ease, in Granta's sluggish shade; 50
Where on Cam's sedgy banks supine they lie,
Unknown, unhonour'd live,—unwept for, die;
Dull as the pictures, which adorn their halls,
They think all learning fix'd within their walls;
In manners rude, in foolish forms precise, 55

26 lift] lifts *FP*, *POT*, *HI1820*, *1831*, *1832*, *C*, *More* 31 The manner of the speech
is nothing, since *FP*, *POVO*

All modern arts, affecting to despise;
Yet prizing BENTLEY'S, BRUNCK'S, or PORSON's note,
More than the verse, on which the critic wrote;
Vain as their honours, heavy as their Ale,
Sad as their wit, and tedious as their tale,				60
To friendship dead, though not untaught to feel,
When Self and Church demand a Bigot zeal.
With eager haste, they court the lord of power,
Whether 'tis PITT or P[E]TTY rules the hour:
To him, with suppliant smiles, they bend the head,		65
While distant mitres, to their eyes are spread;
But, should a storm o'erwhelm him with disgrace,
They'd fly to seek the next, who fill'd his place.
Such are the men, who learning's treasures guard,
Such is their practice, such is their reward;			70
This much, at least, we may presume to say;
The premium can't exceed the price they pay.

1806

59			To the Earl of [Clare]

Tu semper amoris
Sis memor, et cari comitis ne abscedat Imago.

VALERIUS FLACCUS.

[1.]
Friend of my youth! when young we rov'd,
Like striplings mutually belov'd,
	With Friendship's purest glow;
The bliss, which wing'd those rosy hours,
Was such as Pleasure seldom showers			5
	On mortals here below.

59–62 added in POT	63 lord] tool FP, POVO	64 P[e]tty] Petty FP, POVO
66 While distant mitres] Whilst mitres, prebends FP, POVO	72 Th' reward's scarce
equal, to the price they pay. FP

59. Copy text: POT, collated with MS. T (lines 73–81), HI1820

2.

The recollection seems, alone,
Dearer than all the joys I've known,
   When distant far from you;
Though pain, 'tis still a pleasing pain,   10
To trace those days and hours again,
   And sigh again, adieu!

3.

My pensive mem'ry lingers o'er,
Those scenes to be enjoy'd no more,
   Those scenes regretted ever;   15
The measure of our youth is full,
Life's evening dream is dark and dull,
   And we may meet—ah! never!

4.

As when one parent spring supplies
Two streams, which from one fountain rise,   20
   Together join'd in vain;
How soon, diverging from their source,
Each, murmuring, seeks another course,
   Till mingl'd in the Main.

5.

Our vital streams of weal or woe,   25
Though near, alas! distinctly flow,
   Nor mingle as before;
Now swift or slow, now black or clear,
Till Death's unfathom'd gulph appear,
   And both shall quit the shore.   30

6.

Our souls, my Friend! which once supplied
One wish, nor breath'd a thought beside,
   Now flow in different channels;
Disdaining humbler rural sports,
'Tis yours to mix in polish'd courts,   35
   And shine in Fashion's annals.

7.

'Tis mine to waste on love my time,
Or vent my reveries in rhyme,
    Without the aid of Reason;
For Sense and Reason, (Critics know it,)   40
Have quitted every amorous Poet,
    Nor left a thought to seize on.

8.

Poor LITTLE! sweet, melodious bard!
Of late esteem'd it monstrous hard,
    That he, who sang before all;   45
He who the lore of love expanded,
By dire Reviewers should be branded,
    As void of wit and moral.

9.

And yet, while Beauty's praise is thine,
Harmonious favourite of the nine!   50
    Repine not at thy lot;
Thy soothing lays may still be read,
When Persecution's arm is dead,
    And Critics are forgot.

10.

Still, I must yield those worthies merit,   55
Who chasten, with unsparing spirit,
    Bad rhymes, and those who write them;
And though myself may be the next,
By critic sarcasm to be vext,
    I really will not fight them;   60

11.

Perhaps, they would do quite as well,
To break the rudely sounding shell,
    Of such a young beginner;
He, who offends at pert nineteen,
Ere thirty may become, I ween,   65
    A very harden'd sinner.

12.

Now [Clare] I must return to you,
And sure apologies are due,
   Accept then my concession;
In truth, dear [Clare], in fancy's flight,   70
I soar along from left to right,
   My Muse admires digression.

13.

I think, I said, 'twould be your fate
To add one star to royal state,
   May regal smiles attend you;   75
And should a noble Monarch reign,
You will not seek his smiles in vain,
   If worth can recommend you.

14.

Yet, since in danger, courts abound,
Where specious rivals glitter round,   80
   From snares may Saints preserve you;
And grant, your love or friendship ne'er
From any claim a kindred care,
   But those, who best deserve you.

15.

Not for a moment may you stray   85
From Truth's secure unerring way,
   May no delights decoy;
O'er roses may your footsteps move,
Your smiles be ever smiles of love,
   Your tears be tears of joy.   90

16.

Oh! if you wish, that happiness
Your coming days and years may bless,
   And virtues crown your brow:
Be, still, as you were wont to be,
Spotless as you've been known to me,   95
   Be, still, as you are now.

74 royal] regal *T*   75 regal] Royal *T*   76 should] if *earlier reading, cor. in T*
78 If worth can] *That face* will *earlier reading, cor. in T*   79–81 *cor. in T* [passage
originally begin 'Oh! you will triumph']

17.

And though some trifling share of praise,
To cheer my last declining days,
    To me were doubly dear;
Whilst blessing your beloved name,   100
I'd *wave* at once, a *Poet's* fame,
    To *prove* a *Prophet here.*

[1807]

60   Granta, A Medley

Ἀργυρέαις λόγχαισι μάχου καὶ πάντα κρατήσαις.

[1.]
Oh! could Le SAGE's demon's gift,
    Be realiz'd at my desire;
This night my trembling form he'd lift,
    To place it on St. Mary's spire.

2.

Then would, unroof'd, old Granta's halls   5
    Pedantic inmates full display;
Fellows, who dream on lawn, or stalls,
    The price of venal votes to pay.

3.

Then would I view each rival wight,
    P[e]tty and P[a]lm[er]s[to]n survey;   10
Who canvass there, with all their might,
    Against the next elective day.

60. Copy text: *HI*, collated with *FP, POVO, POT, HI1820*
epigraph   *added in HI*

  4 To] And *FP*   8 venal] hireling *FP*   10 Petty and Palmerston *FP, POVO*
11 there] now *FP*

4.

Lo! candidates and voters lie,
   All lull'd in sleep, a goodly number!
A race renown'd for piety,   15
   Whose conscience won't disturb their slumber.

5.

Lord H[awke] indeed, may not demur,
   Fellows are sage, reflecting, men;
They know preferment can occur,
   But very seldom, now and then.   20

6.

They know, the Chancellor has got
   Some pretty livings, in disposal;
Each hopes, that one may be his lot,
   And, therefore, smiles on his proposal.

7.

Now, from the soporific scene,   25
   I'll turn mine eye, as night grows later,
To view, unheeded, and unseen,
   The studious sons of Alma Mater.

8.

There, in apartments small and damp
   The candidate for college prizes,   30
Sits poring by the midnight lamp,
   Goes late to bed, yet early rises.

9.

He surely well deserves to gain them,
   With all the honours of his college,
Who, striving hardly to obtain them,   35
   Thus seeks unprofitable knowledge:

13–15   One on his power and place depends,
            The other on—the Lord knows what!
         Each to some eloquence pretends,
            But neither will convince by that. *FP, POVO*
17 Lord H[awke]] The first *FP, POVO*   19 They] And *FP*   24 on] at
FP, POVO   25 the soporific] corruption's shameless *FP, POVO*   32 yet] and *FP*
34 With] And *FP*

10.

Who sacrifices hours of rest,
  To scan precisely metres Attic;
Or agitates his anxious breast,
  In solving problems mathematic.   40

11.

Who reads false quantities in Sele,
  Or puzzles o'er the deep triangle;
Depriv'd of many a wholesome meal,
  In barbarous latin, doom'd to wrangle.

12.

Renouncing every pleasing page,   45
  From authors of historic use;
Preferring to the lettered sage,
  The square of the hypothenuse.

13.

Still harmless are these occupations,
  That hurt none but the hapless student,   50
Compar'd with other recreations,
  Which bring together the imprudent.

14.

Whose daring revels shock the sight,
  When vice and infamy combine;
When drunkenness and dice unite,   55
  As every sense is steep'd in wine.

15.

Not so, the methodistic crew,
  Who plans of reformation lay;
In humble attitude they sue,
  And for the sins of others pray.   60

39 Or] And *FP*   43 And robs himself of many a meal *FP*   49 Still] But *FP*
50 That] ⟨Which⟩ *FPM*   55 dice] vice [E. Pigot's MS. cor. in her copy of *POVO*]
unite] invite *HI1820, 1831, 1832, C, More*   56 As] And *FP*

16.

Forgetting that their pride of spirit,
    Their exultation in their trial;
Detracts, most largely, from the merit
    Of all their boasted self-denial.

17.

'Tis morn,—from these I turn my sight,   65
    What scene is this, which meets the eye?
A numerous crowd, array'd in white,
    Across the green in numbers fly.

18.

Loud rings, in air, the chapel bell;   70
    'Tis hush'd; What sounds are these I hear?
The organ's soft celestial swell,
    Rolls deeply on the listening ear.

19.

To this is join'd the sacred song,
    The royal minstrel's hallowed strain;
Though he, who hears the music long,   75
    Will never wish to hear again.

20.

Our choir would scarcely be excus'd,
    Even as a band of raw beginners;
All mercy, now, must be refus'd,
    To such a set of croaking sinners.   80

21.

If David, when his toils were ended,
    Had heard these blockheads sing before him,
To us, his psalms had ne'er descended,
    In furious mood, he would have tore 'em.

62 Their] And *FP*   75 Though] But *FP*   79 All] But *FP*

22.

The luckless Israelites, when taken,   85
   By some inhuman tyrant's order,
Were ask'd to sing, by joy forsaken,
   On Babylonian river's border.

23.

Oh! had they sung in notes like these,
   Inspir'd by stratagem, or fear;   90
They might have set their hearts at ease,
   The devil a soul had stay'd to hear.

24.

But, if I scribble longer now,
   The deuce a soul will stay to read;
My pen is blunt, my ink is low,   95
   'Tis almost time to stop, indeed.

25.

Therefore, farewell, old GRANTA's spires,
   No more, like Cleofas, I fly,
No more thy theme my muse inspires,
   The reader's tir'd and so am I.   100

[28 Oct. 1806]

89 Oh!] But *FP*   93 But if I write much longer now, *FP, POVO*   95 my]
the *FP*
dating *thus in FP;* 1806 *POVO, HI, POT*

61   Lachin Y Gair

LACHIN Y GAIR, or as it is pronounced in the Erse, LOCH NA GARR, towers proudly pre-eminent
in the Northern Highlands, near Invercauld. One of our modern Tourists mentions it as the
highest mountain perhaps in GREAT BRITAIN; be this as it may, it is certainly one of the most
sublime, and picturesque, amongst our 'Caledonian Alps'. Its appearance is of a dusky hue, but
the summit is the seat of eternal snows; near Lachin y Gair, I spent some of the early part of
my life, the recollection of which, has given birth to the following Stanzas.

[1.]
Away, ye gay landscapes! ye gardens of roses!
    In you let the minions of luxury rove;
Restore me the rocks, where the snow-flake reposes,
    Though still they are sacred to freedom and love:
Yet, Caledonia! belov'd are thy mountains,   5
    Round their white summits though elements war,
Though cataracts foam, 'stead of smooth flowing foun-
        tains,
    I sigh, for the valley of dark Loch na Garr.

2.
Ah! there my young footsteps, in infancy, wander'd,
    My cap was the bonnet, my cloak was the plaid;   10
On chieftains, long perish'd, my memory ponder'd,
    As daily I strode through the pine-cover'd glade;
I sought not my home, till the day's dying glory
    Gave place to the rays of the bright polar star;
For Fancy was cheer'd, by traditional story,   15
    Disclos'd by the natives of dark Loch na Garr.

3.
'Shades of the dead! have I not heard your voices
    Rise on the night-rolling breath of the gale?'
Surely the soul of the hero rejoices,
    And rides on the wind, o'er his own Highland vale: 20
Round Loch na Garr, while the stormy mist gathers,
    Winter presides in his cold icy car;
Clouds, there, encircle the forms of my Fathers,
    They dwell in the tempests of dark Loch na Garr:

61. Copy text: *HI*, collated with *POT*, *HI1820*

4.

'Ill starred, though brave, did no visions foreboding,   25
    Tell you that Fate had forsaken your cause?'
Ah! were you destin'd to die at Culloden,
    Victory crown'd not your fall with applause;
Still were you happy in death's earthy slumber,
    You rest with your clan, in the caves of Braemar,   30
The Pibroch resounds, to the piper's loud number,
    Your deeds, on the echoes of dark Loch na Garr.

[5.]

Years have roll'd on, Loch na Garr, since I left you,
    Years must elapse, e'er I tread you again;
Nature of verdure and flowers has bereft you,   35
    Yet still are you dearer than Albion's plain:
England! thy beauties are tame and domestic,
    To one, who has rov'd on the mountains afar;
Oh! for the crags that are wild and majestic,
    The steep, frowning glories of dark Loch na Garr.   40

[1807]

62   To Romance

[1.]

Parent of golden dreams, Romance,
    Auspicious Queen! of childish joys,
Who lead'st along in airy dance,
    Thy votive train of girls and boys;
At length, in spells no longer bound,   5
    I break the fetters of my youth,
No more I tread thy mystic round,
    But leave thy realms for those of Truth.

2.

And, yet, 'tis hard to quit the dreams,
    Which haunt the unsuspicious soul,   10

62. Copy text: *HI*, collated with *MS. N, POT, HI1820*

Where every nymph a goddess seems,
  Whose eyes through rays immortal roll;
While Fancy holds her boundless reign,
  And all assume a varied hue,
When Virgins seem no longer vain,   15
  And even Woman's smiles are true.

3.

And must we own thee, but a name,
  And from thy hall of clouds descend?
Nor find a Sylph in every dame,
  A Pylades in every friend;   20
But leave, at once, thy realms of air,
  To mingling bands of fairy elves;
Confess that Woman's false as fair,
  And friends have feeling for—themselves.

4.

With shame, I own, I've felt thy sway,   25
  Repentant, now thy reign is o'er,
No more thy precepts I obey,
  No more on fancied pinions soar;
Fond fool! to love a sparkling eye,
  And think, that eye to Truth was dear,   30
To trust a passing wanton's sigh,
  And melt beneath a wanton's tear.

5.

Romance! disgusted with deceit,
  Far from thy motley court I fly,
Where Affection holds her seat,   35
  And sickly Sensibility;

11 nymph] Girl N   21 leave] quit N   22 To] Thy N
33–40   Romance! ⟨with this⟩ this last farewell from me,
              Is sent without a parting sigh,
            My early dreams I leave ⟨with⟩ to thee,
              My tears to Sensibility,
            Thy votary, still inclined to steep,
              Her eyes in tears for woes of thine,
            And as, indeed, I cannot weep,
              She now may shed a few for mine. *cancelled in N*
Is . . . sigh] ⟨Receive my parting legacy⟩ N

Whose silly tears can never flow,
  For any pangs excepting thine,
Who turns aside from real woe,
  To steep in dew thy gaudy shrine.   40

6.

Now join with sable Sympathy,
  With cypress crown'd, array'd in weeds,
Who heaves with thee her simple sigh,
  Whose breast for every bosom bleeds;
And call thy sylvan female quire,   45
  To mourn a swain forever gone,
Who once could glow with equal fire,
  But bends not now before thy throne.

7.

Ye genial nymphs! whose ready tears,
  On all occasions swiftly flow,   50
Whose bosoms heave with fancied fears,
  With fancied flames and phrenzy glow;
Say, will you mourn my absent name,
  Apostate from your gentle train?
An infant Bard at least may claim,   55
  From you a sympathetic strain.

8.

Adieu, fond race, a long adieu,
  The hour of fate is hov'ring nigh,
Even now the gulph appears in view,
  Where unlamented you must lie;   60
Oblivion's blackening lake is seen,
  Convuls'd by gales you cannot weather,
Where you, and eke your gentle queen,
  Alas! must perish altogether.

[1807]

41 Now join with] ⟨Invoke too⟩ *N*   42 Who always wears another's weeds, *N*
49 Ye genial nymphs!] Auspicious Band! *N*   57 ⟨Yes let us hail each other's
praise⟩ *N*   59 Even] ⟨Where⟩ *N*   60 Where you are doom'd in Death to lie, *N*
62 by] ⟨with⟩ *N*

63   Elegy on Newstead Abbey

> It is the voice of years that are gone! they roll before me, with all
> their deeds.   OSSIAN.

Newstead! fast falling, once resplendent dome!
   Religion's shrine! repentant HENRY's pride!
Of warriors, monks, and dames the cloister'd tomb;
   Whose pensive shades around thy ruins glide,

Hail! to thy pile! more honour'd in thy fall,   5
   Than modern mansions, in their pillar'd state;
Proudly majestic frowns thy vaulted hall,
   Scowling defiance on the blasts of fate.

No mail-clad Serfs, obedient to their Lord,
   In grim array, the crimson cross demand;   10
Or gay assemble round the festive board,
   Their chief's retainers, an immortal band.

Else might inspiring Fancy's magic eye
   Retrace their progress, through the lapse of time;
Marking each ardent youth, ordain'd to die,   15
   A votive pilgrim, in Judea's clime.

But not from thee, dark pile! departs the Chief,
   His feudal realm in other regions lay;
In thee, the wounded conscience courts relief,
   Retiring from the garish blaze of day.   20

Yes, in thy gloomy cells and shades profound,
   The Monk abjur'd a world, he ne'er could view;
Or blood-stained Guilt, repenting solace found,
   Or Innocence, from stern Oppression, flew.

A Monarch bade thee, from that wild arise,   25
   Where Sherwood's outlaws, once, were wont to prowl;
And Superstition's crimes of various dyes,
   Sought shelter in the Priest's protecting cowl.

63. Copy text: *HI*, collated with *POVO*, *POT*, *HI1820*
epigraph *added in HI*
  23 Guilt, repenting] Guilt repenting, *C*; Guilt repenting *1831*, *1832*, *More*

Where, now, the grass exhales a murky dew,
   The humid pall of life-extinguish'd clay;   30
In sainted fame, the sacred fathers grew,
   Nor raised their pious voices but to pray.

Where, now, the bats their wavering wings extend,
   Soon as the Gloaming spreads her waning shade;
The choir did, oft, their mingling vespers blend,   35
   Or matin orisons to Mary paid.

Years roll on years; to ages, ages yield;
   Abbots to Abbots, in a line succeed;
Religion's charter, their protecting shield,
   Till royal sacrilege their doom decreed.   40

One holy HENRY, rear'd the gothic walls,
   And bade the pious inmates rest in peace;
Another HENRY the kind gift recalls,
   And bids devotion's hallow'd echoes cease.

Vain is each threat, or supplicating prayer,   45
   He drives them, exiles, from their blest abode;
To roam a dreary world, in deep despair,
   No friend, no home, no refuge, but their God,

Hark! how the hall, resounding to the strain,
   Shakes with the martial music's novel din!   50
The heralds of a warrior's haughty reign,
   High crested banners, wave thy walls within.

Of changing sentinels, the distant hum,
   The mirth of feasts, the clang of burnish'd arms,
The braying trumpet, and the hoarser drum,   55
   Unite in concert, with increas'd alarms.

34 Soon . . . her] Soon as the twilight winds a *POVO*

An abbey once, a regal fortress now,
    Encircled by insulting rebel powers;
War's dread machines o'erhang thy threat'ning brow,
    And dart destruction, in sulphureous showers.   60

Ah! vain defence! the hostile traitor's siege,
    Though oft repuls'd, by guile o'ercomes the brave;
His thronging foes oppress the faithful Liege,
    Rebellion's reeking standards o'er him wave.

Not unaveng'd, the raging Baron yields,   65
    The blood of traitors smears the purple plain;
Unconquer'd, still, his faulchion there he wields,
    And days of glory, yet, for him remain.

Still, in that hour, the warrior wish'd to strew,
    Self-gather'd laurels, on a self-sought grave;   70
But Charles' protecting genius hither flew,
    The monarch's friend, the monarch's hope, to save.

Trembling she snatch'd him from the unequal strife,
    In other fields, the torrent to repel;
For nobler combats, here, reserv'd his life,   75
    To lead the band, where god-like FALKLAND fell.

From thee, poor pile! to lawless plunder given,
    While dying groans, their painful requiem sound,
Far different incense, now, ascends to heaven,
    Such victims wallow on the gory ground.   80

There, many a pale and ruthless Robber's corse,
    Noisome and ghast, defiles thy sacred sod;
O'er mingling man, and horse commix'd with horse,
    Corruption's heap, the savage spoilers trod.

Graves, long with rank and sighing weeds o'erspread,   85
    Ransack'd, resign, perforce, their mortal mould;
From ruffian fangs, escape not e'en the dead,
    Rak'd from repose, in search for buried gold.

Hush'd is the harp, unstrung the warlike lyre,
    The minstrel's palsied hand reclines in death;   90
No more he strikes the quivering chords with fire,
    Or sings the glories of the martial wreath.

At length the sated murderers, gorged with prey,
    Retire, the clamour of the fight is o'er;
Silence, again, resumes her awful sway,   95
    And sable Horror guards the massy door.

Here, Desolation holds her dreary court,
    What satellites declare her dismal reign!
Shrieking their dirge, ill omen'd birds resort,
    To flit their vigils, in the hoary fane.   100

Soon, a new Morn's restoring beams dispel
    The clouds of Anarchy from Britain's skies:
The fierce Usurper seeks his native hell,
    And Nature triumphs, as the Tyrant dies.

With storms she welcomes his expiring groans,   105
    Whirlwinds, responsive, greet his labouring breath;
Earth shudders, as her caves receive his bones,
    Loathing the offering of so dark a death.

The legal Ruler, now, resumes the helm,
    He guides thro' gentle seas, the prow of state;   110
Hope cheers, with wonted smiles, the peaceful realm,
    And heals the bleeding wounds of wearied Hate.

The gloomy tenants, Newstead! of thy cells,
    Howling, resign their violated nest;
Again, the Master on his tenure dwells,   115
    Enjoy'd, from absence, with enraptur'd zest.

Vassals, within thy hospitable pale,
    Loudly carousing bless their Lord's return;
Culture, again, adorns the gladdening vale,
    And matrons, once lamenting, cease to mourn.   120

92 martial] laurell'd *POVO*   96 sable Horror] horror stalking *POVO*
114 resign] forsake *POVO*

A thousand songs, on tuneful echo, float,
  Unwonted foliage mantles o'er the trees;
And, hark! the horns proclaim a mellow note,
  The hunter's cry hangs lengthening on the breeze.

Beneath their coursers' hoofs the valleys shake,   125
  What fears! what anxious hopes! attend the chace!
The dying stag seeks refuge in the lake,
  Exulting shouts announce the finish'd race.

Ah! happy days! too happy to endure!
  Such simple sports, our plain forefathers knew;   130
No splendid vices glitter'd to allure,
  Their joys were many, as their cares were few.

From these descending, Sons to Sires succeed,
  Time steals along, and Death uprears his dart;
Another Chief impels the foaming steed,   135
  Another Crowd pursue the panting hart.

Newstead! what saddening change of scene is thine!
  Thy yawning arch betokens slow decay;
The last and youngest of a noble line,
  Now holds thy mouldering turrets in his sway.   140

Deserted now, he scans thy grey worn towers;
  Thy vaults, where dead of feudal ages sleep;
Thy cloisters, pervious to the wintry showers;
  These, these he views, and views them but to weep.

Yet are his tears, no emblem of regret,   145
  Cherish'd affection only bids them flow;
Pride, Hope, and Love, forbid him to forget,
  But warm his bosom, with empassion'd glow.

Yet, he prefers thee, to the gilded domes,
  Or gewgaw grottos, of the vainly great;   150
Yet, lingers mid thy damp and mossy tombs,
  Nor breathes a murmur 'gainst the will of fate.

132 Their] There *HI*   145 emblem] emblems *POVO, HI*

Haply thy sun, emerging, yet, may shine,
  Thee to irradiate, with meridian ray;
Hours, splendid as the past, may still be thine,   155
  And bless thy future, as thy former day.

[1804?]

64   The Death of Calmar and Orla, An Imitation of Macpherson's Ossian

Dear are the days of youth! Age dwells on their remembrance through the mist of time. In the twilight he recalls the sunny hours of morn. He lifts his spear with trembling hand. 'Not thus feebly did I raise the steel before my fathers!' Past is the race of heroes!
5 but their fame rises on the harp; their souls ride on the wings of the wind! they hear the sound through the sighs of the storm; and rejoice in their hall of clouds! Such is Calmar. The grey stone marks his narrow house. He looks down from eddying tempests; he rolls his form in the whirlwind; and hovers on the blast of the mountain.
10 In Morven dwelt the chief. A beam of war to Fingal. His steps in the field were marked in blood; Lochlin's sons had fled before his angry spear! but mild was the eye of Calmar; soft was the flow of his yellow locks; they streamed like the meteor of the night. No maid was the sigh of his soul; his thoughts were given to friendship!
15 to dark-hair'd Orla; destroyer of heroes! Equal were their swords in battle: but fierce was the pride of Orla! gentle alone to Calmar. Together they dwelt in the cave of Oithona.

From Lochlin, Swaran bounded o'er the blue waves. Erin's sons fell beneath his might. Fingal roused his chiefs to combat. Their
20 ships cover the ocean! Their hosts throng on the green hills. They come to the aid of Erin.

Night rose in clouds. Darkness veils the armies. But the blazing oaks gleam through the valley. The sons of Lochlin slept: their

155–6 Fortune may smile, upon a future line, | And heaven restore an ever cloudless day. *POVO, HI*

64. Copy text: *HI*, collated with *MS. Y, POT, HI1820*
1 of youth] of ⟨our⟩ youth *Y*   2–4 In the . . . did I raise] He lifts the spear with trembling hand, 'thus did I raise *Y*   5 rises] ⟨dwells⟩ rises *Y*   their souls] ⟨our⟩ their Souls *Y*   6 they hear] they ⟨catch⟩ hear *Y*   7 is] was *Y*   8 He] ⟨but⟩ he *Y*   11 Lochlin's] Erin's *Y*   19 Fingal . . . combat] the horn of Fingal . . . ⟨fight⟩ combat *Y*   22–3 blazing oaks] fires *Y*

dreams were of blood. They lift the spear in thought, and Fingal
flies. Not so the Host of Morven. To watch was the post of Orla.   25
Calmar stood by his side. Their spears were in their hands. Fingal
called his chiefs: they stood around. The king was in the midst.
Grey were his locks, but strong was the arm of the king. Age
withered not his powers. 'Sons of Morven' said the hero, 'to-
morrow we meet the foe; but where is Cuthullin, the shield of Erin?   30
He rests in the halls of Tura; he knows not of our coming. Who will
speed through Lochlin to the hero? And call the chief to arms. The
path is by the swords of foes, but many are my heroes. They are
thunderbolts of war! Speak ye chiefs, Who will arise?'
    'Son of Trenmor! mine be the deed,' said dark-haired Orla,   35
'and mine alone. What is death to me? I love the sleep of the mighty,
but little is the danger. The sons of Lochlin dream. I will seek car-
borne Cuthullin. If I fall, raise the song of bards; and lay me by
the stream of Lubar.'—'And shalt thou fall alone?' said fair-haired
Calmar. 'Wilt thou leave thy friend afar? Chief of Oithona! not   40
feeble is my arm in fight. Could I see thee die, and not lift the spear?
No, Orla! ours has been the chase of the roebuck, and the feast of
shells; ours be the path of danger; ours has been the cave of Oithona; ours be the narrow dwelling on the banks of Lubar.' 'Calmar!'
said the chief of Oithona, 'Why should thy yellow locks be darkened   45
in the dust of Erin? Let me fall alone. My father dwells in his hall
of air: he will rejoice in his boy: but the blue-eyed Mora spreads
the feast for her son in Morven. She listens to the steps of the
hunter on the heath, and thinks it is the tread of Calmar. Let him
not say, "Calmar has fallen by the steel of Lochlin! he died with   50
gloomy Orla; the chief of the dark brow." Why should tears dim
the azure eye of Mora? Why should her voice curse Orla, the
destroyer of Calmar? Live Calmar. Live to raise my stone of moss;
live to revenge me in the blood of Lochlin. Join the song of bards
above my grave. Sweet will be the song of Death to Orla, from the   55
voice of Calmar. My ghost shall smile on the notes of Praise.'
'Orla!' said the son of Mora, 'could I raise the song of death, to my
friend? Could I give his fame to the winds? No, my heart would
speak in sighs; faint and broken are the sounds of sorrow. Orla!

25 flies] flies ⟨before them⟩ *Υ*   33 by] ⟨through⟩ *Υ*   36 I love] ⟨'tis⟩ *Υ*
37 dream] ⟨sleep⟩ *Υ*   42 Orla! ours] Orla ⟨we have liv'd together,⟩ ours *Υ*   51 Why
should tears] let not tears *Υ*   54 Join the] ⟨And⟩ join thou the *Υ*   57 *new
paragraph in Υ*   58–9 heart . . . broken] ⟨voice⟩ . . . ⟨lonely⟩ *Υ*

60 our souls shall hear the song together. One cloud shall be ours on
high; the bards will mingle the names of Orla and Calmar.'
   They quit the circle of the chiefs. Their steps are to the Host of
Lochlin. The dying blaze of oak dim-twinkles through the night.
The northern star points the path to Tura. Swaran, the king, rests
65 on his lonely hill. Here the troops are mixed: they frown in sleep.
Their shields beneath their heads. Their swords gleam, at distance,
in heaps. The fires are faint; their embers fail in smoke. All is hushed;
but the gale sighs on the rocks above. Lightly wheel the heroes
through the slumbering band. Half the journey is past, when
70 Mathon, resting on his shield, meets the eye of Orla. It rolls in
flame, and glistens through the shade: his spear is raised on high.
'Why dost thou bend thy brow, chief of Oithona?' said fair-haired
Calmar, 'we are in the midst of foes. Is this a time for delay?' 'It is a
time for vengeance,' said Orla of the gloomy brow. 'Mathon of
75 Lochlin sleeps: seest thou his spear? Its point is dim with the gore
of my father. The blood of Mathon shall reek on mine; but shall I
slay him sleeping, Son of Mora? No: he shall feel his wound; my
fame shall not soar on the blood of slumber: rise, Mathon, rise!
The son of Connal calls, thy life is his; rise to combat.' Mathon
80 starts from sleep, but did he rise alone? No: the gathering chiefs
bound on the plain. 'Fly, Calmar, fly,' said dark-hair'd Orla, 'Mathon is mine; I shall die in joy, but Lochlin crowds around; fly
through the shade of night.' Orla turns, the helm of Mathon is
cleft; his shield falls from his arm: he shudders in his blood. He
85 rolls by the side of the blazing oak. Strumon sees him fall: his
wrath rises; his weapon glitters on the head of Orla; but a spear
pierced his eye. His brain gushes through the wound, and foams on
the spear of Calmar. As roll the waves of Ocean, on two mighty
barks of the North, so pour the men of Lochlin on the chiefs. As
90 breaking the surge in foam, proudly steer the barks of the North,
so rise the Chiefs of Morven, on the scattered crests of Lochlin.
The din of arms came to the ear of Fingal. He strikes his shield:
his sons throng around; the people pour along the heath. Ryno,
bounds in joy. Ossian, stalks in his arms. Oscar, shakes the spear.

63 dying blaze of oak] fires ϒ   64 rests] ⟨sleeps / reposes⟩ ϒ   67 fail] die ϒ
68 but the gale . . . above] ⟨save the crackling of faggots,⟩ but the ⟨sighing⟩ gale ⟨of sought?
heaven⟩ ϒ   73 delay] ⟨Rage⟩ ϒ   74–5 'Mathon . . . sleeps] ⟨there sleeps Mathon
of Lochlin⟩ ϒ   79 rise to combat] ⟨he gives it thee—defend it⟩ ϒ   83 shade of]
⟨coat? of the⟩ ϒ   84 shudders] trembles ϒ   85 by . . . oak] convulsive ϒ
89 pour] ⟨rage⟩ ϒ   90 surge] ⟨waves⟩ ϒ   94 in joy] ⟨along⟩ ϒ   shakes] ⟨lifts⟩ ϒ

The eagle wing of Fillan floats on the wind. Dreadful is the clang of 95
death! many are the widows of Lochlin. Morven prevails in its
strength.

Morn glimmers on the hills: no living foe is seen; but the sleepers
are many; grim they lie on Erin. The breeze of ocean lifts their
locks; yet they do not awake. The hawks scream above their prey. 100
Whose yellow locks wave o'er the breast of a chief? bright as the
gold of the stranger, they mingle with the dark hair of his friend.
'Tis Calmar, he lies on the bosom of Orla. Theirs is one stream of
blood. Fierce is the look of the gloomy Orla. He breathes not; but
his eye is still a flame. It glares in death unclosed. His hand is 105
grasped in Calmar's; but Calmar lives! he lives, though low. 'Rise,'
said the king, 'rise, Son of Mora; 'Tis mine to heal the wounds of
heroes. Calmar may yet bound on the mountains of Morven.'

'Never more shall Calmar chase the deer of Morven with Orla,'
said the hero, 'what were the chase to me alone? Who would share 110
the spoils of battle with Calmar? Orla is at rest! rough was thy
soul, Orla! yet soft to me as the dew of morn. It glared on others,
in lightning: to me a silver beam of night. Bear my sword to blue-
eyed Mora; let it hang in my empty hall. It is not pure from blood;
but it could not save Orla. Lay me with my friend: raise the song 115
when I am dark.'

They are laid by the stream of Lubar. Four grey stones mark
the dwelling of Orla and Calmar.

When Swaran was bound, our sails rose on the blue waves. The
winds gave our barks to Morven. The bards raised the song.   120
'What form rises on the roar of clouds, whose dark ghost gleams
on the red stream of tempests? his voice rolls on the thunder;
'tis Orla. The brown chief of Oithona. He was unmatched in war.
Peace to thy soul, Orla! thy fame will not perish. Nor thine, Calmar! Lovely wast thou, Son of blue-eyed Mora; but not harmless 125
was thy sword. It hangs in thy cave. The ghosts of Lochlin shriek
around its steel. Hear thy praise, Calmar! It dwells on the voice of

95 Fillan] ⟨Fillan's helmet⟩ *Υ*   98 sleepers] ⟨Earth / Dead⟩ *Υ*   100 scream
above] ⟨hover round⟩ *Υ*   102 wave] ⟨float⟩ *Υ*   105 he breathes] he ⟨yet⟩
breathes *Υ*   106 flame. It] flame, ⟨nor yet is it dead in Death,⟩ it *Υ*   107 Rise]
⟨but⟩ rise *Υ*   108 'Tis . . . heal] ⟨and have healed⟩ *Υ*   112 Orla] ⟨his friend⟩ *Υ*
113 morn] ⟨Heaven⟩ *Υ*   120–1 our sails . . . Morven] we ⟨strung⟩ sailed the blue
waves to Morven. *Υ*   122 roar of clouds] ⟨the clouds of Heaven / the roar of winds⟩ *Υ*
123 on the. . .tempests] ⟨in the lightnings⟩ *Υ*   his voice rolls] ⟨whose voice rises⟩ *Υ*
127 sword] ⟨Steel⟩ *Υ*   128 the voice of *B's MS.* ends here. *The poem's conclusion is
written in E. Pigot's hand.*

the mighty. Thy name shakes on the echoes of Morven. Then raise
thy fair locks, son of Mora. Spread them on the arch of the rainbow;
130 and smile through the tears of the storm.'

[1807]

65   To E[dward] N[oel] L[ong] Esq.

Nil ego contulerim jucundo sanus amico.
                                    Hor[ace, *Satires*, I. v. 44]

Dear L[ong], in this sequester'd scene,
    While all around in slumber lie,
The joyous days, which ours have been,
    Come rolling fresh on fancy's eye:
Thus, if amidst the gathering storm,   5
While clouds the darken'd noon deform,
Yon heaven assumes a varied glow,
I hail the sky's celestial bow;
Which spreads the sign of future peace,
And bids the war of tempests cease.   10
Ah! though the present brings but pain,
I think those days may come again;
Or if, in melancholy mood,
Some lurking envious fear intrude;
To check my bosom's fondest thought,   15
    And interrupt the golden dream;
I crush the fiend with malice fraught,
    And still indulge my wonted theme;
Although we ne'er again can trace

65. Copy text: *HI*, collated with *MSS. T* and *P, POT, HI1820*
title   To E. N. Long *T, P*
epigraph   *not in MSS.*

    1 ⟨Alone,⟩ in *T*   4 fresh] ⟨back⟩ *T*   5 if ... the] ⟨while the Clouds in⟩ *T*
6 ⟨The blushing Noon with rain deform⟩ ⟨While darkened Clouds / The Clouds / The Noon⟩ *T*
7-8   ⟨I view the Lightning's livid Glow
                        And / The Heaven assumes a varied glow⟩
                        ⟨I hail the skies celestial bow
                        I view the lightning's livid glow⟩ *T*
9 Which spreads] ⟨Spreads, with⟩ *T*   14 fear] ⟨thought⟩ *T*   intrude] obtrude *P,*
cancelled T   16 dream] ⟨Scheme⟩ *T*   18 theme] ⟨Scheme⟩ *T*

In Granta's vale, the pedant's lore,   20
Nor through the groves of IDA chase
Our raptur'd visions as before;
Though Youth has flown on rosy pinion,
And Manhood claims his stern dominion,
Age will not every hope destroy,   25
But yield some hours of sober joy.

Yes, I will hope that Time's broad wing,
Will shed around some dews of spring;
But if his scythe must sweep the flowers,
Which bloom among the fairy bowers,   30
Where smiling Youth delights to dwell,
And hearts with early rapture swell;
If frowning Age with cold controul,
Confines the current of the soul,
Congeals the tear of Pity's eye,   35
Or checks the sympathetic sigh,
Or hears unmoved Misfortune's groan,
And bids me feel for self alone;
Oh! may my bosom never learn,
    To soothe its wonted heedless flow,   40
Still, still, despise the censor stern,
    But ne'er forget another's woe;
Yes, as you knew me in the days,
O'er which Remembrance yet delays,
Still may I rove untutor'd, wild,   45
And ev'n in age, at heart a child.

Though, now, on airy visions borne,
    To you my soul is still the same,
Oft has it been my fate to mourn,
    And all my former joys are tame;   50
But, hence! ye hours of sable hue,

23 rosy] ⟨daring⟩ T   25 Age] ⟨Time⟩ T   30 among] ⟨around⟩ T   31 smiling]
glowing T, P   40 To soothe its young romantic glow T, P   44 Remembrance]
my fancy T, P
45–6   Still may my breast to Boyhood cleave
                 With every early passion heave T, P
                 Still may I rove ⟨untutored,⟩ unawed and wild P
                 But never cease to seem a child. T, P
49 Since we have met, I learn'd to mourne T; ⟨I learned⟩ twas mine to mourne P

Your frowns are gone, my sorrow's o'er,
   By every bliss my childhood knew,
I'll think upon your shade no more:
   Thus when the whirlwind's rage is past,   55
   And caves their sullen roar enclose;
We heed no more the wint'ry blast,
   When lull'd by zephyr to repose.

Full often has my infant Muse,
   Attun'd to love, her languid lyre,   60
But, now, without a theme to chuse,
   The strains in stolen sighs expire:
My youthful nymphs, alas! are flown,
   E——is a wife, and C——a mother,
And Carolina sighs alone,   65
   And Mary's given to another;
And Cora's eye, which roll'd on me,
   Can now no more my love recal,
In truth, dear L[ong], 'twas time to flee,
   For Cora's eye will shine on all.   70
And though the Sun with genial rays,
His beams alike to all displays,
And every lady's eye's a *sun*,
These last should be confin'd to one;
The soul's meridian don't become her,   75
Whose Sun displays a general *summer*.
Thus faint is every former flame,
And Passion's self is now a name;
As when the ebbing flames are low,
   The aid which once improv'd their light,   80
And bade them burn with fiercer glow,
   Now quenches all their sparks in night;
Thus has it been with Passion's fires,
   As many a boy, and girl, remembers,

---

52 my] ⟨your⟩ T   53 By ⟨Cora's smiling orbs of Blue⟩ T   54 shade] shades T
56 And caves ⟨the murmur⟩ their sullen ⟨storm⟩ roar enclose T   roar] ⟨beam⟩ P
63 alas] thank heaven T, P   64 ⟨This is⟩ a wife, and ⟨that⟩ a mother T
66 Mary's] Mary T   69 truth] ⟨faith⟩ T   72 alike to all] to all alike T, P
74 ⟨Yet these should⟩ be T   75 ⟨I do not then⟩ The ⟨glancing⟩ Glances really don't
become her T   soul's meridian] ⟨glances really⟩ P   76 Sun] ⟨eye⟩ T   77–8 Thus
faint ⟨are all my former flames | For passion's self will sometimes tame⟩ T   79 ⟨And
I linger / No more I linger on the / But still I linger⟩ T

While all the force of love expires,   85
Extinguish'd with the dying embers.

But, now, dear L[ong], 'tis midnight's noon,
And clouds obscure the watery moon,
Whose beauties I shall not rehearse,
Describ'd in every stripling's verse;   90
For why should I the path go o'er,
Which every bard has trod before?
Yet, ere yon silver lamp of night,
  Has thrice perform'd her stated round,
Has thrice retrac'd her path of light,   95
  And chas'd away the gloom profound,
I trust, that we, my gentle Friend,
Shall see her rolling orbit wend,
Above the dear lov'd peaceful seat,
Which once contain'd our youth's retreat,   100
And, then, with those our childhood knew,
We'll mingle in the festive crew;
While many a tale of former day,
Shall wing the laughing hours away,
And all the flow of soul shall pour,   105
The sacred intellectual shower,
Nor cease till Luna's waning horn,
Scarce glimmers through the mist of Morn.

[1807]

66   To [George, Earl Delawarr]

[1.]

Oh! yes, I will own we were dear to each other,
  The friendships of childhood, tho' fleeting, are true;

85 all the force] ⟨every hope⟩ T   87 'tis ... noon] ⟨the winking Moon⟩ T
90 stripling's] ⟨Rhymer's⟩ T   92 Which ⟨love⟩ every T   And what much worse than
this I find, | Have left their deepen'd tracks behind. *couplet after line 92 in* T, P   93 yon
silver lamp] ⟨their⟩ silver ⟨orb⟩ T   94 perform'd] ⟨retraced⟩ T   96 And chased ⟨the
night⟩ away the ⟨shady⟩ gloom profound T   97 trust] ⟨hope⟩ T   99 dear lov'd]
⟨that blest and⟩ T   100 Which ⟨formed our⟩ once T   101 those] ⟨many⟩ T
102 We'll ⟨join the laughter loving⟩ crew T   in] with P   103 While] And P
104 wing] ⟨chase⟩ T   105 And many a present Joy shall pour T, P   soul] souls
HI1820, 1831, 1832, C, *More*   106 Its pleasure with increasing Shower T, P
107 waning] ⟨fading⟩ T   108 Scarce] ⟨Is⟩ T

66. Copy text: *HI,* collated with *POT, HI1820*

The Love which you felt, was the love of a brother,
  Nor less the affection I cherish'd for you.

2.

But Friendship can vary her gentle dominion,   5
  Th' attachment of years in a moment expires;
Like Love too, she moves on a swift-waving pinion,
  But glows not, like Love, with unquenchable fires.

3.

Full oft have we wander'd through Ida together,
  And blest were the scenes of our youth, I allow;   10
In the spring of our life, how serene is the weather,
  But winter's rudes tempests are gathering now.

4.

No more with Affection shall Memory blending
  The wonted delights of our childhood retrace,
When pride steels the bosom, the heart is unbending,   15
  And what would be Justice, appears a disgrace.

5.

However, dear [George], for I still must esteem you,
  The few, whom I love, I can never upbraid,
The chance, which has lost, may in future redeem you,
  Repentance will cancel the vow you have made.   20

6.

I will not complain, and tho' chill'd is affection,
  With me no corroding resentment shall live;
My bosom is calm'd by the simple reflection,
  · That both may be wrong, and that both should forgive.

7.

You knew that my soul, that my heart, my existence,   25
  If danger demanded were wholly your own;
You knew me unalter'd, by years or by distance,
  Devoted to love and to friendship alone.

17 [George]] S—— *HI, POT, HI1820, 1831*

8.

You knew,——but away with the vain retrospection,
    The bond of affection no longer endures;   30
Too late you may droop o'er the fond recollection,
    And sigh for the friend who was formerly yours.

9.

For the present, we part,—I will hope not forever,
    For time and regret will restore you at last;
To forget our dissention we both should endeavour,   35
    I ask no atonement, but days like the past.

[1807]

67   Stanzas

1.

I would I were a careless child,
    Still dwelling in my Highland cave,
Or roaming through the dusky wild,
    Or bounding o'er the dark blue wave;
The cumbrous pomp of Saxon pride,   5
    Accords not with the freeborn soul,
Which loves the mountain's craggy side,
    And seeks the rocks where billows roll.

2.

Fortune! take back these cultur'd lands,
    Take back this name of splendid sound!   10
I hate the touch of servile hands,
    I hate the slaves that cringe around:
Place me along the rocks I love,
    Which sound to Ocean's wildest roar,
I ask but this—again to rove   15
    Through scenes my youth hath known before.

67. Copy text: *POT*, collated with *HI1820*

3.

Few are my years, and, yet, I feel
  The World was ne'er design'd for me,
Ah! why do dark'ning shades conceal
  The hour when man must cease to be?   20
Once I beheld a splendid dream,
  A visionary scene of bliss;
Truth!—wherefore did thy hated beam
  Awake me to a world like this?

4.

I lov'd—but those I lov'd, are gone,   25
  Had friends—my early friends are fled,
How cheerless feels the heart alone,
  When all its former hopes are dead!
Though gay companions, o'er the bowl,
  Dispel awhile the sense of ill,   30
Though Pleasure stirs the maddening soul,
  The heart—the heart is lonely still.

5.

How dull! to hear the voice of those
  Whom Rank, or Chance, whom Wealth, or
    Power,
Have made; though neither Friends or Foes,   35
  Associates of the festive hour;
Give me again, a faithful few,
  In years and feelings still the same,
And I will fly the midnight crew,
  Where boist'rous Joy is but a name.   40

6.

And Woman! lovely Woman, thou!
  My hope, my comforter, my all!
How cold must be my bosom now,
  When e'en thy smiles begin to pall.
Without a sigh would I resign   45
  This busy scene of splendid Woe;
To make that calm Contentment mine,
  Which Virtue knows, or seems to know.

7.

Fain would I fly the haunts of men,
  I seek to shun, not hate mankind,   50
My breast requires the sullen glen,
  Whose gloom may suit a darken'd mind;
Oh! that to me the wings were given,
  Which bear the Turtle to her nest!
Then would I cleave the vault of Heaven,   55
  To flee away, and be at rest.

[1807 or 1808]

68   Lines Written Beneath an Elm,
         in the Churchyard of
         Harrow on the Hill

September 2d, 1807

Spot of my youth! whose hoary branches sigh,
Swept by the breeze that fans thy cloudless sky,
Where now alone, I muse, who oft have trod,
With those I lov'd, thy soft and verdent sod;
With those, who scatter'd far, perchance, deplore,   5
Like me the happy scenes they knew before;
Oh! as I trace again thy winding hill,
Mine eyes admire, my heart adores thee still,
Thou drooping Elm! beneath whose boughs I lay,
And frequent mus'd the twilight hours away;   10
Where, as they once were wont, my limbs recline,
But, ah! without the thoughts, which, then, were
    mine;
How do thy branches, moaning to the blast,
Invite the bosom to recall the past,
And seem to whisper, as they gently swell,   15
'Take, while thou canst, a ling'ring, last farewell!'

When Fate shall chill at length this fever'd breast,
And calm its cares and passions into rest;

68. Copy text: *POT*, collated with *HI1820*

Oft, have I thought, 'twould soothe my dying hour,
If aught may soothe, when Life resigns her power;   20
To know, some humbler grave, some narrow cell,
Would hide my bosom, where it lov'd to dwell;
With this fond dream, methinks 'twere sweet to die,
And here it linger'd, here my heart might lie.
Here might I sleep, where all my hopes arose,   25
Scene of my youth, and couch of my repose;
Forever stretch'd beneath this mantling shade,
Prest by the turf, where once my childhood play'd;
Wrapt by the soil, that veils the spot I lov'd,
Mix'd with the earth, o'er which my footsteps   30
    mov'd;
Blest by the tongues, that charm'd my youthful ear,
Mourn'd by the few, my soul acknowledg'd here;
Deplor'd by those, in early days allied,
And unremember'd by the world beside.

                                                    [1807]

69   To E.——

        Let Folly smile, to view the names
            Of thee and me in friendship twin'd,
        Yet virtue will have greater claims
            To love, than rank with vice combin'd.

        And though unequal is *thy* fate,   5
            Since title deck'd my higher birth;
        Yet envy not this gaudy state,
            Thine is the pride of modest worth.

        Our *souls* at least congenial meet,
            Nor can *thy* lot *my* rank disgrace;   10
        Our intercourse is not less sweet,
            Since worth of rank supplies the place.

                                            [1802, 1805]

69. Copy text: *FP*, collated with *MS. G, POVO*
    2 me] ⟨I⟩ *cor. by hand in* FPN, FPM, FPA   8 modest] simple *G*
dating   November, 1802 *FP, POVO*

70   On the Death of a Young Lady, Cousin to the Author and Very Dear to Him

[1.]

Hush'd are the winds, and still the evening gloom,
  Not e'en a zephyr wanders through the grove,
Whilst I return to view my Margaret's tomb,
  And scatter flowers on the dust I love.

2.

Within this narrow cell reclines her clay,   5
  That clay where once such animation beam'd;
The king of terrors seiz'd her as his prey,
  Not worth, nor beauty, have her life redeem'd.

3.

Oh! could that king of terrors pity feel,
  Or Heaven reverse the dread decree of fate!   10
Not here the mourner would his grief reveal,
  Not here the muse her virtues would relate.

4.

But wherefore weep! her matchless spirit soars
  Beyond where splendid shines the orb of day;
And weeping angels lead her to those bowers,   15
  Where endless pleasures virtuous deeds repay.

5.

And shall presumptuous mortals Heaven arraign!
  And, madly, God-like Providence accuse!
Ah! no, far fly from me attempts so vain,
  I'll ne'er submission to my God refuse.   20

6.

Yet is remembrance of those virtues dear,
  Yet fresh the memory of that beauteous face;
Still they call forth my warm affection's tear,
  Still, in my heart, retain their wonted place.

[1802]

70. Copy text: *FP*, collated with *POVO*
24 (Such sorrow brings me honour, not disgrace) *FPM*

71   To D[elawarr]

[1.]
In thee, I fondly hop'd to clasp
    A friend, whom death alone could sever,
Till envy, with malignant grasp,
    Detach'd thee from my breast for ever.

2.

True, she has forc'd thee from my *breast*,   5
    Yet, in my *heart*, thou keep'st thy seat;
There, there, thine image still must rest,
    Until that heart shall cease to beat.

3.

And, when the grave restores her dead,
    When life again to dust is given,   10
On *thy dear* breast I'll lay my head,
    Without *thee! where* would be *my Heaven?*

Feb. 1803

72   To Caroline

Think'st thou, I saw thy beauteous eyes,
    Suffus'd in tears, implore to stay;
And heard *unmov'd*, thy plenteous sighs,
    Which said far more than words can say?

Though keen the grief, *thy* tears exprest,   5
    When love, and hope, lay *both* o'erthrown,
Yet still, my girl, *this* bleeding breast,
    Throbb'd, with deep sorrow, as *thine own*.

71. Copy text: *FP*, collated with *MSS. N, NP, G,* and *POVO*
title   To D.—— *G, FP, POVO; untitled in N, NP*
    1 clasp] find *G*   3 Till] But *FP, N, NP*   4 Detach'd] Has torn *FP, N, NP*
6 Yet,] But *FP, N, NP*

72. Copy text: *FP*, collated with *POVO*
title   To ——. *FP*
    4 can] could *FP*   5 keen] deep *FP*

But, when our cheeks with anguish glow'd,
　　When *thy* sweet lips were join'd to mine;　　10
The tears, that from *my* eye-lids flow'd,
　　Were lost in those which fell from *thine*.

Thou could'st not feel my burning cheek,
　　Thy gushing tears had quench'd its flame,
And as thy tongue essay'd to speak,　　　　　15
　　In *sighs alone* it breath'd my name.

And yet, my girl, we weep in vain,
　　In vain our fate in sighs deplore;
Remembrance only can remain,
　　But *that*, will make us weep the more.　　20

Again, thou best belov'd, adieu!
　　Ah! if thou canst o'ercome regret,
Nor let thy mind past joys review,
　　Our only *hope* is, to *forget*.

　　　　　　　　　　　　　　　　1805

73   To Caroline

[1.]

You say you love, and yet your eye
　　No symptom of that love conveys,
You say you love, yet know not why
　　Your cheek no sign of love betrays.

2.

Ah! did that breast with ardour glow,　　　5
With me alone it joy could know,
Or feel with me the listless woe,
　　Which racks my heart when far from you.

73. Copy text: *FPM*, as corrected
　8 you] ⟨thee⟩ *FPM*

3.

Whene'er we meet, my blushes rise,
    And mantle through my purpled cheek,   10
But yet no blush to mine replies,
    Nor do those eyes your love bespeak.

4.

Your voice alone declares your flame,
And though so sweet it breathes my name,
Our passions still are not the same,   15
    Though Love and Rapture still are new.

5.

For e'en your lip seems steep'd in snow,
    And, though so oft it meets my kiss,
It burns with no responsive glow,
    Nor melts, like mine, in dewy bliss.   20

6.

Ah! what are words to love like mine,
Though uttered by a voice divine,
I still in murmurs must repine,
    And think that love can ne'er be true,

7.

Which meets me with no joyous sign;   25
    Without a sigh which bids adieu:
How different is that love from mine,
    Which feels such grief when leaving you.

8.

Your image fills my anxious breast,
Till day declines adown the West,   30
And when, at night, I sink to rest,
    In dreams your fancied form I view.

12 do those] ⟨e'en your⟩ *FPM*   18 oft it meets] soft it melts *cor. by hand in FPT*,
FPM   22 divine] ⟨like thine⟩ *FPM*   27 that ... mine] ⟨my ... thine⟩ *FPM*
28 Which feels such] ⟨How keen my⟩ *FPM*

9.

'Tis then, your breast, no longer cold,
    With equal ardour seems to burn,
While close your arms around me fold,   35
    Your lips my kiss with warmth return.

10.

Ah! would these joyous moments last!
Vain HOPE! the gay delusion's past;
That voice!—ah! no, 'tis but the blast,
    Which echoes through the neighbouring grove!   40

11.

But, when *awake*, your lips I seek,
    And clasp, enraptur'd, all your charms,
So chills the pressure of your cheek,
    I fold a statue in my arms.

12.

If thus, when to my heart embrac'd,   45
No pleasure in your eyes is trac'd,
You may be prudent, fair, and chaste,
    But ah! my girl, you *do not love!*

[1806]

74   To Emma

Since now the hour is come at last,
    When you must quit your anxious lover,
Since now, our dream of bliss is past,
    One pang, my girl, and all is over.

Alas! that pang will be severe,   5
    Which bids us part, to meet no more;
Which tears me far from *one* so dear,
    Departing for a distant shore.

74. Copy text: *FP*, collated with *POVO*
title   To Maria——. *FP*

Well! we have pass'd some happy hours,
   And joy will mingle with our tears;   10
When thinking on these ancient towers,
   The shelter of our infant years.

Where from this gothic casement's height,
   We view'd the lake, the park, the dell,
And still, though tears obstruct our sight,   15
   We lingering look a last farewell.—

O'er fields, through which we us'd to run,
   And spend the hours in childish play,
O'er shades, where, when our race was done,
   Reposing on my breast you lay.   20

Whilst I, admiring, too remiss,
   Forgot to scare the hovering flies,
Yet envied every fly the kiss,
   It dar'd to give your slumbering eyes.

See still the little painted *bark*,   25
   In which I row'd you o'er the lake;
See there, high waving o'er the park,
   The *elm*, I clamber'd for your sake.

These times are past, our joys are gone,
   You leave me, leave this happy vale: 30
These scenes, I must retrace alone;
   Without thee, what will they avail?

Who can conceive, who has not prov'd,
   The anguish of a last embrace?
When torn from all you fondly lov'd,   35
   You bid a long adieu to peace.

This is the deepest of our woes,
   For *this*, these tears our cheeks bedew,
This is of love the final close,
   Oh GOD! the fondest, *last* adieu!   40

1805

75   Lines Written in 'Letters of an Italian Nun and an English Gentleman', by J. J. Rousseau, Founded on Facts

'Away, away, your flattering arts
May now betray some simpler hearts;
And you will smile at their believing,
And they shall weep at your deceiving.'

Answer to the Foregoing, Address'd to Miss [Pigot]

Dear simple girl, those flattering arts,
From which thou'dst guard frail female hearts,
Exist but in imagination,
Mere phantoms of thine own creation;
For he who views that witching grace,   5
That perfect form, that lovely face,
With eyes admiring, oh! believe me,
He never wishes to deceive thee:
Once in thy polish'd mirror glance,
Thou'lt there descry that elegance,   10
Which from our sex demands such praises,
But envy in the other raises.
Then he, who tells thee of thy beauty,
Believe me, only does his duty;
Ah! fly not from the candid youth,   15
It is not flattery, 'tis truth.

July 1805

---

75. Copy text: *FP*, collated with *POVO*

title etc.   Lines Written in] Lines in *FP*, *MS. cor. in FPM*   Foregoing] ⟨above⟩ *FPM*

2 thou'dst] ⟨you'd⟩ *FPM*   4 thine] ⟨your⟩ *FPM*   5 views] ⟨sees⟩ *FPM*
9 ⟨Once let you at your⟩ mirror glance *FPM*   10 Thou'lt] ⟨You'll⟩ *FPM*   13 thee
of thy] ⟨you of your⟩ *FPM*   16 'tis] but *FP*

76   On a Change of Masters, at a Great Public School

Where are those honours, IDA! once your own,
When Probus fill'd your magisterial throne?
As ancient Rome, fast falling to disgrace,
Hail'd a Barbarian, in her Caesar's place:
So you, degenerate, share as hard a fate,   5
And seat Pomposus, where your Probus sate.
Of narrow brain, yet of a narrower soul,
Pomposus holds you, in his harsh controul;
Pomposus, by no social virtue sway'd,
With florid jargon, and with vain parade;   10
With noisy nonsense, and new fangled rules,
Such, as were ne'er, before, enforc'd in schools;
Mistaking pedantry, for learning's laws,
He governs, sanction'd but by self applause.
With him, the same dire fate, attending Rome,   15
Ill-fated IDA! soon must stamp your doom;
Like her o'erthrown, forever lost to fame,
No trace of science left you, but the name.

Harrow, July 1805

77   To Mary

[1.]

Rack'd by the flames of jealous rage,
By all her torments deeply curst,
Of hell-born passions far the worst,
What hope my pangs can now assuage?

76. Copy text: FP, collated with POVO
   7 yet] but FP   12 enforc'd] ⟨beheld⟩ FPM
dating   July, 1805 POVO

77. Copy text: FPM, as corrected

2.

I tore me from thy circling arms,   5
   To madness fir'd by doubts and fears,
   Heedless of thy suspicious tears,
Nor feeling for thy feign'd alarms.

3.

Resigning every thought of bliss,
   Forever, from your love I go,   10
   Reckless of all the tears that flow,
Disdaining thy polluted kiss.

4.

No more that bosom heaves for me,
   On it another seeks repose,
   Another riots on its snows,   15
Our bonds are broken, both are free.

5.

No more with mutual love we burn,
   No more the genial couch we bless,
   Dissolving in the fond caress;
Our love o'erthrown will ne'er return.   20

[6.]

Though love than ours could ne'er be truer,
   Yet flames too fierce themselves destroy,
   Embraces oft repeated cloy,
Ours came too *frequent*, to endure.

7.

You quickly sought a second lover,   25
   And I too proud to share a heart,
   Where once I held the *whole*, not *part*,
Another mistress must discover.

18 we bless] ⟨we press⟩ *MS. cor. in FPM*   25 You quickly sought] ⟨Thou quickly
sought'st⟩ *MS. cor. in FPM*

8.

Though not the *first* one, who has blest me,
  Yet I will own, you was the dearest,   30
  The one, unto my bosom nearest;
So I conceiv'd, when I possest thee.

9.

Even now I cannot well forget thee,
  And though no more in folds of pleasure,
  Kiss follows kiss in countless measure,   35
I hope *you* sometimes will regret me.

10.

And smile to think how oft we've done,
  What prudes declare a sin to act is,
  And never but in darkness practice,
Fearing to trust the tell-tale sun.   40

11.

And wisely therefore night prefer,
  Whose dusky mantle veils their fears,
  Of *this*, and *that*, of eyes and ears
Affording shades to those that err.

12.

Now, by my soul, 'tis most delight   45
  To view each other panting, dying,
  In love's *extatic posture* lying,
Grateful to *feeling*, as to *sight*.

13.

And had the glaring God of Day,
  (As formerly of Mars and Venus)   50
  Divulg'd the joys which pass'd between us,
Regardless of his *peeping* ray,

14.

Of love admiring such a *sample*,
  The Gods and Goddesses descending,
  Had never fancied us offending,   55
But *wisely* followed *our example*.

[1806]

78   To Caroline

1.

Oh! when shall the grave hide forever my sorrow?
  Oh! when shall my soul wing her flight from this clay?
The present is hell! and the coming to-morrow,
  But brings with new torture, the curse of to-day.

2.

From my eye flows no tear, from my lips fall no curses,   5
  I blast not the fiends, who have hurl'd me from bliss,
For poor is the soul which bewailing rehearses
  Its querulous grief, when in anguish like this——

3.

Was my eye, 'stead of tears, with red fury flakes bright'ning,
  Would my lips breathe a flame, which no stream could   10
    assuage,
On our foes should my glance launch in vengeance its
    lightning,
  With transport my tongue give a loose to its rage.

4.

But now tears and curses alike unavailing,
  Would add to the souls of our tyrant's delight;
Could they view us, our sad separation bewailing,   15
  Their merciless hearts would rejoice at the sight.

78. Copy text: *FP*, collated with *POVO*
title   To ——. *FP, cor. in FPM*
  5 fall] flow *1831, 1832, C, More*

5.

Yet still though we bend with a feign'd resignation,
   Life beams not for us with one ray that can cheer,
Love and hope upon earth bring no more consolation,
   In the grave is our hope, for in life is our fear.   20

6.

Oh! when, my ador'd, in the tomb will they place me,
   Since in life, love and friendship, for ever are fled,
If again in the mansion of death I embrace thee,
   Perhaps they will leave unmolested—the dead.

1805

79   To Caroline

1.

When I hear you express an affection so warm,
   Ne'er think, my belov'd, that I do not believe;
For your lip, would the soul of suspicion disarm,
   And your eye beams a ray, which can never deceive.

2.

Yet, still, this fond bosom regrets, whilst adoring,   5
   That love, like the leaf, must fall into the sear;
That age will come on, when remembrance deploring,
   Contemplates the scenes of her youth, with a tear.

3.

That the time must arrive, when, no longer retaining
   Their auburn, those locks must wave thin to the   10
      breeze;
When a few silver hairs of those tresses remaining,
   Prove nature a prey to decay and disease.

79. Copy text: *FP*, collated with *POVO*
title   *untitled in FP but added in MS. in FPM*
   10 those] these *FP*

4.

'Tis this, my belov'd, which spreads gloom o'er my
    features,
    Tho' I ne'er shall presume to arraign the decree,
Which God has proclaim'd, as the fate of his creatures,   15
    In the death, which one day will deprive you of me.

5.

Mistake not, sweet sceptic, the cause of emotion,
    No doubt can the mind of your lover invade;
He worships each look, with such faithful devotion,
    A smile can enchant, or a tear can dissuade.   20

6.

But as death, my belov'd, soon or late, shall o'ertake us,
    And our breasts, which alive, with such sympathy
    glow,
Will sleep in the grave, till the blast shall awake us,
    When calling the dead, in earth's bosom laid low.

7.

Oh! then let us drain, while we may, draughts of   25
    pleasure,
    Which from passion, like ours, must unceasingly flow;
Let us pass round the cup of love's bliss, in full measure,
    And quaff the contents, as our nectar below.

1805

16 you of me] ⟨me of thee⟩ *FPM*
17–20   No jargon of priests o'er our union was mutter'd,
          To rivet the fetters of husband and wife;
          By our lips, by our hearts, were our vows alone utter'd,
          To perform them, in full, would ask more than a life. *FP*
26 must] ⟨will⟩ *FPM*

80   On a Distant View of the Village and School, of Harrow, on the Hill

Oh! mihi praeteritos referat si Jupiter annos.

[1.]

Ye scenes of my childhood, whose lov'd recollection,
　Embitters the present, compar'd with the past;
Where science first dawn'd on the powers of reflection,
　And friendships were form'd, too romantic to last.

2.

Where fancy, yet, joys to retrace the resemblance,　　　　5
　Of comrades, in friendship and mischief allied;
How welcome to me, your ne'er fading remembrance,
　Which rests in the bosom, though hope is deny'd.

3.

Again I revisit the hills where we sported,
　The streams, where we swam, and the fields, where　10
　　we fought;
The school, where loud warn'd, by the bell, we resorted,
　To pore o'er the precepts by Pedagogues taught.

4.

Again I behold, where for hours I have ponder'd,
　As reclining, at eve, on yon tombstone I lay;
Or round the steep brow of the churchyard I wander'd,　15
　To catch the last gleam of the sun's setting ray.

5.

I once more view the room, with spectators surrounded,
　Where, as Zanga, I trod on Alonzo o'erthrown;
While, to swell my young pride, such applauses re-
　　sounded,
　I fancied that Mossop himself was outshone.　　　　20

80. Copy text: *HI*, collated with *FP*, *POVO*
epigraph   *added in HI*
　7 to me] once more *FP*

6.

Or, as Lear, I pour'd forth the deep imprecation,
  By my daughters, of kingdom and reason depriv'd;
Till, fir'd by loud plaudits, and self adulation,
  I regarded myself, as a Garrick reviv'd.

7.

Ye dreams of my boyhood, how much I regret you,   25
  Unfaded your memory dwells in my breast;
Though sad and deserted, I ne'er can forget you,
  Your pleasures may still be, in fancy, possest.

8.

To Ida, full oft may remembrance restore me,
  While Fate shall the shades of the future unroll,   30
Since Darkness o'ershadows the prospect before me,
  More dear is the beam of the past to my soul.

9.

But, if through the course of the years which await me,
  Some new scene of pleasure should open to view,
I will say, while with rapture the thought shall elate me,   35
  'Oh! such were the days, which my infancy knew.'

1806

24 regarded] considered *FP*   26–8 As your memory beams through this agoniz'd breast; | Thus sad and deserted, I ne'er can forget you, | Though this heart throbs to bursting by anguish possest. *FP*   28 Your memory beams through this agonized breast *POVO cor. for FP; MS. cor. in FPM and FPT to HI text*
29–36   I thought this poor brain, fever'd even to madness,
      Of tears as of reason for ever was drain'd;
     But the drops which now flow down *this* bosom of sadness,
      Convince me the springs have some moisture retain'd.

     Sweet scenes of my childhood! your blest recollection,
      Has wrung from these eyelids, to weeping long dead,
     In torrents, the tears of my warmest affection,
      The last and the fondest, I ever shall shed. *FP, POVO*

81   To a Lady, Who Presented to the Author a Lock of Hair, Braided with his Own, and Appointed a Night, in December, to Meet him in the Garden

These locks, which fondly thus entwine,
In firmer chains our hearts confine,
Than all th' unmeaning protestations,
Which swell with nonsense, love orations.
Our love is fix'd, I think we've prov'd it,   5
Nor time, nor place, nor art, have mov'd it;
Then, wherefore, should we sigh, and whine,
With groundless jealousy repine;
With silly whims, and fancies frantic,
Merely to make our love romantic?   10
Why should you weep, like Lydia Languish,
And fret with self-created anguish?
Or doom the lover you have chosen,
On winter nights, to sigh half frozen;
In leafless shades, to sue for pardon,   15
Only because the scene's a garden?
For gardens seem, by one consent,
Since SHAKESPEARE set the precedent,
Since Juliet first declar'd her passion,
To form the place of assignation.   20
Oh! would some modern muse inspire,
And seat her by a sea-coal fire;
Or had the bard at Christmas written,
And laid the scene of love in Britain;
He surely, in commiseration,   25
Had chang'd the place of declaration.
In Italy, I've no objection;
Warm nights are proper for reflection;
But, here, our climate is so rigid,
That love, itself is rather frigid.   30
Think on our chilly situation,
And curb this rage for imitation;

81. Copy text: *FP*, collated with *POVO*
title   Presented to] Presented *FP*

Then, let us meet, as oft we've done,
Beneath the influence of the sun;
Or, if, at midnight, I must meet you,   35
Within your mansion, let me greet you;
There, we can love for hours together,
Much better, in such snowy weather,
Than plac'd in all th' Arcadian groves,
That ever witness'd rural loves;   40
There, if my passion fail to please,
Next night I'll be content to freeze;
No more I'll give a loose to laughter,
But curse my fate, for ever after.

[1805]

82   To a Beautiful Quaker

Sweet girl! though only once we met,
That meeting I shall ne'er forget;
And though we ne'er may meet again,
Remembrance will thy form retain;
I would not say, 'I love', but still,   5
My senses struggle with my will;
In vain, to drive thee from my breast,
My thoughts are more and more represt;
In vain, I check the rising sighs,
Another to the last replies: 10
Perhaps, this is not love, but yet,
Our meeting I can ne'er forget.

What, though we never silence broke,
Our eyes a sweeter language spoke;
The tongue in flattering falsehood deals,   15
And tells a tale, it never feels;
Deceit, the guilty lips impart,
And hush the mandates of the heart;

36 Oh! let me in your chamber greet you *FP*

82. Copy text: *HI*, collated with *FP*, *POVO*, *RM1816*
   14 a] in *RM1816*   15 falsehood] language *RM1816*

But soul's interpreters, the eyes,
Spurn such restraint, and scorn disguise.   20
As thus our glances oft convers'd,
And all our bosoms felt rehears'd;
No spirit, from within, reprov'd us,
Say rather, ' 'twas the spirit mov'd us'.
Though, what they utter'd, I repress,   25
Yet, I conceive, thou'lt partly guess;
For, as on thee, my memory ponders,
Perchance, to me, thine also wanders.
This, for myself, at least, I'll say,
Thy form appears, through night, through day: 30
Awake, with it my fancy teems,
In sleep, it smiles in fleeting dreams;
The vision charms the hours away,
And bids me curse Aurora's ray;
For breaking slumbers of delight,   35
Which make me wish for endless night.
Since, oh! whate'er my future fate,
Shall joy or woe my steps await;
Tempted by love, by storms beset,
Thine image, I can ne'er forget.   40

      Alas! again, no more we meet,
No more our former looks repeat;
Then, let me breathe this parting prayer
The dictate of my bosom's care:
'May Heaven so guard my lovely quaker,   45
That anguish never can o'ertake her;
That peace and virtue ne'er forsake her,
But bliss be aye, her heart's partaker.
Oh! may the happy mortal, fated
To be, by dearest ties, related;   50
For her, each hour, new joy discover,
And lose the husband, in the lover.

29 This] Thus *RM1816*   40–1 *no paragraph in RM1816*   44 dictate]
dictates *RM1816*   46 can] may *RM1816*   48 bliss] bless'd *RM1816*
48   No jealous passion shall invade,
                         No envy that pure breast pervade;
                         For he that revels in such charms,
                         Can never seek another's arms; *in FP after line 48*
51 joy] joys *1831, 1832, C, More*

May that fair bosom never know,
What 'tis to feel the restless woe,
Which stings the soul, with vain regret,   55
Of him, who never can forget.'

[1806]

83   To Lesbia

[1.]

Lesbia! since far from you I've rang'd,
    Our souls, with fond affection, glow not;
You say, 'tis I, not you, have chang'd,
    I'd tell you why,—but yet I know not.

2.

Your polish'd brow, no cares have crost,   5
    And Lesbia! we are not much older,
Since, trembling, first my heart I lost,
    Or told my love, with hope grown bolder.

3.

Sixteen was, then, our utmost age,
    Two years have lingering pass'd away, love!   10
And, now, new thoughts our minds engage,
    At least, I feel disposed to stray, love!

4.

'Tis I, that am alone to blame,
    I, that am guilty of love's treason;
Since your sweet breast is still the same,   15
    Caprice must be my only reason.

5.

I do not, love! suspect your truth,
    With jealous doubt, my bosom heaves not;
Warm was the passion of my youth,
    One trace of dark deceit it leaves not.   20

83. Copy text: *FP*, collated with *POVO*
title   To Julia. *FP*
    1 Lesbia] Julia *FP*   6 Lesbia] Julia *FP*

6.

No, no, my flame was not pretended,
    For, oh! I lov'd you most sincerely;
And though our dream at last is ended,
    My bosom still esteems you dearly.

7.

No more we meet in yonder bowers;   25
    Absence has made me prone to roving;
But older, firmer hearts than ours,
    Have found monotony in loving.

8.

Your cheek's soft bloom is unimpair'd,
    New beauties, still, are daily bright'ning,   30
Your eye, for conquest, beams prepar'd,
    The forge of love's resistless lightning.

9.

Arm'd thus, to make their bosoms bleed,
    Many will throng, to sigh like me, love!
More constant they may prove, indeed,   35
    Fonder alas! they ne'er can be, love!

[1806]

84   To Miss E[lizabeth] P[igot]

I.

Eliza! what fools are the Mussulman sect,
    Who to woman deny the soul's future existence,
Could they see thee, Eliza! they'd own their defect,
    And this doctrine would meet with a general resistance.

26 Perhaps my soul's too prone to roving, *FP*   30 New] Your *FP*   31 beams]
comes *FP*

84. Copy text: *FP*, collated with *POVO*, *MS. T*
title   To Miss E. P. *FP*; To Eliza *1832, C, More*
    1 what fools] how weak *T*   3 Did they know but yourself, they would bend with
Respect, *T*

2.

Had their Prophet possess'd half an atom of sense,   5
   He ne'er would have *woman* from Paradise driven,
Instead of his *Houris* a flimsy pretence,
   With *woman alone*, he had peopled his Heaven.

3.

Yet still to increase your calamities more,
   Not content with depriving your bodies of spirit,   10
He allots one poor husband to share amongst four,
   With *souls* you'd dispense—but this last who could bear it.

4.

His religion to please neither *party* is made,
   On *husbands* 'tis *hard*, to the wives most uncivil;
Still I can't contradict what so oft has been said,   15
   'Though women are angels, yet wedlock's the devil.'

5.

This terrible truth, even Scripture has told,
   Ye Benedicks! hear me, and listen with rapture;
If a glimpse of redemption you wish to behold,
   Of St. MATT.—read the second and twentieth chapter.   20

6.

'Tis surely enough upon earth to be vex'd,
   With wives who eternal confusion are spreading;
'But in Heaven' (so runs the Evangelist's Text,)
   'We neither have giving in marriage, or wedding.'

7.

From this we suppose, (as indeed well we may,)   25
   That should Saints after death, with their spouses put up
     more,
And wives, as in life, aim at absolute sway,
   All Heaven would ring with the conjugal uproar.

5 half] but *FP*   7 Instead] But instead *FP*; ⟨And⟩ But instead *T*   9 Yet]
But *T, FP*   11 one poor husband] but *one husband FP*   amongst] between *T*
15 Still] But *T, FP*   17–40 *not in POVO and crossed out in FPM*   19 you]
ye *T*   20 Go back to St. Matthew the 17th Chapter. *T*   27 in life] on earth *T*
28 ring] shake *T*

8.

Distraction and discord would follow in course,
  Nor MATTHEW, nor MARK, nor St. PAUL, can deny it,   30
The only expedient is general divorce,
  To prevent universal disturbance and riot.

9.

But though husband and wife, shall at length be disjoin'd
  Yet woman and man ne'er were meant to dissever,
Our chains once dissolv'd, and our hearts unconfin'd,   35
  We'll love without bonds, but we'll love you forever.

10.

Though souls are denied you by fools and by rakes,
  Should you own it yourselves, I would even then doubt
    you,
Your nature so much of *celestial* partakes,
  The Garden of Eden would wither without you.   40

Southwell, 9 Oct. 1806

85   Reply to Some Verses of J. M. B. Pigot, Esq.
       on the Cruelty of his Mistress

[1.]

Why, PIGOT, complain,
Of this damsel's disdain,
Why thus in despair, do you fret?
For months you may try,
Yet, believe me, a sigh   5
Will never obtain a coquette.

2.

Would you teach her to love,
For a time seem to rove,

29 Distraction and] ⟨But horrible⟩ *T*   in] of *T*   40 would] must *T*

85. Copy text: *FP*, collated with *POVO*
  5 Yet,] But *FP*

At first she may frown in a pet;
  But leave her awhile,   10
  She shortly will smile,
And then you may kiss your coquette.

3.

For such are the airs,
  Of these fanciful fairs,
They think all our homage a debt;   15
  Yet a partial neglect,
  Soon takes an effect,
And humbles the proudest coquette.

4.

Dissemble your pain,
  And lengthen your chain,   20
Nor seem her hauteur to regret;
  If again you shall sigh,
  She no more will deny,
That yours is the rosy coquette.

5.

If still from false pride,   25
  Your pangs she deride,
This whimsical virgin forget;
  Some other admire,
  Who will melt with your fire,
And laugh at the little coquette.   30

6.

For me I adore,
  Some twenty or more,
And love them most dearly, but yet,
  Though my heart they enthral,
  I'd abandon them all,   35
Did they act like your blooming coquette.

16 Yet] But *FP*   21 Nor] And *1831, 1832, C, More*   25 If still] But if *FP*

7.

No longer repine,
Adopt this design,
And break through her slight woven net;
　　Away with despair,   40
　　No longer forbear,
To fly from the captious coquette.

8.

Then quit her, my friend!
Your bosom defend,
Ere quite with her snares you're beset;   45
　　Lest your deep wounded heart,
　　When incens'd by the smart,
Should lead you to curse the coquette.

27 Oct. 1806

86   To the Sighing Strephon

[1.]

Your pardon my friend,
If my rhymes did offend,
Your pardon a thousand times o'er,
　　From friendship I strove,
　　Your pangs to remove,   5
But I swear I will do so no more.

2.

Since your *beautiful* maid
Your flame has repaid,
No more I your folly regret;
　　She's now most divine,   10
　　And I bow at the shrine,
Of this quickly reformed coquette.

38 Adopt] But form *FP*
dating   Byron, October 27, 1806. *FP*

86. Copy text: *FP*, collated with *POVO*

3.

Yet still, I must own,
I should never have known,
From *your verses* what else she deserv'd,   15
Your pain seem'd so great,
I pitied your fate,
As your fair was so dev'lish reserv'd.

4.

Since the balm-breathing kiss,
Of this magical Miss,   20
Can such wonderful transports produce,
Since the '*world you forget*,
When your lips once have met,'
My Counsel will get but abuse.

5.

You say 'when I rove   25
I know nothing of love',
'Tis true I am given to range,
If I rightly remember,
I've lov'd a good number,
Yet there's pleasure, at least, in a change.   30

6.

I will not advance,
By the rules of romance,
To humour a whimsical fair,
Though a smile may delight,
Yet a *frown* won't *affright*,   35
Or drive me to dreadful despair.

[7.]

Whilst my blood is thus warm,
I ne'er shall reform,
To mix in the Platonist's school;

13 Yet] But *FP*   19 Since the balm-breathing kiss] But since the chaste kiss, *FP*
21 Can such] ⟨Such⟩ *FPM*   29 lov'd] kiss'd *FP*   30 Yet] But *FP*   31 will
not] ne'er will *FP*   35 won't] will *C*   39 Platonist's] Platonists' *1831, 1832, C,*
More

Of this I am sure,   40
Was my passion so pure,
My mistress must think me *a fool*.

8.

Though the kisses are sweet,
Which voluptuously meet,
Of kissing I ne'er was so fond,   45
As to make me forget,
Though our lips oft have met,
That still there was *something beyond*.

9.

And if I should shun,
Every *woman* for *one*,   50
Whose *image* must fill my whole breast;
Whom I must *prefer*,
And *sigh* but for *her*,
What an *insult* 'twould be to the *rest!*

10.

Now, Strephon, good bye,   55
I cannot deny,
Your passion appears most absurd,
Such *love* as you plead,
Is *pure* love indeed,
For it *only* consists in the *word*.   60

[1806]

87   The Cornelian

[1.]

No specious splendour of this stone,
Endears it to my memory ever,
With lustre *only once* it shone,
But blushes modest as the giver.

42 *My . . . must*] Thy . . . would *1831, 1832, C, More*   43–8 *not in POVO*

87. Copy text: *FP*, collated with *POVO*
4 But] And *1831, 1832, C, More*

2.

Some who can sneer at friendship's ties,   5
   Have for my weakness oft reprov'd me,
Yet still the simple gift I prize,
   For I am sure, the giver lov'd me.

3.

He offered it with downcast look,
   As *fearful* that I might refuse it,   10
I told him when the gift I took,
   My *only fear* should be to lose it.

4.

This pledge attentively I view'd,
   And *sparkling* as I held it near,
Methought one drop the stone bedew'd,   15
   And ever since I've *lov'd a tear.*

5.

Still to adorn his humble youth,
   Nor wealth nor birth their treasures yield,
But he who seeks the flowers of truth,
   Must quit the garden for the field.   20

6.

'Tis not the plant uprear'd in sloth,
   Which beauty shews, and sheds perfume,
The flowers which yield the most of both,
   In nature's wild luxuriance bloom.

7.

Had Fortune aided nature's care,   25
   For once forgetting to be blind,
His would have been an ample share,
   If well proportioned to his mind.

8.

But had the Goddess clearly seen,
   His form had fixed her fickle breast,   30
Her countless hoards would *his* have been,
   And none remain'd to give the rest.

[1806]

88   Lines Addressed to a Young Lady.

As the Author Was Discharging His Pistols in a
Garden, Two Ladies Passing Near the Spot, Were
Alarmed by the Sound of a Bullet Hissing Near
Them, to One of Whom the Following Stanzas
Were Addressed the Next Morning

1.
Doubtless, sweet girl, the hissing lead,
  Wafting destruction near thy charms,
And hurtling o'er thy lovely head,
  Has fill'd that breast with fond alarms.

2.
Surely some envious Demon's force,   5
  Vex'd to behold such beauty here,
Impell'd the bullet's viewless course,
  Diverted from its first career.

3.
Yes! in that nearly fatal hour,
  The ball obey'd some hell-born guide,   10
But Heaven, with interposing power,
  In pity, turn'd the death aside.

4.
Yet, as perchance, one trembling tear
  Upon that thrilling bosom fell,
Which I, th' unconscious cause of fear,   15
  Extracted from its glistening cell;—

5.
Say, what dire penance can atone
  For such an outrage, done to thee?
Arraign'd before thy beauty's throne,
  What punishment wilt thou decree?   20

88. Copy text: *FP*, collated with *POVO*
title   As the Author ... Following Verses on the Occasion, Were Addressed ... *FP*
2 near] o'er *1831, 1832, C, More*

6.

Might I perform the Judge's part,
  The sentence I should scarce deplore,
It only would restore a heart,
  Which but belong'd to *thee* before.

7.

The least atonement, I can make,   25
  Is to become no longer free;
Henceforth, I breathe but for thy sake,
  Thou shalt be *all in all* to me.

8.

But thou, perhaps, may'st now reject
  Such expiation of my guilt,   30
Come then—some other mode elect!
  Let it be death—or what thou wilt.

9.

Choose then, relentless! and I swear,
  Nought shall thy dread decree prevent,
Yet hold—one little word forbear!   35
  Let it be aught but *banishment*.

[1806]

89   Imitation of Tibullus.
            'Sulpicia Ad Cerintum.' Lib. Quart.

Cruel Cerintus! does this fell disease,
Which racks my breast, your fickle bosom please?
Alas! I wish'd but to o'ercome the pain,
That I might live for love, and you again;
But now I scarcely shall bewail my fate,   5
By Death alone, I can avoid your hate.

[1806]

89. Copy text: FP, collated with MS. G, POVO
  1 this] the *1831*, *1832*, C, *More*

90 ## To M. S. G.

1.

Whene'er I view those lips of thine,
  Their hue invites my fervent kiss;
Yet, I forego that bliss divine,
  Alas! it were—unhallow'd bliss.

2.

Whene'er I dream of that pure breast,   5
  How could I dwell upon its snows;
Yet, is the daring wish represt,
  For that,—would banish its repose.

3.

A glance, from thy soul-searching eye,
  Can raise with hope, depress with fear;   10
Yet, I conceal my love, and why?
  I would not force a painful tear.

4.

I ne'er have told my love, yet thou
  Hast seen my ardent flame, too well;
And shall I plead my passion, now,   15
  To make thy bosom's heaven, a hell?

5.

No! for thou never can'st be mine,
  United by the priest's decree;
By any ties but those divine,
  Mine, my belov'd, thou ne'er shalt be.   20

6.

Then let the secret fire consume,
  Let it consume, thou shalt not know;
With joy I court a certain doom,
  Rather than spread its guilty glow.

90. Copy text: *POVO*

7.

I will not ease my tortur'd heart,   25
    By driving dove-ey'd peace from thine;
Rather than such a sting impart,
    Each thought presumptuous, I resign.

8.

Yes! yield those lips, for which I'd brave,
    More than I here shall dare to tell;   30
Thy innocence, and mine to save,
    I bid thee now, a last farewell.

9.

Yes! yield that breast, to seek despair;
    And hope no more thy soft embrace;
Which to obtain, my soul would dare,   35
    All, all reproach, but thy disgrace.

10.

At least from guilt, shalt thou be free,
    No matron shall thy shame reprove;
Though cureless pangs may prey on me,
    No martyr shalt thou be to love.   40

[1806]

91   Horace, Ode 3. Lib. 3

Translation

[1.]

The man of firm, and noble soul,
No factious clamours can controul;
No threat'ning tyrant's darkling brow,
    Can swerve him from his just intent;
Gales the warring waves which plow,   5
    By Auster on the billows spent,
To curb the Adriatic main,
    Would awe his fix'd determined mind in vain.

91. Copy text: *POVO*
title   Translation from Horace *1831*, *1832*, C, *More*

2.Aye, and the red right arm of Jove,
Hurtling his lightnings from above, 10
With all his terrors there unfurl'd,
    He would, unmov'd, unaw'd, behold;
The flames of an expiring world,
    Again in crashing chaos roll'd
In vast promiscuous ruin hurl'd, 15
Might light his glorious funeral pile,
Still dauntless midst the wreck of earth he'd smile.

[1806 ?]

92   The First Kiss of Love

Ἁ Βάρβιτος δε χορδαῖς
Ἔρωτα μοῦνον ἠχεῖ.

ANACREON.

[1.]
Away, with your fictions of flimsy romance,
    Those tissues of falsehood which Folly has wove;
Give me the mild beam of the soul-breathing glance,
    Or the rapture, which dwells on the first kiss of love.

2.
Ye rhymers, whose bosoms with fantasy glow, 5
    Whose pastoral passions are made for the grove;
From what blest inspiration your sonnets would flow,
    Could you ever have tasted the first kiss of love.

3.
If Apollo should e'er his assistance refuse,
    Or the Nine be dispos'd from your service to rove, 10
Invoke them no more, bid adieu to the muse,
    And try the effect, of the first kiss of love.

92. Copy text: HI, collated with POVO, MS. N
epigraph added in HI

2 ⟨Whose air drawn webs by Moria are wove⟩ Moriah those air drawn tissues has wove N
falsehood which] fancy Moriah POVO   3 soul-⟨telling⟩ N   5 Ye rhymers, who
sing, as if seated on snow, N, POVO   7 From] With POVO

4.

I hate you, ye cold compositions of art,
    Tho' prudes may condemn me, and bigots reprove;
I court the effusions, that spring from the heart,   15
    Which throbs, with delight, to the first kiss of love.

5.

Your shepherds, your flocks, those fantastical themes,
    Perhaps, may amuse, yet they never can move;
Arcadia displays but a region of dreams,
    What are visions like these, to the first kiss of love?   20

6.

Oh! cease to affirm, that man, since his birth,
    From Adam, till now, has with wretchedness strove;
Some portion of Paradise still is on earth,
    And Eden revives, in the first kiss of love.

7.

When age chills the blood, when our pleasures are past,   25
    For years fleet away with the wings of the dove;
The dearest remembrance will still be the last,
    Our sweetest memorial, the first kiss of love.

[23 Dec. 1806]

93   Childish Recollections

I cannot but remember such things were,
And were most dear to me.   MACBETH.

When slow Disease with all her host of Pains,
Chills the warm tide, which flows along the veins;

16 ⟨That⟩ Which *N*   17 Your Shepherds, your pipes, your fantastical themes *N*,
POVO   19 displays] yields *N*   21 since] from *N*, *POVO*
dating   *in MS. N only*

93. Copy text: *HI*, collated with *MS. T*, *MS. Y*, *MS. M*, *POVO*, *POT* (original state)
epigraph   *not in POVO*; Et dulces moriens reminiscitur Argos. Virgil. *second epigraph
intended for POT printing*
    1–28   Hence! thou unvarying song, of varied loves,
                      Which youth commends, maturer age reproves;
                      Which every rhyming bard repeats by rote,
                      By thousands echo'd to the self same note;   [*Cont. on p. 158*
2 flows along] riots through *T*

When Health affrighted spreads her rosy wing,
And flies with every changing gale of spring;
Not to the aching frame alone confin'd,   5
Unyielding pangs assail the drooping mind:
What grisly forms, the spectre train of woe!
Bid shuddering Nature shrink beneath the blow,
With Resignation wage relentless strife,
While Hope retires appall'd, and clings to life.   10
Yet less the pang, when, through the tedious hour,
Remembrance sheds around her genial power,
Calls back the vanish'd days to rapture given,
When Love was bliss, and Beauty form'd our heaven;
Or dear to youth, pourtrays each childish scene,   15
Those fairy bowers, where all in turn have been.
As when, through clouds that pour the summer storm,
The orb of day unveils his distant form,

Tir'd of the dull, unceasing, copious strain,
My soul is panting to be free again.
Farewell! ye nymphs, propitious to my verse,
Some other Damon, will your charms rehearse;
Some other paint his pangs, in hope of bliss,
Or dwell in rapture, on your nectar'd kiss,
Those beauties grateful, to my ardent sight,
No more entrance my senses in delight.
Those bosoms, form'd of animated snow,
Alike are tasteless and unfeeling now.
These, to some happier lover, I resign;
The memory of those joys alone is mine.
Censure no more shall brand my humble name,
The child of passion, and the fool of fame.
Weary of love, of life, devour'd with spleen,
I rest, a perfect Timon, not nineteen;
World! I renounce thee! all my hope's o'ercast;
One sigh I give thee, but that sigh's the last,
Friends, foes, and females, now alike, adieu!
Would I could add, remembrance of you, too.
Yet, though the future, dark and cheerless gleams,
The curse of memory, hovering in my dreams,
Depicts, with glowing pencil, all those years,
Ere yet, my cup, empoison'd flow'd, with tears,
Still rules my senses with tyrannic sway,
The past confounding with the present day.

Alas! in vain I check the maddening thought,
It still recurs, unlook'd for, and unsought; *POVO*

5 frame] Breast *T*   6 drooping] pensive *T*   7 spectre train] hideous-Train *T*
8 Bid ... beneath] Make ... before *T*   9 wage ⟨a lasti⟩ relentless *T*   10 And bid
the trembling victim cling to Life *T*   14 form'd our] was our *T*   15 Or not less
dear recalls each childish Scene *T*   16 ⟨And paints our childhood as it once has been⟩ *T*
17 through ... pour] at times amid *T*

Gilds with faint beams the chrystal dews of rain,
And dimly twinkles o'er the watery plain;   20
Thus, while the future dark and cheerless gleams,
The Sun of Memory, glowing through my dreams,
Though sunk the radiance of his former blaze,
To scenes far distant points his paler rays,
Still rules my senses with unbounded sway,   25
The past confounding with the present day.

Oft does my heart indulge the rising thought,
Which still recurs, unlook'd for, and unsought;
My soul to Fancy's fond suggestion yields,
And roams romantic o'er her airy fields;   30
Scenes of my youth, develop'd, croud to view,
To which I long have bade a last adieu!
Seats of delight, inspiring youthful themes;
Friends lost to me, for aye, except in dreams;
Some, who in marble prematurely sleep,   35
Whose forms I now remember, but to weep;
Some, who yet urge the same scholastic course
Of early science, future fame the source:
Who, still contending in the studious race,
In quick rotation, fill the senior place!   40
These, with a thousand visions, now unite,
To dazzle, though they please, my aching sight.

IDA! blest spot, where Science holds her reign,
How joyous, once, I join'd thy youthful train;
Bright, in idea, gleams thy lofty spire,   45
Again, I mingle with thy playful quire;
Our tricks of mischief, every childish game,
Unchang'd by time or distance, seem the same;
Through winding paths, along the glade I trace,
The social smile of ev'ry welcome face,   50
My wonted haunts, my scenes of joy or woe,
Each early boyish friend, or youthful foe,

21 while] ⟨though⟩ T   22 glowing] ⟨hovering⟩ T   23 blaze] ⟨rays⟩ T   24 ⟨Points
to / Far distant⟩ T   43–98 *added in HI*   47 Our tricks] Each trick T
48 seem] seems T   49 ⟨Each path⟩ Through winding paths ⟨each former scene⟩
along the Glades I trace T   50 Each ⟨lov'd⟩ old Companion, every former Face T
52 ⟨My much lov'd youthful friends⟩ T

Our feuds dissolv'd, but not my friendship past,
I bless the former, and forgive the last.
Hours of my youth, when nurtur'd in my breast,   55
To Love a stranger, Friendship made me blest;
Friendship, the dear peculiar bond of youth,
When every artless bosom throbs with truth;
Untaught by worldly wisdom how to feign,
And check each impulse with prudential rein;   60
When, all we feel, our honest souls disclose,
In love to friends, in open hate to foes;
No varnish'd tales the lips of youth repeat,
No dear bought knowledge purchas'd by deceit;
Hypocrisy, the gift of lengthen'd years,   65
Matur'd by age, the garb of Prudence wears;
When, now, the Boy is ripen'd into Man,
His careful Sire chalks forth some wary plan;
Instructs his Son from Candour's path to shrink,
Smoothly to speak, and cautiously to think;   70
Still to assent, and never to deny,
A patron's praise can well reward the lie;
And who, when Fortune's warning voice is heard,
Would lose his opening prospects for a word?
Although, against that word, his heart rebel,   75
And Truth, indignant, all his bosom swell.

Away with themes like this, not mine the task,
From flattering fiends to tear the hateful mask;

53 ⟨My / Our former feuds dissolved, our hatred past⟩ T   54 bless] love T
55 ff.   Lives there a man ?
                    Whose soul no dream of present love inspires
                    Of if the glowing Hour has ceased at last
                    ? with Joy ? to the past,
                    Owns that his breast was once by rapture swayed
                    And ? the image of some ? maid
                    Still to the dear Idea fondly clings
                    Yet sighing owns that only Love has wings
                    Ah no ! we all alike have felt the same
                    Hours of delight when Friendship was my aim *cancelled in* T
60 ⟨To ? unless delight, a smoother pain⟩ T   64 ⟨Whatever⟩ The faults of youth let
⟨heartless censors⟩ age with envy view | We're heedless ⟨headstrong, wild—still we're true⟩
fiery, still our Souls are true ! *cancelled in* T   65 lengthen'd] ⟨riper⟩ T   66 Matur'd
by] ⟨When cunning⟩ Cunning with T   68 Sire] ⟨parent⟩ T   70 cautiously] ⟨silently⟩
T   72 can] ⟨will⟩ T   73 Fortune's] Plutus T   74 opening prospects] ⟨wealth
of Honour⟩ opening fortune T   77 ⟨Away—I'll think of arts like these no more⟩ Away
⟨I'll think no more—⟩ not mine the task T   78 the hateful] ⟨away the⟩ T

Let keener bards delight in Satire's sting,
My Fancy soars not on Detraction's wing;   80
Once, and but once, she aim'd a deadly blow,
To hurl Defiance on a secret Foe;
But, when that Foe, from feeling or from shame,
The cause unknown, yet still to me the same,
Warn'd by some friendly hint, perchance, retir'd,   85
With this submission, all her rage expir'd.
From dreaded pangs that feeble Foe to save,
She hush'd her young resentment, and forgave:
Or, if my Muse a Pedant's portrait drew,
Pomposus' virtues are but known to few;   90
I never fear'd the young usurper's nod,
And he who wields, must, sometimes, feel the rod.
If since, on Granta's failings, known to all,
Who share the converse of a college hall,
She sometimes trifled in a lighter strain,   95
'Tis past, and thus she will not sin again.
Soon must her early song forever cease,
And, all may rail, when I shall rest in peace.

Here, first remembered be the joyous band,
Who hail'd me chief, obedient to command;   100
Who join'd with me, in every boyish sport,
Their first adviser, and their last resort.
Nor shrunk before the upstart pedant's frown,
Or all the sable glories of his gown;

79–84   By mightier bards be Satire's ⟨thunder⟩ lightning hurled
And launch ⟨their lightnings⟩ in thunder oer ⟨a
          guiltier⟩ the guiltier world
Mine is the ⟨dear⟩ fond yet melancholy part
To sooth the anguish of a lonely Heart,
A Heart which once affection's rapture knew,
⟨Now lost / Forever⟩ And lingers still, my early friends,
          with you *cancelled in* T
87 dreaded] keenest T
89–92   If once my muse a harsher portrait drew,
Warm with her wrongs, and deem'd the likeness true,
By cooler judgment taught, her fault she owns,—
With noble minds a fault confess'd, atones. M
91 young usurper's] ⟨? despot's⟩ T   98 And ⟨foe⟩ pedants, foes, & Granta ⟨sleep⟩ rest in
peace. T   103 before] beneath *1831, 1832*, C, *More*
103–4   Careless to soothe the pedant's furious frown,
Scarcely respecting his majestic gown;
By which, in vain, he gain'd a borrow'd grace,
Adding new terror to his sneering face. *POVO*

Who, thus transplanted from his father's school,   105
Unfit to govern, ignorant of rule,
Succeeded him, whom all unite to praise,
The dear preceptor of my early days;
Probus, the pride of science, and the boast,
To IDA, now, alas! for ever lost.   11
With him, for years, we search'd the classic page,
And fear'd the Master, though we lov'd the Sage;
Retir'd at last, his small, yet peaceful seat,
From learning's labour is the blest retreat.
Pomposus fills his magisterial chair;   115
Pomposus governs,—but my Muse forbear:
Contempt, in silence, be the pedant's lot,
His name and precepts be alike forgot;
No more his mention shall my verse degrade,
To him my tribute is already paid.   120

High, thro' those elms with hoary branches crown'd,
Fair IDA's bower adorns the landscape round;
There Science from her favour'd seat surveys
The vale, where rural Nature claims her praise;
To her awhile resigns her youthful train,   125
Who move in joy, and dance along the plain,
In scatter'd groupes each favoured haunt pursue,
Repeat old pastimes, and discover new;
Flush'd with his rays, beneath the noon-tide Sun,
In rival bands, between the wickets run,   130
Drive o'er the sward the ball with active force,
Or chace with nimble feet its rapid course.

---

111 we] I *POVO* Beneath his sway we searched each classic page *M*   112 Culling
the treasures of the letter'd sage; *POVO*

115–20   Another fills his magisterial chair;
          Reluctant Ida owns a stranger's care;
          Oh! may like honours crown his future name:
          If such his virtues, such shall be his fame.
          Here on this spot, if Probus' name is dear,
          Let Ida's sons behold it, and revere. *M*

118 Soon shall his shallow precepts be forgot; *POVO*   119 verse] pen *POVO*
120 My tribute to his name's already paid. *POVO*   121–243 *added in HI*
121 (High on the hill with ancient / High on thy / the hill, where yonder turrets / gleams
yon lofty Spire) *T*   124 vale] ⟨charms⟩ *T*   128 Repeat] ⟨Explore⟩ *T*
129 Embrowned ⟨beneath the glowing⟩ with play beneath the noontide Sun, *T*   131 sward]
green *T*   132 chace] trace *T*

But these with slower steps direct their way,
Where Brent's cool waves in limpid currents stray;
While yonder few search out some green retreat,   135
And arbours shade them from the summer heat;
Others, again, a pert, and lively crew,
Some rough, and thoughtless stranger plac'd in view,
With frolic quaint, their antic jests expose
And tease the grumbling rustic as he goes;   140
Nor rest with this, but many a passing fray,
Tradition treasures for a future day;
' 'Twas here the gather'd swains for vengeance fought,
And here we earn'd the conquest dearly bought,
Here have we fled before superior might,   145
And here renew'd the wild tumultuous fight.'
While thus our souls with early passions swell,
In lingering tones resounds the distant bell;
Th' allotted hour of daily sport is o'er,
And Learning beckons from her temple's door.   150
No splendid tablets grace her simple hall,
But ruder records fill the dusky wall;
There, deeply carv'd, behold! each Tyro's name
Secures its owner's academic fame;
Here, mingling view the names of Sire and Son,   155
The one long grav'd, the other just begun,
These shall survive alike when Son and Sire,
Beneath one common stroke of fate expire,
Perhaps, their last memorial these alone,
Denied, in Death, a monumental stone,   160
Whilst to the gale, in mournful cadence wave,
The sighing weeds, that hide their nameless grave.
And, here, my name and many an early friend's
Along the wall in lengthened line extends,
Though, still, our deeds amuse the youthful race,   165
Who tread our steps, and fill our former place,
Who young obeyed their lords in silent awe,

135 green] ⟨cool⟩ T   138 Some ⟨hapless Rustic⟩ rough T   139 frolic quaint]
⟨antics quaint⟩ frolic big T   140 tease the grumbling] scare the ⟨passing⟩ T   141 with
this] ⟨they here⟩ T   142 Tradition ⟨treasures / tells tales of⟩ treasures T
148 lingering] ⟨distant⟩ T   149 daily] playful T   151 No ⟨splendid statues /
pomp of words⟩ splendid T   159 ⟨When these perhaps ? and these alone⟩ T
161–2 *supplied by E. Pigot in* T   165 deeds ⟨a many / a youthful / inspire⟩ amuse T
167 obeyed their lords] ⟨beheld their lords⟩ obeyed a power T

Whose nod commanded, and whose voice was law:
And now, in turn, possess the reins of power,
To rule the little Tyrants of an hour;   170
Though sometimes, with the Tales of ancient day,
They pass the dreary Winter's eve away:
'And, thus, our former rulers stemm'd the tide,
And, thus, they dealt the combat, side by side;
Just in this place, the mouldering walls they scaled,   175
Nor bolts, nor bars, against their strength availed;
Here, Probus came, the rising fray to quell,
And, here, he faultered forth his last farewell,
And, here, one night, abroad they dared to roam,
While bold Pomposus bravely staid at home.'   180
While thus they speak, the hour must soon arrive,
When names of these, like ours, alone survive;
Yet a few years, one general wreck will whelm
The faint remembrance of our fairy realm.

Dear honest race, though now we meet no more,   185
One last, long look on what we were before;
Our first kind greetings, and our last adieu!
Drew tears from eyes unus'd to weep with you;
Through splendid circles, Fashion's gaudy world,
Where Folly's glaring standard waves unfurl'd,   190
I plung'd to drown in noise my fond regret,
And all I sought or hop'd, was to forget:
Vain wish! if, chance, some well remember'd face,
Some old companion of my early race,
Advanc'd to claim his friend with honest joy,   195
My eyes, my heart proclaim'd me still a boy;
The glittering scene, the fluttering groupes around,
Were quite forgotten, when my friend was found;
The smiles of Beauty, (for, alas! I've known
What 'tis to bend before Love's mighty throne;)   200
The smiles of Beauty, though those smiles were dear,
Could hardly charm me, when that friend was near;

168 Whose ⟨voice ? / arm was⟩ nod T   169 possess] ⟨to wield⟩ T   171 ancient]
⟨former⟩ T   173 tide] ⟨storm⟩ T   175 the ⟨lofty⟩ walls we scaled T
176 ⟨And against the scattered foe prevailed⟩ T   177 ⟨Yet a few years our names alone
shall tell⟩ T   185 Dear friendly Band, though ⟨now no more we meet⟩ T   187 ⟨Revives
my drooping⟩ T   189 ⟨For you in splendid ? I heave the sigh / I think of you⟩ T
191 I ⟨move regardless⟩ plung'd T   200 Love's mighty] a female T

My thoughts bewilder'd in the fond surprise,
The woods of Ida danc'd before my eyes;
I saw the sprightly wand'rers pour along,   205
I saw, and join'd again the joyous throng;
Panting again, I trac'd her lofty grove,
And Friendship's feelings triumph'd over Love.

Yet, why should I alone with such delight,
Retrace the circuit of my former flight?   210
Is there no cause beyond the common claim,
Endear'd to all in childhood's very name?
Ah! sure some stronger impulse vibrates here,
Which whispers friendship will be doubly dear
To one, who thus for kindred hearts must roam,   215
And seek abroad, the love denied at home:
Those hearts, dear Ida, have I found in thee,
A home, a world, a paradise to me.
Stern Death, forbade my orphan youth to share,
The tender guidance of a Father's care;   220
Can Rank, or ev'n a Guardian's name supply,
The Love, which glistens in a Father's eye?
For this, can Wealth, or Title's sound atone,
Made, by a Parent's early loss, my own?
What Brother springs a Brother's love to seek?   225
What Sister's gentle kiss has prest my cheek?
For me, how dull the vacant moments rise,
To no fond bosom link'd by kindred ties;
Oft, in the progress of some fleeting dream,
Fraternal smiles, collected round me seem,   230
While still the visions to my heart are prest,
The voice of Love will murmur in my rest;
I hear, I wake, and in the sound rejoice,
I hear again,—but ah! no Brother's voice.

203 ⟨All other dreams⟩ T   204 woods] ⟨greens⟩ T   205 sprightly] ⟨little⟩ T
207 ⟨Again I tread / Again with smiles I panting tread⟩ T   212 ⟨Which all unite⟩ T
214 Why Friendship thus to me is doubly dear T   215 To distant scenes for kindred
heart I roam T   217 ⟨My fate forbade a father's⟩ T   219 Stern Death] ⟨My fate⟩
T   222 The ⟨fostering / prospects⟩ love T   223 For ⟨such a loss can titled⟩ this,
can Title's splendid sound atone T   225 springs] ⟨moves⟩ T   227 ⟨Alone I look
on crowds / In misery / I sleep in misery and in anguish rise / Alone you ? unblest by social
ties / Neer know the paradise of social ties / A Hermit amidst / I sleep in sorrow and in anguish
rise / Alone, unseen, unblest⟩ T   230 ⟨A social⟩ Fraternal T   231 ⟨My heart
feelings⟩ T   232 ⟨The voices of love still⟩ T

A Hermit, midst of crowds, I fain must stray   235
Alone, though thousand pilgrims fill the way;
While these a thousand kindred wreaths entwine,
I cannot call one single blossom mine:
What then remains? in solitude to groan,
To mix in friendship, or to sigh alone?   240
Thus, must I cling to some endearing hand,
And none more dear, than Ida's social band.

Alonzo! best and dearest of my friends,
Thy name ennobles him, who thus commends;
From this fond tribute, thou can'st gain no praise,   245
The praise is his, who now that tribute pays.
Oh! in the promise of thy early youth,
If hope anticipate the words of truth;
Some loftier bard shall sing thy glorious name,
To build his own, upon thy deathless fame.   250
Friend of my heart, and foremost of the list
Of those, with whom I liv'd supremely blest;
Oft have we drain'd the font of antient lore,
Though, drinking deeply, thirsting still the more.
Yet, when confinement's lingering hour was done,   255
Our sports, our studies, and our souls were one;
Together we impell'd the flying ball,
Together waited in our tutor's hall;
Together join'd in cricket's manly toil,
Or shar'd the produce of the river's spoil;   260
Or, plunging from the green, declining shore,
Our pliant limbs the buoyant waters bore;
In every element, unchang'd, the same,
All, all, that brothers should be, but the name.

Nor, yet, are you forgot, my jocund Boy!   265
DAVUS, the harbinger of childish joy;

236 fill] ⟨wind⟩ T   237 these] ⟨see⟩ T   241 ⟨Alone I look on woods / in misery in
? / Alone amidst / This this endears each⟩ T   242 And seek relief in Ida's social Band. T
243 Alonzo] Joannes *POVO*
250   Could aught inspire me with poetic fire,
                                   For thee, alone, I'd strike the hallow'd lyre;
                                   But, to some abler hand, the task I wave,
                                   Whose strains immortal may outlive the grave.
                                                       POVO, between lines 250–1
          262 pliant] lusty *POVO*   waters] billows *1831, 1832, C, More*

For ever foremost in the ranks of fun,
The laughing herald of the harmless pun;
Yet, with a breast, of such materials made,
Anxious to please, of pleasing half afraid;   270
Candid and liberal, with a heart of steel
In danger's path, though not untaught to feel.
Still, I remember, in the factious strife,
The rustic's musket aim'd against my life;
High pois'd in air, the massy weapon hung,   275
A cry of horror burst from every tongue;
Whilst I, in combat with another foe,
Fought on, unconscious of th' impending blow;
Your arm, brave Boy, arrested his career,
Forward you sprung, insensible to fear;   280
Disarm'd, and baffled, by your conquering hand,
The groveling Savage roll'd upon the sand;
An act, like this, can simple thanks repay?
Or all the labours of a grateful lay?
Oh! no! whene'er my breast forgets the deed,   285
That instant, DAVUS, it deserves to bleed.

LYCUS! on me, thy claims are justly great
Thy milder virtues could my Muse relate,
To thee, alone, unrivall'd, would belong,
The feeble efforts of my lengthen'd song.   290
Well canst thou boast, to lead in senates fit,

283–5 Thus, did you save that life I scarcely prize, | A life unworthy such a sacrifice; |
Oh! when my breast forgets the generous deed, *POVO*
291–4   For ever to possess a friend in thee,
            Was bliss, unhop'd, though not unsought, by me;
            Thy softer soul was form'd for love alone,
            To ruder passions, and to hate unknown;
            Thy mind, in union with thy beauteous form,
            Was gentle, but unfit to stem the storm;
            That face, an index of celestial worth,
            Proclaim'd a heart, abstracted from the earth;
            Oft, when depress'd with sad, foreboding gloom,
            I sat reclin'd upon our favourite tomb,
            I've seen those sympathetic eyes o'erflow,
            With kind compassion for thy comrade's woe;
            Or when less mournful subjects form'd our themes,
            We try'd a thousand fond romantic schemes;
            Oft hast thou sworn, in friendship's soothing tone,
            Whatever wish was mine, must be thine own.

            The next can boast to lead in senates fit,
            A Spartan firmness, with Athenian wit;

A Spartan firmness, with Athenian wit;
Tho' yet, in embryo, these perfections shine,
LYCUS! thy father's fame, will soon be thine.
Where Learning nurtures the superior mind,   295
What may we hope, from genius thus refin'd!
When Time, at length, matures thy growing years,
How wilt thou tower, above thy fellow peers!
Prudence and sense, a spirit bold and free,   .
With honour's soul, united, beam in thee.   300

　　Shall fair EURYALUS, pass by unsung?
From ancient lineage, not unworthy, sprung:
What, though one sad dissention bade us part,
That name is yet embalm'd, within my heart;
Yet, at the mention, does that heart rebound,   305
And palpitate, responsive to the sound:
Envy dissolv'd our ties, and not our will,
We once were friends,—I'll think, we are so still.
A form unmatch'd, in Nature's partial mould,
A heart untainted, we, in thee, behold;   310
Yet, not the Senate's thunder thou shalt wield,
Nor seek for glory, in the tented field;
To minds of ruder texture, these be given,
Thy soul shall nearer soar its native heaven.
Haply, in polish'd courts, might be thy seat,   315
But, that thy tongue could never forge deceit;
The courtier's supple bow, and sneering smile,
The flow of compliment, the slippery wile,
Would make that breast, with indignation, burn,
And, all the glitttering snares, to tempt thee, spurn.   320
Domestic happiness, will stamp thy fate;
Sacred to love, unclouded e'er by hate;
The world admire thee, and thy friends adore,
Ambition's Slave, alone, would toil for more.

　　Now last, but nearest, of the social band,   325
See, honest, open, generous CLEON stand;

Tho' yet, in embryo, these perfections shine,
CLARUS! thy father's fame, will soon be thine. *POVO*
324 Where is the restless fool, would wish for more?

With scarce one speck, to cloud the pleasing scene,
No vice degrades that purest soul serene.
On the same day, our studious race begun,
On the same day, our studious race was run;   330
Thus, side by side, we pass'd our first career,
Thus, side by side, we strove for many a year,
At last, concluded our scholastic life,
We neither conquer'd in the classic strife:
As Speakers, each supports an equal name,   335
And crouds allow to both a partial fame;
To soothe a youthful Rival's early pride,
Though Cleon's candour would the palm divide;
Yet Candour's self compels me now to own,
Justice awards it to my Friend alone.   340

Oh! Friends regretted, Scenes for ever dear,
Remembrance hails you, with her warmest tear!
Drooping, she bends, o'er pensive Fancy's urn,
To trace the hours, which never can return,
Yet, with the retrospection loves to dwell,   345
And soothe the sorrows of her last farewell!
Yet, greets the triumph, of my boyish mind,
As infant laurels round my head were twin'd:
When Probus' praise repaid my lyric song,
Or plac'd me higher in the studious throng;   350
Or, when my first harangue receiv'd applause,
His sage instruction the primaeval cause,
What gratitude, to him, my soul possest,
While hope of dawning honours fill'd my breast.
For all my humble fame, to him alone,   355
The praise is due, who made that fame my own.

POVO 329-30 begun ... run] began ... ran POVO
335-8   As speakers, each supports a rival name,
             Though neither seeks to damn the other's fame.
             Pomposus sits, unequal to decide,
             With youthful candour, we the palm divide; POVO
345-6   Yet, in the retrospection, finds relief,
             And revels, in the luxury of grief; POVO
355-412   When, yet a novice, in the mimic art,
             I feign'd the transports of a vengeful heart;
             When, as the ROYAL SLAVE, I trod the stage,
             To vent in Zanga, more than mortal rage;
             The praise of Probus, made me feel more proud,
             Than all the plaudits of the list'ning croud.

Oh! could I soar above these feeble lays,
These young effusions of my early days,
To him my Muse her noblest strain would give,
The song might perish, but the theme must live;   360
Yet, why for him the needless verse essay?
His honour'd name requires no vain display;
By every son of grateful Ida blest,
It finds an echo in each youthful breast;

> Ah! vain endeavour, in this childish strain,
> To soothe the woes, of which I thus complain;
> What can avail this fruitless loss of time,
> To measure sorrow, in a jingling rhyme!
> No social solace, from a friend, is near,
> And heartless strangers drop no feeling tear.
> I seek not joy, in woman's sparkling eye,
> The smiles of beauty cannot check the sigh.
> Adieu! thou world! thy pleasure's still a dream,
> Thy virtue, but a visionary theme;
> Thy years of vice, on years of folly roll,
> 'Till grinning death assigns the destin'd goal;
> Where all are hastening to the dread abode,
> To meet the judgement of a righteous God;
> Mix'd in the concourse of the thoughtless throng,
> A mourner, 'midst of mirth, I glide along;
> A wretched, isolated, gloomy thing,
> Curst by reflection's deep corroding sting:
> But not that mental sting, which stabs within,
> The dark avenger of unpunish'd sin;
> The silent shaft, which goads the guilty wretch,
> Extended on a rack's untiring stretch;
> Conscience that sting, that shaft to him supplies,
> His mind the rack, from which he ne'er can rise.
> For me, whate'er my folly, or my fear,
> One chearful comfort still is cherish'd here;
> No dread internal, haunts my hours of rest,
> No dreams of injur'd innocence infest;
> Of hope, of peace, of almost all bereft,
> Conscience my last, but welcome, guest is left.
> Slander's empoison'd breath, may blast my name,
> Envy delights to blight the buds of fame;
> Deceit may chill the current of my blood,
> And freeze affection's warm impassion'd flood;
> Presaging horror, darken every sense,
> Even here will conscience be my best defence;
> My bosom feeds 'no worm which ne'er can die',
> Not crimes I mourn; but happiness gone by.
> Thus, crawling on with many a reptile vile,
> My heart is bitter, though my cheek may smile;
> No more, with former bliss, my breast is glad,
> Hope yields to anguish, and my soul is sad:
> From fond regret, no future joy can save,
> Remembrance slumbers only in the grave. *POVO*

360 must live] might live *1831*, *1832*, C, *More*   362 honour'd . . . vain] ⟨name . . .
pompous vain⟩ *T*   363 ⟨It lives by every son of Ida blest⟩ *T*   364 It . . . youth-
ful] ⟨And . . . grateful⟩ *T*

A fame beyond the glories of the proud,   365
Or all the plaudits of the venal crowd.

IDA, not yet exhausted is the theme,
Nor clos'd the progress of my youthful dream;
How many a friend deserves the grateful strain!
What scenes of childhood still unsung remain!   370
Yet let me hush this echo of the past,
This parting song, the dearest and the last;
And brood in secret o'er those hours of joy,
To me a silent, and a sweet employ,
While future hope and fear alike unknown,   375
I think with pleasure on the past alone;
Yes, to the past alone, my heart confine,
And chase the phantom of what once was mine.

IDA! still o'er thy hills in joy preside,
And proudly steer through time's eventful tide;   380
Still, may thy blooming Sons thy name revere,
Smile in thy bower, but quit thee with a tear;
That tear, perhaps, the fondest which will flow,
O'er their last scene of happiness below:
Tell me, ye hoary few, who glide along,   385
The feeble Veterans of some former throng;
Whose friends, like Autumn leaves by tempests whirl'd,
Are swept forever from this busy world;
Revolve the fleeting moments of your youth,
While Care as yet withheld her venom'd tooth;   390
Say, if Remembrance days like these endears,
Beyond the rapture of succeeding years?
Say, can Ambition's fever'd dream bestow
So sweet a balm, to soothe your hours of woe?
Can Treasures, hoarded for some thankless Son,   395

365 fame] ⟨praise⟩ *T*   366 venal] ⟨heartless / wondering?⟩ *T*   368 clos'd]
⟨faint / ceased⟩ *T*   370 ⟨These many⟩ scenes of childhood ⟨yet⟩ unsung remain *T*
372 parting] feeble *T*   373 secret . . . hours] ⟨silence . . . scenes⟩ *T*   376 I ⟨wish⟩
think *T*   379 in] ⟨may⟩ *T*   380 ⟨Nor ? by storms⟩ *T*   381 ⟨May Science
still her favoured site revere⟩ Still may thy rosy Sons their Queen revere, *T*   382 in]
⟨oer⟩ *T*   384 their] the *T*   385 ye ⟨who hoary still⟩ *T*   386 The ⟨feeble⟩
veteran remnants of some former throng, *T*   387 ⟨Revolves the moment⟩ *T*
388 busy] rolling *T*   390 as] has *T*, *1831*, *1832*, *C*, *More*   her] his *T*   391 ⟨Say,
were the days of Boyhood far more dear⟩ *T*   395 ⟨Can hoarded Wealth, or Wreathes by
Conquest won⟩ *T*   thankless] slothful *T*

Can Royal Smiles, or Wreaths by slaughter won,
Can Stars, or Ermine, Man's maturer Toys,
(For glittering baubles are not left to Boys,)
Recall one scene, so much belov'd, to view,
As those, where Youth her garland twin'd for you?   400
Ah, no! amidst the gloomy calm of age,
You turn with faultering hand life's varied page,
Peruse the record, of your days on earth,
Unsullied only, where it marks your birth;
Still, ling'ring, pause above each chequer'd leaf,   405
And blot with Tears the sable lines of grief;
Where Passion o'er the theme her mantle threw,
Or weeping Virtue sigh'd a faint adieu;
But bless the scroll which fairer words adorn,
Trac'd by the rosy finger of the Morn;   410
When Friendship bow'd before the shrine of Truth,
And Love, without his pinion, smil'd on Youth.

[1806]

93a, b, c [Three Poems Associated With 'Childish Recollections']

93a   [Portrait of Pomposus]

Just half a Pedagogue, and half a Fop,
Not formed to grace the Pulpit, but the shop;
The *Counter*, not the *Desk*, should be his place,
Who deals out precepts, as if dealing lace;
Servile in mind, from Elevation proud,   5
In argument, less sensible than loud,
Through half the Continent, the Coxcomb's been,
And stuns you with the Wonders he has seen:

396 Can Titles glare or wreathes by ⟨conquest⟩ slaughter won *T*   397 Can Stars ⟨and ? / titles⟩ or Ermine *T*   398 Baubles as frail and vain as those of Boys, *T* 400 where . . . twin'd] when . . . wove *T*   401 amidst] amid *C*   402 varied] early *T* 403 days] deeds *T*   404 where it marks your] ⟨nearest to⟩ where ⟨they⟩ it marks your *T* 407–8, 411–12 *supplied by* E. Pigot *in T*   409 ⟨But hail with smiles the joyous time of Morn⟩ ⟨Smile oer⟩ the page which ⟨brighter trace?⟩ adorn *T*

93a. Copy text: *C*, collated with *MS*. *Y*

'*How* in Pompeii's vault he found the page
Of some long lost, and long lamented Sage,   10
And doubtless he the *Letters* would have trac'd,
Had they not been by age and dust effac'd':
This single specimen will serve to show,
The mighty lessons of this reknowned Beau,
Bombast in vain would want of Genius cloke,   15
For feeble fires evaporating in smoke,
A Boy, o'er boys he holds a trembling reign,
More fit than they to seek some School again.

93b   [A Dialogue on Pomposus]

Says Edward to George, 'poor Pomposus forgive,
Or else in your lines his remembrance will live';
Says George, 'it is just the reverse:
Oblivion should ever be Pedantry's lot;
As I wish that his name should at once be forgot   5
I give it a place in my verse'.—

93c   [Youth and Age]

Ah, why should hoary age complain
Of ills he cannot suffer long,
While youth must hide each secret pain
Which years but threaten to prolong?

12 age] ⟨time⟩ *Υ*   14 mighty] weighty *C*   15 ⟨Such Tinsel served his native
weakness Cloke⟩ *Υ*   16 For] ⟨His / But⟩ *Υ*   evaporating] evaporate *C*   17 ⟨Such
ostentation his commencement marks⟩ *Υ*   18 to seek some] ⟨to get to⟩ *Υ*

93b. Copy text: *MS. T*, collated with *Pratt*
                    ⟨Oblivion should ever be pedantry's lot
                    So the faults of Pomposus rehearse.
                    As I wish that his name should at once be forgot
                    I give it a place in my verse⟩ *initial stanza cancelled in T*
1 George, 'poor] George ⟨if you notice⟩ poor *T*   2 ⟨The notice of bards makes / If you
notice / Or else with your own lines⟩ *T*

93c. Copy text: *MS. T*, collated with *Pratt*
2 ills] ⟨age⟩ *T*   3 each] ⟨his⟩ *T*

Delight is sure the gift of Age,   5
  He smiles on pangs which scarce can last,
While Memory unfolds her page,
  . And soothes the present, by the past.—

94   Answer to a Beautiful Poem, Written by Montgomery, Author of 'The Wanderer in Switzerland', &c. &c. Entitled 'The Common Lot'

[1.]
Montgomery! true, the common lot
  Of mortals lies in Lethe's wave;
Yet some shall never be forgot,
  Some shall exist beyond the grave.

2.
'Unknown the region of his birth',   5
  The hero rolls the tide of war;
Yet not unknown his martial worth,
  Which glares a meteor from afar.

3.
His joy, or grief, his weal, or woe,
  Perchance, may 'scape the page of fame;   10
Yet nations, now unborn, will know
  The record of his deathless name.

4.
The patriot and the poet's frame,
  Must share the common tomb of all;
Their glory will not sleep the same;   15
  That will arise, though empires fall.

5 Delight is sure] ⟨Oh joy should be⟩ *T*   7 ⟨In him perchance⟩ *T*

94. Copy text: *POVO*
  13 patriot] patriot's *1831, 1832, C, More*

5.

The lustre of a Beauty's eye,
    Assumes the ghastly stare of death;
The fair, the brave, the good must die,
    And sink the yawning grave beneath.   20

6.

Once more, the speaking eye revives,
    Still beaming through the lover's strain;
For Petrarch's Laura still survives,
    She died, but ne'er will die again.

7.

The rolling seasons pass away,   25
    And time, untiring, waves his wing;
Whilst honour's laurels ne'er decay,
    But bloom in fresh, unfading spring.

8.

All, all, must sleep in grim repose,
    Collected in the silent tomb;   30
The old, the young, with friends and foes,
    Festering alike in shrouds consume.

9.

The mouldering marble lasts its day,
    Yet falls, at length, an useless fane;
To ruin's ruthless fangs a prey,   35
    The wrecks of pillar'd pride remain.

10.

What, though the sculpture be destroy'd,
From dark oblivion meant to guard;
A bright renown shall be enjoy'd,
    By those, whose virtues claim reward.   40

11.

Then do not say, the common lot
    Of all, lies deep in Lethe's wave;
Some few who, ne'er will be forgot,
    Shall burst the bondage of the grave.

[1806]

95   Love's Last Adieu!

Ἀεὶ δ' ἀεί με φεύγει.

ANACREON.

[1.]

The roses of love, glad the garden of life,
    Though nurtur'd 'mid weeds dropping pestilent dew,
Till Time crops the leaves, with unmerciful knife,
    Or prunes them for ever, in love's last adieu!

2.

In vain, with endearments, we soothe the sad heart,   5
    In vain, do we vow, for an age to be true;
The chance of an hour, may command us to part,
    Or death disunite us, in love's last adieu!

3.

Still, Hope breathing peace, through the grief-swollen
        breast,
    Will whisper, 'our meeting we yet may renew';   10
With this dream of deceit, half our sorrow's represt,
    Nor taste we the poison, of love's last adieu!

4.

Oh! mark you yon pair, in the sunshine of youth,
    Love twin'd round their childhood, his flow'rs, as
        they grew;
They flourish awhile, in the season of truth,   15
    Till chill'd by the winter of love's last adieu!

5.

Sweet lady! why thus doth a tear steal its way,
    Down a cheek, which outrivals thy bosom in hue?
Yet, why do I ask? to distraction a prey,
    Thy reason has perish'd, with love's last adieu!   20

95. Copy text: HI, collated with POVO
epigraph added in HI
    2 dropping] breathing POVO   9 Hope breathing] hope-beaming POVO

6.

Oh! who is yon Misanthrope, shunning mankind?
  From cities to caves of the forest he flew:
There, raving, he howls his complaint to the wind,
  The mountains reverberate love's last adieu!

7.

Now, hate rules a heart, which in love's easy chains,   25
  Once, passion's tumultuous blandishments knew;
Despair, now, enflames the dark tide of his veins,
  He ponders, in frenzy, on Love's last adieu!

8.

How he envies the wretch, with a soul wrapt in steel,
  His pleasures are scarce, yet his troubles are few;   30
Who laughs at the pang, that he never can feel,
  And dreads not the anguish of Love's last adieu!

9.

Youth flies, life decays, even hope is o'ercast,
  No more, with love's former devotion, we sue;
He spreads his young wing, he retires with the blast,   35
  The shroud of affection is Love's last adieu!

10.

In this life of probation, for rapture divine,
  Astrea declares that some penance is due;
From him, who has worship'd at love's gentle shrine,
  The atonement is ample, in Love's last adieu!   40

11.

Who kneels to the God, on his altar of light,
  Must myrtle and cypress, alternately, strew;
His myrtle, an emblem of purest delight,
  His cypress, the garland of Love's last adieu!

[1806]

24 The] And the *POVO; cor. by hand by B in the copy of POVO sent to his sister (location: Princeton—Taylor)*

96   To the Rev. J. T. Becher

[1.]

Dear BECHER, you tell me, to mix with mankind,
  I cannot deny such a precept is wise;
But, retirement accords with the tone of my mind,
  I will not descend to a world I despise.

2.

Did the Senate, or Camp, my exertions require,   5
  Ambition might prompt me, at once, to go forth;
When infancy's years of probation expire,
  Perchance, I may strive to distinguish my birth.

3.

The fire, in the cavern of Aetna, conceal'd,
  Still mantles unseen, in its secret recess,   10
At length, in a volume terrific, reveal'd,
  No torrent can quench it, no bounds can repress.

4.

Oh! such the desire, in my bosom, for fame,
  Bids me live, but to hope for posterity's praise,
Could I soar with the Phoenix, on pinions of flame;   15
  With him, I would wish, to expire in the blaze.

5.

For the life of a FOX, of a CHATHAM the death,
  What censure, what danger, what woe would I brave?
Their lives did not end, when they yielded their breath,
  Their glory illumines the gloom of the grave.   20

6.

Yet why should I mingle in fashion's full herd?
  Why crouch to her leaders, or cringe to her rules?
Why bend to the proud, or applaud the absurd?
  Why search for delight, in the friendship of fools?

96. Copy text: *POVO*
title   Lines Addressed to the Rev. J. T. Becher, on his Advising the Author to Mix More
with Society *1832, C, More*
  13 such] thus *1831, 1832, C, More*   20 the] their *1831, 1832, C, More*

7.

I have tasted the sweets, and the bitters, of love,   25
    In friendship, I early was taught to believe;
My passion, the matrons of prudence reprove,
    I have found, that a friend may profess, yet deceive.

8.

To me what is wealth? it may pass in an hour,
    If Tyrants prevail, or if Fortune should frown;   30
To me what is title? the phantom of power;
    To me what is fashion? I seek but renown.

9.

Deceit, is a stranger, as yet, to my soul,
    I, still, am unpractis'd to varnish the truth;
Then, why should I live in a hateful controul?   35
    Why waste, upon folly, the days of my youth?

                                                    [1806]

97   Answer to Some Elegant Verses,
                    Sent by
          A Friend to the Author,
complaining that one of his descriptions was
          rather too warmly drawn

> 'But, if any old Lady, Knight, Priest, or Physician,
> Should condemn me for printing a second edition;
> If good Madam Squintum my work should abuse,
> May I venture to give her a smack of my muse?'
> ANSTEY's NEW BATH GUIDE [A New Edition, 1797], page 169.

Candour compels me, Becher! to commend,
The verse, which blends the censor with the friend;
Your strong, yet just, reproof extorts applause,
From me, the heedless and imprudent cause;

97. Copy text: *HI*, collated with *POVO*
epigraph *added in HI*
    1 Becher] B—H—R *POVO*   4 imprudent] unworthy *POVO*

For this wild error, which pervades my strain,   5
I sue for pardon,—must I sue in vain?
The wise, sometimes, from Wisdom's ways depart;
Can youth then hush the dictates of the heart?
Precepts of prudence curb, but can't controul,
The fierce emotions of the flowing soul.   10
When Love's delirium haunts the glowing mind,
Limping Decorum lingers far behind;
Vainly the dotard mends her prudish pace,
Outstript and vanquish'd in the mental chace;
The young, the old, have worn the chains of love,   15
Let those, they ne'er confin'd, my lay reprove:
Let those, whose souls contemn the pleasing power,
Their censures on the hapless victim shower;
Oh! how I hate the nerveless, frigid song,
The ceaseless echo of the rhyming throng;   20
Whose labour'd lines, in chilling numbers flow,
To paint a pang the author ne'er can know.
The artless Helicon, I boast, is Youth;
My Lyre, the Heart;—my Muse, the simple Truth:
Far be't from me, the 'virgin's mind' to 'taint',   25
Seduction's dread, is here no slight restraint:
The maid, whose virgin breast is void of guile,
Whose wishes dimple in a modest smile;
Whose downcast eye disdains the wanton leer,
Firm in her virtue's strength, yet not severe;   30
She, whom a conscious grace shall thus refine,
Will ne'er be 'tainted' by a strain of mine.
But, for the nymph, whose premature desires
Torment her bosom with unholy fires,
No net to snare her willing heart is spread,   35
She would have fallen, tho' she ne'er had read.
For me, I fain would please the chosen few,
Whose souls, to feeling, and to nature true,
Will spare the childish verse, and not destroy
The light effusions of a heedless boy.   40
I seek not glory from the senseless crowd,
Of fancied laurels, I shall ne'er be proud;

5 wild] sole *POVO*   18 censures] curses *POVO*   40 a heedless] an amorous
POVO

Their warmest plaudits I would scarcely prize,
Their sneers, or censures, I alike despise.

26 Nov. 1806

98   [Pignus Amoris]

1.

As by the fix'd decrees of Heaven,
    'Tis vain to hope that Joy will last;
The dearest boon that Life has given,
    To me is—visions of the past.

2.

For these this toy of blushing hue   5
    I prize with zeal before unknown,
It tells me of a Friend I knew,
    Who loved me for myself alone,

3.

It tells me what how few can say
    Though all the social tie commend;   10
Recorded in my heart 'twill lay,
    It tells me mine was once a Friend.

4.

Through many a weary day gone by,
    With Time the gift is dearer grown;
And still I view in Memory's eye   15
    That teardrop sparkle through my own.

5.

And heartless Age perhaps will smile,
    Or wonder whence these feelings sprung;

dating   *not in HI*

98. Copy text: *C*, collated with *MS. Ba*, *MS. B*
title   *untitled in B, Ba*

1 ⟨As through the fleeting maze of years⟩ *B*   fix'd] ⟨firm⟩ *B*   4 is visions] ⟨Re-
membrance⟩ *B*   5 For . . . of] ⟨Cornelian when⟩ *B*   6 prize] ⟨love⟩ *B*   9 say]
⟨boast⟩ *B*   10 ⟨Though now perchance forever lost⟩ *B*   11 ⟨That once / Deep in
my heart the⟩ *B*   13 ⟨Though many a weary day has past⟩ *B*   17 perhaps . . .
smile] ⟨will smile at this⟩ *B*   18 Or] ⟨And⟩ *B*

Yet let not sterner souls revile,
  For Both were open, Both were young.   20

6.

And Youth is sure the only time,
  When Pleasure blends no base alloy;
When Life is blest without a crime,
  And Innocence resides with Joy.

7.

Let those reprove my feeble Soul,   25
  Who laugh to scorn Affection's name;
While these impose a harsh controul,
  All will forgive who feel the same.

8.

Then still I wear my simple toy,
  With pious care from wreck I'll save it;   30
And this will form a dear employ
  For dear I was to him who gave it.

[1807]

99   The Adieu.

Written under the impression that the author would soon die

Adieu, thou Hill! where early joy
  Spread roses o'er my brow;
Where Science seeks each loitering boy
  With knowledge to endow.
Adieu my youthful friends or foes,   5
Partners of former bliss or woes;
  No more through Ida's paths we stray;
Soon must I share the gloomy cell,
Where ever-slumbering inmates dwell
  Unconscious of the day.   10

19 sterner] ⟨marble⟩ *B*   25–8 *not in B*

99. Copy text: see Addenda page

Adieu, ye hoary Regal Fanes,
  Ye spires of Granta's vale,
Where Learning robed in sable reigns,
  And Melancholy pale.
Ye comrades of the jovial hour,   15
Ye tenants of the classic bower,
  On Cama's verdant margin placed,
Adieu! while memory still is mine,
For, offerings on Oblivion's shrine,
  These scenes must be effaced.   20

Adieu, ye mountains of the clime
  Where grew my youthful years;
Where Loch na Garr in snows sublime
  His giant summit rears.
Why did my childhood wander forth   25
From you, ye regions of the North,
  With sons of pride to roam?
Why did I quit my Highland cave,
Marr's dusky heath, and Dee's clear wave,
  To seek a Sotheron home?   30

Hall of my Sires! a long farewell—
  Yet why to thee adieu?
Thy vaults will echo back my knell,
  Thy towers my tomb will view:
The faltering tongue which sung thy fall,   35
And former glories of thy Hall
  Forgets its wonted simple note—
But yet the Lyre retains the strings,
And sometimes, on Aeolian wings,
  In dying strains may float.   40

Fields, which surround yon rustic cot,
  While yet I linger here,
Adieu! you are not now forgot,
  To retrospection dear.
Streamlet! along whose rippling surge,   45
My youthful limbs were wont to urge

11 Fanes] Towers *N* [recorded in *C*]

At noontide heat their pliant course;
Plunging with ardour from the shore,
Thy springs will lave these limbs no more,
    Deprived of active force.   50

And shall I here forget the scene,
  Still nearest to my breast?
Rocks rise, and rivers roll between
  The spot which passion blest;
Yet, Mary, all thy beauties seem   55
Fresh as in Love's bewitching dream,
    To me in smiles display'd:
Till slow disease resigns his prey
To Death, the parent of decay,
    Thine image cannot fade.   60

And thou, my Friend! whose gentle love
  Yet thrills my bosom's chords,
How much thy friendship was above
  Description's power of words!
Still near my breast the gift I wear,   65
Which sparkled once with Feeling's tear,
    Of love the pure, the sacred gem;
In that dear moment quite forgot
Our souls were equal, and our lot
    Let Pride alone condemn!   70

All, all, is dark and cheerless now!
  No smile of Love's deceit,
Can warm my veins with wonted glow,
  Can bid Life's pulses beat:
Not e'en the hope of future fame,   75
Can wake my faint, exhausted frame,
    Or crown with fancied wreaths my head.
Mine is a short inglorious race,—
To humble in the dust my face,
    And mingle with the dead.   80

65 thy] the *N* [recorded in *C*

Oh Fame! thou goddess of my heart;
  On him who gains thy praise,
Pointless must fall the Spectre's dart,
  Consumed in Glory's blaze;
But me she beckons from the earth,   85
My name obscure, unmark'd my birth,
  My life a short and vulgar dream:
Lost in the dull, ignoble crowd,
My hopes recline within a shroud,
  My fate in Lethe's stream.   90

When I repose beneath the sod,
  Unheeded in the clay,
Where once my playful footsteps trod,
  Where now my head must lay;
The meed of Pity will be shed   95
In dew-drops o'er my narrow bed,
  By nightly skies, and storms alone;
No mortal eye will deign to steep
With tears the dark sepulchral deep
  Which hides a name unknown.   100

Forget this world, my restless sprite,
  Turn, turn thy thoughts to Heaven:
There must thou soon direct thy flight,
  If errors are forgiven.
To bigots and to sects unknown,   105
Bow down beneath th' Almighty's Throne;
  To him address thy trembling prayer:
He, who is merciful and just,
Will not reject a child of dust,
  Although his meanest care.   110

Father of Light! to Thee I call,
  My soul is dark within:
Thou, who canst mark the sparrow's fall,
  Avert the death of sin.
Thou, who canst guide the wandering star,   115
Who calm'st the elemental war,
  Whose mantle is yon boundless sky,

My thoughts, my words, my crimes forgive;
And, since I must forebear to live,
    Instruct me how to die.   120

[1807]

100   To ——

1.

Oh! well I know your subtle Sex,
    Frail daughters of the wanton Eve,—
While jealous pangs our Souls perplex,
    No passion prompts you to relieve.

2.

From Love, or Pity ne'er you fall,   5
    By *you*, no mutual Flame is felt,
'Tis Vanity, which rules you all,
    Desire alone which makes you melt.

3.

I will not say no *souls* are yours,
    Aye, ye have *Souls*, and dark ones too,   10
Souls to contrive those smiling lures,
    To snare our simple hearts for you.

4.

Yet shall you never bind me fast,
    Long to adore such brittle toys,
I'll rove along, from first to last,   15
    And change whene'er my fancy cloys.

5.

Oh! should I be a *baby* fool,
    To sigh the dupe of female art—
Woman! perhaps thou hast a *Soul*,
    But where have *Demons hid* thy *Heart?*   20

Jan. 1807

119 must forebear] soon must cease *all ebitions.*
dating *in MS. CM, 1832*

100. Copy text : *C*, collated with *MS. N*

101   [To Harriet]

1.

Harriet! to see such Circumspection,
In Ladies I have no objection
    Concerning what they read;
An ancient Maid's a sage adviser,
Like *her*, you will be much the wiser,   5
    In word, as well as Deed.

2.

But Harriet, I don't wish to flatter,
And really think 'twould make the matter
    More perfect if not quite,
If certain Ladies when they preach,   10
Would certain Damsels also teach
    More cautiously to *write*.

[1807]

102   On the Eyes of Miss A[nne] H[ouson]

1.

Anne's Eye is liken'd to the *Sun*,
    From it such Beams of Beauty fall;
And *this* can be denied by none,
    For like the *Sun*, it shines on *All*.—

2.

Then do not admiration smother,   5
    Or say these glances don't become her;
To *you*, or *I*, or *any other*
    Her *Sun*, displays perpetual Summer.—

14 Jan. 1807

101. Copy text: *C*, collated with *MS. N*
    8 make] ⟨mend⟩ *N*   10 certain] other *C, Mor*

102. Copy text: *C*, collated with *MS. H*

103   On Finding a Fan
            Of Miss A[nne] H[ouson]

In one who felt as once he felt,
    This might, perhaps, have fann'd the flame;
But now his heart no more will melt,
    Because that heart is not the same.

As when the ebbing flames are low,   5
    The aid which once improved their light
And bade them burn with fiercer glow,
    Now quenches all their blaze in night,

Thus has it been with passion's fires—
    As many a boy and girl remembers—   10
While every hope of love expires,
    Extinguish'd with the dying embers.

The *first*, though not a spark survive,
    Some careful hand may teach to burn;
The *last*, alas! can ne'er survive;   15
    No touch can bid its warmth return.

Or, if it chance to wake again,
    Not always doom'd its heat to smother,
It sheds (so wayward fates ordain)
    Its former warmth around another.   20

                                              [1807]

104   [To a Vain Lady]

AH, heedless girl! why thus disclose
    What ne'er was meant for other ears?
Why thus destroy thine own repose
    And dig the source of future tears?

103. Copy text: *1832*, collated with *C*, *More*
title   On Finding a Fan *1832*, *C*, *More*

104. Copy text: *1832*, collated with *C*, *More*
title   To A Young Lady (Miss Anne Houson) whose vanity induced her to repeat the
compliments paid her by some young men of her acquaintance. *MS. N* [recorded in *C*]
dating   *from 1832*

Oh, thou wilt weep, imprudent maid,   5
   While lurking envious foes will smile,
For all the follies thou hast said
   Of those who spoke but to beguile.

Vain girl! thy ling'ring woes are nigh,
   If thou believ'st what striplings say: 10
Oh, from the deep temptation fly,
   Nor fall the specious spoiler's prey.

Dost thou repeat, in childish boast,
   The words man utters to deceive?
Thy peace, thy hope, thy all is lost,   15
   If thou can'st venture to believe.

While now amongst thy female peers
   Thou tell'st again the soothing tale,
Can'st thou not mark the rising sneers
   Duplicity in vain would veil?   20

These tales in secret silence hush,
   Nor make thyself the public gaze:
What modest maid without a blush
   Recounts a flattering coxcomb's praise?

Will not the laughing boy despise   25
   Her who relates each fond conceit—
Who, thinking Heaven is in her eyes,
   Yet cannot see the slight deceit?

For she who takes a soft delight
   These amorous nothings in revealing,   30
Must credit all we say or write,
   While vanity prevents concealing.

Cease, if you prize your beauty's reign!
   No jealousy bids me reprove:
One, who is thus from nature vain,   35
   I pity, but I cannot love.

                          15 Jan. 1807

105   To A[nne Houson]

[1.]

Oh, Anne! your offenses to me have been grievous;
   I thought from my wrath no atonement could save you;
But woman is made to command and deceive us—
   I look'd in your face, and I almost forgave you.

2.

I vow'd I could ne'er for a moment respect you,   5
   Yet thought that a day's separation was long:
When we met, I determin'd again to suspect you—
   Your smile soon convinced me suspicion was wrong.

3.

I swore, in a transport of young indignation,
   With fervent contempt evermore to disdain you: 10
I saw you—my anger became admiration;
   And now, all my wish, all my hope's, to regain you.

4.

With beauty like yours, oh, how vain the contention!
   Thus lowly I sue for forgiveness before you;—
At once to conclude such a fruitless dissension,   15
   Be false, my sweet Anne, when I cease to adore you!

16 Jan. 1807

106   To Anne

Oh say not, sweet Anne, that the Fates have decreed
   The heart which adores you should wish to dissever;
Such Fates were to me most unkind ones indeed,—
   To bear me from love and from beauty for ever.

105. Copy text: *1832*, collated with *C* and *MS. N*, *More*
title   To Anne *1832*, *C*, *More*
   13 contention] ⟨endeavour⟩ *N*

106. Copy text: *1832*, collated with *C*, *More*
title   To the Same *1832*
dating   *from 1832*

Your frowns, lovely girl, are the Fates which alone   5
  Could bid me from fond admiration refrain;
By these, every hope, every wish were o'erthrown,
  Till smiles should restore me to rapture again.

As the ivy and oak, in the forest entwined,
  The rage of the tempest united must weather,   10
My love and my life were by nature design'd
  To flourish alike, or to perish together.

Then say not, sweet Anne, that the Fates have decreed,
  Your lover should bid you a lasting adieu;
Till Fate can ordain that his bosom shall bleed   15
  His soul, his existence, are centred in you.

[1807]

107   A Valentine

1.

When Beauty lends her aid to Youth,
  And varied charms in one combine,
Then Love is praise, and praise is truth,
  To mark the virgin Valentine.

2.

But Youth once gone, and Beauty fled   5
  Ah! maids no longer seem divine,
But ugliness and spleen instead
  Surround the aged Valentine.

3.

Such are the trophies thou dost wear,
  Fit offering on ill nature's shrine,   10
The winds to thee no raptures bear
  For thou art not my Valentine.

107. Copy text: *MS. B*

4.

Perhaps the captain, Dearest name!
  Inspired by Jones's generous wine,
May love, or feign—'tis *all the same*—   15
  And hail thee for his Valentine.

5.

Say, didst thou not prepare a dart
  On which the Swain might sup, or dine,
Of Apricots, to win the heart
  Of him, thy Martial Valentine?   20

6.

Didst thou with culinary taste
  Adorn this dish with emblems fine—
Cupids and Doves engraved on paste,—
  To win thy winsome Valentine?

7.

Who kisses thee no Nectar sips,   25
  Such kisses taste like Neptune's wine;
May those who sigh for arid Lips
  Choose such as thee for Valentine.

8.

Not that I e'er those lips have tried—
  Heaven shield me back from Lips like thine!   30
Let fiends with lips in sulphur fried
  Claim *such*, from *such* a Valentine.

9.

And yet report most strongly tells
  That they possess a smack saline;
Such as in Ocean's bosom dwells   35
  Embues thy lips, Oh Valentine!

10.

Tho' flattery flies my humble Muse
  Yet truth presides o'er every line;
Then do not with a frown refuse
  This tribute 'stead of Valentine.   40

5 in . . . bosom] ⟨the breast of Ocean⟩ *B*

11.

To waste the words of love on thee
  Were surely casting pearls to swine,
When words of love are sent by me
  May I have such a Valentine.

12.

When ancient Maids affect such airs   45
  May they *for ever maids* repine
When folly crowns such silvery hairs
  Youth laughs at such a Valentine.

13.

But hold! I know thou wear'st a wig
  A *Chestnut Wig* of gay design,   50
Each curl appears an artful twig
  To catch some heedless Valentine.

14.

Venus from thee has parted long,
  No flowers for thee the Loves entwine,
By me they send this warning Song,   55
  And seek some Younger Valentine.

15.

Now from myself a fond Adieu,
  May no such ancient maid be mine;
Thy Years are many, mine are few,
  Farewell thou hoary Valentine.   60

1807

108 The Edinburgh Ladies' Petition to Doctor
     Moyes, and his Reply

The Petition

Dear Doctor, let it not transpire
How much your Lectures we admire,

43 of love] ⟨like these⟩ *B*

108. Copy text: *MS. M*, collated with *New Monthly Mag.* and *Steffan*

How at your Eloquence we wonder
When you explain the cause of Thunder;
Of Lightning and of Electricity,   5
With so much plainness and simplicity,
The origin of Rocks and Mountains,
Of seas and rivers, Lakes and Fountains,
Of Rain and Hail, of Frost and snow,
And all the Winds and Storms that blow;   10
Besides an hundred wonders more,
Of which we never heard before.
But now, dear Doctor, not to flatter,
There is a most important matter,
A matter which you never touch on,   15
A matter which our thoughts run much on,
A Subject, if we right conjecture
Which well deserves a long, long lecture,
Which all the ladies would approve,
The Natural History of Love!   20
Oh! list to our united voice,
Deny us not dear Doctor Moyes;
Tell us why our poor tender hearts
So willingly admit Love's darts;
Teach us the marks of Love's beginning,   25
What is it makes a Beau so winning;
What is it makes a Coxcomb witty,
A Dotard wise, a red Coat pretty;
Why we believe such horrid lies,
That we are Angels from the skies,   30
Our Teeth are pearl, our Cheeks are Roses,
Our Eyes are Stars, such charming Noses;
Explain our Dreams waking and sleeping,
Explain our laughing and our weeping;
Explain our hoping and our doubting,   35
Our blushing, simpering and pouting;
Teach us all the enchanting arts,
Of winning and of keeping hearts;
Teach us, dear Doctor, if you can,
To humble that proud Creature Man,   40
To turn the wise ones into fools,
The proud and insolent to Tools;

To make them all run helter skelter,
Their necks into the Marriage halter;
Then leave us to ourselves with these,   45
We'll rule and turn them as we please;
Dear Doctor, if you grant our wishes,
We promise you five hundred kisses;
And rather than the affair be blunder'd,
We'll give you *six score to the hundred*.   50
              Approved by 300 Ladies.

The Reply

To explain The Natural History of Love.—This 'Petition', a sprightly
little Poem, was put into my hands by a Lady for whom I entertain
a very *great respect*, accompanied by a wish that I would reply in the
Doctor's name; Though by no means adequate to the Task, I have
endeavoured in the following lines to give such answers to the questions, as my own *trifling* experience suggested, more from my dislike
to refuse *any* request of a *female*, than the most distant hope of affording a perspicuous or Satisfactory *Solution* of the different *queries*.

In all the arts without Exception,
The Moderns shew a vast perception,
From morbid symptoms diagnostic
Each Doctor draws a sage prognostic,
Whilst each professor forms a project   5
From Diagrams, or subtle Logic.
Herchell improves us in Astronomy,
Lavater writes on Physionomy,
The Principles of Nature's history
To Man appear no more a Mystery;   10
Monboddo says that once a tail huge
Adorned man before the Deluge,
And that at length Mankind got rid of 'em
Because they stood no more in need of 'em.
Since *we* on *fours* no longer went all,   15
Clothes were declared more *ornamental*.
Religion split in many a Schism,
Lectures commence on Galvanism,
The marvellous phantasmagoria,

Work on the optics, and *Sensoria*.   20
But not content with common things—
Behold some daily wonder springs,
An Infant Billington, or Banti,
Squalls out Adagio, or Andante.
The Town to view the veteran Kemble,   25
In nightly crowds no more assemble;
The House is crammed in every place full
To see the Boy, of action Graceful;
While Roscius lends his name to Betty
Tully must yield the palm to Petty;   30
And last though not the least in Crime,
A sucking *Peer* pretends to rhyme—
Though many think the noble Fool
Had better far return to School,
And there improve in Learning faster,   35
Instead of *libelling* his Master.
Such Trifles now amuse the Age,
Infant Attempts are all the Rage,
Knowledge is daily more prolific,
Babes will soon be scientific.   40
Yet in the midst of general Science
One theme to *Sophists* bids defiance,
Which *some* condemn, but most approve,
The *Natural History of Love*.
In Water, Fire, Earth, or Air,   45
Love holds his general empire there;
The Birds who cleave yon azure Sky
Breathe amorous warblings as they fly;
In Water even the very Fishes
Are periodically vicious;   50
And Fire all elements above
Is emblematical of Love;
On Earth, since first the Earth begun,
We know the miracles he's done.
But why should I Romances tell,   55
Which every damsel knows so well.

25 The Town] ⟨Cockneys⟩ *M*   29 lends] ⟨yiel⟩ *M*   37–8 *not in New Monthly*
Mag.   40 Babes will soon be] ⟨And all alike are⟩ *M*   45–70 *Misplaced after*
line 119 in New Monthly Mag.

To these just now I shan't recall 'em—
But may the very same befall 'em!
And this I think, with all due Deference,
In fact with maids would have the preference,   60
Because the best detailed Narration
Falls very short of Demonstration.—
This truth requires no great Rehearsal—
That Love indeed is universal,
From things with animation rife   65
To things of vegetable life.
Shells and their inmates also feel it,
There's not an Oyster can conceal it.
The Loves of plants are all the Fashion,
And Cabbage tastes the tender *passion*.—   70
That Love exists! sure none can doubt it,
Indeed, where should we be without it?
'Tis in the Catalogue of Sins,
But *when*, or *where*, this Love begins
Is perfectly incomprehensible,   75
Though *all* to its approach are sensible.
'Tis pleasure, pain, 'tis *old*, 'tis *new*,
'Tis *Alpha* and *Omega* too,
'Tis subject to no jurisdiction,
But burns the fiercer for restriction.   80
Some call it *Passive*, others active,
We all agree, that 'tis attractive;
Others declare, when first this World,
In dark promiscuous Chaos hurl'd,
Through Elements yet undigested,   85
Of shape and sense lay quite divested,
That *Form* and *Matter* join'd in Marriage,
And happily without Miscarriage,
In blissful Bonds at once uniting,
Produced this *Earth* we draw the light in;   90
And hence in fable allegorical,
The Bards of Yore most Metaphorical,
Have drawn (the simile must strike Ye)
The *Pretty* Tale of *Love* and *Psyche*.

61 best ... Narration] ⟨very best Relation⟩ *M*   detailed] ⟨displayed⟩ *M*   66 of
vegetable] ⟨that hardly⟩ *M*

Thus *Form* is the first I heard of,   95
(Or rather ever *read* a word of)
If *he*, as I *have stated*, be Male,
Who talk'd on Love, or kiss'd a Female.
We'll therefore call *him Love*, or rather,
Of *Love* at least the mighty Father;   100
For this to *Matrons* must appear,
And *Husbands* also very clear,
That we are under obligation
To *those*, who first produced *Creation*,
For had they never given Birth,   105
To this our general parent Earth,
We might have trod some other Sphere,
Or been just now, *the Lord knows where!*—
This *Origin* we'll take for granted,
Because *some Origin* was wanted;   110
Yet still I shall be much the Debtor
Of any one who finds a better;
Though *Love* be Sprung of very *great* degree,
I know but little of his *Pedigree*,
Yet as his *Family* was *thought* about,   115
A Circumstance which I knew nought about,
To settle this I have been *bold* enough
To give *him*, one at least, that's *old* enough.—
Why Ladies' young, and tender hearts,
So readily admit Love's darts,   120
Requires no Seraph from on high
To make at once an apt reply.
This faith, is *orthodox* forever,
A Damsel's *Heart* is *Cupid's Quiver*,
For never placed *he there* an Arrow,   125
Which found its residence too narrow
But gently was at once admitted,
The Shaft and all most nicely fitted.
Why they suppose a Coxcomb witty,
A Dotard wise, a red coat pretty,   130
Are questions that would pose the Sages
Of these, or any former Ages.
Some wicked wretches who peruse
The Patriarchs' Lives but to abuse,

Have said that very ancient Story,   135
Concerning *Eve*, is *Allegory*,
That Satan was no fiery Dragon,
But a *fine Youth*, without a *rag* on,
And held as good a claim as Adam
To be the *Spouse* of *Eve*, a sad Dame!   140
And consequently 'tis pretended
Some are from *Lucifer* descended.—
This parentage I shan't dispute,
Or what was the *forbidden Fruit*;
The ancient Texts have all agreed   145
The *Devil* was of *Reptile Breed*.
Proceeding on their grave decision,
We'll form from *thence* this Supposition:
As *Serpents* it is often *said*
Are caught with any thing that's *red*,   150
Perchance *some females* may inherit
A *Secret Sympathetic Spirit*,
Which binds them to this prediliction,
And *Scarlet is to them perfection*.
Why *Wit* in Coxcombs they discern   155
Is hardly worth our while to learn,
Why *fools* are oft prefer'd to wise men
I *know*, but *never* shall advise them;
We really can't explain the reason,
Because to *mention* it, were *Treason*.   160
Why all the charming easy creatures
Believe that heaven, to deck their features,
Has lent her *Stars*, that Earth has given
Her *roses*, to *outrival* Heaven;
Or why the *Sea*, to please the *Girl*,   165
Bids *oysters* mourn their absent *Pearl*,
Requires but little Explanation—
Their own *mistakes* are the *occasion;*
While *Vanity* shall hold the Glass,
All this will daily come to pass.—   170
To cure their laughing, and their weeping,
Their *wandering* Dreams, or *ev'n* their *Sleeping*,
'Tis known by Men of nice precision
That *Hymen* is the best *Physician*.

He will unravel hopes and doubting,   175
And put an end to fits of pouting;
But how to tame the other Sex
Would any Saint or *Sage* perplex.
Ladies! I think you can't complain,
You hold a wide extensive reign;   180
First learn to rule *Yourselves*, and then,
Perhaps, you'll quite *subdue the Men.*
As for that Word, the '*Marriage Halter*',
The very mention makes me falter,
The texture is so monstrous coarse,   185
It drags us into *Heaven* by *Force.*
Though much disposed to sin in Rhyming,
The *Muses* never *speak* of Hymen.
I'm therefore almost doubtful whether
I'd best be silent altogether,   190
Or with a Compliment conclude,
Since all *before* is downright *rude;*
But when I read the blest reward
Awaits the *Doctor*, or his Bard,
'*Five hundred Kisses*'*!* Oh ye Gods,   195
For *half* I'd dare all Mortal odds;
Though I can never be victorious,
To fall in such a *Cause* is *glorious.*
I'll therefore, since I've made beginning,
Conclude with scarce a hope of winning.—   200
To make my Deities propitious,
I'll *wish*, what *each* in Secret *wishes*,
Though much I fear that ev'n veracity
Can ne'er atone for such audacity.
'May each amongst you find a Mate   205
Content at home in peace to wait,
Grateful for each connubial Blessing
And *quite* enough in Spouse possessing,
A cheerful, constant, kind and free one,
But Heaven forbid, that *I* should *be One.*'   210

1807

109   Egotism.—'Εαυτὸν Βύρων ἀείδει

1.

If Fate should seal my Death to-morrow,
   (Though much *I* hope she will *postpone* it,)
I've held a share of *Joy* and *Sorrow*,
   Enough for *Ten;* and *here I own it.*

2.

I've lived, as many other men live,   5
   And yet, I think, with more Enjoyment;
For could I through my days again live,
   I'd pass them in the *same* employment,

3.

That *is to* say, with *some exception,*
   For though I will not make confession,   10
I've seen too much of man's deception
   Ever again to trust profession.

4.

Some sage *Mammas* with gesture haughty,
   Pronounce me quite a youthful Sinner—
But *Daughters* say, 'although he's naughty,   15
   You must not check a *young Beginner*'!

5.

I've loved, and many damsels know it—
   But whom I don't intend to mention,
As *certain stanzas* also show it,
   Some say *deserving Reprehension.*   20

6.

Some ancient Dames, of virtue fiery,
   (Unless Report does much belie them,)
Have lately made a sharp Enquiry,
   And much it *grieves* me to *deny* them.

109. Copy text: *C*, collated with *MS. N, More*
title   Egotism. A Letter to J. T. Becher. *C, More*

7.

Two whom I lov'd had *eyes* of *Blue*,   25
   To which I hope *you've* no objection;
The *Rest* had eyes of *darker Hue*—
   Each Nymph, of course, was *all perfection*.

8.

But here I'll close my *chaste* Description,
   Nor *sow the Seeds* of *Animosity*,   30
For *silence* is the best prescription,
   To *physic* idle curiosity.

9.

Of *Friends* I've known a *goodly Hundred*—
   For finding *one* in each acquaintance,
By *some deceived*, by *others plunder'd*,   35
   Friendship, to me, was but *Repentance*.

10.

At *School* I thought like other *Children*,
   Instead of *Brains*, a fine Ingredient,
Romance, my *youthful Head bewildering*,
   To *Sense* had made me disobedient.   40

11.

A victim, *nearly* from affection,
   To certain *very precious scheming*,
The still recurring recollection,
   Has *cured* my *boyish soul* of *Dreaming*.

12.

By Heaven! I rather would foreswear   45
   This Earth, and all the joys reserved me,
Than dare again the *specious Snare*,
   From which *my Fate* and *Heaven preserved* me.

13.

Still I possess some Friends who love me—
   In each a much esteemed and true one,   50
The Wealth of Worlds shall never move me
   To quit their Friendship, for a new one.

14.

But Becher! you're a *reverend pastor*,
    Now take it in consideration,
Whether for penance I should fast, or   55
    Pray for my *sins* in expiation.

15.

I own myself the child of *Folly*,
    But not so wicked as they make me—
I soon must die of melancholy,
    If *female* Smiles should e'er forsake me.   60

16.

Philosophers have *never doubted*,
    That *Ladies' Lips* were made for *Kisses!*
For *Love!* I could not live without it,
    In such a *cursed* place as *This is.*

17.

Say, Becher, shall I be forgiven?   65
    If *you* don't *warrant* my salvation,
I must resign *all Hopes of Heaven!*
    For, *Faith*, I can't withstand *Temptation.*

25 Feb. 1807

110   To the Author of a Sonnet Beginning Thus,
'Sad is Thy Verse You Cry and Yet No Tear
Etc. Etc.'

1.

Thy verse is 'sad' enough, no doubt:
    A devilish deal more sad than witty!
Why we should weep I can't find out,
    Unless for *thee* we weep in pity.

110. Copy text: *1832*, collated with *MS. T, C, More*
title   To The Author of a Sonnet Beginning, 'Sad is My Verse', You say, 'And Yet No
Tear' *1832, C, More*
    3 we] ⟨she⟩ *T*

2.

Yet there is one I pity more;   5
And much, alas! I think he needs it:
For he, I'm sure, will suffer sore,
Who, to his own misfortune, reads it.

3.

Thy rhymes, without the aid of Magic,
May *once* be read—but never after: 10
Yet their effect's by no means tragic,
Although by far too dull for laughter.

4.

But would you make our bosoms bleed,
And of no common pang complain—
If you would make us weep indeed,   15
Tell us, you'll read them o'er again.

                                                8 Mar. 1807

111   To an Oak in the Garden of Newstead Abbey, planted by the Author in the 9th Year of his age; this tree at his last visit was in a state of decay, though perhaps not irrecoverable.—15th March 1807

[1.]

Young Oak! when I planted thee deep in the ground,
  I hoped that thy days would be longer than mine;
That thy dark-waving branches would flourish around,
  And ivy thy trunk with her mantle entwine.
Such, such was my hope, when, in infancy's years,   5
  On the land of my fathers I viewed thee with pride:
They are past, and I water thy stem with my tears,—
  Thy decay not the weeds that surround thee can hide.

9 rhymes] ⟨strains⟩ T   12 Although] ⟨In sooth⟩ T

111. Copy text: *1832*, collated with *MSS. Na, Nb, Nc, C, More*
  4 her] its *Nc, 1832, C, More*   her mantle] ⟨affection⟩ *Na*   6 viewed] rear'd *Nc,*
1832, C, More,   pride] ⟨joy⟩ *Na*   7 They] ⟨Now⟩ They *Na*   8 Thy . . .] ⟨And
For the weeds that⟩ *Na*

2.

I left thee, my Oak, and, since that fatal hour,
    A stranger has dwelt in the hall of my sire;   10
Till manhood shall crown me, not mine is the power,
    But his, whose neglect may have bade thee expire.
Oh! hardy thou wert—even now little care
    Might revive thy young head, and thy wounds gently heal:
But thou wert not fated affection to share—   15
    For who could suppose that a Stranger would feel?

3.

Ah, droop not, my Oak! lift thy head for a while;
    Ere twice round yon Glory, this planet shall run,
The hand of thy Master will teach thee to smile,
    When Infancy's years of probation are done.   20
Oh, live then, my Oak! tower aloft from the weeds,
    That clog thy young growth, and assist thy decay,
For still in thy bosom are life's early seeds,
    And still may thy branches their beauty display.

4.

Oh! yet, if maturity's years may be thine,   25
    Though *I* shall lie low in the cavern of death,
On thy leaves yet the day-beam for ages may shine,
    Uninjured by time, or the rude winter's breath.
For centuries still may thy boughs lightly wave
    O'er the corse of thy lord, in the canopy laid;   30
While the branches thus gratefully shelter his grave,
    The chief who survives may recline in thy shade.

5.

And as he, with his boys, shall revisit the spot,
    He will tell them in whispers more softly to tread.

9–10 since . . . dwelt] ⟨a stranger has dwelt Since that hour⟩ *Na*   14 gently] ⟨lightly⟩
Na   15 But . . .] ⟨Ah! / But none but thy masters⟩ *Na*   16 could . . . would]
⟨would . . . could⟩ *Na*   21 tower . . . weeds] ⟨and if thou canst in weather⟩ *Na*
22 and . . . decay] ⟨but resist not the weather⟩ *Na*   26 death] ⟨Fate⟩ *Na*   27 On . . .
for] ⟨Thy leaves in the Sunbeam of⟩ *Na*   for] of *Nc, 1832, C, More*   28 rude
winter's] ⟨Winter's rude⟩ *Na*   29 For . . . boughs lightly] ⟨And . . . Canopy / Boughs
gently⟩ *Na*   30 lord] ⟨Planter⟩ *Na*   31 thus gratefully] ⟨in gratitude⟩ *Na*
32 The . . . survives] ⟨Some Chief of that hour⟩ *Na*   33 with] ⟨oer⟩ *Na*   the] this
1832, C, More

Ah! surely, by these I shall ne'er be forgot: 35
Remembrance still hallows the dust of the dead.
And here, will they say, when in life's glowing prime,
Perhaps he has pour'd forth his young simple lay,
And here must he sleep, till the moments of time
Are lost in the hours of Eternity's day.   40

15 Mar. 1807

112   Adieu to the Muse

1.

Thou Power! who hast ruled me through infancy's days,
Young offspring of Fancy, 'tis time we should part;
Then rise on the gale this the last of my lays,
The coldest effusion which springs from my heart.

2.

This bosom, responsive to rapture no more,   5
Shall hush thy wild notes, nor implore thee to sing;
The feelings of childhood, which taught thee to soar,
Are wafted far distant on Apathy's wing.

3.

Though simple the themes of my rude flowing Lyre,
Yet even those themes are departed for ever;   10
No more beam the eyes which my dream could inspire,
My visions are flown, to return,—ah never!

4.

When drain'd is the nectar which gladdened the bowl,
How vain is the effort delight to prolong!

35 Ah] Oh *1832, C, More*   36 dust] ⟨name⟩ *Na*   37, 40 *punctuation supplied*
from Nc

112. Copy text: *1832*, collated with *MS. T, MS. Ta, Pratt*
title   Farewell to the Muse *Ta, 1832, C, More*

3 ⟨Thou shalt not perish⟩ ⟨Direct / Protect I implore thee⟩ this last of my lays *T*
4 The coldest] ⟨Then ? / Nor spurn / The swift light⟩ *T*   5 ⟨The heart which I saw⟩ *T*
8 Are ⟨chilled by⟩ *T*   10 those] these *Ta, 1832, C, More*   11 ⟨The eyes are no more which
once⟩ could inspire *T*   12 ah] alas *Ta, 1832, C, More*   13–14 ⟨When the glow is no /cold
which awakened the Soul | How vain is the effort my / the strain to prolong⟩ *T*   13 glad-
dened] gladdens *Ta, 1832, C, More*

When cold is the beauty which dwelt in my soul,   15
What magic of Fancy can lengthen my song?

5.

Can the lips sing of Love in the desert alone,
    Of kisses and smiles which they now must resign?
Or dwell with delight on the hours that are flown?
    Ah, no! for those hours can no longer be mine.   20

6.

Can they speak of the friends whom I lived but to love?
    Ah, surely affection ennobles the strain!
But how can my numbers in sympathy move,
    When I scarcely can hope to behold them again?

7.

Can I sing of the deeds which my Fathers have done,   25
    And raise my loud harp to the fame of my Sires?
For glories like theirs, oh, how faint is my tone!
    For Heroes' exploits how unequal my fires!

8.

Untouch'd, then, my Lyre shall reply to the blast—
    'Tis hush'd; and my feeble endeavours are o'er;   30
And those who have heard it will pardon the past,
    When they know that its murmurs shall vibrate no more.

9.

And soon shall its wild erring notes be forgot,
    Since early affection and love is o'ercast:
Oh! blest had my fate been, and happy my lot,   35
    Had the first strain of love been the dearest, the last.

18 ⟨When Beauty no longer ? with a smile / When a smile or a passion no longer be mine⟩ T
19 flown] ⟨gone⟩ T   21 whom] ⟨that⟩ T; that *1832*, C, *More*   22 ⟨Affection
demands / Ah ah! no for affection too weak is / No ah! Friendship no more can awaken my
strain⟩ T   ennobles] ⟨is worthy⟩ T   23 ⟨But how can the heart with affection / the
harp in unison move⟩ But how ⟨the Harpstrings⟩ in ⟨ecstacy⟩ move T   24 ⟨To those
whom I hope to behold⟩ T   25 ⟨Can I sing of the few who are low in the dust⟩ T
27 ⟨Too faint is my voice, and enfeebled the tone⟩ T   30 my] ⟨its⟩ T   33 wild
erring] ⟨faults and its⟩ T   34 ⟨For few ? and hopes of the / When Friendship and Love⟩ T
is] are C, *More*   35 had ⟨I been⟩ my T   36 Had the first ⟨simple strain of my Love
been⟩ the last T

10.

Farewell, my young Muse! since we now can ne'er meet;
  If our songs have been languid, they surely are few:
  Let us hope that the present at least will be sweet—
  The present—which seals our eternal Adieu.   40

[1807]

113   Stanzas to Jessy

1.

There is a mystic thread of life
  So dearly wreath'd with mine alone,
That destiny's relentless knife
  At once must sever both, or none.

2.

There is a Form on which these eyes   5
  Have fondly gaz'd with such delight—
By day, that Form their joy supplies,
  And dreams restore it through the night.

3.

There is a voice whose tones inspire
  Such soften'd feelings in my breast,   10
I would not hear a seraph choir,
  Unless that voice could join the rest.

4.

There is a face whose blushes tell
  Affection's tale upon the cheek,
But pallid at our fond farewell   15
  Proclaims more love than words can speak.

37 since . . . meet] ⟨our offences are oer / we shall neer meet again⟩ T   38 If our
⟨efforts were feeble, at least they⟩ are few T   39 ⟨We will ? that our Song is more ? /
To none but ourselves⟩ T   40 ⟨Repent and atone / And atone for / And repent of a
sin / fault⟩ T   eternal] ⟨lasting⟩ T

113. Copy text: *Monthly Literary Recreations*; collated with *MS. BM*, the unauthorized
editions of *RM1816* and *Phil1820*

  6 Have often gazed with fond delight *Phil1820*   7 joy] joys *Phil1820*   10 Such
. . . feelings] Such thrills of Rapture *Phil1820*

5.

There is a Lip which mine has prest,
  But none had ever prest before;
It vowed to make me sweetly blest,
  That mine alone should press it more.   20

6.

There is a bosom all my own,
  Has pillow'd oft this aching head,
A mouth, which smiles on me alone,
  An eye, whose tears with mine are shed.

7.

There are two hearts whose movements thrill   25
  In unison so closely sweet,
That pulse to pulse responsive still,
  They both must heave, or cease to beat.

8.

There are two souls whose equal flow
  In gentle stream so calmly run,   30
That when they part—they part?—ah no!
  They cannot part—those souls are one.

                                        [1807]

114   Epitaph on John Adams of Southwell, A Carrier Who Died of Drunkenness

John Adams lies here, of the parish of Southwell,
A *Carrier* who *carried* his Can to his mouth well;
He *carried* so much, and he *carried* so fast,
He could *carry* no more—so was *carried* at last;
For, the liquor he drank, being too much for one,   5
He could not *carry off*,—so he's now *carri-on*.

                              Sept. 1807

17 has] hath *RM1816*, *Phil1820*   18 But] And *Phil1820*   20 That mine
alone] And mine—mine only *Phil1820*   22 Has] Hath *Phil1820*   28 They]
That *Phil1820*   30 stream] streams *RM1816*, *Phil1820*   32 those] their *RM1816*

114. Copy text: *Life*, collated with *MS. M*

115   [On Revisiting Harrow]

1.

Here once engaged the Stranger's view
　Young Friendship's record simply traced;
Few were her words,—but yet though few,
　Resentment's hand the line defaced.

2.

Deeply she cut—but, not erased,　　　　　　　　5
　The characters were still so plain,
That Friendship once return'd, and gazed,—
　Till Memory hail'd the words again.

3.

Repentence placed them as before;
　Forgiveness join'd her gentle name;　　　　　10
So fair the inscription seem'd once more,
　That Friendship thought it still the same.

4.

Thus might the Record now have been;
　But, ah, in spite of Hope's endeavour,
Or Friendship's tear, Pride rush'd between,　　15
　And blotted out the line for ever!

B. Sept. 1807.

116   To My Son

1.

Those flaxen locks, those eyes of blue,
Bright as thy mother's in their hue;
Those rosy lips, whose dimples play
And smile to steal the heart away,
Recall a scene of former joy,　　　　　　　　5
And touch thy father's heart, my Boy!

115. Copy text: *Life*, collated with *MS. M*
title　*from 1831*
　13 now] ⟨yet⟩ *M*　　　15 tear] tear⟨s⟩ *M*; tears *Life, 1831, 1832, C, More*
116. Copy text: *Life*, collated with *MS. M*
　2 thy . . . in their] ⟨their . . . azure⟩ *M*

2.

And thou canst lisp a father's name—
Ah, William, were thine own the same,
No self-reproach—but, let me cease—
My care for thee shall purchase peace;   10
Thy mother's shade shall smile in joy,
And pardon all the past, my Boy!

3.

Her lowly grave the turf has prest,
And thou hast known a stranger's breast.
Derision sneers upon thy birth,   15
And yields thee scarce a name on earth;
Yet shall not these one hope destroy,—
A Father's heart is thine, my Boy!

4.

Why, let the world unfeeling frown,
Must I fond Nature's claim disown?   20
Ah, no—though moralists reprove,
I hail thee, dearest child of love,
Fair cherub, pledge of youth and joy—
A Father guards thy birth, my Boy!

5.

Oh, 'twill be sweet in thee to trace,   25
Ere age has wrinkled o'er my face,
Ere half my glass of life is run,
At once a brother and a son;
And all my wane of years employ
In justice done to thee, my Boy!   30

6.

Although so young thy heedless sire,
Youth will not damp parental fire;
And, wert thou still less dear to me,
While Helen's form revives in thee,
The breast, which beat to former joy,   35
Will ne'er desert its pledge, my Boy!

[1807]

15 sneers] ⟨smiles⟩ M   23 Fair ⟨Thou⟩ M

117   Verses, Written in Compliance with a Lady's Request to Contribute to her Album

They say that Love had once a book,
  (The urchin loves to copy you)
Where all who came a pencil took,
  And wrote, perhaps, a word or two.

'Twas Innocence, that maid divine,   5
  Who kept this volume bright and fair,
And watch'd that no unhallow'd line
  Should ever find admittance there.

And sweetly did the pages fill
  With fond device of loving lore,   10
Till every line she wrote was still
  More bright than that she wrote before.

Beneath the touch of Hope how soft,
  How swift the magic pencil ran,
Till Fear would come, alas! as oft,   15
  And, trembling, close what Hope began.

A tear or two had dropp'd from Grief,
  And Jealousy would now and then
Ruffle in haste a snowy leaf,
  Which Love had still to smooth again.   20

But oh! there was a blooming boy
  Who sometimes turn'd the pages o'er,
And wrote therein such lines of joy,
  That all who read them wish'd for more.

And Pleasure was the spirit's name;   25
  And tho' so soft his voice and look,
Yet Innocence, whene'er he came,
  Would tremble for her spotless book.

117. Copy text: *The Casket* (1829)

For well she knew his rosy fingers
   Were fill'd with sweet and wanton joys,   30
And well she knew the stain that lingers
   After sweets from wanton boys.

And so it happ'd—one luckless night
   He let his honey'd goblet fall
O'er the poor book, so fair and white,   35
   And sullied lines, and marge, and all.

In vain he strove, with eager lip,
   The honey from the book to drink,
But oh! the more the boy would sip,
   The deeper still the blot would sink.   40

Oh! it would make you weep to see
   The progress of the honey'd flood
Steal o'er a page where Modesty
   Had freshly drawn a rose's bud.

And Fancy's emblems lost their hue,   45
   And Hope's sweet lines were all defac'd,
And Love himself now scarcely knew
   The lines that he had lately trac'd.

The index now alone remains
   Of all the pages spoilt by Pleasure,   50
And though it bears some honey stains,
   Yet Memory counts this leaf a treasure.

And oft, they say, she scans it o'er;
   And oft, by this memorial aided,
Recalls those scenes, alas! no more,   55
   And brings back lines which long had faded.

I know not if the tale be true,
   But thus the simple facts are stated,
And I refer the truth to you,
   For *Love* and *you* are near related.   60

[1808?]

118 ['There Was a Time I Need Not Name']

There was a time, I need not name,
    Since it will ne'er forgotten be,
When all our feelings were the same,
    As still my soul hath been to thee.

And from that hour when first thy tongue   5
    Confess'd a love which equall'd mine,
Though many a grief my heart hath wrung,
    Unknown, and thus unfelt, by thine:

None, none, hath sunk so deep as this,
    To think how all that love hath flown;   10
Transient as every faithless kiss,
    But transient in thy breast alone.

And yet my heart some solace knew,
    When late I heard thy lips declare,
In accents once imagin'd true,   15
    Remembrance of the days that were.

Yes! my adored, yet most unkind!
    Though thou wilt never love again,
To me 'tis doubly sweet to find
    Remembrance of that love remain.   20

Yes! 'tis a glorious thought to me,
    Nor longer shall my soul repine,
Whate'er thou art, or e'er shalt be,
    Thou hast been dearly, solely mine.

[1808]

118. Copy text: *IT*, collated with *MS. M*

title *1832*; To G.J.F.S.D. *M*; Stanzas to the Same *IT*; Stanzas to—. *1831*

4 my soul hath] *my heart has M*   10 flown] ⟨past⟩ *M*   20 Remembrance] The Memory *M*

119   ## Song

1.

Breeze of the night! in gentler sighs
  More gently murmur o'er the billow;
For Slumber seals my Fanny's eyes,
  And Peace must never shun her pillow.

2.

Oh breathe those sweet Aeolian strains   5
  Stolen from celestial spheres above,
To charm her ear while sense remains
  And soothe her soul to dreams of love.

3.

But Breeze of Night! again forebear,
  In softest murmurs only sigh;   10
Let not a Zephyr's pinion dare
  To lift those auburn locks on high.

4.

Chill is thy Breath, thou breeze of night!
  Oh! ruffle not those lids of Snow;
For only Morning's cheering light   15
  May wake the beam that lurks below.

5.

Blest be that lip and azure eye!
  Sweet Fanny, hallowed be thy Sleep!
Those lips shall never vent a sigh,
  Those eyes may never wake to weep.   20

23 July 1808

119. Copy text: *C*, collated with *MS. M*

1 in gentler sighs] ⟨more softly sigh⟩ *M*   2 gently] softly *C*   billow] pillow *C*
5 Oh] Or *C*   7 sense] some *C*   19 lips ... vent a] ⟨eyes ... ope to⟩ *M*

120   ['And Wilt Thou Weep When I Am Low']

And wilt thou weep when I am low?
　　Sweet lady! speak those words again;
Yet if they grieve thee, say not so,
　　I would not give that bosom pain.

My heart is sad, my hopes are gone,   5
　　My blood runs coldly thro' my breast;
And when I perish, thou alone
　　Wilt sigh above my place of rest.

And yet methinks a gleam of peace
　　Doth thro' my cloud of anguish shine,   10
And for awhile my sorrows cease
　　To know thy heart hath felt for mine.

Oh, lady! blessed be that tear,
　　It falls for one who cannot weep;
Such precious drops are doubly dear   15
　　To those whose eyes no tear may steep.

Sweet lady! once my heart was warm,
　　With every feeling soft as thine,
But beauty's self hath ceas'd to charm
　　A wretch created to repine.   20

Yet wilt thou weep when I am low?
　　Sweet lady! speak those words again;
Yet if they grieve thee, say not so,
　　I would not give that bosom pain.

                                        [1808]

120. Copy text: *IT*, collated with *MS. M, MS. T*
title *1831*; To the Same *IT*; Stanzas *M*; *untitled T*
　15–16 For one whose life is torment here | And only in the dust may sleep. *M*
16 may] can *T*   17 heart] soul *M*   18 soft] ⟨pure⟩ *M*   *In M is an uncancelled
stanza between present stanzas 5 and 6:*
　　　　　　　　　　Lady! I will not tell my tale
　　　　　　　　　　　For it would rend thy melting heart
　　　　　　　　　　Twere pity, sorrow should prevail
　　　　　　　　　　　Oer one so gentle as thou art.

121   ['Remind Me Not, Remind Me Not']

Remind me not, remind me not,
    Of those belov'd, those vanish'd hours,
    When all my soul was given to thee;
Hours that may never be forgot
    Till time unnerves our vital powers,   5
    And thou and I shall cease to be.

Can I forget? canst thou forget?
    When playing with thy golden hair
    How quick thy fluttering heart did move?
Oh! by my soul, I see thee yet,   10
    With eyes so languid, breast so fair,
    And lips, though silent, breathing love.

When thus reclining on my breast
    Those eyes threw back a glance so sweet,
    As half reproach'd, yet rais'd desire,   15
And still we near, and nearer prest,
    And still our glowing lips would meet,
    As if in kisses to expire.

And then those pensive eyes would close,
    And bid their lids each other seek,   20
    Veiling the azure orbs below;
While their long lashes' darkening gloss
    Seemed stealing o'er thy brilliant cheek,
    Like raven's plumage smooth'd on snow.

I dreamt last night our love return'd,   25
    And sooth to say that very dream
    Was sweeter in its phantasy

121. Copy text: *IT*, collated with *MS. M*
title   *1831*; To D.D.W.D.G. *M*; A Love Song. To——*IT*; To Mary *Paris 1828*
    2 belov'd, those vanish'd] beloved, vanished   25–30 *Not in MS.; a different stanza
appears in the MS. but is entirely cancelled:*
                    Remind me not, remind me not
                    Though hours like these no more we know
                ⌠ Since most of pleasures ever flee
                ⌡ Yet cherished in my heart they be

Than if for other hearts I burn'd,
   For eyes that ne'er like thine could beam
      In rapture's wild reality.   30

Then tell me not, remind me not
   Of hours which, though for ever gone,
      Can still a pleasing dream restore,
Till thou and I shall be forgot;
   And senseless as the mouldering stone,   35
      Which tells that we shall be no more.

[1808]

122   To a Youthful Friend

1.

Few years have pass'd since thou and I
   Were firmest friends, at least in name,
And childhood's gay sincerity
   Preserv'd our feelings long the same.

2.

But now, like me, too well thou know'st   5
   What trifles oft the heart recall;
And those who once have lov'd the most
   Too soon forget they lov'd at all.

Whatever joy may be my lot
All present rapture I'd forego
In hours long past, but past with thee.

31 Remind me not, remind me not *M*   33 ⟨Must still recall / Can summon our for-
gotten⟩ *M*   34 shall be] are both *M*   36 tells . . . no] ⟨hides our bones forever⟩ *M*

122. Copy text: *CHP(7)*, collated with *MS. M, Proof M, Proof H, IT, CHP(2)–CHP(6), CHP(8)–CHP(10)*

title   *all printed texts;* To Sir W. D. on his using the expression 'Soyez bien constant en Amitie'. *M; Proof M cancels M title and adds received title in MS.*

1–4   Twere well my friend if still with thee
                               Through every scene of joy or woe,
                               That thought could ever cherished be
                               As warm as it was wont to glow. *M, cancelled in Proof M*
5 now] ⟨yet⟩ *Proof M*   8 Forget they ever lov'd at all. *IT, CHP(2)–CHP(6)*

3.

And such the change the heart displays,
     So frail is early friendship's reign,   10
A month's brief lapse, perhaps a day's,
     Will view thy mind estrang'd again.

4.

If so, it never shall be mine
     To mourn the loss of such a heart;
The fault was Nature's fault not thine,   15
     Which made thee fickle as thou art.

5.

As rolls the ocean's changing tide,
     So human feelings ebb and flow;
And who would in a breast confide
     Where stormy passions ever glow?   20

6.

It boots not, that together bred,
     Our childish days were days of joy;
My spring of life has quickly fled;
     Thou, too, hast ceas'd to be a boy.

7.

And when we bid adieu to youth,   25
     Slaves to the specious world's controul,
We sigh a long farewell to truth;
     That world corrupts the noblest soul.

8.

Ah, joyous season! when the mind
     Dares all things boldly but to lie;   30
When thought ere spoke is unconfin'd,
     And sparkles in the placid eye.

10 frail] short *M, cor. in Proof M*   11 perhaps] perchance *IT*   12 Will send my
friendship back again. *M*   20 Where ever transient passions glow. *M*; stormy passions
Proof M   23 has quickly] at length has *M*, Proof *M*   24 hast] has *Proof M*
28   Courage is manhood's proudest boast,
                     Cold Prudence cautious Age employs,
                     Affection woman feels the most,
                     Sincerity is left for boys. *printed after line 28 in Proof M*
29–36 *Not in M, added to Proof M in MS.*   29 joyous] pleasing *Proof M*   31 thought
ere spoke] ⟨every thought⟩ *Proof M*

9.

Not so in Man's maturer years,
   When Man himself is but a tool,
When interest sways our hopes and fears,   35
   And all must love and hate by rule.

10.

With fools in kindred vice the same,
   We learn at length our faults to blend,
And those, and those alone may claim
   The prostituted name of friend.   40

11.

Such is the common lot of man:
   Can we then 'scape from folly free?
Can we reverse the general plan,
   Nor be what all in turn must be?

12.

No, for myself so dark my fate   45
   Through every turn of life hath been;
Man and the world I so much hate,
   I care not when I quit the scene.

13.

But thou, with spirit frail and light,
   Wilt shine awhile and pass away,   50
As glow-worms sparkle through the night,
   But dare not stand the test of day.

14.

Alas! whenever folly calls
   Where parasites and princes meet,
(For cherish'd first in royal halls,   55
   The welcome vices kindly greet)

37–9   Each fool whose vices are the same
                 Whose faults with ours may chance to blend
                 With open arms received will claim *M, cor. in Proof M*
39 And specious spoilers inly, claim *Proof M*   45 dark] ⟨murk⟩ *M*   47 I so much] so much I *M*   49 with spirit] whose mind is *M, Proof M*   53 ⟨Then go, where gaudy⟩ folly calls *M*

15.

Ev'n now thou'rt nightly seen to add
One insect to the fluttering crowd;
And still thy trifling heart is glad,
To join the vain, and court the proud.   60

16.

There dost thou glide from fair to fair,
Still simpering on with eager haste,
As flies along the gay parterre,
That taint the flowers they scarcely taste.

17.

But say, what nymph will prize the flame   65
Which seems, as marshy vapours move,
To flit along from dame to dame,
An ignis-fatuus gleam of love?

18.

What friend for thee, howe'er inclin'd,
Will deign to own a kindred care?   70
Who will debase his manly mind,
For friendship every fool may share.

19.

In time forbear; amidst the throng
No more so base a thing be seen;
No more so idly pass along: 75
Be something, any thing, but—mean.

[1808]

123   ['Well! Thou Art Happy']

1.

Well! thou art happy, and I feel
That I should thus be happy too;

57 Ev'n] CHP(7)–CHP(10), 1831, 1832; E'en M, Proof M, IT, CHP(2)–CHP(6)
58 fluttering] Proof M, IT, CHP(7)–CHP(10), 1831, 1832; flattering M, CHP(2)–CHP(6)
61 glide] fleet M   73 In time] Oh! then M   75 pass] glide M

123. Copy text: CHP(7), collated with MS. M, the Proof, IT, and CHP(2)–CHP(6) and CHP(8)–CHP(10)
title from 1831; To Mrs. M— M cancelled; To —— IT and printings to 1831

For still my heart regards thy weal
  Warmly, as it was wont to do.

2.

Thy husband's blest—and 'twill impart   5
  Some pangs to view his happier lot:
But let them pass—Oh! how my heart
  Would hate him, if he lov'd thee not!

3.

When late I saw thy favourite child,
  I thought my jealous heart would break;   10
But when th' unconscious infant smil'd,
  I kiss'd it, for its mother's sake.

4.

I kiss'd it, and repress'd my sighs
  Its father in its face to see;
But then it had its mother's eyes,   15
  And they were all to love and me.

5.

Mary, adieu! I must away:
  While thou art blest I'll not repine;
But near thee I can never stay;
  My heart would soon again be thine.   20

6.

I deem'd that time, I deem'd that pride
  Had quench'd at length my boyish flame;
Nor knew, till seated by thy side,
  My heart in all, save hope, the same.

7.

Yet was I calm: I knew the time   25
  My breast would thrill before thy look;
But now to tremble were a crime—
  We met, and not a nerve was shook.

6 view . . . lot] see my rival's lot *M*
16   Poor little Pledge of mutual love!
                  I would not hurt a hair of thee,
              Although thy birth should chance to prove
                  Thy parents' Bliss! —my misery!— *stanza after line 16 in M*

26 look] ⟨gaze⟩ *M*

8.

I saw thee gaze upon my face,
    Yet meet with no confusion there: 30
One only feeling could'st thou trace;
    The sullen calmness of despair.

9.

Away! away! my early dream
    Remembrance never must awake:
Oh! where is Lethe's fabled stream?   35
    My foolish heart be still, or break.

[1808]

124   Lines inscribed upon a Cup formed from a
        Skull

1.

Start not!—nor deem my spirit fled:
    In me behold the only skull,
From which, unlike a living head,
    Whatever flows is never dull.

2.

I lived—I loved—I quaff'd like thee;   5
    I died—let earth my bones resign.
Fill up—thou canst not injure me;
    The worm hath fouler lips than thine.

3.

Better to hold the sparkling grape
    Than nurse the earth-worm's slimy brood;   10
And circle in the goblet's shape
    The drink of Gods, than reptile's food.

32 sullen calmness] ⟨Resignation⟩ M

124. Copy text: CHP(7), collated with MSS. M, Ma, the Proof, CHP(8)–CHP(10)
    3 which] whom M   10 earth-worm's] Slowworm's M

4.

Where once my wit perchance hath shone,
  In aid of others' let me shine;
And when, alas! our brains are gone,
  What nobler substitute than wine!   15

5.

Quaff while thou canst—another race,
  When thou and thine like me are sped,
May rescue thee from earth's embrace,
  And rhyme and revel with the dead.   20

6.

Why not? since through life's little day
  Our heads such sad effects produce;
Redeemed from worms and wasting clay,
  This chance is theirs to be of use.

                              Newstead Abbey, 1808

125   Inscription on the Monument of a
              Newfoundland Dog

When some proud son of man returns to earth,
Unknown to glory, but upheld by birth,
The sculptor's art exhausts the pomp of woe,
And storied urns record who rests below;
When all is done, upon the tomb is seen,   5
Not what he was, but what he should have been:
But the poor dog, in life the firmest friend,
The first to welcome, foremost to defend,
Whose honest heart is still his master's own,
Who labours, fights, lives, breathes for him alone,   10

18–20 ⟨To thee as thou to me unknown | May give thy head my genial place | Then—
empty mine, and Fill thine own!⟩ M   21–4 added in M   21 life's little day] ⟨this
little life⟩ M   22 Our] ⟨So many⟩ M   23 ⟨For once then try one⟩ M   wasting]
⟨rotting / mouldering⟩ M   24 This . . . theirs] ⟨This / One chance they have⟩ M

125. Copy text: Corsair(7), collated with MS. M, Proofs a and b, IT, and Corsair(2)–
Corsair(9)

title   Epitaph on a favourite Newfoundland Dog, born in Newfoundland in March 1803
died at Newstead Notts. Nov. 10th 1808. M   Newfoundland] Favourite IT, Proof a,
cor. in Proof b

Unhonoured falls, unnoticed all his worth,
Denied in heaven the soul he held on earth:
While man, vain insect! hopes to be forgiven,
And claims himself a sole exclusive heaven.
Oh man! thou feeble tenant of an hour,   15
Debased by slavery, or corrupt by power,
Who knows thee well must quit thee with disgust,
Degraded mass of animated dust!
Thy love is lust, thy friendship all a cheat,
Thy smiles hypocrisy, thy words deceit!   20
By nature vile, ennobled but by name,
Each kindred brute might bid thee blush for shame.
Ye! who perchance behold this simple urn,
Pass on—it honours none you wish to mourn:
To mark a friend's remains these stones arise,   25
I never knew but one, and here he lies.

                                                    1808

126   The Farewell to a Lady

When man expell'd from Eden's bowers,
    A moment linger'd near the gate,
Each scene recall'd the vanish'd hours,
    And bade him curse his future fate.

But wandering on through distant climes,   5
    He learnt to bear his load of grief;
Just gave a sigh to other times,
    And found in busier scenes relief.

Thus, lady! will it be with me,
    And I must view thy charms no more;   10
For while I linger near to thee
    I sigh for all I knew before.

20 Thy tongue hypocrisy, thy heart deceit *M*   26 I . . . one] I knew but one unchang'd *IT, cor. in MS. in ITB*

126. Copy text: *IT*, collated with *MS. M, MS. JH. ITB, ITBa, Paris 1826*
title   To Mrs.——, on being asked my Reason for quitting England in the Spring *M, 1831;* To Mrs. M. C. *JH;* To a Lady, on . . . Spring *1832, More*
5 through] to *JH*   9 lady] Mary *M, JH*   11 while *JH, MS. cor. in ITBa, 1831, 1832* whilst *M, IT, Paris1826*

In flight I shall be surely wise,
   Escaping from temptation's snare;
I cannot view my Paradise   15
   Without the wish of dwelling there.

[1808]

127   [Verses Found in a Summer House at
Hales-Owen]

When Dryden's fool, 'unknowing what he sought',
His hours in whistling spent, 'for want of thought',
This guiltless oaf his vacancy of sense
Supplied, and amply too by innocence;
Did modern swains, possess'd of Cymon's powers,   5
In Cymon's manner waste their leisure hours,
Th' offended guests would not, with blushing, see
These fair green walks disgraced by infamy.
Severe the fate of modern fools, alas!
When vice and folly mark them as they pass.   10
Like noxious reptiles o'er the whiten'd wall,
The filth they leave still points out where they crawl.

[1808?]

128   [Three Epigrams]

128a On the King's Speech to the Bishop of Bristol

When royal George the mitre placed
   Upon the sprightliest head of Cam,
Thus spoke the King his high behest
   'Doctor, we've done with Epigram!'

16 *cor. MS. reading in ITB, ITBa;* Without a wish to sojourn there. *cancelled MS. cor. in ITB;* Without a wish to enter there. *M, JH, IT, Paris1826*

127. Copy text: *1832*

128. Copy text: *MS. M*

Alas! my liege thy maddest fits 5
Could hardly conjure such a wish up,
For Christ-sake! make thy *Bishops* wits,
Not sink a *wit* into a—*Bishop.*—

128b On the Same

From Crown and Mitre Wit alike hath flown,
George damped poor Mansel's and hath lost his own.

128c · · ·

Grieve, Grieve no more, whom no high honours wait,
But view the evils of exalted State:
Cares of a Crown have addled George's skull,
And lo! a Mitre makes our Mansel dull.

[1808]

129 English Bards and Scotch Reviewers.

A Satire

I had rather be a kitten, and cry, mew!
Than one of these same metre ballad-mongers.
Shakespeare [*I Henry IV*, iii. i. 128–9].

Such shameless Bards we have; and yet 'tis true,
There are as mad, abandon'd Critics too.
Pope [*Essay on Criticism*, 610–11].

PREFACE

ALL my friends, learned and unlearned, have urged me not to
publish this Satire with my name. If I were to be 'turn'd from the
career of my humour by quibbles quick, and paper bullets of the

129. Copy text: *EBSR5*, collated with *MSS. M* (comprising *MF*, *MQ*, *MB*), *BB*, the
series of MS. fragments *A* and *L*, and all the early authorized editions of *EBSR*, and *EBSR5a*
title The British Bards, a satire *BB*
epigraphs *not in MSS.*
Preface [*MS. M* does not have the Preface, nor does *EBSR1* or *EBSR5*. Text of the Preface
here taken from *EBSR5a. MS. BB* and *EBSR1a* have only the last paragraph of the Preface

brain', I should have complied with their counsel. But I am not to be
5 terrified by abuse, or bullied by reviewers, with or without arms.
I can safely say that I have attacked none *personally* who did not
commence on the offensive. An Author's works are public property:
he who purchases may judge, and publish his opinion if he pleases;
and the Authors I have endeavoured to commemorate may do by
10 me as I have done by them: I dare say they will succeed better in
condemning my scribblings, than in mending their own. But my
object is not to prove that I can write well, but, *if possible*, to make
others write better.

As the Poem has met with far more success than I expected, I
15 have endeavoured in this Edition to make some additions and
alterations to render it more worthy of public perusal.

In the First Edition of this Satire, published anonymously,
fourteen lines on the subject of Bowles's Pope were written and
inserted at the request of an ingenious friend of mine, who has now
20 in the press a volume of Poetry. In the present Edition they are
erased, and some of my own substituted in their stead; my only
reason for this being that which I conceive would operate with
any other person in the same manner: a determination not to
publish with my name any production which was not entirely and
25 exclusively my own composition.

With regard to the real talents of many of the poetical persons
whose performances are mentioned, or alluded to in the following
pages, it is presumed by the Author that there can be little difference of opinion in the Public at large; though, like other sectaries,
30 each has his separate tabernacle of proselytes, by whom his abilities
are overrated, his faults overlooked, and his metrical canons
received without scruple and without consideration. But the
unquestionable possession of considerable genius by several of the
writers here censured, renders their mental prostitution more to be
35 regretted. Imbecility may be pitied, or, at worst, laughed at and
forgotten; perverted powers demand the most decided reprehension. No one can wish more than the Author, that some known
and able writer had undertaken their exposure, but Mr. GIFFORD
has devoted himself to Massinger, and in the absence of the regular
40 physician, a country practitioner, may in cases of absolute necessity,
be allowed to prescribe his nostrum to prevent the extension of so
deplorable an epidemic, provided there be no quackery in his

27 mentioned ... to] discuss(ing)ed *BB*   28–9 that there ... in] there ... among *BB*

treatment of the malady. A caustic is here offered, as it is to be feared nothing short of actual cautery can recover the numerous patients afflicted with the present prevalent and distressing *rabies* 45 for rhyming.—As to the *Edinburgh Reviewers;* it would, indeed, require a Hercules to crush the Hydra; but if the Author succeeds in merely 'bruising one of the heads of the serpent', though his own hand should suffer in the encounter, he will be amply satisfied.

Still must I hear?—shall hoarse FITZGERALD bawl
His creaking couplets in a tavern hall,
And I not sing, lest, haply, Scotch Reviews
Should dub me scribbler, and denounce my Muse?
Prepare for rhyme—I'll publish, right or wrong: 5
Fools are my theme, let Satire be my song.

  Oh! Nature's noblest gift—my grey goose-quill!
Slave of my thoughts, obedient to my will,
Torn from thy parent bird to form a pen,
That mighty instrument of little men!   10
The pen! foredoom'd to aid the mental throes
Of brains that labour, big with Verse or Prose,
Though Nymphs forsake, and Critics may deride
The Lover's solace, and the Author's pride.
What Wits! what Poets, dost thou daily raise!   15
How frequent is thy use, how small thy praise!
Condemned at length to be forgotten quite,
With all the pages which 'twas thine to write.
But thou, at least, mine own especial pen!
Once laid aside, but now assumed again,   20
Our task complete, like Hamet's shalt be free;
Tho' spurned by others, yet beloved by me:

---

43 treatment of] ⟨mode of treating⟩ *BB*   48 heads of the serpent] serpent's heads *BB*

1–96 *not in EBSR1, EBSR1a*   1 ⟨Prepare for rhyme⟩—shall ⟨dull⟩ Fitzgerald bawl *A*
Still must I] Must I still *A*   2 creaking] ⟨maudlin⟩ *A, MB*   4 scribbler] ⟨block-
head⟩ *A, MB*   5 I'll publish] away then *A;* I'll ⟨scribble⟩ *MB*   6 Truth be my
Muse, and censure ⟨be⟩ guide my song. *A;* Truth be my theme, and Censors guide my song!
MB   8 Slave of] Bound to *A, MB*   11 Foredoomed to aid the agonizing throes *A,*
MB   12 brains that] all ⟨who⟩ in *A*; all who *MB*   13–14 *transposed in A*
15 What ⟨great immortals / numbers of immortals hast thou raised⟩ *A*   16 How ⟨often
? ⟩ frequent *A*   19 pen] quill *A, MB*   20 Besprent with dew from Heliconian
Hill *A;* Dipt in the dewdrops of Parnassus' Hill *MB, cor. from A*   21–2 Shalt ever
honoured and regarded be | By more beside no doubt, yet still by me, *A, MB*

Then let us soar to-day, no common theme,
No Eastern vision, no distempered dream
Inspires—our path, though full of thorns, is plain;   25
Smooth be the verse, and easy be the strain.

When Vice triumphant holds her sov'reign sway,
Obey'd by all, who nought beside obey;
When Folly, frequent harbinger of crime,
Bedecks her cap with bells of every Clime,   30
When Knaves and Fools combined o'er all prevail,
And weigh their Justice in a Golden Scale,
E'en then the boldest start from public sneers,
Afraid of Shame, unknown to other fears,
More darkly sin, by Satire kept in awe,   35
And shrink from Ridicule, though not from Law.

Such is the force of Wit! but not belong
To me the arrows of satiric song;
The royal vices of our age demand
A keener weapon, and a mightier hand.   40
Still there are follies, e'en for me to chase,
And yield at least amusement in the race:
Laugh when I laugh, I seek no other fame,
The cry is up, and scribblers are my game:
Speed Pegasus!—ye strains of great and small,   45
Ode! Epic! Elegy!—have at you all!
I, too, can scrawl, and once upon a time
I poured along the town a flood of rhyme,
A school-boy freak, unworthy praise or blame;
I printed—older children do the same.   50
'Tis pleasant, sure, to see one's name in print;
A Book's a Book, altho' there's nothing in't.
Not that a Title's sounding charm can save
Or scrawl or scribbler from an equal grave:

---

25 Inspires] ⟨Demands / ? ⟩ A   26 ⟨Though⟩ Rude be the song, yet simple be the strain
A   28 And men through life her willing slaves obey MB, EBSR2, 3, 4, 4a   30 Unfolds
her motley store to suit the time MB, EBSR2, 3, 4, 4a   32 When Justice halts, and
Right begins to fail MB, EBSR2, 3, 4, 4a   34 of] ⟨from⟩ MB   35 darkly] secret
MB   39–40 Yet though I dare not try Ulysses' bow | Lest the keen shaft recoil and
lay me low A   40 ⟨The mortal purpose of / deathblow from a mightier hand⟩ MB
keener] mortal MB   41–6 not in MB   43 seek] ⟨ask⟩ A   47 scrawl] ⟨scribble⟩
A   48 along] upon MB   53 Yet names of noble lineage cannot save A; Yet
⟨names of⟩ Title's sounding lineage cannot save MB

This LAMB must own, since his Patrician name   55
Failed to preserve the spurious Farce from shame.
No matter, GEORGE continues still to write,
Tho' now the name is veiled from public sight.
Moved by the great example, I pursue
The self-same road, but make my own review: 60
Not seek great JEFFREY's yet like him will be
Self-constituted Judge of Poesy.

A man must serve his time to every trade
Save Censure; Critics all are ready made.
Take hackneyed jokes from MILLER, got by rote,   65
With just enough of learning to misquote;
A mind well skilled to find, or forge a fault,
A turn for punning, call it Attic salt;
To JEFFREY go, be silent and discreet,
His pay is just ten sterling pounds per sheet: 70
Fear not to lie, 'twill seem a sharper hit,
Shrink not from blasphemy, 'twill pass for wit;
Care not for feeling—pass your proper jest,
And stand a Critic hated, yet caress'd.

And shall we own such judgment? no—as soon   75
Seek roses in December, ice in June;
Hope constancy in wind, or corn in chaff,
Believe a woman, or an epitaph,
Or any other thing that's false, before
You trust in Critics who themselves are sore;   80
Or yield one single thought to be misled
By JEFFREY's heart, or LAMB's Boeotian head.

To these young tyrants, by themselves misplaced,
Combined usurpers on the Throne of Taste;
To these when Authors bend in humble awe,   85
And hail their voice as Truth, their word as Law;

55 ⟨Bard of the purple prose⟩ A; Lamb had his farce, but that Patrician name A, MB
56 Farce] brat A, MB   60 road] path A, MB   68 call it] ⟨called⟩ MB
69 ⟨Stick⟩ To A   70 pay is] hire of A, cor. MB   71 sharper] lively MB; lucky
EBSR2, 3, 4, 4a   72 blasphemy] impudence A   73 for ⟨truth, at random⟩ feeling A
74 hated, yet caress'd] to the world confest A   75–80 not in MB   81 Or yield ⟨a
manly⟩ your powers of mind to be misled MB   83 ⟨Such are / If⟩ To these ⟨the ? ⟩ young
tyrants A   84 on] of A   85 humble] silent A, cor. MB

While these are Censors, 'twould be sin to spare;
While such are Critics, why should I forbear?
But yet so near all modern worthies run,
'Tis doubtful whom to seek, or whom to shun: 90
Nor know we when to spare, or where to strike,
Our Bards and Censors are so much alike.

Then should you ask me, why I venture o'er
The path, which POPE and GIFFORD trod before?
If not yet sickened, you can still proceed;   95
Go on; my rhyme will tell you as you read.

But hold! exclaims a friend,—here's some neglect:
This—that—and 'tother line seem incorrect.
What then? the self-same blunder Pope has got,
And careless Dryden—aye—but Pye has not,—   100
Indeed!—'tis granted faith!—but what care I?
Better to err with POPE, than shine with PYE.

Time was, ere yet in these degenerate days
Ignoble themes obtained mistaken praise,
When Sense and Wit with Poesy allied,   105
No fabled Graces, flourished side by side,
From the same fount their inspiration drew,
And, reared by Taste, bloomed fairer as they grew.
Then, in this happy Isle, a POPE's pure strain
Sought the rapt soul to charm, nor sought in vain;   110
A polished nation's praise aspired to claim,
And rais'd the people's, as the poet's fame.
Like him great DRYDEN poured the tide of song,
In stream less smooth indeed, yet doubly strong.
Then CONGREVE's scenes could cheer, or OTWAY's
        melt;   115
For Nature then an English audience felt—

90 or whom] or what *MB*   93 ⟨But ? go oer⟩ *MB*   But should you ask me why I
then go oer *A, cor. MB*   95 ⟨If *then?* as I rhyme you care not to read⟩ *A*   96 tell]
⟨teach⟩ *A*   97–102 *added EBSR5*   97 But] Yet *L*   98 seem] seems *L*
101 'tis granted faith] ⟨then 'tis a fault⟩ 'tis bad enough *L*   109 happy] fairer *BB*
113 great] ⟨had⟩ *BB*   114 indeed] ⟨than his⟩ *BB*   115–16 [MS. addition in *BB*]:
Otway and Congreve mimic scenes had wove, | And Waller tun'd his lyre to mighty Love
[this couplet plus another, indecipherable, in pencil on margin of *BB*]

But why these names, or greater still, retrace,
When all to feebler Bards resign their place?
Yet to such times our lingering looks are cast,
When taste and reason with those times are past.   120
Now look around, and turn each trifling page,
Survey the precious works that please the age;
This truth at least let Satire's self allow,
No dearth of Bards can be complained of now:
The loaded Press beneath her labour groans,   125
And Printer's devils shake their weary bones,
While SOUTHEY's Epics cram the creaking shelves,
And LITTLE's Lyrics shine in hot-pressed twelves.

    Thus saith the Preacher; 'nought beneath the sun
Is new', yet still from change to change we run.   130
What varied wonders tempt us as they pass!
The Cow-pox, Tractors, Galvanism, and Gas
In turns appear to make the vulgar stare,
Till the swoln bubble bursts—and all is air!
Nor less new schools of poetry arise,   135
Where dull pretenders grapple for the prize:
O'er Taste awhile these Pseudo-bards prevail;
Each country Book-club bows the knee to Baal,
And, hurling lawful Genius from the throne,
Erects a shrine and idol of its own;   140
Some leaden calf—but whom it matters not,
From soaring SOUTHEY, down to groveling STOTT.

    Behold! in various throngs the scribbling crew,
For notice eager, pass in long review:
Each spurs his jaded Pegasus apace,   145
And Rhyme and Blank maintain an equal race;
Sonnets on sonnets crowd, and ode on ode;
And Tales of Terror jostle on the road;

118 feebler] ⟨feebler / modern⟩ feebler BB   121 Now look] ⟨Look now⟩ BB
123 let ... self] ⟨een ... will⟩ BB   124 Bards] Rhyme MQ, cor. BB   125 loaded
Press] Press oppressed MQ, cor. BB   127 cram] load MQ, cor. BB   129–42 added
EBSR2   129 ⟨The Prophet saith that⟩ Thus saith the Prophet MB   131 ⟨Behold
what varied wonders⟩ MB   134 Till ⟨bursts⟩ MB   135–6 And dull Pretenders
grapple for the prize | ⟨Till Taste and Sense at length no more arise⟩ MB   137 Pseudo-
bards] Infidels MB   140 Erects ... its] Erect ... their MB   146 And] ⟨Verse,⟩
BB

Immeasurable measures move along,
For simpering Folly loves a varied song,   150
To strange, mysterious Dullness still the friend,
Admires the strain she cannot comprehend.
Thus Lays of Minstrels—may they be the last!—
On half-strung harps, whine mournful to the blast,
While mountain spirits prate to river sprites,   155
That dames may listen to the sound at nights;
And goblin brats of Gilpin Horner's brood
Decoy young Border-nobles through the wood,
And skip at every step, Lord knows how high,
And frighten foolish babes, the Lord knows why,   160
While high-born ladies, in their magic cell,
Forbidding Knights to read who cannot spell,
Dispatch a courier to a wizard's grave,
And fight with honest men to shield a knave.

        Next view in state, proud prancing on his roan,   165
The golden-crested haughty Marmion,
Now forging scrolls, now foremost in the fight,
Not quite a Felon, yet but half a Knight,
The gibbet or the field prepared to grace;
A mighty mixture of the great and base.   170
And think'st thou, SCOTT! by vain conceit perchance,
On public taste to foist thy stale romance,
Though MURRAY with his MILLER may combine
To yield thy muse just half-a-crown per line?
No! when the sons of song descend to trade,   175
Their bays are sear, their former laurels fade.
Let such forego the poet's sacred name,
Who rack their brains for lucre, not for fame:
Still for stern Mammon may they toil in vain!
And sadly gaze on Gold they cannot gain!   180

---

149 Immeasurable] Unmeasurable *MB, cor. BB*   151 To strange] ⟨To strange⟩ And
to *BB*   168 Felon] Footpad *MB, cor. BB*   172 stale] ⟨dull⟩ *MB*   176 sear]
seared *MB*   178 lucre] ⟨profit⟩ *MB*
179–80   Low may they stoop beneath deserved Contempt
        And scorn remunerate the ⟨base⟩ mean attempt—*MB, cor. BB*
        Low may they sink to merited contempt,
        And scorn remunerate the mean attempt. *BB, EBSR1, 1a, 2, 3, 4, 4a; cor.*
        EBSR4a (Hunt copy)

Such be their meed, such still the just reward
Of prostituted Muse, and hireling bard!
For this we spurn Apollo's venal son,
And bid a long, 'good night to Marmion'.

These are the themes, that claim our plaudits now;
These are the Bards to whom the Muse must bow: 186
While MILTON, DRYDEN, POPE, alike forgot,
Resign their hallow'd Bays to WALTER SCOTT.

The time has been, when yet the Muse was young,
When HOMER swept the lyre, and MARO sung,   190
An Epic scarce ten centuries could claim,
While awe-struck nations hailed the magic name:
The work of each immortal Bard appears
The single wonder of a thousand years.
Empires have mouldered from the face of earth,   195
Tongues have expired with those who gave them birth,
Without the glory such a strain can give,
As even in ruin bids the language live.
Not so with us, though minor Bards content,
On one great work a life of labour spent: 200
With eagle pinion soaring to the skies,
Behold the Ballad-monger SOUTHEY rise!
To him let CAMOENS, MILTON, TASSO, yield,
Whose annual strains, like armies, take the field.
First in the ranks see Joan of Arc advance,   205
The scourge of England, and the boast of France!
Though burnt by wicked BEDFORD for a witch,
Behold her statue placed in Glory's niche;
Her fetters burst, and just released from prison,
A virgin Phoenix from her ashes risen.   210
Next see tremendous Thalaba come on,
Arabia's monstrous, wild, and wond'rous son;
Domdaniel's dread destroyer, who o'erthrew
More mad magicians than the world e'er knew.
Immortal Hero! all thy foes o'ercome,   215
For ever reign—the rival of Tom Thumb!

185–6 These . . . These] Such . . . Such *MA, BB*   199 minor] lesser *MA, cor. BB*
203 ⟨Let Camoens, Milton, Tasso yield to thee⟩ *MA*   204 ⟨Who thence has struck⟩
MA

Since startled Metre fled before thy face,
Well wert thou doomed the last of all thy race!
Well might triumphant Genii bear thee hence,
Illustrious conqueror of common sense!   220
Now, last and greatest, Madoc spreads his sails,
Cacique in Mexico, and Prince in Wales:
Tells us strange tales, as other travellers do,
More old than Mandeville's, and not so true.
Oh! SOUTHEY, SOUTHEY! cease thy varied song!   225
A Bard may chaunt too often, and too long:
As thou art strong in verse, in mercy spare!
A fourth, alas! were more than we could bear.
But if, in spite of all the world can say,
Thou still wilt verseward plod thy weary way;   230
If still in Berkeley-Ballads most uncivil,
Thou wilt devote old women to the devil,
The babe unborn thy dread intent may rue:
'God help thee', SOUTHEY, and thy readers too.

    Next comes the dull disciple of thy school,   235
That mild apostate from poetic rule,
The simple WORDSWORTH, framer of a lay
As soft as evening in his favourite May;
Who warns his friend 'to shake off toil and trouble,
And quit his books, for fear of growing double';   240
Who, both by precept and example, shows
That prose is verse, and verse is merely prose,
Convincing all by demonstration plain,
Poetic souls delight in prose insane;
And Christmas stories tortured into rhyme,   245
Contain the essence of the true sublime:
Thus when he tells the tale of Betty Foy,
The idiot mother of 'an idiot Boy';
A moon-struck silly lad who lost his way,
And, like his bard, confounded night with day,   250
So close on each pathetic part he dwells,
And each adventure so sublimely tells,
That all who view the 'idiot in his glory',
Conceive the Bard the hero of the story.

240 books] book *EBSR5, 5a*   247 tale] tales *EBSR5, 5a*   251 on] ⟨in⟩ *BB*

Shall gentle COLERIDGE pass unnoticed here,   255
To turgid ode, and tumid stanza dear?
Though themes of innocence amuse him best,
Yet still obscurity's a welcome guest.
If inspiration should her aid refuse,
To him who takes a Pixy for a Muse,   260
Yet none in lofty numbers can surpass
The bard who soars to elegize an ass:
So well the subject suits his noble mind,
He brays the Laureat of the long-ear'd kind!

Oh! wonder-working LEWIS! Monk, or Bard,   265
Who fain would'st make Parnassus a church-yard!
Lo! wreaths of yew, not laurel, bind thy brow,
Thy Muse a Sprite, Apollo's sexton thou!
Whether on ancient tombs thou tak'st thy stand,
By gibb'ring spectres hailed, thy kindred band;   270
Or tracest chaste descriptions on thy page,
To please the females of our modest age,
All hail, M.P.! from whose infernal brain
Thin sheeted phantoms glide, a grisly train;
At whose command, 'grim women' throng in crouds,
And kings of fire, of water, and of clouds,   276
With 'small grey men',—'wild yagers', and what-not,
To crown with honour, thee, and WALTER SCOTT:
Again, all hail! If tales like thine may please,
St. Luke alone can vanquish the disease: 280
Even Satan's self with thee might dread to dwell,
And in thy skull discern a deeper hell.

Who in soft guise, surrounded by a choir
Of virgins melting, not to Vesta's fire,
With sparkling eyes, and cheek by passion flush'd,   285
Strikes his wild Lyre, whilst listening dames are hush'd?
'Tis LITTLE! young Catullus of his day,
As sweet, but as immoral in his lay!

255–64 *not in MA*   263 So] How *all edns. except EBSR5, 5a, cor. EBSR4a (Hunt copy)*   264 A fellow feeling makes us wond'rous kind. *all edns. except EBSR5, 5a, cor. EBSR4a (Hunt and Murray copies)*   266 Sublime alike in Novel, or Churchyard *MA* 267–8 *not in MA*

Griev'd to condemn, the Muse must still be just,
Nor spare melodious advocates of lust.   290
Pure is the flame which o'er her altar burns;
From grosser incense with disgust she turns:
Yet, kind to youth, this expiation o'er,
She bids thee, 'mend thy line, and sin no more.'

    For thee, translator of the tinsel song,   295
To whom such glittering ornaments belong,
Hibernian STRANGFORD! with thine eyes of blue,
And boasted locks of red, or auburn hue,
Whose plaintive strain each love-sick Miss admires,
And o'er harmonious fustian half expires,   300
Learn, if thou can'st, to yield thine author's sense,
Nor vend thy sonnets on a false pretence.
Think'st thou to gain thy verse a higher place
By dressing Camoens in a suit of lace?
Mend, STRANGFORD! mend thy morals and thy taste;   305
Be warm, but pure, be amorous, but chaste:
Cease to deceive; thy pilfer'd harp restore,
Nor teach the Lusian Bard to copy MOORE.

    Behold—Ye Tarts! one moment spare the text!—
HAYLEY'S last work and worst—until his next.   310
Whether he spin poor couplets into plays,
Or damn the dead with purgatorial praise,
His style in youth or age is still the same;
For ever feeble and for ever tame.
Triumphant first see 'Temper's Triumphs' shine!   315
At least I'm sure they triumph'd over mine.
Of 'Music's Triumphs' all who read may swear
That luckless Music never triumph'd there.

---

293 Yet] But *MA, cor. BB*   294 line] life *MA, BB*; ⟨song⟩ *BB*   300 fustian]
nonsense *MA, BB, EBSR1, 1a*   306 but] but be *MA, BB*   307 pilfer'd]
⟨borrowed⟩ *MA*
309–12   In many marble cover'd volumes view,
     Hayley, in vain attempting something new,
     Whether he spins his comedies in rhyme,
     Or scrawls, as Wood and Barclay walk, 'gainst time; *MA, BB, EBSR1, 1a, 2,*
3, 4, 4a, cor. EBSR4a (Murray copy)
309 the] his *L, A*

Moravians, rise! bestow some meet reward
On dull devotion—lo! the Sabbath Bard,   320
Sepulchral GRAHAME, pours his notes sublime,
In mangled prose, nor e'en aspires to rhyme,
Breaks into blank the Gospel of St. Luke,
And boldly pilfers from the Pentateuch;
And, undisturbed by conscientious qualms,   325
Perverts the prophets, and purloins the Psalms.

Hail, Sympathy! thy soft idea brings
A thousand visions of a thousand things,
And shows, still whimpering thro' threescore of years,
The maudlin prince of mournful sonneteers.   330
And art thou not their prince? harmonious Bowles!
Thou first, great oracle of tender souls!
Whether thou sing'st with equal ease and grief,
The fall of empires, or a yellow leaf;
Whether thy muse most lamentably tells   335
What merry sounds proceed from Oxford bells,
Or, still in bells delighting, finds a friend
In every chime that jingled from Ostend?
Ah! how much juster were thy Muse's hap,
If to thy bells thou would'st but add a cap!   340
Delightful BOWLES! still blessing, and still blest,
All love thy strain, but children like it best.
'Tis thine with gentle LITTLE's moral song,
To soothe the mania of the amorous throng!
With thee our nursery damsels shed their tears,   345
Ere Miss, as yet, completes her infant years:

319–26   In verse most stale, unprofitable, flat,
                    Come let us change the scene, and glean with Pratt,
                    In him an author's luckless lot behold,
                    Condemned to make the books which he once sold.
                    Degraded man, again resume thy trade,
                    The votaries of the muse are ill repaid,
                    Though daily puffs once more invite to buy,
                    A new edition of thy 'Sympathy'. *MA, cor. BB*
323 Breaks into mawkish lines each holy book *BB, EBSR1, 1a*   327 Hail,] Thy *MA,
cor. BB*   329 And shows dissolved in sympathetic tears *MA*; And shows, dissolved
in thine own melting tears *BB, all edns. except EBSR5, 5a, cor. EBSR4a (Hunt copy)*
333–4   Whether in sighing winds thou seek'st relief, | Or consolation in a yellow leaf;
MA, BB, all edns. except EBSR5, 5a, cor. EBSR4a (Hunt copy)   336 merry] pretty
MA, BB   340 would'st but] fain would'st *MA, BB*   342 strain] *cor. to* rhyme
in EBSR4a (Hunt copy)

But in her teens thy whining powers are vain;
She quits poor BOWLES, for LITTLE's purer strain.
Now to soft themes thou scornest to confine
The lofty numbers of a harp like thine: 350
'Awake a louder and a loftier strain',
Such as none heard before, or will again;
Where all discoveries jumbled from the flood,
Since first the leaky ark repos'd in mud,
By more or less, are sung in every book,   355
From Captain NOAH down to Captain COOK.
Nor this alone, but pausing on the road,
The Bard sighs forth a gentle episode;
And gravely tells—attend each beauteous Miss!—
When first Madeira trembled to a kiss.   360
BOWLES! in thy memory let this precept dwell:
Stick to thy Sonnets, man! at least they sell.
But if some new-born whim, or larger bribe
Prompt thy crude brain, and claim thee for a scribe,
If 'chance some bard, though once by dunces fear'd,   365
Now, prone in dust, can only be rever'd;
If POPE, whose fame and genius from the first
Have foil'd the best of critics, needs the worst,
Do thou essay; each fault, each failing scan;
The first of poets was, alas! but man!   370
Rake from each ancient dunghill ev'ry pearl,
Consult Lord Fanny, and confide in CURLL;
Let all the scandals of a former age,
Perch on thy pen and flutter o'er thy page;
Affect a candour which thou can'st not feel,   375
Clothe envy in the garb of honest zeal;
Write, as if St. John's soul could still inspire,
And do from hate what MALLET did for hire.

349 Now] But *MA*, *BB*, *EBSR1*, *1a*   358 sighs forth] ⟨has wove⟩ *BB*   362 [Hob-
house passage after this line in *BB*, *EBSR1*, *1a*; see notes]   363–417 *not in MA, BB*
363 whim] ⟨zeal⟩ *A*   364. brain, and] ⟨pen, and⟩ Brain, or *A*   365 some ⟨glorious⟩
name though *A*   366 Yet prone in dust can never but be ⟨feared⟩ revered *A*, *cor. MB*
(*first copy*)   367 whose . . . first] ⟨yet blending first from Nature's / though mighty /
godlike / not untaught to err *A*, *cor. MB* (*first copy*)   368 Demands ⟨a dull Biographer
again⟩ / ⟨another / a second⟩ again a dull Biographer *A*, *cor. MB* (*first copy*)   369 each
. . . each] ⟨the task, his⟩ *A*   372 Lord Fanny] Oldmixon *A*, *cor. MB* (*first copy*)
373 ⟨Raise the⟩ *A*   374 ⟨Sit⟩ in thy pen, and grace thy teeming page *A*   flutter
o'er] float along *MB* (*fair copy*)   375 Affect] ⟨Then ? ⟩ *A*   376 Clothe . . . garb]
⟨Let Envy wear the mark⟩ *A*   377 St. John's . . . still] ⟨St. John could thy heart⟩ *A*

Oh! had'st thou liv'd in that congenial time,
To rave with Dennis, and with Ralph to rhyme,   380
Throng'd with the rest around his living head,
Not rais'd thy hoof against the lion dead,
A meet reward had crown'd thy glorious gains,
And link'd thee to the Dunciad for thy pains.

Another Epic! who inflicts again   385
More books of blank upon the sons of men?
Boeotian Cottle, rich Bristowa's boast,
Imports old stories from the Cambrian coast,
And sends his goods to market—all alive!
Lines forty-thousand, Cantos twenty-five!   390
Fresh fish from Hippocrene! who'll buy? who'll buy?
The precious bargain's cheap—in faith, not I.
Your turtle-feeder's verse must needs be flat,
Though Bristol bloat him with the verdant fat,
If Commerce fills the purse, she clogs the brain,   395
And Amos Cottle strikes the Lyre in vain.
In him an author's luckless lot behold!
Condemned to make the books which once he sold.
Oh! Amos Cottle!—Phoebus! what a name
To fill the speaking-trump of future fame!—   400
Oh! Amos Cottle! for a moment think
What meagre profits spring from pen and ink!
When thus devoted to poetic dreams,
Who will peruse thy prostituted reams?
Oh! pen perverted! paper misapplied!   405
Had Cottle still adorned the counter's side,
Bent o'er the desk, or, born to useful toils,
Been taught to make the paper which he soils,
Plough'd, delv'd, or plied the oar with lusty limb,
He had not sung of Wales, nor I of him.   410

As Sisyphus against the infernal steep
Rolls the huge rock, whose motions ne'er may sleep,

379 Oh! ⟨that the Bard⟩ A   381 ⟨And / With these ? gainst⟩ Assailing with the
rest his living head A   384 link'd] ⟨joined⟩ A   385–417 added EBSR2
391 Hippocrene] Helicon MB (both copies), cor. L, EBSR4a (Hunt and Murray copies)
393–4 Too much in turtle Bristol's sons delight, | Too much o'er bowls of Rack prolong
the night; MB (both copies), EBSR2, 3, 4, 4a   o'er] in EBSR4a

So up thy hill, ambrosial Richmond! heaves
Dull MAURICE all his granite weight of leaves:
Smooth, solid monuments of mental pain!   415
The petrifactions of a plodding brain,
That ere they reach the top fall lumbering back
          again.

With broken lyre and cheek serenely pale,
Lo! sad ALCAEUS wanders down the vale!
Though fair they rose, and might have bloomed at
          last,   420
His hopes have perished by the northern blast:
Nipped in the bud by Caledonian gales,
His blossoms wither as the blast prevails!
O'er his lost works let *classic* SHEFFIELD weep:
May no rude hand disturb their early sleep!   425

Yet, say! why should the Bard, at once, resign
His claim to favour from the sacred Nine?
For ever startled by the mingled howl
Of Northern wolves that still in darkness prowl;
A coward brood, which mangle as they prey,   430
By brutal instinct, all that cross their way:
Aged or young, the living or the dead,
No mercy find,—these felons must be fed.
Why do the injured unresisting yield
The calm possession of their native field?   435
Why tamely thus before their fangs retreat,
Nor hunt the hell-hounds back to ARTHUR'S seat?

Health to immortal JEFFREY! once, in name,
England could boast a judge almost the same:

421 perished] ⟨withered⟩ *MA*   426 Yet, say!] And yet *MA, cor. BB*   430 which]
who *MA, cor. to* that *in BB*   431 brutal] hellish *all MSS. and edns.* [cor. in letter
to Murray]   432 Aged] Or old *MA, cor. BB*   433 find] ⟨claim⟩ *BB*   felons]
harpies *all MSS. and edns.* [cor. in letter to Murray]   437 hell-hounds] bloodhounds
all MSS. and edns. [cor. in letter to Murray]
438–559   Who has not heard, in this enlightened age,
               When all can criticize th' historic page,
               Who has not heard, in James's bigot reign,
               Of Jeffries! monarch of the scourge and chain?
               Jeffries the wretch whose pestilential breath,
               Like the dread Simoom, wing'd the shaft of Death,
               The ⟨young⟩ old, the ⟨old⟩ young, to Fate remorseless gave
               Nor spared one victim from the common grave.

In soul so like, so merciful, yet just,   440
Some think that Satan has resigned his trust,
And given the Spirit to the world again,
To sentence Letters, as he sentenced men.
With hand less mighty, but with heart as black,
With voice as willing to decree the rack;   445
Bred in the Courts betimes, though all that law
As yet hath taught him is to find a flaw,
Since well instructed in the patriot school
To rail at party, though a party tool,
Who knows? if chance his patrons should restore   450
Back to the sway they forfeited before,
His scribbling toils some recompence may meet,
And raise this Daniel to the Judgment Seat.
Let JEFFRIES' shade indulge the pious hope,
And greeting thus, present him with a rope;   455
'Heir to my virtues! man of equal mind!
Skilled to condemn as to traduce mankind,
This cord receive! for thee reserv'd with care,
To wield in judgment, and at length to wear.'

Health to great JEFFREY! Heaven preserve his life,   460
To flourish on the fertile shores of Fife,
And guard it sacred in his future wars,
Since authors sometimes seek the field of Mars!

> Such was the Judge of James's iron time,
> When Law was Murder, Mercy was a crime,
> Till from his throne by weary millions hurled
> The Despot roamed an Exile through the World.
>
> Years have rolled on; in all the lists of Shame,
> Who now can parallel a Jeffries' name?
> With hand less mighty, but with heart as black,
> With voice as willing to decree the Rack,
> With tongue envenomed, with intentions foul
> The same in name, in character, in Soul. *MA, cor. BB*
> [see notes]

443 sentence] ⟨censure⟩ *BB*
460   ⟨Health to great Jeffrey, can his Country boast
                    A Son more genial on her barren Coast⟩ /
                    ⟨Health to great Jeffrey—leader of the Band
                    The proudest Bulwark of her sterile Strand
                    In him conjoined these various functions view
                    Critic,—Philosopher, Attorney too⟩
                    So much for him, yet Heaven preserve his life *A*
462 in . . . wars] ⟨from the vengeful bard⟩ *A*   463 ⟨For bards too⟩ sometimes *A*

Can none remember that eventful day,
That ever glorious, almost fatal fray,   465
When LITTLE's leadless pistol met his eye,
And Bow-street Myrmidons stood laughing by?
Oh! day disastrous! on her firm set rock,
Dunedin's castle felt a secret shock;
Dark roll'd the sympathetic waves of Forth,   470
Low groan'd the startled whirlwinds of the North;
TWEED ruffled half his waves to form a tear,
The other half pursued its calm career;
ARTHUR's steep summit nodded to its base,
The surly Tolbooth scarcely kept her place;   475
The Tolbooth felt—for marble sometimes can,
On such occasions, feel as much as man—
The Tolbooth felt defrauded of his charms,
If JEFFREY died, except within her arms:
Nay, last not least, on that portentous morn   480
The sixteenth story where himself was born,
His patrimonial garret fell to ground,
And pale Edina shuddered at the sound:
Strewed were the streets around with milk-white
        reams,
Flowed all the Canongate with inky streams;   485
This of his candour seemed the sable dew,
That of his valour shewed the bloodless hue,
And all with justice deemed the two combined
The mingled emblems of his mighty mind.
But Caledonia's Goddess hovered o'er   490
The field, and saved him from the wrath of MOORE;
From either pistol snatched the vengeful lead,
And strait restored it to her favourite's head.
That head, with greater than magnetic power,
Caught it, as Danae caught the golden shower,   495

464 Can none] We all *BB alternate reading*   that ... day] yes I'm sure all may *A, cor. in BB*
471 Low ... startled] ⟨Loud ... bleakest⟩ *A*   472–3 *not in A*   472 ⟨Half Tweed
combined his waves⟩ to form a tear *BB*   474 its] his *A*   475 ⟨And / Even Nature
sympathised for Jeffrey's hopeless case⟩ / All Nature felt for Jeffrey's hopeless case *A*
476–89 *not in A*   486–7 *transposed in BB, then cor.*   489 The] Were *BB alternate
reading*   490–1 ⟨But Caledonia's ? / Scotland's Genius saved his ? head | And from his
pistol snatched the dreadful / mindless lead⟩ *A*   490 Caledonia's] ⟨Scotland's⟩ *A*
494–7 *not in A, MS. insertion in BB*

And, though the thickening dross will scarce refine,
Augments its ore, and is itself a mine.
'My son,' she cried, 'ne'er thirst for gore again,
Resign the pistol, and resume the pen;
O'er politics and poesy preside,   500
Boast of thy country, and Britannia's guide!
For long as Albion's heedless sons submit,
Or Scottish taste decides on English wit,
So long shall last thine unmolested reign,
Nor any dare to take thy name in vain.   505
Behold a chosen band shall aid thy plan,
And own thee chieftain of the critic clan.
First in the oat-fed phalanx shall be seen
The travelled Thane! Athenian Aberdeen.
HERBERT shall wield THOR'S hammer, and some-
    times   510
In gratitude thou'lt praise his rugged rhymes.
Smug SYDNEY too thy bitter page shall seek,
And classic HALLAM, much renowned for Greek.
SCOTT may perchance his name and influence lend,
And paltry PILLANS shall traduce his friend.   515
While gay Thalia's luckless votary LAMBE,
Damned like the Devil—Devil-like will damn.
Known be thy name! unbounded be thy sway!
Thy HOLLAND'S banquets shall each toil repay;
While grateful Britain yields the praise she owes,   520
To HOLLAND'S hirelings, and to Learning's foes.
Yet mark one caution, ere thy next Review
Spread its light wings of Saffron and of Blue,
Beware lest blundering BROUGHAM destroy the
    sale,
Turn Beef to Bannocks, Cauliflowers to Kail.'   525
Thus having said, the kilted Goddess kist
Her son, and vanished in a Scottish mist.

496 scarce] ⟨neer⟩ BB   498 gore] ⟨blood⟩ A   501 ⟨Thy Scotlan⟩ The boast of
Scotland, and ⟨proud England's⟩ guide A   504 So long thy name shall ever ? reign A
505 thy] that A   506 shall aid] ⟨thy ?⟩ shall curse A   508 oat-fed phalanx] ranks
illustrious all MSS. and edns. except EBSR5, 5a, cor. EBSR4a (Hunt and Murray copies)
516 While] And L   gay . . . votary] ⟨Cloacina's holy Pontiff⟩ BB   517 As he
himself was damn'd, shall try to damn. BB, all edns. except EBSR5, 5a   Devil-like will]
⟨like the Devil would / Devil-like shall⟩ L   523 Spread] ⟨Spreads⟩ BB   524 destroy]
⟨spoils⟩ BB; spoil BB, EBSR1, 1a   525 Turn] ⟨Turns⟩ BB

Then prosper JEFFREY! pertest of the train!
Whom Scotland pampers with her fiery grain!
Whatever blessing waits a genuine Scot,   530
In double portion swells thy glorious lot,
For thee, Edina culls her evening sweets,
And showers their odours on thy candid sheets,
Whose Hue and Fragrance to thy work adhere,
This scents its pages, and that gilds its rear,   535
Lo! blushing Itch, coy nymph, enamoured grown,
Forsakes the rest, and cleaves to thee alone,
And, too unjust to other Pictish men,
Enjoys thy person, and inspires thy pen!

Illustrious HOLLAND! hard would be his lot,   540
His hirelings mentioned, and himself forgot!
HOLLAND, with HENRY PETTY at his back,
The whipper-in and huntsman of the pack.
Blest be the banquets spread at Holland House,
Where Scotchmen feed, and Critics may carouse!   545
Long, long beneath that hospitable roof,
Shall Grub-street dine, while duns are kept aloof.
See honest HALLAM lay aside his fork,
Resume his pen, review his Lordship's work,
And grateful for the dainties on his plate,   550
Declare his landlord can at least translate!
Dunedin! view thy children with delight,
They write for food, and feed because they write:
And lest, when heated with the unusual grape,
Some glowing thoughts should to the press escape,   555
And tinge with red the female reader's cheek,
My lady skims the cream of each critique;
Breathes o'er the page her purity of soul,
Reforms each error, and refines the whole.

528–39 *added EBSR5*   528 Oh! happy thou! beyond the happiest Swain *L*   529 fiery favourite *L*   530 waits . . . Scot] hails the name of ⟨Scott⟩ Scot *L*   531 swells thy glorious] crowns thy ⟨joyous⟩ *L*   532 evening] nightly *L*   534–5 *not in L*   537 cleaves] clings *L*   546 Long,] ⟨Lo!⟩ *BB*   547 Shall . . . dine] Grubstreet shall dine *MB, cor.* *BB*   550–1 And grateful to the founder of the feast, | Declare his landlord can translate, at least! *all MSS. and edns. except EBSR5, 5a*   553 and feed] are fed *MB, cor. BB*
559   Ah! virtuous Vassal! exemplary dame!
          ⟨Nay—blush not, Lady, at thy maiden name⟩
          On thy fair fame let ⟨Satire⟩ Libel do its worst,
          True to thy second husband and—thy first. *L, unincorporated*
               addition intended after 559

Now to the drama turn—oh! motley sight!   560
What precious scenes the wondering eyes invite!
Puns, and a Prince within a barrel pent,
And Dibdin's nonsense yield complete content.
Though now, thank Heaven! the Rosciomania's o'er,
And full-grown actors are endured once more;   565
Yet, what avails their vain attempts to please,
While British critics suffer scenes like these?
While REYNOLDS vents his 'dammes, poohs', and
        'zounds',
And common place, and common sense confounds?
While KENNY's 'World', ah! where is Kenny's wit?   570
Tires the sad gallery, lulls the listless Pit;
And BEAUMONT's pilfered Caratach affords
A tragedy complete in all but words?
Who but must mourn, while these are all the rage,
The degradation of our vaunted stage?   575
Heavens! is all sense of shame, and talent gone?
Have we no living Bard of merit?—none?
Awake, GEORGE COLMAN, CUMBERLAND, awake!
Ring the alarum bell, let folly quake!
Oh! SHERIDAN! if aught can move thy pen,   580
Let Comedy assume her throne again,
Abjure the mummery of German schools,
Leave new Pizarros to translating fools;
Give as thy last memorial to the age,
One classic drama, and reform the stage.   585
Gods! o'er those boards shall Folly rear her head
Where GARRICK trod, and SIDDONS lives to tread?
On those shall Farce display buffoonery's mask,
And HOOK conceal his heroes in a cask?
Shall sapient managers new scenes produce   590
From CHERRY, SKEFFINGTON, and Mother GOOSE?

562 Princes in barrels, counts in arbours pent *MA, cor. BB*   567 While] If *MA,
cor. BB*   568 'dammes' 'damme' *MA*; 'damme *EBSR1, 1a*   570–1 While Kenny's
World just suffer'd to proceed, | Proclaims the audience very kind indeed? *MA, EBSR1–
EBSR4, cor. EBSR4a (Hunt and Murray copies)*   listless] listening *EBSR4a (Murray copy)*
570–1 *BB, EBSR5, 5a*   581 Let Comedy resume her ⟨long lost reign⟩ *MA* assume]
resume *MA, BB, EBSR1–EBSR4a, cor. EBSR4a (Hunt copy)*   584 age] ⟨Stage⟩ *MA*
587 SIDDONS] Kemble *MA, BB, EBSR1–EBSR4a, cor. EBSR4a (Hunt copy)*   590–1 *transposed in MA, cor. BB*

While SHAKESPEARE, OTWAY, MASSINGER, forgot,
On stalls must moulder, or in closets rot?
Lo! with what pomp the daily prints proclaim,
The rival candidates for Attic fame!   595
In grim array though LEWIS' spectres rise,
Still SKEFFINGTON and GOOSE divide the prize.
And sure *great* SKEFFINGTON must claim our praise,
For skirtless coats, and skeletons of plays
Renowned alike; whose genius ne'er confines   600
Her flight to garnish GREENWOOD's gay designs;
Nor sleeps with 'Sleeping Beauties', but anon
In five facetious acts comes thundering on,
While poor John Bull, bewildered with the scene,
Stares, wondering what the devil it can mean;   605
But as some hands applaud, a venal few!
Rather than sleep, why John applauds it too.

Such are we now, ah! wherefore should we turn
To what our fathers were, unless to mourn!
Degenerate Britons! are ye dead to shame,   610
Or, kind to dullness, do you fear to blame?
Well may the nobles of our present race
Watch each distortion of a NALDI's face;
Well may they smile on Italy's buffoons,
And worship CATALANI's pantaloons,   615
Since their own Drama yields no fairer trace
Of wit than puns, of humour than grimace.

Then let AUSONIA, skill'd in ev'ry art
To soften manners, but corrupt the heart,
Pour her exotic follies o'er the town,   620
To sanction Vice and hunt decorum down:
Let wedded strumpets languish o'er DESHAYES,
And bless the promise which his form displays;
While Gayton bounds before th' enraptured looks
Of hoary Marquises and stripling Dukes: 625

592-3 *transposed in MA, cor. BB*   595 The] ⟨New⟩ *MA*   597 ? and Goody
Goose divide the prize *BB alternate reading*   601 Her humble flight to splendid panto-
mimes *MA, cor. BB*   605 Stares,] Keeps *MA, BB, EBSR1, 1a*   610 ye] you
MA, BB   618-706 *not in MA*   618-37 *in BB as MS. addition*

Let high-born letchers eye the lively Presle
Twirl her light limbs that spurn the needless veil;
Let Angiolini bare her breast of snow,
Wave the white arm and point the pliant toe;
Collini trill her love-inspiring song,   630
Strain her fair neck, and charm the listening throng!
Raise not your scythe, Suppressors of our Vice!
Reforming Saints! too delicately nice!
By whose decrees, our sinful souls to save,
No Sunday tankards foam, no barbers shave;   635
And beer undrawn, and beards unmown, display
Your holy rev'rence for the Sabbath-day.

   Or, hail at once the patron and the pile
Of vice and folly, Greville and Argyle!
Where yon proud palace Fashion's hallowed fane,   640
Spreads wide her portals for the motley train,
Behold the new Petronius of the day,
Our Arbiter of pleasure and of play!
There the hired Eunuch, the Hesperian choir,
The melting lute, the soft lascivious lyre,   645
The song from Italy, the step from France,
The midnight orgy, and the mazy dance,
The smile of beauty, and the flush of wine,
For fops, fools, gamesters, knaves, and Lords combine:
Each to his humour,—Comus all allows;   650
Champaign, dice, music, or your neighbour's spouse.
Talk not to us, ye starving sons of trade!
Of piteous ruin, which ourselves have made:
In Plenty's sunshine Fortune's minions bask,
Nor think of Poverty, except 'en masque',   655
When for the night some lately titled ass
Appears the beggar which his grandsire was.
The curtain dropped, the gay Burletta o'er,
The audience take their turn upon the floor;
Now round the room the circling dow'gers sweep,   660
Now in loose waltz the thin-clad daughters leap:

632 Raise] ⟨Raise⟩ Whet *cor. EBSR4a (Murray copy)*   scythe] ⟨knife⟩ *BB*   633 too]
so *BB*   638–706 *not in BB*   642 day] times *MB, A*   643 The skilful
arbiter of modern crimes *MB, A*   Our] The *EBSR1–EBSR4a*   644 Hesperian]
⟨Etruscan⟩ *A*   649 gamesters] ⟨females⟩ *A*   656 When ⟨newly clad⟩ for the
night some ⟨lately titled⟩ newly titled *A*

The first in lengthened line majestic swim,
The last display the free, unfettered limb:
Those for Hibernia's lusty sons repair
With art the charms which Nature could not   665
    spare;
These after husbands wing their eager flight,
Nor leave much mystery for the nuptial night.

    Oh! blest retreats of infamy and ease!
Where, all forgotten but the power to please,
Each maid may give a loose to genial thought,   670
Each swain may teach new systems, or be taught:
There the blithe youngster, just returned from
    Spain,
Cuts the light pack, or calls the rattling-main;
The jovial Caster's set, and seven's the nick,
Or—done!—a thousand on the coming trick!   675
If, mad with loss, existence 'gins to tire,
And all your hope or wish is to expire,
Here's POWELL's pistol ready for your life,
And, kinder still, two PAGETS for your wife:
Fit consummation of an earthly race   680
Begun in folly, ended in disgrace,
While none but menials o'er the bed of death,
Wash thy red wounds, or watch thy wavering
    breath;
Traduced by liars, and forgot by all,
The mangled victim of a drunken brawl,   685
To live like CLODIUS, and like FALKLAND fall.

    Truth! rouse some genuine Bard, and guide his
    hand
To drive this pestilence from out the land.

664 Those] These *MB*   665 art . . . Nature could not] ⟨rouge . . . Time forgot to⟩ *A*
666 These] Those *MB*   667 nuptial] wedding *A*   671 Each Swain ⟨obtain a patron,
all for nought⟩ may teach love's learning, or be taught— *A, cor. in MB*   672 blithe]
⟨gay⟩ *A*   674 jovial] jolly *A*   679 two PAGETS] a Paget *A, MB, EBSR1–EBSR4a,
cor. in EBSR4a (Murray copy)*   680 Fit . . . an] ⟨Blest . . . our⟩ *A*   682 ⟨Without
one friend to⟩ *A*   death] ⟨pain⟩ *A*   683 ⟨To soothe thy ? on the bed of death⟩ *A*
watch thy wavering] ⟨catch thy ? ⟩ *A*   684 ⟨Without one friend to hold thy ? ⟩ *A*
685 ⟨To perish⟩ *A*   686 CLODIUS] ⟨Parnell / Clodius⟩ Wilmot / Barry / Sackville /
Townsend *A alternate readings*

Even I—least thinking of a thoughtless throng,
Just skilled to know the right and chuse the   690
    wrong,
Freed at that age when Reason's shield is lost
To fight my course through Passion's countless
    host,
Whom every path of pleasure's flowery way
Has lured in turn, and all have led astray—
E'en I must raise my voice, e'en I must feel   695
Such scenes, such men destroy the public weal:
Altho' some kind, censorious friend will say,
'What art thou better, meddling fool, than they?'
And every Brother Rake will smile to see
That miracle, a Moralist in me!   700
No matter—when some Bard in virtue strong,
GIFFORD perchance, shall raise the chastening
    song,
Then sleep my pen for ever! and my voice
Be only heard to hail him and rejoice;
Rejoice, and yield my feeble praise, though I   705
May feel the lash that Virtue must apply.

    As for the smaller fry, who swarm in shoals
From silly HAFIZ up to simple BOWLES,
Why should we call them from their dark abode,
In broad St. Giles's, or in Tottenham Road?   710
Or (since some men of fashion nobly dare
To scrawl in verse) from Bond-street or the Square?
If things of ton their harmless lays indite,
Most wisely doomed to shun the public sight,
What harm? in spite of every critic elf,   715
Sir T. may read his stanzas to himself;
MILES ANDREWS still his strength in couplets try,
And live in prologues, though his dramas die.
Lords too are Bards: such things at times befall,
And 'tis some praise in Peers to write at all.   720
Yet, did or taste or reason sway the times,
Ah! who would take their titles with their rhymes?

709 dark] ⟨blest⟩ *MA*   712 from . . . the] from Grosvenor place or *MA, cor. BB*
718 his] ⟨their⟩ *MA*

ROSCOMMON! SHEFFIELD! with your spirits fled,
No future laurels deck a noble head;
No Muse will cheer with renovating smile,   725
The paralytic puling of CARLISLE:
The puny Schoolboy and his early lay
Men pardon, if his follies pass away;
But who forgives the Senior's ceaseless verse,
Whose hairs grow hoary as his rhymes grow worse? 730
What heterogeneous honours deck the Peer!
Lord, rhymester, petit-maitre, pamphleteer!
So dull in youth, so drivelling in his age,
His scenes alone had damned our sinking stage;
But Managers for once cried, 'hold, enough!'   735
Nor drugged their audience with the tragic stuff.
Yet at their judgment let his Lordship laugh,
And case his volumes in congenial calf:
Yes! doff that covering where Morocco shines,
And hang a calfskin on those recreant lines.   740

   With you, ye druids! rich in native lead,
Who daily scribble for your daily bread;
With you I war not: GIFFORD's heavy hand
Has crushed, without remorse, your numerous band.
On 'all the Talents' vent your venal spleen,   745
Want is your plea, let Pity be your screen.
Let Monodies on Fox regale your crew,
And Melville's Mantle prove a Blanket too!
One common Lethe waits each hapless Bard,
And peace be with you! 'tis your best reward.   750

723–46 *not in MA*
723   In ⟨times like these⟩ these our times with daily wonders big
             A lettered Peer is like a lettered pig,
             Both know their Alphabet, but who from thence
             Infers that Peers or pigs have manly sense,
             Still less that such should woo the graceful Nine,
             Parnassus was not made for Lords and Swine. (*BB*, unincorporated
                   MS. addition intended to follow 722]
723–6   ⟨On one alone Apollo deigns to smile |
             And crowns a new Roscommon in Carlisle.⟩ *BB*
725–6 Nor e'en a hackney'd Muse will deign to smile | On minor BYRON, or mature
CARLISLE. *EBSR1, 1a*   727–36 *BB MS. addition*   728 Men] We *BB*   734 had
damned] ⟨might damn⟩ *BB*; had ⟨damned / sunk⟩ damned *A*   737–40 *BB MS. addition*
737 judgment] nausea fiat *BB alternate readings*   746 plea] defence *BB, EBSR1–*
EBSR4a, cor. EBSR4a (Hunt copy)   749 hapless] hopeless *MA*

Such damning fame as Dunciads only give
Could bid your lines beyond a morning live;
But now at once your fleeting labours close,
With names of greater note in blest repose.
Far be't from me unkindly to upbraid   755
The lovely ROSA's prose in masquerade,
Whose strains, the faithful echoes of her mind,
Leave wondering comprehension far behind.
Though Crusca's bards no more our journals fill,
Some stragglers skirmish round the columns still,   760
Last of the howling host which once was Bell's,
Matilda snivels yet, and Hafiz yells,
And Merry's metaphors appear anew,
Chained to the signature of O. P. Q.

When some brisk youth, the tenant of a stall,   765
Employs a pen less pointed than his awl,
Leaves his snug shop, forsakes his store of shoes,
St. Crispin quits, and cobbles for the Muse,
Heavens! how the vulgar stare! how crowds applaud!
How ladies read! and Literati laud!   770
If chance some wicked wag should pass his jest,
'Tis sheer ill-nature; don't the world know best?
Genius must guide when wits admire the rhyme,
And CAPEL LOFFT declares 'tis quite sublime.
Hear then, ye happy sons of needless trade!   775
Swains! quit the plough, resign the useless spade:
Lo! BURNS and BLOOMFIELD, nay, a greater far,
GIFFORD was born beneath an adverse star,
Forsook the labours of a servile state,
Stemmed the rude storm, and triumphed over Fate: 780

751 damning] sneering *MA, cor. BB*; Only such damning fame as Dunciads give *BB*
759–98 *not in MA*
759–64   Though BELL has lost his nightingales and owls,
                  MATILDA snivels still, and HAFIZ howls,
                  And CRUSCA's spirit, rising from the dead,
                  Revives in LAURA, QUIZ, and X. Y. Z. *BB, EBSR1–EBSR4*
                  ⟨Though Crusca's host were once defended still
                  Some straggling bards the daily columns fill,
                  Sad tortures of consonants and vowels!
                  Matilda snivels yet, and Hafiz howls,
                  And Merry's metaphors as good as new,
                  Proud in the signature of O. P. Q.⟩ *L*
759 bards] ⟨host⟩ *L*   760 the] their *EBSR4a*   761 host] ⟨band⟩ *L*   762 yet]
⟨still⟩ *L*   765–98 *added EBSR2*

Then why no more? if Phoebus smiled on you,
BLOOMFIELD! why not on brother Nathan too?
Him too the Mania, not the Muse, has seized;
Not inspiration, but a mind diseased:
And now no Boor can seek his last abode,   785
No common be enclosed without an ode.
Oh! since increased refinement deigns to smile
On Britain's sons, and bless our genial Isle,
Let Poesy go forth, pervade the whole,
Alike the rustic, and mechanic soul: 790
Ye tuneful cobblers! still your notes prolong,
Compose at once a slipper and a song;
So shall the fair your handy work peruse,
Your sonnets sure shall please—perhaps your shoes.
May Moorland weavers boast Pindaric skill,   795
And taylors' lays be longer than their bill!
While punctual beaux reward the grateful notes,
And pay for poems—when they pay for coats.

     To the famed throng now paid the tribute due,
Neglected Genius! let me turn to you.   800
Come forth, oh CAMPBELL! give thy talents scope;
Who dares aspire if thou must cease to hope?
And thou, melodious ROGERS! rise at last,
Recal the pleasing memory of the past;
Arise! let blest remembrance still inspire,   805
And strike to wonted tones thy hallowed lyre;
Restore Apollo to his vacant throne,
Assert thy country's honour and thine own.
What! must deserted Poesy still weep
Where her last hopes with pious COWPER sleep?   810
Unless perchance, from his cold bier she turns,
To deck the turf that wraps her minstrel, BURNS!
No! tho' contempt hath marked the spurious brood,
The race who rhyme from folly, or for food;
Yet still some genuine sons 'tis hers to boast,   815
Who least affecting, still affect the most;

---

799 Now since the past have claimed the tribute due *MA*   claimed] ⟨claim'd⟩ found *BB*
816–17 From Albion's Cliffs to Caledonia's Coast, | Some few who know to write as well
as feel, *MA*

Feel as they write, and write but as they feel—
Bear witness GIFFORD, SOTHEBY, MACNEIL.

'Why slumbers GIFFORD?' once was asked in
    vain:
Why slumbers GIFFORD? let us ask again.   820
Are there no follies for his pen to purge?
Are there no fools whose backs demand the scourge?
Are there no sins for Satire's Bard to greet?
Stalks not gigantic Vice in every street?
Shall Peers or Princes tread pollution's path,   825
And 'scape alike the Law's and Muse's wrath?
Nor blaze with guilty glare through future time,
Eternal beacons of consummate crime?
Arouse thee, GIFFORD! be thy promise claimed,
Make bad men better, or at least ashamed.   830

    Unhappy WHITE! while life was in its spring,
And thy young Muse just waved her joyous wing,
The Spoiler swept that soaring Lyre away,
Which else had sounded an immortal lay.
Oh! what a noble heart was here undone,   835
When Science' self destroyed her favourite son!
Yes! she too much indulged thy fond pursuit,
She sowed the seeds, but Death has reaped the fruit;
'Twas thine own Genius gave the final blow,
And helped to plant the wound that laid thee low: 840
So the struck Eagle stretched upon the plain,
No more through rolling clouds to soar again,
Viewed his own feather on the fatal dart,
And winged the shaft that quivered in his heart:
Keen were his pangs, but keener far to feel   845
He nursed the pinion which impell'd the steel,
While the same plumage that had warmed his nest
Drank the last life-drop of his bleeding breast.

819–90 [not in *MA*, *BB*, but in margin of *BB* is a note by B: 'Unhappy White /
Crabbe / Tr. of Gr. Anthology.']   833–4 The spoiler came; and all thy promise fair |
Has sought the grave, to sleep for ever there. *A*, *EBSR1–EBSR4a*, *cor. EBSR4a (Hunt
and Murray copies)*   843 feather] ⟨plumage⟩ *A*   846 which] ⟨that⟩ *A*
847 plumage] ⟨feather⟩ *A*

There be, who say in these enlightened days
That splendid lies are all the poet's praise;   850
That strained Invention, ever on the wing,
Alone impels the modern Bard to sing:
'Tis true, that all who rhyme, nay, all who write,
Shrink from that fatal word to Genius—Trite;
Yet Truth sometimes will lend her noblest fires,   855
And decorate the verse herself inspires:
This fact in Virtue's name let CRABBE attest,
Though Nature's sternest Painter, yet the best.

And here let SHEE and Genius find a place,
Whose pen and pencil yield an equal grace;   860
To guide whose hand the sister Arts combine,
And trace the Poet's or the Painter's line;
Whose magic touch can bid the canvas glow,
Or pour the easy rhyme's harmonious flow,
While honours doubly merited attend   865
The Poet's rival, but the Painter's friend.

Blest is the man! who dares approach the bower
Where dwelt the Muses at their natal hour;
Whose steps have pressed, whose eye has marked afar,
The clime that nursed the sons of song and war,   870
The scenes which Glory still must hover o'er;
Her place of birth, her own Achaian shore:
But doubly blest is he, whose heart expands
With hallowed feelings for those classic lands;
Who rends the veil of ages long gone by,   875
And views their remnants with a poet's eye!
WRIGHT! 'twas thy happy lot at once to view
Those shores of glory, and to sing them too;
And sure no common Muse inspired thy pen
To hail the land of Gods and Godlike men.   880

And you, associate Bards! who snatched to light
Those Gems too long withheld from modern sight;

859–80 *added EBSR2*   859 And ⟨should⟩ here *MB*   861 ⟨With other ? /
In whose ? ⟩ *MB*   862 or] ⟨and⟩ *MB*   865 ⟨One Scion may ? honour still
attend⟩ *MB*   866 but] and *MB*   881 associate] ⟨ye nameless⟩ united / associate
BB MS. addition

Whose mingling taste combined to cull the wreath
Where Attic flowers Aonian odours breathe,
And all their renovated fragrance flung, 885
To grace the beauties of your native tongue;
Now let those minds that nobly could transfuse
The glorious Spirit of the Grecian Muse,
Though soft the echo, scorn a borrowed tone:
Resign Achaia's lyre, and strike your own. 890

Let these, or such as these, with just applause,
Restore the Muse's violated laws;
But not in flimsy DARWIN's pompous chime,
That mighty master of unmeaning rhyme;
Whose gilded cymbals, more adorned than clear, 895
The eye delighted, but fatigued the ear;
In show the simple lyre could once surpass,
But now worn down, appear in native brass;
While all his train of hovering sylphs around
Evaporate in similies and sound: 900
Him let them shun, with him let tinsel die:
False glare attracts, but more offends the eye.

Yet let them not to vulgar WORDSWORTH stoop,
The meanest object of the lowly group,
Whose verse of all but childish prattle void, 905
Seems blessed harmony to LAMB and LLOYD:
Let them—but hold my Muse, nor dare to teach
A strain, far, far beyond thy humble reach;
The native genius with their being given
Will point the path, and peal their notes to heaven. 910

And thou, too, SCOTT! resign to minstrels rude
The wilder Slogan of a Border feud:
Let others spin their meagre lines for hire;
Enough for Genius if itself inspire!

889–90 Translation's servile work at length disown | And quit ACHAIA's Muse, to court your
own. *BB*   889 Though sweet the sound, disdain a borrowed tone *A* [this version and
received text sent as alternates in *A*]   891 Let these arise, and conscious of applause
MA, cor. BB   893 flimsy] heavy *MA, cor. BB*   909 being] feeling *MA, BB,
EBSR1–EBSR4a*   913–30 Let Lewis fill our nurseries with alarm, | With tales that
oft disgust, and never charm; *MA, cor. BB*   914 itself] ⟨the Muse⟩ *BB*

Let SOUTHEY sing, altho' his teeming muse,   915
Prolific every spring, be too profuse;
Let simple WORDSWORTH chime his childish verse,
And brother COLERIDGE lull the babe at nurse;
Let Spectre-mongering LEWIS aim, at most,
To rouse the Galleries, or to raise a ghost;   920
Let MOORE still sigh; let STRANGFORD steal from
        MOORE,
And swear that CAMOENS sang such notes of yore;
Let HAYLEY hobble on; MONTGOMERY rave;
And godly GRAHAME chaunt a stupid stave;
Let sonneteering BOWLES his strains refine,   925
And whine and whimper to the fourteenth line;
Let STOTT, CARLISLE, MATILDA, and the rest
Of Grub-street, and of Grosvenor-Place the best,
Scrawl on, 'till death release us from the strain,
Or Common sense assert her rights again;   930
But Thou, with powers that mock the aid of
        praise,
Should'st leave to humbler Bards ignoble lays:
Thy country's voice, the voice of all the Nine,
Demand a hallowed harp—that harp is thine.
Say! will not Caledonia's annals yield   935
The glorious record of some nobler field,
Than the vile foray of a plundering clan,
Whose proudest deeds disgrace the name of man?
Or Marmion's acts of darkness, fitter food
For SHERWOOD's outlaw tales of ROBIN HOOD?   940
Scotland! still proudly claim thy native Bard,
And be thy praise his first, his best reward!
Yet not with thee alone his name should live,
But own the vast renown a world can give;
Be known perchance, when Albion is no more,   945
And tell the tale of what she was before;
To future times her faded fame recall,
And save her glory, though his country fall.

915 Let ⟨potent⟩ prurient Southey cease, his teeming Muse BB   916 be] is BB
918 lull] still BB   921 still sigh] be lewd BB, EBSR1–EBSR4a, cor. EBSR4a
(Hunt copy)   929 Scrawl ⟨Rhyme⟩ BB   937 a] ⟨some⟩ MA   940 For . . .
tales] For outlaw'd Sherwood's tales MA, BB, EBSR1–EBSR4a   942 his best] and
best MA, cor. BB   943 Yet . . . name] ⟨But . . . fame⟩ MA

Yet what avails the sanguine Poet's hope
To conquer ages, and with time to cope?   950
New eras spread their wings, new nations rise,
And other Victors fill th' applauding skies;
A few brief generations fleet along,
Whose sons forget the Poet and his song: 954
E'en now, what once-loved Minstrels scarce may claim
The transient mention of a dubious name!
When Fame's loud trump hath blown its noblest blast
Though long the sound the echo sleeps at last;
And glory, like the Phoenix midst her fires,
Exhales her odours, blazes, and expires.   960

Shall hoary Granta call her sable sons,
Expert in science, more expert at puns?
Shall these approach the Muse? ah no! she flies,
Ev'n from the tempting ore of Seaton's prize;
Though Printers condescend the press to soil   965
With rhyme by HOARE, and epic blank by HOYLE:
Not him whose page, if still upheld by whist,
Requires no sacred theme to bid us list.
Ye! who in Granta's honours would surpass,
Must mount her Pegasus, a full-grown ass: 970
A foal well worthy of her ancient dam,
Whose Helicon is duller than her Cam.

There CLARKE, still striving piteously 'to please',
Forgetting doggrel leads not to degrees,
A would-be satirist, a hired Buffoon,   975
A monthly scribbler of some low Lampoon,
Condemned to drudge, the meanest of the mean,
And furbish falsehoods for a magazine,

949–60 added in EBSR2   963 these] such L   964 And even spurns the great
Seatonian prize, MA, BB, EBSR1–EBSR4a, cor. EBSR4a (Hunt and Murray copies)
tempting] sterling L   966 With odes by Smythe and epic songs by Hoyle. MA, cor. BB
967 Not . . . page] Hoyle, whose learn'd page MA, BB   968 Requires] Requir'd MA,
BB
972   ⟨Yet hold, as when by Jove's divine behest,
                         If found, ten righteous had preserved the rest,
                         In Sodom's fated town, for Granta's name
                         Let Hodgson's genius plead and save her fame.⟩ MA, BB after 972
Jove's divine] Heaven's supreme BB   973–80 added EBSR2   974 Forgetting]
⟨Forgot that⟩ A   975 A . . . a] ⟨A / The . . . this / the⟩ A   976 A] ⟨This⟩ A

Devotes to scandal his congenial mind;
Himself a living libel on mankind.   980

Oh dark asylum of a Vandal race!
At once the boast of learning, and disgrace;
So lost to Phoebus that nor Hodgson's verse
Can make thee better, or poor Hewson's worse:
But where fair Isis rolls her purer wave,   985
The partial Muse delighted loves to lave,
On her green banks a greener wreath she wove,
To crown the Bards that haunt her classic grove,
Where RICHARDS wakes a genuine poet's fires,
And modern Britons glory in their Sires.   990

For me, who thus unasked have dared to tell
My country, what her sons should know too well,
Zeal for her honour bade me here engage
The host of idiots that infest her age.
No just applause her honoured name shall lose,   995
As first in freedom, dearest to the Muse.
Oh! would thy Bards but emulate thy fame,
And rise, more worthy, Albion, of thy name!
What Athens was in science, Rome in power,
What Tyre appeared in her meridan hour,   1000
'Tis thine at once, fair Albion! to have been;
Earth's chief dictatress, Ocean's lovely queen:
But Rome decayed, and Athens strewed the plain,
And Tyre's proud piers lie shattered in the main;
Like these thy strength may sink in ruin hurled,   1005
And Britain fall, the bulwark of the World.
But let me cease, and dread Cassandra's fate,
With warning ever scoffed at, 'till too late;
To themes less lofty still my lay confine,
And urge thy Bards to gain a name like thine.   1010

981–4 BB MS. addition   983–4 So sunk in dullness and so lost in shame | That SMYTHE
and HODGSON scarce redeem thy fame. BB, EBSR1–EBSR4a, cor. EBSR4a (Hunt copy)
987 she] is MA, BB, EBSR1–EBSR4a, cor. EBSR4a (Hunt copy)   990 glory in]
justly praise MA, BB, EBSR1–EBSR4a, cor. in EBSR4a (Hunt copy)   991 unasked]
⟨unask'd⟩ unknown BB; unknown EBSR1, 1a   992 should] must MA, cor. BB
993–4 Zeal for her honour, no malignant rage, | Has bade me spurn the follies of her age.
MA, BB, EBSR1, 1a   1002 lovely] lonely MA, cor. BB; mighty / lovely BB alternate
readings; mighty EBSR1–EBSR4a   1005 strength] ⟨cliffs⟩ MA, cor. BB   1006 The
last white ramparts of a falling world. MA, cor. BB   1009 themes] ⟨lays⟩ MA

Then, hapless Britain! be thy rulers blest,
The senate's oracles, the peoples's jest!
Still hear thy motley orators dispense
The flowers of rhetoric, though not of sense,
While CANNING's colleagues hate him for his wit,   1015
And old dame PORTLAND fills the place of PITT.

Yet once again adieu! ere this the sail
That wafts me hence is shivering in the gale;
And Afric's coast and Calpe's adverse height,
And Stamboul's minarets must greet my sight: 1020
Thence shall I stray through beauty's native clime,
Where Kaff is clad in rocks, and crowned with snows
    sublime.
But should I back return, no tempting press
Shall drag my Journal from the desk's recess:
Let coxcombs printing as they come from far,   1025
Snatch his own wreath of Ridicule from Carr;
Let ABERDEEN and ELGIN still pursue
The shade of fame through regions of Virtu;
Waste useless thousands on their Phidian freaks,
Mis-shapen monuments, and maimed antiques;   1030
And make their grand saloons a general mart
For all the mutilated blocks of art:
Of Dardan tours let Dilettanti tell,
I leave topography to rapid GELL;
And, quite content, no more shall interpose   1035
To stun the public ear—at least with Prose.

Thus far I've held my undisturbed career,
Prepared for rancour, steeled 'gainst selfish fear:

1011–70 *added EBSR2*   1011 Then ... be] ⟨Ah! happy Britain! in⟩ *MB*
1013 ⟨How sweet to hear thy orators dispense⟩ *MB*   1017 ere this] ⟨for me⟩ *A*
1018 That ... hence] ⟨Now half unfurled⟩ That bears me hence *A*   1021 Thence
shall I] And thence I *A*
1023–6   But should I back return, no lettered rage
                Shall drag my common-place book on the stage:
                Let vain Valentia rival luckless Carr,
                And equal him whose work he sought to mar. *A, EBSR2–EBSR4a*
luckless] libelled *A*   1027–30 *not in A*   1032 For] In *A*   1033 ⟨Of Troy
let other dilettanti tell⟩ *A*   Dardan] Trojan *A*   1034 rapid] coxcomb *A*; classic
EBSR2–EBSR4a   1036 To stun mankind with poesy or prose. *A, EBSR2–EBSR4a*
1038 steeled] ⟨armed⟩ *MB*

This thing of rhyme I ne'er disdained to own,
Though not obtrusive, yet not quite unknown: 1040
My voice was heard again, though not so loud;
My page, though nameless, never disavowed;
And now at once I tear the veil away:—
Cheer on the pack! the Quarry stands at bay,
Unscared by all the din of MELBOURNE house,   1045
By LAMBE'S resentment, or by HOLLAND'S spouse,
By JEFFREY'S harmless pistol, HALLAM'S rage,
EDINA'S brawny sons and brimstone page.
Our men in buckram shall have blows enough,
And feel, they too are 'penetrable stuff':   1050
And though I hope not hence unscathed to go,
Who conquers me, shall find a stubborn foe.
The time hath been, when no harsh sound would fall
From lips that now may seem inbued with gall;
Nor fools nor follies tempt me to despise   1055
The meanest thing that crawled beneath my eyes:
But now, so callous grown, so changed since youth,
I've learned to think, and sternly speak the truth;
Learned to deride the critic's starch decree,
And break him on the wheel he meant for me;   1060
To spurn the rod a scribbler bids me kiss,
Nor care if courts and crowds applaud or hiss:
Nay more, through all my rival rhymesters frown,
I too can hunt a Poetaster down;
And, armed in proof, the gauntlet cast at once   1065
To Scotch marauder, and to Southern dunce.
Thus much I've dared; if my incondite lay
Hath wronged these righteous times let others say;
This, let the world, which knows not how to spare,
Yet rarely blames unjustly, now declare.   1070

[1808–12]

POSTSCRIPT

I have been informed, since the present edition went to the Press,
that my trusty and well beloved cousins, the Edinburgh Reviewers,

1046 or] ⟨and⟩ MB   1053 sound] ⟨word⟩ MB   1058 and sternly] ⟨with
freedom⟩ MB   1067 Thus much I've dared to do; how far my lay MB, EBSR2–EBSR4a
Postscript   added EBSR2

are preparing a most vehement critique on my poor, gentle, *un-resisting* Muse whom they have already so bedeviled with their ungodly ribaldry: 5

'Tantaene animis coelestibus Irae!'

I suppose I must say of JEFFREY as Sir ANDREW AGUE-CHEEK saith, 'an I had known he was so cunning of fence, I had seen him damned ere I had fought him.' What a pity it is that I shall be beyond the Bosphorus, before the next number has passed the   10
Tweed. But I yet hope to light my pipe with it in Persia.

My Northern friends have accused me, with justice, of personality towards their great literary Anthropophagus JEFFREY; but what else was to be done with him and his dirty pack, who feed 'by lying and slandering', and slake their thirst by 'evil-speaking'?   15
I have adduced facts already well known, and of JEFFREY's mind I have stated my free opinion, nor has he thence sustained any injury;—what scavenger was ever soiled by being pelted with mud? It may be said that I quit England because I have censured there 'persons of honour and wit about town', but I am coming back   20
again, and their vengeance will keep hot till my return. Those who know me can testify that my motives for leaving England are very different from fears, literary or personal; those who do not, may one day be convinced. Since the publication of this thing, my name has not been concealed; I have been mostly in London, ready to   25
answer for my transgressions, and in daily expectation of sundry cartels; but, alas! 'the age of chivalry is over', or, in the vulgar tongue, there is no spirit now-a-days.

There is a youth ycleped Hewson Clarke (subaudi, Esq.) a Sizer of Emanuel College, and I believe a Denizen of Berwick upon   30
Tweed, whom I have introduced in these pages to much better company than he has been accustomed to meet: he is, notwithstanding, a very sad dog, and for no reason that I can discover, except a personal quarrel with a bear, kept by me at Cambridge to sit for a fellowship, and whom the jealousy of his Trinity cotem-   35
poraries prevented from success, has been abusing me, and what is worse, the defenceless innocent above mentioned, in the Satirist for one year and some months. I am utterly unconscious of having given him any provocation; indeed I am guiltless of having heard his name, till it was coupled with the Satirist. He has, therefore, no   40
reason to complain, and I dare say that, like Sir Fretful Plagiary, he is rather *pleased* than otherwise. I have now mentioned all who

have done me the honour to notice me and mine, that is, my
Bear and my Book, except the Editor of the Satirist, who, it seems,
45   is a gentleman, God wot! I wish he could impart a little of his
gentility to his subordinate scribblers. I hear that Mr. JERNING-
HAM is about to take up the cudgels for his Maecenas, Lord Carlisle;
I hope not: he was one of the few, who, in the very short inter-
course I had with him, treated me with kindness when a boy, and
50   whatever he may say or do, 'pour on, I will endure.' I have nothing
further to add, save a general note of thanksgiving to readers,
purchasers, and publisher, and in the words of SCOTT, I wish

> 'To all and each a fair good night,
> And rosy dreams and slumbers light.'

129a   Lines Associated With *English Bards and Scotch Reviewers*

Like reptiles hatched from out the mud of Nile,
Congenial spawn of Bigotry and Bile
Behold crawl forth from Grub Street's inkiest kennel
The eldest born of Diet and Dr. Rennel!
Groveling in toil and trouble from the first,   5
Since from its slime the half-formed witling burst
With dwarfish mimicry of little works
In infant spleen his petty venom lurks—
Since schoolboy fame the pigmy copyist led
To Eton essays and a broken head—   10
When issuing *weekly* from the astonished press
He made 'George Canning's' little world a less.
Reduced the 'Microcosm' to 'Miniature'
And scrawled till cudgeled to a perfect cure—
For blackened 'Rusticus' repaid his hue   15
With interest, and left him black and blue.

129a. 1 from out] within *A, alternate reading*   6 slime] ⟨shell⟩ *A*   7 With]
⟨In⟩ *A*   8 his] ⟨the⟩ *A*

130   Song

Fill the goblet again! for I never before
Felt the glow which now gladdens my heart to its core;
Let us drink! who would not? since thro' life's varied round
In the goblet alone no deception is found.

I have tried in its turn all that life can supply;   5
I have bask'd in the beam of a dark rolling eye;
I have lov'd! who has not? but what heart can declare
That pleasure existed while passion was there?

In the days of my youth, when the heart's in its spring,
And dreams that affection can never take wing,   10
I had friends! who has not? but what tongue will avow
That friends, rosy wine! are so faithful as thou?

The breast of a mistress some boy may estrange,
Friendship shifts with the sunbeam—thou never canst
        change;
Thou grow'st old, who does not? but on earth what appears 15
Whose virtues, like thine, still increase with its years?

Yet if blest to the utmost that love can bestow,
Should a rival bow down to our idol below,
We are jealous! who's not?—thou hast no such alloy,
For the more that enjoy thee, the more we enjoy.   20

Then the season of youth, and its vanities past,
For refuge we fly to the goblet at last;
There we find, do we not, in the flow of the soul,
That truth, as of yore, is confin'd to the bowl?

When the box of Pandora was open'd on earth,   25
And Misery's triumph commenc'd over Mirth;
Hope was left, was she not? but the goblet we kiss,
And care not for Hope, who are certain of bliss.

130. Copy text: *IT*, collated with *Paris 1828*.
title   *IT, 1831*; A Drinking Song *Paris 1828*; Fill the Goblet Again. A Song. *1832*
    7 heart] tongue *Paris 1828*   9 days of my] bright days of *Paris 1828*   16 still ...
its] but ... their *Paris 1828*   21 vanities] jollities *Paris 1828*

Long life to the grape! for when summer is flown
The age of our nectar shall gladden our own;   30
We must die, who shall not? may our sins be forgiven,
And Hebe shall never be idle in heaven.

[1808–9]

131   Stanzas to [Mrs. Musters] On Leaving
England

'Tis done—and shivering in the gale
The bark unfurls her snowy sail;
And whistling o'er the bending mast
Loud sings on high the fresh'ning blast;
And I must from this land begone,   5
Because I cannot love but one.

But could I be what I have been,
And could I see what I have seen,
Could I repose upon the breast
Which once my warmest wishes blest,   10
I should not seek another zone
Because I cannot love but one.

'Tis long since I beheld that eye
Which gave me bliss or misery;
And I have striven, but in vain,   15
Never to think of it again;
For tho' I fly from Albion
I still can only love but one.

As some lone bird without a mate,
My weary heart is desolate;
I look around, and cannot trace   20
One friendly smile or welcome face;
And ev'n in crowds am still alone,
Because I cannot love but one.

131. Copy text: *IT*, collated with *ITB*, *ITBa*, *Paris 1828*

title   *IT*, *1831*; Stanzas to a Lady, On Leaving England *1832*, *C*, *More*; On Leaving England *Paris 1828*; to Mrs. Musters *MS. insertion in ITBa*

23 ev'n] e'en *IT*, *Paris 1828* [MS. cor. to received text made in *ITBa*]

And I will cross the whit'ning foam,   25
And I will seek a foreign home,
Till I forget a false fair face,
I ne'er shall find a resting place;
My own dark thoughts I cannot shun,
But ever love, and love but one.   30

The poorest, veriest wretch on earth
Still finds some hospitable hearth,
Where friendship's or love's softer glow
May smile in joy or soothe in woe;
But friend or leman I have none,   35
Because I cannot love but one.

I go—but wheresoe'er I flee
There's not an eye will weep for me;
There's not a kind, congenial heart
Where I can claim the meanest part: 40
Nor thou, who hast my hopes undone,
Wilt sigh although I love but one.

To think of every early scene,
Of what we are, and what we've been,
Would whelm some softer hearts with woe,   45
But mine, alas! has stood the blow;
Yet still beats on as it begun,
And never truly loves but one.

And who that dear lov'd one may be
Is not for vulgar eyes to see;   50
And why that early love was crost,
Thou knowst the best, I feel the most;
But few that dwell beneath the sun
Have loved so long, and loved but one.

I've tried another's fetters too,   55
With charms perchance as fair to view;
And I would fain have lov'd as well,
But some unconquerable spell

35 leman] lover *IT, Paris 1828* [MS. cor. to received text in *ITB, ITBa*]   57 fain]
feign *IT* [MS. cor. to received text made in *ITB*]

Forbade my bleeding breast to own
A kindred care for aught but one.   60

'Twould soothe to take one lingering view,
And bless thee in my last adieu;
Yet wish I not those eyes to weep
For him that wanders o'er the deep;
His home, his hope, his youth are gone,   65
Yet far away he loves but one.

[1809]

132   [Lines to Mr. Hodgson]

1.

Huzza! Hodgson, we are going,
    Our embargo's off at last,
Favourable Breezes blowing
    Bend the canvass o'er the mast;
From aloft the signal's streaming,   5
    Hark! the farewell gun is fired,
Women screeching, Tars blaspheming,
    Tells us that our time's expired.
            Here's a rascal
            Come to task all   10
    Prying from the custom house,
            Trunks unpacking
            Cases cracking
    Not a corner for a mouse
'Scapes unsearched amid the racket   15
Ere we sail on board the Packet.—

2.

Now our boatmen quit their mooring
And all hands must ply the oar;

65–6 Tho' wheresoe'er my bark may run, | I love but thee, I love but one. *IT, Paris 1828*
The land recedes, his bark is gone, | Yet still he loves, and loves but one. *MS. cor. in ITBa;*
in ITB the ITBa MS. cor. is corrected to received text. 1831 and later edns. follow ITBa.

132. Copy text: *MS. T,* collated with *Life, BLJ*
title *1831, 1832; untitled in T, Life, BLJ*

Baggage from the quay is low'ring,
  We're impatient—push from shore—   20
'Have a care! that Case holds liquor—'
'Stop the boat—I'm sick—oh Lord!'
Sick Maam! damme, you'll be sicker
  Ere you've been an hour on board.'
    Thus are screaming   25
    Men and women,
  Gemmen, Ladies, servants, Jacks,
    Here entangling
    All are wrangling
  Stuck together close as wax,   30
Such the genial noise and racket
Ere we reach the Lisbon Packet.

3.

Now we've reached her, lo! the Captain,
  Gallant Kidd commands the crew,
Passengers *now* their berths are clapt in   35
  Some to grumble, some to spew.
Heyday! call you that a Cabin?
  Why 'tis hardly three feet square,
Not enough to stow Queen Mab in,
  Who the deuce can harbour there?   40
    Who Sir? plenty,
    Nobles twenty
  Did at once my vessel fill
    Did they—Jesus!
    How you squeeze us   45
  Would to God, they did so still,
Then I'd scape the heat and racket
Of the good ship, Lisbon Packet.

4.

Fletcher, Murray, Bob, where are you?
  Stretched along the deck like logs.   50
Bear a hand—you jolly tar you!
  Here's a rope's end for the dogs.
Hobhouse muttering fearful curses
  As the hatchway down he rolls,

31 genial] general *Life*, *1831*, *1832*, C, *More*

Now his breakfast, now his verses   55
   Vomits forth and damns our souls.
    Here's a stanza
    On Braganza;
   Help!—a couplet—no, a cup
    Of warm water—   60
    What's the matter?
   Zounds! my liver's coming up.
I shall not survive the racket
Of this brutal Lisbon Packet.—

5.

Now at length we're off for Turkey,   65
   Lord knows when we shall come back.
Breezes foul, and tempests murkey,
   May unship us in a crack.
But since life at most a jest is,
   As Philosophers allow,   70
Still to laugh by far the best is,
   Then laugh on—as I do now.
    Laugh at all things,
    Great and small things,
   Sick or well, at sea or shore,   75
    While we're quaffing
    Let's have laughing,
   Who the Devil cares for more?
Save good wine, and who would lack it,
Even on board the Lisbon Packet?   80

[1809]

133   [Song. The Girl of Cadiz]

I.

Oh never talk again to me
Of Northern charms and British ladies;

69 since] ⟨as⟩ *T*

133. Copy text: *1832*, collated with *MS. M*, *MS. T*, *MS. L*
title   *untitled in* T, *1832*; Song *M, L*; The Girl of Cadiz *C*
  2 charms] climes *1832, C, More*

It has not been your lot to see,
   Like me, the lovely Girl of Cadiz.
Although her eyes be not of blue,   5
   Nor fair her locks, like English lasses,
How far its own expressive hue
   The languid azure eye surpasses!

2.

Prometheus-like, from heaven she stole
   The fire, that through those silken lashes   10
In darkest glances seems to roll
   From eyes that cannot hide their flashes:
And as along her bosom steal,
   In lengthen'd flow her raven tresses,
You'd swear each clustering lock could feel,   15
   And curl'd to give her neck caresses.

3.

Our English maids are long to woo,
   And frigid even in possession;
And if their charms be fair to view,
   Their lips are slow at Love's confession: 20
But born beneath a brighter sun,
   For love ordain'd the Spanish maid is,
And who,—when fondly, fairly won,—
   Enchants you like the Girl of Cadiz?

4.

The Spanish maid is no coquette,   25
   Nor joys to see a lover tremble,
And if she love, or if she hate,
   Alike she knows not to dissemble.
Her heart can ne'er be bought or sold—
   Howe'er it beats, it beats sincerely;   30
And, though it will not bend to gold,
   'Twill love you long and love you dearly.

   3 ⟨For thou hast never lived to see⟩ T   lot] fate T   9 Prometheus-like] ⟨You'd
swear it was⟩ T   11 In darkest glances seems] ⟨At every glance appears⟩ T
12 ⟨Whene'er her speaking dark eye flashes⟩ T   cannot hide their] ⟨speak in darkening⟩ T
13 along] ⟨adown⟩ T   14 raven] ⟨teeming⟩ T   15 swear ... clustering] ⟨think ...
raven⟩ T   17 English] ⟨English⟩ Saxon T   20 slow] ⟨cold⟩ M   24 Enchants]
⟨Adores⟩ T   26 joys] ⟨likes⟩ T

5.

The Spanish girl that meets your love
   Ne'er taunts you with a mock denial,
For every thought is bent to prove   35
   Her passion in the hour of trial.
When thronging foemen menace Spain,
   She dares the deed and shares the danger;
And should her lover press the plain,
   She hurls the spear, her love's avenger!   40

6.

And when, beneath the evening star,
   She mingles in the gay Bolero,
Or sings to her attuned guitar
   Of Christian knight or Moorish hero,
Or counts her beads with fairy hand   45
   Before the twinkling rays of Hesper,
Or joins Devotion's choral band,
   To chaunt the sweet and hallow'd vesper;—

7.

In each, her charms the heart must move
   Of all, who venture to behold her;   50
Then let not maids less fair reprove,
   Because her bosom is not colder:
Through many a clime 'tis mine to roam
   Where many a soft and melting maid is,
But none abroad, and few at home,   55
   May match the dark-eyed Girl of Cadiz!

[1809]

33 that] who *T*   35 For] ⟨And⟩ *T*   41 beneath] ⟨beneath / as gleams⟩ *T*
42 mingles in] dances to *T* ; *M cancelled*   44 knight or] ⟨or of⟩ *T*   45 counts
her beads with] ⟨tells with light and / reckons with her⟩ *T*   46 ⟨Her beads beneath
the beams / rays of Hesper⟩ *T*   Before] Beneath *1832, C, More*
49–52   In each alike she wins the heart
              And triumphs oer the youthful bosom
              And who from her can bear to part
              Who seems so fair ⟨and yet⟩ so loth to lose him? *cancelled in T*
49 her . . . must] her ⟨winning⟩ charms the heart can *T*   50–1 ⟨The willing heart of
each ? | Though maids less fair will bid reprove⟩ *T*   53 clime] shore *T*
54 ⟨And I have sailed⟩ *T*   soft] fair *T*   56 dark-eyed] ⟨lovely⟩ *T*

134   Written in an Album

1.

As o'er the cold sepulchral stone
    Some name arrests the passer-by;
Thus when thou view'st this page alone
    May mine attract thy pensive eye!

2.

And when by thee that name is read,   5
    Perchance in some succeeding year,
Reflect on me as on the dead,
    And think my heart is buried here.

14 Sept. 1809

135   To Florence

Oh Lady! when I left the shore,
    The distant shore, which gave me birth,
I hardly thought to grieve once more,
    To quit another spot on earth:
Yet here amidst this barren isle,   5
    Where panting Nature droops the head,
Where only thou art seen to smile,
    I view my parting hour with dread.
Though far from Albin's craggy shore,
    Divided by the dark-blue main;   10
A few, brief, rolling seasons o'er,
    Perchance I view her cliffs again:
But wheresoe'er I now may roam,
    Through scorching clime, and varied sea,

134. Copy text: *CHP*(7), collated with *MSS.* M, T, D, and G, the proof copy, *CHP(1)*–*CHP*(6) and *CHP*(8)–*CHP(10)*

title   *all CHP texts, 1831, G;* Written at Mrs. S. S.'s request in her Memorandum Book *T, D cancelled;* Written at Mrs. ⟨Spencer⟩ S.'s request in her memorandum book *M;* Written at the request of a Lady in her Memorandum Book *D;* Lines Written in an Album, at Malta *1832*

135. Copy text: *CHP*(7), collated with *MS.* M, *MS. H,* the proof copy, *CHP(1)*–*CHP*(6) and *CHP*(8)–*CHP(10)*

title   *1832; untitled in M and H;* To——*all editions from CHP(1) to 1831*

    2 which] that *M, H*   4 quit] ⟨leave⟩ *M*   6 Where ⟨droop⟩ panting Nature *M*
8 my] the *M, H*   9 Albin's] Albion's *M*   12 her cliffs] ⟨my house⟩ *M*
13 I now may] ⟨my footsteps⟩ *M*   14 Through foreign clime and distant sea *M, H*

Though Time restore me to my home,   15
    I ne'er shall bend mine eyes on thee:
On thee, in whom at once conspire
    All charms which heedless hearts can move,
Whom but to see is to admire,
    And, oh! forgive the word—to love.   20
Forgive the word, in one who ne'er
    With such a word can more offend;
And since thy heart I cannot share,
    Believe me, what I am, thy friend.
And who so cold as look on thee,   25
    Thou lovely wand'rer, and be less?
Nor be, what man should ever be,
    The friend of Beauty in distress?
Ah! who would think that form had pass'd
    Through Danger's most destructive path,   30
Had brav'd the death-wing'd tempest's blast,
    And 'scap'd a tyrant's fiercer wrath?
Lady! when I shall view the walls
    Where free Byzantium once arose;
And Stamboul's Oriental halls   35
    The Turkish tyrants now enclose;
Though mightiest in the lists of fame,
    That glorious city still shall be;
On me 'twill hold a dearer claim,
    As spot of thy nativity: 40
And though I bid thee now farewell,
    When I behold that wond'rous scene,

16 shall] ⟨can⟩ *M*   17 in] ⟨for⟩ *M*   18 which] that *M, H*   23 ⟨And let me claim a ? share⟩ *M*   thy] that *M, H*   25 so cold] alas *M, H*   30 Through ⟨stern Misfortune's⟩ distant danger's rugged path *M, H, cancellation in M*   31 death-wing'd] ⟨howling⟩ *M*   33 Lady . . . view] ⟨Oh Lady when I view⟩ *M*   35 And] ⟨And⟩ Where *M*

41–4 *B made three failed attempts at these lines in M:*
    (*a*) ⟨Adieu a first a last adieu
        From thee be sorrow far removed⟩
    (*b*) ⟨Now fare thee well and may thy sail / breeze
        That wafts thee to those other climes
        Convey thee safe⟩
    (*c*) For me who thus have dared to lay
        ⟨My tribute at so fair a shrine
        I ask / Think not of me when far away
        Unworthy thoughts so pure as thine⟩
41 bid thee now] ⟨bid thee now⟩ could then say *M*   42 When I behold] ⟨ Yet when I view⟩ *M*   wond'rous] hallowed *M*

Since where thou art I may not dwell,
'Twill soothe to be, where thou hast been.

Sept. 1809

136   Stanzas

*Composed October 11th 1809, during the night; in a thunder-storm, when
the guides had lost the road to Zitza, near the range of mountains formerly
called Pindus, in Albania.*

1.

Chill and mirk is the nightly blast,
    Where Pindus' mountains rise,
And angry clouds are pouring fast
    The vengeance of the skies.

2.

Our guides are gone, our hope is lost,   5
    And lightnings, as they play,
But show where rocks our path have crost,
    Or gild the torrent's spray.

3.

Is yon a cot I saw, though low?
    When lightning broke the gloom—   10
How welcome were its shade!—ah, no!
    'Tis but a Turkish tomb.

4.

Through sounds of foaming waterfalls
    I hear a voice exclaim—
My way-worn countryman, who calls   15
    On distant England's name.

44 soothe] ⟨please⟩ *M*

136. Copy text: *CHP(7)*, collated with *MS. M*, *MS. D*, the proof, *CHP(1)–CHP(10)*
title   Stanzas Composed during a Thunder Storm *1832*, *C*, *More*
5 guides] ⟨path⟩ *M*

5.

A shot is fir'd—by foe or friend?
  Another—'tis to tell
The mountain-peasants to descend,
  And lead us where they dwell.   20

6.

Oh! who in such a night will dare
  To tempt the wilderness?
And who 'mid thunder peals can hear
  Our signal of distress?

7.

And who that heard our shouts would rise   25
  To try the dubious road?
Nor rather deem from nightly cries
  That outlaws were abroad.

8.

Clouds burst, skies flash, oh, dreadful hour!
  More fiercely pours the storm!   30
Yet here one thought has still the power
  To keep my bosom warm.

9.

While wand'ring through each broken path,
  O'er brake and craggy brow;
While elements exhaust their wrath,   35
  Sweet Florence, where art thou?

10.

Not on the sea, not on the sea,
  Thy bark hath long been gone:
Oh, may the storm that pours on me,
  Bow down my head alone!   40

11.

Full swiftly blew the swift Siroc,
  When last I pressed thy lip;
And long ere now with foaming shock
  Impell'd thy gallant ship.

28 were] ⟨are⟩ M   38 bark] ⟨ship⟩ M

12.

Now thou art safe; nay, long ere now   45
   Hast trod the shore of Spain;
'Twere hard if aught so fair as thou
   Should linger on the main.

13.

And since I now remember thee
   In darkness and in dread,   50
As in those hours of revelry
   Which mirth and music sped;

14.

Do thou amidst the fair white walls,
   If Cadiz yet be free,
At times from out her lattic'd halls   55
   Look o'er the dark blue sea;

15.

Then think upon Calypso's isles
   Endear'd by days gone by,
To others give a thousand smiles,
   To me a single sigh.   60

16.

And when the admiring circle mark
   The paleness of thy face,
A half form'd tear, a transient spark
   Of melancholy grace,

17.

Again thou'lt smile, and blushing shun   65
   Some coxcomb's raillery;
Nor own for once thou thought'st of one,
   Who ever thinks on thee.

18.

Though smile and sigh alike are vain,
   When sever'd hearts repine,   70
My spirit flies o'er mount and main,
   And mourns in search of thine.

[1809]

68 on] of *M*   71 flies o'er] ⟨passest⟩ *M*

137

Stanzas

Written in passing the Ambracian Gulph,
November 14th, 1809

1.

THROUGH cloudless skies, in silvery sheen,
    Full beams the moon on Actium's coast:
And on these waves for Egypt's queen
    The ancient world was won and lost.

2.

And now upon the scene I look,   5
    The azure grave of many a Roman;
Where stern Ambition once forsook
    His wavering crown to follow woman.

3.

Florence! whom I will love as well
    As ever yet was said or sung,   10
(Since Orpheus sang his spouse from hell)
    Whilst thou art fair and I am young;

4.

Sweet Florence! those were pleasant times,
    When worlds were staked for ladies' eyes:
Had bards as many realms as rhymes,   15
    Thy charms might raise new Anthonies.

5.

Though Fate forbids such things to be,
    Yet, by thine eyes and ringlets curl'd!
I cannot lose a world for thee,
    But would not lose thee for a world!   20

[1809]

137. Copy text: *CHP(7)*, collated with *MSS. L, M,* and *D,* the proof copy, *CHP(1)–CHP(6)* and *CHP(8)–CHP(10)*

title   *thus in all forms, except the date was dropped in 1831, 1832*

5 scene] ⟨spot⟩ *L*   6 ⟨Stain'd with Egyptian gore and Roman⟩ *L*   9 Florence . . . love] ⟨Sweet Florence, whom I love⟩ *L*   11 *parentheses around lines 10–11 in M*
15–16 ⟨I bring ? rhymes | But here my only kingdom lies⟩ *L*   15 as . . . as] but realms along with *L, M, D*   along with] ⟨instead of⟩ *M*   16 Again we'd see some Anthonies *M, cancelled in D*; ⟨I leave? the world like Anthony⟩ *L*   17 Fate] Jove *M, D cancelled*
18 Yet] ⟨But⟩ *L*

138   [Lines in the Travellers' Book of the Macri Family]

In this book a traveller had written:—
'Fair Albion, smiling, sees her son depart
To trace the birth and nursery of art:
Noble his object, glorious is his aim;
He comes to Athens, and he writes his name.'

Beneath which Lord Byron inserted the following:—
The modest bard, like many a bard unknown,
Rhymes on our names, but wisely hides his own;
But yet, whoe'er he be, to say no worse,
His name would bring more credit than his verse.

[1810]

139   Substitute for an Epitaph

Kind Reader! take your choice to cry or laugh;
A Man here lies—but where's his Epitaph?
If such you seek, try Westminster, and view
Ten thousand just as fit for him as you.

12 J[anuar]y 1810

140   Written at Athens

January 16, 1810

The spell is broke, the charm is flown!
Thus is it with life's fitful fever:

138. Copy text: *1831*, collated with *Williams, 1832, C,*
title   *untitled in Williams*; Lines Written in the Travellers' Book at Orchomenus *all editions*

139. Copy text: *1832* collated with *MS. T, New Monthly*
   2 A Man here lies] Here Harold lies *1832, C, More*; Here lies a man *New Monthly*
dating   Feb. 12, 1810 *New Monthly*

140. Copy text: *CHP(7)*, collated with *MS. T, MS. M, MS. D,* the proof copy, *CHP(1)–CHP(6)* and *CHP(8)–CHP(10)*
title   *thus in the MSS. and all editions up to 1831*; The Spell is Broke, the Charm is Flown! Written at Athens, January 16. 1810 *1831, 1832, C, More*

We madly smile when we should groan;
   Delirium is our best deceiver.
Each lucid interval of thought   5
   Recalls the woes of Nature's charter,
And he that acts as wise men ought,
   But lives, as saints have died, a martyr.

                                        [1810]

141   Song

                Ζώη μοῦ, σάς ἀγαπῶ

                 Athens, 1810.

                       1.

Maid of Athens, ere we part,
Give, oh, give me back my heart!
Or, since that has left my breast,
Keep it now, and take the rest!
Hear my vow before I go,   5
Ζώη μοῦ, σάς ἀγαπῶ.

                       2.

By those tresses unconfin'd,
Woo'd by each Aegean wind;
By those lids whose jetty fringe
Kiss thy soft cheeks' blooming tinge;   10
By those wild eyes like the roe,
Ζώη μοῦ, σάς ἀγαπῶ.

                       3.

By that lip I long to taste;
By that zone-encircl'd waist;
By all the token-flowers that tell   15
What words can never speak so well;

5 Each lucid] ⟨But each cool⟩ T   7 acts as wise] ⟨thinks as good⟩ T ; ⟨thinks⟩ as wise M

141. Copy text: *CHP(7)*, collated with *MS. K*, the proof, *CHP(1)–CHP(6)* and *CHP(8)–CHP(10)*

title   *thus in all editions until 1831*; Maid of Athens, Ere We Part *1831, 1832, C, More*
   1 Maid] Girl *K*   15–16 ⟨By each charm beheld by me |By those alas ! I may not see⟩ *K*
15 ⟨By every charm so well espi⟩ *K*

Painted by Thos. Stothard R.A.

Engraved by A. Smith ARA.

SONG 7.

MAID OF ATHENS, ERE WE PART,

GIVE, AH, GIVE ME BACK MY HEART!

PUBLISHED BY JOHN MURRAY, ALBEMARLE STREET, DECR 1.1814.

'Song' (poem no. 141), lines 1–2

(*Reproduced with the permission of the British Library*)

By Love's alternate joy and woe,
Ζώη μοῦ, σάς ἀγαπῶ.

4.

Maid of Athens! I am gone:
Think of me, sweet! when alone.   20
Though I fly to Istambol,
Athens holds my heart and soul:
Can I cease to love thee? No!
Ζώη μοῦ, σάς ἀγαπῶ.

[1810]

142 Written after swimming from Sestos to Abydos

May 9, 1810

1.

If in the month of dark December
Leander, who was nightly wont
(What maid will not the tale remember?)
To cross thy stream, broad Hellespont!

2.

If when the wintry tempest roar'd   5
He sped to Hero, nothing loth,
And thus of old thy current pour'd,
Fair Venus! how I pity both!

3.

For *me*, degenerate modern wretch,
Though in the genial month of May,   10
My dripping limbs I faintly stretch,
And think I've done a feat to-day.

17 ⟨Yet still I hope and say not so⟩ By all that makes our joy and woe *K*   19 Maid]
Girl *K*

142. Copy text: *CHP(7)*, collated with *MS. T*, proof, *CHP(1)*–*CHP(6)* and *CHP(8)*–
CHP(10)

title   Written After Swimming from Sestos to Abydos—May 3rd 1810 *T*

3 (If I the tale aright remember) *T*
12   Though Hero and a hundred such
                       Were waiting on these welcome banks—
                       But I've already done too much
                       Confound Leander's gooselike pranks! *T, between stanzas 3 and 4*

4.

But since he cross'd the rapid tide,
   According to the doubtful story,
To woo,—and—Lord knows what beside,   15
   And swam for Love, as I for Glory;

5.

'Twere hard to say who fared the best:
   Sad mortals! thus the Gods still plague you!
He lost his labour, I my jest:
   For he was drown'd, and I've the ague.   20

[1810]

143   Farewell Petition to
J[ohn] C[am] H[obhouse] Esq.

Oh thou yclep'd by vulgar sons of men
Cam Hobhouse! but by wags Byzantian Ben!
Twin sacred titles, which combined appear
To grace thy volume's front, and gild its rear,
Since now thou put'st thyself and work to Sea   5
And leav'st all Greece to *Fletcher* and to me,
Oh hear my single muse our sorrows tell,
One song for *self*, and Fletcher quite as well.—

First to the *Castle* of that man of woes
Dispatch the letter which *I must* enclose;   10
And when his lone Penelope shall say,
Why, where, and *wherefore* doth my William stay?
Spare not to move her pity, or her pride—
By all that Hero suffered, or defied;
The *chicken's toughness,* and the *lack* of *Ale,*   15
The *stoney mountain,* and the *miry vale,*
The *Garlick* steams, which *half* his meals enrich,
The *impending vermin,* and the threatened *Itch*;
That *ever-breaking* Bed, beyond repair!
The hat too *old,* the coat too *cold* to wear;   20

15 woo] kiss *T*   17 In vain ⟨we both did⟩ we've dared to swim and soak *T*   19 He
lost his ⟨lass and⟩ labour, I my joke *T*

143. Copy text: *MS. M,* collated with *Murray's Magazine* and *C,*

The hunger, *which, repulsed from Sally's door,*
Pursues her grumbling half from shore to shore;
Be these the themes to greet his faithful Rib,
So may thy pen be smooth, thy tongue be glib!

This duty done, let me in turn demand   25
Some friendly office in my native land;
Yet let me ponder well, before I ask,
And set thee swearing at the tedious task.

First the Miscellany!—to Southwell town
Per coach for Mrs. *Pigot* frank it down;   30
So may'st thou prosper in the paths of Sale,
And Longman smirk and critics cease to rail.

All hail to Matthews! wash his reverend feet,
And in my name the man of Method greet,
Tell him, my guide, Philosopher, and Friend,   35
Who cannot love me, and who will not mend,
Tell him, that not in vain I shall essay
To tread and trace our 'old Horatian way',
And be (with prose supply my dearth of rhymes)
What better men have been in better times.   40

Here let me cease, for why should I prolong
My notes, and vex a *Singer* with a *Song*?
Oh thou with pen perpetual in thy fist!
Dubbed for thy sins a stark Miscellanist,
So pleased the printer's orders to perform,   45
For Messrs. *Longman, Hurst,* and *Rees* and *Orme,*
Go, get thee hence to Paternoster Row,
Thy patrons wave a duodecimo!
(Best form for *letters* from a distant land,
It fits the pocket, nor fatigues the hand.)   50
Then go, once more the joyous work commence
With stores of anecdote, and grains of sense.
Oh may Mammas relent, and Sires forgive!
And scribbling Sons grow dutiful and live!

Constantinople, 7 June 1810

21 *repulsed*] (exiled) *M*   37 essay] assay *Murray's Magazine, C, More*

144   [Translation of the Nurse's Dole
in the Medea of Euripides]

Oh how I wish that an embargo
Had kept in port the good ship Argo!
Who, still unlaunch'd from Grecian docks,
Had never pass'd the Azure rocks;
But now I fear her trip will be a   5
Damn'd business for my Miss Medea, &c. &c.

[1810]

145   [On his Sickness. A Parody]

On a cold room's cold floor, within a bed
Of iron, with three coverlids like lead,
A coat and breeches dangling o'er a nook,
Where sits a doctor, and prescribes a puke,
Poor B-r-n sweats—alas! how changed from him   5
So plump in feature, and so round in limb,
Grinning and gay in Newstead's monkish fane,
The scene of profanation and Champagne;
Or just as gay with scribblers in a ring
Of twenty hungry authors banqueting.   10
No whore to fondle left of half a score,
Yet one thing left him, which he values more:
Here victor of a fever, and its friends,
Physicians and their art, his lordship *mends*.

[1810]

146   [Epitaph from a Sickbed]

Odious! in boards, 'twould any Bard provoke,
(Were the last words that dying Byron spoke).

144. Copy text: *Life*
title   *untitled in Life*

145. 146. Copy text: *MS. M*, collated with *LBC*, *BLJ*

No, let some charming cuts and frontispiece
Adorn my volume, and the sale increase;
One would not be unpublished when one's dead,   5
And, Hobhouse, let my works be bound in *Red*.

[1810]

147   [My Epitaph]

Youth, Nature, and relenting Jove,
To keep my lamp *in* strongly strove;
But Romanelli was so stout
He beat all three—and *blew* it *out*.

[1810]

148   The Monk of Athos

Oh ye, whose lips have touch'd the Sacred Stream
That from the Mount of classic Sweetness flows,
Whose gen'rous Souls have drunk the vital Beam
Of ardent Glory which resistless glows
Through ev'ry page of Grecian lore, and throws   5
A lustre mellowed by the hand of Time
Around the bleeding Hero's laurell'd Brows—
To you I sing, though all uncouth my rhyme,
And far unmeet I ween for audience so sublime.

Yet deem I not unwelcome to your Ear   10
The feeble strain shall prove which thus essays
To wake Remembrance to a theme so dear,
And mourne in simple and incondite lays
The fate of Greece in those disastrous days,
When late, though sunk beneath a tyrant's might,   15
She boldly ventured (Oh immortal praise)
In arms to reassert her ancient light,
And Freedom's standard rear'd, and dared the unequal fight.

147. Copy text: *Life*, collated with *MS.*
title   *untitled in MS. and Life*

148. Copy text: *MS. B*, lines 55–81 collated with *Roden Noel*
   5 Grecian] ⟨antient⟩ *B*   7 Hero's] ⟨patriot's⟩ *B*   15 might] ⟨pow'r⟩ *B*

Alas, that with the ever-blooming meed
Which Virtue wreathes around the Patriot's head,   20
The Muse must intertwine the mournful weed
That crowns the ashes of the Glorious Dead.
Alas, that clouds of woe should overspread
The blush of Freedom's renovated Dawn,
While Desolation stalks with blasting tread   25
Mid scenes of Honour wasted and forlorn,
And waves her lurid torch, and smiles in baleful scorn.

Ah, who unmoved had seen both field and flood
With undistinguished carnage all defiled,
And vengeance gorg'd with unoffending Blood,   30
Or heard the widow's shriek of Anguish wild
When from her arms was torn her only child,
Sad pledge of him whom death so lately reft;
As yet unconscious of her grief it smil'd,
Her only Hope of earthly solace left,   35
Now on the Spear impaled, or by the Sabre cleft.

Full well I know how ev'ry gen'rous Heart
Shares in the ills which desolate Mankind,
Yet are there private woes that oft impart
A deeper Sorrow to the feeling mind,   40
That wake the sense of sympathy refined
And bid the tide of wild Emotion roll,
Thrilling those chords which Nature has entwined
In closest union with the Human Soul,
With now resistless force and absolute controul.   45

Of such I tell; of fond domestic ties
Asunder torn by War's relentless Hand
(Like Blossoms withered by inclement Skies
That perish ere their tender sweets expand),
Proscription's sword and Persecution's brand,   50
The hopeless Exile's Anguish and Despair,
As he still lingers near his native Land,
Or drags a weary load of Grief and Care
From clime to clime astray, forlorn, and reckless where.

28 had seen] ⟨could see⟩ *B*   35 Hope] ⟨pledge⟩ *B*

Beside the confines of the Aegean main   55
Where northward Macedonia bounds the flood
And views opposed the Asiatic Plain
Where once the pride of lofty Ilion stood,
Like the great father of the giant Brood,
With lowering port Majestic Athos stands,   60
Crowned with the verdure of Eternal wood
As yet unspoil'd by sacrilegious Hands,
And throws his Mighty shade o'er seas and distant lands.

And deep embosomed in his shady groves
Full many a Convent rears its glittering spire   65
Mid scenes where heav'nly Contemplation loves
To kindle in the soul her hallowed fire;
Where Air and Sea with Rocks and Woods conspire
To breathe a sweet religious calm around,
Weaning the thoughts from every low desire;   70
And the wild waves that break with Murm'ring Sound
Along the rocky shore proclaim it Holy Ground.

Sequestered shades where Piety has given
A quiet refuge from each Earthly care,
Whence the rapt Spirit may ascend to Heaven   75
In holy strains of Penitence and Prayer—
Oh ye, condemn'd the ills of life to bear,
As with advancing age your woes increase,
What bliss amidst these solitudes to share
The happy foretaste of Eternal Peace,   80
Till Heaven in mercy bids your pains and sorrows cease.

[1811]

149   Written Beneath a Picture

I.

Dear object of defeated care!
Though now of Love and thee bereft,

73 Piety ⟨Penitence⟩ B

149. Copy text: *CHP(7)*, collated with *MS. M*, *MS. D*, proof, *CHP(1)–CHP(6)* and *CHP(8)–CHP(10)*

title   *thus in all editions to 1831*; Lines Written Beneath a Picture *1832*; Written Beneath a Picture of J. V. D. *M, D*

1 of ⟨my⟩ defeated *M*

To reconcile me with despair
Thine image and my tears are left.

2.

'Tis said with Sorrow Time can cope;   5
But this I feel can ne'er be true:
For by the death-blow of my Hope
My Memory immortal grew.

[1811]

150   Hints from Horace:

Being an Allusion in English Verse to the Epistle 'Ad Pisones de
Arte Poetica' and Intended as a Sequel to 'English Bards and Scotch
Reviewers'

> Ergo fungar vice cotis, acutum
> Reddere quae ferrum valet, exsors ipsa secandi.
> HOR. *De Arte Poet.*, ll. 304, 305

> Rhymes are difficult things—they are stubborn things, Sir.
> FIELDING's *Amelia*, Vol. III, Book and Chap. v.

PREFACE

HOWEVER little this poem may resemble the Latin, it has been
submitted to one of the great rules of Horace, having been kept
in the desk for more than *nine* years. It was composed at Athens
in the Spring of 1811, and received some additions after the auth-
or's return to England in the same year.

[1821]

7 death-blow of] ⟨Stroke that crushed⟩ *M*
dating   Athens 1811 *M, cancelled in D*

150. Copy text: Preface *BLÿ*; 1–276, 583–804 *Proof M*; 277–582 *MS. T*; collated
with *MSS. LA, LB, M, T* and (fragments) *MA, LC, Υ, B, H, TX*; Proofs *BMA, BMB*;
1831, C.
title   Imitation of Horace. De Arte Poetica in English Verse. *LA*;
Hints from Horace. Athens March 12 1811. Imitation in English Verse of Horace De Arte
. . . Reviewers. *LB*; Hints . . . Poetica' from Horace (to be printed with the Original Latin).
M; Hints from Horace: being a Partial Imitation in . . . *Reviewers*. Proof *BMB*; Hints
from Horace. *Proof M*
epigraphs   *not in LA, Proof M*

Who would not laugh, if Lawrence, skilled to grace
His classic canvass with each flatter'd face,
Abused his art, till Nature with a blush
Saw cits grow centaurs underneath his brush?
Or should some limner join, for show or sale,   5
A maid of honour to a mermaid's tail?
Or low Dubost, as once the world has seen,
Degrade God's creatures in his graphic spleen?
Not all that forced politeness which defends
Fools in their faults, could gag his grinning friends.   10
Believe me, Moschus, like that picture seems
The book, which, sillier than a sick man's dreams,
Displays a crowd of figures incomplete,
Poetic night-mares, without head or feet.

Poets and painters as all artists know,   15
May shoot a little with a lengthen'd bow;
We claim this mutual mercy for our task,
And grant in turn the pardon which we ask;
But make not monsters spring from gentle dams,
Birds breed not vipers, tigers nurse not lambs.   20

A labour'd, long exordium sometimes tends
(Like patriot speeches) but to paltry ends;
And nonsense in a lofty note goes down,
As pertness passes with a legal gown:

1–8   If West or Lawrence (take whicheer you will)
           ⟨These mighty masters of Pictorial skill⟩
           Sons of the Brush, ⟨and peers⟩ supreme in graphic skill,
           Should clap a human headpiece on a mare,
           How would ⟨the⟩ our Exhibition loungers stare!
           Or should some dashing limner set to sale,
           My Lady's likeness with a ⟨fish's⟩ Mermaid's tail, *LA*
1 skilled] paid *LB, cor. in M*; hired *M, T, Proof BMB, 1831, cor. in Proof M*   2 classic]
costly *LB, M, T, Proof BMB, 1831, 1832, C, More, cor. in Proof M*   each] a *LB*
3 The features finished, should ⟨proceed to⟩ / superbly deck *LB*   Abused his] Embellished
Art *M*; ⟨Embellished / Distorted art⟩ *T*   4 ⟨Your portly person with—a Horse's neck⟩
My Lady's likeness with—a Filly's neck! *LB*   9 forced politeness] ⟨starch decorum⟩ *LA*
10 Fools . . . faults] ⟨Een fools from fools⟩ *LA*   11 Moschus] Hobhouse *LA, LB, M*
cor. in T: thus for all subsequent lines with 'Moschus'   12 sillier than] hideous as *LA,*
cor. in LB   13 ⟨Is filled with nightmare spectres / figures horrible and pale⟩ *LA*
14 ⟨Yet all confusing without head and tail *LA*⟩   15 Painters and Poets—as we scribblers know *LA, LB, M*   19 make . . . spring] ⟨savage sons spring not⟩ *LA*   make]
⟨bid⟩ *LB*   20 Birds] ⟨Doves⟩ *LA*   22 patriot] Wardle's *LA, cor. in LB*   23 ⟨And
trifles sounded / And nonsense passes⟩ *LA*   24 Which covers all things like a Parson's
gown *LA*   Parson's] Prelate's *LB*; ⟨Which wraps presumption⟩ with a legal gown *M*

Thus many a bard describes in pompous strain   25
The clear brook babbling through the goodly plain;
The groves of Granta, and her gothic halls—
King's Coll.—Cam's streams—stain'd windows, and old
    walls:
Or, in adventurous numbers neatly aims
To paint a rainbow, or—the river Thames.   30

You sketch a tree, and so perhaps may shine,
But daub a shipwreck like an ale-house sign;
You plan a vase—it dwindles to a pot—
Then glide down Grub-street—fasting, and forgot;
Laughed into Lethe by some quaint Review,   35
Whose wit is never troublesome, till true.
In fine, to whatsoever you aspire,
Let it at least be simple and entire.

The greater portion of the rhyming tribe—
(Give ear, my friend, for thou hast been a scribe)   40

25–8   ⟨Such genial bards description / to ostentation yields⟩
As when ⟨sage⟩ the poet describes in fustian [*sic*]
Of waters gliding through the goodly fields,
⟨Of hoary⟩ The groves of Granta and her gothic halls,
Oxford and Christchurch, London and St. Paul's *LA*
29 Or with a nobler flight he feebly aims *LA*
31–6   ⟨But you perhaps young sir can paint⟩
Perhaps you ⟨paint a tree with⟩ draw a fir tree or a beech,
But then a landscape is beyond your reach,
Or if that ⟨simile should⟩ allegory please you not
Take this,—you'd ⟨make⟩ form a vase, but make a pot. *LA, LB, cor. in M*
31–2 Although you sketch a tree which Taste endures | Your ill-daubed Shipwreck shocks
the Connoisseurs *M, cor. in T*   33–4 *MS. MA shows the following series of attempts at
the couplet:*

    a. ⟨Beware the Bathos—Grubstreet and the lot | Of him whose vase⟩
    b. ⟨You'd ? a vase and made it end a pot⟩
    c. You've planned ⟨an Urn⟩ a Vase—⟨and next it ends a pot⟩ why end it in a pot?
    d. ⟨Observe the⟩ Beware the Bathos of the Grubstreet lot
    e. ⟨Avoid / Reject / Complete with care—for if the end's forgot
        A polished urn will dwindle to a pot⟩
    f. ⟨Neer let the ? of polish be forgot
        With grand beginnings / Your valued vase will dwindle to a pot⟩
    g. Beware the Bathos of the Grubstreet lot | Who ⟨planned a vase⟩ fain would mould a
        vase but make a pot

33 plan] form *LA*; mould *LB*; Why plan a vase which dwindles to a pot *Proof BMB*
34 Then] You *Proof BMB*   38 at least] ⟨my friend / young man⟩ *LA*   39 rhyming
tribe] ⟨rhyming race⟩ *LA*; men of rhyme *LA, LB, M, cor. in T*   40 Father and children as their Sire sublime *LA, LB*; Parents . . . Sires *M, cor. in T*

Are led astray by some peculiar lure;
I labour to be brief—become obscure:
One falls while following elegance too fast,
Another soars, inflated with bombast;
Too low a third crawls on, afraid to fly,   45
He spins his subject to satiety;
Absurdly wavering, he at last engraves
Fish in the woods, and boars beneath the waves!

Unless your care's exact, your judgment nice,
The flight from folly leads but into vice;   50
None are complete, all wanting in some part,
Like certain tailors, limited in art;
For galligaskins Slowshears is your man,
But coats must claim another artisan.
Now this to me, I own, seems much the same   55
As Vulcan's feet to bear Apollo's frame;
Or, with a fair complexion to expose
Black eyes, black ringlets, but—a bottle nose!

Dear authors! suit your topics to your strength,
And ponder well your subject and its length,   60
Nor lift your load before you're quite aware
What weights your shoulders will or will not bear.
But lucid order, and wit's siren voice,
Await the poet skilful in his choice;

41 ⟨Are led astray by striving to be sure⟩ But change the malady they strive to cure *LA*, *cor. in LB*   42 brief] terse *LA*   43 ⟨In following graces strength and spirit fail / Strength, Spirit fail by following grace too fast⟩ *LA*   falls] fails *LA, LB, M, Proof BMB* while] ⟨by⟩ *T*   44 ⟨He strives to soar but bursts into bombast⟩ *LA*   46 spins] twists *LA, LB, M;* ⟨twirls⟩ *T*   47 wavering] varying *LA, LB, M, Proof BMB, 1831, 1832, C, More*   48 Fish] ⟨Dolphins⟩ *LA*   boars beneath] wild boars in *LA, LB, M, cor. in T*   49 care's exact⟩ ⟨art be just⟩ *LA*   52 certain tailors] ⟨matchless Hoby / London⟩ *LA*   53 For coat and waistcoat ⟨Allen⟩ Switzer is your man *LA, LB, M*   galligaskins] *T, Proof BMB*   54 coats must] breeches *LA, LB, M, Proof BMB, cor. in T*   56 As one leg perfect, and the other lame *LA, LB, M;* ⟨As one too perfect, and the other lame⟩ *T*   58 ringlets] ⟨curls⟩ *LA*   but] and *Proof BMB* 59 Dear] ⟨Suit / Oh⟩ *LA*   60 well ⟨on all their⟩ your *LA*   61 quite] well *LA, LB*   62 weights] weight *LA, LB, M, Proof BMB, 1831, 1832 C, More*

63–7   Him, who hath sense to make a skilful choice
                            Nor lucid order, nor the ⟨enchanting⟩ Siren voice
                            Of eloquence, shall ⟨quit⟩ shun, and wit and grace
                            ⟨Or I'm deceived⟩ shall aid him in the race.
                            These too will teach him to defer or join *LA, LB, M, cor. in T*

With native eloquence he soars along,   65
Grace in his thoughts, and music in his song!
Let judgment teach him wisely to combine
With future parts the now omitted line,
This shall the author choose, and that reject,
Precise in style, and cautious to select;   70
Nor slight applause will candid pens afford
To him who furnishes a *wanting* word;
Then fear not, if 'tis needful, to produce
Some term unknown, or obsolete in use:
(As Pitt has furnish'd us a word or two,   75
Which lexicographers declined to do),
So you indeed, with care, (but be content
To take this licence rarely) may invent.

New words find credit in these latter days,
If neatly grafted on a Gallic phrase;   80
What Chaucer, Spenser did, we scarce refuse
To Dryden's, or to Pope's maturer muse.
If you can add a little, say, why not?
As well as William Pitt and Walter Scott;
Since they by force of rhyme and force of lungs   85
Enrich'd our islands' ill-united tongues;
'Tis then, and shall be, lawful to present
Reforms in writing, as in Parliament.

As forests shed their foliage by degrees,
So fade expressions, which in season please;   90
And we and ours, alas! are due to fate,
And works and words but dwindle to a date;

68 With] To *LA*, *LB*, *M*, *cor. in T*   69 shall] let *LA* choose] like *LA*, *LB*, *M*, *cor. in T*   and] or *M*, *Proof BMB*, *1831*, *1832*, *C*, *More*   70 Precise in style] Sparing in words *LA*, *LB*, *M*, *cor. in T*   71 will ... afford] ⟨the public will⟩ / will critic ⟨tongues⟩ pens avoid *LA*, *cor. in LB*   72 furnishes] ⟨will / skilfully⟩ well compounds ⟨new⟩ *LA*, *LB*, *M*, *cor. in T*   To ... furnishes] The dextrous coiner of *Proof BMB*   73 Then fear not, if] And if by chance *LA*, *LB*, *M*, *cor. in T*   74 unknown] long hid *LA*, *LB*, *cor. in M*   76 Which ⟨Sheridan and Johnson never knew⟩ *LA*   77 So you ⟨but sparingly such licence take⟩ with care a little be content *LA*   78 For once, with circumspection may invent *LA*   80 neatly] ⟨nicely / slightly⟩ *LA*   If neatly] Adroitly *Proof BMB*   81 ⟨To Pope and Dryden⟩ *LA*   we scarce] then why *LA*, *cor. in LB*   83 you] I *LA*   85–6 ⟨If⟩ Since they enriched our language in their time | In modern speeches or Blackletter rhyme, *LA*, *cor. in LB*   87 'Tis lawful then, and shall be, to invent *LA*, *LB*   90 in season] ⟨at present / for a season⟩ *LA*   in] a *M*, *cor. in T*   91 alas ... fate] ⟨alike ... death⟩ *LA*   92 And works ⟨of the mighty / labours⟩ and words alike but have their date *LA*

Though as a monarch nods, and commerce calls,
Impetuous rivers stagnate in canals;
Though swamps subdued, and marshes drain'd, sustain   95
The heavy ploughshare and the yellow grain,
And rising ports along the busy shore
Protect the vessel from old Ocean's roar;—
All, all must perish—but, surviving last,
The love of letters half preserves the past;   100
True—some decay, yet not a few revive,
Though those shall sink, which now appear to thrive,
As custom arbitrates, whose shifting sway
Our life and language must alike obey.

The immortal wars which gods and angels wage,   105
Are they not shown in Milton's sacred page?
His strain will teach what numbers best belong
To themes celestial told in epic song.

The slow, sad stanza will correctly paint
The lover's anguish or the friend's complaint,   110
But which deserves the laurel, rhyme or blank,
Which holds on Helicon the higher rank?
Let squabbling critics by themselves dispute
This point, as puzzling as a Chancery suit.

93 ⟨Een Nature yields⟩ Though Nature changes, and at Commerce' call *LA*; Though at a
Monarch's beck and Commerce' / Traffic's call *LB*   beck . . . call] nod, and Traffic's /
Nation's call *M*   94 ⟨The new taught⟩ Reluctant rivers dwindle to canal *LA*
stagnate in] deviate to *M*   canals] canal *LB*   95 drain'd] dried *Proof BMB*
sustain] ⟨receive⟩ *LA*   96 heavy ploughshare] ⟨grateful burthen⟩ *LA*   97 along
. . . shore] ⟨with many a laboured ? ⟩ along the busy ⟨pier⟩ *LA*   99 All all ⟨shall
perish, but from mortal hands / half immortal stands⟩ *LA*   100 ⟨The fame, the grace of
letters long hath stood / The grace of poets in a lettered land⟩ *LA*   101 True—some
decay] ⟨Though⟩ some have fallen *LA, cor. in LB*   102 sink] ⟨fall⟩ *LA*   101–2
Thus—future years dead volumes shall revive, | And those shall sink which now appear
to thrive; *Proof BMB*   103 As ⟨use determ / arbitrates⟩ Custom fluctuates ⟨that second
Law⟩ whose Iron sway *LA*   shifting] Iron *LB, M, cor. in T*   104 Though ever changing
mortals must obey *LA, LB, M, cor. in T*   105 immortal] glorious *LA*   106 Why
need I state? are shown in Milton's page *LA, LB, M, cor. in T*   107 ⟨Nor need I state
what I⟩ *LA*   108 To ⟨suit⟩ match the majesty of epic Song. *LA*   109 will correctly]
most is used to *LA, LB, M, cor. in T*   110 lover's] ⟨soul's deep⟩ *LA*   111 deserves
the laurel] is preferable *LA*   112 on Helicon] in poesy *LA*   113 ⟨On common
subjects / I leave to squabbling critics to divine⟩ *LA*   by] 'mongst *LA, LB, M, cor. in T*
114 This point ⟨as tedious as argue as refute⟩ *LA*   114a–b Satiric rhyme first sprang
from selfish spleen. | You doubt—see Dryden, Pope, St. Patrick's dean. *cancelled in Proof M*
selfish *M, T, Proof BMB, 1831, 1832, C, More*; jealous *LA, LB*

Blank verse is now with one consent allied   115
To Tragedy, and rarely quits her side;
Though mad Almanzor rhymed in Dryden's days,
No singsong hero rants in modern plays;
While modest Comedy her verse foregoes
To jest and pun in very middling prose;   120
Not that our Bens or Beaumonts show the worse,
Or lose one point because they wrote in verse;
But, so Thalia pleases to appear—
Poor virgin! damn'd some twenty times a year!

Whate'er the scene, let this advice have weight;   125
Adapt your language to your hero's state:
At times Melpomene forgets to groan,
And brisk Thalia takes a serious tone;
Nor unregarded will the act pass by
Where angry Townly lifts his voice on high;   130
Again—our Shakspeare limits verse to kings,
When common prose will serve for common things,
And lively Hal resigns heroic ire
To 'hollowing' Hotspur and the sceptred sire.

'Tis not enough, ye bards, with all your art,   135
To polish poems—they must touch the heart!
Where'er the scene be laid, whate'er the song,
Still let it bear the hearer's soul along;
Command your audience, or to smile or weep,
Whiche'er may please you, any thing but sleep.   140
The poet claims our tears—but, by his leave,
Before I shed them, let me see him grieve:

116 rarely] never *LA*   117 Though ⟨Dryden's dread Almanzor raved in rhymes⟩ *LA*
days] ⟨age⟩ *LA*   118 singsong...modern] ⟨rhyming Hero whines in our chaster⟩ *LA*
119 her...foregoes] at last hath chose *LA*   120 To] For *T, Proof BMB, 1831, 1832,*
C, More, cor. in Proof M   121 Bens...the] Beaumonts comedies are *LA*   comedies]
dramas *LB*   123 Thalia pleases] ⟨it seems⟩ Thalia pleases *LA*; Thalia ⟨pleases⟩ ventures
Proof BMB   124 Poor ⟨Lady drooping with the weight of years⟩ *LA*   125 the
scene] ⟨your theme / plot⟩ *LA*   127 Melpomene] ⟨our tragedy⟩ *LA*   131-2 ⟨Again
in tragedy we can / in certain dramas we dispense | With verse and take a turn with common
sense⟩ *LA*   132 When...serve] And...do *LA*   133 And Harry Monmouth
⟨in his youthful fire⟩ till the scenes require *LA, cor. in LB*   134 Resigns heroics to
his sceptred Sire *LA*   the] ⟨his⟩ *Proof BMB*; his C   137 ⟨Whateer⟩ the scene ⟨or⟩
whateer the song *LA*   be] is *LA*   138 soul] heart *LA*   141 ⟨Feel for my woe /
You'd have me feel your woes,—but by your leave⟩ *LA*   142 Before I] ⟨If I must⟩ *LA*

If banish'd Romeo feign'd nor sigh, nor tear,
Lull'd by his languor, I should sleep or sneer.
Sad words, no doubt, become a serious face, 145
And men look angry in the proper place;
At double meanings folks seem wondrous sly,
And sentiment prescribes a pensive eye;
For Nature form'd at first the inward man,
And actors copy Nature when they can; 150
She bids the beating heart with rapture bound,
Raised to the stars, or levell'd with the ground;
And for expression's aid, 'tis said or sung,
She gave our mind's interpreter, the tongue,
Who, worn with use, of late would fain dispense, 155
At least in theatres, with common sense;
O'erwhelm with sound the boxes, gallery, pit,
And raise a laugh with any thing but wit.

To skilful writers it will much import,
Whence spring their scenes, from common life or court; 160
Whether they seek applause by smile or tear,
To draw a 'Lying Valet' or a 'Lear',
A sage or rakish youngster wild from school,
A wandering 'Peregrine', or plain 'John Bull'.
All persons please when Nature's voice prevails, 165
Scottish or Irish, born in Wilts or Wales;
Or follow common fame, or forge a plot,
Who cares if mimic heroes lived or not?
One precept serves to regulate the scene,
Make it appear as if it *might* have been. 170
If some Drawcansir you aspire to draw,
Present him raving, and above all law;
If female furies in your scheme are plann'd,
Macbeth's fierce dame is ready to your hand;

143 Romeo ⟨seemed to ? ⟩ feigned *LA*   144 Lull'd . . . languor] Dull as an opera *LA*, *LB*, *M*, *cor. in T*   146 men] ⟨folks⟩ *LA*   147 seem] ⟨look⟩ *LA*   148 And . . . prescribes] While . . . ⟨demands⟩ *LA*   150 copy] follow *LA*, *cor. in LB*   151 beating] ⟨varying / changing *LA*   153 expression's . . . or] emotion's . . . and *LA*   154 ⟨The mind's best dragoman⟩ *LA*   155 ⟨But / Though many with that minister might dispense⟩ *LA*   157 ⟨Yet / And touch⟩ *LA*   160 spring] ⟨come⟩ *LA*   161 ⟨Whom seek they to delineate⟩ *LA*   163 ⟨A rakish Author, a pedantic fool⟩ *LA*   164 'Peregrine'] merchant *LA*   166 Scottish] English *LA*, *LB*, *M*, *cor. in T*   167 forge] form *Proof BMB*   168 We care not if your heroes lived or not *LA*, *LB*   cares if mimic] ⟨careth if your⟩ *M*   170 it appear] ⟨them exist⟩ *LA*   171 some Drawcansir] ⟨mad Almanzor⟩ *LA*   173 scheme] ⟨mind⟩ *LA*

For tears and treachery, for good and evil,   175
Constance, King Richard, Hamlet, and the devil!
But if a new design you dare essay,
And freely wander from the beaten way,
True to your characters till all be past,
Preserve consistency from first to last.   180

'Tis hard to venture where our betters fail,
Or lend fresh interest to a twice-told tale;
And yet perchance 'tis wiser to prefer
A hackney'd plot, than choose a new, and err:
Yet copy not too closely, but record   185
More justly thought for thought, than word for word;
Nor trace your prototype through narrow ways,
But only follow where he merits praise.

For you, young bard! whom luckless fate may lead
To tremble on the nod of all who read,   190
Ere your first score of cantos time unrolls,
Beware—for God's sake don't begin like B[owle]s!
'Awake a louder and a loftier strain',
And pray, what follows from his boiling brain?
He sinks to Southey's level in a trice,   195
Whose epic mountains never fail in mice!
Not so of yore awoke your mighty sire,
The temper'd warblings of his master lyre;
Soft as the gentler breathing of the lute,
'Of man's first disobedience, and the fruit',   200

175 good and evil] ⟨wiles and woes⟩ *LA*   and evil] or evil *LB*, *Proofs BMA*, *BMB*,
1831, cor. in M   176 and the] ⟨Milton's⟩ *LA*   177 new design] ⟨nobler track⟩ *LA*
178 freely . . . beaten] ⟨boldly⟩ nobly . . . ⟨vulgar⟩ *LA*   179 True to your ⟨character⟩
hero till his part be past *LA*
181–2   ⟨Whatever critics say, or scribblers write
                             Tis hard to sketch with skill from vulgar life⟩
                             ⟨Wheneer our Bards and Critics talk of 'Trite,'
                             Of common things tis difficult to write⟩ *LA*
                             Whateer the critic says or poet sings
                             Tis no slight task to write on common things *LA, cor. in LB*
181 venture] ⟨follow⟩ *M*   183 perchance] perhaps *LA, LB*   184 hackney'd] ⟨well-
known⟩ *LA*   186 More justly] The rather *LA*   189 fate] ⟨lot⟩ *LA*   191 Ere
oer our heads your Muse's thunder rolls *LA, cor. in LB*   195 sinks ⟨like⟩ to *LA*
197 your] our *LA*   198 temper'd . . . master] ⟨first born / glorious⟩ tempered . . . ⟨tem-
pered⟩ solemn *LA, cor. in LB*

He speaks; but as his subject swells along,
Earth, Heaven, and Hades echo with the song:
Still in the midst of things he hastens on,
As if he witness'd all already done;
Leaves on his path whatever seems too mean   205
To raise the subject, or adorn the scene;
Gives, as each page improves upon the sight,
Not smoke from brightness, but from darkness light;
And truth and fiction with such art compounds,
We know not where to fix their several bounds.   210

If you would please the public, deign to hear
What soothes the many-headed monster's ear;
If your heart triumph when the hands of all
Applaud in thunder at the curtain's fall;
Deserve those plaudits—study Nature's page,   215
And sketch the striking traits of every age;
While varying man and varying years unfold
Life's little tale, so oft so vainly told,
Observe his simple childhood's dawning days,
His pranks, his prate, his playmates, and his plays; 220
Till time at length the mannish tyro weans,
And prurient vice outstrips his tardy teens!

Behold him freshman! forced no more to groan
O'er Virgil's devilish verses, and—his own;
Prayers are too tedious, lectures too abstruse,   225
He flies from T[a]v[e]ll's frown to 'Fordham's Mews';
(Unlucky T[a]v[e]ll! doom'd to daily cares,
By pugilistic pupils and by bears!)

201 speaks] ⟨tells⟩ *LA*   202 Hades echo] Hell are shaken *LA, cor. in LB*   203 in
. . . things] ⟨to the great event⟩ *LA*   in] to *LA, LB, M, Proofs BMA, BMB, 1831, 1832,*
C, More   204 he] we *LA, LB, M, Proofs BMA, BMB, 1831, 1832, C, More*
207–8 *not in LA*   209 ⟨And feigns so well, so mixes false and true⟩ *LA*   212 ⟨What
most / best delights the critic's skilful ear⟩ *LA*; What soothes the people's, peers' or pedant's
ear *LA, cor. in LB*   214 Applaud in] ⟨Wake changing⟩ *LA*   217 and] ⟨with⟩
LA   219 ⟨And first the pleasures of his boyish days⟩ *LA*   220 prate] wants
LA, LB   221 tyro] stripling *LA, LB, cor. in M*   222 And budding Vice
developed with his teens *LA*; And Vice buds forth developed with his teens *LB, cor. in
M*   223–4 The heedless ⟨stripling⟩ tyro freed at length from school, | ⟨Hot with
the ?⟩ And dreaded birch disdains ⟨his⟩ all College rule *LA, LB*   heedless] beardless *M*
dreaded] blushing *M*   225 Prayers . . . tedious] ⟨Escaped from chapel⟩ *LA*   227 doom'd]
⟨damned⟩ *M*   228 pupils] freshmen *LA*

Fines, tutors, tasks, conventions threat in vain,
Before hounds, hunters, and Newmarket plain.   230
Rough with his elders, with his equals rash,
Civil to sharpers, prodigal of cash,
Constant to nought—save hazard and a whore,
Yet cursing both, for both have made him sore:
Unread (unless, since books beguile disease,   235
The p[o]x becomes his passage to degrees);
Fool'd, pillaged, dunn'd, he wastes his terms away,
And unexpell'd, *perhaps*, retires M.A.
Master of Arts! as *hells* and *clubs* proclaim,
Where scarce a blackleg bears a brighter name!   240

Launch'd into life, extinct his early fire,
He apes the selfish prudence of his sire;
Marries for money, chooses friends for rank,
Buys land, and shrewdly trusts not to the Bank!
Sits in the senate, gets a son and heir,   245
Sends him to Harrow, for himself was there;
Mute, though he votes, unless when call'd to cheer,
His son's so sharp—he'll see the dog a peer!

Manhood declines, age palsies every limb,
He quits the scene, or else the scene quits him;   250
Scrapes wealth, o'er each departing penny grieves,
And avarice seizes all ambition leaves;
Counts cent per cent. and smiles, or vainly frets
O'er hoards diminish'd by young Hopeful's debts;
Weighs well and wisely what to sell or buy,   255
Complete in all life's lessons—but to die;

230 hounds] dogs *LA, cor. in LB*   231 Rough to his ⟨master, prodigal of cash⟩
seniors, ⟨in all his friendships rash⟩ with his equals rash *LA, cor. in LB*   232 to
⟨Black⟩ sharpers *LA*   233–4 Ready to quit whateer he loved before | Constant to
nought save hazard and a whore *LA, cor. in LB*   235–6 *not in LA*   237 The
better years of youth he wastes away *LA, cor. in LB*   terms] term *1831*   238 And
unexpell'd, *perhaps,*] And, unexpell'd perhaps, *1831, 1832, C, More*   239–40 *not in LA*
239 *hells* and] all the *LB, cor. in M*   241 life, extinct] ⟨the world⟩, and quenched *LA, LB,
M, cor. in T*   242 selfish] ⟨prudent⟩ *LA*   244 shrewdly] wisely *LA, cor. in LB*
247 unless] except *LA*   249 ⟨So passes Manhood, stealing Age comes on⟩ *LA*   palsies]
quakes in *LA*   250 ⟨He shifts the scene before his hateful son⟩ *LA*   251 ⟨To /
Seeks money / wealth of every other thought bereft⟩ *LA*   Scrapes] Seeks *LA*   254 ⟨All
/ For father's⟩ Oer Grandam's mortgage, or young Hopeful's debts *LA*   Grandam's] Uncle's
LB   hoards . . . by] ⟨endless mortgages or⟩ *M*   255 ⟨Abstains from what he wished,
he knows not why⟩ *LA*   256 ⟨Forgetting nothing but / except that he must die⟩ *LA*

Peevish and spiteful, doting, hard to please,
Commending every time, save times like these;
Crazed, querulous, forsaken, half forgot,
Expires unwept—is buried: let him rot!   260

But from the drama let me not digress,
Nor spare my precepts, though they please you less;
Though woman weep, and hardest hearts are stirr'd,
When what is done is rather seen than heard;
Yet many deeds preserved in history's page   265
Are better told than acted on the stage;
The ear sustains what shocks the timid eye,
And horror thus subsides to sympathy:
True Briton all beside, I here am French,
Bloodshed 'tis surely better to retrench;   270
The gladiatorial gore we teach to flow,
In tragic scene disgusts though but in show;
We hate the carnage while we see the trick,
And find small sympathy in being sick.
Not on the stage, the regicide Macbeth   275
Appals an audience with a monarch's death;
To gaze, when sable Hubert threats to sear
Young Arthur's eyes, can *ours*—or *Nature* bear?
A halter'd heroine Johnson sought to slay,
We saved Irene, but half damned the play;   280
And (Heaven be praised) our tolerating times
Stint Metamorphoses to Pantomimes,
And Lewis' self with all his sprites would quake,
To change Earl Osmond's negro to a snake!
Because in scenes exciting joy or grief,   285
We loathe the action which exceeds belief:
And yet, God knows, what may not authors do?

258 save] ⟨but⟩ *LA*   259 Crazed] ⟨Complaining⟩ *LA*   260 Expires] He dies *LA*, *cor. in LB*   262 The ⟨scene⟩ plot is told, as stated, more or less *LA* ; Your plot is told, or acted, more or less *LB, M*   263–4 ⟨With⟩ To greater sympathy the feelings rise | When what is done is done before our eyes *LA, cor. in LB*   265 But many deeds which ? the historic page *LA*   preserved] described *M*   267–8 *not in LA* 269 True Briton] ⟨English in⟩ *LA*   270 ⟨And scenes with these tis wiser to retrench⟩ *LA*   271 gladiatorial ⟨shows of blood and⟩ gore *LA*   272 ⟨In the scenes⟩ *LA* scene] scenes *C*   273–4 *not in LA*   277 sable Hubert] Hubert simply *LA, LB* 278 or] and *LA*   279 sought] thought *LA*   280 Irene] ⟨the heroine⟩ *LA* 281 ⟨But ⟩ Heaven be praised even our ⟨foolish⟩ good natured times *LA*   285–8 *not in LA*

Whose Postscripts prate of dyeing 'heroines Blue'!

Above all things,—*Dan* Poet,—if you can—
Eke out your acts, I pray, with mortal man,   290
Nor call a ghost, unless some cursed scrape
Must open ten trap-doors for your escape!
Of all the monstrous things I'd fain forbid,
I loathe an Opera worse than Dennis did;
Where good and evil persons, right or wrong,   295
Rage, love, and aught—but moralise in song.—
Hail last memorial of our foreign friends!
Which Gaul allows, and still Hesperia lends,
Napoleon's edicts no embargo lay
On whores, spies, singers, wisely shipped away.   300
Our giant Capital, whose squares are spread,
Where Rustics earned, and now may beg their bread;
In all iniquity is grown so nice,
It scorns amusements which are not of price.
Hence the pert shopkeeper whose throbbing ear   305
Aches with Orchestras which he pays to hear,
Whom shame, not sympathy, forbids to snore,
His anguish doubling by his own 'Encore';
Squeezed in 'Fop's Alley', jostled by the Beaux,
Teased with his hat, and trembling for his toes;   310
Scarce wrestles through the night, nor tastes of Ease,
Till the dropp'd curtain gives a glad release:
Why this and more he suffers—can ye guess?
Because it costs him dear—and makes him dress!

So prosper Eunuchs from Etruscan schools,   315
Give us but fiddlers, and they're sure of fools!

289 ⟨Now that we speak of ?⟩ *LA*   291 scrape] hitch *LA, cor. in LB*   292 Requires a trap door goblin, or a Witch *LA, cor. in LB;* ⟨Must ? Hell for help in your escape⟩
LB   296 and . . . moralise] and moralize forsooth *LA, cor. in LB*   aught] ⟨all⟩ *M*
297–8 This comes from commerce with our foreign friends | These are the passions first
Ausonia lends *LA, cor. in LB*   297 Hail] ⟨That⟩ *M*   298 Which Gaul] ⟨And
all⟩ *M*   301 squares are spread] ⟨monstrous head⟩ streets still spread *LA;* streets ⟨still⟩
are spread *LB;* squares ⟨bespread⟩ *M*   302 Our fields where once our simple sires were
bred *LA, cor. in LB*   304 It scorns] ⟨And⟩ We loathe *LA;* We hate *LB;* It ⟨hates⟩ *M*
305 pert shopkeeper] ⟨dull cit⟩ *LA*   306 Orchestras] the Orchestra *LA, cor. in T*
308 ⟨Who⟩ Sense kept awake by roaring out 'Encore' *LA, cor. in LB*   310 Teased]
Plagued *LA, cor. in LB*   311 Scarce wrestles] He ⟨suffers⟩ wrestles *LA, cor. in LB*
312 dropp'd] fall'n *LA*   315 Etruscan] ⟨Ausonian⟩ *LA*

Ere scenes were played by many a reverend Clerk,
(What harm, if David danced before the Ark?)
In Christmas revels, simple country folks
Were pleased with Morrice-mumm'ry, and coarse jokes; 320
Improving years with things no longer known,
Produced blithe Punch, and merry Madame Joan,
Who still frisk on with feats so lewdly low,
'Tis strange Benvolio suffers such a show;
Suppressing Peer! to whom each Vice gives place, 325
Oaths, Boxing, Begging, all save Rout and Race.

Farce followed Comedy, and reached her prime
In ever-laughing Foote's fantastic time,
Mad Wag! who pardoned none, nor spared the best,
And turned some very serious things to jest. 330
Nor Church nor State escaped his public sneers,
Arms nor the Gown, Priests, Lawyers, Volunteers:
'Alas, poor Yorick!' now forever mute!
Whoever loves a laugh must sigh for Foote!

We smile perforce when histrionic scenes 335
Ape the swoln dialogue of Kings and Queens,
When 'Crononhotonthologos must die'
And Arthur struts in mimic majesty.

Moschus, with whom once more I hope to sit
And smile at Folly, if we can't at Wit, 340

317 Ere theatres were built, and reverend Clerks *LA, cor. in LB*   318 Performed,
wrote plays (as some old book remarks) *LA, cor. in LB* ⟨Like David's pantomimes before
the Ark⟩ *LB*   318a–b Who did what Vestris, yet at least, can not, | And cut
his kingly capers 'Sans Culotte' *M, cancelled in T*   320 Morrice-mumm'ry]
Morrice-⟨dancing⟩ *LB*   322 Madame] Mistress *LA*   323 Who yet ⟨despite of all
things helps his ground⟩ squeaks on nor fears to be forgot *LA, cor. in LB*   lewdly] ⟨vastly⟩
M, T   324 If great Earl Grosvenor suppressed them not *LA, cor. in LB*   Benvolio]
Earl Grosvenor *LB, M, cor. in T*   325 each] all *LB, M, cor. in T, Υ*   326 Save
gambling—for his Lordship loves a race! *LA, LB, M, cor. in T, Υ*   330 And . . . very]
⟨Forever turning⟩ And turned at times een *LA, cor. in LB*   331 sneers] ⟨jeers⟩ *LA*
332 Sons of the ⟨Church⟩ Gown, or city Volunteers *LA*   334 Yet all who love a laugh
still laugh with Foote. *LA*   335 Nor less we smile when ⟨Fielding's⟩ histrionic scenes *LA*
336 Ape the swoln] Abuse the *LA*   337 ⟨And Arthur, 'scaped from Cottle and from
Pye⟩ *LA*   338 And . . . struts] ⟨Struts with Tom Thumb⟩ *LA*
339–52   Hobhouse, since we have roved through Eastern climes
                While all the Aegean echoed to our rhymes—
                And bound to Momus by some pagan spell
                Laughed sang and quaffed to 'Vive la Bagatelle'—
                Now free to think the broadest farce delights
                Our clownish *masters?* more than melting sights *LA*
340–52   And smile at what our stage retails for wit
                Since few, I know, enjoy a laugh so well

Yes, Friend! for thee I'll quit my Cynic cell,
And bear Swift's motto 'Vive la Bagatelle!'
Which charmed our days in each Aegean clime,
As oft at home, with Revelry—and Rhyme.
Then may Euphrosyne, who sped the past,   345
Soothe thy life's scenes, nor leave thee in the last!
But find in thine,—like Pagan Plato's bed,
Some merry Manuscript of Mimes,—when dead.

Now to the drama let us bend our eyes
Where fettered by Whig Walpole low she lies.   350
Corruption foiled her,—for she feared her glance;
Decorum—left her for an Opera Dance!
Yet Chesterfield, whose polished pen inveighs
'Gainst laughter, fought for freedom to our plays,
Unchecked by Megrims of Patrician brains,   355
And damning Dullness of Lord Chamberlains.
Repeal that act!—again let Humour roam
Wild o'er the stage!—we've time for tears at home:
Let 'Archer' plant the horns on 'Sullen's' brows
And Estifania gull her 'Copper' spouse,   360
The moral's scant—but that may be excused,
Men go not to be lectured, but amused.
He, whom our plays dispose to Good or Ill,
Must wear a head in want of Willis' skill,
Aye—but Macheath's example—Psha—no more,   365
It formed no Thieves, the Thief was formed before,
And spite of Puritans and 'Collier's' curse,
Plays make mankind no better, and no worse.
Then spare our Stage ye Methodistic men!
Nor burn damn'd Drury if it rise again.   370

Sardonic slave to 'Vive la Bagatelle'!
So that in yours, like Pagan Plato's bed,
They'll find some book of epigrams—when dead. LB

342 Swift's] ⟨thy⟩ M   343 Words we have proved in ⟨many a distant⟩ clime M
344 with] in M   345-6 ? wayward spirit weakly yields to gloom, | But thine will waft
thee lightly to the tomb M   353 Yet] ⟨Why⟩ Since LA; If LB   355-6 not in LA
357 Once more unfettered then let freedom roam LA; Accord not you? that Humour
still should roam LB, cor. in M   358 Wild] Free LA   361 scant] bad LB
362 Men] We LA   363-80 not in LA   363-4 ⟨He who's seduced by plays must
be a fool, | If boys want teaching—can't they learn at school?⟩ LB   366 formed . . .
formed] ⟨made . . . made⟩ LB   367 Puritans] Methodism LB, M, cor. in T
369-80 not in LB, M   369 Then . . . our Stage] ⟨Yet . . . my verse⟩ MA   370 damn'd
. . . it] ⟨or damn should Drury⟩ MA

But why to brain-scorched Bigots thus appeal?
Can heavenly Mercy dwell with earthly Zeal?
For times of fire and faggot let them hope,
Times, dear alike to Puritan, or Pope.
As pious Calvin saw Servetus blaze   375
So would new sects on newer victims gaze;
E'en now the Songs of Solyma begin,
Faith cants, perplexed Apologist of Sin!
While the Lord's servant chastens whom he loves
And Simeon kicks where Baxter only 'shoves'.   380

Whom Nature guides, so writes, that every dunce
Enraptured thinks to do the same at once,
But after inky thumbs and bitten nails
And twenty scattered quires, the Coxcomb fails.

Let Pastoral be dumb! for who can hope   385
To match the youthful eclogues of our Pope?
Yet his and Phillips' faults of different kind,
For Art—too rude, for Nature—too refined,
Instruct how hard the medium 'tis to hit
Twixt too much polish, and too coarse a Wit.   390

A vulgar scribbler certes stands disgraced
In this nice age, when all aspire to Taste,
The dirty language, and the noisome jest,
Which pleased in Swift of yore, we now detest,
Proscribed not only in the World polite   395
But even too nasty for a City Knight.

371 But ... brain-scorched] Yet ... ⟨blazing / brainless⟩ MA   372 Can heavenly]
⟨When felt thy⟩ Υ   ⟨When felt they aught their Master bid them feel⟩ MA   ⟨When
felt they⟩ Υ   374 Times ... to] ⟨Dear to souls of⟩ MA   375 As] ⟨So⟩ MA
377 Songs ... begin] song of Sion sons begins MA; of ⟨Sion⟩ Solyma Υ   378 Faith ...
perplexed] ⟨And Faith stalks / smirks the soft⟩ MA   379 While] ⟨Yet / Though⟩ MA
381 every dunce] he who sees LA, LB, M, cor. in T   382 at once] with ease LA, LB,
M, cor. in T   383 inky] inked LA   384 Scratched head, torn quires, the easy
scribbler fails LA   385 be dumb] ⟨sleep in peace⟩ LA   386 youthful ... our]
⟨meanest, earliest lines of⟩ LA   youthful] early LA, LB, M, cor. in T   387 faults of
different] faulty in their LA, LB   388 The one too rustic, t'other too refined LA, cor.
in M   389 Instruct] May teach LA   392 this nice] such an LA
393 ⟨When all our critics, men with home and lands⟩ LA   noisome] brutal LA
395-6   ⟨All are offended, men with home and lands,
               Peers / High, low, Lords, Ladies, squires with bloody hands.⟩
               Offensive must be men with home and land,
               Possessed of Pedigree and bloody hand. LA

Peace to Swift's faults, his Wit hath made them pass,
Unmatched by all save matchless Hudibras,
Whose Author is perhaps the first we meet
Who from our couplet lopped two final feet;   400
Nor less in merit than the longer line,
This measure moves a favourite of the Nine.
Though at first view—eight feet may seem in vain
Formed, save in Ode, to bear a serious strain,
Yet Scott has shown our wondering isle of late   405
This measure shrinks not from a theme of weight,
And varied skilfully, surpasses far
Heroic rhyme, but most in Love and War,
Whose fluctuations, tender or sublime,
Are curbed too much by long recurring rhyme.   410

But many a skilful judge abhors to see—
What few admire—Irregularity.
This some vouchsafe to pardon—but 'tis hard,
When such a word contents a British Bard.

And must the Bard his glowing thoughts confine?   415
Lest Censure hover o'er some faulty line,
Remove whate'er a Critic may suspect,
To gain the paltry suffrage of 'Correct'!
Or prune the spirit of each daring phrase
To fly from Error—not to merit praise?   420

Ye who seek finished models, never cease
By day and night, to read the works of Greece,
But our good fathers never bent their brains
To heathen Greek, content with native strains.

397 Peace . . . made] ⟨From Swift we note⟩ his wit shall make *LA, cor. in LB*   faults]
⟨thoughts⟩ *T*   398 save matchless] except our *LA*   399 perhaps] (I deem) *LA,
cor. in LB*   400 Who mulcht'd our couplet of its final feet *LA, LB, M, cor. in T*
402 moves] ⟨lives⟩ *LA*   404 Composed for any but the lightest strain *LA, cor. in
LB*   405 has ⟨lately taught⟩ shown *LA*   407 surpasses far] ⟨resounds afar⟩ *LA*
408 rhyme]⟨verse⟩ *LA*   409 fluctuations] quick transitions *LB*   411 skilful judge
abhors] judge of verse dislikes *LA*   412 few admire] ⟨others praise⟩ *LA*   413 This
some vouchsafe] ⟨Some condescend⟩ *LA*   415 the Bard his] I then my *LA, cor. in LB*
417 ⟨Or shall I wander careless of defect⟩ *LA*   418 suffrage] ⟨praise⟩ *LA*   419 Or
prune . . . each] ⟨And let . . . some⟩ *LA*   420 Error] ⟨faults / censure *LA*   421 ⟨He
who the fruits of ? seeks / Who by example would his fame increase⟩ *LA*   seek finished
models] require improvement *LA*   422 to . . . Greece] ⟨must study in the Greeks⟩ *LA*
423 bent] clogged *LA, cor. in LB*   424 To] With *LA*

The few who read a page, or used a pen,   425
Were satisfied with Chaucer and old Ben,
The jokes and numbers, suited to their taste
Were quaint and careless—anything but chaste.
Yet whether right or wrong the ancient Rules
It will not do to call our Fathers—Fools!   430
Though you, and I, who eruditely know
To separate the elegant and low,
Can also, when a hobbling line appears,
Detect with fingers—in default of ears.

In sooth I do not know or greatly care   435
To learn, who our first English Strollers were,
Or if—till Roofs received the vagrant Art—
Our Muse—like that of Thespis—kept a Cart.
But this is certain, since our Shakspeare's days
There's pomp enough, if little else in plays;   440
Nor will Melpomene ascend her Throne,
Without high heels, white plume, and Bristol-Stone.

Old Comedies still meet with much applause,
Though too licentious for Dramatic Laws;
At least, we moderns—wisely 'tis confest   445
Curtail, or silence, the lascivious jest!

Whate'er their follies, and their faults beside,
Our enterprising Bards pass nought untried,
Nor do they merit slight applause who choose
An English subject for an English Muse,   450
And leave to Minds which never dare invent,
French flippancy, and German sentiment.
Where is that living language which could claim
Poetic more, as Philosophic fame?

426 satisfied] better pleased *LA*   427 numbers] language *LA*, *cor. in LB*
432 elegant and] ⟨witty and the⟩ *LA*   433 ⟨When any hobbling⟩ *LA*   436 learn]
⟨trace⟩ ask *LA*   437 ⟨Or have till Drury⟩ *LA*   439 is certain] we're sure of *LA*,
LB   441 ⟨And Tragedy, whatever stuff be spoke⟩ *LA*   will] can *LA*   442 ⟨Neer
wants high heels, long sword, and velvet cloak⟩ *LA*   443 Comedies] Comedy *LA*
446 lascivious] offensive *LA, LB, M, cor. in T*   448 pass] leave *LA, cor. in LB*
450 subject] story *LA*   451 ⟨Disdaining with their ? to invent / Nor lend our serious
language to invent⟩ *LA*   which never dare] too futile to *LA, cor. in LB*   453 Where
. . . living] ⟨Nor could there be a⟩ / I know no living *LA, cor. in LB*

If all our Bards, more patient of delay,   455
Would stop like Pope—to polish by the way.

Lords of the quill! whose critical assaults
O'erthrow whole quartos, with their quires of faults,
Who soon detect, and mark where'er we fail,
And prove our Marble with too nice a nail,   460
Democritus himself was not so bad,
He only *thought*—but *you* would make us—mad!

But truth to say, most rhymers rarely guard
Against that ridicule they deem so hard.
In person negligent, they wear from sloth   465
Beards of a week, and nails of annual growth;
Reside in garrets, fly from those they meet,
And walk in Alleys, rather than the street.
With little rhyme, less reason, if you please,
The name of Poet may be got with ease,   470
So that not tuns of Helleboric juice
Shall ever turn your head to any use.
Write but like Wordsworth,—live beside a lake
And keep your bushy locks a year from Blake,
Then print your book, once more return to Town,   475
And boys shall hunt your Bardship up and down.

Am I not wise? if such some poet's plight
To purge in spring (like Bayes) before I write?
If this precaution softened not my Bile,
I know no scribbler with a madder style;   480
But since (perhaps my feelings are too nice)
I cannot purchase fame at such a price,

455 ⟨If that thy / all English / our Bards, impatient of delay⟩ *LA*   all our Bards] every
Bard *LA*   457 Lords ... quill] ⟨You too, my friend⟩ *LA*   Lords] ⟨Sons⟩ *LA*
458 quartos ... quires] books with all their host *LA, cor. in LB*   459 soon detect, and]
⟨armed in science⟩ *LA*   460 too nice a] ⟨your polished⟩ *LA*   463 rhymers]
rhymsters *LA*   465 negligent, they wear] ⟨slovenly⟩, they bear *LA*   467 Reside
in ⟨alleys, walk in byway paths⟩ *LA*   fly from] shy ⟨of⟩ to *LA*   468 walk] ⟨found⟩
LA   469 With ... less] Without or rhyme or *LA, LB, cor. in M*   470 of ⟨crazy⟩
poet *LA*   471 So that not Hellebore with all its juice *LA, cor. in M*   tuns] Isles /
Seas / Tuns *M*; ⟨Isles⟩ Tuns / Seas *T*   474 locks] ⟨skull / head⟩ *LA*   475 ⟨Publish
your book, return again⟩ to town *LA*   476 shall] will *LA*   477 ⟨If such are
certain poets, am I right⟩ *LA*

I'll labour gratis as a Grinder's wheel,
And blunt myself, give edge to others' steel,
Nor write at all, unless to teach the Art   485
To those, rehearsing for the Poet's part,
From Horace, show the pleasing paths of song,
And from my own example—what is wrong.

Though modern practice sometimes differs quite,
'Tis just as well to think before you write,   490
Let every Book that suits your theme be read
So shall you trace it to the Fountain head.

He, who has learn'd the duty which he owes
To friends, and country—and to pardon foes,
Who models his deportment, as may best   495
Accord with Brother, Sire, or Stranger-guest,
Who takes our Laws, and Worship, as they are,
Nor roars reform for Senate, Church, and Bar,
In practice rather than loud precept wise,
Bids not his tongue, but heart—philosophize;   500
Such is the man, the poet should rehearse
As joint exemplar of his life and verse.

Sometimes a sprightly wit, and tale well told,
Without much grace, or weight, or art, will hold
A longer empire o'er the public mind,   505
Than sounding trifles, empty, though refined.

Unhappy Greece! thy Sons of ancient days
The Muse may celebrate with perfect praise,
Whose generous children narrowed not their hearts
With Commerce, given alone to Arms, and Arts.   510

483–4 I'll act instead of whetstone, blunted, but | Of use to make another's razor cut
LA, cor. in LB   485 at . . . to] myself, but try to *LA, cor. in LB*   486 rehearsing]
who practise *LA, M, cor. in T*   487–8 ⟨Show sucking rhymers how to keep in
health | And ? (like Horace) ? rhyme for wealth⟩ *LA*   487 pleasing paths] better
arts *LA, cor. in LB*   488 from] by *LA*   490 think before] ⟨know / study what⟩
LA   491 ⟨Remake your⟩ *LA*   492 to] from *LA*   493 has learn'd] ⟨can
pay / yield⟩ *LA*   494 to pardon] ⟨despises / to forgive his⟩ *LA*   496 Brother,
Sire] ⟨father, friend⟩ *LA*   500 ⟨By silent ? to philosophize⟩ *LA*   501 ⟨Thy
peace and peaceful arts a friend / Prompt at her call his country to⟩ *LA*   502 ⟨The
master of⟩ *LA*   503 tale well told] ⟨well told tale⟩ *LA*   506 empty,
though refined] ⟨of another kind⟩ *LA*   509 Whose] ⟨Thy⟩ *LB*   children] ⟨youth⟩ *LA*
510 With Trade, but gave their brains to arms or arts *LA*   Commerce] traffic *LB*

Our boys (save those whom public schools compel
To 'Long and Short' before they're taught to spell)
From frugal fathers soon imbibe by rote
'A penny saved, my Lad, 's a penny got.'
Babe of a city-birth! from sixpence take   515
The third—how much will the remainders make?
A groat—Ah bravo! Dick hath done the sum,
He'll swell my fifty thousand to a Plum!

They whose young souls receive this rust betimes
'Tis clear, are fit for any thing but rhymes,   520
And Locke will tell you that the Father's right,
Who hides all verses from his children's sight.
For Poets (says this Sage, and many more)
Make sad Mechanics with their Lyric lore,
And Delphi now, however rich of old,   525
Discovers little silver, and less gold,
Because Parnassus though a mount divine,
Is poor as Irus or—and Irish mine!

Two objects always should the poet move
Or one, or both, to please, or to improve.   530
Whate'er you teach be brief—if you design
For our remembrance your didactic line,
Redundance places Memory on the rack,
For brains may be o'erloaded,—like the back.

Fiction does best when taught to look like Truth,   535
And fairy fables bubble none but Youth.

515 a city-birth] old Thelasson *LA*, *LB*   517 Dick ... sum] Dick's the boy for
sums *LA*, *LB*   518 ⟨My fifty thousand soon will be a plum⟩ He'll turn my fifty thousand
all to Plums *LA*; He'll ⟨turn⟩ swell my fifty thousand all to Plums *LB*   523 and] with
LA, *cor. in LB*   524 Are idle dogs, and ⟨damn them⟩ always poor *LA*, *cor. in LB*
525–6 Then adds, that man is crazy or undone | Who ⟨hopes⟩ looks for profit from a rhyming
son. *LA*   525 Delphi ... rich] ⟨Delphi's shame—whateer it was⟩ *LB*   526 Dis-
covers] ⟨Hath now but⟩ *LB*   527 though] ⟨albeit⟩ *LA*   528 Unlike Potosi holds
no silver mine *LA*; Is rather costive—like an Irish mine *LB*   Is ... like *LB*] Keeps back her
ingots—like / Is poor as Irus—or / Is no Potosi—but *LB alternate versions*   533 ⟨From
all redundancy the mind⟩ *LA*   535 ⟨Fiction pleases most, when most like to Truth⟩ *LA*
535a, b, c, d   ⟨Write but recite not, e'en Apollo's song
                  Mouthed in a mortal ear would seem too long,
                  Long as the last year of a lingering lease,
                  When Revel pauses until rents increase.⟩ *M*

Expect no credit for too wondrous tales
Since Jonas only springs alive from Whales!

Young men with aught but elegance dispense,
Maturer years require a little sense.   540
To end at once—that Bard for all is fit,
Who mingles well Instruction with his Wit;
For him Reviews shall smile, for him o'erflow
The Patronage of Paternoster Row;
His book with Longman's liberal aid shall pass   545
(Who ne'er despises books that bring him brass);
Through three long weeks the taste of London lead,
And cross St. George's Channel, and the Tweed.

But every thing has faults, nor is't unknown
That harps and fiddles often lose their tone,   550
And wayward voices, at their owner's call,
With all his best endeavours only squall;
Dogs blink their covey, flints with-hold the spark,
And double-barrels (damn them) miss their mark!

Where frequent Beauties strike the reader's view,   555
We must not quarrel for a blot or two,
But pardon equally to books, or men,
The slips of Human Nature—and the Pen.

Yet if an Author spite of foe, or friend,
Despises all advice too much to mend,   560
But ever twangs the same discordant string,
Give him no quarter—howsoe'er he sing.
Let Havard's fate o'ertake him, who for once,
Produced a play too dashing for a Dunce.

537 too wondrous] ⟨too gross a⟩ LA   538 Since] For LA   539 ⟨All men love
poems with⟩ LA   aught] all LA, cor. in LB   541 To end all short, that Bard the mark
will hit LA   To . . . once] To finish all LB   543 shall smile] ⟨will praise⟩ LA
545 with . . . aid] ⟨through liberal Longman's aid⟩ LA   547 Through . . . weeks] Through
⟨six⟩ long months LA; For three long months LB   548 St. George's] the Irish LA
549 nor is't unknown] ⟨and 'tis well known⟩ LA   553–4 Revenge defeats its object in
the dark, | And pistols (courage ⟨Jeffrey⟩ bullies !) miss their mark. LA, cor. in LB   bullies
LA] duellist LB   555 strike . . . view] ⟨deck the scene, 'tis true⟩ LA   556 must]
will LA   557 or] ⟨and⟩ M   559 Yet] But LA, LB   561 ⟨But always / to the
last⟩ And always strike the same ⟨untuneful chord⟩ LA, cor. in LB   But] And M
562 quarter]⟨glory⟩ LA   563 Let Havard's fate be his, whose pen for once LA, cor. in
LB   564 play too dashing] ⟨strain⟩ too able LA, cor. in LB

At first none deemed it his—but when his name   565
Announced the fact—what then?—it lost its fame.
Though all deplore when Milton deigns to doze,
In a long work, 'tis fair to steal repose.

As Pictures so shall Poems be, some stand
The Critic eye, and please when near at hand,   570
But others at a distance strike the sight.
This seeks the shade, but that demands the light
Nor dreads the Connoisseur's fastidious view,
But ten times scrutinized is ten times new.

Parnassian Pilgrims—Ye! whom chance, or choice,   575
Hath led to listen to the Muse's voice,
Receive this counsel, and be timely wise;
Few reach the summit which before you lies.
Our Church, and State, our Courts and Camps concede
Reward to very moderate heads indeed!   580
In these plain common Sense will travel far,
All are not Erskines who mislead the Bar,
But Poesy, between the best and worst
No medium knows,—you must be last or first;
For middling poets' miserable volumes   585
Are damn'd alike by gods, and men, and columns.

As if at table some discordant dish
Should shock our optics, such as frogs for fish,

566 fact] truth *LA*   567 all deplore] much displeased *LA*, *LB*, *cor. in M*
568 steal] take *LA*, *cor. in LB*   569 be] ⟨please⟩ *LA*   570 The Critic eye] Our
scrutiny *LA*; The Scrutiny *LB*, *M*, *cor. in T*   572 seeks] loves *LA*, *LB*
574 scrutinized] ⟨criticised⟩ *T*   ten times new] ⟨always⟩ new *LA*   575 Oh ⟨then⟩
you aspiring youths, whom fate or choice *LA*, *cor. in LB*   fate *LA*] ⟨want⟩ *LB*
576 Hath] Has *LA*   577 ⟨Remember this⟩ *LA*   578 Few . . . summit] ⟨And shun
the danger⟩ / Nor tempt the peril *LA*   579–80 ⟨In Church and State, in camps and
courts we grant | A middle course may lead to all you want⟩ *LA*, *LB*   581 plain . . . will]
⟨will common talents⟩ *LA*   582 mislead] adorn *LA*, *LB*, *M*, *cor. in T*   583 best]
⟨last⟩ *LA*   584 knows] ⟨holds⟩ *LA*
585–6   With very middling verses to offend
               The Devil and Jeffrey grant but to a friend. *LA*
               Though what Gods, Men, and Columns interdict,
               The Devil and Jeffrey pardon in a Pict! *LB*, *M*, *cor. in T*
586–7 [Jeffrey passage inserted between these lines by amanuensis in *MS. T*. See 'Associated Lines' at the end of the poem.]   587 if] ⟨when⟩ *LB*   588 optics] ⟨eyesight⟩
LA

As oil instead of butter men decry,
And poppies please not in a modern pie,   590
If all such mixtures then be half a crime,
We must have excellence to relish rhyme;
Mere roast or boil'd no epicure invites,
Thus poetry disgusts—or else delights.

Who shoot not flying rarely touch a gun;   595
Will he who swims not to the river run?
And men unpractised in exchanging knocks
Must go to Jackson ere they dare to box;
Whate'er the weapon—cudgel, fist, or foil,
None reach expertness without years of toil;   600
But fifty dunces can, with perfect ease,
Tag twenty thousand couplets when they please.
Why not?—Shall I, thus qualified to sit
For rotten boroughs, never show my wit?
Shall I, whose fathers with the quorum sate,   605
And lived in freedom on a fair estate,
Who left me heir, with stables, kennels, packs,
To *all* their *income*, and to—*twice* its *tax*!
Whose form and pedigree have scarce a fault—
Shall I, I say, suppress my Attic salt?   610

Thus think 'the mob of gentlemen', but you
Besides all this must have some genius too;
Be this your sober judgment, and a rule,
And print not piping hot from Southey's school,
Who, ere another Thalaba appears,   615
I trust will spare us for at least nine years;
And, harkee, Southey! pray—but don't be vext—
Burn all your last three works—and half the next.

589 instead] in lieu *M, 1831, 1832, C, More*   590 And pepper rarely pleases
in a pie *LA, LB*   pepper *LA*] mustard *LB*   591 all such mixtures] ⟨such a mixture⟩
LA   593 or] and *LA, LB, M, 1831, 1832, C, More*   595 touch] use *LA*
599 fist, or] ⟨broadsword⟩ *LA*   600 expertness . . . years] ⟨its use . . . a wealth⟩ *LA*
601 ⟨But every sluggish fool ? ⟩ *LA*   can] dare *LA*   602 Tag] To tag *LA*
605 with . . . sate] at the sessions sate *LB alternate reading*   606 lived in . . . on] left me
. . . and *LA, cor. in LB*   607–8 *not in LA*   609 Whose character contains no
glaring fault *LA, LB*   612 ⟨Young⟩ Besides *LA*   613 your sober . . . and a] ⟨to you
a⟩ . . . and your *LA*   614 ⟨And don't come⟩ Nor ⟨print⟩ publish *LA*   615 ⟨Ere his
next epic from his name appears⟩ *LA*   616 trust . . . at least] hope . . . ⟨the next⟩ *LA*

But why this vain advice? once publish'd books
Can never be recall'd—from pastry cooks!   620
Though 'Madoc', with 'Pucelle', instead of punk,
May travel back to Quito—on a trunk!

Orpheus, we learn from Ovid and Lempriere,
Led all wild beasts, but women, by the ear,
And had he fiddled at the present hour,   625
We'd seen the lions waltzing in the Tower;
And old Amphion, such were minstrels then,
Had built St. Paul's without the aid of Wren.
Verse too was justice, and the bards of Greece
Did more than constables to keep the peace;   630
Abolish'd cuckoldom with much applause,
Call'd county-meetings, and enforc'd the laws;
Cut down crown influence with reforming scythes,
And served the church, without demanding tythes;
And hence, throughout all Hellas and the East,   635
Each poet was a prophet and a priest,
Whose old establish'd board of joint controuls
Included kingdoms in the care of souls.

Next rose the martial Homer, Epic's prince!
And fighting's been in fashion ever since;   640
And old Tyrtaeus, when the Spartans warr'd,
(A limping leader, but a lofty bard),
Though wall'd Ithome had resisted long,
Reduced the fortress by the force of song.

When oracles prevail'd in times of old,   645
In song alone Apollo's will was told,

619–20 But why this hint, what author eer could stop | His poems' progress in a grocer's
shop *LA alternate reading*   621–2 *not in LA*   621 instead of] ⟨by way of⟩ *M*
624 all . . . but] ⟨men and beasts and⟩ *LA*   627 were minstrels] were ⟨Muses⟩ fiddlers *LA*
628 Had built] ⟨Could build⟩ *LA*   629 too was justice] then was ⟨virtue⟩ justice *LA*
630 Did more than] Served 'stead of *LA, cor. in LB*   631 Abolish'd] ⟨Proscribed all⟩ *LA*
632 Call'd county-meetings] ⟨And / Constructed cities⟩ *LA*   enforc'd the] enacted *LA*
633 crown influence . . . reforming] ⟨Oppression . . . unsparing⟩ *LA*   636 They joined
the names of Poet and of Priest *LA*   and a] or a *M*   637–8 *not in LA*
639 martial] ⟨grand / immortal⟩ *LA*   640 fighting's] ⟨War has⟩ *LA*   642 (As lame
as I am, but a better bard) *LA, LB, M, cor. in T*   645 oracles] ⟨Orpheus⟩ *T*
646 ⟨In some the fate of men and statesmen told⟩ Apollo's song the fate of man foretold
LA, cor. in LB

Then if your verse is what all verse should be,
And gods were not ashamed on't—why should we?

The Muse, like mortal females, may be woo'd,
In turn she'll seem a Paphian, or a prude;   650
Fierce as a bride, when first she feels—affright!
Mild as the same, upon the second night!
Her eyes beseem, her heart belies, her zone;
Ice in a crowd, and lava when alone:
Wild as the wife of alderman of peer,   655
Now for his Grace, and now a grenadier!
If verse be studied with some show of art,
Kind Nature always will perform her part;
Though without genius, and a native vein
Of wit, we loathe an artificial strain,   660
Yet Art and Nature join'd will win the prize,
Unless they act like us and our allies.

The youth who trains to ride, or run a race,
Must bear privations with unruffled face,
Be call'd to labour, when he thinks to dine,   665
And, harder still, leave wenching and his wine;
Ladies who sing, at least who sing at night,
Have follow'd Music through her farthest flight;
But rhymers tell you neither more or less,
'I've got a pretty poem for the press',   670
And that's enough—then write and print so fast,
If Satan take the hindmost, who'd be last?
They storm the types, they publish one and all,
They leap the counter, and they leave the stall.
Provincial maidens, men of high command,   675
Yea! baronets have ink'd the bloody hand!
Cash cannot quell them—Pollio play'd this prank,
(Then Phoebus first found credit in a bank!)

647 verse . . . verse] ⟨rhyme / song . . . song⟩ *LA*   649–56 *not in LA*, *LB*
650 turn] turns *1831*, *1832*, *C*, *More*   653–6 *lines 653–4 not in M but were*
added by B in T; *the two couplets are transposed in T*, *1831*,*1832*, *C*, *More*   661 But both
combined may win the wished for prize *LA*   664 Must suffer hardships with ⟨a decent⟩
face *LA*, *cor. in LB*   667 at night] at sight *LA*, *LB*, *M*   668 Have studied with a
master day and night *LA*, *cor. in LB*   669 rhymers] rhymsters *LA*   or] nor *1831*,
1832, *C*, *More*   672 take] takes *LA*, *cor. in LB*   673–718 *not in LA*, *LB*
673 the types] Bolt Court *MA*, *cor. in M*   676 Yea] Nay *MA*   677 Pollio]
Rogers *MA*, *M*

Not all the living only, but the dead,
Fool on—as fluent as an Orpheus' head!   680
Damn'd all their days, they posthumously thrive,
Dug up from dust, though buried when alive!
Reviews record this epidemic crime,
Those books of martyrs to the rage for rhyme,
Alas! woe worth the scribbler! often seen   685
In Morning Post, or Monthly Magazine,
There lurk his earlier lays—but soon—hot-prest,
Behold a quarto!—Tarts must tell the rest!
Then leave, ye wise, the lyre's precarious chords
To Muse-mad Baronets, or madder lords,   690
Or country Crispins, now grown somewhat stale,
Twin Doric minstrels, drunk with Doric ale!
Hark to those notes, narcotically soft!
The cobbler-laureats sing to Capel Lofft!
Till, lo! that modern Midas, as he hears,   695
Adds an ell-growth to his egregious ears!

There lives one Druid, who prepares in time,
'Gainst future feuds his poor revenge of rhyme;
Racks his dull memory, and his duller muse,
To publish faults which friendship should excuse;   700
If friendship's nothing, self-regard might teach
More polish'd usage of his parts of speech;
But what is shame, or what is aught to him?
He vents his spleen, or gratifies his whim;
Some fancied slight has roused his lurking hate,   705
Some folly crost, some jest, or some debate;
Up to his den Sir Scribbler hies, and soon
The gather'd gall is voided in lampoon.

679 ⟨The living / As the sad land like Orphic   ? spread⟩ *MA*   680 Fool . . . an]
Are found as fluent as ⟨old⟩ *MA*   681 Bear witness ye who posthumously thrive
MA   682 Before unheard of—would you see alive? *MA*   683 Allow we then
to ? the young in time *MA*   record] ⟨scarce stop⟩ *M*   684 Against this rage of epidemic
rhyme *MA*   685 Ah me, how narrow are the bounds between *MA*   scribbler]
Sinner *M*   687 There see their sonnets first—but spring—hot prest *MA, cor. in*
M   688 Behold] Beholds *MA*   690 To fuddled Esquires, or to flippant Lords
MA, M, cor. in T   692 drunk] dazed *MA*   695-6 Till Capel, modern Midas
of the Swains, | Feels his ears lengthen with the lengthening Strains. *MA, cor. in M*
696 ⟨Adds a week's growth to his enormous ears⟩ *M*   697 Druid] ⟨scribbler⟩ *LC*
701-2 ⟨But what are these? Benefits might bind | Some decent ties around a manly mind.⟩
M, T   701-4 If Friendship's nothing, benefits might bind | Some decent ties around
a manly mind, *LC*   707 Scribbler] Rhymster *LC*

Perhaps at some pert speech you've dared to frown,
Perhaps, your poem may have pleased the town!   710
If so, alas! 'tis nature in the man:
May Heav'n forgive you, for he never can!
Then be it so, and may his withering bays
Bloom fresh in satire! though they fade in praise;
While his lost songs no more shall steep and stink,   715
The dullest, fattest weeds on Lethe's brink;
But springing upward from the sluggish mould,
Be (what they never were before) be—sold!

Should some rich bard—(but such a monster now
In modern physics we can scarce allow)—   720
Should some pretending scribbler of the court,
Some rhyming peer,—we have several of the sort,
All but one poor dependent priest withdrawn,
(Ah! too regardless of his chaplain's yawn!)
Condemn the unlucky curate to recite   725
His last dramatic work by candle-light,
How would the preacher turn each rueful leaf,
Dull as his sermons, but not half so brief;
Yet since 'tis promised at the rector's death,
He'll risk no living for a little breath;   730
Then spouts and foams, and cries at every line
(The Lord forgive him) Bravo! Grand! Divine!
Hoarse with those praises (which, by Flatt'ry fed,
Dependence barters for her bitter bread),
He strides and stamps along with creaking boot,   735
Till the floor echoes his emphatic foot;

717 upward] upwards *LC*, *1831*, *1832*, *C*, *More*   719 but ⟨that's⟩ such *LA*   720 ⟨Which⟩ Our modern sceptics can no more allow *LA*   can scarce] can not *LB*, *M*, *cor. in T* 722 we have . . . sort] Carlisle or Carysfort *LA*, *LB*, *M*, *cor. in T* ; there's plenty of the sort *T*, *1831*, *1832*, *C*, *More*, *cor. in Proof M*   723 All . . . poor] When all but one *LA*, *LB*, *M*, *cor. in T*   724 ⟨Ah! too] ⟨Alas⟩ *LA*   725 Condemn] Compel *LA* 726 Their last ⟨dull drama⟩ dramatic ⟨arts / verses⟩ work for half a night *LA*, *cor. in LB* His] Their *LB*, *M*, *T*, *1831*, *1832*, *C*, *More*, *cor. in Proof M*   727 the ⟨agonizing⟩ preacher *LA*   728 Dull] ⟨Sad⟩ *LA*   729 ⟨Spout every ? metaphor till out of breath⟩ Yet since ⟨he bears it⟩ he's sure on't at the ⟨vicar's⟩ rector's death *LA*, *cor. in LB* 730 ⟨He will not⟩ *LA*   733–4 ⟨Till⟩ Hoarse with ⟨praising⟩ bepraising, and half choaked with lies | Sweat on his brow, and ⟨tears⟩ teardrops in ⟨both⟩ his eyes *LA*, *cor. in LB* 735 He strides along as may the action suit *LA*, *LB*   736 Till the floor trembles to his ⟨thundering⟩ tiger's boot *LA*, *cor. in LB*

Then sits again, then rolls his pious eye,
As when the dying vicar will not die!
Nor feels, forsooth, emotion at his heart—
But all dissemblers overact their part.   740

Ye, who aspire to build the lofty rhyme,
Believe not all who laud your false 'sublime';
But if some friend shall hear your work and say,
'Expunge that stanza, lop that line away',
And after fruitless efforts you return   745
Without amendment, and he answers 'Burn!'
That instant throw your paper in the fire,
Ask not his thoughts, or follow his desire:
But if (true bard) you scorn to condescend,
And will not alter what you can't defend,   750
If you will breed this bastard of your brains,
We'll have no words—I've only lost my pains.

Yet if you only prize your favourite thought,
As critics kindly do, and authors ought;
If your cool friend annoy you now and then,   755
And cross whole pages with his plaguy pen,
No matter—throw your ornaments aside,
Better let him, than all the world, deride.
Give light to passages too much in shade,
Nor let a doubt obscure one verse you've made;   760

737–8 Then sits again, then shakes his piteous head | As if the vicar were already dead
LA, cor. in LB   739 Nor . . . forsooth] Not that he feels LA; Nor feels, withall LB,
M, cor. in T   742 laud your false] tell you 'tis LA, LB, M, cor. in T   743 some]
a LA   744 Correct that ⟨line, amend that stanza⟩ stanza LA   745 after ⟨toils⟩
fruitless LA   746 he ⟨tells⟩ answers LA   749 But if ⟨you love the offspring of
your brains⟩ you're too converted to amend LA, cor. in LB   But if (true bard)] But (if
true bard !) 1832, C   751 you . . . bastard] ⟨so you love this offspring⟩ LA   752 We'll
. . . words] ⟨I'll say no more⟩ LA   753 Yet] But LA, cor. in LB   754 kindly
. . . authors] ⟨always⟩ really do, and poets LA, LB, M, cor. in T
755–6   ⟨Then let thy ponderous Quarto steep and stink
                     The dullest fattest weed on Lethe's brink
                     Down with that volume to the depths of Hell
                     Oblivion seems rewarding it too well,
                     Yet there thy Quarto still / rooted rhyme may steep and stink
                     The dullest fattest weeds on Lethe's brink⟩ LC
756 ⟨By crossing⟩ pages LA   757 throw your] ⟨cut⟩ all LA, cor. in LB   758 let
him] ⟨your friends⟩ LA   759 too . . . shade] ⟨that most it need⟩ LA   760 obscure
. . . made] ⟨hang oer / cloud⟩ obscure the verse you've made LA, cor. in LB

Your friend's 'a Johnson', not to leave a word,
However trifling, which may seem absurd;
Such erring trifles lead to serious ills,
And furnish food for critics, or their quills.

As the Scotch fiddle with its touching tune,   765
Or the mad influence of the angry moon,
All men avoid bad writers' angry tongues,
As yawning waiters fly Fitzscribble's lungs;
Yet on he mouths—ten minutes—tedious each
As prelate's homily, or placeman's speech,   770
Long as the last years of a lingering lease,
When riot pauses, until rents increase.
While such a minstrel, muttering fustian, strays
O'er hedge and ditch, through unfrequented ways,
If by some chance he walks into a well,   775
And shouts for succour with Stentorian yell,
'A rope! help, Christians, as ye hope for grace!'
Nor woman, man, or child will stir a pace.
For there his carcase he might freely fling
From frenzy, or the humour of the thing!   780
Though this has happen'd to more bards than one;
I'll tell you Budgell's story—and have done.
Budgell, a rogue and rhymester,—for no good,
(Unless his case be much misunderstood)
When teased with creditors' continual claims,   785
'To die like Cato'—leapt into the Thames!
And therefore be it lawful through the town
For any bard to poison, hang, or drown:

761 a word] one word T, *1831, 1832*, C, *More, cor. in Proof M*   764 for] to LB, M
or] and LA, *cor. in T*   766 mad] sad LA, M, *1831, 1832*, C, *More*   angry] ⟨wand /
rising⟩ LA   767 All ⟨fear and fly the ? ⟩ fly ⟨inveterate⟩ unlucky scribblers' evil tongues
LA   angry] ready M, *1831, 1832*, C, *More*   768 On pain of suffering from their pen
or lungs LA, LB, *cor. in M*   Fitzscribble's] Fitzgerald's M, *cor. in T*   769–72 *not
in LA, LB*   769 ⟨Ah! when Bards mouth, from sympathetic ? ⟩ M   770 ⟨Stagnates,
and Hours stand still to ? ⟩ M   773 ⟨These⟩ Such while ⟨they⟩ he mutters strange
bombast, and strays LA, LB, *cor. in M*   minstrel] scribbler M, *cor. in T*   775 walks]
⟨pops⟩ LA   776 shouts] roars LA, LB   777 A rope, ⟨dear⟩ Christians! ⟨for the
Virgin's⟩ grace LA   778 or] nor LA, LB, *1831, 1832*, C, *More*   779 Besides how
know ye? that he did not fling LA, LB, M, *cor. in T*   780 Himself ⟨on purpose in the
bitter spring⟩ there for the humour of the thing? LA, LB, M, *cor. in T*   781 Though
this has] ⟨Such things have⟩ LA   788 to . . . hang] that likes to hang LA

Who saves the intended suicide, receives
Small thanks from him who loathes the life he leaves;   790
And, sooth to say, mad poets must not lose
The glory of that death they freely choose.

Nor is it certain, that some sorts of verse
Prick not the poet's conscience as a curse;
Dosed with vile drams, on Sunday he was found,   795
Or gat a child on consecrated ground!
And hence is haunted with a rhyming rage,
Fear'd like a bear just bursting from his cage;
If free, all fly his versifying fit,
Fatal at once to simpleton or wit.   800
But *him* unhappy! whom he seizes, *him*!
He flays with recitation limb by limb,
Probes to the quick, where'er he makes his breach,
And gorges, like a lawyer, or a leech.

                                                                        1811

150a   Lines Associated with *Hints from Horace*

Again, my Jeffrey—as that sound inspires,
How wakes my bosom to its wonted fires!
Fires, such as gentle Caledonians feel
When Southrons writhe upon their critic wheel,
Or mild Eclectics, when some worse than Turks   5
Would rob poor Faith to decorate 'Good Works'.
Such are the genial feelings thou canst claim—
My falcon flies not at ignoble game.

790 Small thanks, ⟨if the poor maniac really grieves⟩ unwelcome life he quickly leaves *LA*
LB, *M*, *cor. in T*   791 And ⟨poets in particular would lose⟩ raving poets really should
not lose *LA*, *LB*, *M*, *cor. in T*   793–5 Nor is it clearly understood that verse |
Has not been given the poet for a curse, | Perhaps he sent the parson's pig to pound— *LA*,
cor. in LB   796 gat] got *1831, 1832, C, More*   797–8 But be this as it may, his
rhyming rage | ⟨Is like⟩ Exceeds a Bear's who strives to break his cage, *LA*, *cor. in LB*
799 If ⟨once his⟩ free *LA*   800 The young, the old, the simpleton, and wit *LA*   at
once] alike *LB*   803 ⟨Strikes to the last, where first he makes / plants⟩ his breach *LA*
804 gorges ... lawyer] ⟨sucks his blood like lawyers⟩ *LA*

150a. Copy text: *MS. B*, collated with *MS. T, 1831, 1832, C*. These lines have hitherto
been printed as part of *Hints*, after line 586 above. See commentary.
    6 rob ... decorate] ⟨pilfer Faith's poor spoils to deck⟩ *B*

Mightiest of all Dunedin's beasts of chase!
For thee my Pegasus would mend his pace.   10
Arise, my Jeffrey! or my inkless pen
Shall never blunt its edge on meaner men;
Till thee or thine mine evil eye discerns,
'Alas! I cannot strike at wretched kernes.'
Inhuman Saxon! wilt thou then resign   15
A Muse and heart by choice so wholly thine?
Dear d——d contemner of my schoolboy songs,
Hast thou no vengeance for my Manhood's wrongs?
If unprovoked thou once could bid me bleed,
Hast thou no weapon for my daring deed?   20
What! not a word?—and am I then so low?
Wilt thou forebear who never spared a foe?
Hast thou no wrath, or wish to give it vent,
No wit for Nobles, Dunces by descent,
No jest on 'minors', quibbles on a name,   25
Nor one facetious paragraph of blame?
Is it for this on Ilion I have stood,
And thought of Homer less than Holyrood?
On shore of Euxine or Aegean sea,
My hate, untravelled, fondly turned to thee.   30
Ah! let me cease! in vain my bosom burns,
From Corydon unkind Alexis turns—
Thy rhymes are vain, thy Jeffrey then forego,
Nor woo that anger which he will not show.
What then? Edina starves some lanker son,   35
To write an article thou canst not shun;
Some less fastidious Scotchman shall be found,
As bold in Billingsgate, though less renowned.

11 ⟨Or then⟩ Arise *B*   19 could] couldst *T*   35 lanker] ⟨less fastidious⟩ *B*
36 ⟨Shall⟩ To *B*   37 shall] ⟨may⟩ *B*

151　　　　　The Curse of Minerva

'Pallas te hoc vulnere, Pallas
Immolat, et poenam scelerato ex sanguine sumit.'
AENEID, 12th [948–9]

Athens: Capuchin Convent, *March 17, 1811*

Slow sinks, more lovely ere his race be run,
Along Morea's hills the setting Sun;
Not as in Northern climes obscurely bright,
But one unclouded blaze of living light;
O'er the hush'd deep the yellow beam he throws, 　　　5
Gilds the green wave that trembles as it glows;
On old Aegina's rock and Hydra's isle,
The God of gladness sheds his parting smile;
O'er his own regions lingering loves to shine,
Though there his altars are no more divine. 　　　10
Descending fast the mountain-shadows kiss
Thy glorious Gulph, unconquer'd Salamis!
Their azure arches through the long expanse
More deeply purpled meet his mellowing glance,
And tenderest tints, along their summits driven, 　　　15
Mark his gay course and own the hues of Heaven;
Till darkly shaded from the land and deep,
Behind his Delphian rock he sinks to sleep.

On such an Eve, his palest beam he cast
When, Athens! here thy wisest looked his last: 　　　20

151. Copy text: *Curse1812*, collated with *MSS. S, B, Υ*, MS. fragments *A, M, P*, partial proof *H*, and *Corsair*, III. 1–54 with lines 1–54.

1 Slow ⟨sinking⟩ more ⟨glorious⟩ . . . be ⟨done⟩ *S*　　　2 Along] ⟨Behind⟩ *S*　　　3 as in Northern] ⟨such as in our⟩ *S*　　　5 Oer the ⟨blue ocean many a⟩ beam he throws *S* 6 green] ⟨hushed / long⟩ *S*　　that] ⟨and⟩ *S*　　7 On] ⟨Oer⟩ *S*　　8 sheds] gleams *S, cor. in B* 9 ⟨And / Oer mountains / regions all his own he loves to shine⟩ *S*　　10 ⟨Though there no more he finds each wonted shrine⟩ / Nor yet forebears each long abandoned shrine *S*; ⟨Where once each Altar wooed him to its shrine⟩ *B*　　11–12 *added in margin of S* 13–14　　　Their ⟨Mountains / deepening⟩ varying azure mingled with the sky
　　　　　Beneath his ⟨brightness⟩ rays assume a deeper die *S*
　　　　　Their azure arches ⟨curving oer the sky
　　　　　Beneath his rays reflects a deeper dye⟩ *B*
13 varying azure mingled *S*]; ⟨azure summit mingles⟩ *S*　　　14 ⟨More deeply dyed receive him from on High⟩ *B*　　　15 And tenderest tints] Each tender tint *S*; And ⟨each bright tint⟩ *B*　　　17 darkly shaded] ⟨lost / slowly / darkly shrouded⟩ *S*　　　18 ⟨To seek his Delphic cave he seems to seek⟩ *S*　　sinks] ⟨seems⟩ *S*　　rock] cliff *Corsair*　　　19 an Eve a night *S*　　palest . . . cast] ⟨last pale beam he threw⟩ *S*

How watch'd thy better Sons his farewell ray,
That clos'd their murder'd Sage's latest day!
Not yet—not yet—Sol pauses on the hill,
The precious hour of parting lingers still;
But sad his light to agonizing eyes,   25
And dark the mountain's once delightful dyes:
Gloom o'er the lovely land he seem'd to pour,
The land where Phoebus never frown'd before;
But ere he sunk below Cithaeron's head
The cup of Woe was quaff'd—the spirit fled;   30
The Soul of Him, that scorn'd to fear or fly,
Who liv'd and died, as none can live or die.

But lo! from high Hymettus to the plain
The Queen of Night asserts her silent reign:
No murky vapour, herald of the storm,   35
Hides her fair face, or girds her glowing form:
With cornice glimmering as the Moon-beams play
There the white column greets her grateful ray,
And bright around with quivering beams beset
Her emblem sparkles o'er the Minaret: 40
The groves of Olive scatter'd dark and wide,
Where meek Cephisus sheds his scanty tide,
The Cypress saddening by the sacred mosque,
The gleaming turret of the gay Kiosk,
And sad and sombre 'mid the holy calm,
Near Theseus' fane, yon solitary palm;
All tinged with varied hues arrest the eye,
And dull were his that pass'd them heedless by.

Again the Aegean, heard no more afar,
Lulls his chaf'd breast from elemental war;   50

21 farewell] ⟨parting⟩ S   22 their] thy S   23 Sol pauses] ⟨he⟩ lingers S; Sol
⟨lingers⟩ B   24 ⟨An hour⟩ The precious ⟨moment of twilight⟩ pauses still S   lingers]
⟨pauses⟩ B   25 ⟨Then⟩ sad ⟨the⟩ light S   29 ⟨But eer his stream of⟩ S   31 scorn'd
. . . fly] ⟨never ? a sigh⟩ S   that] ⟨who⟩ B; who Corsair   33 from] ⟨oer⟩ S   34 asserts
her silent] ⟨descending claims her⟩ asserts her silver S   35–6 How sweet and silent,
not a ⟨single⟩ passing cloud | Hides her fair face with intervening shroud S   37 ⟨There
/ Oer the white / tall column through its lengthening shone / on the mountains drew⟩ S
38 ⟨With an / The cornice glimmering to her grateful light / near its marble head⟩ S
39 ⟨Brighter with quivering streams⟩ S   42 ⟨The darker cypress⟩ Where meek
Cephisus rolls his S   43–6 not in S   44 gleaming] ⟨whiter⟩ B   45 sombre]
lonely A, cor. in B   47 ⟨All shone their varied / tinged with varied hues adorn the
scene⟩ / ⟨The Dome of Pallas on her sacred rock⟩ S   arrest] ⟨invite⟩ S   49 heard
no more] ⟨gleaming from⟩ S   50 Lulls . . . breast] ⟨Rests his lulled care⟩ S

Again his waves in milder tints unfold
Their long expanse of sapphire and of gold,
Mixt with the shades of many a distant isle
That frown, where gentler Ocean deigns to smile.

As thus within the walls of Pallas' fane   55
I mark'd the beauties of the land and main,
Alone, and friendless on the magic shore,
Whose arts revive, whose arms avenge no more;
Oft, as the matchless dome I turn'd to scan
Sacred to Gods, but not secure from man,   60
The past return'd, the present seem'd to cease,
And Glory knew no clime beyond her Greece.

Hours roll'd along, and Dian's orb on high
Had gain'd the centre of her softest sky,
And yet unwearied still my footsteps trod   65
O'er the vain shrine of many a vanish'd God:
But chiefly, Pallas! thine; when Hecate's glare,
Check'd by thy columns, fell more sadly fair
O'er the chill marble, where the startling tread
Thrills the lone heart like echoes from the dead.   70
Long had I mused and treasured every trace
The wreck of Greece recorded of her race,
When lo! a giant-form before me strode,
And Pallas hail'd me in her own abode!

Yes, 'twas Minerva's self—but ah! how chang'd   75
Since o'er the Dardan field in arms she rang'd!

51 waves] ⟨foam⟩ S   53 ⟨Begirt / ? along by / Checquered / And the dark / And oer
the Shadows / bosoms of their distant isles⟩ S   54 gentler Ocean deigns] ⟨all besides
appears⟩ gentler Ocean seems S; gentler Ocean ⟨seems⟩ B; gentler Ocean seems *Corsair*
57 the magic] ⟨that foreign⟩ S   58 Whose arts and arms but live in poets' lore S, B,
Υ, *proof H, 1831, 1832, C, More; cor. in M*   59 ⟨With sad yet soothing ? of the days⟩ S
matchless] ⟨Goddess / perfect⟩ S   60 ⟨When Greece possessed / Glory knew no clime
beyond her grave⟩ S   63–4 ⟨But soon a vision, if it bear the name | Recalled me back
to truth⟩ S   66 vain] sad S   67 But chiefly ⟨thine Minerva's, when the⟩ glare S
68 ⟨Along thy columns shone severely fair⟩ Between thy columns fell more sadly fair S
69 ⟨Oft at / Then⟩ S   where the startling] ⟨and the echoing⟩ S   70 echoes] ⟨voices /
whispers⟩ S   71 ⟨I stood, or stumbling / moved along with slow and solemn pace⟩ S
72 ⟨That records / time has left of young and gallant race⟩ / ⟨The wreck of ages left of such
a race⟩ S   75 ⟨Yet⟩ S   76 the . . . arms] the fated Dardan field S

Not such as erst by her divine command
Her form appear'd from Phidias' plastic hand:
Gone were the terrors of her awful brow,
Her idle Aegis bore no Gorgon now;   80
Her helm was dinted, and the broken lance
Seem'd weak and shaftless e'en to mortal glance;
The olive branch, which still she deign'd to clasp,
Shrunk from her touch and wither'd in her grasp;
And ah! tho' still the brightest of the sky,   85
Celestial tears bedimm'd her large blue eye;
Round the rent casque her owlet circled slow,
And mourned his mistress with a shriek of woe!

'Mortal!' ('twas thus she spake) 'that blush of shame
Proclaims thee Briton, once a noble name;   90
First of the mighty, foremost of the free,
Now honoured *less* by all, and *least* by me:
Chief of thy foes shall Pallas still be found—
Seek'st thou the cause of loathing?—look around.
Lo! here, despite of war and wasting fire,   95
I saw successive tyrannies expire:
'Scap'd from the ravage of the Turk and Goth,
Thy country sends a spoiler worse than both.
Survey this vacant, violated fane;
Recount the relics torn that yet remain: 100
These Cecrops placed, *this* Pericles adorn'd,
That Adrian rear'd when drooping Science mourn'd.
What more I owe let Gratitude attest—
Know Alaric and Elgin did the rest.
That all may learn from whence the plunderer came   105
The insulted wall sustains his hated name:

---

77 ⟨Gone were the⟩ *S*   80 And even her Aegis held no Gorgon now *S, cor. in B*
81 the . . . lance] ⟨her broken spear⟩ / the ⟨shaftless spear⟩ *S*   82 Seemed ⟨harmless⟩ *S*
84 Shrunk . . . touch] ⟨Forgot its power⟩ *S*   85 tho' . . . of] ⟨no more the mightiest in⟩ /
⟨but⟩ still the brightest in *S*   87 the . . . her] her ⟨high⟩ tall head ⟨the⟩ her *S*   rent]
⟨plumed⟩ *B*   89 Mortal] Stranger *S*   91 First . . . mighty] ⟨Welcome to slaves,
when⟩ *S*   93 ⟨Why⟩ Chief *S*   94 the ⟨reason⟩ cause of ⟨loathing⟩ hatred *S*
97–8 Ah Athens! scarce escaped from Turk and Goth | Hell sends a paltry Scotchman
worse than both. *S*   99 Survey this vacant] Survey ⟨the / his deeds / this fragment⟩
this falling *S*   101 placed] built *S*   102 ⟨And⟩ Adrian *S*   105 learn] know *S*
106 insulted] ⟨wounded⟩ *B*   his hated] the ⟨Scotchman's⟩ Scot's dull *S*

For Elgin's fame thus grateful Pallas pleads,
Below, his name; above, behold his deeds!
Be ever hail'd with equal honour here
The Gothic monarch and the Pictish peer: 110
Arms gave the first his right, the last had none,
But basely stole what less barbarians won.
So when the Lion quits his fell repast
Next prowls the Wolf, the filthy Jackall last:
Flesh, limbs and blood the former make their own,   115
The last poor brute securely gnaws the bone.
Yet still the Gods are just, and crimes are crost:
See here what Elgin won, and what he lost!
Another name with *his* pollutes my shrine:
Behold where Dian's beams disdain to shine!   120
Some retribution still might Pallas claim,
When Venus half aveng'd Minerva's shame.'

       She ceas'd awhile, and thus I dar'd reply,
To soothe the vengeance kindling in her eye:
'Daughter of Jove! in Britain's injur'd name,   125
A true-born Briton may the deed disclaim.
Frown not on England; England owns him not:
Athena! no; thy plunderer was a Scot.
Ask'st thou the difference? From fair Phyle's towers
Survey Boeotia; Caledonia's ours.   130
And well I know within that bastard land
Hath Wisdom's goddess never held command:
A barren soil where Nature's germs confin'd
To stern sterility can stint the mind,
Whose thistle well betrays the niggard earth,   135
Emblem of all to whom the land gives birth;

108 ⟨Above⟩ Below *S*   109 Be] ⟨Oh⟩ *S*   110 Pictish] ⟨British⟩ *S*   114 filthy]
sneaking *S*   116 brute] thief *S*   119 ⟨Lo / Look a name⟩ *S*   his . . . shrine]
⟨this insults my call⟩ *S*   120 ⟨Of one who fell and dragged him in his fall⟩ *S*
122 When . . . half] ⟨For⟩ And . . . ⟨hath⟩ *S*   124 To . . . kindling] ⟨And⟩ . . . swelling
S, cor. in B   125 in . . . name] ⟨whose worth is now a jest / in Greek celestial minds / no
son⟩ / in Britain's ⟨honoured⟩ guilty name *S*   126 ⟨No true-born Briton ?⟩ / ⟨A Briton
dares this outrage to disclaim⟩ *S*   128 No Greece, thy Glory's plunderer was a Scot *S*
Athena . . . thy] ⟨No, Greece, thy paltry⟩ *B*   131 within . . . land] ⟨that never in that
land / in that abandoned land⟩ *S*   132 never] ⟨ever⟩ *S*   133 ⟨A land expunged /
Proud were her children⟩ *S*   soil . . . germs] ⟨land . . . self⟩ *S*   134 ⟨Even stints in
stern sterility⟩ *S*   135 ⟨One plant alone⟩ betrays *S*

Each genial influence nurtur'd to resist,
A land of meanness, sophistry and mist:
Each breeze from foggy mount and marshy plain
Dilutes with drivel every drizzly brain,   140
Till burst at length each watery head o'erflows,
Foul as their soil and frigid as their snows:
Then thousand schemes of petulance and pride
Dispatch her scheming children far and wide,
Some East, some West, some every where but North,   145
In quest of lawless gain they issue forth.
And thus, accursed be the day and year!
She sent a Pict to play the felon here.
Yet Caledonia claims some native worth,
As dull Boeotia gave a Pindar birth;   150
So may her few, the letter'd and the brave,
Bound to no clime and victors of the grave,
Shake off the sordid dust of such a land,
And shine like children of a happier strand.
As once, of yore, in some obnoxious place,   155
Ten names (if found) had saved a wretched race.'

'Mortal!' the blue-eyed maid resum'd, 'once more
Bear back my mandate to thy native shore;
Though fallen, alas! this vengeance yet is mine,
To turn my counsels far from lands like thine.   160
Hear then in silence Pallas' stern behest;
Hear and believe, for Time will tell the rest.

'First on the head of him who did this deed
My curse shall light, on him and all his seed:
Without one spark of intellectual fire,   165
Be all the sons as senseless as the sire:

137 nurtur'd] ready S   138 meanness, sophistry] Liars, Mountebanks S, B, ϒ
139 The ⟨sea⟩ fogs they breathe from ⟨every⟩ many a marshy plain S, cor. in B   141 Till
burst] With froth S
143–4   ⟨This flood of Folly pours from thousand tongues,
               Till / And pens at length relieve the weary lungs / imbibe the deluge
                  of the lungs⟩
               ⟨The flood of Nothing / Nonsense pours from Nature's rills
               Diffused an example through ten thousand quills⟩ S
143 schemes ... pride] ⟨projects float along the tide⟩ S   144 Dispatch] ⟨And send⟩ S
145 West] ⟨South⟩ S   146 quest] search S   149–56 not in S; added in margin of B
162 will] shall B, ϒ   164 all] ⟨on⟩ S   166 senseless] ⟨silly⟩ S

If one with wit the parent brood disgrace,
Believe him bastard of a brighter race:
Still with his hireling artists let him prate,
And Folly's praise repay for Wisdom's hate;   170
Long of their Patron's gusto let them tell,
Whose noblest, *native* gusto is—to sell:
To sell, and make, may Shame record the day,
The State receiver of his pilfer'd prey:
Meantime, the flattering, feeble dotard West,   175
Europe's worst dauber, and poor Britain's best,
With palsied hand shall turn each model o'er,
And own himself an infant of fourscore:
Be all the bruisers cull'd from all St. Giles,
That art and nature may compare their styles;   180
While brawny brutes in stupid wonder stare,
And marvel at his Lordship's "stone shop" there.
Round the throng'd gate shall sauntering coxcombs creep,
To lounge and lucubrate, to prate and peep;
While many a languid maid, with longing sigh,   185
On giant statues casts the curious eye:
The room with transient glance appears to skim,
Yet marks the mighty back and length of limb;
Mourns o'er the difference of *now* and *then*,
Exclaims, "these Greeks indeed were proper men!"   190
Draws sly comparisons of *these* with *those*,
And envies Lais all her Attic beaux.
When shall a modern maid have swains like these!
Alas! Sir Harry is no Hercules!
And last of all amidst the gaping crew   195
Some calm spectator, as he takes his view
In silent indignation mix'd with grief,
Admires the plunder, but abhors the thief.

---

167 wit ... disgrace] ⟨sense disgrace the parent brood⟩ *S* 168 brighter] ⟨better⟩ *S*
170 Folly's praise] praise of Fools *S* 173 ⟨To sell the produce of a plundered⟩ *S*
Shame ... day] ⟨may Heaven avert⟩ the day *S* 174 of his ⟨stolen goods⟩ *S*
176 ⟨The worst of Europe's painters / daubers⟩ *S* 178 infant of fourscore] ⟨idiot at
threescore⟩ *S* 180 That art may measure old and modern styles *S* 181 While
brawny] ⟨That / While as the⟩ *S* 182 marvel] ⟨wonder⟩ *S* 183 the] his *S*
184 to] ⟨and⟩ *S* 190 Exclaims] ⟨And says / cries⟩ *S* 191 ⟨Ah me ? must yield to
those⟩ *S* sly] slight *C* 192 Lais] ⟨Phryne⟩ *S* 193 In sooth the nymph
twere no slight task to please *S* modern maid] modern nymph *B* 194 ⟨And⟩ Since
young Sir *S*; Ah would Sir Harry you were Hercules *B, Y* 195 gaping crew] gazing
⟨throng⟩ *S* 197 In silent] ⟨In / With active⟩ *S*

Oh, loath'd in life, nor pardon'd in the dust,
May Hate pursue his sacrilegious lust!   200
Link'd with the fool that fired the Ephesian dome
Shall vengeance follow far beyond the tomb,
And Eratostratus and Elgin shine
In many a branding page and burning line:
Alike reserv'd for aye to stand accurst,   205
Perchance the second blacker than the first.

'So let him stand through ages yet unborn,
Fix'd statue on the pedestal of Scorn;
Though not for him alone revenge shall wait,
But fits thy country for her coming fate: 210
Hers were the deeds that taught her lawless son
To do what oft Britannia's self had done.
Look to the Baltic—blazing from afar,
Your old ally yet mourns perfidious war:
Not to such deeds did Pallas lend her aid,   215
Or break the compact which herself had made;
Far from such councils, from the faithless field
She fled—but left behind her Gorgon shield:
A fatal gift that turn'd your friends to stone,
And left lost Albion hated and alone.   220

'Look to the East, where Ganges' swarthy race
Shall shake your tyrant empire to its base;
Lo, there Rebellion rears her ghastly head,
And glares the Nemesis of native dead;
Till Indus rolls a deep purpureal flood,   225
And claims his long arrear of northern blood.
So may ye perish! Pallas when she gave
Your free-born rights, forbade ye to enslave.

'Look on your Spain, she clasps the hand she hates,
But coldly clasps, and thrusts you from her gates.   230
Bear witness, bright Barossa! thou canst tell
Whose were the sons that bravely fought and fell.

200 his] ⟨thy⟩ S   202 the] his S   203–64 not in S   207 stand through]
⟨pass to⟩ B   209 Though] ⟨But⟩ B   210 ⟨Thy Country totters on the verge of
Fate⟩ B

But Lusitania, kind and dear ally,
Can spare a few to fight, and sometimes fly.
Oh glorious field! by Famine fiercely won,   235
The Gaul retires for once, and all is done!
But when did Pallas teach that one retreat
Retriev'd three long Olympiads of defeat?

'Look last at home, ye love not to look there
On the grim smile of comfortless despair: 240
Your city saddens, loud though revel howls,
Here Famine faints, and yonder Rapine prowls:
See all alike of more or less bereft,
No misers tremble when there's nothing left.
"Blest paper credit", who shall dare to sing?   245
It clogs like lead Corruption's weary wing:
Yet Pallas pluck'd each Premier by the ear,
Who gods and men alike disdain'd to hear;
But one, repentant o'er a bankrupt state,
On Pallas calls, but calls, alas! too late: 250
Then raves for [Stanhope], to that Mentor bends,
Though he and Pallas never yet were friends:
Him Senates hear whom never yet they heard,
Contemptuous once, and now no less absurd:
So once of yore, each reasonable frog   255
Swore faith and fealty to his sovereign "log".
Thus hail'd your rulers their Patrician clod,
As Egypt chose an Onion for a God.

'Now fare ye well, enjoy your little hour,
Go grasp the shadow of your vanish'd power;   260
Gloss o'er the failure of each fondest scheme,
Your strength a name, your bloated wealth a dream:
Gone is that Gold, the marvel of mankind,
And Pirates barter all that's left behind.
No more the hirelings, purchas'd near and far,   265
Crowd to the ranks of mercenary war.
The idle merchant on the useless quay,
Droops o'er the bales no bark may bear away;

249 one] ⟨now⟩ B   251 Then raves for Stanhope B, Υ   256 sovereign] ⟨leader⟩ B
261 ⟨Gone is that Gold the marvel of each scheme⟩ B   267 useless] ⟨vacant⟩ S

Or back returning sees rejected stores
Rot piecemeal on his own encumber'd shores: 270
The starv'd mechanic breaks his rusting loom,
And desperate mans him 'gainst the common doom.
Then in the Senate of your sinking state,
Show me the man whose counsels may have weight.
Vain is each voice where tones could once command,   275
E'en factions cease to charm a factious land;
Yet jarring sects convulse a sister isle,
And light with maddening hands the mutual pile.

' 'Tis done, 'tis past, since Pallas warns in vain,
The Furies seize her abdicated reign: 280
Wide o'er the realm they wave their kindling brands,
And wring her vitals with their fiery hands.
But one convulsive struggle still remains,
And Gaul shall weep ere Albion wear her chains.
The banner'd pomp of war, the glittering files,   285
O'er whose gay trappings stern Bellona smiles;
The brazen trump, the spirit-stirring drum,
That bid the foe defiance ere they come;
The hero bounding at his country's call,
The glorious death that decorates his fall,   290
Swell the young heart with visionary charms,
And bid it antedate the joys of arms.
But know, a lesson you may yet be taught,
With death alone are laurels cheaply bought:
Not in the conflict Havoc seeks delight,   295
His day of mercy is the day of fight.

271 breaks his rusting] quits his ⟨vacant⟩ S, cor. in B   273 Then in the ⟨conquests /
jarring / ? ⟩ Senates of your ⟨jarring⟩ state S   274 may] ⟨thus⟩ S   275 ⟨Past is
the ? of each ? and head⟩ S   276 E'en ... charm] ⟨And factions charm no more⟩ S
277 ⟨While stern Religion shakes⟩ a sister isle S   278 maddening ... mutual] ⟨mutual
... funeral⟩ S   281 Wide] ⟨Dark⟩ S   282 vitals ... fiery] ⟨entrails ... scorching⟩ S
282a–b Fallen is each dear bought friend on foreign coast, | Or leagued to add you to the
World you lost. S   Or ... to] ⟨And Conquest joins you with⟩ S   283 But] ⟨Yet⟩ S
284 lines 299–304 were first written, then cancelled, after 284   285 pomp ⟨the glittering
ranks / file⟩ of war ... file S   286 The martial sounds that animate the while S, cor.
in B; ⟨That please the eye but not defend your isle⟩ B   where] whose pen correction by
Samuel Rogers in his copy of Curse1812   287 brazen] ⟨sounding⟩ S   288 ⟨That
/ Strikes to each heart⟩ That seem to say oh would the foe were come! S, cor. in B   were
S] ⟨but⟩ B   290 decorates] consecrates 1831, 1832, C, More   291 Swell] ⟨Spark⟩ S
292 bid it] bids him S; bids it B, Y

But when the field is fought, the battle won,
Though drench'd with gore, his woes are but begun;
His deeper deeds as yet ye know by name,
The slaughter'd peasant, and the ravish'd dame,   300
The rifled mansion, and the foe-reap'd field,
Ill suit with souls at home untaught to yield.
Say with what eye along the distant down
Would flying burghers mark the blazing town?
How view the column of ascending flames,   305
Shake his red shadow o'er the startl'd Thames?
Nay frown not, Albion! for the torch was thine
That lit such pyres from Tagus to the Rhine:
Now should they burst on thy devoted coast,
Go, ask thy bosom who deserves them most.   310
The law of Heaven and Earth is life for life,
And she who rais'd, in vain regrets the strife.'

[1811]

151a   Lines Associated With *The Curse of Minerva*
[Carmina Byronis in C. Elgin]

Aspice, quos Scoto Pallas concedit honores,
    Subter stat nomen—facta superque vide!—
Scote miser! quamvis nocuisti Palladis aedi
    Infandum facinus vindicat ipsa Venus;
Pygmalion statuam pro sponsa arsisse refertur,   5
    Tu statuam rapias, Scote, sed uxor abest.

1811

152 Translation of the Famous Greek War Song
Δεῦτε παῖδες τῶν Ἑλλήνων,
written by Riga, who perished in the attempt to revolutionize

299 deeper] ⟨gentler⟩ S   305 ascending] ⟨avenging⟩ B   306 his] ⟨the⟩ S
307 torch] ⟨gold⟩ S   308 fires ⟨as Fates and⟩ from S   309 ⟨If now they spread
within thy wanton coast⟩ S   312 in vain regrets] ⟨may well repay⟩ S

151a. Copy text: *MS. L*, collated with *MS. P, Paris1826*
title   *Paris1826*

    3 quamvis nocuisti] ⟨dum tu nocuistis⟩ L

152. Copy text: *CHP(7)*, collated with *MS. T*, proof, *CHP(1)–CHP(6)* and *CHP(8)–CHP
(10)*
title   Translation of the Famous Greek War Song. *1831, 1832, C, More*

Greece. The following translation is as literal as the author could
make it in verse, which is of the same measure with that of the
original.

1.

Sons of the Greeks, arise!
    The glorious hour's gone forth,
And, worthy of such ties,
    Display who gave us birth.

CHORUS

Sons of Greeks! let us go   5
In arms against the foe,
Till their hated blood shall flow
    In a river past our feet.

2.

Then manfully despising
    The Turkish tyrant's yoke,   10
Let your country see you rising,
    And all her chains are broke.
Brave shades of chiefs and sages,
    Behold the coming strife!
Hellenes of past ages,   15
    Oh, start again to life!
At the sound of my trumpet, breaking
    Your sleep, oh, join with me!
And the seven-hill'd city seeking,
    Fight, conquer, till we're free.   20
        Sons of Greeks, &c.

3.

Sparta, Sparta, why in slumbers
    Lethargic dost thou lie?
Awake, and join thy numbers
    With Athens, old ally!
Leonidas recalling,   25
    That chief of ancient song,

6 against] gainst *T*   9 despising] ⟨disdaining⟩ *T*   10 The ⟨Yoke of⟩ Turkish *T*
21–36 *not in T*

Who sav'd ye once from falling,
  The terrible! the strong!
Who made that bold diversion
  In old Thermopylae,   30
And warring with the Persian
  To keep his country free;
With his three hundred waging
  The battle, long he stood,
And like a lion raging,   35
  Expir'd in seas of blood.
            Sons of Greeks, &c.

                                    [1811]

153   On Parting

                    1.

The kiss, dear maid! thy lip has left,
  Shall never part from mine,
Till happier hours restore the gift
  Untainted back to thine.

                    2.

Thy parting glance, which fondly beams,   5
  An equal love may see:
The tear that from thine eyelid streams
  Can weep no change in me.

                    3.

I ask no pledge to make me blest
  In gazing when alone;   10
Nor one memorial for a breast,
  Whose thoughts are all thine own.

153. Copy text: *CHP(7)*, collated with *MSS. T, P, H*, the proof, *CHP(1)–CHP(6)* and *CHP(8)–CHP(10)*

title *untitled in T*

  5 Thy ⟨glance thy parting eye has⟩ beamed *T*   6 ⟨Once / Has bound my soul to thee⟩
may] ⟨should / might⟩ *T*   7 streams] streamed *T*   8 Can] ⟨Should / Could⟩ *T*
9 ⟨I will not ask one pledge to ⁊ ⟩ *T*   10 ⟨When wandering forth⟩ alone *T*
11 ⟨There needs no token⟩ for a breast *T*

4.

Nor need I write—to tell the tale
  My pen were doubly weak:
Oh! what can idle words avail,   15
  Unless the heart could speak?

5.

By day or night, in weal or woe,
  That heart, no longer free,
Must bear the love it cannot show,
  And silent ache for thee.   20

[1811]

154   Translation of a Romaic Love Song

1.

Ah! Love was never yet without
The pang, the agony, the doubt,
Which rend my heart with ceaseless sigh,
While day and night roll darkling by.

2.

Without one friend to hear my woe,   5
I faint, I die beneath the blow.
That Love had arrows, well I knew;
Alas! I find them poison'd too.

3.

Birds, yet in freedom, shun the net,
Which Love around your haunts hath set;   10
Or circled by his fatal fire,
Your hearts shall burn, your hopes expire.

13 ⟨But yet methinks one tender ? ⟩ T   14 ⟨Which words but feign⟩ T   15 idle
words] ⟨tongue / words or pen⟩ T   16 the] my T   20 ache] ⟨droop⟩ turn T

154. Copy text: CHP(7), collated with proof, CHP(8)–CHP(10), Hobhouse
3 rend] Hobhouse; rends all other printings

4.

A bird of free and careless wing
Was I, through many a smiling spring;
But caught within the subtle snare,   15
I burn, and feebly flutter there.

5.

Who ne'er have loved, and loved in vain,
Can neither feel, nor pity pain;—
The cold repulse—the look askance—
The lightning of Love's angry glance.   20

6.

In flattering dreams I deemed thee mine;
Now hope, and he who hoped, decline;
Like melting wax, or withering flower,
I feel my passion, and thy power.

7.

My light of life! ah, tell me why   25
That pouting lip, and alter'd eye?
My bird of love! my beauteous mate!
And art thou chang'd, and canst thou hate?

8.

Mine eyes like wintry streams o'erflow:
What wretch with me could barter woe?   30
My bird! relent: one note would give
A charm, to bid thy lover live.

9.

My curdling blood, my madd'ning brain,
In silent anguish I sustain;
And still thy heart, without partaking   35
One pang, exults—while mine is breaking.

10.

Pour me the poison; fear not thou!
Thou canst not murder more than now:
I've lived to curse my natal day,
And Love, that thus can lingering slay.   40

31 would] *CHP*(7), *Hobhouse*; could *all other printings*

11.

My wounded soul, my bleeding breast,
Can patience preach thee into rest?
Alas! too late, I dearly know,
That joy is harbinger of woe.

[1811]

155   Translation. τι θελεις Ματ[ια μ']

Matiam! what want you?
    Something my lover!
What can I grant you?
    You may discover—
Gold or a jewel?   5
    No, no, no.—
Tell me then cruel!
    Tell [MS. torn]— wh [MS. torn]
Ohimia, ohimia
Milai, milai.   10

Want you a gay ring—
    Surely not.
Garments or fair ring—
    These I have got.
Matiam, what wish you   15
    Greek, till you know—
Come, shall I kiss you
    Go, go, go.
Ohimia, ohimia
Milai, milai.   20

[1811?]

155. Copy text: MS. M

11 ⟨Garments or playthings / fair rings⟩ M   12 ⟨No not those⟩ / ⟨No not them /
that⟩ M   13 ⟨Turban or ? ⟩ / ⟨Pistol—for what⟩ M

156 Translation of the Romaic Song,

Μπένω μεσ' τὸ περιβόλι,
'Ωραιοτάτη Χαηδή, etc.

The song from which this is taken is a great favourite with the young girls of Athens of all classes. Their manner of singing it is by verses in rotation, the whole number present joining in the chorus. I have heard it frequently at our χόροι in the winter of 1810–11. The air is plaintive and pretty.

1.

I enter thy garden of roses,
  Beloved and fair Haideé,
Each morning where Flora reposes,
  For surely I see her in thee.
Oh, Lovely! thus low I implore thee,   5
  Receive this fond truth from my tongue,
Which utters its song to adore thee,
  Yet trembles for what it has sung;
As the branch, at the bidding of Nature,
  Adds fragrance and fruit to the tree,   10
Through her eyes, through her every feature,
  Shines the soul of the young Haideé.

2.

But the loveliest garden grows hateful
  When Love has abandon'd the bowers—
Bring me hemlock—since mine is ungrateful, 15
  That herb is more fragrant than flowers.
The poison, when pour'd from the chalice,
  Will deeply embitter the bowl;
But when drunk to escape from thy malice,
  The draught shall be sweet to my soul.   20
Too cruel! in vain I implore thee
  My heart from these horrors to save:
Will nought to my bosom restore thee?
  Then open the gates of the grave!

156. Copy text: CHP(7), collated with MS., proof, CHP(1)–CHP(6) and CHP(8)–CHP (10)

3.

As the chief who to combat advances   25
  Secure of his conquest before,
Thus thou, with those eyes for thy lances,
  Hast pierc'd through my heart to its core.
Ah, tell me, my soul! must I perish
  By pangs which a smile would dispel?   30
Would the hope, which thou once bad'st me cherish,
  For torture repay me too well?
Now sad is the garden of roses,
  Beloved but false Haideé!
There Flora all wither'd reposes,   35
  And mourns o'er thine absence with me.

[1811]

157   Imitation of Horace

                            Satire 4

Dryden and Buckingham in Charles's reign,
And Foote in George's,—took men's names in vain.
All evil doers doomed to be described,
Were lashed along, however high they bribed,
And every Indian thief and English rogue,   5
Or other follower of the Vice in vogue,
Adulteress or duellist—felt the rowell,
No matter which,—two Pagets or one Powell!—
Whate'er was done—the Cat escaped the bag—
And Peers found small protection in Scan. Mag.!—   10
These and their followers laughed at great and small
Till desperate Churchill's Muse outthundered all,
Whose verse by turns half angry, half facete
Moves or must run on most unpolished feet.
But all this roughness of his rhyming prose   15
We pardon (like a Poodle) for his nose,
Than which there never was Satiric snout
So sharp at smelling mortal foibles out.—

[1811]

157. Copy text: *MS. M*
  5 And every] ⟨If any⟩   7 or] ⟨and⟩   9 Whate'er was done] ⟨To all and each⟩
13 by turns half] ⟨alternately⟩   16 like a] ⟨as to⟩   17 Satiric] ⟨a cultured⟩

158   Epitaph for Mr. Joseph Blackett,
          Late Poet and Shoemaker

          Stranger! behold, interr'd together,
          The *souls* of learning and of leather.
          Poor Joe is gone, but left his *all:*
          You'll find his relics in a *stall.*
          His works were neat, and often found   5
          Well stitch'd, and with *morocco* bound.
          Tread lightly—where the bard is laid
          He cannot mend the shoe he made;
          Yet is he happy in his hole,
          With verse immortal as his *sole.*   10
          But still to business he held fast,
          And stuck to Phoebus to the last.
          Then who shall say so good a fellow
          Was only 'leather and prunella?'
          For character—he did not lack it;   15
          And if he did, 'twere shame to 'Black-it'.

                              Malta 16 May 1811

159   Farewell to Malta

          Adieu, ye joys of La Valette!
          Adieu, sirocco, sun, and sweat!
          Adieu, thou palace rarely enter'd!
          Adieu, ye mansions where—I've ventured!
          Adieu, ye cursed streets of stairs!   5
          (How surely he who mounts you swears!)
          Adieu, ye merchants often failing!
          Adieu, thou mob for ever railing!

158. Copy text: *1832* collated with *MS.* ϒ
title   Mr. Joseph] Joseph *1832*, *C*
       1 ⟨Here rests, what long had held together⟩ ϒ   2 *souls*] ⟨bones⟩ ϒ   11 still ...
held] ⟨true ... holds⟩ ϒ   12 stuck] ⟨staunch⟩ ϒ

159. Copy text: *1832*, collated with *MS.* and *Hone*
       1 ye] the *Hone*   6 you] them *Hone*

Adieu, ye packets—without letters!
Adieu, ye fools—who ape your betters!   10
Adieu, thou damned'st quarantine,
That gave me fever, and the spleen!
Adieu that stage which makes us yawn, Sirs,
Adieu his Excellency's dancers!
Adieu to Peter—whom no fault's in,   15
But could not teach a colonel waltzing;
Adieu, ye females fraught with graces!
Adieu red coats, and redder faces!
Adieu the supercilious air
Of all that strut 'en militaire!'   20
I go—but God knows when, or why,
To smoky towns and cloudy sky,
To things (the honest truth to say)
As bad—but in a different way.—

Farewell to these, but not adieu,   25
Triumphant sons of truest blue!
While either Adriatic shore,
And fallen chiefs, and fleets no more,
And nightly smiles, and daily dinners,
Proclaim you war and women's winners.   30
Pardon my Muse, who apt to prate is,
And take my rhyme—because 'tis 'gratis'.

And now I've got to Mrs. Fraser,
Perhaps you think I mean to praise her—
And were I vain enough to think   35
My praise was worth this drop of ink,
A line—or two—were no hard matter,
As here, indeed, I need not flatter:
But she must be content to shine
In better praises than in mine,   40
With lively air, and open heart,
And fashion's ease, without its art;
Her hours can gaily glide along,
Nor ask the aid of idle song.—

21 when] where *Hone*   34 I mean] ⟨I'm going⟩ *MS.*

And now, O Malta! since thou'st got us,   45
Thou little military hothouse!
I'll not offend with words uncivil,
And wish thee rudely at the Devil,
But only stare from out my casement,
And ask, for what is such a place meant?   50
Then, in my solitary nook,
Return to scribbling, or a book,
Or take my physic while I'm able
(Two spoonfuls hourly by the label),
Prefer my nightcap to my beaver,   55
And bless the gods—I've got a fever!

                                        26 May 1811

160   [A Mouthful of Saltwater Poetry]

          If I had an E*di*cation
          I'd sing your praise *more large*,
          But I'm only a common foremast Jack
          On Board of *the le Volage*!!!

                                        [1811]

161   [Loneliness and Death. A Fragment]

                          1.
          What, am I better than my Sires?
              The load of life grows heavier still;
          Each hour some early hope retires
              And yields its place to coming ill.

                          2.
          Well then, 'tis done, and I will die,   5
              But not with Superstition's gloom,

54 the] this *Hone*
dating   *not in Hone*

160. Copy text: *MS. M*, collated with *LBC, BLJ*

161. Copy text: *MS. TP*
   6 Superstition's] ⟨Bigot's⟩ *TP*

Nor will I ask a single sigh
To breathe of sadness o'er my tomb.

3.

For who exists so much alive
To me and mine as mourne my fall?   10
Alone I stand, alone survive
The deaths of some, the hearts of all.

[1811?]

162   [Newstead Abbey]

1.

In the dome of my Sires as the clear moonbeam falls
Through Silence and Shade o'er its desolate walls,
It shines from afar like the glories of old;
It gilds, but it warms not— 'tis dazzling, but cold.

2.

Let the Sunbeam be bright for the younger of days: 5
'Tis the light that should shine on a race that decays,
When the Stars are on high and the dews on the ground
And the long Shadow lingers the ruin around.

3.

And the step that o'erechoes the gray floor of stone
Falls sullenly now, for 'tis only my own;   10
And sunk are the voices that sounded in mirth,
And empty the goblet, and dreary the hearth.

9 ⟨For I have now outlived⟩ *TP*   so much] ⟨to whom⟩ *TP*

162. Copy text: *C*, collated with *MSS. M, N, T,* and *L, Mirror, Hodgson*
title   *Mirror, Hodgson, C; untitled in all MSS.*

2 Through . . . Shade] Through the silence of night *M, N cancelled*   5 ⟨Tis the light
that should shine on a race that decays⟩ *M*   Let] ⟨While⟩ *M*   6 the light] a light *T*
7 When . . . high] ⟨With the stars in the sky⟩ *M*   8 long . . . lingers] ⟨dark . . . lengthens/
darkens⟩ *M*   9 And] ⟨But⟩ *N*   o'erechoes] ⟨I hear in⟩ *M*   gray floor of] floor of
gray *M*   10 Falls] ⟨Is heavy⟩ Sounds *M*; ⟨Sounds⟩ *N*

4.

And vain was each effort to raise and recall
The brightness of old to illumine our Hall;
And vain was the hope to avert our decline,   15
And the fate of my fathers has faded to mine.

5.

And theirs was the wealth and the fulness of Fame,
And mine to inherit too haughty a name;
And theirs were the times and the triumphs of yore,
And mine to regret, but renew them no more.   20

6.

And Ruin is fixed on my tower and my wall,
Too hoary to fade, and too massy to fall;
It tells not of Time's or the tempest's decay,
But the wreck of the line that have held it in sway.

[1811]

163 Parody on Sir William Jones's Translation from Hafiz—'Sweet Maid etc.'

[1.]

Bar Maid, if for this shilling white,
   Thou'dst let me love, nor scratch or scold,
That ruddy cheek and ruddier hand
   Would give my Bardship more delight
Than all the ale that e'er was sold,   5
   Than even a pot of 'Cyder-And'.

---

13 each . . . and] ⟨the⟩ each effort again to *M*   14 our] my *M*; the *L*   15 our] ⟨the⟩ *M*   16 has faded to] ⟨sits darkly on⟩ *M*   has] had *C*, *More*   18 And mine was the pride and the wreck of a name *M*   to inherit] ⟨was the wreck of⟩ *N*   23 ⟨To the ages that come the decay it records / it shall speak of decay⟩ *M*   Time's or] time nor *M*   24 wreck] fall *M*, *N cancelled*

163. Copy text: *MS. M*

2.

Girl, let your stupid booby go
And bid him bring a pint of Beer—
Whate'er the droning Vicar swear
Tell him, his Living cannot show   10
A tap at once so strong and clear,
A sofa like this Elbow chair.

3.

Oh! when these ogling Chambermaids
Whose fingers fumble beds of down,
Their dear expensive charms display,   15
Each glance my dwindling cash invades
And robs my purse of half a crown,
As footpads on the Turnpike way.

4.

Speak not of pay:—oh! change the theme,
And talk of Bitters, talk of Gin,   20
Talk of the Beef that begs thy coin,
'Tis all a scent, 'tis all a steam;
[To] bread and cheese restrict thy din,
Nor hope to touch the dear Sirloin.

5.

Brown Stout has such resistless power   25
That even the pious Parish Priest
Swore at the sauntering Pot Boy.
To him how jovial is the hour
When quaffing at the vestry's feast
The Punch that kills, but cannot cloy.   30

6.

What devilish answer have I heard?
And yet, by Jove, I'll kiss thee still.
Can aught be cruel from thy lip?
Yet say, why be so damned absurd
As box my ears—(unpaid my Bill)   35
And let such execrations slip!—

23 [To] *MS. torn*   25 Brown Stout] ⟨Liquor⟩ *M*   27 ⟨Calls answer from the
loud Pot Boy⟩ *M*   28 jovial is] ⟨fatal was⟩ *M*   29–30 ⟨When at the vestry's
worthy feast | Came Punch his stomach to annoy.⟩ *M*

7.

Go boldly forth my Parody,
   Whose stanzas flow just as I please
Like—Lord knows what—to any tune,
   My Notes are brisk, as brisk can be.   40
But ah! much brisker might I seize
   The maid for whom I turn buffoon.

[1811]

164   On Moore's late *Operatic Farce*,
       or *Farcical Opera*

Good plays are scarce
So Moore writes farce:
   The poet's fame grows brittle—
We knew before
That 'Little's' Moore,
   But now 'tis *Moore* that's *little*.—   5

14 Sept. 1811

165   [Epistle to a Friend,
In Answer to Some Lines Exhorting the Author
to be Cheerful, and to 'Banish Care']

'Oh! Banish care'—such ever be
The motto of *thy* Revelry!
Perchance of *mine*, when wassail nights
Renew those riotous delights,

39 to any tune] ⟨(for I'm in haste)⟩ *M*   40 brisk can be] ⟨you may see⟩ *M*
42 ⟨The Barmaid by her swelling waist⟩ *M*

164. Copy text: *Life*, collated with *MS. M*
   3 ⟨To *fame* like *his* there⟩ *M*   Is fame like his so brittle? *MS. variant recorded in C*

165. Copy text: *Life*, collated with *MS. H*
title   *1831, 1832, C, More*; Answer. *H; untitled in Life*

Wherewith the children of Despair   5
Lull the lone heart, and 'banish care'.
But not in morn's reflecting hour,
When present, past, and future lower,
When all I loved is changed or gone,
Mock with such taunts the woes of one,   10
Whose every thought—but let them pass—
Thou know'st I am not what I was.
But, above all, if thou would'st hold
Place in a heart that ne'er was cold,
By all the powers that men revere,   15
By all unto thy bosom dear,
Thy joys below, thy hopes above,
Speak—speak of anything but love.

'Twere long to tell, and vain to hear,
The tale of one who scorns a tear;   20
And there is little in that tale
Which better bosoms would bewail.
But mine has suffer'd more than well
'Twould suit philosophy to tell.
I've seen my bride another's bride,—   25
Have seen her seated by his side,—
Have seen the infant, which she bore,
Wear the sweet smile the mother wore,
When she and I in youth have smiled,
As fond and faultless as her child;—   30
Have seen her eyes, in cold disdain,
Ask if I felt no secret pain;
And I have acted well my part,
And made my cheek belie my heart,
Return'd the freezing glance she gave,   35
Yet felt the while *that* woman's slave;—
Have kiss'd, as if without design,
The babe which ought to have been mine,
And show'd, alas! in each caress
Time had not made me love the less.   40

But let this pass—I'll whine no more,
Nor seek again an eastern shore;

29 in youth have] ⟨together⟩ H   39 each] ⟨the⟩ H

The world befits a busy brain,—
I'll hie me to its haunts again.
But if, in some succeeding year,   45
When Britain's 'May is in the sere',
Thou hear'st of one, whose deepening crimes
Suit with the sablest of the times,
Of one, whom love nor pity sways,
Nor hope of fame, nor good men's praise,   50
One, who in stern ambition's pride
Perchance not blood shall turn aside,
One rank'd in some recording page
With the worst anarchs of the Age,
Him wilt thou *know*—and *knowing* pause,   55
Nor with the *effect* forget the cause.

                                        11 Oct. 1811

166   To Thyrza

Without a stone to mark the spot,
    And say, what Truth might well have said,
By all, save one, perchance forgot,
    Ah, wherefore art thou lowly laid?
By many a shore and many a sea   5
    Divided, yet belov'd in vain;
The past, the future fled to thee
    To bid us meet—no—ne'er again!
Could this have been—a word—a look
    That softly said, 'We part in peace',   10
Had taught my bosom how to brook,
    With fainter sighs, thy soul's release.
And didst thou not, since Death for thee
    Prepar'd a light and pangless dart,
Once long for him thou ne'er shalt see,   15
    Who held, and holds thee in his heart?

51 stern] ⟨high⟩ *H*

166. Copy text: *CHP(7)*, collated with *MS.*, proof, *CHP(1)–CHP(6)* and *CHP(8)–CHP(10)*
title   On the death of——Thyrza. *MS.*

    2 ⟨And soothe—if such could soothe thy shade⟩ *MS.*   5 shore] land *MS.*   6 yet
. . . vain] ⟨Hope would still remain⟩ *MS.*   8 no—ne'er] ⟨neer meet⟩ *MS.*   9 this have
been] ⟨we have met⟩ *MS.*

Oh! who like him had watch'd thee here?
  Or sadly mark'd thy glazing eye,
In that dread hour ere death appear,
  When silent Sorrow fears to sigh,   20
Till all was past? But when no more
  'Twas thine to reck of human woe,
Affection's heart-drops, gushing o'er,
  Had flow'd as fast—as now they flow.
Shall they not flow, when many a day   25
  In these, to me, deserted towers,
Ere call'd but for a time away,
  Affection's mingling tears were ours?
Ours too the glance none saw beside;
  The smile none else might understand;   30
The whisper'd thought of hearts allied,
  The pressure of the thrilling hand;
The kiss so guiltless and refin'd
  That Love each warmer wish forbore;
Those eyes proclaim'd so pure a mind,   35
  Ev'n passion blush'd to plead for more.
The tone, that taught me to rejoice,
  When prone, unlike thee, to repine
The song, celestial from thy voice,
  But sweet to me from none but thine;   40
The pledge we wore—I wear it still,
  But where is thine?—ah, where art thou?
Oft have I borne the weight of ill,
  But never bent beneath till now!
Well hast thou left in life's best bloom   45
  The cup of woe for me to drain.

25 Shall . . . flow,] And shall they not? *MS.*   29 glance . . . beside] thought, the
walk aside *MS.*
33–6   The kiss that left no sting behind
           So ⟨pure that⟩ guiltless Passion thus forebore
           Those eyes bespoke so pure a mind
           That love forgot to ⟨ask⟩ plead for more. *MS. version a, in pencil*

           The kiss that left no sting behind
           So guiltless love each wish forebore
           Those eyes proclaimed so pure a mind
           That Passion blushed to plead for more. *MS. version b, in pencil*
33–4 The kiss ⟨that left no sting behind | So guiltless Love each⟩ wish forebore *MS. version
c, in ink*   45 left] ⟨fled⟩ *MS.*   46–7 ⟨If judging from my present pain | That rest
shall never quit⟩ the tomb *MS.*

If rest alone be in the tomb,
　　I would not wish thee here again;
But if in worlds more blest than this
　　Thy virtues seek a fitter sphere,　　　　　　　50
Impart some portion of thy bliss,
　　To wean me from mine anguish here.
Teach me—too early taught by thee!—
　　To bear, forgiving and forgiv'n:
On earth thy love was such to me,　　　　　　　55
　　It fain would form my hope in heav'n!

　　　　　　　　　　　　　　　　　　　[1811]

167　[What News, What News Queen Orraca]

What news, what news Queen Orraca?
　　What news of the Scribblers five?
Southey, Wordsworth, Coleridge, Lloyd and Lambe
　　All damned, though yet Alive!

　　　　　　　　　　　　　　　　　　　[1811]

168　The Composite Merits of Hervey's Fish Sauce and Hervey's Meditations

Two Herveys had a mutual wish
　　To shine in separate stations;
The one converted sauce for fish,
　　The other meditations.
Each has his different powers applied　　　　　　5
　　To aid the dead and dying;
This relishes a *sole* when fried,
　　That saves a *soul* from frying.

　　　　　　　　　　　　　　　　　　　1811

47 be] is *MS.*　　49 worlds] ⟨realms⟩ *MS.*　　55 such] ⟨all⟩ *MS.*　　56 It . . .
orm] ⟨So let it be⟩ *MS.*

167. Copy text: *MS.*, collated with *Life*, *Paris1831*, *Pratt*, *BLJ*
title　*supplied in More*

168. Copy text: *The New Monthly Belle Assemblée*

THYRZA.

THE VOICE THAT MADE THOSE SOUNDS MORE SWEET

IS HUSH'D AND ALL THEIR CHARMS ARE FLED;

PUBLISHED BY JOHN MURRAY, ALBEMARLE STREET, DEC^{R}1,1814.

'Stanzas' (poem no. 170), lines 9–10

(Reproduced with the permission of the British Library)

169   [Lucietta. A Fragment]

Lucietta my dear,
That fairest of faces!
Is made up of kisses;
But, in love, oft the case is
Even stranger than this is—   5
There's another, that's slyer,
Who touches me nigher,—
A Witch, an intriguer,
Whose manner and figure
Now piques me, excites me,   10
Torments and delights me—

[1811]

170   Stanzas

1.

Away, away, ye notes of woe!
     Be silent thou once soothing strain,
Or I must flee from hence, for, oh!
     I dare not trust those sounds again.
To me they speak of brighter days: 5
     But lull the chords, for now, alas!
I must not think, I may not gaze
     On what I am, on what I was.

2.

The voice that made those sounds more sweet
     Is hush'd, and all their charms are fled;   10
And now their softest notes repeat
     A dirge, an anthem o'er the dead!

169. Copy text: *C*, collated with *MS. M*

  1 dear] deary *C*   11 [The poem breaks off after B began the next line with 'And']

170. Copy text: *CHP(7)*, collated with *MSS. H, T, B, proof, CHP(1)–CHP(6)* and *CHP(8)–CHP(10)*

title   *thus all forms except MS. T, where the poem is untitled; and in C and More, where the first line is the title*

  3 flee] ⟨fly⟩ *H*   4 trust] ⟨hear⟩ *H*   6 lull] ⟨hush⟩ *H*   7 may] ⟨dare⟩ *H*
9 those sounds] ⟨that song⟩ *H*   10 charms are] ⟨power is⟩ *T*   11 And . . . notes]
⟨Their softest notes to me⟩ *H*

Yes, Thyrza! yes, they breathe of thee,
    Beloved dust! since dust thou art;
And all that once was harmony   15
    Is worse than discord to my heart!

                        3.
'Tis silent all!—but on my ear
    The well-remember'd echoes thrill;
I hear a voice I would not hear,
    A voice that now might well be still.   20
Yet oft my doubting soul 'twill shake:
    Ev'n slumber owns its gentle tone,
Till consciousness will vainly wake
    To listen, though the dream be flown.

                        4.
Sweet Thyrza! waking as in sleep,   25
    Thou art but now a lovely dream;
A star that trembled o'er the deep,
    Then turn'd from earth its tender beam.
But he, who through life's dreary way
    Must pass, when heav'n is veil'd in wrath,   30
Will long lament the vanish'd ray
    That scatter'd gladness o'er his path.

                                                    [1811]

171   To Thyrza

                        1.
One struggle more, and I am free
    From pangs that rend my heart in twain;
One last long sigh to love and thee,
    Then back to busy life again.

16 worse than discord] hideous discord *H, T*   17 all] now *H, cor. in T*   24 flown]
gone *T, cor. in B*   27 star that trembled] ⟨beam that glided⟩ *H*   28 ⟨As bright and
transient in thy gleam / Celestial yet a shadowy gleam⟩ *H*   29 who through] ⟨that treads⟩
H   30 ⟨When darkness veils the skies in wrath⟩ *H*

171. Copy text: *CHP(7)*, collated with *MSS. H, BM, Proof M, Proof H, CHP(1)–
CHP(6) and CHP(8)–CHP(10)*
title   Stanzas. To Thyrza *H; title is the first line in C, More*
   2 From . . . rend] From ⟨secret pangs⟩ pangs that tear *H*

It suits me well to mingle now   5
  With things that never pleas'd before:
Though every joy is fled below,
  What future grief can touch me more?

2.

Then bring me wine, the banquet bring;
  Man was not form'd to live alone: 10
I'll be that light unmeaning thing
  That smiles with all, and weeps with none.
It was not thus in days more dear,
  It never would have been, but thou
Hast fled, and left me lonely here;   15
  Thou'rt nothing, all are nothing now.

3.

In vain my lyre would lightly breathe!
  The smile that sorrow fain would wear
But mocks the woe that lurks beneath,
  Like roses o'er a sepulchre.   20
Though gay companions o'er the bowl
  Dispel awhile the sense of ill;
Though pleasure fires the madd'ning soul,
  The heart—the heart is lonely still!

4.

On many a lone and lovely night   25
  It sooth'd to gaze upon the sky;
For then I deem'd the heav'nly light
  Shone sweetly on thy pensive eye:
And oft I thought at Cynthia's noon,
  When sailing o'er the Aegean wave,   30
'Now Thyrza gazes on that moon—'
  Alas, it gleam'd upon her grave!

6 never pleas'd] ⟨moved me not⟩ H   8 What . . . can] ⟨Yet Sorrow cannot⟩ H
13 thus . . . dear] ⟨so in dearer days⟩ H   14 It ⟨could not be so hadst not thou⟩ / ⟨never
would have been till / but⟩ would not be so hadst not thou H   15 ⟨Art gone⟩ / ⟨Withdrew
so soon and left⟩ Withdrew and left me lonely here H   stanza 3 added to H at end, marked
st. 6 by B   17 ⟨But vain the struggle, doubly vain⟩ H   21–3 ⟨And such is sure the
lonely heart | That holds the wreck of all it loved | The last, the dearest till it break⟩ H
26 ⟨Unknown / Twas ? ⟩ H   27 For well I knew the rolling light H   then] ⟨well⟩
BM   28 Shone . . . on] ⟨Would oft arrest⟩ H   29 And oft ⟨at⟩ I thought in ⟨Mi⟩
Cynthia's noon H   31 Now . . . gazes on] ⟨Doth . . . gaze upon⟩ H

5.

When stretch'd on fever's sleepless bed,
  And sickness shrunk my throbbing veins,
' 'Tis comfort still', I faintly said,   35
  'That Thyrza cannot know my pains':
Like freedom to the time-worn slave,
  A boon 'tis idle then to give;
Relenting nature vainly gave
  My life, when Thyrza ceas'd to live.   40

6.

My Thyrza's pledge in better days,
  When love and life alike were new!
How different now thou meet'st my gaze!
  How ting'd by time with sorrow's hue!
The heart that gave itself with thee   45
  Is silent—ah, were mine as still!
Though cold as e'en the dead can be,
  It feels, it sickens with the chill.

7.

Thou bitter pledge! thou mournful token!
  Though painful, welcome to my breast!   50
Still, still, preserve that love unbroken,
  Or break the heart to which thou'rt prest!
Time tempers love, but not removes,
  More hallow'd when its hope is fled:
Oh! what are thousand living loves   55
  To that which cannot quit the dead?

                                                          [1811–12]

172   Euthanasia

1.

When Time, or soon or late, shall bring
  The dreamless sleep that lulls the dead,

33 fever's] ⟨Sickness'⟩ H   34 And ⟨Fever⟩ fired my throbbing veins H   35 I
faintly] ⟨how oft⟩ H; I sadly H, BM   36 cannot know] knows not of H
37–9 ⟨But Health and Life returning gave | A boon twas idle then to give | Like Freedom
to a⟩ H   39 Relenting Health and Nature gave H, cor. in BM; ⟨Relenting Health in
mockery gave⟩ BM   40 My life] ⟨To live⟩ H   41 My . . . pledge] ⟨Dear simple gift⟩ H
172. Copy text: CHP(7), collated with Byron's draft of lines 33–6 (from printed version
in American Art Assoc. Catalogue), Augusta's MS. copy (fragment), Huntington proof,
Clarke printed copy, CHP(2)–CHP(6) and CHP(8)–CHP(10)

Oblivion! may thy languid wing
  Wave gently o'er my dying bed!

2.

No band of friends or heirs be there,   5
  To weep, or wish, the coming blow:
No maiden, with dishevell'd hair,
  To feel, or feign, decorous woe.

3.

But silent let me sink to Earth,
  With no officious mourners near: 10
I would not mar one hour of mirth,
  Nor startle friendship with a fear.

4.

Yet Love, if Love in such an hour
  Could nobly check its useless sighs,
Might then exert its latest power   15
  In her who lives and him who dies.

5.

'Twere sweet, my Psyche! to the last
  Thy features still serene to see:
Forgetful of its struggles past,
  E'en Pain itself should smile on thee.   20

6.

But vain the wish—for Beauty still
  Will shrink, as shrinks the ebbing breath:
And woman's tears, produc'd at will,
  Deceive in life, unman in death.

7.

Then lonely be my latest hour,   25
  Without regret, without a groan!
For thousands Death hath ceas'd to lower,
  And pain been transient or unknown.

8.

'Ay, but to die, and go', alas!
   Where all have gone, and all must go!   30
To be the nothing that I was
   Ere born to life and living woe!

9.

Count o'er the joys thine hours have seen,
   Count o'er thy days from anguish free,
And know, whatever thou hast been,   35
   'Tis something better not to be.

[1811 or 1812]

173   Edleston

Te, te, care puer! veteris si nomen amoris
   Iam valeat, socium semper amare voco.
Te, fatumque tuum, quoties carissime! plango,
   Et toties haeret fortior ipse dolor.
Dulcis at ipse dolor, quam dulcis! dulcior ardet   5
   Vanus amor, credens te tenuisse sinu.
Me miserum! frustra pro te vixisse precatum,
   Cur frustra volui te moriente mori?—
Heu quanto minus est iam serta, unguenta, puellas
   Carpere cum reliquis quam meminisse tui?   10
Quae mihi nunc maneant? gemitus, vaga somnia fratris,
   Aut sine te lacrymis pervigilare toro.
Ah Libitina veni, invisae mihi parcere Parcae!
   Mortua amicitia Mors sit amica mihi.

[1811 or 1812]

---

34 thy] the *MS. copy*   35 know] own *MS. copy*

173. Copy text: *MS. M*, collated with *Exhibition Catalogue*

   3 fatumque] ⟨nomenque⟩ *M*   6 credens . . . sinu] ⟨poscens / fingens revocare gradum⟩ *M*
9 iam] ⟨aut⟩ *M*   12 sine te] ⟨vacuo⟩ *M*

COMMENTARY

1. *MS. and Publishing History.* No MS.; first printed in *Life*, I. 28; collected in *Paris1831*, *C*, and *More*. Moore had the lines orally from B's nurse May Gray, and though he raised a question about their originality, he allowed them to be collected. *C* was the first to note that the place mentioned in the first line was Swine Green, not Swan Green, but *C* did not emend the line. The green was about a quarter mile from B's lodgings (in 1799) at Mr. Gill's house in St. James's Lane.

2. *MS.* B's fair copy, untitled, undated (location: Yale). Unpublished. The subject of the poem is probably the same as no. 32 (see commentary below). The style is very early Byron, without the intensity of B's elegies for Edleston written in 1811 or 1812. Dated conjecturally 1803.

3. *MS. and Publishing History.* B's fair copy (*MS. N*, location: Newstead); another holograph fair copy (*MS. M*, the so-called Musters copy, location: unknown. Reproduced B. Halliday Sale Catalogue 42, Dec. 1915). Published first in *Paris1831*, *Paris1835*; collected *C1905* only.
The earliest known verses to B's idealized youthful love, Mary Chaworth. Written at his parting from her late in 1804 (see *Marchand*, I. 87–8, 99–100). Elizabeth Pigot's note with *MS. N* states that he was '14 or 15 years of age' when he wrote it, but in 1804 he was 16. Mary Chaworth was B's fourth cousin, and two years his senior. She died in 1832. For further details see B's other poems to her, below.

4. *MS. and Publishing History.* B's draft fragment, undated (*MS. N*, location: Newstead). Unpublished.
The location of the MS. and the style both point to a very early date, though 1804 is only a conjecture. The fragment's subject is the famous duel in 1765 between the grand-uncles of B and Mary: William, fifth Lord Byron (the 'Wicked Lord') and William Chaworth (see *Marchand*, I. 7–8).

5. *MS. and Publishing History.* Unpublished; B's pencil draft on the inside front cover of his copy of *Homeri Ilias . . .* , ed. Samuel Clarke (1760), vol. I (location: Murray). The book has various notes by B indicating he used it while a pupil of Dr. Drury's, at Harrow. One note is dated 23 Oct. 1804. For Dr. Drury see no. 76, commentary.

6. *MS. and Publishing History.* At one time there must have been two holograph MSS. (one held by B, one owned by Mrs. Chaworth-Musters), a copy of the latter by E. Pigot (from which *Life* text was made), and—the only surviving MS.—Teresa Guiccioli's fair copy (*MS. G*) from B's MS. (location: Keats–Shelley Memorial House, Rome). Published first in *Life*, I. 56–7, collected thereafter.

Miss Pigot said the poem was written in 1804 (see *C* I. 210–11 n.) but she must have been mistaken. Mary Chaworth was married in Aug. 1805. The impetus for the poem came from B's reading Richard Gall's 'Farewell to Ayrshire', a poem then attributed to Burns.

2. Echoes Gray's 'Ode on . . . Eton College', 13.

7. *MS*. None. The couplet was printed in *Recollections of the Table-Talk of Samuel Rogers*, ed. A. Dyce (1856), 242 n. It was told to Rogers, Moore, and some others by B's schoolfellow William Harness (1790–1869). Dyce's note to the poem reads: 'When B was at Harrow he, one day, seeing a young acquaintance at a short distance who was a violent admirer of Bonaparte, roared out the following lines.'

8. *MS. and Publishing History*. The corrected draft, originally at Newstead, is now at Texas (*MS. T*); the poem was first published from *MS. T* in *C*; Pratt, 121–2 gives a transcription. It should be noted that the poem collected in *C* and *More*, 'A Version of Ossian's Address to the Sun' ('O Thou! who rollest in yon azure field'), is not genuine. It is a forgery copied into B's (1806) edition of Ossian.

For commentary on the Ossianic qualities of the piece see *Wilmsen*, 11–13, where the poem is dated, as in *C*, 1805. The original 'Address' is the concluding paragraph of 'Carthon'.

9. *MS. and Publishing History*. Teresa Guiccioli's fair copy (*MS. G*, location: Keats–Shelley Memorial House, Rome). First published *1832*, probably from *MS. G*. The date, from *1832*, is approximate.

The poem's subject is probably the marriage of Mary Chaworth.

10. *MS. and Publishing History*. B's corrected fair copy (*MS. N*, location: Newstead). First published *1832* with eight final lines which do not belong to the poem. *More* reprints *1832*, but *C* removes the eight lines to make a separate poem. All previous printings are in quatrains. According to E. Pigot's note with *MS. N*, the *1832* text is based on her copy of *MS. N*, which she sent to Thomas Moore. Her copy has not been found. The extra lines in *1832* comprise the separate poem immediately below.

The poem's subject is apparently the 'naughty Mary' of no. 77.

11. *MS. and Publishing History*. B's fair copy, in pencil, written into the fourth vol. of E. Pigot's copy of Burns's *Works*, 4 vols. (1802, 3rd edn.), with Miss Pigot's note below the poem: 'The above lines were written by

Lord Byron's *own* hand in 1806—EP.' Miss Pigot's fair copy from *MS. N*
(*MS. NP*, which is, along with *MS. N*, in the Nottingham Public Library),
with her endorsement: 'copied from the fly leaf in a vol. of my Burns books,
which is written in pencil by himself—copied for T. Moore Oct. 1830.'
First published in *1832*, from *MS. NP*, as sts. 5–6 of the previous poem; first
published as a separate poem, *C*. The lines are evidently addressed to Miss
Pigot.

12. *MS.* Corrected draft, untitled, undated (location: Murray). Never
published. The first line (see 'To a Lady . . . ' no. 10, line 4) establishes the
probable date of this piece as 1806. See previous commentaries.

13 and 14. *MS. and Publishing History.* B's apparently fair copy (*MS. F*, loca-
tion: Folger Library, Washington D.C.). Both nos. 13 and 14 are unpublished.
The MSS. are in in B's Commonplace Book made up largely of extracts from
Shakespeare. The Folger dates the book *c.* 1810, but it is certainly earlier.

15. *MS. and Publishing History.* B's draft, originally at Newstead, is now at
Texas (*MS. T*), undated. First published from the MS. in *C* (Pratt, 33 gives a
correct printing). The MS. has a note by E. Pigot (see *Pratt*, 33 n.).

16. *MS. and Publishing History.* B's fair copy, dated 1806 (*MS. T*, location:
Yale). Unpublished. The date of this MS. establishes the probable date of
nos. 17 and 18.

17 and 18. *MS. and Publishing History.* B's draft MSS. for these poems are
at Texas, with an endorsement by E. Pigot. Undated. First published *Pratt*,
34 from the MSS. Uncollected.

19. *MS. and Publishing History.* B's fair copy (*MS. NP*, location: Newstead).
Unpublished.
    This is doubtless the 'epitaph on his mother composed in a game which
he was playing at the Pigots' in 1806 or 1807 (*Mayne*, 59 n.). B's mother was
notoriously loud and volatile. For a salutary correction of the traditional,
one-sided view of her character see Doris Langley Moore, *Lord Byron.
Accounts Rendered* (1974).

20. *MS. and Publishing History.* Unpublished; B's draft MS. (*MS. NP*, location:
Newstead). Probable date: late 1806.
    6. *Hall.* Capt. Basil Hall (1788–1844) shipped for a tour in American
waters in 1802 (see *LJ* IV. 252–3).

21. *MS. and Publishing History.* First published by Henry T. Wake in *Notes
and Queries*, Sept. 1891, pp. 182–3; from B's pencil MS. of the lines in a copy

of Anna Seward's *Memoirs of the Life of Dr. Darwin* (1804), on the end flyleaf. Uncollected. The present location of this book is not known to the editor, but from Wake's description there is no good reason to doubt the authenticity of the lines. DeGibler forgeries, which often appear in the flyleaves or endpapers of books, are never written in pencil, whereas B's genuine poems written into books are normally in pencil. The book belonged to Julia Leacroft, who lent it to Mrs. Byron in Oct. 1806, which is the probable date of the verses. For Lord Falkland see *EBSR 686* and n.

22. *MS. and Publishing History.* First published *Pratt*, 51 from B's autograph fair copy MS. at Texas (*MS. T*), where there is also an untitled, undated, unsigned fair copy MS. of the poem in B's hand (*MS. Ta*). The date at the end of *MS. T* is 15 Nov., not 10 Nov., as *Pratt* records. Uncollected.

The poem is a parody of Southey's 'Father William'. Anne Houson, to whom the poem is addressed, was three years younger than B.

14. *Captain*: either John Leacroft or Captain Lightfoot (see no. 23).

23. *MS. and Publishing History.* Uncollected. First published in *Pratt*, 54–9, from the draft holograph (*MS. T*, location: Texas). The present text is that of E. Pigot's fair copy, with B's autograph corrections, and signed and dated by him 30 Nov. 1806 (*MS. S*, sold at Christie's 23 June 1976, Lot 166). *MS. S* has Miss Pigot's cover note: 'written by Ld. B upon hearing the report that he had made Miss Bristoe an offer: *Which* report it was shrewdly conjectured she had *herself* raised.—The *Copy* is corrected by himself and *sign'd* by himself—The whole is a *true* tale put into *verse* for the very *dress* she wore is accurate. The *copy is signed* by *himself.*'

The verses parody Henry Bunbury's 'The Little Grey Man', published in the *Tales of Wonder* (1801), which was wrongly attributed to M. G. Lewis.

13. *one Lover*: a Captain Lightfoot (see commentary for no. 107).

32. (*A tempest impending*). Echoes Matthew Prior, 'The Lady's Looking Glass', 14.

82. *poles*: pole (or poll) means the head, or the nape of the neck (*OED*).

97. *Mrs. Wylde*: the wife of a Southwell banker.

24. *MS. and Publishing History.* B's corrected draft, signed and dated (*MS. Y*, location: Yale). Published by Ward Pafford in *K–SJ* 1 (1952), 67–9. Uncollected.

For the subject see comment on 'To Mary' (no. 77).

25. *MS. and Publishing History.* B's corrected fair copy, originally at Newstead, now at Texas (*MS. T*, watermark 1805, dated 1 Dec. 1806; with a transcript by E. Pigot dated Dec. 1806). First published from *MS. T* in *C*; first accurate transcription in *Pratt*, 125–7.

Another piece occasioned by the criticisms levelled at *FP* by Southwell society. (See 'Answer to Some Elegant Verses . . . ', no. 97, and *BLJ* I. 102–4.) The identity of the 'portly Female', who also appears in this poem's companion piece, 'Soliloquy of a Bard in the Country', no. 27, is not known.

41. See *Paradise Lost*, IV. 810–12.

82. See Pope's 'Epistle to Dr. Arbuthnot', 307–8.

26. *MS. and Publishing History.* B's draft (*MS. N*) and E. Pigot's fair copy made from it (*MS. NM*) for Moore in 1828; both at Newstead, *MS. NM* dated Dec. 1806 by E. Pigot. First published complete in *1831*, *1832*, and thereafter; *Life*, I. 103 printed three stanzas.

Compare 'Childish Recollections' (no. 93).

41. Harrow.

51. *Lycus*: the Earl of Clare (see no. 59).

61–70. The stanza refers to B's falling out with George, Earl Delawarr (*BLJ* I. 106, 134). See no. 66.

27. *MS. and Publishing History.* B's rough draft, originally at Newstead, now at Texas (*MS. T*) along with E. Pigot's fair copy (*MS. Ta*) dated by her Dec. 1806. First published, *C*, from *MS. Ta*.

See commentary on 'To a Knot of Ungenerous Critics' (no. 25). E. Pigot's note on *MS. Ta* identifies the physician as Dr. Smith, apparently a local Southwell doctor. The parson is the Revd. John Becher.

title See *The Works of George, Lord Lyttlelton* . . . , ed. George E. Ayscough, 3rd edn. (1776), III. 73.

32. *Wilmot's*: John Wilmot, Earl of Rochester (1648–80).

77–9. Edmund Curll the bookseller (1675–1747), and John Dennis (1657–1734); William Mason (1725–97), poet and divine, and friend of Gray, both of whose odes are parodied by Robert Lloyd (1733–64): see *The Poetical Works of Robert Lloyd*, ed. Dr. William Henrick (1774), I. 120–31; Luke Milbourne (d. 1720) attacked Dryden in his *Notes on Dryden's Virgil* (1698).

28. *MS. and Publishing History.* First published in *C* from an autograph MS. then at Newstead, and said to be watermarked 1805. MS. location now unknown. The date is conjectural, but the poem certainly belongs to 1805–7.

29. *MS. and Publishing History.* E. Pigot's fair copy with B's corrections (*MS. B*, location: Berg). Miss Pigot's note with the poem states that she copied it for Moore in 1828. Thus the first published text, *Life*, I. 106, is from a copy made from *MS. B*. The 1828 copy is not forthcoming. *1832* printed the poem in quatrains, but otherwise followed *Life* and *1831*, which vary substantively from *MS. B*.

The poem deliberately recalls Pope's 'The Universal Prayer'.

1–2. Cf. James 1 : 17.

17–18. Cf. Acts 17 : 24.

30. *MS. and Publishing History.* Unpublished, from a rough draft MS. at Texas (*MS. T*) on three sheets. The first sheet (watermark 1803) has eighteen cancelled lines. The other two sheets (watermark 1806) have the text as given. Though the identity of the woman is not known, she probably belonged to Southwell society. B seems to be imitating Pope's portrait of Belinda at her toilet. Not all the lines on the first sheet are recoverable, but the first twelve run as follows:

> And must the hag Lucina's power invoke
> A fountain issuing from barren smoke
> Each plan—each charm she heaps with eager care
> Each magick rite and incantation rare
> What shagged spectre or what wizard dame
> Ere felt the anguish of her mutual flame
> Ere *?* learned or in Matron pride
> Sin youth and pleasure weary by her side
> Sooner, dire prodigy, will marble glow
> Or flaming ashes melt in winter snow
> Nor rest nor quiet in her mind can dwell
> The very restlessness of fervid *?* Hell

Lucina was the Roman goddess of childbirth. At the top of the first sheet, in another hand, is the note: 'MSS by Byron. From a vol belonging to the Hon. Augusta Leigh Lord Byron's half Sister'.

31–97. *MS. and Proofs.* A fair number of MSS. survive of the poems published in B's first four volumes, which are here treated, as traditionally, under the title-heading of the third volume (for descriptions see the individual commentaries). According to Elizabeth Pigot, B's friend and amanuensis at Southwell, the printer's copies for almost all of these poems were the copies she transcribed from B's MSS. But printer's copy for the new poems added to *POVO* was probably B's own fair copies, and for the new poems in *POT* printer's copy was certainly B's own MSS. An interesting late MS. copy of some of these poems (as well as a few other lyrics) is Theresa Guiccioli's fair copy (*MS. G*, location: Keats–Shelley Memorial House, Rome). *MS. G* is undated, but was probably made in 1821 or 1822. It is clear from *MS. G* that the copies were not made from available printed texts, and the presumption must be that these copies were made from MSS. which B had with him. At the end of *MS. G* Teresa has written: 'Lord Byron scripsit. Th. Guiccioli amanuens.' Below this B has written: 'Vu. Byron'.

No proofs survive. But B's copy of *FP* (see below) is heavily corrected by him and may well have served as printer's copy for *POVO*.

Publishing History. Of B's first, privately printed volume, *Fugitive Pieces* (*FP*), only four copies survive: (*a*) *FPT*, the copy at Texas, with a number of

MS. corrections, apparently B's presentation copy to E. Pigot; (*b*) FP*A*, copy owned by the Revd. J. T. Becher, now in the Ashley Collection (*BM*, Ashley 2604). Twice published in facsimile, in 1886 (a type facsimile) and in 1933 (a photo-facsimile for the Facsimile Text Society); (*c*) FP*M*, B's copy, with extensive corrections. This may have been printer's copy for *POVO* (location: Morgan); (*d*) FP*N*, presentation copy to John Pigot, lacking pp. 17–20 ('To Mary') and everything after p. 58 (location: Newstead).

B began preparations to publish *FP* in July 1806. He left a MS. with his printer Ridge at the beginning of August, and John and Elizabeth Pigot assisted with the printing of the poems during the month while B was away from Southwell. At the end of August B asked that '*every* Copy' then printed be sent to him 'as I have several alterations and some additions to make' (*BLJ* I. 99). Pratt (27–8) conjectures that the August printing represented an earlier form of *FP*, which B destroyed, and that the book was printed again in the received format during September and October, when further revisions and additions were made. This is possible but unlikely. The four copies of *FP* show that a considerable number of corrections were made in the texts (particularly in the earlier parts of these books), often in ink. The likelihood is that these are the corrections B refers to. None the less, it is certain that the book grew in size between August and early October (when the first copies were ready for distribution); and furthermore, that more poems were added in late October and November, for the latest date on one of the poems in the book is 16 November. Some of the poems in *FP* were printed in separate formats (see *Pratt*, 27–30), the most likely of these being 'The Tear' (no. 34) and 'Reply to Some Verses of J. M. B. Pigot . . . ' (no. 85). The fact of these separate printings led to the broadside forgery of 'To a Beautiful Quaker', described by Wise (I. xxii–xxiii, 13–14). FP*N* may lack everything after p. 58 because Pigot was in Edinburgh at the time the book was being augmented and may not have received the late pages containing the subsequent poems. The poems added after August are probably those after pp. 40–1 in *FP* (*Pratt*, loc. cit.). Some were new, some were earlier pieces which B had only just found among his papers (*BLJ* I. 100). The earlier pieces were probably nos. 50, 51, 89, and perhaps 81.

When B decided to suppress and destroy *FP*, he also planned to issue a new, revised version of the book. This was *Poems on Various Occasions* (1807: *POVO*), which appeared after 23 Dec. 1806 and before 13 Jan. 1807, and probably around 10 Jan. This book was also privately printed. The changes introduced into *POVO* made the new book, B ironically observed, 'miraculously chaste' (*BLJ* I. 103). The epigraph from Horace on the title-page first appeared in *POVO*.

By March B was working on the third volume of his early poems, *Hours of Idleness* (1807: *HI*), which was issued for the public. *HI* shows further extensive changes and it was published in the last week of June 1807. (The

so-called second issue of *HI* is spurious, and probably dates from around
1825.) There is a cancel leaf at sig. D3, with two textual corrections, in some
copies of *HI*. All three epigraphs are on the title-page.

   HI sold well and was favourably received for the most part. A second
edition was being planned by Ridge in Nov. 1807, but without B's approval,
and it was finally published in Mar. 1808 as *Poems Original and Translated*
(1808: *POT*). This was the first of B's early volumes for which he did not
receive or correct a complete proof. Ridge printed from a corrected copy of
HI which B sent to him, and the Revd. J. T. Becher saw the book through
the press. B did, however, correct proof for 'every *new* piece in the volume'
(*BLJ* I. 155). Further changes were made from Nov. 1807 to the end of Feb.
1808, but when B decided to remove 'Childish Recollections' in February,
the whole edition may have been reset (*BLJ*, loc. cit.). It is more likely,
however, that Ridge kept intact what he had printed up to p. 150. In any
case, publication was delayed until late March. The title-page has only the
Homer and Dryden epigraphs.

   The only further authorized printings of these early poems made in B's
lifetime were published by Galignani, in Paris (the first of these appeared in
1819). B did not supervise these printings in any way, and they are 'authorized' only in the sense that B assigned to Galignani the legal right to publish
his works in Paris. Ridge published an unauthorized edition in 1814, and
again in 1820. The so-called 'genuine authorised edition' of 1820 (*Wise*, I.
14) is merely the first issue of the 1820 unauthorized printing (*HI1820*).
All of these later editions (more appeared in the 1820s) are reissues of *POT*.
The principal significance of these later editions lies in the fact that *HI1820*
was copy text for *1831* and *1832*, and hence for all subsequent collected
editions. But *HI1820* introduces a number of changes in the text of *POT*, and
although these changes have been perpetuated in *C* and *More*, they have no
apparent authority. I have relegated them to the apparatus.

   The present edition returns to the original volumes for its texts. *HI* is the
basic copy text because it is the last volume which we know B corrected in
proof. But *POT* is copy text for the poems which first appeared there. For
poems appearing in *FP* and *POVO*, but not in the later volumes, copy text is
FP, into which are incorporated the MS. changes shown in *FPM* and the
substantive changes in *POVO*. Poems appearing only in one of the volumes
use that volume as copy text. All copies of *FP* are collated, and the annotations in E. Pigot's copy of POVO (location: Texas) and in the presentation
copy to Sarah Ann Cam (location: *BM*) are incorporated in the notes, and
so are B's corrections made in the copy he sent to his sister (location: Princeton–Taylor).

   The order of the poems is as follows: (*a*) the poems from *POT*, in sequence
as in *POT*; (*b*) the poems from *FP* not in *POT*, in sequence as in *FP*; (*c*) the
poems in *POVO* or *HI* not in *POT*, in sequence as in *HI*. For those who
wish to reconstruct the complete sequential texts of the four volumes, the

following lists show the contents of each (by their number in the present edition):

FP. 30, 68, 69, 70, 71, 72, 73, 54, 74, 75, 31, 47, 76, 32, 77, 78, 79, 57, 42, 35, 80, 81, 82, 38, 34, 83, 33, 84, 59, 85, 86, 37, 87, 48, 49, 88, 50, 51. Total: 38 pieces.

POVO. 30, 79, 70, 31, 32, 54, 68, 84, 85, 33, 83, 74, 86, 69, 73, 89, 71, 78, 77, 36, 42, 82, 38, 37, 87, 39, 81, 80, 47, 48, 49, 88, 50, 51, 90, 55 (early version), 75, 57, 34, 35, 59, 91, 92, 93, 94, 95, 96, 62. Total: 48 pieces.

HI. 30, 79, 31, 32, 33, 34, 35, 36, 91, 37, 38, 39, 81, 41, 42, 94, 43, 44, 80, 47, 48, 49, 50, 51, 52, 53, 54, 55, 56, 57, 96, 59, 60, 61, 62, 92, 63, 64, 65. Total: 39 pieces.

POT. 30–67. Total: 38 pieces.

Literary and Historical Background. B's first volume of poems was certainly a juvenile production, but it was often a lively, though slightly ribald, book. Its appearance, however, caused a furore in Southwell society because of certain of its amatory pieces, and B yielded to the urging of friends like the Revd. J. T. Becher to destroy the book. Nevertheless, B was irritated at the reaction, and said so in his letters and a number of poems (most of which did not appear in print at the time). The revised book, *POVO*, was indeed 'miraculously chaste', not to say a little stuffy, and this pretentiousness carried over into the published versions of *HI* and *POT*. *HI* was well received, by and large, but the attacks upon it in the *Satirist* (by Hewson Clarke) and the *Edinburgh Review* (by Henry Brougham), particularly the latter, had a crushing effect (*Satirist*, Oct. 1807 and May 1808; *ER*, Jan. 1808). B certainly was shamed by Brougham's review (*BLJ* I. 159), but he was also resentful that a Whig journal should have cut him up. His anger at Clarke was another matter (see notes and commentary for *EBSR* and *Hints*). These adverse reviews, as well as the one in the *Eclectic Review* (Nov. 1807), caused B to reorganize and expand the satire he had been writing, 'The British Bards', into *EBSR*. It is not always realized, however, that many of the qualities in contemporary poetry which B was attacking in 'The British Bards' are only too plainly apparent in *HI*.

For further comment see: *C* I. xi–xiii, VII. 246–54; *Gleckner*, chap. 1; Marcel Kessel, ed., *Fugitive Pieces*. Facsimile edn. (New York, 1933); *McGann* (*1*), chap. 1; *Pratt*; H. C. Roe, *The Rare Quarto Edition of Lord Byron's 'Fugitive Pieces'* (Nottingham, 1919); W. S. Ward, 'Byron's *Hours of Idleness* and other than Scotch Reviewers', *MLN* 59 (Dec. 1944), 547–50; *Wise*, I. xx–xxiii, 1–16.

Preface As these POEMS were never intended to meet the public eye, no apology is necessary for the form in which they now appear. They are printed merely for the perusal of a few friends to whom they are dedicated; who will look upon them with indulgence; and as most of them were composed between the age of 15 and 17, their defects will be pardoned or forgotten, in the youth and inexperience of the WRITER. [Prefatory note to *FP*]

The only Apology necessary to be adduced, in extenuation of any errors in the following collection, is, that the Author has not yet completed his nineteenth year.

December 23, 1806. [Prefatory note to *POVO*]

Both *FP* and *POVO* were dedicated 'To those Friends, At whose Request They were printed ... These TRIFLES are respectfully Dedicated. ... ' *POT* was dedicated to B's guardian the Earl of Carlisle; it was the only one of B's first four volumes that had no prose Preface at all. B's draft MS. of the *HI* Preface is at Texas (*MS. T*). It was printed, with a selection of variant readings, in *Pratt*, 72–6.

19–20. I ... die. See Suetonius, *Lives of the Caesars*, 'Julius', sec. 32.

23. *words of Cowper*: not located; B may be paraphrasing Cowper's letter to William Unwin, 12 June 1782 (see William Hayley, *The Life and Posthumous Writings of William Cowper* (1806), II. 40–1).

55. *Virum ... ora*: Virgil, *Georgics*, III. 8.

56–7. *dulce ... in loco*: Horace, *Odes*, IV. xii. 28.

59–60. *amongst the mob ... with ease*: Pope, *Imitations of Horace*, Epistles, II. i. 108.

76. *relation of mine*: The Earl of Carlisle, whose works have long received the meed of public applause; to which, by their intrinsic worth, they were well entitled. [B] The note is not in *MS. T.*; see Boswell's *Life of Dr. Johnson* for May 1781; see also *EBSR* 718–39 and nn.

31. *MS. and Publishing History*. No MS.; published *FP, POVO, HI, POT*.

The poem was probably written in Nov. 1803, when B was a guest at Newstead Abbey, which had been leased earlier in the year to Lord Grey de Ruthyn. See below, no. 63.

epigraph   Ossian, 'Carthon: A Poem', *The Poems of Ossian* (1803) I. 269.

6. B's belief in his crusading ancestors is apparently based on an old wooden panel, still at Newstead, which carries the heads of Christian and Saracen soldiers. But the panel seems to have been part of the Abbey before the Byrons took possession.

9. *old Robert*. B seems to be suggesting that Robert de Byron, who lived during the reign of Henry II (1165–89), was the 'minstrel' of John of Horistan's martial deeds.

11. Horistan Castle, in Derbyshire, an ancient seat of the Byron family. [B] John de Horestan was a crusader under Richard I. He was killed in the siege of Askalon (1157).

13. *Paul and Hubert*. There is no record of these 'ancestors' of B.

Cressy: i.e. the battle of Crécy (1346).

14. Edward the Black Prince (1330–76).

17. The Battle of Marston Moor [1644], where the adherents of Charles I were defeated. [B]

Rupert: Son of the Elector Palatine, and related to Charles I. He afterwards commanded the fleet, in the reign of Charles II. [B] Prince Rupert, Duke of Bavaria (1619–82).

18. B has in mind Richard, the second Lord Byron (d. 1679) and his younger brothers, who served Charles loyally in the civil wars. See Karl Elze, *Lord Byron, A Biography* (1872), 436.

32. *MS. and Publishing History*. No MS.; published *FP, POVO, HI, POT*.

Elizabeth Pigot's pencil note to the poem in her copy of *POVO* is 'Southwell, March 17'. This is difficult to understand, if B's date of 1803 is accepted, for Mrs. Byron did not take her house at Southwell, Burgage Manor, until July 1803. The poem may belong to 1804 or 1805. The identity of the 'Friend' is even more uncertain: *1832* says he was 'a boy of Lord Byron's own age, son of one of his tenants at Newstead'.

epigraph   Plato's epitaph, quoted by Diogenes Laertius. (See Shelley's exquisite translation beginning 'Thou wert the morning star / Among the living'.) B misquotes slightly in *HI*.

1. Echoes Pope, *Eloisa to Abelard*, 31.

28. The end date in *FP* is 'Harrow, 1803'.

33. *MS. and Publishing History*. No MS.; published *FP, POVO, HI, POT*.

The poem is Ossianic: see esp. 'Berrathon'.

1. *airy hall*: an Ossianic phrase, but derived from Thomson's *The Seasons*, 'Winter', 896.

6. Cf. Genesis 3: 19.

8. A Byronic thought: see e.g. 'Directions for the Contents of a Will . . . ' (*BLJ* II. 72) and letter to Murray, 9 June 1819.

34. *MS. and Publishing History*. No MS.; published *FP, POVO, HI, POT*.

The poem may have been printed separately as a broadside in Sept. 1806 (*Pratt*, 27–30).

epigraph   Quoting Thomas Gray's 'Alcaic Fragment'.

37. Harrow.

44. Mary Chaworth, married in 1805.

35. *MS. and Publishing History*. No MS.; published *FP, POVO, HI, POT*.

Composed Sept. 1806 when B was travelling from Harrogate to Southwell with John Pigot. The private theatricals were performed in the Leacrofts' drawing-room, in Southwell, Oct. 1806 (see *Pratt*, 29–30 and *Life*, I. 39). B played Penruddock in Richard Cumberland's *Wheel of Fortune* (1775). See B's 'Detached Thoughts', no. 71 (*LJ* v. 445). A note in the Newstead copy of *FP*, by E. Pigot says: '(Spoken by G. Wylde Esqr. London Sept. 1806)'.

11. *Roscii*: Quintus Roscius (*c.* 126–62 B.C.), the greatest Roman actor of his day.

13–14. George Frederick Cooke (1756–1811), Charles Kemble (1775–1854), Sarah Siddons (1755–1831), celebrated actors.

36. *MS. and Publishing History.* No MS.; published *FP, POVO, HI, POT*.

E. Pigot's MS. note in *FPN*: 'Southwell Oct. 1806'. The lines on the death of the Whig statesman Charles James Fox (1749–1806) were in the *Morning Post*, 26 Sept. 1806; B's poem never appeared in the *Morning Chronicle*.

10. Echoes Sophocles, *Antigone*, 1029.

37. *MS. and Publishing History.* MS. G (see *HI* commentary). Published in *POVO, HI, POT*.

Written Nov.–Dec. 1806, to E. Pigot (see copy of *POVO* in *BM*). See also *EBSR* 295–308, 921–2.

title B refers to Lord Viscount Strangford's *Poems . . . of . . . Camoens* (1803). The lyric poems of Luis Vaz de Camoens (1524–80), author of *The Lusiads*, were all published posthumously.

38. *MS. and Publishing History.* Draft MS. of lines 5–8 (*MS. N*, location: Newstead); *MS. G* (see *HI* commentary). Published in *FP, POVO, HI, POT*.

One of the last poems to be included in *FP*, it is addressed to Anne Houson (see E. Pigot's MS. annotation in her copy of *POVO*, in *BM*).

14. Cf. Jude 9.

22. Berenice II, Egyptian princess (*fl.* 3rd century B.C.). Her hair was said to have been transformed into the constellation *Coma Berenices*.

39. *MS. and Publishing History.* No MS.; published in *FP, POVO, HI, POT*.

Undated by B, the poem probably belongs to 1805 or early 1806. It is placed in *FP* as a companion piece to 'To Lesbia' (in *FP*, 'To Julia'), which dates from the autumn, 1806. But 'To Woman' appears before pp. 40–1 in *FP*, and so must antedate Sept. 1806. The poem's sentiments are more appropriate to B's feelings in 1805. It is a derivative piece, echoing Thomas Moore's 'Inconstancy'.

22. The last line is almost a literal translation from a Spanish proverb. [B, added in *HI*]

40. *MS. and Publishing History.* E. Pigot's fair copy (*MS. NP*, location: Newstead), with her note: 'G. G. B. to E. P.' Published in *POVO, HI, POT*. Probably written Nov.–Dec. 1806.

41. *MS. and Publishing History.* No MS.; published in *POT*.

The poem deals with B's memories of Mary Duff, his childhood sweetheart. Date: late 1807 or early 1808. It is one of a series of memory pieces B composed at that time: compare 'Stanzas' ('I would I were a careless child'), no. 67. For the Ossianic elements in the piece see *Wilmsen*, 27–8.

2. Morven, a lofty Mountain in Aberdeenshire: 'Gormal of Snow', is an Expression frequently to be found in Ossian. [B]

4. This will not appear extraordinary to those who have been accustomed to the Mountains; it is by no means uncommon on attaining the top of Ben-e-vis, Ben-y-bourd, etc. to perceive, between the Summit and the Valley, clouds pouring down rain, and, occasionally, accompanied by lightning, while the Spectator, literally, looks down on the Storm, perfectly secure from its Effects. [B]

19. 'Breasting the lofty surge,' Shakespeare. [B] *Henry V*, III, Chorus, 13.

Dee's. The Dee is a beautiful river, which rises near Mar Lodge, and falls into the sea, at New Aberdeen. [B]

34. Colbleen is a mountain near the verge of the Highlands, not far from the ruins of Dee Castle. [B]

42. *MS. and Publishing History*. No MS.; published in *HI*, *POT*.

The poem is a memory piece composed before the 'token' of line 2, the picture of herself which Mary Chaworth had given to B before her marriage in 1805. Lines 25–8, and the fact that the poem was not printed until *HI*, suggest the poem was written late in 1806 or 1807.

1. The opening lines echo Thomas Moore's 'Song' ('Mary, I believed in thee'), 13–16.

43. *MS. and Publishing History*. No MS.; published in *FP*, *POVO*, *HI*, *POT*.

E. Pigot's note in *FPN* reads: 'This poem was to that *naughty* Mary to whom the lines were written which occasioned such a commotion in the State and were the reason of this Edition being put in the fire.' See 'To Mary' (no. 77) and 'To a Lady' (no. 81). Moore said 'she was of a humble, if not equivocal, station in life' and that B showed her picture and a lock of her light golden hair to his friends (*Life*, I. 41 n.). The poem precedes pp. 40–1 in *FP* and so must have been written before Sept. 1806.

44. *MS. and Publishing History*. MS. *G*, Teresa Guiccioli's fair copy (see *HI* commentary) of the first four lines (up to 'adept'). Published in *HI*, *POT*.

C rejected the *1832* description of the poem as an autobiographical sketch, but *MS. G* shows that *1832* was correct. *C* compares *EBSR* 668–86, but *EBSR* 687–706, *Hints*, 223–40, and the opening stanzas of *CHP I* are more appropriate analogues. Date: early 1807, when *HI* was being prepared for the press.

title The name derives from the pastorals of Theocritus, and is proverbial for folly.

1. In Law, every person is an infant, who has not attained the age of 21. [B]

45. *MS. and Publishing History*. MS. *N*, B's corrected fair copy (location: Newstead), signed and dated 'Byron. Jany 10th 1807', untitled. Published in *HI*, *POT*.

E. Pigot's MS. note accompanying the poem reads: 'This was to Harriet Maltby, afterwards Mrs. Nichols, written upon her meeting Byron, and, "being *cold, silent,* and *reserved* to him" by the advice of a Lady with whom she was staying; quite foreign to her *usual* manner, which was gay, lively, and full of flirtation.'

46. *MS. and Publishing History.* The MS. scraps of the poem which survive are from B's draft MS., which he gave to E. Pigot to copy for the *HI* printing. Miss Pigot evidently cut the draft MS. into smaller pieces, and these were subsequently given away or sold. The surviving fragments include: 93–6, 105–8 (*MS. H,* location: Dickie Collection, Johns Hopkins Univ.); 113–23, 125–36 (*MS. Hn,* location: Huntington); 137–68 (*MS. B,* location: Bodmer); 179–84, 193–6 (*MS. P,* location: Pforzheimer); 257–60, 267–72 (*MS. Ne,* location: Trevelyan Papers, Newcastle Univ. Library); 285–8 (*MS. Mo,* location: Morgan); 289–92 (*MS. T,* location: Texas); 293–6 (*MS. S,* location: presently unknown; sold at Sotheby's 14 Dec. 1976, lot 179). Published in *HI, POT.*

E. Pigot's MS. note on verso of *MS. Mo* states that she copied this poem fair for the printer, as she did in the case of all of the poems B printed when he was at Southwell. Her note on the verso of *MS. T* states that B wrote the poem when he 'resided with his mother on Burgage Green, Southwell, in 1807'. B probably wrote the poem early in the year, in Feb. or Mar.: he does not mention it as one of the pieces being worked on in May for the imminent publication of *HI* (see *BLJ* I. 112, 118).

For the Ossianic elements in the poem see *Wilmsen,* 23–4. As B's note to the poem shows, the story is based upon the story of Jeronymo and Lorenzo in the first part of Schiller's *Der Geisterseher* (known to B in a wretched translation called *The Armenian: or, The Ghost-Seer*). The story had a particular fascination for B (see commentary for 'Il Diavolo Inamorato' and *Lara*). See also Emile Turdeanu, *Oscar of Alva de Lord Byron: sources occidentales et reflets roumains* (Sibiu, 1944).

title   The Catastrophe of this tale was suggested by the story of 'Jeronymo and Lorenzo', in the first volume of 'The Armenian, or Ghost-Seer': It also bears some resemblance to a scene in the third act of 'Macbeth'. [B] *The Armenian.* See no. 188, commentary.

42. Brougham's review ridiculed B for confusing certain music of the bag-pipe (pibroch) with the instrument.

54. *hills of wind:* Ossianic.

62. Ossianic.

106. *bounding roe:* Ossianic.

206. *big tear:* Ossianic.

220. Beltane Tree—A Highland festival, on the 1st of May, held near fires, lighted for the occasion. [B]

250. *gleaming form:* Ossianic.

260. Recalls Coleridge, *Rime of the Ancient Mariner*, 436.

47. *MS. and Publishing History.* No MS.; published in *POT*.

The poem is addressed to George John Frederick, fourth Duke of Dorset (1793–1815). B later wrote some elegiac pieces on his death: see nos. 239, 245, 246, 247.

6. At every public School, the junior boys are completely subservient to the upper forms, till they attain a seat in the higher Classes. From this state of probation, very properly, no rank is exempt; but after a certain period, they command, in turn, those who succeed. [B]

13. Allow me to disclaim any personal allusions, even the most distant; I merely mention generally, what is too often the weakness of Preceptors. [B]

68. 'Thomas S[ac]k[vi]lle, Lord B[uc]k[hur]st, created Earl of D[orset] by James the First, was one of the earliest and brightest ornaments to the poetry of his country, and the first who produced a regular drama.' Anderson's British Poets. [B] Thomas Sackville (1536–1608), wrote *Gorboduc* (1561).

74. Charles S[ac]k[vi]lle, Earl of D[orset], esteemed the most accomplished man of his day, was alike distinguished in the voluptuous court of Charles II and the gloomy one of William III. He behaved with great gallantry in the sea-fight with the Dutch, in 1665, on the day previous to which he composed his celebrated song. His character has been drawn in the highest colours by Dryden, Pope, Prior, Congreve. Vide Anderson's British Poets. [B] Charles Sackville, sixth Earl of Dorset (1637–1706). B refers to his song 'To All You Ladies Now at Land'.

48. *MS. and Publishing History. MS. G.* (see *HI* commentary).
Published in *FP, POVO, HI, POT*.

The Emperor Hadrian (75–138) is reputed to have spoken these verses at his death.

49. *MS. and Publishing History.* No MS.; published in *FP, POVO, HI, POT*.
See Catullus, *Carmina*, LI. The date for the translation is conjectural.

13–14. Cf. Psalms 137: 6 and Ezekiel 3: 26.

50. *MS. and Publishing History. MS. G.* (see *HI* commentary). Published in *FP, POVO, HI, POT*.

Domitius Marsus, 'Epitaphium Tibulli' (see e.g. *Poetarum Latinorum . . .*, ed. W. M. Weichert (Leipzig, 1830), 264–5). Dating conjectural.

3. The hand of Death is said to be unjust, or unequal, as Virgil was considerably older than Tibullus, at his decease. [B] Tibullus (*c.* 55–19 B.C.); Virgil (70–19 B.C.).

51. *MS. and Publishing History.* No MS.; published in *FP, POVO, HI, POT*.

See Catullus, *Carmina*, III. Dating conjectural.

13–14. Echoes *Hamlet*, III. i. 78.

52. *MS. and Publishing History.* B's fair copy (*MS. N*, location: Newstead), undated; *MS. G.* (see *HI* commentary). Published in *FP, POVO, HI, POT*.

See Catullus, *Carmina*, XLVIII (B's principal point of imitation; but see also V and VII).

4. Echoes Andrew Marvell, 'To His Coy Mistress', 17–18.

53. *MS. and Publishing History.* B's draft (*MS. T*, location: Texas) is undated, but watermarked 1805. Published in *HI, POT*. The MS. is transcribed in *Pratt*, 32.

See Anacreontea, Ode I. B probably wrote the draft in 1805 or 1806, and polished it for publication in *HI* in April and May 1807 (see *BLJ* I. 115, 118).

54. *MS. and Publishing History.* B's early draft. (*MS. P*, location: Meyer Davis Collection, Univ. of Pennsylvania Library. See their *Library Chronicle*, 33 (1967), 17–19.) Published in *HI, POT*.

See commentary for no. 53.

55. *MS. and Publishing History.* No MS.; published in *FP, POVO, HI, POT*.

B loosely paraphrases lines 528 ff. According to B, 'My first Harrow verses (that is, English, as exercises), a translation of a chorus from the Prometheus of Aeschylus, were received by [Dr. Drury] but coolly' (*Life*, I. 20). See also *BLJ* V. 268.

56. *MS. and Publishing History.* B's draft of lines 19–406 (*MS. B*, location: Berg), headed with a note by E. Pigot: 'The original MS. of Nisus and Euryalus. I gave the first part away —afterwards he made many alterations toward the end when he corrected the proofs.' B's fair copy of lines 373–4, with an endorsement by E. Pigot dated 22 Mar. 1861, was sold at the Charles Hamilton Galleries (N.Y.), 9 Dec. 1971, lot 116. A sixteen-line version was first printed in *POVO* (1–4, eight-line version of 5–14, 15–18). First printed complete in *HI, POT*, collected thereafter.

The *POVO* version was probably composed as a school exercise at Harrow. B decided to include it in *POVO* in Sept. 1806 (see *BLJ* I. 97–100). The complete work was not written until 1807. It was under way by 16 Apr. and was being concluded on 14 May (see *BLJ* I. 115, 118).

140. *Penates:* Household Gods. [B's note, *HI*]

202. *Creusa:* The mother of Iulus, lost on the night when Troy was taken. [B's note, *HI*]

57. *MS. and Publishing History.* No MS.; published in *HI, POT*.

Free translation of lines 627–60. Composed Apr.–May 1807 (*BLJ* I. 118).

45. Medea, who accompanied Jason to Corinth, was deserted by him for the daughter of Creon, king of that city. The Chorus from which this is taken here address Medea: though a considerable liberty is taken with the original, by expanding the idea, as also in some other parts of the translation. [B]

53. The original is 'Καθαραν ἀνοίξαντι Κληῖδα φρενῶν', literally disclosing the bright Key of the mind'. [B]

58. *MS. and Publishing History.* No MS.; except for 59–62 (which B sent in a letter to Ridge, 14 Dec. 1807, while *POT* was in press: location, Yale). Published in *FP, POVO, HI, POT.*

Probably composed between Apr. and July 1806, after B had been made to return unwillingly to Cambridge.

title   No reflection is here intended against the person mentioned under the name of Magnus. He is merely represented, as performing an unavoidable function of his office: indeed, such an attempt could only recoil upon myself; as that gentleman is now as much distinguished by his eloquence, and the dignified propriety with which he fills his situation, as he was in his younger days, for wit and conviviality. [B] William Lort Mansel (1753–1820), appointed Master of Trinity College in 1798. See B's later epigrams on him, nos. 128a, b, c.

15–16. i.e. Edward III and Henry V.

19. *Lycurgus:* legendary lawgiver of Sparta.

20. Sir William Blackstone (1723–1780), author of the *Commentaries on the Laws of England* (1765–9).

30. Demosthenes. [note in *1832*]
Tully: i.e. Cicero.

50. *Granta:* from the Roman name for the town, Grantchester.

57. Celebrated Critics. [B, n. in *FP, POVO, HI*] Richard Bentley (1662–1742), Richard Brunck (1729–1803), Richard Porson (1759–1808).

PORSON: The present Greek Professor [at Cambridge, *FP*] at Trinity College, Cambridge; a man whose powers of mind, and writings, may per-
64 justify their preference. [B, added in *HI*]
haps. Since this was written Lord H[enry] P[ett]y, has lost his place, and subsequently, (I had almost said *consequently*) the honour of representing the University; a fact so glaring requires no comment. [B, added in *HI*] *Petty.* See no. 108, line 30 n.

59. *MS. and Publishing History.* No MS., except B's corrections for lines 73–81 sent in a letter to Ridge, 20 Dec. 1807 (*MS. T,* location: Texas). Published in *POT.*

John Fitzgibbon, second Earl of Clare (1792–1851), one of B's closest friends at Harrow (he is the 'Lycus' of 'Childish Recollections'). The note to 48 dates the poem July–Aug. 1807.

epigraph *Argonauticon, IV. 36.*

48. These Stanzas were written soon after the appearance of a severe critique in a Northern review, on a new publication of the British Anacreon. [B] The *Edinburgh Review* (July 1807) on Moore's *Epistles, Odes, and other Poems* (1806).

60. A Bard, (Horresco referens,) defied his Reviewer to mortal combat; if this example becomes prevalent, our periodical Censors must be dipt in the River Styx, for what else can secure them from the numerous Host of their enraged assailants. [B] See *EBSR* 446 and n.

60. *MS. and Publishing History.* No MS.; published in *FP, POVO, HI, POT.*

B apparently wrote the poem when he was away from Cambridge in the autumn of 1806. For his opinions about life at Cambridge see *BLJ* I. 80–1; and about his poem here, *BLJ* I. 111.

epigraph The reply of the Pythian Oracle to Philip of Macedon: 'Fight with silver spears [i.e. bribes] and you shall prevail in all things.'

1. The Diable Boiteux of Le Sage, where Asmodeus, the Demon, places Don Cleofas on an elevated situation, and unroofs the houses for his inspection. [B] Alain René Le Sage (1668–1747), *Le Diable Boiteux* (1707), chap. 3.

10. Lord Henry Petty defeated Lord Palmerston in the contest for Pitt's parliamentary seat representing Cambridge University (in 1806, after Pitt's death).

17. Edward Harvey Hawke, third Lord Hawke (1774–1824).

36. Echoes Cowper's *The Task* VI. 92.

41. Sele's publication on Greek metres, displays considerable talent and ingenuity, but, as might be expected in so difficult a work, is not remarkable for accuracy. [B, in *HI, POT*]

Sele's publication on Greek metres is not remarkable for its accuracy. [B, in *FP, POVO*] John Barlow Seale, *Analysis of the Greek Metres* (Cambridge, 1785).

44. The Latin of the schools is of the CANINE SPECIES and not very intelligible. [B, in *HI, POT*]

Every Cambridge man will assent to this,—the Latin of the Schools is almost unintelligible. [B, in *FP, POVO*]

48. The discovery of Pythagoras, that the square of the Hypotenuse, is equal to the squares of the other two sides of a right angled triangle. [B]

67. On a Saint Day, the Students wear Surplices, in Chapel. [B] Cf. II Chronicles 5: 12.

61. *MS. and Publishing History.* No MS.; published in *HI, POT.*

Written early in 1807, when B was putting *HI* together. The Ossianic qualities in the poem are noted in *Wilmsen*, 26–7. But the poem is in fact an imitation of Thomas Campbell's 'Exile of Erin' (1801). See also *Island*, II, st. 12.

10. This word is erroneously pronounced PLAD, the proper pronunciation (according to the Scotch) is shown by the Orthography. [B]

19–20. Cf. Job 30: 22.

25. I allude here to my maternal ancestors, the 'Gordons', many of whom fought for the unfortunate Prince Charles, better known by the name of the Pretender. This branch was nearly allied by blood, as well as attachment, to the STEWARTS. George, the 2nd Earl of Huntley, married the Princess Annabella Stewart, daughter of James the 1st of Scotland. By her he left four sons; the 3d Sir William Gordon, I have the honour to claim as one of my progenitors. [B] B seems to have had this romanticized history of the Gordons from his mother. B's *facts* are correct, but he apparently did not know that the Gordons of Gight, from whom his mother was descended, 'had a record of violence and banditry, of feuding and murder, which pales into insignificance the peccadilloes of the Byrons' (*Marchand*, I. 16–17, and see J. M. Bulloch, *The House of Gordon* (1903–12).

27. Whether any perished in the Battle of Culloden [1746], I am not certain; but as many fell in the insurrection, I have used the name of the principal action, 'Pars pro toto'. [B] i.e. the insurrection of 1745 led by Charles Edward Stuart, 'Bonnie Prince Charlie' (1720–88).

30. A Tract in the Highlands so called; there is also a Castle of Braemar. [B]

31. *Pibroch:* The Bagpipe. [B, n. in *HI*, removed in *POT*] See 'Oscar of Alva', 42 and n.

62. *MS. and Publishing History.* B's corrected draft, undated (*MS. N*, location: Newstead). Published in *HI*, *POT*.

Written early in 1807.

8. Echoes Pope, 'Epistle to Dr. Arbuthnot', 340–1.

20. It is hardly necessary to add, that Pylades was the companion of Orestes, and a partner in one of those friendships, which with those of Achilles and Patroclus, Nisus and Euryalus, Damon and Pythias, have been handed down to posterity, as remarkable instances of attachments, which in all probability never existed, beyond the imagination of the Poet, the page of an historian, or modern novelist. [B. In *HI*: 'an ancient historian, or a modern novelist'.]

60. Echoes Pope, 'Ode on Solitude', 18.

63. *MS. and Publishing History.* No MS.; published in *POVO*, *HI*, *POT*.

Written at some time between 1803–6, probably earlier than later. Compare no. 31.

title   As one poem, on this subject, is printed in the beginning, the author had, originally, no intention of inserting the following; it is added now, at the particular request of some friends. [B]

epigraph   'Oina–Morul: A Poem', *Poems of Ossian* (1803) I. 281.

2. Henry II founded Newstead, soon after the murder of Thomas à Becket. [B] It was founded between 1163 and 1173.

9. *Serf.* This word is used by Walter Scott, in his poem, 'The Wild Huntsman': synonymous with Vassal. [B]

10. The Red Cross was the badge of the Crusaders. [B]

34. As 'Gloaming', the Scottish word for Twilight, is far more poetical, and has been recommended by many eminent literary men, particularly Dr. Moore, in his letters to Burns, I have ventured to use it on account of its harmony. [B] The letter from Sir John Moore (1729-1802) to Burns of 10 June 1789 (*Letters of Robert Burns*, ed. Francis H. Allen (New York, 1927), II. 154).

36. The Priory was dedicated to the Virgin. [B, added in *HI*]

41. At the dissolution of the Monasteries, Henry VIII bestowed Newstead Abbey on Sir John Byron. [B] This was in 1540, the year after the dissolution.

57. Newstead sustained a considerable siege, in the war between Charles I and his Parliament. [B] B's remark is not true.

73. Lord Byron, and his brother, Sir William, held high Commands in the Royal Army; the former was General in Chief, in Ireland, Lieutenant of the Tower, and Governor to James, Duke of York; afterwards, the unhappy James II. The latter had a principal share in many Actions. Vide Clarendon, Hume, etc. [B] See Clarendon's *History of the Rebellion*, Books IV, VII, XI.

76. Lucius Cary, Lord Viscount Falkland, the most accomplished man of his age, was killed at the Battle of Newbery, charging in the ranks of Lord Byron's Regiment of Cavalry. [B] He was the second Viscount Falkland (1610–43).

108. This is an historical fact; a violent tempest occurred immediately subsequent to the death, or interment of Cromwell [1658], which occasioned many disputes between his Partizans, and the Cavaliers; both interpreted the circumstance into divine interposition, but whether as approbation or condemnation, we leave to the Casuists of that age to decide; I have made such use of the occurrence as suited the subject of my poem. [B]

109. Charles II. [B]

64. *MS. and Publishing History.* B's corrected draft (*MS. T*, location: Yale). This is the MS. called in *C* 'MS. Newstead'. It carries a note by E. Pigot: 'The original M.S. of the Death of Calmar and Orla—The *End of it* was given to Mr. Dowland who wanted a bit of his writing for his fine collection of autographs.' Missing are the last three sentences, plus the last two words of the fourth-to-last sentence; they have been written in by E. Pigot. Untitled and undated. Published in *HI*, *POT*.

As B's note to the poem indicates, the poem is an Ossianic version of the Nisus and Euryalus story. For detailed discussion of Ossianic elements see *Wilmsen*, 28–30. The names in the piece are all from Ossian. It is sufficient to understand that Calmar and Orla are taken from *Fingal*. Calmar is glossed by

Macpherson as meaning 'a strong man'; Orla, whose name is not glossed, appears first in Book v. Calmar is a warrior in the hosts of Cuthullin, Orla in the army of Fingal. The traditional enemies of Morven are the Scandinavian armies of Lochlin, whose king was Starno. Swaran was the son of Starno. Morven, according to Macpherson's gloss, is 'all the North-west coast of Scotland'. The name, he adds, signifies ' a ridge of very high hills'.

The poem was written early in Apr. 1807 (*BLJ* II. 114–15).

title It may be necessary to observe that the story, though considerably varied in the Catastrophe, is taken from 'Nisus and Euryalus', of which Episode, a translation is already given in the present volume. [B]

5–6. Cf. Psalms 18:10.

17. *Cave of Oithona*: the cave where Dunromath concealed Oithona after he carried her off. See *Oithona. A Poem.*

31. *Tura:* a castle on the Irish coast. [Macpherson's gloss]

35. *Son of Trenmor.* Fingal was actually his great-grandson.

42–3. *feast of shells.* Macpherson has a similar phrase in *Fingal*, Book II which he glosses: 'The ancient Scots, as well as the present Highlanders, drank in shells; hence it is that we so often meet, in the old poetry, with the *chief of shells*, and the *hall of shells*.'

44. *Lubar:* a river in Ulster. [Macpherson's gloss]

70. *Mathon.* See *Fingal*, Book IV.

85. *Strumon:* a stream 'in the neighborhood of Selma', the royal residence of Fingal. [Macpherson's gloss]

93. *Ryno:* the youngest of Fingal's sons.

130. I fear, Laing's late Edition has completely overthrown every hope that Macpherson's Ossian, might prove the Translation of a series of Poems complete in themselves; but, while the Imposture is discovered, the merit of the work remains undisputed, though not without faults, particularly in some parts, turgid and bombastic diction.—The present humble imitation, will be pardoned by the admirers of the original, as an attempt, however inferior, which evinces an attachment to their favourite Author. [B] Malcolm Laing (1762–1818), *The Poems of Ossian . . .* (1805).

65. *MS. and Publishing History.* B's corrected draft, originally at Newstead, is at Texas (*MS. T,* paper watermarked 1806); reproduced with a brief description in *Pratt*, 135–8. E. Pigot's fair copy, with B's corrections, is in Pforzheimer (*MS. P*); reproduced with description in *Shelley and His Circle*, VI. 1113–18. MS. P dated 19 Apr. 1807 and with a prose note by B to lines 64–7 (see below). Published *HI*, *POT*.

Edward Noel Long, one of B's closest friends at Harrow, died at sea in 1809 on his way to fight in the Peninsular War. B's note to the poem may have been written for Long, who would not have been familiar with Southwell society. It reads: 'E——is a west Indian married to a *Creole*, C——is Mrs. Musters *Chaworth*, a former flame; Caroline is her *mother in Law*; Mary is a

Mrs. *Cobourne*, and Cora a *Notts* Girl, her real name is Julia Leacroft, there is a poem addressed to her, under the name of *Lesbia*.' Mary is Mary Duff, who married Robert Cockburn (see *BLJ* III. 222). E——and Caroline have never been certainly identified; B's identifications here of these two women may be jokes: cf. no. 72, commentary.

Michael Cooke (*The Blind Man Traces the Circle* (Princeton, 1969), 18–20) sees in the opening lines a general allusion to Wordsworth's lines on 'Tintern Abbey'.

66. *MS. and Publishing History.* No MS.; published *HI, POT*.

The poem treats, retrospectively, B's falling out with one of his closest friends at Harrow, George, fifth Earl Delawarr (1788–1869). It was written in Feb. 1807 (see B's letter to Clare, *BLJ* I. 106).

19. *chance.* The reading is clear, but not the meaning. B probably wishes 'has lost' to be read 'has been lost'.

67. *MS. and Publishing History.* No MS.; published in *POT*.

Composed late 1807 or early 1808. It was the last poem to be added to *POT* (B sent it to Ridge in Feb. 1808, to help make up for the removal of 'Childish Recollections' a few months earlier). Stanzas 4–5 refer to B's carousings either at Cambridge, in the autumn of 1807, or in London in the winter of 1808 (see *BLJ* I. 155, and 135, 150).

1. Echoes Coleridge, 'Sonnet to the River Otter', 14.
5. Sassenagh, or Saxon, a Gaelic word, signifying either Lowland or English. [B]
21–4. Perhaps recalling Wordsworth's 'Elegiac Stanzas Suggested by a Picture of Peele Castle . . .', esp. 1–32.
49–50. A very Byronic thought: see e.g. *CHP III*, st. 69.
56. Psalm 55, Verse 6.——'And I said, Oh! that I had wings like a dove, then would I fly away and be at rest.' This verse also constitutes a part of the most beautiful anthem in our language. [B]

68. *MS. and Publishing History.* No MS.; published in *POT*.

B described this favourite spot of his in a letter to Murray, 26 May 1822 ('a large tree (bearing the name of Peachie, or Peachy)': see *LJ* VI. 69–72).

69. *MS. and Publishing History.* MS. G. (see *HI* commentary). Published in *FP*, *POVO*.

The poem is almost certainly addressed to John Edleston, the Cambridge choirboy whom B met in Oct. 1805 and of whom he became passionately fond (see *BLJ* I. 124–5). Marchand (I. 109 n.) therefore redates the poem 1805, instead of 1802, as B had specified. But B may very well have written the poem first in 1802 as he said, and addressed it then to the unknown person (also of low birth) eulogized in 'Epitaph on a Friend' (no. 32). B may have deliberately meant the title to refer to Edleston, and the date to the earlier friend, in order to obtain, simultaneously, a double reference.

70. *MS. and Publishing History.* No MS.; published in *FP, POVO.*

An elegy on the death of Margaret Parker (1789–1802). B's first poem (now lost) was apparently written to her (*LJ* v. 449).

7–8. Cf. Job 18: 14.

24. The Author claims the indulgence of the reader, more for this piece, than, perhaps, any other in the collection; but as it was written at an earlier period than the rest (being composed at the age of 14), and his first Essay, he preferred submitting it to the indulgence of his friends in its present state, to making either addition or alteration. [B]

71. *MS. and Publishing History.* B's holograph fair copy, undated, and E. Pigot's copy made from B's draft (*MSS. N* and *NP*, location: Newstead). Also, *MS. G* (see *HI* commentary). At the bottom of her copy E. Pigot wrote: 'Facsimile of the *first* bit of poetry Ld. B. ever wrote down at Southwell.'

The poem is addressed to George, fifth Earl Delawarr (1791–1869), as E. Pigot noted in her copy of *POVO.* Delawarr was one of B's closest friends at Harrow. See also 'Childish Recollections', 301–24 and 'To [George, Earl Delawarr]', no. 66.

72. *MS. and Publishing History.* No MS.; published in *FP, POVO.*

That Caroline is a generic name, and not a particular girl, see *BLJ* I. 103, 157. But for B's mystifying (and perhaps buffooning) identification of Caroline as Mary Chaworth's mother-in-law see *BLJ* I. 116.

73. *MS. and Publishing History.* No MS.; published *FP*, not collected until *C*, where the text is the unrevised *FP*. But B extensively revised the poem in *FPM* when he was preparing for the publication of *POVO.* This poem, and the notorious 'To Mary' (no. 77), were dropped from all later printings by B because both were 'too warmly drawn' (see 'Answer to Some Elegant Verses . . . ', no. 97).

Southwell gossip had it that some of B's most amorous verses in *FP* were addressed to Julia Leacroft. B warded off the suggestion, in the case of 'To a Lady . . . ' (no. 81), by adding a disclaiming note to that poem, and he may have removed this piece altogether simply to silence the gossip (see also *BLJ* I. 104 and n.). The dating of 1806 is conjectural.

74. *MS. and Publishing History.* No MS.; published in *FP, POVO.*

This interesting poem is an imaginary dramatization of B's parting hour with Mary Chaworth. He saw her for the last time before her marriage in 1804 (she was married in Aug. 1805). The formal emphasis which the poem

places upon an imaginative recovery of past events and scenes seems peculiarly appropriate to the subject, especially if B did write the poem in 1805.

75. *MS. and Publishing History.* No MS.; published *FP, POVO.*
    The initial quatrain is by E. Pigot, to whom B's poem is addressed. Miss
Pigot's verses are in her copy of *Letters of an Italian Nun and an English Gentleman. Translated from the French of J. J. Rousseau* (2nd edn., 1784). The book is
at Texas. B's poem had been written on the front flyleaf, but this has been
removed (See *Pratt*, 14–15). *MS. G* (see *HI* commentary) has a copy of the
Pigot verses, but not B's.

76. *MS. and Publishing History.* No MS.; published *FP, POVO.*
    The Probus of the poem is Dr. Joseph Drury, Headmaster at Harrow (1784–
1805), whom B came to respect enormously. B's piece was called forth when
Drury was replaced, in Apr. 1805, by the Revd. Dr. George Butler ('Pomposus'). B and Dr. Butler were later reconciled through Dr. Drury's good
offices, and B suppressed this poem as well as 'Childish Recollections', where
he had carried on his satire of Dr. Butler (see *BLJ* I. 155 and n.).
    4. *Barbarian:* alluding to Theodoric, Emperor of the Ostrogoths (493–526).

77. *MS. and Publishing History.* No MS.; published in *FP*, then suppressed.
In *FPM* the entire poem is crossed through. Uncollected previously.
    This was the poem which so stirred up Southwell society against *FP*, all
copies of which B tried to have destroyed. His anger at the reaction was
expressed in a series of poems: 'Answer to Some Elegant Verses . . . ' (no. 97),
'To a Knot of Ungenerous Critics' (no.25), 'Soliloquy of a Bard in the Country'
(no. 27), 'Egotism . . . ' (no. 109). He recorded his thanks to friends who
supported him at the time in 'To Those Ladies . . . ' (no. 24). For full
details see *Pratt*, 36–43. The identity of this particular Mary is not known,
but she seems to have been from London, and B may have written the poem
while he was in London, 9 Aug. 1806 (*BLJ* I. 97; but see *Pratt*, 28). B's other
poems to her include 'To a Lady . . . ' (no. 81), 'To Mary . . . ' (no. 43), 'To
a Lady . . . ' (no. 10), 'A Woman's Hair' (no. 11).

78. *MS. and Publishing History.* No MS.; published in *FP, POVO.*
    The poem is probably associated with Mary Chaworth.

79. *MS. and Publishing History.* No MS.; published in *FP, POVO.*
    Perhaps addressed to the 'naughty Mary' of 'To Mary' (no. 77).

80. *MS. and Publishing History.* No MS.; published in *FP, POVO, HI.*
    Probably written in the summer or early autumn of 1806.
    title   Recalling Gray's 'Ode on a Distant Prospect of Eton College'.
    epigraph   *Aeneid,* VIII. 560.

20. Mossop, a contemporary of Garrick, famous for his performance of Zanga, in Young's tragedy of the Revenge. [B] Henry Mossop (1729–73). Here and in the next stanza B alludes to his performances on two Speech Days at Harrow, 6 June and 4 July 1805 (see *Marchand*, I. 96–7). Zanga and Alonzo are characters in Young's *The Revenge*.

81. *MS. and Publishing History.* No MS.; published in *FP*, *POVO*.
The subject of the poem is the 'naughty Mary' of 'To Mary' (no. 77; see also no. 43). B's note to line 20 suggests that the poem's date is Dec. 1805, though it could at least conceivably be 1804 (see *Pratt*, 49–50).

11. Sheridan, *The Rivals*, esp. I. ii.

20. In the above little piece, the author has been accused by some *candid readers*, of introducing the name of a lady, from whom he was some hundred miles distant, at the time this was written; and poor Juliet, who has slept so long in 'the Tomb of all the Capulets' has been converted, with a trifling alteration of her name, into an English damsel, walking in a garden of their own creation, during the month of *December*, in a village, where the author never passed a winter; such has been the candour of some ingenious critics: we would advise these *Liberal* commentators on taste, and arbiters of decorum, to read Shakespeare. [B, added in *POVO*] The Southwell gossip was that the poem was written to Julia Leacroft. See 'To Caroline' and 'To Lesbia' (nos. 73, 83).

22. Alluding to Otway, *Venice Preserved*, II. iii.

44. Having heard that a very severe, and indelicate censure has been passed on the above poem, I beg leave to reply in a quotation from an admired work, '*Carr's* Stranger in France', chapter 16.—'As we were contemplating a painting on a large scale, in which, amongst other figures, is the uncovered whole length of a warrior, a prudish looking lady, who seemed to have touched the age of desperation, after having, attentively, surveyed it through her glass, observed to her party, that there was a great deal of indecorum in that picture; Madame S. shrewdly whispered in my ear, "that the indecorum was in the remark".' [B, added in *POVO*] Sir John Carr, *The Stranger in France* (1803).

82. *MS. and Publishing History.* No MS.; published in *FP*, *POVO*, *HI*.
A slightly different text appeared in *Fare The Well . . . by Lord Byron. With Other Poems* (1816, printed for Rodwell and Martin: cited here as *RM1816*). This text is dated '1813', and the nature of the volume strongly suggests that it had been picked up from a newspaper printing, perhaps of that year. But the source of the *RM1816* text is still not known. It is not, in any case, the pamphlet described by Wise (I. xxii–xxiii and 13–14) as having been issued around 1810, for the pamphlet is a forgery.
The poem is one of the new pieces written while he was revising his plans for an augmented edition of *FP* in September 1806 (see *BLJ* I. 100 and n.).

title   Whom the Author saw at Harrowgate. [B's MS. note in *BM* copy of *POVO*] At Harrowgate, Sept. 1806. [E. Pigot's note in *FPN*] That is, Harrogate (see no. 35, commentary).

83. *MS. and Publishing History.* No MS.; published in *FP*, *POVO*.

Addressed to Julia Leacroft, with whom B flirted intermittently between 1804 and 1806, and written in Aug. or Sept. 1806 (see *Pratt*, 29–30 and n. and *Marchand*, I. 117). The poem strongly recalls B's letter to John Pigot of 9 Aug. 1806 (*BLJ* I. 94–5).

title   E. Pigot's MS. note in *FPN* is 'Leacroft', and in the *BM* copy of *POVO* 'Julia L'.

25. It was perhaps this line, in a poem known to be addressed to Julia Leacroft, which fed the gossip that 'To a Lady' (no. 81) was also written to her.

84. *MS. and Publishing History.* B's fair copy, untitled, undated (*MS. T*, location: Texas; this is called the Newstead MS. in *C*). Published complete in *FP*, sts. 1–4 in *POVO*. Collected edns. until *C* and *More* printed only the *POVO* version.

E. Pigot's annotation in *FPN* states the poem was addressed to her. B removed sts. 5–10 because of the adverse reaction to *FP* in Southwell society (see 'To Mary', no. 77).

16. Shakespeare, *Troilus and Cressida*, I. ii. 312–13.
20. Matthew 22: 30.

85. *MS. and Publishing History.* No MS.; published in *FP*, *POVO*. The poem may have been printed separately as a broadside in Sept.–Oct. 1806 (see *Pratt*, 27–30).

E. Pigot's notation in the *BM* copy of *POVO* is: 'C.B.F. J.B.M.P.', the latter four letters referring to her brother John, and the former three letters to 'his Mistress'. B may be referring to her in his letter to John Pigot of 13 Jan. 1807 when he speaks of 'your *adorable* "Caroline"' (*BLJ* I. 103). The identity of the girl is not known; she may have been the daughter of B's mother's landlord, Dr. Falkner (see B's letter to Dr. Falkner, 8 Jan. 1807, *BLJ* I. 102–3).

19. Echoing Goldsmith, *The Traveller*, 9–10. The image of the 'lengthening chain' is one to which B frequently recurs in his verse.

86. *MS. and Publishing History.* No MS.; published in *FP* and *POVO*. B removed st. 8 in *POVO* for the same reason that he removed sts. 5–10 in no. 84 (and for the same reason that he dropped 'To Mary' altogether from *POVO*). *C* and *More* restored sts. 5–10 to no. 84, but they did not restore this dropped stanza. Their procedure seems to have been inconsistent, and the stanza is restored here.

E. Pigot's note in the *BM* copy of *POVO* is: 'J.M.B.P.', i.e. her brother John. This is clearly a companion piece to the previous poem and must have been written in Nov. 1806. B's attitude toward Pigot's alternately cruel and yielding 'Mistress' seems to have been justified, for she turned out a 'complete "*Jilt*" ' (*BLJ* I. 103–4).

87. *MS. and Publishing History.* No MS.; published in *FP, POVO.*

E. Pigot's MS. note in *FPN* reads: 'There was a youth in the Choir, when Ld. Byron was at Cambridge, with whose voice he was so much charmed, that he frequently had him at his rooms, and grew so fond of his society, from his amiable disposition and pleasing manners, that he provided for him by placing him in an advantageous Mercantile concern—he died of a consumption at an early age, his name was *Eddleston*, and this poem was written upon his giving Ld. Byron a small Cornelian heart when he left Cambridge —E.B.P.' B probably wrote the verses when Edleston gave him the Cornelian, either in Dec. 1805 or in July 1806. For further details see commentary on 'To E.——' (no. 69).

88. *MS. and Publishing History.* No MS.; published in *FP, POVO.*

E. Pigot's note in the *BM* copy of *POVO* says the poem was addressed to Anne Houson, the daughter of the Revd. Henry Houson, of Southwell. Its placement in *FP* shows that it must have been written Oct.–Nov. 1806.

3. *hurtling.* This word is used by Gray in his poem to the Fatal Sisters:—
'Iron sleet of arrowy shower,
Hurtles through the darken'd air.' [B]
See 'The Fatal Sisters', 3–4.

89. *MS. and Publishing History. MS. G* (see *HI* commentary). Published in *FP, POVO.*

The original poem (IV. 2) is only attributed to Tibullus.

90. *MS. and Publishing History.* No MS.; published in *POVO* only.

Like the other poem 'To M.S.G.' (no. 40), this was probably addressed to E. Pigot and composed Nov.–Dec. 1806.

91. *MS. and Publishing History.* No MS.; published in *POVO* only.

The original lines from Horace, *Odes*, III. iii were published with the poem in *POVO*. Composed either Nov.–Dec. 1806, or earlier as a school exercise.

92. *MS. and Publishing History.* B's corrected draft (*MS. N*, location: Newstead). Published in *POVO, HI.* In most crown octavo copies of *HI*, sig. D3 is a cancel leaf, the original cancelled leaf having carried the *POVO* text of sts. 1–2, including the note to line 2.

This was probably the last poem added to *POVO*. It should be compared with 'To Romance' (no. 62).

epigraph   Anacreontea, Ode 1.

2. *Moriah:* The Goddess of Folly. [B, in *POVO*]

26. Psalms 55: 6.

93. *MS. and Publishing History.* The original MS. of the poem, written late in 1806 for printing in *POVO*, does not survive. Early in 1807 B revised and augmented the poem for printing in *HI*. All later collected editions ultimately depend upon *HI*, which is copy text here. At the beginning of 1808 B began making further revisions for the *POT* printing, where it was in fact set up in type under the title 'Childish Recollections, written during Illness' and with a second epigraph from Virgil (see *BLJ* 1. 152 and *Wise*, 1. 11). But B was reconciled to Dr. Butler, the Pomposus of the poem, in Feb. 1808, and he therefore decided to remove the work from *POT*, a decision made during the course of printing which forced a delay in publication of *POT* (see *BLJ* 1. 154–5). For further intended revisions see *BLJ* 1. 143 and n. and *MS. M* below.

MS. T, at Texas, contains the corrected draft of the revisions made for the *HI* printing. The MS. is in a folder marked by E. Pigot as 'what remains of "Childish Recollections"—the only copy he ever wrote'. The title is inserted in pencil by Miss Pigot along with a series of her pencil corrections in various lines to make the MS. conform to the *HI* printing. This MS. was printed (without variants) and briefly described in *Pratt*, 128–35. It contains the following: 1–26 (B holograph); 43–84 (fair copy in another hand heavily corrected by B and headed by him '2nd Insertion in Childish Recollections'. Lines 43–54 are in the other hand—not Miss Pigot's—with the remainder of the passage in B's hand); 48–54 (B's draft holograph); 55–98 (55–84 are in the other hand, corrected by B, to which B added 85–98); 121–226 (B's draft holograph headed by Miss Pigot '3rd Insertion'); 227–42 (B's draft holograph); 355–410 (B's draft holograph headed by Miss Pigot '4th Insertion'). Two related poems are also embedded in the MS. The first is entirely cancelled (printed in *Pratt*, 133 n.), while the second, an epigram on Pomposus, is uncancelled (printed incorrectly in *Pratt*, 134 n.). Both are printed here after the text of 'Childish Recollections' along with the better-known satiric portrait of Pomposus (see *C* 1. 91 n.). The MS. of the latter, at Yale (*MS. Y*), is a corrected holograph fair copy. The final MS. to be noted is at Murray (*MS. M*), a holograph sheet dated 1808 containing several of the alterations intended for *POT* (revisions for lines 89–92, 111, 115–20).

'This parting song' (372) is a memorial exercise on the years B spent at Harrow and the most ambitious piece published in B's early volumes. It is obviously indebted to the tradition of 18th-century retrospective poetry, but B seems to have had particularly in mind Henry Kirke White's 'Childhood'. B identified the real models for the poem's different characters in a letter to

E. N. Long (*BLJ* I. 109–10 and n.); Miss Pigot's annotations are in the Texas copy of *POVO* (printed in *Pratt*, 62 n.).

epigraphs *Macbeth*, IV. iii. 222–3 (slightly misquoted); *Aeneid*, X. 781. 35–6. Identities unknown: see *BLJ* I. 112.

90. *Pomposus*: the Revd. Dr. George Butler, who succeeded Dr. Joseph Drury (the Probus of the poem) as Headmaster of Harrow in 1805.

100. See *Life*, I. 29.

109. This most able, and excellent man retired from his situation in Mar. 1805, after having resided 35 years at H[arrow]—the last 20 as Head Master; an office he held with equal honour to himself, and advantage to the very extensive School, over which he presided; panegyric would here be superfluous, it would be useless to enumerate qualifications which were never doubted; a considerable contest took place between three rival candidates for his vacant Chair, of this I can only say

> 'Si mea, cum vestris valuissent Vota, Pelasgi!
> Non foret ambiguus tanti certaminis Haeres.'

[B's note in *HI*] Latin quotation: Ovid, *Metamorphoses*, XIII. 128–9.

120. This alludes to a character printed in a former private edition [i.e. *POVO*] for the perusal of some friends, which with many other pieces is withheld from the present volume; to draw the attention of the public to insignificance would be deservedly reprobated, and another reason, though not of equal consequence, may be given in the following couplet:—

> 'Satire or sense, alas! can Sporus feel?
> Who breaks a Butterfly upon the wheel?'
> Prologue to the Satires. Pope.

[B's note in *HI*] The reference is to poem no. 76. B slightly misquotes Pope's 'Epistle to Dr. Arbuthnot', 307–8.

131. Cf. Gray's 'Ode on . . . Eton College', 30, and line 257 below.

243. *Alonzo*: John Wingfield (Pigot annotation in Texas copy of *POVO*: see also *CHP I*, st. 91). The original portrait of 'Joannes' was Lord Clare (B's annotation in *BM* copy of *POVO*: see also 'To the Earl of Clare', no. 59).

266. *Davus*: John Cecil Tattersall (Pigot annotation in *POVO*; see also *BLJ* I. 109). Tattersall died in 1812.

273. The incident occurred in 1803: see *Life*, I. 25 and *Marchand*, I. 72–3.

287. *Lycus*: traditionally Lord Clare (*C* I. 98 n.) but B said the portrait was of James Wynne de Bathe (1792–1828) (*BLJ* I. 109; also Pigot annotation in *POVO*, where Clarus is identified as Lord Clare).

294. John Fitzgibbon, first Earl of Clare (1749–1802), was Attorney-General and Lord Chancellor of Ireland.

301. *Euryalus*: George John, fifth Earl of Delawarr (Pigot annotation in *POVO*; see also *BLJ* I. 109).

326. *Cleon*: E. N. Long (Pigot annotation in *POVO*; see also *BLJ* I. 109 and no. 65).

335. This alludes to the public speeches, delivered at the school where the author was educated. [B's note in *POVO* and *HI*]

351. See *LJ* V. 415, 453.

393–4. Cf. Jeremiah 8: 22.

412. 'L'Amitie est L'Amour sans Ailes', is a French proverb. [B's note in *HI*] Cf. no. 26.

93a. The MS. has at the end a version of B's note for line 120.

93b. The interlocutors are Edward Noel Long and B.

94. *MS. and Publishing History.* No MS.; published in *POVO* only.

Composed Nov.–Dec. 1806. James Montgomery's poem, 'The Common Lot', was published in *The Wanderer of Switzerland, and Other Poems* (1806).

6. No particular Hero is here alluded to; the exploits of Bayard, Nemours, Edward the Black Prince; and in more modern times, the fame of Marlborough, Frederick the Great, Count Saxe, Charles of Sweden, etc. are familiar to every historical reader, but the exact places of their birth are known to a very small proportion of their admirers. [B] James of Armagnac, Duke of Nemours (1433–77), and Maurice, the Comte de Saxe (1696–1750), are perhaps not so well known any longer.

95. *MS. and Publishing History.* No MS.; published in *POVO*, *HI*.

Composed Nov.–Dec. 1806.

epigraph   Anacreontea, 58. 4.

38. *Astrea*: The Goddess of Justice. [B]

96. *MS. and Publishing History.* No MS.; published in *POVO* only.

It was the Revd. John Thomas Becher (1770–1848) who helped with the publication of *POVO* and who induced B to destroy (almost) all copies of *FP*. Composed Nov.–Dec. 1806.

17. CHATHAM: William Pitt, first Earl of Chatham (1708–78).

36. Cf. Ecclesiastes 12: 7.

97. *MS. and Publishing History.* No MS.; published in *POVO*, *HI*.

See previous poem. For a good insight into B's relations with Becher see B's letter to him of 26 Feb. 1808 (*BLJ* I. 157–8).

37–8. Echoes Thomas Moore, 'To Julia' ('Why let the stingless critic chide'), 5–6.

98. *MS. and Publishing History.* B's corrected draft (*MS. B*) and E. Pigot's fair copy (*MS. Ba*): location, Berg. Both undated, untitled; *MS. B* is watermarked 1806 and lacks lines 25–8. First published C from MS. B (there called Newstead MS.).

The subject is the cornelian heart given B by John Edleston. The date of the piece must be 1807, probably earlier in the year.

11. *lay*: irregular usage.

99. *MS. and Publishing History*. The only MS. to appear is E. Pigot's fair copy of the last four lines, dated 1807 (location: New York Public Library, Montague MS., no. 56). First published *1832* complete (there are excerpts in *Life*, I. 108 which are reprinted in *1831*). These texts presumably derive from a copy given Moore by E. Pigot. C had access to a Newstead MS. (*MS. N*), but like a number of other MSS. once at Newstead, it is no longer there.

If the poem was in fact written in 1807, as *1832* indicates, it probably was written early in the year (see *BLJ* I. 106).

1. Harrow.
29. *Marr*: in Scotland, between the Don and the Dee.
35. 'On Leaving Newstead Abbey', no. 31.
45. *Streamlet*: the Grete, in Southwell.
55. Mary Chaworth; *1832* says Mary Duff.
61. *Friend*: John Edleston.
94. *lay*: irregular usage.
111. Cf. James 1: 17.
113. Cf. Matthew 10: 29.
115. Cf. Jude 13.

100. *MS. and Publishing History*. B's fair copy (*MS. N*, location: Newstead). First published C, from *MS. N*.

Compare 'To Woman' and 'To Miss E[lizabeth] P[igot]' (nos. 39, 84).

101. *MS. and Publishing History*. B's fair copy, untitled, undated (*MS. N*, location: Newstead). First published in C from *MS. N*.

Addressed to Harriet Maltby (see 'To Marion', no. 45).

102. *MS. and Publishing History*. B's fair copy (*MS. H*, location: Huntington). Published first in C, from *MS. H* (called the Newstead MS. in C).

Compare nos. 103–6 below. Anne Houson was one of B's brief amours at Southwell (see *BLJ* I. 104).

103. *MS. and Publishing History*. No MS. forthcoming. First printed in *1832*, presumably from the Newstead MS. to which C also had access, but which is no longer at Newstead. Title herein is the MS. title as recorded in C, where the stanzas are numbered.

5–12. These lines were later plundered for 'To E[dward] N[oel] L[ong] Esq.' (no. 65), lines 79–86.

8118902   O

104. *MS. and Publishing History.* No MS. forthcoming. First published *1832*. C had access to a Newstead MS. (*MS. N*) which is no longer in the collection.
15–16. Cf. Mark 9: 23.

105. *MS. and Publishing History.* B's corrected draft (*MS. N*, location: Newstead). First published *1832*.

106. *MS. and Publishing History.* No MS.; first published *1832*, presumably from a MS. supplied by E. Pigot.

107. *MS. and Publishing History.* Unpublished. E. Pigot's fair copy, with two corrections by B, is at the Berg (*MS. B*).
    The poem is clearly a companion piece to no. 23, where we are told that Mary Ann Bristoe was seven years older than B. The 'captain' in stanza four is the Captain Lightfoot who acted in a pair of plays privately performed in late Jan. 1807, along with Miss Bristoe, B, and some other persons from Southwell. Lightfoot only got through the performances after fortifying himself with several glasses of wine. These were apparently supplied by B's tutor, the Revd. Thomas Jones, who must have come to Southwell for the performances. See *LJ* I. 118 n., *Marchand*, I. 126, and *Pratt*, 35–6.

108. *MS. and Publishing History.* The Morgan MS. (*MS. M*) is in three parts: (*a*) fair copy of the 'Petition' in unknown hand; (*b*) fair copy of the 'Reply' by Ann Bristoe containing lines 1–20, 41–4, 71–210; (*c*) B's draft holograph of lines 21–40, 45–70. The Bristoe fair copy has two marginal notes by Miss Bristoe indicating the proper places for the insertions of B's draft additions to the poem. At the end of B's draft is a note by E. Pigot: 'The above is L——— Byron's *own* writing, and is intended to be put into the "Reply to the Edinburg Ladies Petition" in addition to what Miss A[nn] B[ristoe] already possesses. March 1807.' Published first, probably not from *MS. M*, in the *New Monthly Magazine*, 44 (Aug. 1835), and again, from *MS. M*, by T. G. Steffan in *Texas Studies in English*, 27 (June 1948). Steffan argues the possibility of co-authorship and concludes that B probably wrote only the 'Reply'. But the 'Petition' was surely not written by a woman. If it was not written by B, it was probably written by John Pigot, who was studying medicine in Edinburgh at the time the poem was written. The present editor believes the entire poem is B's, and that it was written partly for the amusement of his friend John Pigot.
    title   *Doctor Moyes*: Dr. Henry Moyes (1750–1807), professional lecturer on various scientific subjects.
The Reply
    7. William Herschel (1738–1822), the astronomer; see *LJ* v. 458.
    8. Johann Kaspar Lavater (1741–1801), Swiss mystic and poet, inventor of the science of Phrenology (which he called Physiognomy).

16. For this ingenious hypothesis vide Monboddo's Works. [n. in *MS. M*] See *Of the Origin and Progress of Language* (1773), I. ii.

18. The work of Aloisio Galvani (1737–98) on animal magnetism and electricity created widespread interest in England. Alessandro Volta (1745–1827) spoke before the Royal Society in London in 1793.

20. Thomas Young (1773–1829) published his *Lectures on Natural Philosophy and the Mechanical Arts* in 1807, a work generally recognized as the most significant advance in optics since Newton's pioneering study.

Sensoria: a favourite 18th-century term for the nervous system.

23. Elizabeth Billington (1768–1818) and Brigitta Giorgi Banti (1759–1806) were both veteran sopranos in the London opera. B seems to have in mind the 'Infant Billington who had made its mark strutting about the stages of Brighton and Worthing', but who was probably not a singer. See Y. Ffrench, *Mrs. Siddons: Tragic Actress* (1936), 242.

29. The celebrated boy actor William Henry West Betty (1791–1874): see *EBSR* 564–5.

Roscius. See no. 35, line 11.

30. Henry Petty, third Marquis of Lansdowne (1780–1863), entered the House of Commons at twenty-two and became Chancellor of the Exchequer at twenty-five.

Tully: i.e. Cicero.

32–6. The MS. has a pencilled n.: 'Earl of Carlisle' (see *EBSR* 719–40). Despite this note, however, the passage here is certainly an ironic reference to B himself. The 'Master' of line 36 was Dr. Butler, who replaced B's beloved Dr. Drury as headmaster at Harrow in 1805. See 'On a Change of Masters . . .', no. 76, and 'Childish Recollections', no. 93, lines 90–4, 103–6, 115–20.

34. *return to School.* B refused to return to school throughout the autumn, winter, and spring of 1806–7.

45–50, 64–70. a joke on Erasmus Darwin's *Loves of the Plants* (1789) and *The Botanic Garden* (1792), where Darwin expatiates on plant sexuality.

87. Timaeus has written on this idea, and on this foundation, I have taken the liberty of *personifying Form, and Matter.* [note in *MS. M*] Timaeus of Locri, said to be a teacher of Plato. The work bearing his name is probably only an abridgement of Plato's *Timaeus.*

94. Vide Ovid.—The Story of Cupid and Psyche is also in Apuleius. See his 'Golden Ass'. [note in *MS. M*] The story is not in Ovid; B was misled by the alternate title of the 'Golden Ass', the *Metamorphoses.*

133–46. The 'wicked wretches' refers to Pierre Bayle, whose article on 'Eve' in the *Dictionnaire* is the source of the details here. See also B's 'Preface' to *Cain.*

153. *prediliction:* spelt thus in the MS.

109. *MS. and Publishing History.* B's draft (*MS. N*, location: Newstead). First published, from *N*, in *C*, where there are, however, several mistranscriptions.

At the end of *N* is B's note to Becher: 'P.S. These were written between 1 and 2 after *Midnight*, I have not *corrected* or *revised*, yours Byron.' The poem is a loose set of reflections on B's friendships and amours at Harrow, Cambridge, and Southwell, with asides on the bad reception in Southwell of *FP*.

title   the Greek tag means: 'Byron sings himself.'

41–8. Alluding to B's relations with Julia Leacroft and her family (see *BLJ* I. 104–6 and *Marchand*, I. 124).

110. *MS. and Publishing History*. B's corrected fair copy at Texas, dated by him and with a note by E. Pigot: 'Cop[ied] for Mr. Moore Jan 26th 1828.' First published *1832* from Pigot copy, and collected thereafter.

The identity of the 'author of a Sonnet' is not known, but was one of B's male Southwell acquaintances, though probably not a close friend like John Pigot.

111. *MS. and Publishing History*. There are three MSS., all at Newstead: (*a*) B's untitled first draft (*MS. Na*) with present title as prose note at the end, and dated 15 Mar. 1807; (*b*) B's fair copy of lines 1–12 (*MS. Nb*), with title as here printed; (*c*) E. Pigot's fair copy (*MS. Nc*), apparently from the draft MS. with her final note: 'Copied for Mr. Moore, Jan. 24, 1828'. First published complete in *1832*, but excerpts were printed in *Life*, I. 101–2 and thence in *1831*. All the MSS. arrange the poem in numbered octaves; *1832* and *C* arrange it in quatrains, with *1832* numbered and *C* unnumbered. The Pigot MS. apparently miscopies from the draft MS., and *1832* and subsequent printings follow the Pigot MS. The text here is *1832*, but with the stanza form and title as in *Nb* and *Nc*, and with the substantive readings of *Na*.

title   The tree, known as 'The Byron Oak', was actually planted in 1798 (*Marchand*, I. 50–1).

10. Newstead was occupied from 1802 to 1808 by (successively) a Mr. Clay, two Misses Launders, and for five years by Lord Grey de Ruthyn. It is the latter whom B has especially in mind (see *Marchand*, I. 73–4).

112. *MS. and Publishing History*. B's draft MS. originally at Newstead, is now at Texas (*MS. T*) along with E. Pigot's fair copy made in 1828 (*MS. Ta*). First published *1832* from *MS. Ta*, and collected thereafter. *Pratt*, 139–40, was the first to print the poem from *MS. T*. The composition was around 14 May 1807 (see *BLJ* I. 118). The text here is *1832*, but with the stanza numbering, the title, and two readings restored from *MS. T*.

113. *MS. and Publishing History*. B's fair copy, signed (*MS. BM*, location: *BM*). Published from the MS. in *Monthly Literary Recreations* (July 1807), a magazine issued by Ben Crosby, the London agent of B's publisher Ridge. Published again, without authorization, in *Fare Thee Well . . . With Other*

Poems (Printed for Rodwell and Martin, New Bond Street, 1816) and *The Works of . . . Lord Byron* (Philadelphia, Printed for M. Thomas, 1820). First published in a Murray edition, *C*, from the *MS*. Published occasionally in Paris editions, and English piracies, between 1820 and 1830; these texts all derive from the M. Thomas text (*Phil1820*) rather than the 1816 piracy noted above (*RM1816*; see no. 82). A MS. copy in the hand of Ann Gould Webb, deriving from *Phil1820*, is in the Cambridge University Library. All texts except the first and *C* carry the following note prefixed to the poem: 'The following stanzas were addressed by Lord Byron to his Lady, a few months before their separation.' *RM1816* is the source of this incorrect description.

B sent the poem to Crosby 21 July 1807 (*BLJ* I. 129). Marchand (ibid.) says the poem seems 'obviously addressed to John Edleston'.

114. *MS. and Publishing History.* B's fair copy (*MS. M*, location: Murray). First published in *Life*, I. 106 from the Murray MS., with title, signature, and date as in the MS.; collected, *1831*, *1832*, and thereafter.

115. *MS. and Publishing History.* Corrected fair copy in bound volume of Miscellaneous Early Poems (*MS. M*, location: Murray). First published, *Life*, I. 102; collected, *1831*, *1832*, and thereafter. The MS. is untitled but carries the following headnote by B: 'Some years ago, when at H[arrow] a Friend of the author's engraved on a particular Spot the names of Both, with a few additional words as a memorial, afterwards on receiving some real or imagined injury the author destroyed the frail record before he left H[arrow]. On revisiting the place in 1807—he wrote under it the following stanzas.'

The poem seems to deal with B's estrangement from the Earl of Delawarr, to whom he had been closely attached at Harrow. See *BLJ* I. 134 and 'To [George, Earl Delawarr]', no. 66.

116. *MS. and Publishing History.* B's corrected fair copy in bound volume of Miscellaneous Early Poems (*MS. M*, location: Murray). First published, *Life*, I. 104–5; collected, *1831*, *1832*, and thereafter.

The poem has sometimes been thought to have been written about B's illegitimate child by his maid Lucy (see, e.g., *BLJ* I. 189 and note). But Lucy was pregnant by B early in 1809, nor did she die an untimely death, but lived to marry. B later told Lady Byron that he had two natural children he meant to provide for (see *C* I. 260 n. and *DJ* XVI. 61).

117. *MS. and Publishing History.* No MS.; uncollected. First published in *The Casket, A Miscellany Consisting of Unpublished Poems* (1829). This book was published by Murray and edited by Francis Hodgson, and it prints the poem as B's. See E. A. Axon, 'Album Verses Attributed to Lord Byron', *The Bookman* (Feb. 1908), 201, where it is printed again.

The date is pure conjecture, but the style is early Byron.

118. MS. and Publishing History. B's corrected fair copy, dated 10 June 1808, in a bound volume of Miscellaneous Early Poems (*MS. M*, location: Murray). First published *IT*; collected *Paris1828, 1831, 1832*, and thereafter.

The title in *IT* suggests the poem was written to 'the same' person addressed in nos. 119–21. *Paris1828* printed all four poems as addressed to Mary Chaworth. But the lady concerned in the poems below was probably the Miss Cameron whom B spent some time with at Brighton (see *BLJ* 1. 167 and n.; *Marchand*, 1. 151, 156, and nos. 119–21 below). Furthermore, as the MS. title of the poem shows, the verses were originally written to George, Earl Delawarr.

119. MS. and Publishing History. B's holograph MS., perhaps a draft but probably a second copy (*MS. M*, location: Murray, in bound volume of Miscellaneous Early Poems). First published in *C* from a MS. in the Lovelace papers, but this MS. is not forthcoming. *C* probably miscopied at line 5, and almost certainly at line 7; and *C* gave the MS. date of the poems as 23 Feb., which must have been a misreading, for it is clearly 23 July 1808 in *MS. M*.

B was in Brighton on 23 July 1808 (hence the 'billow' of line 2). The poem is probably written to the Miss Cameron whom he kept at Brompton and often took with him to Brighton. He said that he had 'parted with Miss Cameron' on 20 July (see *BLJ* 1. 167 and note), but he may have resumed his relations with her, at least for a time. He left Brighton around 14 Aug. and on 12 and 13 Aug. he wrote two melancholy love poems of farewell which may well have marked the definitive end of his relationship with Miss Cameron.

120. MS. and Publishing History. B's corrected fair copy, dated 12 Aug. 1808 (*MS. M*, location: Murray, bound volume of Miscellaneous Early Poems). E. Pigot copied the poem on the end flyleaf of her copy of *POVO* (*MS. T*, location: Texas). *MS. T* differs slightly from the first printed text, and even more considerably from *MS. M*. She may have made her copy from another MS., now lost. First published *IT*, collected *Paris1826, 1831, 1832*.

The poem is almost certainly addressed to Miss Cameron (see nos. 118, 119, 121, commentaries), but B may have later given it to Miss Pigot as if it were addressed to her.

7–8. Cf. Isaiah 34: 14.

121. MS. and Publishing History. B's corrected draft, first five stanzas dated 12 Aug. 1808, final stanza dated 13 Aug., in bound volume of Miscellaneous Early Poems (*MS. M*, location: Murray). First published, *IT*; collected *Paris1828, 1831, 1832*.

Probably addressed to Miss Cameron (see commentaries above).

122. *MS. and Publishing History.* B's corrected draft, dated 20 Aug. 1808, in bound volume of Miscellaneous Early Poems (*MS. M*, location: Murray). Also at Murray, B's heavily corrected proof for *IT* (*Proof M*). There is an uncorrected proof of stanzas 1–7 for *CHP* (*7*) (*Proof H*, location: Huntington). First published *IT*, reprinted *CHP*(*2*), collected thereafter.

In *CHP*(*2*) the poem was preceded by a note: 'This poem and the following were written some years ago.' See no. 123 below. The MS. title of the present poem indicates that it was addressed to Sir James Wynne de Bathe (1792–1828), one of B's Harrow friends and the 'Lycus' of 'Childish Recollections' (see notes to that poem as well as *BLJ* I. 109 and note, and 151).

123. *MS. and Publishing History.* B's corrected draft, dated 2 Nov. 1808 (*MS. M*, location: Murray). Also at Murray: an uncorrected proof, in a bound volume of various proofs for *CHP*(*5*) and *CHP*(*7*). First published *IT*, reprinted *CHP*(*2*) and collected thereafter.

B wrote the poem after having dinner at the home of Mary Chaworth-Musters, whom he had not seen since her marriage in 1805. During the evening he was unnerved at the sight of Mary's two-year-old daughter (see *Marchand*, I. 159–60 and *BLJ* I. 173–4).

124. *MS. and Publishing History. MS. M:* Augusta Leigh's fair copy, untitled, with B's corrections and additions dated 14 Aug. 1811 (B added lines 21–4 in this MS.); *MS. Ma:* Augusta's second fair copy, made from *MS. M*, with title added by B. There is also an uncorrected proof in a bound volume of various proofs for *CHP*(*5*) and *CHP*(*7*). Proof and MSS. are at Murray. First published *CHP*(*7*), collected thereafter.

Composed late Nov. or early Dec. 1808. For circumstances see *Marchand*, I. 163–4. The poem obviously recalls *Hamlet*, V. i.

125. *MS. and Publishing History.* Augusta Leigh's fair copy, dated by B 20 Nov. 1808 and with title in his hand (*MS. M*, location: Murray). Also at Murray, two proofs of *Corsair*(*2*) text, and B's corrected copy of *IT* (*ITB*). First published *IT*, reprinted *Corsair*(*2*) and collected thereafter. Except in *IT*, where the poem is not dated, all printings in B's lifetime were dated 'Newstead Abbey, Oct. 30, 1808'. There has been some confusion about when the dog actually died as well as about the date of the poem's composition (for discussion see *BLJ* I. 176 and note). But it seems clear from the MS. that the dog died on 10 Nov. and that the poem was written on 20 Nov. Boatswain's monument at Newstead Abbey bears the following inscription:

> Near this spot
> Are deposited the Remains of one
> Who possessed Beauty without Vanity,
> Strength without Insolence
> Courage without Ferocity,

And all the Virtues of Man without his Vices.
This Praise, which would be unmeaning Flattery
If inscribed over human ashes,
Is but a just tribute to the Memory of
BOATSWAIN, a Dog,
Who was born at Newfoundland, May, 1803,
And died at Newstead Abbey, Nov. 18, 1808.

126. *MS. and Publishing History.* First fair copy, sent in a letter to Hodgson of 27 Nov. 1808 (*MS. JH*, location: Dickey Collection, Johns Hopkins University). Second fair copy, dated 1 Dec. 1808, in bound volume of Miscellaneous Early Poems (*MS. M*, location: Murray). B's corrected copy of *IT* (*ITB*) is also at Murray, and *1831, 1832, C* had access to the MS. corrections in B's mother's copy of *IT* (*ITBa*). First published, *IT*; collected *Paris 1826, 1831, 1832.*

For the context see *BLJ* I. 173–4, 178–9. B's note to the poem in *MS. JH* reads: 'You perceive the last lines—the "Double Entendre"—are a little too much in English Poesy.'

127. No MS., first published *1832*, collected thereafter.

The poem's subject is the gardens at The Leasowes, near Halesowen, which had been the home of the poet William Shenstone (1714–63). The verses definitely suggest that B had visited Shenstone's estate and that he wrote these lines in response. But no record of such a visit survives, so far as anyone knows. (See also C. J. L. Elwell, 'Byron and the Black Country', *The Blackcountryman* (Spring 1977), 8–10, where Elwell also records 'negative results' from his research into B's possible visit.)

But whenever (or if ever) B was at The Leasowes, this poem is more literary than topical in its orientation. The Leasowes' gardens acquired some celebrity both during and after Shenstone's life, and they are the particular subject of Goldsmith's fine essay, 'The History of a Poet's Garden' (cf. *The Collected Works of Oliver Goldsmith*, ed. Arthur Friedman (Oxford, 1966), III. 203–9). B's poem recapitulates the thoughts of Goldsmith's essay, but shifts from Goldsmith's beautifully plangent reverie to a rather clumsy satiric manner.

The date of the poem is a problem. It is not specifically dated in *1832* or any other edition, but *1832, C* and *More* place it so that we necessarily infer an 1812 date of composition. I think, from internal evidence, that this is too late. In the first place, the allusion to Dryden (*Cymon and Iphigenia*, 84–5) recalls the title page of *HI*; in the second place, the stylistic manner, particularly the last three lines, is close to *EBSR*. An 1808 dating is probably more accurate than 1812.

128. *MS. and Publishing History.* Unpublished. B's draft MS. of the three epigrams is at Murray.

William Lort Mansel (1753–1820), Master of Trinity College (1798–1820), was installed Bishop of Bristol in 1808. He was famous as a wit and epigrammatist. George III's mental derangement was a constant object of Whig jokes.

129. The MS. history of *EBSR* has been unclear in certain respects, largely because of details about this history supplied by R. C. Dallas in his *Recollections* (1824). E. H. Coleridge helped to straighten matters out in several of his commentaries in *C*, and Andrew Rutherford ('An Early MS. of "English Bards and Scotch Reviewers" ', *KSMB* 1956, 11–13) clarified a number of other important points. A more accurate description of the earliest states of the poem is needed, however.

MS. and Proofs

A. B's first draft of *EBSR* was begun in Oct. 1807, as the following MS. note by B indicates (location: Murray): 'The British Bards, A Satire. Nov. 26th 1808. This poem was begun in October 1807 in London and at different intervals composed from that period till Sept. 1808 when it was completed. Newstead Abbey. B. 1808. The poem was intended to have been transcribed here [in a bound volume of MSS. titled *Miscellaneous Poems*], but it is too long for insertion. Dec. 4th 1808.' This chronology seems accurate. The original MS. was '380 Lines' long on 26 Oct. 1807 and 'above four hundred Lines' on 22 Dec. 1807 (*BLJ* I. 136, 141). This draft does not survive, however.

B. The earliest MS. we have of *EBSR* is *MS. M* (location: Murray). This MS. was believed to be the first draft of the poem, until Rutherford showed that it could not have been written before late Feb. 1808. *MS. M* seems clearly to be partly a copy of material contained in the first draft, and partly a new composition altogether, and it was probably begun late in Feb. 1808 shortly after B read Brougham's review of *HI* in the *Edinburgh Review* (see *BLJ* I. 158–60). Much of the MS. is copied fair, but there is a good deal of new material as well in which B expanded his satire, largely to include the 'Reviewers'. The original poem had confined its attack to 'the poetry of the present Day' (*BLJ* I. 141). *MS. M* is divisible into three parts:

1. *MF*, a series of folio leaves numbered 6–25, 28–41, containing 376 lines of verse. The MS. is mutilated in two places so that ten lines are missing. *MF* comprises: 185–254 (70 lines), (255–8; four lines missing, MS. mutilation), 259–66 (8 lines), 269–362 (94 lines), a 16-line passage by J. C. Hobhouse, 418–37 (20 lines), first part of the original lines on Jeffrey (18 lines), 560–617 (58 lines), 707–22 (16 lines), (741–6; six lines missing, MS. mutilation), 747–58 (12 lines), 799–818 (20 lines), 891–912 (22 lines), a couplet on M. G. Lewis, 931–48 (18 lines), 961–2. At this point *MF* breaks off and a series of MS. additions (see *MB* below) are bound into the MS. volume. The contents of the missing leaves 1–5 are not deducible from the evidence; but the missing leaves 26–7, which would have continued the passage on Jeffrey, must have contained 22 lines. The inference is based upon a comparison of

MF with *BB* (see below). Thus, in unmutilated form, the leaves 6–41 of *MF* contained a total of 408 lines.

2. *MQ*, a series of quarto leaves numbered 2–5, 42–6 containing 90 lines of verse. The *MS. M* version of the poem concludes on *MQ*46, and the date 1808 is placed by B at the end. *MQ* comprises: 121–8 (8 lines), 143–84 (42 lines), 963–72 (10 lines), 972a–d (4 lines printed in, then cancelled from, *BB*), 985–1010 (26 lines). This part of *MS. M* is a rewriting of the missing leaves 1–5 in *MF* and of the material which originally followed *MF*41. Leaves 2–5 in *MQ*, ending in the middle of a verso leaf, clearly represent a later correction for *MF*; and leaves 42–6 are similarly corrective, for *MF*41 breaks off *in mediis rebus*. The missing leaf 1 of *MQ* must have contained lines 103–14, 117–20 (16 lines), as a comparison of *MQ* with *BB* shows. *MF* and *MQ* together (*MF/MQ*) made up the copy text for *BB* (see below) and they contain a total of 514 lines. It was *MF/MQ* which B said, on 4 Dec. 1808, was 'too long' to be copied into his notebook of Miscellaneous Poems.

3. Strictly speaking, the MS. leaves comprising *MB*—the third part of *MS. M*—were not part of the poem as B wrote it in 1807–8. *MB* contains MS. additions made in *EBSR* after *BB* was set up in type; the separate leaves of *MB* were bound up later with *MF* and *MQ*. *MB* contains: 1–96 (fair copy), 81–2 (fair copy), 129–42 (draft), 363–84 (draft and fair copy), 385–410 (draft and fair copy), 411–17 (fair copy), 540–59 (fair copy), 638–706 (fair copy), 859–66 (draft), 973–80 (fair copy), 1011–16 (fair copy), 1037–70 (fair copy).

C. *MF/MQ* was copy text for *BB*, a set of heavily corrected and augmented proofs (with proof revises and additional MSS.) entitled *British Bards, A Satire* (location: *BM*, Egerton 2028). R. C. Dallas's note at the head of *BB* reads: 'This is the original Satire which Ld. B. put into my hands. It was printed in the Country, where he had been staying.—He added 110 lines before it was published. R. C. D.' Thus, according to Dallas, B gave him *BB*, not *MF/MQ*, when he began preparations for publishing. Dallas's account has been questioned by several later scholars; none the less, his chief point, about where and when *BB* was printed, is correct. *BB* is divisible into two parts:

1. A series of octavo proof leaves numbered 1–16, 19–29, with the line numbers also printed. Sheets 1–16 contain 284 lines including: 103–14, 117–20 (16 lines), 121–8 (8 lines), 143–362 (220 lines), the Hobhouse passage (16 lines), 418–37 (20 lines), the first four lines of the original passage on Jeffrey. Leaves 19–29 begin with line number [321] and conclude with a line numbered 520. The printed line counts are correct throughout. Leaves 19–29 contain a total of 200 lines including: 560–617 (58 lines), 707–22 (16 lines), 741–64 (only 22 lines: see variants for 759–64), 799–818 (20 lines), 891–912 (22 lines), the couplet on Lewis (see *MF*), 931–48 (18 lines), 961–72 (12 lines), 972a–d (4 lines: see *MQ*), 985–1010 (26 lines). The missing leaves 17–18 are supplemented in *BB* by two revise proofs (see below), but

in their original form these two leaves must have contained a passage of 36 lines, the conclusion of the original passage on Jeffrey of which we have a longer, though not complete, portion in *MF*. The total number of lines in *BB* as originally printed was therefore 520. The six additional lines, not in the copy text *MF/MQ*, are 267–8 and the four lines which originally occupied 759–64 in *BB*.

2. Two separate revise proof insertions paginated in MS. as 17 and 18: (*a*) a quarto proof of two leaves (four sides) containing an 84-line printed version of 438–527. There are two MS. additions on the proof, 472–3 and 494–7 (thus making a total of 90 lines). This proof is set in a different type from the rest of *BB*, and was evidently made in London between 26 Jan. and 5 Feb. 1809 from a MS. no longer extant. It was printed for B by Dallas (see *BLJ* I. 191) to replace the original passage on Jeffrey. (*b*) a quarto revise proof of one leaf, printed on one side only and containing 540–59 (20 lines). Copy text in *MB*. The typeface and printing are exactly the same as in the original *BB* text. This proof was inserted by B into *BB* shortly before he came to London on 19 Jan., and it was printed by Samuel Ridge in Newark, where *BB* had originally been set. This fact is shown not only by the printed proof itself, but by a series of MS. line renumberings on *BB*19–29: the printed line numbers are systematically increased by 20 by B.

Thus, B placed in Dallas's hands, around 21–2 Jan. 1809, a *BB* text totalling 540 lines (possibly 544: see below). On *BB* this final number is twice revised by Dallas, in MS., first to 584 and then to 604 (see *BLJ* I. 191) in order to take account of the removal of the original passage on Jeffrey and the addition of the two revise proofs. B questioned Dallas's count of 604 on 11 Feb. because, in his renumbering, Dallas had not taken account of the MS. additions B had sent to him.

BB also contains a number of MS. additions, some on *BB* itself, some grouped together at the end of *BB*. Those written on *BB* are 115–16, 472–3, 494–7 (not on the revise proof itself, but B has a marginal note calling for their insertion), 722a–b (see apparatus), 981–4. The group of separate MS. additions are: the 'Preface' and 'Argument' (fair copies, corrected), 723–6 (draft), 727–36 (fair copy), 881–90 (fair copy), 913–30 (fair copy).

D. Extensive fragmentary MSS. are also extant, The largest collection of these (*L*) is from the Lovelace Papers (Location: Bodleian) and includes: 97–102 (fair copy), 309–12 (fair copy), 319–20 (draft), 333–4 (fair copy), 391 (a correction), 508–9 (fair copy), 516–17 (fair copy), 528–39 (fair copy, dated 1810), [540–59] (fair copy of 4 lines intended for this section but never used), 570–1 (draft), 759–64 (fair copy), 963–4 (draft), 983–4 (fair copy), 1035–6 (fair copy).

Other fragments, designated *A* in the apparatus, include: 1–26 (draft in pencil: Princeton–Taylor), 39–46 (corrected fair copy, owned by Gordon N. Ray), 47–74 (draft: Berg), 83–8, 93–6 (draft: Kent), 303–6 (fair copy, not seen: sold from Sotheby's Sale Catalogue 28 Nov. 1972),

363–84 (draft: Texas), 460–507 (draft, containing 460–71, 474–5, 490–3, 498–507; location: library of H. F. Oppenheimer, Johannesburg), 508–9 (fair copy: Texas), 638–67 (draft: Berg), 668–86 (draft: Princeton–Taylor), 734–6 (fair copy, in letter to Dallas 12 Feb. 1809: Newstead), 737–40 (fair copy, in letter to Dallas 19 Feb. 1809: Princeton–Taylor), 831–48 (fair copy: Yale), 889–90 (fair copy, in letter to Dallas 7 Feb. 1809: Berg), 973–80 (draft: Central Library Archive, Moscow), 1017–36 (draft, bound up with the draft MS. of *CHP III*: Murray).

B sent revisions for lines 431, 433, 437 in a letter to Murray, 13 June 1813 (MS.: Murray). Two copies of *EBSR4a* (see below) also carry autograph corrections and/or annotations: (*a*) the copy B sent to Leigh Hunt on 18 Oct. 1815 (in Victoria and Albert Museum); (*b*) at Murray's, the copy with textual corrections probably from 1812 and annotations from 1816 (published in facsimile by the Roxburghe Club, 1936). Finally, there is a 16-line passage intended for *EBSR* on Thomas Rennell, but not printed in the poem (location: *BM*, Ashley 2609). Printed here as 'Lines Associated With *EBSR*' (see also *TLS*, 30 Apr. 1931, p. 347).

A number of contemporary MS. copies of the poem were made from different editions and are extant in various libraries. They do not bear upon the text, however, and have not been collated here.

From this rather extensive MS. evidence the original process of composition can be fairly well described. B wrote a first draft, subsequently lost or destroyed, between Oct. 1807 and Feb. 1808. It was over 400 lines long when it was abandoned at that point. *MF/MQ* was then written, and it was ready to be transcribed on 4 Dec. 1808. He had *MF/MQ* set in type by Samuel Ridge (his publisher at the time) in Newark in Dec. 1808 or early Jan. 1809. Then he began a new process of revision. According to Dallas, B added '110 lines' in the period when *EBSR* was being prepared for the first edition (Jan.–Mar. 1809). This is manifestly incorrect. In a letter to Hobhouse of 16 Jan. 1809, B said his poem was 624 lines long, but once again the information is plainly wrong. B compounded the difficulty for later scholars by misdating this letter '1808' so that Coleridge and Rutherford assumed B's original draft MS. was 624 lines long in Jan. 1808. *BLJ* dates the letter correctly, and the most likely explanation of the number 624 is that B meant 524, which is the number of lines in *BB* not counting the first proof revise addition, but counting lines 115–16 and 722a–b: both couplets are marginal MS. additions on *BB* and were probably put in *BB* before B went to London on 19 Jan. (see especially *BLJ* I. 190, where B asks Dallas to 'scratch out' the couplet on Carlisle, i.e. lines 722a–b). The poem B took with him to London had either 540 or 544 lines; on 16 Jan. it may well have comprised 524 lines, with the first proof revise having been added to *BB* at the very end of B's country sojourn.

The existing MSS., plus B's letters to Dallas of Jan.–Feb. 1809, enable us to date B's pre-publication revisions fairly well. Assuming 115–16 and 722a–b were already written on the revised *BB* proof, B made the following additions to the poem: 438–527 (90 lines: date, 26 Jan.–6 Feb.), 618–37 (20 lines: date, 19 Feb.), 723–40 (18 lines: date, 25 Jan., 12 Feb., and 19 Feb.), 819–48 (30 lines: on 15 Feb. 18 lines were added, 831–48; on 16 Feb. the remaining 12 lines were added, 819–30), 849–58 (10 lines: date, 25 Jan.), 881–90 (10 lines: date, before 7 Feb.), 913–30 (18 lines: date, probably 15 Feb.), 981–4 (4 lines: date, probably 15 Feb.). Total additions in Jan.–Feb.: 198 lines. B also deleted some lines from *BB* at this time: the original Jeffrey passage (40 lines), 722a–b (deleted on 25 Jan.), and 972a–d (4 lines, removed when 981–4 were added). Total deletions: 46 lines. The remaining total of lines is 696, which is the number published in the first edition, in early March (see *BLJ* I. 189–97 and Dallas, *Recollections*, 20).

Briefly, subsequent revisions were made in *EBSR* as follows. B returned to London late in April and set about revisions for a second edition. The much augmented *EBSR2* appeared in mid-May (*Marchand*, I. 176–7). *EBSR3* and *EBSR4* were issued when B was in the Levant. When he returned in 1811 he planned a new edition to be published uniformly with *Hints* and *Curse*. The plan was abandoned, however, and B finally suppressed the poem altogether, probably in Jan. 1812. But the revisions he planned for the fifth edition were incorporated in *EBSR4a* and *EBSR5–5a* in Nov. 1811.

Publishing History

With Dallas acting as intermediary, B offered *EBSR* to Longman's late in January; it was refused, then submitted to Cawthorne, who accepted it. Five editions were printed with B's authorization, though the fifth was suppressed just after the first few copies were ready. B suppressed the poem largely out of respect for Henry Richard Vassal Fox, third Lord Holland (1773–1840), with whom he had become friendly in 1812 (*BLJ* IV. 59, 286, 318, 320–1, 332). In 1812, and again later in 1814, the publisher of *EBSR*, James Cawthorne, tried to get B to reconsider his decision to suppress, but in vain. As a result, Cawthorne issued a series of spurious editions between 1812 and 1819, and several piracies also appeared.

Except for *EBSR5a* (see below), only the authorized editions are relevant to the present text. Their sequence shows the process of accretion which the poem underwent between 1809 and 1812.

EBSR1 (1st edn., first issue: published Mar. 1809). Lacking:
Preface, 1–102, 129–42, 363–417, 528–39, 638–706, 765–98, 859–80, 949–60, 973–80, 1011–70, Postscript.
Total lines: 696.

EBSR1a (1st edn., second issue: published Mar.–Apr. 1809).
Added: Preface (first version).

EBSR2 (2nd edn.: published May 1809). Added: Preface (augmented), 1–96, 129–42, 363–417, 638–706, 765–98, 859–80, 949–60, 973–80, 1011–70, Postscript. Deleted: Hobhouse passage.
Total lines: 1,050.

EBSR3, *EBSR4* (3rd and 4th edn., published 1810: no additions).

EBSR4a (4th edn., second issue: published Dec. 1811). Added: 741–6 (replacing earlier 4-line version). Total lines: 1,052.

EBSR5 (5th edn., suppressed: published Dec. 1811 or Jan. 1812). Added: 97–102, 528–39. Total lines: 1,070. Three copies examined: (*a*) Dallas copy (*BM*, C.59G.19, which is present copy text, with title-page stating 'Fourth Edition. 1811' and without Preface and Postscript; (*b*) Murray copies, with MS. title-page stating 'Fifth Edition. 1812' and without Preface and Postscript.

EBSR5a Unauthorized 5th edition, with title-page dated 1816, but text from the 1811–12 sheets). With Preface and Postscript. Only one copy examined (*BM*, Ashley 2611).

Literary and Historical Background

EBSR is a predominantly Horatian exercise throughout its first edition. The satire is generally not impassioned but aloof—either in the genial manner of the *Anti-Jacobin* (and especially Canning's 'New Morality') or in the cooler Horatian manner of Pope ('Epistle to Dr. Arbuthnot' and *Essay on Criticism* particularly). Indeed, 'British Bards' was begun not because B was deeply stirred by his subject, but largely because he was flushed with the critical success of *HI*. He really had no intense satiric quarrel with his age, and he admitted as much later in a letter to Moore (29 Jan. 1812). A reading of Lady Anne Hamilton's *Epics of the Ton* (1807) probably supplied B with many of his initial ideas for the poem. The opening sections of her poem ridicule the same sort of literature which B decided to attack. For his satire on the theatre B drew in particular upon Gifford's *Maeviad* and Churchill's *Rosciad*.

Brougham's attack on *HI* began to work a change in the poem, however. This is particularly signalled in the new opening which he wrote for 'British Bards'. Juvenal is invoked, and the poem began to take fire from B's personal rancour at the ridicule heaped upon him. The Juvenalian tone remained a minor aspect of 'British Bards' and *EBSR1*, however, and it was not until B greatly expanded the poem in *EBSR2*, just before he left England, that the poem achieved its character as a loose imitation of Juvenal, Satire *1* (see also Mary Clearman, 'A Blueprint for *English Bards and Scotch Reviewers:* The First Satire of Juvenal', *K–SJ* 19 (1970), 87–99). Dallas helped to keep *EBSR1* relatively moderate, but B himself handled the press revisions for *EBSR2*, when the Juvenalian pattern achieved its first definitive shape. (For B's later defiant attitude see his letter to Hodgson, 21 Mar. 1809, and contrast his attitude a year earlier in his letter to Hobhouse, 27 Feb. 1808: *BLJ* I. 198, 158.) The chief English model for the poem's Juvenalian shift was Churchill, especially *The Times* (1764) and *Apology Addressed to the Critical Reviewers* (1761).

In its finished form the poem is controlled by that ancient satiric theme: that the times are degenerate—in the poem's dominant (and borrowed) metaphor, 'diseased'. B advances himself as a 'physician' for these disorders because the chief surgeons either have not come forward (like Gifford) or cannot, because they are dead. Certain traces of this ancient satiric topos can be found in 'British Bards', but it did not begin to get exploited until B was preparing his poem for publication. He self-consciously invoked it in his prose preface only after all the textual revisions for the first edition had been made. Even then, however, the Horatian appoach to this traditional theme predominated.

The most energetic verse in *EBSR* distinctly recalls the rugged irregularity and intemperance of Churchill. In the best passages of his less-heated verse, B is chiefly in debt to the *Poetry of the Anti-Jacobin*. Gifford's rather ponderous *Baviad* and *Maeviad* fortunately had no dominant influence upon B's versification, though both poems served B as general formal models for *EBSR*.

For further information see Dallas and Rutherford, op. cit.; *C* I. xiv-xvi, 293–5 and VII. 225–32, 305–13; Fuess, chap. V; C. Konig, *Byrons English Bards and Scotch Reviewers. Entstehung und Beziehungen zur Zeitgenössichen Satire und Kritik* (1914); Ward Pafford, 'English Bards and Scotch Reviewers: A Study of Byron's Development as a Satirist' (Duke Univ. thesis, 1950); Dierdre Pattison, 'A Variorum Edition of Byron's English Bards and Scotch Reviewers' (Univ. of London thesis, 1967); *Wise*, I. 19–49.

title [the following notes by B appear in MS. on the front blank leaf of the Murray copy of *EBSR4a*. The various notes by B in this volume will be designated here as B 1816.] The *binding* of this volume is considerably too valuable for the contents. B.

Nothing but the consideration of its being the property of another prevents me from consigning this miserable record of misplaced anger and indiscriminate acrimony to the flames. [B 1816]

Preface This Preface was written for the Second Edition. [*EBSR5, 5a*] This Preface was written for the Second Edition, and printed with it. The noble author had left this country previous to the publication of that Edition, and is not yet returned. [*EBSR2–EBSR4a*] He is gone again.—1816 [B 1816]

19. John Cam Hobhouse. B replaced Hobhouse's lines with 385–417.

39. *The Plays of Philip Massinger* (1805), ed. William Gifford.

46–8. 'New Morality', *Poetry of the Anti-Jacobin*, l. 42. Cf. also Genesis 3: 15.

Text

1. Imitation.

> 'Semper ego auditor tantum? nunquamne reponam
> Vexatus toties rauci Theseide Codri?'

Juvenal, Satire I, [1]. Mr. Fitzgerald, facetiously termed by Cobbett the 'Small Beer Poet', inflicts his annual tribute of verse on the 'Literary Fund'; not content with writing, he spouts in person after the company have imbibed

a reasonable quantity of bad port, to enable them to sustain the operation. [B] Right enough—but why notice such a mountebank? [B 1816]
William Thomas Fitzgerald (*c.* 1759–1829), one of B's favourite butts.

3–4. A reference to Brougham's attack on *HI* in the *Edinburgh Review*
(Jan. 1808). B thought Jeffrey wrote the review.

7. 'Epistle to Dr. Arbuthnot', 249.

21. Cid Hamet Benengeli promises repose to his pen in the last chapter of
Don Quixote. Oh! that our voluminous gentry would follow the example of
Cid Hamet Benengeli. [B]

24. This must have been written in the Spirit of prophecy. [B 1816]

32. *Dunciad,* I. 52–3.

39. George III and the Prince of Wales were constant targets of B's satire.

47–50. Echoing Gifford's translation of Juvenal (see *The Satires of Juvenal*
[1802], I. 21–5). B characterized himself as 'A Minor' on the title-page of *HI*,
and Brougham pilloried him for it in his *ER* review. See *HI* commentary above.

56. This ingenuous youth is mentioned more particularly, with his production, in another place. [B] See below, 516–17: William Lamb (1779–1848),
later second Viscount Melbourne (1828) and Prime Minister at Queen
Victoria's accession; he was Lady Melbourne's son and married Caroline
Ponsonby in 1805.

Spurious Brat, that is, the farce [B, in *MB*] The play was *Whistle for It*
(see below) by William's brother George.

57. In the *Edinburgh Review.* [B] George Lamb (1784–1834), an early contributor to the review.

55–8. He [William Lamb] is a very good fellow and (except for his
Mother and Sister) the best of the Set—to my mind.—[B 1816] William, his
sister Lady Cowper, and Lady Melbourne did not take Lady Byron's part in
the separation controversy, while George Lamb was expressly critical of her.

61. Francis Jeffrey (1773–1850), editor of the *Edinburgh Review.*

65. 'Joe' Miller (1684–1738). The famous collection of jokes attributed to
him was published in 1739.

70. This sum was considerably more than the other periodicals were paying.

82. Messrs. Jeffrey and Lamb are the Alpha and Omega, the first and last of
the Edinburgh Review; the others are mentioned hereafter. [B] Neither the
heart nor the head of these gentlemen are at all what they are here represented.—at the time this was written (1808) I was personally unacquainted
with either.—This was not just. 1816. [B 1816] See also *BLJ* III. 252–3.

83.   'Stulta est Clementia, cum tot ubique
                  ——occurras periturae parcere chartae.'
                                Juvenal, Sat. I. [17–18]. [B]

93.   'Cur tamen hoc libeat potius decurrere campo
          Per quem magnus equos Auruncae flexit alumnus:
          Si vacat, et placidi rationem admittitis, edam.'
                                Juvenal, Sat. I. [19–21]. [B]

94. William Gifford (1756–1826), scholar, satirist, and editor of the *Quarterly Review*. B was deferential to Gifford throughout his life, and he came to depend upon Gifford to help with the punctuation, and sometimes the substance, of many of his later works.

100. *Careless Dryden*. See Johnson's Life of Dryden.

102. Henry James Pye (1745–1813), Poet Laureate (1790–1813). B's line echoes Milton, *Paradise Lost*, I. 263.

103. The first edn. opened with this line, and B originally intended the following 'Argument' (in MS. in *BB*) to prefix the poem: The Poet considereth times past and their poesy,—maketh a sudden transition to times present—is incensed against Bookmakers—revileth W. Scott for cupidity and balladmongering with notable remarks on Master Southey—complaineth that Master Southey hath inflicted three poems epic and otherwise on the Public,—inveigheth against Wm. Wordsworth but laudeth Mr. Coleridge and his elegy on a young ass—is disposed to vituperate Mr. Lewis—and gently rebuketh Thomas Little (the late) and Lord Strangford,—recommendeth Mr. Hayley to turn his attention to Prose—and exhorteth the Moravians to glorify Mr. Grahame.—Sympathiseth with the Revd. Bowles, and deploreth the melancholy fate of [James] Montgomery, breaketh out into invective against the Edinburgh Reviewers, calleth them hard names, harpies and the like, apostrophizeth Jeffrey and prophesieth—Episode of Jeffrey and Moore, their jeopardy and deliverance, portents on the morn of the combat, the Tweed, Tolbooth, Firth of Forth, and Arthur's Seat severally shocked, descent of a Goddesss to save Jeffrey, incorporation of the bullets with his sinciput and occiput—Edinburgh Reviewers en masse, Lord Aberdeen, Herbert, Scott, Hallam, Pillans, Lambe, Sidney Smith, Brougham, etc.—Lord Holland applauded for dinners and translations.—The Drama—Skeffington, Hook, Reynolds, Kenney, Cherry, etc.—Sheridan, Colman, and Cumberland requested to write,—return to Poesy—Scribblers of all sorts—Lords sometimes rhyme, much better not—Hafiz, Rosa Matilda and X. Y. Z.—Rogers, Campbell, Gifford etc. true poets, ⟨authors of the⟩ Translators of the Greek Anthology, Crabbe,—Darwin's Style—Cambridge—Seatonian prize—Smythe—Hodgson—Oxford—Richards—Poeta Loquitur—Conclusion. [*BB*]

103–10. Recalls opening of *The Dunciad* and Juvenal, Satire VI. 1–20 *passim*; see also Charles Churchill, *The Times*, 13.

127. *creaking shelves*: echoes *Dunciad*, I. 154

128. Thomas Moore's *Poems of the Late Thomas Little, Esq.* (1801), published in duodecimo. See commentary for *HI*.

129. Ecclesiastes, Cap I. [verse 9] [*B*]

132. *Gas:* not the gas used (first in 1805) for street lights, but Dr. Beddoes's nitrous oxide. These four 'wonders' are mentioned in Christopher Caustic's *Terrible Tractoration! A Poetical Epistle Against Galvanising Trumpery and the Perkinistic Institution* (1803).

Tractors: widely advertised medical remedy of the American quack Benjamin Perkins, founder in London of the Perkinean Institution.

138. Echoes *Dunciad*, IV. 93.

142. [Robert] Stott, better known in the 'Morning Post' by the name of Hafiz. The personage is at present the most profound explorer of the Bathos. I remember, when the reigning family left Portugal, a special ode of Master Stott's beginning thus: (Stott loquitur quoad Hibernia)

> 'Princely offspring of Braganza,
> Erin greets thee with a stanza,' etc. etc.

Also a sonnet to Rats, well worthy of the subject, and a most thundering ode, commencing as follows:

> 'Oh! for a Lay! loud as the surge
> That lashes Lapland's sounding shore.'

Lord have mercy on us! the 'Lay of the Last Minstrel' was nothing to this. [B] See Stott's 'Extemporaneous Verse . . .' (*Morning Post*, 30 Dec. 1807).

148. M. G. Lewis published the *Tales of Terror*, 2 vols. (1801), with contributions by himself, Scott, Southey, *et al.*

153. See the 'Lay of the Last Minstrel', *passim*. Never was any plan so incongruous and absurd as the ground-work of this production. The entrance of Thunder and Lightning prologuizing to Bayes's Tragedy, unfortunately takes away the merit of originality from the dialogue between Messieurs the Spirits of Flood and Fell in the first canto. Then we have the amiable William of Deloraine, 'a stark moss-trooper' [I. xxi], *videlicet*, a happy compound of poacher, sheep-stealer, and highwayman. The propriety of his magical lady's injunction not to read, can only be equalled by his candid acknowledgement of his independence of the trammels of spelling, although, to use his own elegant phrase, ' 'twas his neck verse at hairibee', i.e. the gallows [I. xxiii].

The biography of Gilpin Horner, and the marvellous pedestrian page, who travelled twice as fast as his master's horse, without the aid of seven leagued boots, are *chef d'oeuvres* in the improvement of taste. For incident we have the invisible, but by no means sparing, box on the ear bestowed on the page, and the entrance of a Knight and Charger into the castle, under the very natural disguise of a wain of hay. Marmion, the hero of the latter romance, is exactly what William of Deloraine would have been, had he been able to read and write. The poem was manufactured by Messrs. Constable, Murray, and Miller, worshipful Booksellers, in consideration of the receipt of a sum of money, and truly, considering the inspiration, it is a very creditable production. If Mr. Scott will write for hire, let him do his best for his paymasters, but not disgrace his genius, which is undoubtedly great, by a repetition of black-letter Ballad imitations. [B]

B's strictures on Scott, and Southey, recall Lady Anne Hamilton's *Epics of the Ton* (1807).

184. 'Good Night to Marmion'—the pathetic and also prophetic exclamation of Henry Blount, Esq. on the death of honest Marmion. [B] Cf. Scott's *Marmion*, VI, st. 28.

190. Maro is Virgil (P. Virgilius Maro).

194. As the Odyssey is so closely connected with the story of the Iliad, they may almost be classed as one grand historical poem. In alluding to Milton and Tasso, we consider the 'Paradise Lost' and 'Gierusalemme Liberata' as their standard efforts, since neither the 'Jerusalem Conquered' of the Italian, nor the 'Paradise regained' of the English Bard, obtained a proportionate celebrity to their former poems. Query: Which of Mr. Southey's will survive? [B]

211. Thalaba [1801], Mr. Southey's second poem, is written in open defiance of precedent and poetry. Mr. S. wished to produce something novel and succeeded to a miracle. Joan of Arc [1796] was marvellous enough, but Thalaba was one of those poems 'which, in the words of [Richard] Porson, will be read when Homer and Virgil are forgotten, but—*not till then*'. [B] For Porson's remark see A. Dyce, *Recollections of the Table-Talk of Samuel Rogers*, ed. M. Bishop (1953), 183.

212. *wild, and wond'rous.* See prefatory lines to *Madoc* (1805).

213–14. See *Thalaba*, II. 40; IV. 38; VI. 40, and the final destruction scene.

217. See Preface to *Thalaba* (1st edn.).

221. Echoing the prefatory lines to *Madoc*.

222. *Cacique*: a native chief or prince of the aborigines in the West Indies (*OED*).

225. We beg Mr. Southey's pardon: 'Madoc disdains the degraded title of Epic.' See his Preface. Why is Epic degraded? and by whom? Certainly the late Romaunts of Masters Cottle, Laureate Pye, Ogilvy, Hole, and gentle Mistress Cowley, have not exalted the Epic Muse, but as Mr. Southey's poem 'disdains the appellation', allow us to ask—has he substituted anything better in its stead? or must he be content to rival Sir Richard Blackmore, in the quantity as well as quality of his verse. [B] See Joseph Cottle's *Alfred* (1801) and *The Fall of Cambria* (1809), Richard Hole's *Arthur* . . .(1789), Mrs. Hannah Cowley ('Anna Matilda'), *Siege of Acre* (1801). Sir Richard Blackmore (d. 1729), notorious for his dull, imitative 'epics'. In *MA* and *BB* B had Sir J. B. Burgess (author of *Richard the First*, 1801) and Richard Cumberland (co-author with Burgess of the *Exodiad*, 1808, and author of *Calvary*, 1792) in place of Hole.

228. *The Curse of Kehama* appeared in 1810.

230. Echoes Thomas Gray, 'Elegy Written in a Country Church-Yard', 3.

231. See, The Old Woman of Berkeley, a Ballad, by Mr. Southey, wherein an aged gentlewoman is carried away by Beelzebub, on a 'high trotting horse'. [B]

234. The last line, 'God help thee', is an evident plagiarism from the Anti-Jacobin to Mr. Southey, on his Dactylics: 'God help thee, silly one.'—*Poetry of the Anti-Jacobin* [1799], p. 23. [B]

235–54. Unjust. [B 1816]

240. Lyrical Ballads [(1800), I], page 4.—'The Tables Turned.' Stanza 1.

> Up, up, my friend, and clear your looks,
>   Why all this toil and trouble?
> Up, up, my friend, and quit your books,
>   Or surely you'll grow double.

250. Mr. W. in his preface labours hard to prove that prose and verse are much the same, and certainly his precepts and practice are strictly conformable.

> And thus to Betty's question he
> Made answer, like a traveller bold,
> The cock did crow to-whoo, to-whoo,
> And the sun did shine so cold, etc. etc.

Lyrical Ballads [(1800), I], p. [137]. [B] See Wordsworth's 'Preface' to *Lyrical Ballads* and B's prose Preface to *DJ*. B's attack on Wordsworth here should be compared with Richard Mant's in *The Simpliciad* (1808), esp. 295–305.

255–8. Unjust. [B 1816]

260. Coleridge's Poems [3rd edn., 1803], p. 11. Songs of the Pixies, i.e. Devonshire Fairies, page 42, we have, 'Lines to a Young Lady', and page 52, 'Lines to a Young Ass'. [B] Compare *The Simpliciad*, 102–3, 211–12.

265–82. Matthew Gregory ('Monk') Lewis (1775–1818), a central figure in the English Gothic Revival, promoter of German literature, and author of *The Monk* (1795). B later became friendly with him. See *EBSR* 148 n.

273. 'For every one knows little Matt's an M. P.'—See a Poem to Mr. Lewis, in *The [Evening] Statesman*, supposed to be written by Mr. Jekyll. [B] Joseph Jekyll (d. 1837), a newspaper wit of the day. Lewis liked to sign his works, rather pompously, M. G. Lewis, M.P. B's line echoes *Macbeth*, I. iii. 48.

277. Cf. poem no. 23 above, and see also Scott's 'The Wild Huntsman', a translation of Bürger's 'Der wilde Yäger'.

280. St. Luke was a physician. Cf. Colossians 4: 14.

283–94. See *EBSR* 128 n.

294. John 15: 14, 8: 11.

297. The reader who may wish for an explanation of this, may refer to 'Strangford's Camoens', page 127, note to page 56, or to the last page of the Edinburgh Review of Strangford's Camoens. It is also to be remarked, that the things given to the public, as Poems of Camoens, are no more to be found in the original Portuguese, than in the Song of Solomon. [B] See commentary for *HI*, esp. no. 37.

306. Pope, *Dunciad*, IV. 582.

308. *Simpliciad*, 46–7.

309. Compare *Dunciad*, I. 155–6. The ironical suggestion that pages of verse might at least be useful for pastry wrapping was common.

312. See his various Biographisms of defunct Painters, etc. [B] William Hayley (1745–1820). His biographies include those of Milton, Romney, and Cowper.

318. Hayley's two most notorious verse productions are, 'Triumphs of Temper' [1781], and 'Triumphs of Music' [1804]. He has also written much Comedy in rhyme, Epistles, etc. etc. As he is rather an elegant writer of notes, let us recommend Pope's advice to Wycherly, to Mr. H's consideration; viz. 'to convert his poetry into prose', which may be easily done by taking away the final syllable of each couplet. [B] See Pope's letter to Wycherly urging him to imitate La Rochefoucault, 29 Nov. 1707. For Wood and Barclay in 309–12var. see *The Eccentric Review*, I (1812), 133–50.

326. Mr. [James] Grahame [1765–1811] has poured forth two volumes of Cant, under the name of 'Sabbath Walks' [1804], and 'Biblical Pictures' [1807]. [B] The Unity of Moravian Brethren, a Protestant sect which emigrated to England and influenced English Methodism. To 319–26var., B had the following note: 'Mr. Pratt, once a Bath bookseller, now a London author, has written as much to as little purpose, as any of his scribbling contemporaries. Mr. P's *Sympathy* [1788] is in rhyme, but his prose productions are the most voluminous.' Samuel Jackson Pratt (1749–1814), pseud. 'Courtney Melmoth', a Della Cruscan writer.

327–8. Echoes *Sympathy*, I. 201–2.

336. See Bowles's Sonnets, etc.—'Sonnet to Oxford', and 'Stanzas on hearing the Bells of Ostend'. [B] The Revd. William Lisle Bowles (1768–1850), another 'sympathising' poet and editor of Pope's *Works* (10 vols., 1807). B refers to Bowles's 'On Revisiting Oxford' (sonnet XXVII) and the two sonnets 'At Ostend' (X, XI), and later to Bowles's *The Spirit of Discovery by Sea* (1805). Bowles's various attacks on the character and verse of Pope angered B, who later answered Bowles in two long prose pieces: see *LJ* v. 522–92.

341. *Delightful*: a favourite epithet in Bowles's verse.

351. 'Awake a louder, etc. etc' is the first line in Bowles's 'Spirit of Discovery'; a very spirited and pretty dwarf Epic. Among other exquisite lines we have the following:—

> 'A kiss
> Stole on the list'ning silence, never yet
> Here heard; they trembled even as if the power, etc. etc.'

That is, the woods of Madeira trembled to a kiss, very much astonished, as well they might be, at such a phenomenon. [B] In 1816 B annotated this note: 'Misquoted—and misunderstood by me—but not intentionally.—It

was not the "Woods" but the people in them who trembled—*why*—Heaven
only knows—unless they were overheard making this prodigious smack.'

353–6. Echoes Juvenal, I. 81–6.

358. The Episode above alluded to, is the story of 'Robert à Machin', and
Anna d'Arfet', a pair of constant lovers, who performed the kiss above-
mentioned, that startled the woods of Madeira. [B]

363–84. B substituted this passage for 16 lines by Hobhouse, which
appeared in the first edition. For a transcript of Hobhouse's lines see *C* 1.
327 n. In 1816 B annotated the passage: 'Too savage all this on Bowles.' But
he felt little regret later when Bowles stirred up the Pope controversy again.
See esp. B's letter to Murray, 7 Feb. 1821 (quoted at *C* 1. 327 n.).

372. Curll is one of the Heroes of the Dunciad, and was a bookseller. Lord
Fanny is the poetical name of Lord Hervey, author of 'Lines to the Imitator
of Horace'. [B] Edmund Curll (1675–1747) and John Hervey, Baron Hervey
(1696–1743). See 'Epistle to Dr. Arbuthnot', 149.

378. Lord Bolingbroke hired Mallet to traduce Pope after his decease,
because the Poet had retained some copies of a work by Lord Bolingbroke
(the Patriot King) which that splendid, but malignant genius, had ordered to
be destroyed. [B] Henry St. John, First Viscount Bolingbroke (1678–1751)
and David Mallet (1705?–65).

380. Dennis, the critic, and Ralph, the rhymester.

> 'Silence, ye wolves! while Ralph to Cynthia howls,
> Making night hideous, answer him, ye owls!' *Dunciad*

[B] John Dennis (1657–1734) and James Ralph (1705?–62). B slightly misquotes *Dunciad*, I. 165–6. His own line echoes *Dunciad*, I. 104.

382. 'Now that the old lion is dead, every ass thinks he may kick at him':
Samuel Parr of Dr. Johnson (see Boswell's *Life of Dr. Johnson*, ed. G. B. Hill
(1934), IV. 423).

384. See Bowles's late edition of Pope's works, for which he received £300.
—Thus Mr. B. has experienced, how much easier it is to profit by the repu-
tation of another, than to elevate his own. [B] In this note to the deleted
Hobhouse lines B wrote 'Twelve hundred guineas'. (*BB*)

391var. *Helicon* is a *mountain* and not a fishpond—it should have been
Hippocrene. [B 1816]

406. Mr. Cottle, Amos, or Joseph, I don't know which, but one or both,
once sellers of books they did not write, and now writers of books that do not
sell, have published a pair of Epics. 'Alfred' (poor Alfred! Pye has been at him
too!) 'Alfred' and the 'Fall of Cambria'. [B] See *EBSR* 225 n. B's annotation
in 1816: 'I saw some letters of this fellow (Jh. Cottle) to an unfortunate
poetess—whose productions (which the poor woman by no means
thought highly of) he attacked so roughly and bitterly that I could hardly
regret assailing him—even were it unjust—which it is not—for verily

he is an Ass.' The 'poetess' was probably Ann Yearsley (1756–1806), but B's anecdote has never been corroborated.

414. Mr. Maurice hath manufactured the component parts of a ponderous quarto, upon the beauties of 'Richmond Hill' [1807], and the like:—it also takes in a charming view of Turnham Green, Hammersmith, Brentford, Old and New, and the parts adjacent. [B] The Revd. Thomas Maurice (1754–1824).

425. Poor Montgomery! though praised by every English Review, has been bitterly reviled by the Edinburgh. After all, the Bard of Sheffield is a man of considerable genius: his 'Wanderer of Switzerland' [1806] is worth a thousand 'Lyrical Ballads', and at least fifty 'Degraded Epics'. [B] See commentary for no. 94. In 419–20 B alludes to Montgomery's 'The Lyre' (*The Wanderer of Switzerland*, p. 81)

430. *mangle.* B has the image from John Ring, *The Beauties of the Edinburgh Review, alias the Stinkpot of Literature* (1807). The *Anti-Jacobin Review* (June 1807, pp. 199–204) quotes the relevant passage in Ring in its review of the book.

437. Arthur's Seat; the hill which overhangs Edinburgh. [B]

438–59. Too ferocious—this is mere insanity.—[B 1816]

439. George Jefferies (1644–89), who presided at the 'Bloody Assizes' of 1685.

453. *Merchant of Venice*, IV. i. 223.

460–71. All this is bad—because personal.—[B 1816]

460. Echoes Charles Churchill, 'Dedication' to *Sermons*, lines 1, 11.

467. In 1806, Messrs. Jeffrey and Moore met at Chalk Farm. The duel was prevented by the interference of the Magistracy; and, on examination, the balls of the pistols, were found to have evaporated. This incident gave occasion to much waggery in the daily prints. [B. *EBSR1–EBSR4a*]
I am informed that Mr. Moore published at the time a disavowal of these statements in the newspapers as far as regarded himself, and in justice to him I mention this circumstance: as I never heard of it before, I cannot state the particulars, and was only made acquainted with the fact very lately.—Nov. 4th, 1811. [B. *EBSR5, 5a*, and a MS. insertion in Hunt's copy of *EBSR4a*] In fact, it was Jeffrey's pistol that had no ball. See also *Memoirs, Journal, and Correspondence of Thomas Moore*, ed. Lord John Russell (1860), 57–63.

469. *Dunedin:* Edinburgh.

471. Cf. Isaiah 21: 1.

473. The Tweed here behaved with proper decorum: it would have been highly reprehensible in the English half of the River to have shown the smallest symptom of apprehension. [B]

479. This display of sympathy on the part of the Tolbooth, (the principal prison in Edinburgh) which truly seems to have been most affected on the occasion, is much to be commended. It was to be apprehended, that the many unhappy criminals executed in the front, might have rendered the

Edifice more callous. She is said to be of the softer sex, because her delicacy of feeling on this day was truly feminine, though, like most feminine impulses, perhaps a little selfish. [B]

481–2. B implies that Jeffrey was low-born.

486. Jeffrey was famous for his candour.

495. Danae conceived Perseus when Jupiter came to her in the form of a golden shower.

508. The motto of the *Edinburgh Review* was 'Judex damnatur cum nocens absolvitur' but it was suggested that it ought to be 'Musam tenui meditamur avena' ('We celebrate the Muse on a slender pipe').

509. His Lordship has been much abroad, is a member of the Athenian Society, and Reviewer of 'Gell's Topography of Troy'. [B] George Hamilton Gordon, best known for his *Inquiry into the Principles of Beauty in Grecian Architecture* (1812, 1822).

510. Mr. Herbert is a translator of Icelandic and other poetry. One of the principal pieces is a 'Song on the Recovery of Thor's Hammer': the translation is a pleasant chaunt in the vulgar tongue, and endeth thus—

> 'Instead of money and rings, I wot,
> The hammer's bruises were her lot,
> Thus Odin's son his hammer got.'

[B] William Herbert (1778–1847), *Select Icelandic Poetry* (1804), and see Part I, p. 8. B refers in line 511 to Herbert's *Miscellaneous Poems*, 2 vols. (1804), reviewed in the *Edinburgh Review* (Oct. 1806).

512. The Rev. Sydney Smith [1771–1845], the reputed author of Peter Plymley's Letters, and sundry criticisms. [B] Smith was the author of *Letters on the Catholics, from Peter Plymley . . .* (1807–8), and was one of the founders of the *Edinburgh Review*.

513. Mr. Hallam reviewed Payne Knight's *Taste*, and was exceedingly severe on some Greek verses therein: it was not discovered that the lines were Pindar's till the press rendered it impossible to cancel the critique, which still stands an everlasting monument of Hallam's ingenuity. [B. *EBSR1, 1a*]

The said Hallam is incensed, because he is falsely accused, seeing that he never dineth at Holland House.—If this be true, I am sorry—not for having said so, but on his account, as I understand his Lordship's feasts are preferable to his compositions.—If he did not review Lord Holland's performance, I am glad, because it must have been painful to read, and irksome to praise it. If Mr. Hallam will tell me who did review it, the real name shall find a place in the text, provided nevertheless the said name be of two orthodox musical syllables, and will come into the verse: till then, Hallam must stand for want of a better. [B, added in *EBSR2*]

Henry Hallam (1777–1859), the historian. The reviewer of Richard Payne Knight's *Analytical Inquiry into the Principles of Taste* (1805) was Lord Holland's physician, Dr. John Allen (*ER* VII. 1805). B elsewhere praised Henry Hallam's historical style, specifically in Hallam's *A View of the State of Europe During the Middle Ages* (1808).

514. Scott wrote for the *ER* in 1803–6, but its politics drove him to support Gifford's *Quarterly Review* in 1808.

515. Pillans is a tutor at Eton. [B] James Pillans (1778–1864), became Professor of Humanity at the University of Edinburgh. B assumed, correctly, that Pillans reviewed Hodgson's *Translation of Juvenal* (in *ER* X, 1808).

516. The honourable G. Lambe reviewed 'Beresford's Miseries', and is moreover Author of a Farce enacted with much applause at the Priory, Stanmore; and damned with great expedition at the late Theatre, Covent-Garden. It was entitled 'Whistle for It'. [B] See *EBSR* 56–8 and nn. Lamb's review (*ER* VIII, 1806) of James Beresford's *Miseries of Human Life . . .* (1806) was largely favourable. The following continuation of B's note was cancelled in *BB*: 'We have heard of persons, "who when the bagpipe sings in the nose, cannot contain their urine for affection", but Mr. L. carries it a step further than Shakespeare's diuretic amateurs [*Merchant of Venice*, IV. i. 50–1] being notorious at School and College for his inability to contain—any thing. We do not know to what "Pipe" to attribute this additional effect, but the fact is incontrovertible.'

519–21. Holland House was a centre of Whig society and Lord Holland an exponent of the policies of his uncle Charles Fox.

523. 'Buff and Blue', the colours of both the Whig Club and the *ER*.

524. Mr. Brougham, in No. XXV. of the Edinburgh Review, throughout the article concerning Don Pedro de Cevallos, has displayed more politics than policy: many of the worthy Burgesses of Edinburgh being so incensed at the infamous principles it evinces, as to have withdrawn their subscription. [B. all editions] The name of this personage is pronounced Broom in the south, but the truly northern and *musical* pronunciation is Brough-am, in two syllables. [B. *EBSR1*, *1a*] It seems that Mr. Brougham is not a Pict, as I supposed, but a Borderer, and his name is pronounced Broom, from Trent to Tay.—So be it. [B, added in *EBSR2*] Henry Peter Brougham (1778–1868), the brilliant, witty, and headstrong Whig politician. The article in question ('Exposition of the Practices and Machinations which led to the Usurpation of the Crown of Spain . . . ', *ER*, Oct. 1808) was jointly authored by Jeffrey and Brougham and looked forward to constitutional reform.

527. I ought to apologize to the worthy Deities for introducing a new Goddess with short petticoats to their notice: but, alas! what was to be done? I could not say Caledonia's Genius, it being well known there is no Genius to be found from Clackmannan to Caithness: yet without supernatural agency, how was Jeffrey to be saved? The national 'Kelpies', etc. are too unpoetical, and the 'Brownies' and 'gude neighbours', (spirits of a good disposition) refused to extricate him. A Goddess therefore has been called for the purpose, and great ought to be the gratitude of Jeffrey, seeing it is the only communication he ever held, or is likely to hold, with any thing heavenly. [B]

532. Echoes *Dunciad*, III. 72. Edinburgh was notorious at the time for bad sanitation facilities.

535. See the colour of the back-binding of the E. R. [B]

540–59. Bad enough—and on mistaken grounds besides. [B 1816]

542. Henry Petty was Lord Holland's cousin. See also poems nos. 58, line 64; 60, line 10; 108, line 30, and nn.; and compare *Epics of the Ton*, I. 134–7.

551. Lord H. has translated some specimens of Lope de Vega, inserted in his life of the Author: both are bepraised by his *disinterested* guests. [B] See *ER* IX (Oct. 1806), pp. 224–42, the review of Holland's *Life of Lope de Vega* (1806).

559. Certain it is, her Ladyship is suspected of having displayed her match-less wit in the Edinburgh Review: however that may be, we know from good authority, that the manuscripts are submitted to her perusal—no doubt for correction. [B] Elizabeth Vassal, Lady Holland (1770–1845). B's innuendo in 559 is explicit in 559var.: that Lady Holland divorced Lord Webster to marry Lord Holland in 1799, and that her first son by Lord Holland was illegitimate.

562. In the melo-drama of Tekeli, that heroic prince is clapt into a barrel on the stage: a new asylum for distressed heroes. [B] Theodore Hook (1788–1841), *Tekeli; or The Siege of Montgatz* (1806). B's note in *MA*, *BB* continued: '. . . stage, and Count Everard in The Fortress [1807] hides himself in a green house built expressly for the occasion: 'tis a pity that Theodore Hook, who is really a man of talent, should confine his genius to such paltry productions as The Fortress and Music Mad [1807], etc. etc.'

563. Thomas John Dibdin (1771–1841), dramatist, songwriter, librettist. In 591 B refers to his pantomime, *Harelequin and Mother Goose* (1807).

564. William Henry West Betty (1791–1874), 'The Young Roscius', had a sensational career as a boy actor in London (1804–6).

568. All these are favourite expressions of Mr. R. and prominent in his Comedies, living and defunct. [B] Frederick Reynolds (1764–1841), author of over 100 plays.

570. James Kenney (1780–1849), prolific dramatist, author of *The World* (1808).

573. Mr. T. Sheridan, the new Manager of Drury-Lane theatre, stripped the Tragedy of Bonduca of the Dialogue, and exhibited the scenes as the spectacle of Caractacus.—Was this worthy of his sire? or of himself? [B] Thomas Sheridan (1775–1817), son of the great dramatist. His spectacle *Caractacus* (1808) was an adaptation, as B describes, of Beaumont and Fletcher's *Bonduca* (c. 1619).

578. George Colman, the younger (1762–1836), Richard Cumberland (1732–1811), the former a dramatist, the latter a man of various pursuits, including drama.

581–3. Sheridan caught the mania for translating German writers with his *Pizzaro* (1799), the original by Kotzebue. See *Epics of the Ton*, II. 719–20.

587 and var. The great actors David Garrick (1717–79), Sarah Siddons (1755–1831), Charles Kemble (1775–1854).

591. Andrew Cherry (1762–1812), actor; Lumley St. George Skeffington (1768–1850), dramatist, writer, dandy. See also nn. for 563 and 603.

596. M. G. Lewis, *The Castle Spectre* (1797).

597var. We need not inform the reader that we do not allude to the Champion of England who slew the Dragon. Our St. George is content to draw status with a very different kind of animal. [B, MS. note in *BB*]

601. Mr. Greenwood is, we believe, Scene-Painter to Drury-Lane Theatre —as such, Mr. S. is much indebted to him. [B]

603. Mr. S. is the illustrious author of the 'Sleeping Beauty' [1805]: and some Comedies, particularly 'Maids and Bachelors' [*The Maid of Honour*, 1802], Baculaurii baculo magis quam auro digni. [B]

606. The persons in the audience paid by the management to applaud.

615. Naldi and Catalani require little notice,—for the visage of the one, and the salary of the other, will enable us long to recollect these amusing vagabonds; besides, we are still black and blue from the squeeze on the first night of the lady's appearance in trowsers. [B] Giuseppe Naldi (1770–1820) made his London début in 1806; Angelica Catalani (*c.* 1785–1849) was a soprano at the King's Theatre 1806–14.

618. *Ausonia*: an ancient name for Italy.

622–30. André J. J. Des Hayes (*fl.* 1797–1811), dancer and choreographer at the King's Theatre in London. Fortunata Angiolini (1766–1817) danced at the King's Theatre 1809–12 and again in 1814. I have been unable to discover more particular information about the dancers Gayton and Presle, or the soprano Collini. All worked at the King's Theatre in this period. Collini appeared with Naldi in Pucetta's *I Villegiatori Bizarri* in Feb. 1809. B apparently wrote 618–37 after returning from a night at the opera in late Feb. 1809 (see *BLJ* I. 195).

632. The Society for the Suppression of Vice, founded (London) 1802.

632–7. Good [B 1816]

639. A gentleman, with whom I am slightly acquainted, lost in the Argyle Rooms several thousand pounds at Backgammon; it is but justice to the manager in this instance to say, that some degree of disapprobation was manifested, but why are the implements of gaming allowed in a place devoted to the society of both sexes? A pleasant thing for the wives and daughters of those who are blest or curst with such connections, to hear the Billiard-tables rattling in one room, and the dice in another! That this is the case I myself can testify, as a late unworthy member of an Institution which materially affects the morals of the higher orders, while the lower may not even move to the sound of a tabor and fiddle without a chance of indictment for riotous behavior. [B] True—it was Billy Way—who lost the money. I knew him—and was a subscriber to the Argyle at the time of this event.

[B 1816] For B's controversy with Col. Greville, manager of the Argyle Institution, see *BLJ* II. 168–9 and n.

642. Petronius 'Arbiter elegantiarum' to Nero, 'and a very pretty fellow in his day', as Mr. Congreve's Old Bachelor saith of Hannibal. [B] But Capt. Bluffe, not Heartwell, says it: *The Old Bachelor*, II. i.

658. *Burletta:* comic opera.

660–7. Compare *Waltz*.

673–4. Terms in the game of Hazard.

678–9. Sir Arthur Paget eloped with Lady Boringdon, and his brother, Lord Paget, eloped with Lady Charlotte Wellesley. See *The Examiner*, 22 Mar. 1808 and 12 Mar. 1809.

686. *CLODIUS*. Mutato nomine de te Fabula narratur. [B] Allusion to Clodius' dissolute life, and particularly to his liaison with Pompeia, Caesar's wife. Cf. Horace, *Satires* I. 1. 69–70.

FALKLAND. I knew the late Lord Falkland well. On Sunday night I beheld him presiding at his own table, in all the honest pride of hospitality; on Wednesday morning, at three o'clock, I saw stretched before me all that remained of courage, feeling, and a host of passions. He was a gallant and successful officer; his faults were the faults of a sailor; as such, Britons will forgive them. ⟨His behavior on the field was worthy of a better fate, and his conduct on the bed of death evinced all the firmness of a man without the farce of repentance, I say the farce of repentance, for death-bed repentance is a farce, and as little serviceable to the soul at such a moment as the surgeon to the body, though both may be useful if taken in time. Some hireling in the papers forged some facts about an agonized voice etc. On mentioning the circumstance to Mr. Heaviside he exclaimed—'Good God what absurdity to talk in this manner of one who died like a hero. He did more—*MA*⟩ He died like a brave man in a better cause; for had he fallen in like manner on the deck of the frigate to which he was just appointed, his last moments would have been held up by his countrymen as an example to succeeding heroes. [B] Charles John Cary, ninth Viscount Falkland (1768–1809), died from the wound received in his duel with Sir Arthur Powell on 28 Feb. 1809 (see *BLJ* I. 195 and n.).

690. Ovid, *Metamorphoses*, VII. 20–1.

691–4. Yea—and a precious chace they led me. [B 1816]

697–706. Echoes Juvenal, I. 147–71.

698. *Fool* enough certainly *then* and no wiser since, [B 1816]

708. What would be the sentiments of the Persian Anacreon, Hafiz, could he rise from his splendid sepulchre at Sheeraz, where he reposes with Ferdousi and Sadi, the Oriental Homer and Catullus, and behold his name assumed by one Stott of Dromore, the most impudent and execrable of literary poachers for the Daily Prints? [B] Robert Stott wrote for the *Morning Post* under the pseudonym 'Hafiz'.

713. *things of ton:* people of the fashionable world.

717–18. Miles Peter Andrews (d. 1814), minor but prolific playwright. His first work appeared in 1774.

723. Wentworth Dillon, fourth Earl of Roscommon (1633–85); translated Horace's *Ars Poetica* (1680) and wrote verse; John Sheffield, Earl of Mulgrave, Marquis of Normanby, Duke of Buckingham (1649–1721), patron of Dryden who also wrote poetry.

725–40. Wrong also:—the provocation was not sufficient to justify such acerbity. [B 1816]

732. The Earl of Carlisle has lately published an eighteen-penny pamphlet on the state of the Stage, and offers his plan for building a new theatre: it is to be hoped his Lordship will be permitted to forward any thing for the Stage, except his own tragedies. [B] Frederick Howard, fifth Earl of Carlisle (1748–1825), B's guardian, author of *Tragedies and Poems* (1801). B dedicated *POT* to him, but was angered when Carlisle did not introduce him when B took his seat in the House of Lords. See *BLJ* I. 186–94 *passim*.

735. *Macbeth*, V. viii. 34.

740. 'Doff that lion's hide, / And hang a calf-skin on those recreant limbs.' Shak. *King John* [III. i. 128–9]. Lord C.'s works, most resplendently bound, form a conspicuous ornament to his book-shelves: 'The rest is all but leather and prunella' [Pope, *Essay on Man*, IV. 203]. [B]

743–4. In *The Baviad* (1791), a paraphrastic imitation of Persius' first satire, written to correct taste and morals.

745. In 1806 William Wyndham Grenville, Baron Grenville (1759–1834), formed a coalition government known as the Ministry of All the Talents. It was the subject of numerous attacks in print (e.g. E. S. Barrett, *All the Talents; A Satirical Poem in Three Dialogues*, 1807).

748. Melville's Mantle, a parody on 'Elijah's Mantle', a poem. [B] James Sayer, *Elijah's Mantle . . . occasioned by the death of . . . Pitt* (1807) was answered later in the same year by the anonymous poem of B's note. Henry Dundas, first Viscount Melville (1742–1811), one of Pitt's close political associates, was impeached in 1805, but subsequently acquitted. See also 2 Kings 2: 13–14. Fox's death produced a spate of verse, e.g. Richard Payne Knight's *A Monody on the death of . . . Fox* (1807).

751. *Dunciad*, III. 157–8.

758. This lovely little Jessica, the daughter of the noted Jew K[ing], seems to be a follower of the Della Cruscan School, and has published two volumes of very respectable absurdities in rhyme, as times go; besides sundry novels in the style of the first edition of the Monk. [B] She since married the Morning Post—an exceeding good match. [B 1816] B has confused the daughter of the Jewish moneylender King with Charlotte Dacre ('Rosa Matilda'), who later married Byrne, editor of the *Morning Post*. B refers to her *Hours of Solitude . . .* 2 vols. (1805). She dedicated her *Confessions of a Nun of St. Omer* (1805) to Lewis.

759–64. These are the signatures of various worthies who figure in the poetical departments of the newspapers. [B] The attack on the Della Cruscans here follows Gifford's in *The Baviad* and *The Maeviad*. B refers to the publisher John Bell (1745–1831), Charlotte Dacre ('Rosa Matilda'), and Robert Stott ('Hafiz'), all later Della Cruscans; and to Robert Merry (1755–98), a prominent earlier poet of the school, who signed himself 'Della Crusca'. In the var. Laura was 'Perdita' Robinson ('Laura Maria'). See also E. E. Bostetter, 'The Original Della Cruscans and the Florence Miscellany', *HLQ* 19 (1956), 277–300, and W. N. Hargreaves-Mawdsley, *The English Della Cruscans . . .* (The Hague, 1967).

765–70. This was meant at poor Blackett—who was then patronized by A. I. B. [Lady Byron] but that I did not know—or this would not have been written—at least I think not.— [B 1816] See B's 'Epitaph for Joseph Blackett'.

768. *St. Crispin*: the patron saint of cobblers.

774. Capel Lofft, Esq. the Maecenas of shoemakers, and Preface-writer-General to distressed versemen; a kind of gratis Accoucheur to those who wish to be delivered of rhyme, but do not know how to bring it forth. [B] Capel Lofft (1751–1824), the patron of Robert Bloomfield (1766–1823).

777. See Nathaniel Bloomfield's ode, elegy, or whatever he or any one else chooses to call it, on the enclosure of 'Honington Green'. [B] Robert's brother Nathaniel, 'Honington Green, A Ballad', in *Poems* (1803).

784. *Macbeth*, v. iii. 40.

795. Vide 'Recollections of a weaver in the Moorlands of Staffordshire'. [B] T. Bakewell, *The Moorland Bard . . .* 2 vols. (1807).

801. It would be superfluous to recall to the mind of the reader the author of 'The Pleasures of Memory' [1792] and 'The Pleasures of Hope' [1799], the most beautiful poems in our language, if we except Pope's Essay on Man: but so many poetasters have started up, that even the names of Campbell and Rogers are become strange. [B] In 1816 B wrote the verses 'Pretty Miss Jacqueline' (no. 294) at the bottom of the page of his annotated copy. Thomas Campbell (1777–1844) is remembered principally for *The Pleasures of Hope* and for his fine war songs like 'Hohenlinden'. Samuel Rogers (1763–1855), wealthy and well-regarded poet of the day, wrote *The Pleasures of Memory*, *Columbus* (1810), *Italy* (1822–8). See below, commentaries for 186, 202, 212, 213, 294, 323.

803. R[ogers] has not fulfilled the promise of his first poems, but has still very great merit.—[B 1816]

810. William Cowper (1731–1800).

812. See William Collins, *Ode* ('How sleep the brave') and *CHP* I, st. 42.

817. *Feel as they write*. Compare B's review of Wordsworth's *Poems* (1807), *LJ* I. 341.

818. Gifford, author of the Baviad and Maeviad, the first satires of the day, and translator of Juvenal ⟨and one, (though not the best) of the translators of Juvenal *MA*, *BB*⟩. Sotheby, translator of Wieland's Oberon [1798], and Virgil's Georgics [1800], and author of Saul, an epic poem [1807].

Macneil, whose poems are deservedly popular: particularly 'Scotland's Scaith, or the Waes of War' [1795], of which ten thousand copies were sold in one month. [B] William Sotheby (1757–1833): see *Beppo*, 63; *The Blues*; *DJ* I. 116. Hector Macneil (1746–1816). B's judgement on Gifford's translation of Juvenal was made with his friend Hodgson's translation in mind.

819. Mr. Gifford promised publicly that the Baviad and Maeviad should not be his last original works: let him remember; 'Mox in reluctantes Dracones'. [B] The question was asked first in 'New Morality', *Poetry of the Anti-Jacobin*, 25–42, and n. See also the motto to *The Baviad*.

825–8. See Juvenal, I. 49–51.

831. Henry Kirke White died at Cambridge in October, 1806, in consequence of too much exertion in the pursuit of studies that would have matured a mind which disease and poverty could not impair, and which Death itself destroyed rather than subdued. His poems abound in such beauties as must impress the reader with the liveliest regret that so short a period was allotted to talents, which would have dignified even the sacred functions he was destined to assume. [B] The minor poet Henry Kirke White (1785–1806), whose untimely death gave him considerable celebrity, particularly after the appearance of Southey's *Life and Remains* . . . (1808).

835. Cf. *Hamlet*, III. i. 158.

841–4. Echoes Edmund Waller, 'To a Lady', 5–8.

857. I consider Crabbe and Coleridge as the first of these times in point of power and Genius.—[B 1816] George Crabbe (1754–1832).

859. Mr. Shee, author of 'Rhymes on Art' [1805], and 'Elements of Art' [1809]. [B] Sir Martin Archer Shee (1770–1850).

877. Mr. Wright, late Consul-General for the Seven Islands, is author of a very beautiful poem just published: it is entitled, 'Horae Ionicae' [1809], and is descriptive of the Isles and the adjacent coast of Greece. [B.] For Thomas Rodwell Wright see *CHP I-II*, esp. the Preface. The Seven Islands are Corfu, Paxoi, Lefkas, Kefalonia, Ithaki, Zande, Kithira.

881. The translators of the Anthology have since published separate poems, which evince genius that only requires opportunity to attain eminence. [B] *Bland* and *Merivale*. [B 1816] The Revd. Robert Bland (1779–1825) and John Herman Merivale (1779–1844). *Translations Chiefly from the Greek Anthology* . . . (1806) was chiefly their work, though others assisted. They were later members of the circle of wits that included Frere, Rose, and Hodgson, and that congregated at Murray's.

884. *Aonian.* Aonia is the part of Boeotia sacred to the Muses, and containing Mt. Helicon.

893. Erasmus Darwin (1731–1802), *The Botanic Garden* (1789–92), *The Temple of Nature* (1803), etc. Compare B's remarks on Darwin with *ER* II (Apr. 1803), p. 491.

899–900. Compare T. J. Mathias, *The Pursuits of Literature* (1794–7), pp. 14–15.

902. The neglect of the 'Botanic Garden', is some proof of returning taste; the scenery is its sole recommendation. [B]

906. Messrs. Lamb and Lloyd, the most ignoble followers of Southey and Co. [B] Charles Lloyd (1775–1839). B's later opinion of Charles Lamb was very different: see his Preface to *Werner*.

911. By the by, I hope that in Mr. Scott's next poem his hero or heroine will be less addicted to 'Gramarye', and more to Grammar, than the Lady of the Lay, and her Bravo William of Deloraine. [B, added in *EBSR2*. See *EBSR*153 n.]

917. Unjust. [B 1816]

918. Recalling, possibly, Coleridge's 'Frost at Midnight'.

927. It may be asked why I have censured the Earl of Carlisle, my guardian and relative, to whom I dedicated a volume of puerile poems a few years ago. The guardianship was nominal, at least as far as I have been able to discover: the relationship I cannot help, and am very sorry for it; but as his Lordship seemed to forget it on a very essential occassion to me, I shall not burthen my memory with the recollection. I do not think that personal differences sanction the unjust condemnation of a brother scribbler; but I see no reason why they should act as a preventive, when the author, noble or ignoble, has for a series of years beguiled a 'discerning public' (as the advertisements have it) with divers reams of most orthodox, imperial nonsense. Besides, I do not step aside to vituperate the Earl; no—his works come fairly in review with those of other Patrician Literati. If, before I escaped from my teens, I said any thing in favour of his Lordship's paper books, it was in the way of dutiful dedication, and more from the advice of others than my own judgment, and I seize the first opportunity of pronouncing my sincere recantation. I have heard that some persons conceive me to be under obligations to Lord Carlisle: if so, I shall be most particularly happy to learn what they are, and when conferred, that they may be duly appreciated, and publicly acknowledged. What I have humbly advanced as an opinion on his printed things, I am prepared to support if necessary, by quotations from Elegies, Eulogies, Odes, Episodes, and certain facetious and dainty tragedies bearing his name, and mark:

'What can ennoble knaves, or *fools*, or cowards?
Alas! not all the blood of all the Howards!'

so says Pope. Amen! [B, added in *EBSR2*. See *EBSR* 732 and n.] Much too savage—whatever the foundation might be.—[B 1816] B quotes from Pope's *Essay on Man*, IV. 215–16.

952. 'Tollere humo, victorque virum volitare per ora.' Virgil. [B] *Georgics*, III. 8.

959. The devil take that 'Phoenix'. How came it there? [B 1816]

964. The annual prize to a Cambridge M.A. for the best poem, in English, on a religious subject.

968. The 'Games of Hoyle', well known to the votaries of Whist, Chess,

etc. are not to be superseded by the vagaries of his poetical namesake, whose poem comprised, as expressly stated in the advertisement, all the 'Plagues of Egypt'. [B] The Revd. Charles James Hoare (1781–1865) won the Seatonian prize for *The Shipwreck of St. Paul* (1807); The Revd. Charles Hoyle (1773–1848) for *Moses Viewing the Promised Land* (1804), and *Paul and Barnabus at Lystra* (1806); see also Edmund Hoyle (1672–1769).

972. See *EBSR* 391 and n.

980. This person, who has lately betrayed the most rabid symptoms of confirmed authorship, is the writer of a poem denominated the 'Art of Pleasing', as 'Lucus a non lucendo', containing little pleasantry, and less poetry. He also acts as monthly stipendiary and collector of calumnies for the Satirist. If this unfortunate young man would exchange the magazines for the mathematics, and endeavour to take a decent degree in his university, it might eventually prove more serviceable than his present salary. [B] Right enough —this was well deserved and well laid on.— [B 1816] Hewson Clarke (1787–1832?), hack writer who attacked B in *The Scourge* and *The Satirist*. See *EBSR*, Postscript, and *Hints*, Preface (B's long prose note on Clarke, later dropped from the poem).

981. 'Into Cambridgeshire the Emperor Probus transported a considerable body of Vandals.' Gibbon's Decline and Fall, p. 83, vol. 2. There is no reason to doubt the truth of this assertion; the breed is still in high perfection. [B] See *Decline and Fall*, chap. XII.

983. This gentleman's name requires no praise; the man who in translation displays unquestionable genius, may well be expected to excel in original composition, of which it is to be hoped we shall soon see a splendid specimen. [B] Francis Hodgson (1781–1852), B's lifelong friend, translated Juvenal, parts of the Greek Anthology, and wrote original poetry (e.g. *Lady Jane Grey and other Poems*, 1809).

984. Hewson Clarke, Esq. as it is written. [B]

990. The 'Aboriginal Britons' [1792], an excellent poem by Richards. [B] The Revd. George Richards (1767–1837).

999–1004. Compare *CHP IV*. 1–15, 145, 179–82.

1016. A friend of mine being asked why his Grace of P. was likened to an old woman? replied, 'he supposed it was because he was past bearing.'⟨(Even Homer was a punster—a solitary pun.)⟩ *MB*—His Grace is now gathered to his Grandmothers, where he sleeps as sound as ever, but even his sleep was better than his Colleagues' waking. 1811. [B, added in *EBSR5*] William Henry Cavendish, third Duke of Portland (1738–1809), Prime Minister (1807–9). For B's animus against him see *BLJ* 1. 177–8, 192, 202.

1017. B sailed from England 2 July 1809, to return in July 1811.

1019. Gibraltar. [B. *EBSR5*] Calpe is the ancient name of Gibraltar. [B. *EBSR2–4*] Saw it August 1809. [B 1816]

1020. Stamboul is the Turkish word for Constantinople. [B. *EBSR2–4*] Was there the Summer 1810. [B 1816]

1021. Georgia. [B. *EBSR5*] Georgia, remarkable for the beauty of its inhabitants. [B. *EBSR2–4*]

1022. Mount Caucasus. [B] Saw the distant ridge of—1810—1811. [B 1816]

1026var. Lord Valentia (whose tremendous travels are forthcoming with due decorations, graphical, topographical, and typographical) deposed, on Sir John Carr's unlucky suit, that Dubois's satire prevented his purchase of the 'Stranger in Ireland'.—Oh fie, my Lord! has your Lordship no more feeling than a fellow-tourist? but 'two of a trade', they say, etc. [B. *EBSR2–4*] George Annesley, Viscount Valentia (1771–1844), who published his *Voyages and Travels . . . in the Years 1802–6* (1809), and Sir John Carr (1772–1832), author of numerous books of travel. The latter brought an unsuccessful suit against Edward Dubois (1774–1850) in 1808 for his parody of Carr's books (*My Pocket Book . . . to be called 'The Stranger in Ireland in 1805'*). See also *BLJ* I. 217 and *CHP* I. 87var. and n.

1027. Lord Elgin would fain persuade us that all the figures, with and without noses, in his stone-shop, are the work of Phidias! 'Credat Judaeus!' [B] See B's other attacks on Thomas Bruce, seventh Earl of Elgin (1766–1841), in *CHP II.* 11–16 and var. and *Curse*.

1034. 'Rapid', indeed! he topographized King Priam's dominions in three days!—I called him 'Classic', before I saw the Troad, but since have learned better than to tack to his name what don't belong to it. [B. *EBSR5*] Mr. Gell's Topography of Troy and Ithaca cannot fail to ensure the approbation of every man possessed of classical taste, as well for the information Mr. G. conveys to the mind of the reader, as for the ability and research the respective works display. [B. *EBSR2–4*] Passed first [Ithaca] in 1809. Visited both [Troy and Ithaca] in 1810–1811.—Since seeing the plain of Troy my opinions are somewhat changed as to the above note—Gell's survey was hasty and superficial. [B 1816] Sir William Gell (1777–1836) published his works on Troy and Ithaca in 1804 and 1807. See *BLJ* I. 238 and n.

1042. *EBSR1–1a* was published anonymously.

1045. Singular enough—and 'Din' enough—God knows. [B 1816] Cf. *I Henry IV*, II. iv.

1047. See above, 413 and 465 ff., and notes.

1050. *Hamlet*, III. iv. 36.

1070. The greater part of this Satire I most sincerely wish had never been written—not only on account of the injustice of much of the critical and some of the personal part of it—but the tone and temper are such as I cannot approve.—Byron July 14th 1816. Diodati, Geneva. [B 1816]

Postscript   Added in *EBSR2*, removed in *EBSR5*, replaced in *EBSR5a*

3. B was mistaken.

6. Virgil, *Aeneid*, I. 11.

9. *Twelfth Night*, III. iv. 284.

14–15. *Book of Common Prayer. Catechism.*

27. *cartels:* written challenges.

27. Edmund Burke, *Reflections on The Revolution in France* (see *CHP I–II,* 'Addition to the Preface').

34. *bear:* See *Marchand,* I. 102 n.

40–1. See Sheridan's *The Critic,* I. i.

44. *Editor of the Satirist:* George Manners (1778–1853).

47. Edward Jerningham (1727–1812), a Della Cruscan poet.

50. *King Lear,* III. iv. 18.

53–4. *Marmion,* a misquotation of the last lines of the 'Envoy'.

129a. Lines Associated with *EBSR*

11. Erratum—For 'weekly' read 'weakly'. The 'Miniature' edited by Master Rennell is an imitation of its better the 'Microcosm'. The original of the character of 'Rusticus' in the former publication chastised the Editor thereof in a very relentless manner. [B] The reference is to Thomas Rennell (1787–1824), one of the founders of *The (Eton) Miniature* and a contributor to *The British Critic.* Rennell was at Cambridge at the same time as B. He was the son of Dr. Thomas Rennell (1754–1840), Dean of Westminster. *The Microcosm* of George Canning and John Hookham Frere evolved into the *Anti-Jacobin.*

130. *MS. and Publishing History.* No. MS.; first published, *IT*; first collected, *Paris1828*; first collected, English edition, *1831*, and collected thereafter.

The date and specific occasion of this song are not known, but the work was probably written in late 1808 or early 1809. The variants in *Paris1828* indicate the poem was not reprinted there from *IT*, but from some MS. version.

131. *MS. and Publishing History.* No MS.; but B's corrected copy of *IT* (*ITB*) is at Murray, and *1831, 1832, C* had access to B's MS. corrections in his mother's copy of *IT* (*ITBa*). First published, *IT*, collected *Paris1828, 1831, 1832,* and thereafter.

Probably composed at Falmouth in late June 1809. The poem anticipates the opening parts of *CHP I.*

132. *MS. and Publishing History.* Written as a verse letter to Francis Hodgson, 30 June 1809 (*MS. T,* location: Texas). First published, *Life,* I. 190–2, collected *1831, 1832,* and thereafter. First accurate printing from *MS. T,* with numbered stanzas and correct reading at line 31, *BLJ* 1. 211–13.

Written two days before B sailed from Falmouth on the Lisbon packet, for Portugal and his famous trip to the Levant.

34. Note Erratum—For 'gallant' read 'gallows'. [B's note, *MS. T*] Kidd was the captain's name (*Life,* I. 190–2 n.).

49. William Fletcher, 'Old' Joe Murray, and Robert Rushton, whom B
brought with him from Newstead.

57–8. See *EBSR* 142 and B's note.

133. *MS. and Publishing History.* B's draft, dated 25 Aug. 1809 (*MS. T*, location: Princeton–Taylor). B's fair copy (forming a part of the Murray MS. of
CHP I–II, MS. M). Augusta Leigh's fair copy (*MS. L*, location: Bodleian–
Lovelace; paper watermarked 1808). First published *1832* (VIII. 56–8),
apparently from *MS. M*, and collected thereafter.

Composed on board the Townshend packet when B was sailing from Gibraltar to Sardinia.

17–18. Compare 'To a Lady' (no. 81), 27–30.

33–40. Compare *CHP I*, sts. 54–7.

134. *MS. and Publishing History.* B's fair copy (*MS. T*, location: Princeton–
Taylor). B's second fair copy (*MS. M*, location: Murray MS. of *CHP I–II*).
Dallas's fair copy (*MS. D.* location: *BM*, Egerton 2027). Teresa Guiccioli's
fair copy (*MS. G*, location: Keats–Shelley Memorial House, Rome). There
is a corrected proof of *CHP(7)* in the Huntington Library. First published,
CHP(1), collected thereafter.

Addressed to Mrs. Constance Spencer Smith, with whom B had a brief,
'platonic' affair at Malta in Sept. 1809 (see *Marchand*, I. 199–201). For B's
other poems to her see below nos. 135, 136, 137, 142, and *CHP II*, sts. 30–5.

135. *MS. and Publishing History.* B's draft (*MS. M*, location: Murray), dated
17 Sept. 1809; Charles Hanson's fair copy from *MS. M* (*MS. H*, also at
Murray's). A corrected proof for *CHP(7)* is in the Huntington Library.
First published, *CHP(1)*, collected thereafter. The poem is printed in quatrains in *1832* and editions thereafter, including *C* and *More*, but without
authority.

See commentary for no. 134.

32. B's own account of Mrs. Smith's adventures, including her escape
from a French prison, is given in his letter to his mother of 15 Sept. 1809
(*BLJ* I. 224 and n.).

136. *MS. and Publishing History.* B's corrected fair copy (*MS. M*, location:
Murray; in the MS. of *CHP I–II*); the Dallas fair copy (*MS. D*, location:
BM, Egerton 2027). There is a corrected proof of *CHP(7)* in the Huntington
Library. First published *CHP(1)*, collected thereafter. Stanza numbers were
removed in *1832* and later editions.

For the circumstances see *Marchand*, I. 206 and Hobhouse, *Travels in
Albania*, I. 68–72.

54. Cadiz did not fall to the French; see also *CHP I*, st. 85.

137. *MS. and Publishing History*. B's rough draft (*MS. L*, location: Bodleian–Lovelace); another draft (*MS. M*, location: Murray, in the MS. of *CHP I–II*); the Dallas fair copy, with B's corrections (*MS. D*, location: *BM*, Egerton 2027). There is a corrected proof for *CHP*(7) in the Huntington Library. First published, *CHP*(1), collected thereafter.

Another poem to Mrs. Smith; for details of the scene see *Marchand*, I. 217.

1–4. Actium, where the forces of Octavian defeated Anthony and Cleopatra (31 B.C.).

20. Compare '[A Woman's Hair]' (no. 11), 4.

138. *MS. and Publishing History*. No MS.; first published in Hugh W. Williams's *Travels in Italy, Greece, and the Ionian Islands* (Edinburgh, 1820), 2 vols. II. 290–1. First collected, *1831*, and all subsequent editions.

D. M. Low has pointed out that the traditional title of this poem, 'Lines Written in the Travellers' Book at Orchomenus', is incorrect (*TLS*, 10 Dec. 1931, p. 1006). The error, he notes, 'is due to [Moore's] careless reading of the account of the Macri family by the artist H. W. Williams'. B's lines were actually written in a book of travellers' names kept by the Macri family, in Athens. The poem belongs to 1810.

139. *MS. and Publishing History*. B's fair copy (*MS. Y*, location: Yale). First published *1832*, collected thereafter. Printed again apparently from *MS. Y* (but miscopied) in *The New Monthly Belle Assemblée*, 70 (1869) in 'Letters Etc. of Lord Byron', an unsigned essay printing much new MS. material.

140. *MS. and Publishing History*. B's corrected draft (*MS. T*, location: Princeton–Taylor), dated by B incorrectly '1809'. B's corrected copy (*MS. M*, location: Murray, in the MS. of *CHP I–II*). The Dallas fair copy (*MS. D*, location: *BM*, Egerton 2027). An uncorrected proof for *CHP*(7) is in the Huntington Library. First published *CHP*(1), collected thereafter. The poem was divided into two stanzas when its title was changed in *1831*, *1832*.

The poem is traditionally taken to mark the end of his infatuation for Mrs. Constance Spencer Smith (see *Marchand*, I. 227).

141. *MS. and Publishing History*. B's corrected draft, dated from Athens 9 Feb. 1810 (*MS. K*, location: Kent). There is an uncorrected proof of lines 1–18 in the Huntington, for *CHP*(7). First published in *CHP*(1), collected thereafter.

Addressed to Teresa Macri, the twelve-year-old youngest daughter of Mrs. Tarsia Macri, with whom B took lodgings at Athens late in 1809 (see also *Marchand*, I. 219, 232 and *BLJ* I. 240 and II. 13, 46).

title   *Zoë mou, sas agapo, or Ζώη μοῦ, σάς ἀγαπῶ*, a Romaic expression of tenderness: if I translate it I shall affront the gentlemen, as it may seem I supposed they could not; and if I do not I may affront the ladies. For fear of

any misconstruction on the part of the latter I shall do so, begging pardon
of the learned. It means, 'My Life, I love you!' which sounds very prettily
in all languages, and is as much in fashion in Greece at this day as, Juvenal
tells us, the two first words were amongst the Roman ladies, whose erotic
expressions were all Hellenized. [B's note in *CHP(1)*, much expanded from
the MS. version] The Juvenal reference is Satire VI. 195.

15. In the East (where the ladies are not taught to write, lest they should
scribble assignations) flowers, cinders, pebbles, &c. convey the sentiments of
the parties by that universal deputy of Mercury—an old woman. A cinder
says, 'I burn for thee'; a bunch of flowers tied with hair, 'Take me and fly';
but a pebble declares —what nothing else can. [B's note in *CHP(1)*] In *MS. K*
it reads: 'In the East (where Ladies are not taught to read for fear that they
should write Billets doux) Flowers, ⟨coals⟩ cinders and ⟨stones⟩ pebbles
convey the sentiments of the parties by that universal agent 'an old woman'
—a cinder ⟨means⟩ is 'I die for you', a bunch of flowers tied with a ⟨banded⟩
long hair 'Take me and run away with me', and a pebble—is altogether
inexpressible.' Compare *Bride*, I. 295.

21. *Istambol:* Constantinople [B's note in *CHP(1)*]

142. *MS. and Publishing History.* B's fair copy at Texas (*MS. T*), with, however,
only a portion of the prose note B appended to the poem (up to 'four English
miles'). Huntington has a proof for *CHP(7)* uncorrected. First published
CHP(1), collected thereafter.

For a narrative of this famous event see *Marchand*, 1. 236–9.

title   On the 3d of May, 1810, while the Salsette frigate (Captain
Bathurst) was lying in the Dardanelles, Lieutenant Ekenhead of that frigate
and the writer of these rhymes swam from the European shore to the Asiatic
—by-the-by, from Abydos to Sestos would have been more correct. The
whole distance from the place whence we started to our landing on the other
side, including the length we were carried by the current, was computed by
those on board the frigate at upwards of four English miles; though the
actual breadth is barely one. The rapidity of the current is such that no boat
can row directly across, and it may in some measure be estimated from the
circumstance of the whole distance being accomplished by one of the parties
in an hour and five, and by the other in an hour and ten, minutes. The water
was extremely cold from the melting of the mountain-snows. About three
weeks before, in April, we had made an attempt, but having ridden all the
way from the Troad the same morning, and the water being of an icy chill-
ness, we found it necessary to postpone the completion till the frigate anc-
hored below the castles, when we swam the straits, as above stated; entering
a considerable way above the European, and landing below the Asiatic, fort.
Chevalier says that a young Jew swam the same distance for his mistress;
and Oliver mentions its having been done by a Neapolitan; but our consul,
Tarragona, remembered neither of these circumstances, and tried to dissuade

us from the attempt. A number of the Salsette's crew were known to have accomplished a greater distance; and the only thing that surprised me was, that, as doubts had been entertained of the truth of Leander's story, no traveller had ever endeavoured to ascertain its practicability. [B's note in *CHP(1)*]

Bathurst ... *Ekenhead:* Walter Bathurst (1764?–1827), who was made a captain in 1798. Lieutenant William Ekenhead was with the marines aboard Bathurst's *Salsette* frigate.

Chevalier ... *Olivier* ... *Tarragona.* B refers to Jean Baptiste Lechevalier's *Voyage de la Propontide* ... (Paris, 1800), 2 vols.; Guillaume Olivier's *Voyage dans l'Empire Othoman* ... (Paris, [1801]–1807), 3 vols.; Signor Tarragona was a Jew whose family had the English consulate at Dardanelles (Chanàk-Kalessi) for over a century. Chanàk-Kalessi is the fort B refers to. For more particular details see Hobhouse, *Travels in Albania*, II. 189–96. See also *Marchand*, I. 238–9, *BLJ* I. 237, 243–4, and *LJ* v. 246–8.

2. *Leander.* The famous story of Hero and Leander has its traditional literary source in Ovid. Marlowe's *Hero and Leander*, continued by Chapman, is the best-known English version.

143. *MS. and Publishing History.* B's fair copy MS., with one correction, is in the Murray archives (*MS. M*). First published from *MS. M* in *Murray's Magazine*, I (1887), 290–1; printed again from the same MS. in *C*, and collected thereafter.

The lines are a *jeu d'esprit* written in anticipation of Hobhouse's departure from B in Greece. Hobhouse sailed for England on 17 July 1810 (see *Borst*, 125–6).

6. William Fletcher, B's servant, who was quite unhappy during his travels with B in the East (see ll. 9 ff.).

29. A reference to Hobhouse's *Imitations and Translations* ... (1809), to which B contributed nine poems. The volume sold poorly.

30. The mother of Elizabeth Pigot, B's confidante at Southwell (see B's letter to Mrs. Margaret Pigot, 28 Oct. 1811: *BLJ* II. 119–20).

31. *Sale:* a pun on the name of George Sale (1697?–1736), the orientalist and translator of the Koran (1734); see notes to *CHP I–II* and *Giaour*.

33. Charles Skinner Matthews, B's Cambridge friend who drowned in 1811 (see *BLJ* II. 68 and n.).

35. Quoting Pope, *An Essay on Man*, IV. 390.

47. See the first version of *CHP I*, st. 87.

51. Hobhouse returned to England with the MS. of his *A Journey Through Albania* ..., eventually published by Cawthorne in 1813.

53. Apparently a reference to B's troubles at Southwell following the publication of *FP* (see 'To Mary', no. 77, and commentary).

144. *MS. and Publishing History.* B sent the verses in a letter to Henry Drury, from Constantinople, on 17 June 1810, but the MS. of the letter has not appeared. First published in *Life*, I. 227. It was collected in *1831*, overlooked in *1832*, and replaced in the corpus in *1837*, and collected thereafter. See *BLJ* I. 245–6 and Euripides, *Medea*, 1–7.

4. *Azure rocks:* The Cyanean Symplegades, at the entrance to the Bosporus from the Black Sea.

145 and **146**. *MS. and Publishing History*. Uncollected. First published in *LBC* I. 17–18 as part of the letter in which the poems were sent to Hobhouse, 25 Sept. 1810 (*MS. M*, location: Murray); reprinted *BLJ* II. 15.

B sent the poems from Patras, where he was recovering from a fever caught on his visit to Olympia. B's chief physician was Dr. Romanelli (see no. 147 below). No. 146 is a parody of Pope's 'Epistle to Bathurst', 299–314, and no. 145 is a parody of his 'Epistle to Cobham', 242–7.

147. *MS. and Publishing History*. The verses are part of a letter to Hodgson of 3 Oct. 1810 (MS. of the letter in Meyer Davis Collection, Univ. of Pennsylvania Library). First published *Life*, I. 240, collected *1831*, overlooked in *1832*, replaced in *1837* and thereafter.

See nos. 145, 146 above.

148. *MS. and Publishing History*. B's draft MS. (*MS. B*, location: Balliol College Library, watermarked 1808). Lines 1–54 unpublished, lines 55–81 published in Roden Noel's *Life of Byron* (1890), but collected only in *More*.

Composed early in 1811 while B was staying at the Capuchin convent near Athens. The poem resembles the opening and closing stanzas of *CHP* II as well as B's long prose note to *CHP* II dated from the Capuchin Convent, 23 Jan. 1811. See also *CHP* II, st. 27, incorporated into that poem from 'Il Diavolo Inamorato' (no. 188), as well as the latter poem, and commentary.

14: *those disastrous days:* the years immediately after 1774. Forsaken by their Russian allies in their abortive effort for independence from the Turks, 'the Greeks . . . were abandoned to their fate' (*Finlay*, V. 263), nor were the Turks slow to deal their punishment.

66. Echoes Pope's *Eloisa to Abelard*, 1–2.

72. Compare *CHP II*, st. 88.

149. *MS. and Publishing History*. B's corrected draft (*MS. M*, location: Murray); Dallas fair copy, corrected by B (*MS. D*, location: *BM*, Egerton 2027). An uncorrected proof is also in Murray, bound in with a volume of proofs for *CHP*(5) and *CHP*(7). The MS. title appeared on the original leaf signature BB3 of *CHP*(1), but a cancel leaf, with the present title, was inserted in most copies of *CHP*(1).

The traditional date for the poem, first given in *1832*, is Jan. 1812, but it may have been written during the next few months as well. The identity of J. V. D. is not known (see collations).

150. This is a new text for *Hints*. Unlike texts printed hitherto, it is based upon B's last revisions and directions for printing. *MS. and Proofs.* Four complete MSS. of the poem survive, as well as four incomplete sets of proofs and a number of MS. fragments of different parts of the poem. The complete MSS. are: (*a*) The first draft (*MS. LA*) dated at the beginning from Athens, 2 Mar. 1811, and at the end 11, 12 Mar. It contains: 1–8 (only 6 lines), 9–30, 31–6 (only 4 lines), 37–114, 114a–b (2 extra lines), 115–206, 209–38, 241–72, 275–84, 289–338, 339–52 (only 6 lines), 353–4, 357–62, 381–636, 639–48, 657–72, 719–68, 773–804 (total: 704 lines). First corrected copy (*MS. LB*) dated at beginning 12 Mar. 1811, and at end 20 Mar. *LB* added the following lines: 1–8 (a complete version: 2 extra lines), 207–8, 239–40, 273–4, 285–8, 355–6, 363–8, 637–8 (total: 726 lines). *LA* and *LB* are both in the Bodleian, Lovelace papers. (*c*) Second corrected copy (*MS. M*, location: Murray) with *LB* as copy text. B's note at end reads: '722 lines and 4 inserted after and now counted in all 726. B. Copied fair at Malta May 3rd 1811. B. Since this several lines are added. B. June 14th 1811.' The additional lines are: 318a–b, 339–52 (a complete version: 8 extra lines), 649–56, 673–718, 769–72 (total: 796 lines). (*d*) The 1811 printer's copy (*MS. T*, location: Princeton–Taylor) made from *M* by an amanuensis employed by B's intended publisher Cawthorne, with extensive corrections by B and MS. additions by B and the amanuensis. The copy was made in July 1811 and corrections were made until 20 Aug., when it was handed over to Cawthorne for printing (see *BLJ* II. 58, 59, 73–4). Lines 318a–b were deleted and 369–80 and the Jeffrey passage (38 lines) were added (total: 844 lines).

A number of partial MSS. bearing on the poem are also extant: (*a*) *MS. MA* (location: Murray), three rough draft scraps of lines 33–4, 369–80, and 673–96, all bound up with *MS. MB* of *EBSR*; (*b*) *MS. LC* (location: Bodleian–Lovelace) mixed with various additions to *EBSR:* lines 697–718 (corrected fair copy) and 755–6 (cancelled draft); (*c*) *MS. Y* (location: Yale), corrected fair copy of 369–80; fair copy of 327–8; (*d*) *MS. B* (location: Berg), corrected fair copy of the passage on Jeffrey which B dropped from the poem; (*e*) *MS. H* (location: Huntington), rough draft of part of prose note for 617; (*f*) *MS. Tx* (location: Texas), fair copy of the second part of the same prose note; (*g*) *MS. Mo* (location: Morgan), fair copy of prose note for line 191.

MS. T was copy text for several sets of proofs printed by Cawthorne between Aug. and Nov. 1811. Only portions survive (*Proof BM*, location: BM, Egerton 2029). *Proof BM* carries the Latin text on facing pages and is set in type uniform with *EBSR5*, with which B intended to publish *Hints* in one volume in 1811. *Proof BM* is in two parts: (*a*) *Proof BMA*, with B's MS. corrections, beginning at page 113 and running to page 128, containing lines 171–270; (*b*) *Proof BMB*, with B's MS. corrections. This is later than *Proof BMA* and runs from Page [87] to page 128, containing lines 1–270.

Another, crucial set of proofs (*Proof M*, location: Morgan) was set up from *MS. T* at B's direction late in 1820. *Proof M* consists of four double-column galley sheets of the English text only, and contains lines 1–276, 583–804, with B's MS. corrections, as well as a MS. note to Murray with publishing directions. A part of a second copy of this proof, uncorrected, is also extant, containing lines 645–804 (*Proof Ma*, location: Murray). *Proof Ma* was never sent to B.

Publishing History. B wrote the first draft of *Hints* at Athens between 2 and 11 Mar. 1811, copied and corrected the poem twice, and returned to England with *MSS. LA, LB*, and *M* in July. Cawthorne had a copy made from *M* in the middle of July, and B worked on this copy (*MS. T*) into November. After much vacillating, B and Cawthorne decided to publish *Hints* in a uniform edition with *Curse* and *EBSR5* (see *BLJ* II. 131). The project fell through soon afterwards, however, when B decided to suppress *EBSR*.

B's interest in *Hints* revived in June 1820 (*BSP* II. 515–16) and on 23 Sept. he told Murray to send a proof of the poem (*LJ* v. 77). *Proof M* reached B around 11 Jan. 1821 (*LJ* v. 221), and he was satisfied that there was 'little to alter' in a present publication. He corrected *Proof M* and returned it with a request to have a proof of the remainder of the poem sent. After frequent complaints, B finally received another proof on 1 Mar. He protested, however, because these new proofs (which are not extant) contained the Jeffrey passage which B had ordered to be removed from the poem years before (*LJ* v. 255). Murray had also neglected B's instructions to add a prose note on Pope to lines 81–2, and to set the Latin text with the poem. B was still intending to publish the poem in Aug. 1821 (*LJ* v. 343), but by Mar. 1822 he had again pulled back (*LJ* VI. 30).

Portions of the poem were first published from *Proof BM* in Dallas's *Recollections* (1824), 104–13. Moore published further excerpts in his *Life*, I. 263–9, and a complete text was first published in *1831*. *C* states (I. 387) that the *Life* and *1831* texts were probably derived from 'complete proofs . . . in Moore's possession'. These texts, however, do not incorporate any of B's 1821 revisions from *Proof M*. The *1831* text has been the basis for all subsequent printings, and it is closest to *MS. T*. Copy text for *1831* must have been either *MS. T*, or a proof made from that MS. (perhaps the lost proof of March 1821) but without B's late revisions.

Copy text for the present edition is *Proof M*, as corrected by B, for lines 1–276, 583–804; for 277–582 copy text is *MS. T*, which embodies B's latest corrections made for Cawthorne in 1811. The Jeffrey passage is thus removed, as B wished, and the note on Pope added to lines 81–2. B supplied the Preface in his letter to Murray of 11 Jan. 1821; the early, unprinted Preface is placed in the notes. B wanted the poem printed with the parallel Horace passages but it has not been feasible to print them here. Because B felt a proper appreciation of the poem depended upon one's awareness of the closeness of the imitation, the following is a list of the parallel passages. The line numbers of B's text are followed by the corresponding line numbers in the *Ars Poetica*

(in parentheses): 1–14 (1–9), 15–20 (9–13), 21–30 (14–18), 31–8 (19–23),
39–48 (24–30), 49–58 (31–7), 59–78, 79–88 (38–59), 89–104 (60–72), 105–
8, 109–14, 115–24 (73–85), 125–34 (86–98), 135–58 (99–113), 159–80 (114–
27), 181–8 (128–35), 189–210 (136–52), 211–22, 223–40, 241–8, 249–60
(153–78), 261–88 (179–88), 289–380 (189–239), 381–4 (240–3), 385–90 (244–
7), 390–6 (248–50), 397–410 (251–62), 411–14 (263–4), 415–20, 421–34
(265–74), 435–42, 443–6 (275–84), 447–56 (285–94), 457–62, 463–76, 477–88
(295–308), 489–92, 493–502 (309–18), 503–18, 519–28 (319–32), 529–54
(333–50), 555–8, 559–68 (351–60), 569–74 (361–5), 575–86 (366–73), 587–94,
595–610 (374–84), 611–22 (385–90), 623–38 (391–401), 639–44, 645–8
(401–7), 649–740 (408–33), 741–52 (434–44), 753–64 (445–52), 765–92
(453–67), 793–804 (468–76). Some of B's imitations are very free, and in
the case of lines 289–380 and 649–740 so much freedom is taken with
the original that 'imitation' has become 'allusion'.

Literary and Historical Context. As an act of homage to Horace and the Horatian
tradition of satire, *Hints* offers a nice contrast to the Juvenalian *EBSR*. The
only passage which recalls the severer style of *EBSR* is the Jeffrey passage,
which in fact has no parallel text in the *Ars Poetica* and which B only added to
the poem as a late addition in 1811, when he was still nursing a grudge
against the reviewers of *HI*. B soon removed the inappropriate lines.

   Hints was specifically meant to recall Pope's *Satires and Epistles of Horace
Imitated*, as well as his *Essay on Criticism*. It is also part of a long tradition of
English translations of the poem, and specifically of translations which used
Horace for the basic text, but which substituted contemporary references
where appropriate. In this respect *Hints* is, with *EBSR*, a critique of English
society and letters. Only the manner has changed. The subtitle of B's poem
confirms this fact, for it is borrowed from Rochester's similar Horatian
exercise, 'An Allusion to Horace, the Tenth Satire of the First Book'.

   B's renewed interest in the poem in 1820 is significant, for it occured in the
context of his prose defences of Pope and his own *Don Juan*, and also at the
time he was seriously renewing his attack upon contemporary English
social and literary culture. B wanted to issue *Hints* as another part of the
attack, and he associated the poem with his translation of Pulci and with
the Horatian attitudes of *DJ*.

   B always thought well of the imitation, but most later readers find it dull.
Yet the poem is better than criticism has allowed, and as an 'imitation' of
what was for B a radical poetic text, it is remarkable. Much more than
EBSR, *Hints* anticipates certain important subjects and aspects of *DJ*. For
further comment see *Fuess*, 77–85 and *McGann*(2), 15–17, 69–73.

Preface   Though it be one of the obnoxious egotisms of authorship to state
when or where a work was composed, I ⟨cannot⟩ must incur this censure by
stating that the following Imitation was begun and finished at Athens the
only spot on earth which may partly apologize for such a declaration. It

is necessary for me to mention this to account for the postscript unconnected as it ⟨is⟩ otherwise appears with the poem.

Two years have passed and many countries have been traversed since circumstance converted me into a Satirist. If my first volume of Rhyme had been suffered to pass quickly into mental obscurity, I would have quietly passed along with it. But a ⟨Mr. Jeffrey⟩ celebrated Editor would be witty, and a variety of other factious Gentlemen must needs be waggish and angry too with such perseverance, that after waiting a long time for a cessation of buffoonery and abuse, it became necessary for me to convince these persons how very easy it is to say illnatured things and to sell it also. A Satire if not very bad indeed will generally meet with temporary success because it administers to the malignant or ? propensities of our Nature. My literary pursuits were not very aspiring and I hoped they would have been tranquil —if it has passed otherwise the fault is with the aggressors. ⟨But Time and Reflection teach that nothing can make amends for having inflicted a pang on others. It may seem vain to suppose that anything I have said or could say has affected the security of my neighbours, were it not known how easy it is to wound the 'Genius Irritabile'. These Reflections come to [sic] late, but let them pass, however fruitless—I should not shrink from the consequences of anything I have said or sung.⟩

To those on whose compositions only I have animadverted, I have but written (for the most part) in verse what had been very often said of them before in plain prose.—Had the attacks on me been merely confined to my rhymes, I should have been silent.—⟨The present 'Imitation' will be found to contain as little satire as could be avoided by an author speaking of an enemy. After my former work⟩ For the present I have nothing to claim from Candour or Criticism. If this makes its way, it must be by its own merits, for it has no mercy to ask, or to expect.—

The Latin text is printed with the Imitation, not only to show where I have left Horace, but where Horace has left me. The English example adduced will be found I hope with their merits justly estimated however awkwardly expressed. [MS. M. The postscript to which B refers was removed from the MS. of Hints in Aug. 1811 and appended as one of the notes to CHP II (the note dealing with the article in the Edinburgh Review). See BLJ II. 75. The personal attack which most galled B was by his old enemy of The Satirist, Hewson Clarke (see EBSR 973–80). It appeared in The Scourge (Mar. 1811). B wanted to bring suit against Clarke but was in the end persuaded not to do so (see BLJ II. 65, 68 and nn.). He vented his spleen against Clarke in the following long prose note, now part of MS. M, which he later removed from Hints.]

Note to 'Hints from Horace'.—It is with considerable regret I feel once more compelled to speak of Hewson Clarke (Esqr.) of whom mention is made in 'English Bards etc.' in ⟨such terms⟩ some lines which don't appear to be at all to his liking.—He moreover even places (or somebody very like him in a magazine which on other accounts I leave to the Law) that their insertion was deferred till I had left the country for the East.—The second edition was not published till after my departure,—for the best of reasons viz.—the first was not sold off, and consequently an addition of nearly 400 lines—and there are Hewson's among the rest—were obliged to wait till it came to their turn.—I neither hastened nor delayed my voyage on their account, and now that I have seen the lands I had determined to see long before I ever heard of Hewson, I am here ready to answer all whom it may concern in the way most answerable to their imaginations—it rests with themselves, my separation leaves *me* no choice. If Mr. Clarke, or any given member of Grubstreet (as he speaks of his 'friends' who like 'Legion' it should seem are many) think proper to come forward, though I never did consider him as a Gentleman, but a skulking scribbler, yet if he wished to elevate himself in the scale of society, by supporting anonymous sensibility, with open courage, he shall find that I will not refuse reparation for any fancied injury brought by his own misconduct upon himself.

In July 1808 when I took my degree of A.M. my friends Capt. Hobhouse of the Royal Cornish and Mr. Scrope Davies and Mr. D. Browne then of St. Johns can bear witness that I sought for this traducer in his own college,—the answer first was, he was not at home, the next, he was not in college, the next—when I wanted his address elsewhere—(for I went then with the Note) he was nobody knew where; and at present (it seems he has quitted Emanuel) I neither know nor care where he is, but my own address is left with my publisher for his convenience.

The man I never saw, but for upwards of four years, his lucubrations in 'The Satirist' and since in a miserable imitation of that Magazine were principally directed against Sir G[odfrey] W[ebster] and myself, this at least led to the lines which have thrown him into such hysterics. Of the last magazine and its attacks on my ('British Parentage and Education') family, I will say nothing, as the Attorney General will probably say enough next November.—Of Clarke I can only say I have known him to be foolish and malignant—and it remains with himself to prove whether he be truly entitled to his late assumption of '*Armiger*'. But to him and others of the same stamp I am indebted for the share of approbation (however undeserved) bestowed on the work in which they are mentioned. My Eclectic friends [i.e. *The Eclectic Review*] with some compliments to sweeten their sentence, have told me 'I am an angry schoolboy.' It is true—I was 'angry' and almost (though not quite) 'a schoolboy', and having been flagellated (as they tell me also ?) I broke my Master's head with a brickbat.—I had hoped that Nature meant me for something better than a Satirist, but the kindness of criticism decreed otherwise.

> 'I had a heart oerflowing with good thoughts
> For all mankind, one fatal fatal turn
> Has poisoned all . . . '

This 'turn' the facetious reader will readily interpret to be a 'turn' for rhyming.—I have here rhymed the theme of Magazines, the anti-hero of a novel, the mark of anonymous letters, and Slander of every description in various periodical publications. Certes I have reason to love Mankind, and particularly my fellow rhymers, and after all I have only told them what others have *said*(?) in my peroration.—I have been rambling upwards of two years and heard nothing like the voice of Hewson Clarke, except the yell of the jackalls in the ruins of Ephesus. I also saw one Wolf, and five and twenty pirates near Cape Colonna in Attica, (separately, for the Wolf kept better company), and an Editor and his gang, but excepting these I saw little to remind me of Criticism—except Ali Pacha's Fool with a brimstone coloured Jacket—at Tepaleen in Albania.—

Now being 'back again' I throw them 'the Glove' (as Lord K[ilworth] did to Mr. Wellesley Pole in his letter) and they may put it on and play in their Caledonian Cremona.

If Hewson be injured there be two remedies—the Law of the Land and of Honour,—as he has not had recourse to the one, let him try the other, or one or both, though he will not find a Jury of his Peers in either.—

After the indefatiguable perseverence of his anonymous attacks, the monthly iteration of falsehoods and flippancy, without a shadow of provocation, can he wonder that I dragged him into daylight in these lines which I shall quote in my own defence and defy him to disprove their truth. [B quotes *EBSR* 973–80] To a respectable body of men it is proper I should disclose that Hewson Clarke errs when he insinuates that I speak of his 'Sizarship' as a mark of reproach. I do not mention the 'Sizar' as a disgrace to him, but him as a Sizar [MS. torn] I state that H. C. is a Sizar as I would say he was a Gentleman (as a Sizar may doubtless be) if I could with any shadow of a truth.

I annexed the word Sizar as I would in other instances the letters M.A., M.P., D.D. or any similar supplementary initials.—I despise or affect to despise no man for his profession, from a Secretary of State to a Secretary of legation, from him who instructs the Envoy himself down to the poorest thing that rings bells and writes notes for an ambassador. I honour them all. It is H. Clarke who insults the Sizars by supposing that the name could be for an instant attached as a depreciation, more particularly to one who wanted neither to lower him beyond the mention of the appellation bestowed on him by his Godfather and Godmother.—He asserts roundly that he '*knows* that I have written for money'—'tis false; but I excuse him on account of the covert compliment as it implies that my writings are not unsaleable. My Publisher can set him right as to my receipts, as to them I never inquired. C's labours I trust are well requited according to their average of abuse; no man is at a greater expense of *unclear*(?) imagination.

Mr. Hewson Clarke was (I believe) an author at a very early period of life; the recollection might have taught him forebearance towards one who had never offended him; who knew him not, but after having borne his abuse for some years, did he imagine that I should overlook the first opportunity of painting him in his true colours?

Those friends to whom he supposes the lines were shown previous to their publication would have witheld me from noticing one in their avowed opinion so utterly despicable, but though my contempt was consonant with theirs, I did not conceive him less worthy of Chastisement. But I have committed another insuperable offence, I have seized upon 'those topics' in which he conceives himself 'peculiarly to excel'. [MS. torn] I did before there was nothing common between such a man and me, and had I been aware that he 'excelled' in anything but scurrility, I would have complimented him with the 'Pas' and rejoiced in my proof of his praiseworthy preeminence.—

Genius Irritabile: Horace, *Epistles*, II. ii. 102.

The second edition . . . 400 lines. See *EBSR* commentary.

'Legion': Mark 5: 9.

Mr. Scrope Davies: Scrope Berdmore Davies (1783–1852). B met him at Cambridge and they became good friends. Davies was famous for his wit and fast living (see *BLJ* I. 184 n.).

D. Browne: Dominick Browne: with B, a member of the Cambridge Whig Club. (See *BLJ* I. 158 n.).

Lord K[ilworth] . . . Wellesley Pole: alluding to the duel fought by Lord Kilworth and William Pole-Wellesley (nephew of the Duke of Wellington) on 15 Aug. 1811. It was precipitated by Kilworth's letter in the *Morning Post* of 14 Aug. For details see *C* I. 484–5 n. and see also *Waltz,* 21–2 and n.

Godfrey Webster (1788–1836): see *BLJ* II. 28, 241 and nn.

'Armiger': Latin for 'one who bears arms'.

'I had a heart . . . poisoned all': unidentified.

jackalls . . . Ephesus: see *BLJ* III. 218.

I also saw . . . in Albania: *BLJ* I. 226–35.

Caledonian Cremona: i.e. Edinburgh. Cremona is a town in Lombardy famous for its violin makers. B's joke here does not seem especially pointed. Cf. *Waltz,* 21 n.

Sizar: the designation for an undergraduate admitted to study at Cambridge with an allowance from his college.

1. *Lawrence.* Sir Thomas Lawrence (1769–1830) succeeded Benjamin West (1738–1820) as President of the Royal Academy in 1820. B's note in *LB* (cancelled) is: 'I have been obliged to dive into the "Bathos" for the simile, as I could not find a description of these painters' merits above ground.

Si liceat parvis
Componere magna—
Like London's column pointing to the skies
Like a *tall Bully,* lifts itself and lies—

I was in hopes might bear me out, if the monument be like a Bully. West's glory may be reduced by the scale of comparison. If not, let me have recourse to *Tom Thumb the Great* [Fielding's play] to keep my simile in countenance.' B quotes Virgil, *Georgics*, IV. 176.

7. In an English newspaper, which finds its way abroad wherever there are Englishmen, I read an account of this dirty dauber's caricature of Mr. H[ope] as a 'beast', and the consequent action, etc. The circumstance is, probably, too well known to require further comment. [B's note, *T*] A French painter, Antoine Dubost, had ridiculed Thomas Hope and his wife in a caricature of them as Beauty and the Beast. Mrs. Hope mutilated the picture, and Dubost brought suit. See also Antoine Dubost, *Hunt and Hope. An Appeal . . . Against the Calumnies of the Editor of the Examiner* (1810).

22var. G. L. Wardle (1762–1834), M.P. for Okehampton 1807–12.

20. 'Where pure description held the place of Sense.' Pope. [B's note, *M*, *T*] B quotes the 'Epistle to Dr. Arbuthnot', 148.

30.   'While Mr. Sol decked out all so glorious
                        Shines like a Beau in his Birthday Embroidery.'
'*Fas est et ab Hoste doceri.*' In the 7th Art. of the 31st No. of the *Edinburgh Review* (vol xvi Ap[ril] 1810) the 'Observations' of an Oxford Tutor are compared to 'Children's Cradles' (page 181), then to a 'Barndoor fowl flying' (page 182), then the man himself to 'a Coach-horse on the Trottoir' (page 185) etc. etc., with a variety of other conundrums all tending to prove that the ingenuity of comparison increases in proportion to the dissimilarity between the things compared. [B's note, *LB*, cancelled] B quotes Fielding's *Tom Thumb* I. i and Ovid, *Metamorphoses*, IV. 428.

53. *galligaskins:* more or less ludicrous term for loose breeches (*OED*).

54. Mere common mortals were commonly content with one Taylor and with one bill, but the more particular gentlemen found it impossible to confide their lower garments to the makers of their body clothes. I speak of the beginning in 1809: what reform may have since taken place I neither know nor desire to know. [B's note, *LB*, kept in *Proof M*]

76. Mr. Pitt was liberal in his additions to our parliamentary tongue [B's note, *Proof M*]; as may be seen in many publications, particularly the *Edinburgh Review*. [B's note, *LB*, *M*, *T*, *Proof BMB*]

101. Old ballads, old plays, and old women's stories are at present in as much request as old wine or new speeches. 1811. [B's note, *Proof M*] In fact, this is the millenium of black letter: thanks to our Hebers, Webers, and Scotts! [B's note, *M*, *T*, *Proof BMB*] Richard Heber (1773–1833) and W. H. Weber (1783–1818) were editors of early English poetry.

114a–b. *MacFlecknoe*, and the *Dunciad*, and all Swift's lampooning ballads. Whatever their other works may be, these originated in personal feelings, and angry retort on unworthy rivals; and though the ability of these satires elevates the poetical, their poignancy detracts from the personal character of the writers. [B's note *LA*, cancelled in *Proof M*]

117. *Almanzor:* John Dryden, *Almanzor, or The Conquest of Granada* (1670), whose hero was severely criticized for extravagance.

120. With all the vulgar applause and critical abhorrence of *puns*, they have Aristotle on their side; who permits them to orators, and gives them consequences by a grave disquisition. [B's note, *M–Proof M*]

123. *Thalia:* Muse of Comedy.

127. *Melpomene:* Muse of Tragedy.

130. See Vanbrugh and Cibber's comedy, *The Provoked Husband* (1728)

134. 'And in his ear I'll hollow Mortimer.'—*1st Henry IV* [I. iii. 222]. [B's note, *LB–Proof M*]

162. I have Johnson's authority for making Lear a monosyllable—

> 'Perhaps where Lear rav'd or Hamlet died
> On flying cars new sorcerers may ride.'

—and (if it need be mentioned) the *authority* of the epigram on Barry and Garrick. [B's note in *Proof BMB*, cancelled] B misquotes Johnson's 'Prologue Spoken at the Opening of the Theatre in Drury Lane, 1747', 43–4, which reads 'Lear has rav'd'. Johnson wrote no epigram on Barry and Garrick.

162–4. See Garrick's *The Lying Valet* (1741) and George Colman's *John Bull, or An Englishman's Fire-Side* (1803).

167–8. Pope, *Essay on Criticism*, 68–73.

171. See George Villiers, second Duke of Buckingham, *The Rehearsal* (1671), esp. IV. i. From the play the name Drawcansir became a byword for braggadocio.

181.

> 'Difficile est proprie communia dicere; tuque
> Rectius Iliacum carmen deducis in actus,
> Quam si proferres ignota indictaque primus.'
>
> HOR: DE ARTE POET: 128–130.

Mons. Dacier, Mons. de Sévigné, Boileau, and others, have left their dispute on the meaning of this sentence in a tract considerably longer than the poem of Horace. It is printed at the close of the eleventh volume of Madame de Sévigné's Letters, edited by Grouvelle, Paris, 1806. Presuming that all who can construe may venture an opinion on such subjects, particularly as so many who *can't* have taken the same liberty, I should have held 'my farthing candle' as awkwardly as another, had not my respect for the wits of Louis 14th's Augustan 'Siècle' induced me to subjoin these illustrious authorities. I therefore offer firstly Boileau: 'Il est difficile de traiter des sujets qui sont à la portée de tout le monde d'une manière qui vous les rende propres, ce qui s'appelle s'approprier un sujet par le tour qu'on y donne.' 2dly, Batteux: 'Mais il est bien difficile de donner des traits propres et individuels aux êtres purement possibles.' 3dly, Dacier: 'Il est difficile de traiter convenablement

ces caractères que tout le monde peut inventer.' Mr. Sévigné's opinion
and translation consisting of some thirty pages, I omit, particularly as Mr.
Grouvelle observes, 'La chose est bien remarquable, aucune de ces diverses
interpretations ne parait être la véritable.' But, by way of comfort, it seems,
fifty years afterwards, 'Le lumineux Dumarsais' made his appearance, to set
Horace on his legs again, 'dissiper tous les nuages, et concilier tous les dis-
sentiments'; and I suppose some fifty years hence, somebody, still more
luminous, will doubtless start up and demolish Dumarsais and his system on
this weighty affair, as if he were no better than Ptolemy or Copernicus and
comments of no more consequence than astronomical calculations. I am happy
to say, 'la longueur de la dissertation' of Mr. D. prevents Mr. G. from saying
any more on the matter. A better poet than Boileau, and at least as good a
scholar as Mr. de Sévigné, has said,

> 'A little learning is a dangerous thing.'

And by the above extract, it appears that a good deal may be rendered as
useless to the Proprietors. [B's note, *LB–Proof M*] B's better poet is, of
course, Pope, *Essay on Criticism*, 215.

189. About two years ago a young man named Townsend was announced
by Mr. Cumberland, in a review (since deceased) [the *London Review*], as being
engaged in an epic poem to be entitled 'Armageddon'. The plan and specimen promise much; but I hope neither to offend Mr. Townsend, nor his
friends, by recommending to his attention the lines of Horace to which these
rhymes allude. If Mr. Townsend succeeds in his undertaking, as there is
reason to hope, how much will the world be indebted to Mr. Cumberland
for bringing him before the public! But, till that eventful day arrives, it may
be doubted whether the premature display of his plan (sublime as the ideas
confessedly are) has not,—by raising expectation too high, or diminishing
curiosity, by developing his argument,—rather incurred the hazard of
injuring Mr. Townsend's future prospects. Mr. Cumberland (whose talents
I shall not depreciate by the humble tribute of my praise) and Mr. Townsend
must not suppose me actuated by unworthy motives in this suggestion. I
wish the author all the success he can wish himself, and shall be truly happy
to see epic poetry weighed up from the bathos where it lies sunken with
Southey, Cottle, Cowley (Mrs. or Abraham), Ogilvy, Wilkie, Pye, and all
the 'dull of past and present days'. Even if he is not a *Milton*, he may be better
than *Blackmore*; if not a *Homer*, an *Antimachus*. I should deem myself presumptuous, as a young man, in offering advice, were it not addressed to one
still younger. Mr. Townsend has the greatest difficulties to encounter; but in
conquering them he will find employment; in having conquered them, his
reward. I know too well 'the scribbler's scoff, the critic's contumely'; and I am
afraid time will teach Mr. Townsend to know them better. Those who succeed, and those who do not, must bear this alike, and it is hard to say which
have most of it. I trust that Mr. Townsend's share will be from *envy*; he will

soon know mankind well enough not to attribute this expression of malice. This note was written before the author was apprised of Mr. Cumberland's death. 1811. [B's note, *LB–Proof M*, last sentence added to *M*] The Revd. George Townsend (1788–1857), author of *Poems* (1810) and *Armageddon* (1815). Richard Cumberland died in May 1811. See also *EBSR*, 225 and B's note.

193. Opening line of Bowles's *Spirit of Discovery by Sea* (1805).

200. Milton, *Paradise Lost*, I. 1.

208. Milton, *Paradise Lost*, I. 63.

224. Harvey, the *circulator* of the *circulation* of the blood, used to fling away Virgil in his ecstacy of admiration and say, 'the book had a devil'. Now such a character as I am copying would probably fling it away also, but rather wish that 'the devil had the book'; not from dislike to the poet, but a well-founded horror of hexameters. Indeed, the public school penance of 'Long and Short' is enough to beget an antipathy to poetry for the residue of a man's life, and, perhaps, so far may be an advantage. [B's note, *T*, *Proof BMB*, *Proof M*]

227. *Infandum, regina, jubes renovare dolorem.* I dare say Mr. T[a]v[e]ll (to whom I mean no affront) will understand me; and it is no matter whether any one else does or no.—To the above events, 'quaeque ipse miserrima vidi, et quorum pars magna fui', all times and terms bear testimony. [B's note, *LB–Proof M*] The Revd. G. F. Tavell was a fellow and tutor at Trinity during B's residence. B alludes to his famous bear (see *BLJ* I. 135), and quotes from Virgil, *Aeneid*, II. 3.

239. 'Hell', a gaming-house so called, where you risk little, and are cheated of a good deal. 'Club', a pleasant purgatory, where you lose more, and are not supposed to be cheated at all. [B's note, *M–Proof M*]

277–8. See Shakespeare's *King John*.

279–80. 'Irene had to speak two lines with the bowstring round her neck; but the audience cried out "Murder!" and she was obliged to go off the stage alive.' *Boswell's Johnson* [B's note, *LB*, *M*, *T*] See Boswell's *Life of Dr. Johnson* for 6 Feb. 1749.

288. In the postscript to *The Castle Spectre*, Mr. Lewis tells us, that though blacks were unknown in England at the period of his action, yet he has made the anachronism to set off the scene: and if he could have produced the effect 'by making his heroine blue',—I quote him—'blue he would have made her!' [B's note, *LB*, *M*, *T*] B quotes from Lewis's 'Address to the Reader', where he defended his character Hassan from the attacks of the critics.

294. See John Dennis, *An Essay on the Opera's After the Italian Manner* . . . (1706), and see *EBSR* 608–37.

309. *Fop's Alley:* a gangway at the Opera House (see letter to Murray, 9 Nov. 1820).

314. In the year 1808, happening at the opera to tread on the toes of a very well-dressed man, I turned round to apologize, when, to my utter

astonishment, I recognized the face of the porter of the very hotel where I then lodged in Albemarle Street. So here was a gentleman who ran every morning forty errands for half a crown, throwing away half a guinea at night, besides the expense of his habiliments, and the hire of his 'Chapeau de Bras'. [B's note, *LB*, *M*, *T*]

317. The first theatrical representations, entitled 'Mysteries and Moralities', were generally enacted at Christmas, by monks (as the only persons who could read), and latterly by the clergy and students of the universities. The dramatis personae were usually Adam, Pater Coelestis, Faith, Vice, and sometimes an angel or two; but these were eventually superseded by *Gammer Gurton's Needle*.—Vide Warton's *History of English Poetry* (*passim*). [B's note, *LB*, *M*, *T*]

318. 2 Samuel 6: 14.

326. *Benvolio* ['Lord Grosvenor' in *MS. LB*] does not bet; but every man who maintains racehorses is a promoter of all the concomitant evils of the turf. Avoiding to bet is a little pharisaical. Is it an exculpation? I think not. I never yet heard a bawd praised for chastity, because *she herself* did not commit fornication. [B's note, *LB*, *M*, *T*] Robert, second Earl Grosvenor (1767–1845), a horse-breeder and patron of the turf, argued in the House of Lords in 1799 and 1807 for the suppression of Sunday newspapers.

328. Samuel Foote (1720–77), actor and playwright.

333. *Hamlet*, v. i. 184.

337. See Henry Carey, *Chrononhotonthologos* (1734).

339–48. Addressed directly to Hobhouse who, B said, was to 'fill the same part [in *Hints*] that the "Pisones" do in Horace' (*BLJ* II. 43 and see also 45–6). Hobhouse had left B in Greece in 1810.

347. Under Plato's pillow a volume of the *Mimes* of Sophron was found the day he died.—Vide Barthélemi, De Pauw, or Diogenes Laërtius, if agreeable. De Pauw calls it a jest-book. Cumberland, in his *Observer*, terms it moral, like the sayings of Publius Syrus. [B's note, *LB*, *M*, *T*] B lifted his information from Richard Cumberland's *The Observer* (4th edn., 1791), III. 262, which B practically quotes verbatim.

353. His speech on the Licensing Act, is reckoned one of his most eloquent efforts. [B's note *LB*, *M*, *T*] In 1737 Sir Robert Walpole brought in the Licensing Act which, among other things, subjected dramatic writing to censorship by the Lord Chamberlain. Lord Chesterfield's speech against the act was famous. It was not liberalized until 1857. For Chesterfield ''gainst laughter' see his *Letters to his Son*, 9 Mar. O.S. 1748.

360. Michael Perez, the 'Copper Captain' in *Rule a Wife and Have a Wife*. [B's note *M*, *T*] The play is by Fletcher (1624). Archer and Sullen are characters in Farquhar's *The Beaux' Strategem* (1707).

364. The Revd. Dr. Francis Willis (1717–1807), one of George III's physicians.

365. See Gay's *The Beggar's Opera*.

368. Jeremy Collier's controversy with Congreve, etc., on the subject of the drama, is too well known to require further comment. [B's note *LB*, *M*, *T*] Collier's famous pamphlet, *A Short View of the Immorality . . . of the English Stage* (1697). Congreve did not fare well in the controversy.

375. Michael Servetus: burned for heresy in 1553. Calvin turned him over to the authorities.

379. Hebrews 12: 6.

380. *Baxter's Shove to heavy-a——d Christians*, the veritable title of a book once in good repute, and likely enough to be so once again.—Mr. Simeon is the very bully of beliefs, and castigator of 'good works'. He is ably supported by John Stickles, a labourer in the same vinyard:—but I say no more, for, according to Johnny in full congregation, '*No hopes for them as laughs.*' [B's note *Y*, *T*] *An Effectual Shove to the heavy-arse Christian* (1768) was by William Bunyan. Charles Simeon (1758–1836), a fiery evangelical leader; Stickles: see *BLJ* v. 144.

387. Ambrose Phillips (1675?–1749); see his *Pastorals* (1709).

405–6. See B's remarks on the octosyllabic couplet in *Corsair*, 'Dedication'.

421–2. Pope, *Essay on Criticism*, 124–5.

430. ibid. 438.

442. *Bristol-Stone*: i.e. paste jewellery.

461. *Democritus*: of Abdera (b. 470? 490? B.C.), the celebrated philosopher. His low opinion of the generality of men earned him the epithets 'laughing philosopher' and 'the mocker' (see Juvenal, *Satires* X. 33–4 and Seneca, *De Ira*, ii. 10).

474. As famous a tonsor as Licinus himself, and better paid, and may, like him, be one day a senator, having a better qualification than one half of the heads he crops, viz.—Independence. [B's note *LB*, *M*, *T*; and may. . . Independence: and may be like him a senator, one day or other: no disparagement to the High Court of Parliament. *LB*] Caesar made his barber Licinus a senator; Blake is the London perfumer, Benjamin Blake.

478. See *The Rehearsal*, II. i.

506. 1 Corinthians 13: 1.

515var. Peter I. Thellusson (d. 1797), a banker.

518. *Plum*: cant term for £100,000.

523. I have not the original by me, but the Italian translation runs as follows: 'E una cosa a mio creder molto stravagante, che un Padre desideri, o permetta, che suo figliuolo coltivi e perfezione questo talento.' A little further on: 'Si trovano di rado nel Parnaso le miniere d'oro e d'argento', —*Educazione dei Fanciulli del Signor Locke* [Venice, 1782], II. 87. [B's note *LB*, *M*, *T*] See Locke's *Some Thoughts Concerning Education* (1693).

528. 'Iro pauperior': a proverb: this is the same beggar who boxed with Ulysses for a pound of kid's fry, which he lost and half a dozen teeth besides. [B's note *LB*, *M*, *T*] See the *Odyssey*, XVIII. 98: Irus was the huge beggar who kept watch over Penelope.

The Irish gold mine in Wicklow, which yields just ore enough to swear by, or gild a bad guinea. [B's note, *T*]

554. As Mr. Pope took the liberty of damning Homer, to whom he was under great obligations—'*And Homer (damn him!) calls*'—it may be presumed that anybody or anything may be damned in verse by poetical license; and, in case of accident, I beg leave to plead so illustrious a precedent. [B's note *LB*, *M*, *T*; it may be . . . licence: I shall suppose one may damn anything else in verse with impunity. *LB*] The quotation is not from Pope.

555–6. Pope, *Essay on Criticism*, 235–6.

563. For the story of Billy Havard's tragedy, see Davies's *Life of Garrick* [(1808) II. 205]. I believe it is *Regulus*, or *Charles the First*. The moment it was known to be his the theatre thinned, and the bookseller refused to give the customary sum for the copyright. [B's note, *LB*, *M*, *T*]

582. Thomas Erskine (1750–1823), famous orator and advocate.

586var. The Devil and Jeffrey are here placed antithetically to gods and men, such being their usual position, and their due one—according to the facetious saying, 'If God won't take you, the Devil must'; and I am sure no one durst object to his taking the poetry, which, rejected by Horace, is accepted by Jeffrey. That these gentlemen are in some cases kinder,—the one to countrymen, and the other from his odd propensity to prefer evil to good,—than the 'gods, men, and columns' of Horace, may be seen by a reference to the review of Campbell's *Gertrude of Wyoming* [1809]; and in No. 31 of the *Edinburgh Review* (given to me the other day by the captain of an English frigate off Salamis), there is a similar concession to the mediocrity of Jamie Graham's *British Georgics* [1809]. It is fortunate for Campbell, that his fame neither depends on his last poem, nor the puff of the *Edinburgh Review*. The catalogues of our English are also less fastidious than the pillars of the Roman librarians. A word more with the author of *Gertrude of Wyoming*. At the end of a poem, and even of a couplet, we have generally 'that unmeaning thing we call a thought'; so Mr. Campbell concludes with a thought in such a manner as to fulfil the whole of Pope's prescription, and be as 'unmeaning' as the best of his brethren:—

> 'Because I may not *stain* with grief
> The death-song of an Indian chief.'

When I was in the fifth form, I carried to my master the translation of a chorus in Prometheus, wherein was a pestilent expression about 'staining a voice', which met with no quarter. Little did I think that Mr. Campbell would have adopted my fifth form 'sublime'—at least in so conspicuous a situation. 'Sorrow' has been 'dry' (in proverbs), and 'wet' (in sonnets), this many a day; and now it '*stains*', and stains a sound, of all feasible things! To be sure, death-songs might have been stained with that same grief to very good purpose, if Outalissi had clapped down his stanzas on wholesome paper for the *Edinburgh Evening Post*, or any other given hyperborean gazette; or if the said Outalissi had been troubled with the slightest second sight of his own notes embodied on the last proof of an overcharged quarto; but as he is supposed to have been an improvisatore on this occasion, and probably to the last tune he ever chanted in this world, it would have done him no discredit to have made his exit with a mouthful of common sense. Talking of 'staining' (as Caleb Quotem says) 'put me in mind' of a certain couplet, which Mr. Campbell will find in a writer for whom he, and his school, have no small contempt:—

'E'en copious Dryden wanted, or forgot,
The last and greatest art—the art to *blot!*'

[B's note in *M, T*] unmeaning . . . thought: Pope, *Essay on Criticism*, 355; the final couplet is from Pope, *Imitations of Horace*, 'Epistle II', 280–1. See also *EBSR* 321 and n.

598. John ('Gentleman') Jackson (1769–1845), boxing champion of England (1795–1803), was a good friend of B; his rooms in Bond Street were headquarters of the Pugilistic Club. See *DJ* XI. st. 19.

611. Cf. Pope, *Imitations of Horace*, 'Epistle II', 108.

616. Recalls Pope's *Eloisa to Abelard*, 228.

617. Mr. Southey has lately tied another canister to his tail, in the 'Curse of Kehama'. 1811. [B's note, *Proof M*] maugre the neglect of *Madoc*, etc., and has in one instance had a wonderful effect. A literary friend of mine, walking out one lovely evening last summer, on the eleventh bridge of the Paddington canal, was alarmed by the cry of 'one in jeopardy': he rushed along, collected a body of Irish haymakers (supping on butter-milk in an adjacent paddock), procured three rakes, one eel-spear and a landing net, and at last (*horresco referens*) pulled out—his own publisher. The unfortunate man was gone for ever, and so was a large quarto wherewith he had taken the leap, which proved, on inquiry, to have been Mr. Southey's last work. Its 'alacrity of sinking' was so great, that it has never since been heard of; though some maintain that it is at this moment concealed at Alderman Birch's pastry premises, Cornhill. Be this as it may, the coroner's inquest brought in a verdict of '*Felo de bibliopolâ*' against a 'quarto unknown'; and circumstantial evidence being since strong against *The Curse of Kehama* [1810] (of which the above words are an exact description), it will be tried by its peers next session in Grub-street—Arthur, Alfred, Davideis, Richard Cœur de Lion, Exodus, Exodiad, Epigoniad, Calvary, Fall of Cambria, Siege of Acre, Don Roderick, and Tom Thumb the Great, are the names of the twelve jurors. The judges are Pye, Bowles, and the bell-man of St. Sepulchre's.

The same advocates, pro and con, will be employed as are now engaged in Sir F. Burdett's celebrated cause in the Scotch courts. The public anxiously await the result, and all *live* publishers will be subpoenaed as witnesses.— But Mr. Southey has published *The Curse of Kehama*,—an inviting title to quibblers. By the bye, it is a good deal beneath Scott and Campbell, and not much above Southey, to allow the booby Ballantyne to entitle them, in the *Edinburgh Annual Register* (of which, by the bye, Southey is editor) 'the grand poetical triumvirate of the day'. But, on second thoughts, it can be no great degree of praise to be the one-eyed leaders of the blind, though they might as well keep to themselves 'Scott's thirty thousand copies sold', which must sadly discomfort poor Southey's unsaleables. Poor Southey, it should seem, is the 'Lepidus' of this poetical triumvirate. I am only surprised to see him in such good company.

> 'Such things, we know, are neither rich nor rare,
> But wonder how the devil *he* came there.'

The trio are well defined in the sixth proposition of Euclid:—'Because, in the triangles D B C, A C B; D B is equal to A C; and B C common to both; the two sides D B, B C, are equal to the two A C, C B, each to each, and the angle D B C is equal to the angle A C B: therefore, the base D C is equal to the base A B, and the triangle D B C (Mr. Southey) is equal to the triangle A C B, the *less* to the *greater*, which is *absurd*,' etc.—The editor of the *Edinburgh Register* will find the rest of the theorem hard by his stabling; he has only to cross the river; 'tis the first turnpike t' other side *Pons Asinorum*.*

*This Latin has sorely puzzled the University of Edinburgh. Ballantyne said it meant the 'Bridge of Berwick', but Southey claimed it as half English; Scott swore it was the 'Brig o' Stirling': he had just passed two King James's and a dozen Douglasses over it. At last it was decided by Jeffrey, that it meant nothing more nor less than the 'counter of Archy Constable's shop'. [B's note in *T*]

alacrity of sinking: Merry Wives of Windsor, III. v. 13; for *Alfred*, *Exodus*, and *Fall of Cambria* see *EBSR* 406 and 966 and nn.; Richard Hole, *Arthur, or the Northern Enchantment* (1789), Abraham Cowley, *Davideis* (1656), Sir James Bland Burges, *Richard the First* (1801), and Burges and Richard Cumberland, *Exodiad* (1808), W. Wilkie, *Epigoniad* (1757), Cumberland, *Calvary* (1792), Hannah Cowley, *Siege of Acre* (1801), and Scott's *Vision of Don Roderick* (1811); Pye, Bowles: see *EBSR* 102, 327 ff.; *Sir. F. Burdett's celebrated cause:* Sir F. Burdett v. William Scott (cf. *Courier*, 16 July 1811, for details); *booby Ballantyne:* James Ballantyne (1772–1833), Scott's publisher; *one-eyed leaders of the blind:* proverbial; *Lepidus:* M. Aemelius Lepidus (d. 13 B.C.), the least significant of the triumvirs (with Octavian and Anthony); couplet: Pope. 'Epistle to Dr. Arbuthnot', 171–2; *Archy Constable:* Archibald Constable, the bookseller (see *EBSR* 153 n.).

620. See *EBSR* 309 n.

621. Voltaire's *Pucelle* is not quite so immaculate as Mr. Southey's *Joan of Arc* [1796], and yet I am afraid the Frenchman has both more truth and poetry too on his side—(they rarely go together)—than our patriotic minstrel, whose first essay was in praise of a fanatical French strumpet, whose title of witch would be correct with the change of the first letter. [B's note, *M*, *T*]

622. Like a poem by a celebrated author, the first book of which I read at Malta, on a trunk of Eyre's, 19, Cockspur Street. If this be doubted, I shall buy a portmanteau to quote from. 1811. [B's note, *M*, *T*, *Proof M*; Like... of which: Like Sir Bland Burges's *Richard*, the tenth book of which *M*, *T*] For B's revision of this note, in deference to Burges, see his letter to Hobhouse, 21 Sept. 1820. See also 617 n.

622. *Quito:* capital of Ecuador.

623. Ovid, *Metamorphoses*, X, XI; J. Lemprière (d. 1824), classicist: see his famous *Bibliotheca Classica* (*Classical Dictionary*) (1788).

641–4. *Tyrtaeus ... Ithome:* Spartan elegiac poet (mid-7th cent B.C.) whose songs inspired the Greeks to victory over the Messenians at Ithome.

662. The reference is to the British role in the Peninsular war. B's sarcasm was out of date after Waterloo.

677. *Pollio:* Samuel Rogers.

680.   'Tum quoque marmorea caput a cervice revulsum,
              Gurgite cum medio portans Oeagrius Hebrus,
              Volveret Eurydicen vox ipsa, et frigida lingua;
              Ah, miseram Eurydicen! anima fugiente vocabat;
              Eurydicen toto referebant flumine ripae.'

Georgic [IV. 523–7] [B's note, *T*, *Proof M*]

694. This well meaning gentleman has spoiled some excellent shoemakers, and being accesory to the poetical undoing of many of the industrious poor. Nathaniel Bloomfield and his brother Bobby have set all Somersetshire singing; nor has the malady confined itself to one county. Pratt too (who once was wiser) has caught the contagion of patronage, and decoyed a poor fellow named Blackett into poetry; but he died during the operation, leaving one child and two volumes of 'Remains' utterly destitute. The girl, if she don't take a poetical twist, and come forth as a shoemaking Sappho, may do well; but the 'tragedies' are as ricketty as if they had been the offspring of an Earl or a Seatonian prize poet. The patrons of this poor lad are certainly answerable for his end; and it ought to be an indictable offence. But this is the least they have done: for, by a refinement of barbarity, they have made the (late) man posthumously ridiculous, by printing what he would have had sense enough never to print himself. Certes these rakers of 'Remains' come under the statute against 'resurrection men'. What does it signify whether a poor dear dead dunce is to be stuck up in Surgeons' or in Stationers' Hall? Is it so bad to unearth his bones as his blunders? Is it not better to gibbet his body on a heath, than his soul in an octavo? 'We know what we are, but we know not what we may be'; and it is to be hoped we never shall know, if a man who has passed through life with a sort of éclat is to find himself a mountebank on the other side of Styx, and made, like poor Joe Blackett, the laughing-stock of purgatory. The plea of publication is to provide for the child; now, might not some of this *Sutor ultra Crepidam's* friends and seducers

have done a decent action without inveighling Pratt into biography? And then his inscription split into so many modicums!—'To the Duchess of Somuch, the Right Hon. So-and-So, and Mrs. and Miss Somebody, these volumes are,' etc. etc.—why, this is doling out the 'soft milk of dedication' in gills,—there is but a quart, and he divides it among a dozen. Why, Pratt, hadst thou not a puff left? Dost thou think six families of distinction can share this in quiet? There is a child, a book, and a dedication: send the girl to her grace, the volumes to the grocer, and the dedication to the devil.

I beg Nathaniel's pardon: he is not a cobbler; *it* is a *tailor*, but begged Capel Lofft to sink the profession in his preface to two pair of panta—psha! —of cantos, which he wished the public to try on; but the sieve of a patron let it out, and so far saved the expense of an advertisement to his country customers—Merry's 'Moorfields whine' was nothing to all this. The 'Della Cruscans' were people of some education, and no profession; but these Arcadians ('Arcades ambo'—bumpkins both) send out their native nonsense without the smallest alloy, and leave all the shoes and small-clothes in the parish unrepaired, to patch up Elegies on Enclosures, and Paeans to Gunpowder. Sitting on a shopboard, they describe the fields of battle, when the only blood they ever saw was shed from the finger; and an 'Essay on War' is produced by the ninth part of a 'poet';

'And own that *nine* such poets made a Tate.'

Did Nathan ever read that line of Pope? and if he did, why not take it as his motto? [B's note, *T*, cancelled in Proof *M*]

For Pratt, Bloomfield, Blackett, Capel Lofft, and Merry see *EBSR* 319var. and n., 759–98 and nn. Blackett's *Remains* was published by Pratt in 1811.

   Sutor ultra Crepidam: slightly misquoted from Pliny the Elder, *Historia Naturalis*, XXXV. 10, 36.

   Arcades ambo: Virgil, *Eclogues*, VII. 4.

   And own . . . Tate: Pope, 'Epistle to Dr. Arbuthnot', 190.

   697. *Druid:* i.e. scribbler; see *EBSR* 741.

   722. Here will Mr. Gifford allow me to introduce once more to his notice the sole survivor, the 'ultimus Romanorum', the last of the Cruscanti— 'Edwin' the 'profound' by our Lady of Punishment! here he is, as lively as in the days of 'well said Baviad the Correct'. I thought Fitzgerald had been the tail of poesy; but, alas! he is only the penultimate. [B then quotes 'A Familiar Epistle' and 'On Some Modern Quacks and Reformists'. The note is in *T*, and cancelled in *Proof M*.] The poems are by T. Vaughan, published in the *Morning Chronicle* 7 Oct. 1811. In the *Baviad*, 350, Gifford ridicules 'Edwin's mewlings' by the 'profound Mr. T. Vaughan'.

   722var. Of 'John Joshua, Earl of Carysfort', I know nothing at present, but from an advertisement in an old newspaper of certain Poems and Tragedies by his Lordship, which I saw by accident in the Morea. Being a rhymer himself, he will forgive the liberty I take with his name, seeing, as he must, how very commodious it is at the close of that couplet; and as for what follows and goes before, let him place it to the account of the other Thane; since I cannot, under these circumstances, augur pro or con the contents of his 'foolscap crown octavos'. [B's note in *M*] John Joshua Proby, first Earl of Carysfort, published *Dramatic and Miscellaneous Works* (1810).

741. Echoes Milton, 'Lycidas', 11.

751. Minerva being the first by Jupiter's head-piece, and a variety of equally unaccountable parturitions upon earth, such as Madoc, etc., etc. [B's note, *M*, *T*, cancelled in *Proof M*]

764. 'A crust for the critics.' Bayes, in '*The Rehearsal*'. [II. ii] [B's note, *M*, *T*, cancelled in *Proof M*]

768. And the 'waiters' are the only fortunate people who can 'fly' from them; all the rest, viz. the sad subscribers to the 'Literary Fund', being compelled, by courtesy, to sit out the recitation without a hope of exclaiming, 'Sic' (that is, by choking Fitz. with bad wine, or worse poetry) 'me servavit Apollo!' [B's note, *LB*, *M*, *T*, cancelled in *Proof M*] For W. J. Fitzgerald see *EBSR* 1 and n.

770. *placeman:* one who holds a government sinecure.

786. On his table were found these words:—'What Cato did, and Addison approved, cannot be wrong.' But Addison did not 'approve'; and if he had, it would not have mended the matter. He had invited his daughter on the same water-party; but Miss Budgell, by some accident, escaped this last paternal attention. Thus fell the sycophant of 'Atticus', and the enemy of Pope! 1811. [B's note, *LB*, *M*, *T*, *Proof M*] Eustace Budgell (1686–1737), a friend and relative of Addison.

795. If 'dosed with', etc. be censured as low, I beg leave to refer to the original for something still lower; and if any reader will translate 'Minxerit in patrios cineres', etc. into a decent couplet, I will insert said couplet in lieu of the present. 1811. [B's note, *LB*, *M*, *T*, *Proof M*]

150A. This is the 'Jeffrey passage' discussed in the previous commentary.

5. To the Eclectic or Christian Reviewers I have to return thanks for the fervour of that charity which, in 1809, induced them to express a hope that a thing then published by me might lead to certain consequences, which, although natural enough, surely came but rashly from reverend lips. I refer them to their own pages, where they congratulated themselves on the prospect of a tilt between Mr. Jeffrey and myself, from which some great good was to accrue, provided one or both were knocked on the head. Having survived two years and a half those 'Elegies' which they were kindly preparing to review, I have no peculiar gusto to give them 'so joyful a trouble', except, indeed, 'upon compulsion, Hal'; but if, as David says in *The Rivals*, it should come to 'bloody sword and gun fighting', we 'won't run, will we, Sir Lucius?' I do not know what I had done to these Eclectic gentlemen: my works are their lawful perquisite, to be hewn in pieces like Agag, if it seem meet unto

them: but why they should be in such a hurry to kill off their author, I am ignorant. 'The race is not always to the swift, nor the battle to the strong': and now, as these Christians have 'smote me on one cheek', I hold them up the other; and, in return for their good wishes, give them an opportunity of repeating them. Had any other set of men expressed such sentiments, I should have smiled, and left them to the 'recording angel'; but from the pharisees of Christianity decency might be expected. I can assure these brethren, that, publican and sinner as I am, I would not have treated 'mine enemy's dog thus'. To show them the superiority of my brotherly love, if ever Reverend Messrs. Simeon or Ramsden should be engaged in such a conflict as that in which they requested me to fall, I hope they may escape with being 'winged' only, and that Heaviside may be at hand to extract the ball.—[B's note in *B, T*]

> *so . . . trouble:* recalling *Macbeth*, II. iii. 48.
> *upon compulsion, Hal:* recalling *I Henry IV*, II. iv. 236–8.
> *David.* The words are spoken by Acres.
> *The race . . . the strong :* Ecclesiastes 9: 11.
> *smote me on one cheek:* Matthew 5: 39.
> *mine . . . thus:* King Lear, IV. vii. 35.
> *Simeon or Ramsden.* See line 380 n.; Richard Ramsden, D.D. (1762–1831), Senior Dean, Trinity College, Cambridge (1798), and a famous preacher.
> *Heaviside:* a surgeon, see *EBSR* 686 n. The article B has in mind appeared in the *Eclectic Review* for May 1809.
> 14. *Macbeth*, V. vii. 17.
> 25. See Brougham's review of *HI* (*LJ* I. 344).
> 32. 'Invenies alium, si te hic fastidit, Alexin.' [B's note, *M, T*] Virgil, *Eclogues*, II. 73.

151. *MSS. and Proofs.* Three textually relevant MSS. of the poem exist. First is B's draft, the so-called Stanhope MS. (*MS. S*, location: Kent) which lacks lines 43–6, 149–56, 203–64 and the notes to the poem. *MS. S* is undated, but carries the title and the epigraph, both added at a later stage. The text contains the following: 1–32 (on a single folded quarto sheet, numbered 1); 33–42, 47–54 (on both sides of an unnumbered half sheet); 55–122 (a single foolscap sheet folded into four pages, numbered 2: the handwriting shows that 63–122 were written later than 55–62); 123–48, 157–202 (another foolscap sheet folded into four pages, numbered 3); 265–312 (another foolscap sheet as above, numbered 5). Lines 203–64 were evidently written on the missing fourth sheet. *MS. S* also contains—in the hand of Arthur Philip, sixth Earl Stanhope (1838–1905)—a cover title-page and a three-page MS. description of the circumstances of the poem and how Stanhope acquired the MS. The substance of the provenance data is as follows. The MS. (comprising only pages 1, 2, 3, and 5) was purchased at auction in 1848 by John Murray, who then sold it to Stanhope, at the latter's request. Stanhope purchased the half-sheet page separately, in May 1851, at a Sotheby auction. Stanhope adds a postscript saying that in April 1856 he saw another holograph MS. of the poem owned by the Duke of Newcastle.

The Duke's MS. is *MS. B* (present location: Berg) It is complete, though 149–56 are plainly a late addition. It carries a head-note by R. C. Dallas stating that it is the 'original, written at Athens', and B has dated the MS. at the top of the first page: 'Nov. 17, 1811 (Athens, March 1811).'

Finally, there is an amanuensis copy made from *MS. B* with lines 157–62 added by Dallas after having been accidentally omitted by the copyist. This was copy text for *Curse1812* (see below) and is here designated *MS. Υ* (location: Yale). A few changes were made between *B* and *Υ* and between *Υ* and *Curse1812*. Henry Drury's MS. of the poem at Harvard, and Dallas's at Murray's (in a copy of *EBSR5*), were both made from *Curse1812* and hence do not bear on the text.

The surviving MS. scraps include: lines 45–6 (*MS. A*, from the collection of Francis Lewis Randolph on deposit at the Univ. of Pennsylvania Library); a correction for line 58 (*MS. MA*, a letter to Murray of 4 Oct. 1813; location, Murray: see *BLJ* III. 132); lines 149–56 (*MS. P*, in a letter to Hodgson, 4 Dec. 1811; location: Pforzheimer).

Two separate MSS. exist for the 'Lines Associated with *The Curse of Minerva*', sometimes called 'Carmina Byronis in C. Elgin': B's first fair copy dated 10 Mar. 1811 (*MS. P*, location: Pforzheimer), and his second fair copy dated 'Athens 1810, 1811' (*MS. L*, location: Bodleian–Lovelace).

Three proofs exist under the title 'A Fragment'. They were printed in 1813, when B intended to place such a piece among the short poems at the end of *CHP(7)*: see *BLJ* II. 228, 234. Two of these proofs contain lines 1–54 (location: Huntington and Murray), and the Huntington proof carries accidental corrections at lines 29 and 32, and a typographical correction in the n. to line 44. At the end of this proof B writes: 'As thus etc. Add to line 92 [*sic*: B means 62] and then leave some asterisks thus ★ ★ ★ ★.' (The note means that the printer should add from line 55, which begins 'As thus', to line 62.) Also at the Huntington are four pages from *Curse1812* numbered 7–10 and containing lines 49–103. They are marked at the end in an unknown hand 'June 1813'. These pages carry various printing directions and are evidently what remains of the copy text for the proofs of 'A Fragment'. The 54-line proof of 'A Fragment' at Murray's is uncorrected. Also at Murray's is an uncorrected 62-line proof, same title. This was printed from the directions on the Huntington proof, and it carries B's revision for line 58.

Composition and Publishing History. Every critic and editor of B has accepted the dating of the poem which B indicated in the note he placed before the text in *Curse1812*: Athens. Capuchin Convent, 17 Mar., 1811. But this date is quite misleading. In fact, most of *Curse* was written in Nov. 1811, after B had returned from the Levant. The dating on *MS. B* itself suggests two phases of composition (i.e. begun in Athens in Mar. 1811, finished in London in November, around the 17th). The truth of this general dating scheme is corroborated by internal evidence. Lines 239–78 contain topical references to events that occurred between June and Dec. 1811 (see notes below).

The sequence of composition can be more particularly described. Between Aug. and Nov. 1811 B had to mollify Cawthorne, the publisher of *EBSR*, because B had chosen Murray as his publisher for *CHP I–II* (see *BLJ* II. 83–131 *passim*). B gave Cawthorne *Hints* to publish, in a new edition with *EBSR*, but the project was hanging fire because B wanted someone to correct the printing of *Hints* to make certain that the Latin text was put in accurate parallel. Furthermore, Cawthorne was pressing B for a less literary, not to say less pedantic, work than *Hints*. On 17 Nov.—the date on *MS. B* —B wrote to Hobhouse with the first mention of *Curse:* 'Cawthorne is also at work with a fifth Edition of [*EBSR*]; this and the [*Hints*], with a thing on Ld. Elgin, called the "Curse of Minerva" which you have never seen . . . will make a monstrous vol. of Crown Octavo' (*BLJ* II. 131). B was probably finishing *MS. B* on 17 Nov. *MS. Y* was made from *MS. B* at some time after 4 Dec., when B completed the text by adding lines 149–56. *MS. Y* was probably not made until early in 1812.

The condition of *MS. S* strongly suggests that only lines 1–42, 47–62 were written in March in Athens. Moreover, the MS. clearly indicates that this famous passage was itself not written as a single unit. Lines 1–32, 55–62 made up one fragmentary piece of verse written in Athens, and 33–42, 47–54 comprise another, distinct piece. B probably joined them together in November when he took it into his head to use both pieces for the introductory portion of his satire. It should be observed, however, that when B wrote 1–32, 55–62, he already seems to have intended the lines to introduce a 'truthful' rather than a 'romantic' poem. After line 62 in *MS. S* is the following cancellation: 'But now a Vision if it bear the name / Recalled me back to Truth.' At this point the March 1811 stage of the poem breaks off.

B's plans to publish *Curse* with *Hints* and *EBSR* fell through in Dec. 1811 and Jan. 1812, largely because B was now friendly with people like Moore and Lord Holland, whom he had attacked in *EBSR* (see commentaries for *EBSR* and *Hints*). Nevertheless, B did not want to abandon *Curse* altogether, so when he broke with Cawthorne early in 1812 he had Murray print eight copies of *Curse* for private circulation. This is *Curse1812*, and it seems to have been printed in May (see *BLJ* II. 178). Later in 1812 (*BLJ* II. 228, 234) B thought he would print lines 1–54 (or, later still, 1–62) separately as 'A Fragment', but this project was also abandoned. Instead, lines 1–54 were published in 1814 as the opening of Canto III of *Corsair* (see *Corsair* commentary).

B's wish not to publish the satire was thwarted when extensive excerpts appeared as 'The Malediction of Minerva; or, The Athenian Marble Merchant' (*New Monthly Magazine*, III, 1815), the first of a series of piracies. The first complete pirated text appeared under a Philadelphia imprint in 1815, but it was probably published in London. None of the pirated texts carry any authority; they derive from copies made from *Curse1812*. The first authorized English printing after *Curse1812* was in *1831*, and it has been collected thereafter. But no printed text has carried the corrected version of line 58 until now (see apparatus).

The 'Lines Associated' with the *Curse* were first printed in *Paris1826*. The authorized English editions append the first two lines in the notes for *Curse*, 107–8 in *1832*, and C first printed all six lines in its notes to the poem.

For further bibliography see *Borst*, 161–2; *C* I. 452–6 and VII. 207–8; *Wise*, I. 69–70. Copy text here is Samuel Rogers's copy of *Curse1812* (location: *BM*, Ashley 4725). Earlier bibliographers have suggested that 100 copies of *Curse1812* were printed, but this is not so (see above). In fact, though *Fugitive Pieces*, B's first (privately printed) book, has always been regarded as the rarest item in the bibliography, *Curse1812* may be even more rare. I have seen only three copies (the present copy text, and the copies at Texas and Pforzheimer).

Literary and Historical Background. The poem has B's most sustained attack upon Thomas Bruce, seventh Earl of Elgin (1766–1841), who brought the famous Elgin Marbles to England from Greece, at his own expense, and who eventually (1816) sold them to the government. *Curse* is anticipated, however, by *EBSR* (1007 and n.) and especially by *CHP II*, sts. 11–15 and notes.

The most thorough treatment of the historical circumstances surrounding the Elgin Marbles is in William St. Clair's *Lord Elgin and the Marbles* (1967). As St. Clair shows, the controversy over the Marbles (which arrived in England in 1804) actually began in mid-1807, when Elgin displayed the first part of the collection. But the controversy at first chiefly concerned 'the dry academic question of whether the marbles were truly "Phidian" or not'. With the appearance of B's attacks everything changed:

Now the question was what right had Elgin to remove the precious remains of a weak and proud nation. . . . The Elgin Marbles had now become a symbol—of Greece's ignominious slavery, of Europe's failure to help her, and of Britain's overweening pride. Whatever view one might take of Lord Elgin's activities the whole basis of public opinion was altered. *Childe Harold* [and, by extension, the relevant parts of *Curse*] has dominated all discussion of the Elgin Marbles ever since. (St. Clair, 189.)

But so much attention has been given to the most prominent figure in *Curse* that readers have tended to lose sight of the poem's main subject, of which Lord Elgin is only the chief symbol. As with *Waltz* later, *Curse* uses its focusing symbol as an emblem of more general evils, which B specifies in his attack upon England's foreign and domestic policies in the third section of the poem (211–312). The first section (1–54), a celebrated descriptive passage, has been thought out of place, but it evidently serves as a symbolic introduction to the theme of temporal spoliation of cultural values.

Of the literary influences on the poem, Fuess (pp. 88–9) argues plausibly for Churchill's *Prophecy of Famine* (1763), in particular on the passages which vilify the Scottish climate and people. St. Clair shows B's debt in *Curse* to John Galt's *Atheniad* (published in 1820 but written in Athens in 1810). B borrowed and read Galt's MS. when they were in Greece together (see St. Clair, 187–202 *passim*). Finally, *Curse* may have been written with Cicero's *Verrine Orations* somewhere in B's mind. It is true that the *Orations* are principally concerned with corruption in government, and that Cicero is even a little contemptuous of the art works stolen by Verres. Nevertheless, the *Orations* and *Curse* have obvious parallels, and B's expansion of his attack from Elgin to the English political scene in general only emphasizes these parallels.

For further comment see *Fuess*, 85–92; *Marchand*, I. 221–6; *Borst*, 96–100.

title Minerva: 'the goddess of wisdom, war, and all the liberal arts' (Lemprière); her Greek name was Athena, the protectress of Athens.

epigraph Virgil, *Aeneid*, XII. 948–9.

ATHENS . . . 1811 See commentary.

1–62. See commentary.

7. Aegina, an island 20 miles from the Piraeus in the Saronic Gulf; Hydra, 4 miles off the SE. coast of Argolis.

12. *Salamis:* in the Gulf of Aegina where the Greek fleet defeated the Persians (480 B.C.)

22. Socrates drank the hemlock a short time before sunset (the hour of execution), notwithstanding the entreaties of his disciples to wait till the sun went down. [B] See Xenophon, *Memorabilia*, IV. 8 and Plato's *Phaedrus*.

29. *Cithaeron:* mountain north of Corinth, in Boeotia.

33. *Hymettus:* mountain near Athens, famous for its honey.

34. The twilight in Greece is much shorter than in our own country; the days in winter are longer, but in summer of less duration. [B]

44. The kiosk is a Turkish summer-house; the palm is without the present walls of Athens, not far from the temple of Theseus, between which and the tree the wall intervenes. Cephisus' stream is indeed scanty, and Ilissus has no stream at all. [B] See *Corsair*, III. 44 n.

59. *dome:* the Parthenon. B characteristically uses the word 'dome' in this generic sense (see, e.g., no. 63, line 1).

67. *Hecate:* the moon goddess (see line 63) in her more foreboding form. As Hecate she was the attendant of Persephone in the underworld, and goddess of ghosts. Hence, B's shift of names here from Dian to Hecate prepares for the appearance of Minerva.

76. *Dardan field:* i.e. the plains of Troy (cf. the *Iliad*).

80. See line 218. Minerva's shield was emblazoned with the Gorgon's head, which turned those who looked upon it to stone. The olive branch and owl (lines 83, 87) are associated with her.

95. Cf. *CHP II*. 4.

101. This is spoken of the city in general, and not of the Acropolis in particular. The temple of Jupiter Olympius, by some supposed the Pantheon, was finished by Hadrian; sixteen columns are standing, of the most beautiful marble and architecture. [B] Hadrian, Roman emperor (117–38) was a patron of the arts. The temple of Olympian Zeus is only one of his many public works.

Cecrops: founder and first king of Athens.

Pericles: Athenian statesman (495–429 B.C.), whose public works were so magnificent that his period of ascendancy is called the Golden Age of Athens.

104. Alaric (*c.* 370–410), king of the Visigoths, ravaged Attica (395–6) but spared Athens.

107 ff. See below, 'Lines Associated with *The Curse of Minerva*'.

118. An ironic allusion to the title of Dryden's play *All for Love, or The World Well Lost*.

122. His lordship's name, and that of one who no longer bears it, are carved conspicuously on the Parthenon; above, in a part not far distant, are the torn remnants of the basso-relievos, destroyed in a vain attempt to remove them. [B] 'The names Elgin and Mary Elgin with the date 1802 were carved deeply and clearly about half-way up one of the columns' (St. Clair, 193). B's lines allude to the breakup of Elgin's marriage to Mary Nisbet. Elgin's divorce action for adultery was successful (1808) but extremely unpleasant. Lady Elgin's lover was Robert Ferguson of Raith (see St. Clair, 144–6).

129. *Phyle's towers:* an Attic fortress just below Boeotia, that part of ancient Greece north of the Gulf of Corinth. Boeotia became proverbial (via Athenian sources) for a land of uncivilized and uncultivated people.

131. 'Irish bastards', according to Sir Callaghan O'Brallaghan. [B] In *Love à la Mode* (1759), by Charles Macklin (1697?–1797).

150. Pindar (*c.* 522–433 B.C.), Greece's greatest lyric poet, was born near Thebes, the capital of Boeotia.

153. Matthew 10: 14.

155–6. Genesis 18: 32.

164. Biblical; see, e.g., Deuteronomy 28: 46.

166. 'Perhaps a cruel allusion to the fact that Elgin's son was an epileptic' (St. Clair, 196 n.).

169. Principally William Richard Hamilton, Elgin's private secretary, and Giovanni Battista Lusieri, Elgin's chief painter. (See *CHP II*, sts. 11–12.) Hamilton and Lusieri were commissioned by Elgin to hire other artists.

178. Mr. West, on seeing the 'Elgin Collection' (I suppose we shall hear of the 'Abershaw' and 'Jack Shephard' collection), declared himself a 'mere tyro' in art. [B] Benjamin West (1738–1820), American historical painter. See West's letters to Elgin of 6 Feb. and 20 March 1811 in Hamilton's *Memorandum on the Subject of the Earl of Elgin's Pursuits in Greece* (1811).

Abershaw and Jack Shephard: 'Jerry' Abershaw (1773?–95) and 'Jack' Sheppard (1702–24), highwaymen.

182. Poor Crib was sadly puzzled when the marbles were first exhibited at Elgin House [1807]; he asked if it was not 'a stone shop'—He was right; it *is* a shop. [B] Crib: thieves' slang for a shop; hence, here, a shopman. See above, lines 172–4. B is especially contemptuous of Elgin for his efforts to sell the marbles to the government. The first attempt was made in 1810, but the marbles were not sold until 1816.

192. *Lais:* the name of two Greek courtesans (of the 5th and 4th centuries B.C.) celebrated for their beauty.

201. A direct echo of Galt's *Atheniad* (see St. Clair, 189 n.).

203. Herostratus set fire to the temple of Diana at Ephesus in 356 B.C. in order to immortalize himself.

213–20. B refers to England's bombardment of Copenhagen in Sept. 1807 and the ensuing diplomatic and military manœuvres. England had attacked Denmark in order to prevent Napoleon from gaining control of the Danish fleet. After the bombardment of Copenhagen, which was set ablaze for three days, England made a truce agreement with Denmark. But in 1808 she broke the terms of the truce by supporting the Swedish invasion of Denmark. Twelve thousand English troops, under Sir John Moore, were sent to support the Swedes. But England and Sweden subsequently fell out, and Moore was forced to return home without even landing his men. The sequence of events left England without any European bases, and without European allies as well ('hated and alone'). The Parliamentary opposition loudly decried the entire affair. See Steven Watson, *The Reign of George III, 1760–1815* (Oxford, 1960), 455–8.

221–8. B's reference is to the depredations of the Pindaris, under Chitu, which recurred in Central India from 1806. (See Charles Macfarlane, *The History of British India* (1881), 392.) But B's point may be even more subtle. If the 'Rebellion' refers to the notorious mutiny of English officers at Madras, which erupted in 1809, then the prophesied 'long arrear of northern blood' is presented as the necessary consequence of England's own 'lawless deeds' (cf. lines 209–12). The mutiny, in this reading, would be a sign of factional strife in England, which would itself be interpreted as the fatal consequence of a whole series of 'lawless deeds', particularly against India. Those deeds bring their 'Nemesis'. See, for details of the mutiny, Macfarlane, 356–61, and compare *CHP IV*, sts. 132–5 (and apparatus and notes), where B gives his most famous pronouncement on his 'particular favourite', Nemesis.

229–38. The victory of Barossa on 5 Mar. 1811. See *CHP I*, st. 90 and notes. The fact that the victory was 'won' by famished English troops is obviously a satiric thrust at the government and military leaders. The troops were in fact badly short of food. B's other irony here is that the Spanish and Portuguese at Barossa proved themselves reluctant and not very helpful allies. See William Napier, *History of the War in the Peninsula . . .* (1890) III. 26, 98, 102–7.

238. *Olympiads:* periods of four years. B uses the phrase 'six past Olympiads' in a letter to Hobhouse of 16 Nov. 1811 (*BLJ* II. 130).

242. The costs of maintaining the war against Napoleon were particularly hard on the labouring classes, who bore the worst burdens of a spiralling inflation. See Watson, op. cit. 469. For the 'Rapine' B refers to, see below, 271–6.

245.   'Blest paper credit! last and best supply,
             That lends Corruption lighter wings to fly.'

Pope, ['Epistle to Bathurst', III. 39–40]. [B]

247–54. *C* has a long note attempting to explain the topical allusions in this passage (see *C* I. 470–1 n.). His speculations are developed out of his text's asterisks at line 251, where Stanhope's name ought to have been. *MS. S* (the only one seen by *C*) does not have the name at 251, and the early editions all have asterisks. But in *MSS. B* and *T* the name is Stanhope.

The passage deals with the Gold Coin and Bank Note Bill, the so-called Stanhope Bill because it was proposed by Charles Stanhope, Lord Mahon and third Earl of Stanhope (1735–1813). Stanhope was an eccentric Radical peer more celebrated for his scientific pursuits than for his political views. Yet many of his ideas were enlightened and far in advance of his age, and he was particularly astute in financial matters. Among his fellow parliamentarians he was an object of distrust and antagonism; and, indeed, he often found it difficult to work with others. Stanhope's disgust at the proceedings of Parliament towards the end of the eighteenth century made him withdraw from all the proceedings for five years.

When Stanhope's bill was introduced in June 1811 a vigorous series of debates ensued in both houses (see the *Parliamentary Debates*, XX. 762–1116 *passim*). The bill was an effort to save the country from an extremely serious financial crisis. Briefly, it proposed making bank notes legal tender; it was an 'anti-bullionist' measure. Many opposed the bill, including Lord Holland, but it was eventually passed in mid July.

The two premiers referred to in line 247 are Henry Addington (1757–1844), first Viscount Sidmouth (1805), who was Prime Minister from 1801 to 1804, and William Henry Cavendish Bentinck, third Duke of Portland (1738–1809), Prime Minister from 1807 to 1809. Both listened to the wisdom of Athena, in B's view, because they would not support anti-bullionist legislation, which Pitt himself had to resort to in 1797 as a temporary measure. Nevertheless, B also alludes to the notorious mediocrity of both men in the general conduct of their office. The 'one' premier in line 249 is Sir Spencer Perceval (1762–1812), Prime Minister when the Stanhope Bill was passed. That Perceval sought the aid of Stanhope in the financial crisis is seen as an act of desperate folly. The 'he' and 'Him' in lines 252–3 refer to Stanhope.

248. Horace, *Ars Poetica*, 373.

255–8. B alludes to Aesop's fable, 'The Frogs Choose a King', and implies that England's lawmakers have followed the lead of a fool. The problem with deciphering the meaning of the passage involves line 258. *C* suggests that the 'Patrician clod' is Perceval, and implies that 'onion' is a reference to Perceval's head, which gives the impression of an almost transparent paleness (see his portrait in the National Gallery). Since Egyptian mythology and symbology nowhere show any inclination to divinize onions, *C* goes on to say that B took this image from Lady Ann Hamilton's *Epics of the Ton* (1807), specifically, from the following passage:

> Say, shall we bend to titles thus bestowed,
> And like the Egyptians, hail the calf a god?
> With toads, asps, onions, ornament the shrine,
> And reptiles own and pot-herbs things divine?

This passage does indeed seem to lie behind B's lines 251–8. The problem arises from seeing 'patrician clod' as a reference to Perceval, who was not an aristocrat. But in his governmental office he was 'First Lord of the Treasury and Chancellor of the Duchy of Lancaster', which may (cf. 'titles ... bestowed') be B's justification for calling him a patrician. I am inclined to think this reading is the most plausible. Nevertheless, the general syntactic organization of 250–8 leaves some doubt in my mind: for 255–8, syntactically considered, ought to refer to Stanhope, not to Perceval. Moreover, if Stanhope is the person referred to, 'patrician clod' makes perfect sense. But in that case, the divine onion again becomes problematic.

264. The Deal and Dover traffickers in specie. [B]

271–4. 'On November the 10th, a number of weavers assembling near Nottingham, began forcibly to enter houses in which there were [weaving frames], and destroy them' (*Annual Register* for 1811, 93). These actions escalated into mob violence when the authorities interposed. The military was eventually called in to quell the disturbances. See *LJ* II. 97, and B's speech of 1812 against the frame-breaking bill, ibid. 424–30; see also below, no. 181.

277–8. i.e. the Protestants and Catholics in Ireland. Trouble between these 'jarring sects' was increasing in recent years, largely because of the astute political manœuvring by Daniel O'Connell against the Act of Union. See Denis Gwyn, *Daniel O'Connell* (1929), 95–107.

286. *Bellona:* Roman goddess of war.

308. The war fires from the Iberian Peninsula to Germany are England's responsibility, B is saying, because she maintained hostilities against France. B was always sympathetic towards Napoleon—partly because he was attracted by the magnetism of the man, partly because he wanted to see the European monarchies replaced by republics.

311. Exodus 21: 23.

152. *MS. and Publishing History.* B's incomplete fair copy (*MS. T*, location:

Texas), which was printer's copy for CHP(1). A corrected proof is in the Murray archives, in a bound volume of various proofs for CHP(5) and CHP(7). First published CHP(1), collected thereafter. B printed the original in an appendix to CHP(1).

Composed early in 1811 while B was working on various poems at the Capuchin Convent near Athens. Constantine Rhigas (variously spelt) was put to death in 1798 by the Turks, to whom he had been betrayed by the Austrians. He was 38. Hobhouse also translated the song (*Travels in Albania*, II. 3) and notes that B's translation is not in the same measure as the original.

19. *seven-hill'd*: Constantinople. ''Ἑπτάλοφος.' [B's note in CHP(1)]

153. *MS. and Publishing History*. B's draft MS. (*MS. T*, watermarked 1811, location: Texas; this is the *MS. M* in *C*); B's fair copy, used as copy text for CHP(1) (*MS. P*, location: Pforzheimer; reproduced with comment in *Shelley and His Circle*, VI. 1124–5). John Hanson made a transcript of the last two stanzas (*MS. M*, location: Murray). Also in Murray: an uncorrected proof in a bound volume of various proofs for CHP(5) and CHP(7). First published, CHP(1); collected, all editions. *1832* is the first to date the poem 'March, 1811', which all later editions have followed. The date is meant to indicate that the poem is a farewell lyric written just before B sailed from Greece for home, in Apr. 1811. This inference is supported by B's placement of the poem in CHP(1), i.e. as the last of the shorter poems in that volume which were written on his travels. The poem was almost certainly written to Teresa Macri, whom B was 'near bringing away' with him when he left Athens (see *BLJ* II. 46).

154. *MS. and Publishing History*. No MS.; an uncorrected proof, in a bound volume of various proofs for CHP(5) and CHP(7): location, Murray. First published in 1813 by Hobhouse in *Travels in Albania*, (edn. of 1813), pp. 1148–50; republished, CHP(7), collected thereafter. The poem is a translation of the modern Greek song Ἀγάπη δὲν ἐστάθη ποτε χωρὶς καιμους. B may have heard the song during his travels in 1809–11, but he probably used, for his translation, the text provided in F. C. H. L. Pouqueville, *Voyage en Morée, à Constantinople, en Albanie . . .* (Paris, 1805), I. 281–6. See C. M. Dawson and A. E. Raubitschek, 'A Greek Folksong Copied for Lord Byron', *Hesperia*, 14 (1945), 46–50, and Roy P. Basler, 'The Publication, Date, and Source of Byron's "Translation of a Romaic Love Song"', *MLN* 52 (1937), 503. Hobhouse (op. cit.) says that 'the following translation . . . has just been transmitted to me by my friend Lord Byron'. His book was published on 23 May 1813 (*Marchand*, I. 389). The translation may have been written in 1813, but it is much more likely that B composed it early in 1811, when he was making his other translations from the modern Greek.

155. *MS. and Publishing History*. Unpublished; B's draft MS.; undated (location: Murray). The MS. title in Greek is slightly abbreviated; it means: 'what do you want, my eyes?' The phrase '*μάτιά μου*' ('my eyes') is a term of endearment. The refrain (*ὄχι μία μιλαῖ*) means: 'not one speaks'. The translation is obviously from the modern Greek, but the original has not been found. The date of the translation is conjectural. It is, of course, a dialogue poem.

156. *MS. and Publishing History.* B's fair copy, with epigraph and prose note (location: Yale); uncorrected proof in bound volume of various proofs for *CHP(5)* and *CHP(7)* at Murray. First published *CHP(1)*, collected thereafter; stanza numbering removed in *1831* and subsequent editions. Dudu Roque's copy of the Greek song is also at Yale, with B's note on verso stating she copied it for him on 19 Apr. 1811. B's prose translation of the end of the song is in Pforzheimer (printed in *Shelley and His Circle*, IV. 901): 'I have loved thee, maid with a sincere soul, but thou hast left me like a withered leaf.'

B sailed for England on 22 Apr., so that he probably made the translation after he left Greece, perhaps on his return voyage. See C. M. Dawson and A. E. Raubitschek, 'A Greek Folksong Copied for Lord Byron', *Hesperia*, 14 (1945), 36–47 esp.

157. *MS. and Publishing History.* Unpublished; text from B's corrected holograph fair copy, undated, on a single leaf bound up with *MS. M* of *Hints from Horace*, in Murray. The imitation was almost certainly written between Mar. and June 1811, when B was writing and revising the *Hints*. See especially *Hints*, 328–30.

1. *Buckingham:* George Villiers, second Duke of Buckingham (1628–87). B is thinking of Villiers's satire on Dryden in *The Rehearsal*.

2. *Foote:* Samuel Foote (1720–77), actor and dramatist.

7–8. See *EBSR* 678–9 and n.

10. *Scan. Mag.:* scandal, slang for *scandalum magnatum*.

158. *MS. and Publishing History.* B's corrected fair copy, signed and dated (*MS. Y*, location: Yale); first published, *1832*, and collected thereafter, though *C* questioned the poem's authenticity. Joseph Blackett (1786–1810), the cobbler-poet, was patronized by the Della Cruscan poet S. J. Pratt, as well as by B's literary friend R. C. Dallas and Annabella Milbanke. B believed Blackett was ruined by this sort of patronage. See *EBSR* 765–70; *Hints*, 731–4 and notes; *BLJ* II. 53, 76, 80, 82.

14. Echoing Pope's *Essay on Man*, IV. 204.

159. *MS. and Publishing History.* B's fair copy, titled and dated (owned by Mme. Teresita de la Puente de Nicolini, Lima, Peru); a photographic facsimile of this MS is in *BM*. First published in *Poems on His Domestic Circumstances . . . By Lord Byron . . .* (sixth edn., printed for W. Hone, 1816), and reprinted from this text in various other piracies; first authoritative printing, *1832*, evidently from B's MS., and collected thereafter. See also *BLJ* II. 126 for B's comments on the poem.

14. *his Excellency:* Maj. Gen. Hildebrand Oakes (1754–1822), His Majesty's Commissioner for the Affairs of Malta.

25–30. Referring to the English defeat of a combined Italian and French fleet early in 1811 off the Dalmatian coast.

33. Mrs. Susan Fraser, wife of Commander Fraser, to whom B gave the original MS. of this poem. In a letter to Hobhouse of 2 Nov. 1811 B wrote: 'Just before I left Malta, I wrote during my Ague, a copy of Hudibrastics as an Adieu to La Valette, which I gave to Com[mander] Fraser because it contained a compliment to Mrs. F[raser] without intending the thing to be bandied about. No sooner were we sailed than they were set in circulation, & I am told by a lately arrived traveller, that they are all, but particularly *Oakes*, in a pucker, and yet I am sure there is nothing to annoy any body, or a single personal allusion throughout, as far as I remember, for I kept no copy' (*BLJ* II. 126; see also ibid. 132).

160. *MS. and Publishing History.* Sent in a lettter to Hobhouse, 19 June 1811 (*MS. M,* location: Murray). First published *LBC,* reprinted *BLJ* II. 51; uncollected.

B was sailing from Malta to England on the frigate *Volage.*

161. *MS. and Publishing History.* Unfinished draft MS., no date, no watermark (*MS. TP,* location: Princeton–Taylor); unpublished.

An early poem, but the date is conjectural for B flirted with the idea of suicide a number of times. That it is a suicide poem, and not one written during an illness, seems clear, especially from the *Hamlet* allusion in line 5. Likely date: Aug. 1811.

162. *MS. and Publishing History.* Four MSS. are extant—B's holograph rough draft, corrected, untitled, dated at beginning 'August 26ᵗʰ', in the Murray archives (*MS. M*); B's holograph fair copy, corrected, untitled, dated at beginning 'Newstead—August 26ᵗʰ 1811', in the Newstead collection (*MS. N*); Augusta's fair copy, apparently from *MS. N,* untitled, and misdated 'Newstead Abbey Aug. 26 1814' (*MS. T,* location: Texas, in Augusta Leigh's Commonplace Book); Lady Byron's fair copy, apparently from *MS. N,* untitled, misdated at the beginning 'Newstead—August 26ᵗʰ 1814', in the Lovelace collection (*MS. L*). The stanzas are numbered in *MS. M* and *MS. N,* but not in *MS. L.* First published in *The Mirror of Literature,* XXIII (11 Jan. 1834), p. 26, from a MS. sent by John Galt; published again in *Memoir of the Rev. Francis Hodgson,* by the Revd. James T. Hodgson (1878), 2 vols. II. 187–8; first collected, *C,* using *Hodgson* as copy text. The poem is a gloomier continuation of the Newstead Abbey poems which B wrote for his *HI* volumes.

It was written in one of the bleakest periods of B's life (see *BLJ* II. 69–84 *passim* and commentary to *CHP I–II*).

163. *MS. and Publishing History*. B's corrected draft, undated (*MS. M*, location: Murray); unpublished.

The parody is of Jones's 'A Persian Song of Hafiz' ('Sweet Maid, if thou would'st charm my sight'), *Works of Sir William Jones*, ed. Lord Teignmouth (1807), X. 251–4. B quotes from the poem in a letter to Dallas of 7 Sept. 1811 (*BLJ* II. 91), and the parody probably dates from about that time.

164. *MS. and Publishing History*. B's fair copy dated (*MS. M*, location: Murray). C's variant for line 3 indicates there was another MS. (not seen by this editor). First published *Life*, I. 295 from the Murray MS.; collected *1831*, *1832*, and thereafter. The epigram refers to Moore's *M.P.; or, The Blue Stocking*, which opened at the Lyceum Theatre on 9 Sept. 1811. The last three lines refer to Moore's early volume, *Poems of the Late Thomas Little, Esq.* (1801).

165. *MS. and Publishing History*. Fair copy, corrected, in B's hand, signed and dated at the end. In the MS., Francis Hodgson crossed out lines 47–56 and added two notes: 'From here to the end to be left out.—N.B. the poor dear Lord *meant* nothing of this.' The MS. is in the Huntington Library. First published, *Life*, I. 301–2; first collected, *1831*, and all later editions. The self-portrait in this poem clearly anticipates B's later portraits of his fictitious Byronic heroes, just as it parallels the portrait of Childe Harold, the 'poetical Zeluco' of *CHP I–II*, which was being prepared for the press when this poem was written (see the original Preface for *CHP I–II*). Moore's note to this poem, in the *Life*, is to the point: 'It seemed as if, with the power of painting fierce and gloomy personages, he had also the ambition to be, himself, the dark "sublime he drew", and that in his fondness for the delineation of heroic crime, he endeavored to fancy, where he could not find, in his own character, fit subjects for his pencil.' The poem was written to Francis Hodgson.

19. Compare *Giaour*, 136.
25–40. Alluding to his love for Mary Chaworth. See nos. 123, 126, 131.
44. Compare no. 172, line 4.
46. Echoing *Macbeth*, V. iii. 23.

166. *MS. and Publishing History*. B's corrected fair copy, dated 27 Oct. 1811 (location: Huntington); an uncorrected proof in a bound volume of various proofs for *CHP*(5) and *CHP*(7), in Murray. In the MS., lines 33–6 are a late addition: MS. shows two pencil versions and a corrected version in ink. MS. facsimile in *Poems and Letters of Lord Byron, edited from the original MSS of . . . W. K. Bixby*, by W. N. C. Carlton (Chicago, Society of Dofobs, 1912). Moore probably saw the draft MS., for he dates the poem 11 Oct. 1811 in

1832. First published, *CHP(1)*, collected thereafter. *1815* broke the poem into octaves, much to B's annoyance (see *BLJ* IV. 308); *C* was the first edition after *1815* to print the poem in its proper form.

The poem is one in the so-called 'Thyrza cycle', a series of verses written in memory of the Trinity choirboy John Edleston, who died in May 1811. B first heard of his death on 9 or 10 Oct. (see *Marchand*, I. 107–9, 295–7). B wrote to Mrs. Margaret Pigot on 28 Oct. asking her if she would have Elizabeth Pigot return B the cornelian heart which Edleston had given to B at Cambridge (see no. 87). B had asked Elizabeth Pigot to hold it for him (see *BLJ* II. 119–20). For many years the identity of 'Thyrza' was a subject of perplexed scholarly controversy. That B wrote the Thyrza poems with Edleston in mind is beyond question, but it seems also true that the poems represent a more generalized lament for a series of lost loves and friends, like John Wingfield and Mary Chaworth (see no. 165 and *CHP I–II*, and the commentaries). B said that he took the name of Thyrza from *The Death of Abel* (1758) by Solomon Gessner (1730–88) (see *C* III. 30–2, notes).

26. *towers*. Newstead Abbey.

41. *The pledge*. B seems to be referring to the cornelian, though in fact he did not have it when he wrote these verses. But the day after he wrote this poem he sent a letter (see commentary above) by which he meant to recover the 'pledge'.

167. *MS. and Publishing History*. The epigram is in a letter to William Harness of 6 Dec. 1811, now at Texas. First published with part of the Harness letter in *Life*, I. 316; first collected, *Paris 1831*, from the *Life* text; first collected in a standard edition, *More*. The full letter was first published in *Pratt*, 95–6, and again in *BLJ* II. 137–8.

The lines are a parody of Southey's 'Queen Orraca and the Five Martyrs of Morocco', Part II, stanza 1. The epigram should be compared with B's similar remarks in *EBSR* 903 ff. B later revised his opinions of Charles Lamb (see his Preface to *Werner*). Lloyd is Charles Lloyd (1775–1839), a minor writer of the Lake School. It should be recalled that the epigram was written shortly after B had heard Coleridge lecture on Shakespeare, a performance which did not please B.

168. *MS. and Publishing History*. Published from B's MS. in anon., 'Letters Etc. of Lord Byron', *The New Monthly Belle Assemblée*, 70 (Jan.–June 1869). The article published a large number of B's letters to Augusta and two other early epigrams by B. All are genuine, though, as in the case of this poem, the locations of some of the MSS. printed in the article are not now known.

B refers to James Hervey (1714–58), author of *Meditations and Contemplations*, 2 vols. (1745–6). and to Hervey's Fish Sauce, a popular prepared sauce of the day (cf. *Beppo*, st. 8).

169. *MS. and Publishing History.* First published in *C* from *MS. M*, B's untitled, undated, draft fragment at Murray's.

C's placement of the poem implies a late date of composition, around 1822. But the poem almost certainly belongs to late 1811 or early 1812. 'Lucietta' is Lucy, one of the maids at Newstead to whom B refers in his letter to Hobhouse of 17 Nov. 1811 (*BLJ* II. 131). The 'intriguer' who most caught B's fancy was Susan Vaughan (see commentary, no. 176).

170. *MS. and Publishing History.* The earliest surviving MS. is a holograph corrected draft copy, undated, in the Huntington Library (*MS. H*). This was one of the Bixby MSS. reproduced in facsimile by the Society of Dofobs (see commentary for no. 166). A second MS. is not forthcoming (*MS. T*), but a facsimile of part of it (stanzas 1–3) was published in the Terry sale catalogue, Anderson Galleries, 2 May 1934, p. 41. This facsimile is of the first page of a letter B wrote to Francis Hodgson on 8 December 1811, in which B sent his verses. A third MS., a holograph fair copy, undated and signed 'B', is in the Berg (*MS. B*). The MSS. were written in the above order, and *MS. B* may well have been printer's copy for *CHP(1)*. An uncorrected proof is in the Murray archives, in a bound volume of various proofs for *CHP(5)* and *CHP(7)*. First published, *CHP(1)*; collected thereafter. The poem is another in the Thyrza cycle. In his letter to Hodgson of 8 Dec. B said that he wrote the poem 'a day or two ago on hearing a song of former days'.

14. Genesis 3: 19

19. Echoing Thomas Tickell's 'Colin and Lucy', 25.

171. *MS. and Publishing History.* B's draft, undated (*MS. H*, location: Huntington; reproduced in facsimile for Society of Dofobs, see no. 166); B's fair copy, used as copy text for *CHP(1)* (*MS. BM*, location: BM, Egerton 2027). An uncorrected proof is in Murray (*Proof M*) in a bound volume of various proofs for *CHP(5)* and *CHP(7)*; an uncorrected proof for *CHP(7)* of st. 4–7 (*Proof H*) at Huntington. First published *CHP(1)*, collected thereafter.

Another Thyrza/Edleston poem. The date of composition is not precisely determinable, but it was written in Dec. 1811 or Jan. 1812. The 'pledge' of line 41 is, again, the cornelian heart which Edleston gave to B.

172. *MS. and Publishing History.* B's draft copy of the last three stanzas (written on verso of a bill charged to B) was sold at the Anderson Galleries (American Art Association, Cat. 4249, 8–9 April 1936, Lot 128). The present location of this MS. is not known; the catalogue prints the final stanza (with the var. 'the' for 'thy' in line 34). Another (extant) fragmentary MS. is Augusta Leigh's copy of the final stanza, in her Commonplace Book (location: BM; see no. 249, commentary). Huntington has an uncorrected proof for *CHP(7)*. The William Andrew Clark Library (Los Angeles) has another separate printing of this poem, followed by 'Stanzas' (no. 178) on eight numbered letterpress leaves. Wise (I. xx–xxiii) argues that this is a proof copy for *CHP*(*1*), where B originally intended the two poems to be published, according to Wise. The Clark printing was, however, sold to that library as a first edition, separate printing, of the two poems. The Clark printing of 'Euthanasia' is identical to the Huntington proof. But the 'Stanzas' in the Clark copy differs noticeably in its accidentals from both the Huntington proof and the *CHP* printings of the poem (see commentary on 'Stanzas'). In the absence of more evidence, for example, printer's copy MSS., the issue cannot be definitely settled. But the fact that Elkin Matthews, Ltd. once had a contemporary pen-facsimile copy of four pages of the same printing of the poems argues for the theory of a separate printing (see the letter from R. E. Gathorne-Hardy, of Elkin Matthews, Ltd., to Clark Librarian, 24 July 1930, in the Clark Library). First published either as a small pamphlet, with 'Stanzas', in 1812, or in *CHP*(*2*); see above. Collected thereafter. The poem is often placed with the Thyrza poems, but it seems only loosely associated with that cycle. It is not written directly to or about 'Thyrza', but it is written out of B's melancholy moods of late 1811 and early 1812. The exact date of composition is not known for certain; but see commentary below for no. 178. It was probably composed in Dec. 1811 or Jan. 1812.

29. Recollecting *Hamlet*, III. i. 60 ff.

173. *MS. and Publishing History*. B's MS., apparently a draft, headed 'Edleston Edleston Edleston' (location: Murray). Uncollected, published once in *Byron. Exhibition Catalogue*, by Anthony Burton and John Murdoch (Victoria and Albert Museum, 1974), p. 26, with a translation.

The *Exhibition Catalogue* dates the poem 1811, but it may have been written either in late 1811 or early 1812. The verses are obviously part of the cycle of Thyrza poems (compare, e.g., lines 9–12 with the epigraph to no. 178). B's principal model here is Catullus, especially nos. 68, lines 15–24, and 101. Line 11 here specifically echoes Catullus, 8. 15. Translation: 'Beloved youth, if the name of our former love still means anything to you, I beg you to love your friend always. As often as I lament you, dearest one, and your fate, this grief of mine grows more strongly upon me. Yet how sweet, how very sweet, that grief is; and my empty love burns more sweetly still when I imagine I have held you in my arms. I am wretched; once frustrated in my prayers to have lived for you, why now have I longed in vain to die when you died? Oh how much less it means to me to go with the others seeking garlands, perfumes, and girls, than merely to remember you. What remains for me now?—only groans, or a brother's vague dreams, or else to lie awake on my bed in tears, without you. Ah Libitina [the goddess of death] come, free me from the Fates who hate me. Since our friendship is dead, let Death be my friend.'

INDEX OF FIRST LINES

ADDENDA

Additional Apparatus and Commentary for no. 99

99. Copy text: lines 1–100, *MS. EP*; lines 101–16, *MS. CM*; lines 117–20, *Montague MS.; collated with 1831, 1832.*

9 Where] Whose *all edns.*　　　　11 Fanes] towers *MSS. EP, CM*
52 Still] The *MS. CM*　　57 in smiles] ⟨again⟩ *MS. EP*　　65 the]
thy *all edns.*　　　　68–9 *lines transposed in all edns.*　　　　73 warm]
wake *MS. EP, cor. in MS. CM*　　76 wake] shake *MS. EP, cor. in
MS. CM*　　90 in] is *all edns.*　　106 th'] the *all edns.* Almighty's]
Almighty *MS. CM*　　113 sparrow's] sparrow *MS. CM*

99. *Commentary.* The Pforzheimer Library recently acquired two MSS. of this poem. Neither is holograph, but the first of these (*MS. EP*) was copied by Elizabeth Pigot from B's lost holograph. It comprises lines 1–100 of the poem, in numbered stanzas. Evidently the MS. was at one time complete, for the final four lines are extant as the fragmentary *Montague MS* (see original commentary). *MS. EP* was copied 24 Jan. 1828 for Thomas Moore and carries this headnote by E. Pigot: 'Copy by E P—made *fair* by C M.—The *original* I sent to Moore, it was so *dreadfully ill* written as to be *almost* unintelligible, & I sent it to Moore to show my industry for him in making it out after such a lapse of years, when I had nearly forgotten the intricate *up's and down's* of his pen.' The fair copy she refers to is *MS. CM*, made from *MS. EP*. Also in numbered stanzas, it is dated '1807' at the end and is endorsed: 'Copied by C M—& sent to Murray Novr 1830.' In *MS. CM* line 2 is added by E. Pigot, who also corrects the readings in lines 73 and 76. In printing the poem in *1832*, Moore evidently had these two MSS. as well as B's 'unintelligible' holograph to work from. Some of the *1832* emendations from the MS. copies carry conviction (e.g. at lines 11, 106, 113), but others seem either mistakes (lines 68–9 and 90) or deliberate 'improvements' of the sort Moore frequently made in *1832* (e.g. lines 9 and 119). *MS. CM* carries the following marginal glosses in the copyist's hand: 1–4: Harrow; 11–12: Cambridge; 21: Scotland; 31: Newstead; 41: Miss Pigot's cottage; 45: River Greet; 55: Mary Duff; 63: Eddleston.